A HISTORY OF
HUNGARY

The crown of Saint István.

A HISTORY OF HUNGARY

PETER F. SUGAR, General Editor

PÉTER HANÁK, Associate Editor

TIBOR FRANK, Editorial Assistant

INDIANA UNIVERSITY PRESS
Bloomington and Indianapolis

First Paperback Edition 1994

© 1990 by Indiana University Press

The paper used in this publication meets the minimum requirements of American
National Standard for Information Sciences—Permanence of Paper for Printed
Library Materials, ANSI Z39.48-1984.

∞™

Manufactured in the United States of America

Library of Congress Cataloging-in-Publication Data

A History of Hungary / Peter F. Sugar, general editor : Péter Hanák,
associate editor : Tibor Frank, editorial assistant.

p. cm.

Includes bibliographical references.

ISBN 0-253-35578-8

1. Hungary—History.   I. Sugar, Peter F.   II. Hanák, Péter.
III. Frank, Tibor.

DB925.3.H57   1990

ISBN 0-253-20867-X (pbk.)

943.9—dc20

88-46215
CIP

3 4 5 00 99 98 97 96 95 94

CONTENTS

Illustrations follow chapter x.

LIST OF MAPS

In memory of György Ránki,
esteemed colleague,
distinguished historian,
beloved friend

PREFACE

When we first submitted a draft of this volume to Indiana University Press, Hungary was preparing for the 1985 Congress of its Communist Party. The deteriorating economic situation in the country demanded drastic reforms, and these were expected from the Congress. As it could not be predicted what these would be or how the country would change as a result, we ended the volume with a rather vague statement looking ahead to the future.

During the last two years of the 1980s Eastern Europe was completely transformed. Poland and Hungary proved to be the countries moving fastest on the road of drastic change. By the end of 1989 János Kádár's People's Republic of Hungary, previously anchored firmly in CMEA and the Warsaw Pact, had become the Republic of Hungary, a multi–party state seeking membership in various West European organizations. The two-tier parliamentary elections of March-April 1990 gave none of the contending parties a clear majority. The Socialists, the party of the erstwhile reform Communists, and the hard-line Communists were practically eliminated from the political scene. Both the Democratic Forum, which received the largest number of votes and which would form the new coalition government, and the Free Democrats, emerging from the elections in second place, as the opposition party, ran on platforms promising a restructuring of the country on the western democratic model.

As this paperback edition goes to press in the beginning of 1994, four years have passed since the epilogue was written and Hungary is again facing elections. The coalition government, led until his death in 1993 by Dr. József Antall, is facing serious challenges. Most experts expect that it will be replaced by another coalition built around either the Young Democrats or the Social Democrats. The government elected in 1990 faced numerous major problems. No government could have solved all of these successfully, but the present one is held responsible for not fulfilling the unrealistic and overly optimistic expectations of the population. Introducing parliamentary democracy, replacing a centralized Soviet-type economy with a market economy and fitting it into the global market, facing the problems of privatization and restitution, maintaining social services, avoiding drastic inflation, attracting foreign investments, and "rejoining Europe" were among the numerous tasks that new government had to tackle.

That the Antall government could not in four years solve all these and other problems to the satisfaction of the majority of the voters is not surprising. The government's task was further complicated by the presence of substantial Hungarian minorities in the neighboring states. The issue of protecting their interests led inevitably to political polarization. Both the economy and the political spectrum began to move toward extremes—new wealth amidst growing poverty, growing sentiment for a return to socialism versus rising chauvinism and anti-

Semitism. Numerous problems continued to plague Hungary well into the 1990s.

Let me now turn to the history of this volume's preparation. In April 1981 the newly established Hungarian Studies chair at Indiana University held an inaugural conference during which several Hungarian scholars and their American colleagues met informally to discuss possible further cooperative ventures. Those present agreed that what the profession needed most was a good, basic one–volume history of Hungary that would serve, first of all, classroom needs in English–speaking universities and colleges but that would also be suited as a reference book for nonspecialist historians and the general reading public. It was also agreed that such a volume had to be scholarly in the sense that it had to reflect the best recent scholarship, but readable in style and free of academic paraphernalia. Finally, it was stressed that the volume should not be a collection of essays, but a work written in accordance with specific uniform guidelines. These were the directives which those involved in the preparation of *A History of Hungary* have followed.

At my colleagues' request, I assumed the task of planning this volume. I am also responsible for the cuts and editorial changes the various authors were asked to make, for the translation into English of the chapters originally written in Hungarian or German, and for the style of the final product. Consequently, I am taking full responsiblity for whatever shortcomings readers might find in this volume. My fellow editors and the authors deserve full credit for the work they have done and for the expertise which they brought to their respective tasks. I am deeply grateful to them for their patience and collaboration. I also wish to thank the relevant authorities for the Fulbright Fellowship and also the University of Washington for the financial support which made work on this volume possible. Further gratitude is due to the Institute of History of the Hungarian Academy of Sciences for the hospitality and support which I enjoyed while working on this volume in Budapest in 1984. Thanks are due also to the Institute of History for providing the illustrations that appear in this book. I acknowledge with deep appreciation the support for publication of this volume provided by the Soros Foundation, the University of Washington, and the Hungarian Chair of Indiana University. I also gratefully acknowledge the assistance of the staff of Indiana University Press. Finally, I wish to thank Ms. Judith Skow, who not only typed the final version of the manuscript, but made enough constructive suggestions to qualify as one of the editors.

PETER F. SUGAR

INTRODUCTION

The Great Plain of Europe, stretching from the Atlantic Coast to the Ural Mountains, is cut off from the southern half of the continent by the Alpine mountain complex and from the east by the northern chains of the Carpathians, which turn south, then west, enclosing a smaller plain known as the Carpathian Basin, the home of the Hungarians. Its largest city, Budapest, is roughly equidistant (approximately 550 miles) from Rostock on the Baltic Sea, Genoa on the Ligurian Sea, and Burgas on the Black Sea and is as far from Moscow (around 1,000 miles) as it is from the mouth of the Loire on the Bay of Biscay. This central location did not escape the interest of the Romans, whose two provinces in the basin, Pannonia and Dacia, subsequently became the meeting place and battle ground of Western (Latin) and Eastern (Greek-Orthodox) Christianity and of the different civilizations identified with them. It was also here that the Avar and Hun Empires were centered and that the Mongol and Ottoman incursions into Europe reached their westernmost point. All these people and civilizations left their mark on the land and on the Hungarians, who have lived in the Carpathian Basin for more than one thousand years.

Like the Avars and Huns before them, the Hungarians could raid areas west of the Carpathians but were unable to establish themselves permanently there. Unlike other peoples, the Hungarians, who came to their present home from the foothills of the Urals, were able to maintain themselves in the Carpathian Basin successfully facing pressures from both west and east. Separated from their neighbors and the other inhabitants of the region by their Finno-Ugric language, they nevertheless learned and borrowed from them and developed a culture of their own that remained unique in many ways, while fitting into the Latin, western European pattern.

The first period of Hungarian history in the Carpathian Basin—896–1301—was dominated by the dynasty of the chief conquering prince, Árpád. Under his successors, Hungarians accepted Latin Christianity and developed economic and political institutions following western European models but always modified them to suit their customs and local conditions. The Hungarian feudal system resembled, but was not the same as, the French and German variants, and the nobility, free cities, and peasantry had rights and obligations which, again, showed local variations. The Árpád family, which gave the Catholic Church five saints in three hundred years, dominated this period but their power was never absolute. In 1222, King Andrew II was forced by the nobility to issue his Golden Bull, often compared with the English Magna Carta, only seven years older. During the reign of Béla IV the first of three major catastrophes in Hungarian history occurred: the invasion of the Mongols in 1241. For more than a year, they remained in the Carpathian Basin, transforming major portions of it into a wasteland. The reconstruction that followed their departure involved the final adaptation of western institutions and the full development of a society divided into distinct classes.

The next historical period, the roughly two hundred years between the death in 1301 of Andrew III, the last Árpád, and Hungary's defeat by the Ottomans in 1526, saw rulers from Bohemia, Bavaria, Luxemburg, Austria, Poland, and Naples on the throne of Hungary. The one exception to this stream of foreign rulers was the reign of Matthias I Corvinus of the Hunyadi family (1458–90). Under Louis I of Anjou (of Naples), known as "the Great" (1342–82), and later under Matthias Corvinus, Hungary became one of Europe's great powers. Under these two rulers, as well as the very powerful Sigismund of Luxemburg (1387–1437), Europe's intellectual and economic influences transformed Hungary. Matthias's court was one of the most brilliant Renaissance courts of the time. His reign was followed by the short, two-year rule of Albert, the first Habsburg on the Hungarian throne. During the second half of this era, Hungarians constantly fought the emerging power of the Ottomans and succeeded in keeping them south of the Danube-Sava line. This period of Hungarian history ended with the Battle of Mohács, in 1526. King Louis II and most of the leading nobles of the realm lost their lives in this conflict, which marked the beginning of the Ottoman-dominated period in Hungary's history. The consequences of this second major catastrophe were much more serious and long lasting than those of the Mongol invasion.

The first major result of the Battle of Mohács was the tripartite division of Hungary. The center of the country, the Great Plains between the Danube and Tisza rivers, together with large areas east and west of them, remained in Ottoman hands for some one hundred and fifty years. During this period the population dropped to less than fifty percent of what it had been in 1526, and soil erosion and other damages occurred whose effects lasted until the middle of the present century. Those living west of the Ottoman lands elected Ferdinand Habsburg as King of Hungary, believing that only the might of this family could arrest further Ottoman advances. Thus began a long period of Habsburg rule, which was not to end until 1918. The population living east of the Ottoman-held lands elected a different king, János Zapolyai. Although his successors, members of several families, gave up the royal title, they effectively ruled an independent state, the Principality of Transylvania, until 1699. The Habsburgs, Ottomans, and Transylvanians were at war with each other repeatedly during the next one hundred fifty years. Even when they were officially at peace, border skirmishes continued practically without interruption.

These conflicts were important not only because they added to the destruction of the country, but also because they involved important religious, cultural, and constitutional issues. The Reformation reached Hungary practically at once and made rapid progress, first in its Lutheran and then Reformed (Calvinist) versions. Unitarianism was born in Transylvania, where one of the earliest comprehensive Edicts of Religious Toleration was issued by the Diet of Torda in 1564. Unfortunately, since it did not apply to Orthodoxy, the religion of the

Romanians who made up the majority of the population, it created problems for the future. Freedom of religion (as far as western Christianity went) was stubbornly defended by every Transylvanian prince, although most of them were Catholics. Their reason was that they considered themselves Hungarian nobles, hoped for the liberation and reunification of the country, and wanted to protect the Hungarians' "constitutional rights" from the centralizing tendencies of the Habsburg rulers, who were staunch Catholics and promoters of the Counterreformation. Some of these Transylvanians played an important role internationally and were able to gain repeated concessions for Habsburg-ruled Hungary as a result of their clashes with its kings.

This "constitutional issue"—often fought over in the religious arena in the sixteenth and seventeenth centuries—became the major problem that the Habsburg rulers of reunified Hungary faced in the next major period of the country's history, lasting from the Peace of Karlowitz (1699) to the conclusion of the Compromise of 1867, which created the Austro-Hungarian Empire. The Habsburgs, trying to create a state on the model of other major European countries, tried to centralize their empire, eliminating the traditional laws and privileges of the various lands and provinces they ruled. The Hungarians defended their historic rights and their constitution, citing the various agreements concluded between ruler and nation, including those extracted from Vienna by the princes of Transylvania. This struggle, which began as an attempt by the nobility to protect its privileges, changed drastically during the second half of the eighteenth and the first half of the nineteenth centuries, when the ideas of the Enlightenment gained a wide following in the country. Incipient nationalism revived awareness of history and literature, widened the concept of the nation, introduced the new idea of democracy, and induced some of the leading nobles to pay attention to the national economy, which was in great need of modernization.

During the revolutionary year of 1848, the democratic wing of Hungarian reformers gained temporary leadership of the country. At first the Habsburgs yielded and approved the "March Laws" of 1848, but they subsequently opposed further concessions either to the spirit of the times or to specific Hungarian demands. The resulting war lasted for over a year and made Hungarians the heroes of democratic Europe and even America. Between 1849 and 1867 the Habsburgs tried to reimpose centralism, but both domestic and international affairs worked against them, leading finally to the Compromise of 1867.

During the "Dualist Period" (1867–1918) Hungary made rapid economic strides, especially in industrialization and urbanization. Her school system, including the universities, met the highest international standards, although admission to its better institutions was still limited. The cultural life of the country also caught up with that of the rest of the world, and in almost all fields Hungarians laid the foundations of remarkable achievements. In music, Béla Bartók, Zoltán Kodály, and Ernest Dohnányi began their activities at the end of these years, later becoming world-renowned composers between the two world wars. In physics, the outstanding contributions of Baron Loránd Eötvös paved the way for America's famous Hungarian trio of nuclear physicists, Edward Teller,

Leó Szilárd, and Eugen Wigner. From sports to the theater, from medicine to literature, Hungarian talent blossomed.

The First World War brought what Hungarians consider the third major catastrophe in their history. The Peace Treaty of Trianon detached from Hungary (excluding Croatia) 67 percent of her territory and 58 percent of her population. This loss, and reaction to the country's short-lived Communist regime in 1919, made inter-war Hungary revisionist and right wing. That under these circumstances Hungary gravitated into first Mussolini's, then Hitler's orbit was anything but surprising, and the country wound up on the losing side of the Second World War as well.

As did most countries of East-Central and Southeastern Europe, Hungary began its most recent historical period as a socialist state, under the thumbs of Stalin and his local satraps. A period of erroneous economic reforms, police terror, and all the other features of typical Stalinist regimes led, finally, to the uprising of 1956. The roughly thirty-three years after the fall of 1956 saw the gradual evolution of the "Hungarian version of Communism," an attempt by regime and population to live with each other, an admission of past mistakes coupled with serious endeavors to rectify them. Of these, the best known was the "New Economic Mechanism" introduced in 1968. In spite of its successes as well as the numerous other reforms introduced after 1956, numerous problems plagued Hungary well into the 1980s.

A HISTORY OF
HUNGARY

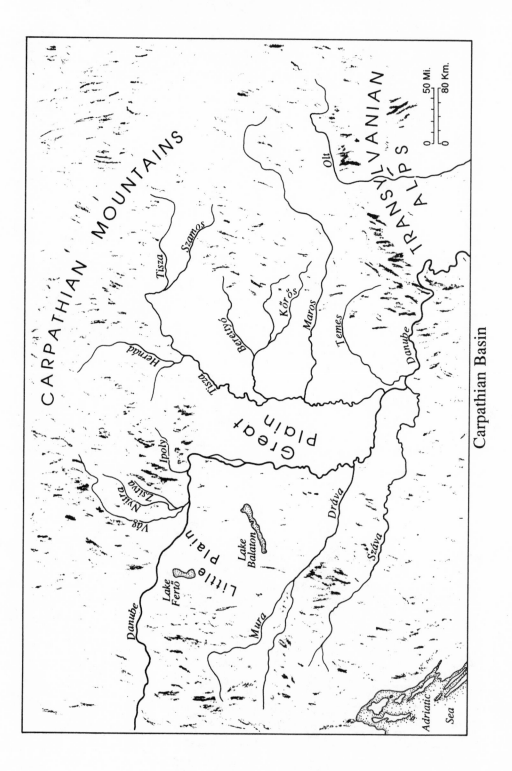

Carpathian Basin

I

HUNGARY BEFORE
THE HUNGARIAN CONQUEST

László Makkai

The Region and Its Geography

For a thousand years prior to 1918, historical Hungary extended over the entire central Danubian Basin. This region is surrounded by the semicircular Carpathian mountains, which leave the Danube in the north near the present-day Moravian-Slovak border and rejoin the river in the south not far from the Iron Gate. The region is, therefore, also known as the Carpathian Basin. Smaller ranges divide it into three sub-basins: the Little Plain in western Hungary, the Great Plain in the center, and Transylvania in the east. Although geologically it belongs to the South European system of basins, its vegetation is not Mediterranean in character, but composed of mixed forests and grasslands. Storms spawned by Atlantic cyclones and Asiatic monsoons occasionally bring rain, but the distances from the sea (about five hundred miles in each direction) and the blocking effect of the mountains limit precipitation to from sixteen to twenty four inches per year. The latitude of the basin is the same as that of central France, New York, and Washington State. While the basin's 1,750 to 2,000 hours of yearly sunshine are sufficient to ripen grapes, its continental location produces great variations in temperature, ranging from well below the freezing point in winter to about 90° Fahrenheit in the summer.

Because of these extremes and the uneven distribution of precipitation, most abundant in June and October, crops are often endangered by drought and only seldom by excessive moisture. While in Western Europe a rainy autumn presages a bad harvest, fall rains are indispensible in the Carpathian Basin for the autumn sowings that must survive until the unpredictable spring rains. These circumstances force the tiller of the land to supplement his work by increased reliance on animal husbandry.

The grasslands of the Carpathian Basin suitable for raising lifestock are not as extensive as those near the Black Sea, but a somewhat higher precipitation produces abundant grass, rendering nomadic grazing unnecessary. (The higher precipitation, however, requires the use of dry fodder in winter.)

1

Even before the region acquired its final characteristics, humans appeared in the Carpathian Basin. Near today's Budapest were found the remnants of a *Homo erectus* group that lived there about a half million years ago. They appear to have hunted the eohippus, primitive bison, and rhinoceros. To judge from the burnt bones, they must have been familiar with fire and must, therefore, be regarded as distant relatives of Sinanthropus. The Ice Age, which began around 200,000 B.C., turned the Carpathian Basin into a forested tundra region, where Neanderthals hunted mammoths, reindeer, and bear. Their material culture was of the Moustier type. Some time around 8,000 B.C., when the region gradually acquired its present-day features, the wild horse, the auroch, the bison, the red deer, and the brown bear appeared, and *Homo sapiens* was soon to bring his Mesolithic culture to the Carpathian Basin.

Early Settlers

Around 4,500 B.C., new inhabitants entered the region. They came from the Balkans and brought with them the skills of animal husbandry, hoeing, spinning and weaving, ceramics, and polishing stone. The old inhabitants, though pushed northward, also learned the skills of agriculture and especially animal husbandry. Abundant game in the Carpathian Basin facilitated the domestication of cattle and pigs and the extension of agriculture westward along the Danube, exploiting the sheep, goats, and cereals that came from the Balkans. Around 2,500 B.C., the use of copper was introduced to the region; because of the rich copper resources in the basin, the Copper Age lasted a thousand years. Toward the end of this period the ox-cart, borrowed from civilizations further south, came into use. This revolution in transportation increased trading activities. Wine and oil from Mycenae were exchanged for amber from the north. The growing population began to use the plow and to breed horses. The introduction of bronze brought the production of better tools and the manufacture of arms for the dominant aristocracy who wore gold and silver jewelry, lived in fortified strongholds, and used chariots in the numerous wars between power centers. Newcomers from the west and east intervened repeatedly in these conflicts, among them the first Indo-Europeans and Indo-Iranians.

When, around 700 B.C., the bronze culture reached its fullest development, people using the shoddier but mass-produced iron weapons overran the Carpathian Basin. Nomadic Scythians advanced from the Pontic Steppes to the Great Plains. They employed, with great success, the military methods they had developed a few hundred years earlier using the speed of massed cavalry armed with the reflex bow. Their short reign was ended by the Illyrians coming from the west. Using iron swords, they destroyed the strongholds of the Bronze Age aristocrats and replaced them with earthwork forts large enough to hold entire clans of their new servitors. Southern Illyrians along the Sava River were called Pannons by the Greeks and Romans. Further to the east, the Thracians settled, and one of their tribes, the Dacians, occupied Transylvania. Around 400 B.C., the Celts appeared. They had made the iron sword even more effective by adapting it for cavalry use. They forced the Pannons and the Dacians to submit.

The Dacians, showing amazing adaptability, were the first people to establish political power by creating their own synthesis of the material achievements of their neighbors. They combined the techniques of Celtic and Hellenistic fortifications in the extensive system of forts in their Transylvanian homeland. One of their kings, Burebista, supported by the high priest of the Dacians, not only united the Dacian and other Thracian tribes around 50 B.C., but extended his rule even over the Celts. While his kingdom broke up into small tribal states after his death, his conquests induced the Romans to take measures to prevent a renewed Dacian attack.

The Period of the Romans

In 8 B.C., the emperor Tiberius succeeded in duplicating along the Danube the *limes* already built along the Rhine, having overcome the resistance of the Pannons. The area north of the Sava and west of the Danube was soon organized into a new province, known as Pannonia. Legions were encamped on its northern, western, and southern limits. Along the line of the Danube, fortified military camps were established, among others Aquincum, the site of which is within the city limits of today's Budapest.

The *limes* along the Danube was fortified to arrest renewed Dacian attacks. The same purpose was served by the settling of some Iranian Sarmatian horsemen as allies in the valley of the Tisza River. To ensure the loyalty of their allies and to repulse attacks, the Romans built a triple line of earthen ramparts. These stretched from the bend of the Danube north of today's Budapest to the location of today's Debrecen and from there along the western slopes of the Transylvanian ranges to the lower Danube. All these preparations proved insufficient to parry the Dacian danger and German raids, which became especially acute when the Dacian king, Decebal, reestablished the unity of the Dacian tribes living north of the Danube. At first he was successful. He annihilated a Roman army and concluded peace with the emperor Domitian, retaining and putting to work the captured Roman military engineers. The attack of the Emperor Trajan, in 101 A.D., led to a temporary settlement. The Roman attack in 104 A.D. ended with the fall of the Dacians' main fortification Sarmisegetuza (today's Grădiște-Várhely) and Decebal's suicide in 106 A.D. Some of the Dacians who survived retreated into the eastern and northern mountains, from where they conducted campaigns against the Romans for many years to come. To replace them, Trajan brought to Dacia soldiers and city dwellers "from the entire Roman world," from as far as Britain and Syria, according to a contemporary historian. The legion of the new province was stationed in Apulum (today's Alba Iulia-Gyulafehérvár). The entire Carpathian Basin—except the mountains in the north—fell under Roman rule, though only Pannonia and Dacia became provinces where legions and auxiliary troops were stationed and cities were built.

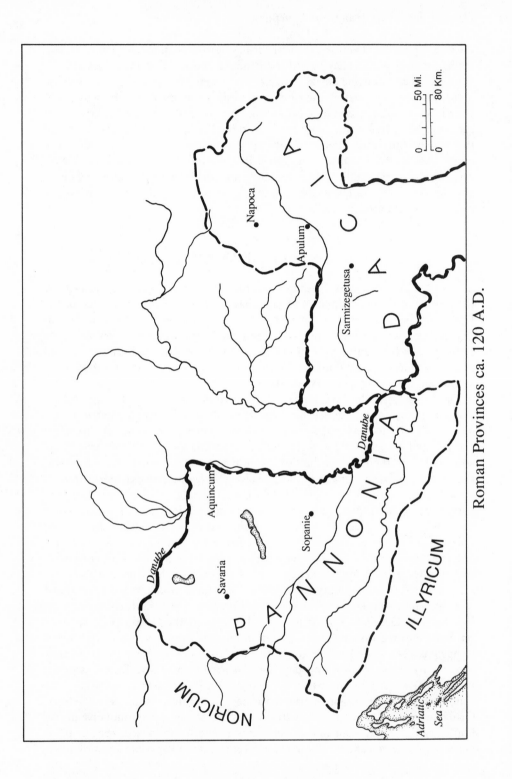

Roman Provinces ca. 120 A.D.

The Roman cities and fortified camps were not erected at earlier sites of settlement, but were built at sites selected by engineers. In these cities, public buildings surrounded forums, built on the Roman model. The cities, whose major structures were temples, embellished with the statues of Jupiter, Juno, and Minerva, also had baths, amphitheaters, running water, and houses with heated floors. In Pannonia, Roman aristocrats lived in the countryside in villas decorated with frescoes, statues, and mosaics. Besides the state religion, the eastern cults of Isis and Mithra were popular in both provinces. Christianity was persecuted until the fourth century, when it became the state religion. Basilicas were erected in the cities, and the pagan temples were destroyed or transformed into churches. No Christian remnants were left in Roman Dacia. The local inhabitants of Pannonia were organized into districts called *civitas,* which were ruled by local leaders. Dacia, whose leaders were killed, had no *civitates.*

Dacia and Pannonia were politically important in the empire (the legions of Pannonia helped Vespasian and later Septimus Severus to gain the throne), yet the permanent establishment of a peaceful and lasting Roman way of life was not possible. Pannonia and Dacia remained border regions to the end, known as the least civilized provinces. The Danubian provinces suffered from constant attacks by the German tribes from north and east as well as by the "free" Dacians who had fled from Roman rule. Between 164 and 167, only campaigns under the direct command of emperors could maintain the *limes,* and, indeed, Marcus Aurelius died at Carnuntum (near Vienna). The series of final attacks began in 258, coming from the lower Danube region, launched by the Goths who had settled on the Pontic Steppe. Around 269, the Germanic Gepids penetrated from the north and established themselves between the Tisza and the Transylvanian border ranges, and in 271, Aurelian had to give up Dacia to the Western Goths. Nonetheless, around 300 Diocletian succeeded in stabilizing the Danubian *limes,* giving Pannonia about another century of relative peace.

Huns, Germanic People, Avars

In 375, the Huns destroyed the Gothic empire. They and their vassals next turned their attention to the Eastern Roman Empire, which proved a rich source of loot and ransom. The Western Roman Emperor considered them allies. Aëtius, born in Pannonia, grew up in the Hun court as a hostage. When he directed Roman politics he yielded Pannonia, in exchange for help against the Visigoths, to Attila who had grown up as a hostage in Rome and became king of the Huns during the same year, 434. Thus the entire Carpathian Basin became an outpost of the Hun empire that stretched to the Urals. Attila, who ruled this state alone after 438, attempted the conquest of the entire Roman Empire. In 474 his armies reached Constantinople, but, satisfied with a huge ransom and yearly tribute, Attila turned towards the west. His erstwhile friend, Aëtius, arrested his advance in 451 at Catalaunum. The next year, advancing on Rome itself, Attila had to turn back to quell revolts in the easternmost regions of his realm. Attila died unexpectedly in 453.

Attila owed his successes and his dreaded reputation to his despotic rule, the power of the Hun heavy cavalry, and the valor of his Germanic and Sarmatian troops. He adopted the Iranian-Sassanid system of centralized power and, as a youth in Rome, had learned the newest methods of bureaucratic and military rule. On the tribal kingdoms he conquered, Attila imposed a government run by Roman, Greek, Hun, and Germanic high officials in accordance with a central- ized imperial concept. Yet the land, with its primitive agrarian economy, could not be transformed within a few years into a bureaucratic state. Economic backwardness as well as the centrifugal forces of fiery tribal loyalties made Attila's attempt to build a centralized state premature and illusory.

After Attila's death, the subject Germanic people attacked the feuding Hun princes, and, under the leadership of the Gepid king, Alaric, routed their armies in Pannonia. The Huns retreated to the Pontic Steppe, where they became part of the peoples of the Turk-Onogur and later the Khazar empire. The Germanic peoples, led by their tribal kings, turned against each other in the Carpathian Basin. In 476, the Herul leader, Odoaker, dethroned the last western Roman emperor, Romulus Augustulus, the son of Orestes, a Roman from Pannonia who had been Attila's chief advisor. In 489, Odoaker was attacked and murdered by the powerful Ostrogothic king, Theodoric, who led his forces from Pannonia to Italy. The remaining Heruls in Pannonia were exterminated by the Longobards, who moved in from the north. By the beginning of the sixth century, only two Germanic states existed in the Carpathian Basin: that of the Longobards in Pannonia and east of the Tisza and that of the Gepids in Transylvania. By this time, the Roman inhabitants of Pannonia had either been killed by the various conquerors or had left. War soon broke out between the Longobards and the Gepids. The Longobards concluded a questionable alliance with the Avars, a Turkic-speaking people who had reached the Lower Danube. The Gepids were destroyed, but the Longobards, now in a vice between Byzantium and the Avars, moved to Italy.

The three-hundred-years-long presence of Germanic people left no lasting trace in the Carpathian Basin. The only possible exception might be the word "teut," which they used to define themselves, and which later the conquering Hungarians used in the form of "tót" to define the Slav population they found in the Carpathian Basin. Nevertheless, they made a lasting contribution for those coming later. The apostle of the Western Goths, Ulfila, translated the New Testament into Gothic. His pupils used it to propagate Aryan Christianity in Pannonia after 456. It was a fateful inheritance. Common religion, which was only that of the leadership, did not preclude wars between the Germanic people, but it prevented the coexistence of the local population and the Germans in the western regions, which were under Roman Catholic ecclesiastic jurisdiction. The Aryan Germans were either annihilated or accepted Roman Catholicism.

The Avars became the masters of the entire Carpathian Basin and opened the region for their allies, the Slavs, whom they settled in the sparsely populated areas, except on the plains. Avar rule differed from that of the Huns in that it was limited to the Carpathian Basin, where they established a new form of government. The conquering chief, Baian, had the title of *kagan* (king of kings) and commanded an army made up not of tribal, but of professional soldiers under his direct command. That important Turkic invention, the stirrup, appeared in Europe with the Avars and, together with the use of Iranian suits of armor, made the relatively small Avar heavy cavalry units unstoppable. The army, with its expensive equipment, could not be supported by the taxes from the small primitively agricultural population of the Carpathian Basin. The military establishment relied instead on booty, and the Avars concentrated their attacks on rich Byzantium, which kept them away by paying tribute. If payments were refused, punitive expeditions appeared. Consequently, large amounts of Byzantine gold found its way to the Avar court, where goldsmiths produced jewelry and decorated weapons and harnesses for the kagan and his followers. After 630, the Byzantine flow of gold suddenly ceased. It appears that the expenses of the army became so high that the free Avars and their Slav allies revolted against the growing tax burden. This revolt diminished the power of the kagan, made the maintenance of his professional army more difficult, allowed the tribal aristocracy to regain some of its lost power, and freed Byzantium of its obligations.

Around 670, some of the Onogurs were displaced by the Khazars and fled to the Avars. This newly arrived and soon dominant population was, according to a recently advanced theory, Hungarian, but there is no proof yet that these newcomers spoke the Finno-Ugric Hungarian language. Another Onogur tribe that moved to the Lower Danube at the same period certainly spoke a Turkic language. This people, who later accepted the Slav language, gave their name to the present-day Bulgarians.

Charlemagne took advantage of the decline of Avar power and destroyed them between 791 and 796, attaching Pannonia to his realm. The district east of the Tisza and parts of Transylvania were conquered, early in the ninth century, by the Bulgarians, while the northwestern corner of the Carpathian Basin became part of the Moravian state. The plains became depopulated. A German source dating from the late ninth century speaks of an uninhabited desert between the Moravian and the Bulgarian borders. The plains between the Danube and the Tisza, as well as the northern steppe-like half of Transylvania, stood empty when the conquering Hungarians appeared in 896.

II

THE HUNGARIANS' PREHISTORY, THEIR CONQUEST OF HUNGARY AND THEIR RAIDS TO THE WEST TO 955

László Makkai

Prehistory

Contemporary Germans considered the Hungarians who conquered the Carpathian Basin to be the descendants of the Huns and Avars, and the Hun tradition was later adopted by the Hungarians (see chapter 4). Byzantine writers called them "Turks," the name they gave to all people living on the steppe. While the Hungarian language contains numerous Turkish loan words, it is not Turkic, but Finno-Ugric. It resembles most closely the speech of several small peoples who live today on the eastern slopes of the Urals. The original home of the Finn-Ugors was probably the region along the Kama river. The common ancestors of the Ugors of the Ob and of the Hungarians lived there during the period of the "neolithic revolution," when they learned to polish stone tools, to make clay pots, and, possibly, to spin and weave. The crucial change, the adoption of agriculture and animal husbandry, occurred about one thousand years later, in the second millennium B.C. At about the same time, they also learned to cast copper and to ride horses, which until then were bred only for their meat. This transition from stone to metal tools and from hunting and gathering to agriculture took about five hundred years. Around 1000 B.C., as the weather became warmer and warmer, the taiga moved further north. The Ugors of the Ob also moved north, looking for a new home. The early Hungarians, living further south, had to travel longer and longer distances on the increasingly dry steppe to find new pastures and eventually became nomads, living in tents. They continued to work the soil only in the river valleys, to which they returned each winter. The Ugric people in the north lived in the taiga and gave up agriculture, while the Hungarians in the south were lured by richer pastures towards the west.

After about 1000 B.C., the early Hungarians' favorite domestic animals became the horse and the sheep, which were best suited for nomadic grazing and were also in demand by the Chinese, the Persians, and Greek traders. From the Scythians and Sarmatians, fellow nomads, the Hungarians learned to work iron, to produce the felt needed for tents, to use the long iron sword and the reflex bow, and to sculpt stylized animals, the religious symbols of a newly learned creed. In about 550 A.D., Turkish Bulgar tribes coming from the east pushed the Hungarians to the regions inhabited at present by the Bashkirs.

It is not likely that the Hungarians gave up agriculture entirely during the Scythian-Sarmatian period of their history. In their new home, nomadism declined because precipitation was more abundant, and the rich grass made migration less necessary. Under the influence of the Khazars, who ruled the area stretching from the Volga to the Black Sea, and of the Alans, the economy of the Bulgars and of the Hungarians now living along the Don underwent considerable change. While animal husbandry remained their chief activity, it now included cattle and swine, and bee keeping and even wine producing became new pursuits. This went hand-in-hand with the permanent inhabitation of winter quarters and the extension of agriculture with the help of plows. Because in Western European languages the Hungarians are known as Onogurs (e.g., *Ungar, Hongrois),* a people that belonged to the Bulgar-Turkish group living on the steppes near the Black Sea, the Hungarians must have belonged to the Onogur tribal alliance before it disintegrated around 670. The Bulgar-Turkish origin of Hungarian tribal names and the survival of two of these to the present among the Bashkirs suggests that the Hungarian tribal alliance also developed in the Bulgar-Turkish milieu.

Tribes, unlike clans, are not based on blood ties, but are created organizations. The leaders of the nomad empires created military units from the various clans living under their jurisdiction and placed them under commanders who were their relatives. The Bulgar-Turkish Onogur tribal alliance included ten tribes (Onogur means "Ten Ogurs"). It is quite possible that the Khazars brought two of the eight Hungarian tribes to the Don to replace the Onogur-Bulgars when their alliance broke up around 670.

Irrespective of when and where Hungarian tribal segments became parts of the Onogur organization, it appears certain that they became its ethnic majority. The culturally Bulgar-Turkish and linguistically Finno-Ugric tribal alliance became a politically independent people and around 830 left the Khazar Kaganate, living first between the Don and the Dnieper, and from 830 to 893 between the Don and the Lower Danube.

In their new home, they were in contact not only with the Khazars, but also with the Greeks and the neighboring Slav people. As the representatives and later the successors of the Khazars, they collected taxes from the Eastern Slav tribes and exchanged their prisoners for household goods, spices, and textiles in Greek colonial cities. In trade and in collecting custom duties, the Iranian-speaking Muslim Khwaresmians, who had joined the Hungarians, played an important role. (They brought with them from their home the Arabian coin, the dirhem, and introduced its use among the Hungarians.) Yet despite this contact,

Islam did not become popular among the Hungarians, mainly because the Khazar kagan did not adopt it. For a long time, he permitted the activity of Orthodox priests and even established Orthodox bishoprics in his cities, but in the end the entire ruling establishment of the Khazars accepted Judaism. This brought the Khazars in conflict with the Muslims and finally facilitated the spread of Orthodox Christianity north of the Black Sea.

The Greek missionaries, it appears, also wrote ecclesiastic treaties for the Hungarians. Constantine-Cyril, one of the two great apostles of the Slavs, mentioned in his writing that the Avars, Khazars, and "Turks" also had ecclesiastic books in their languages. In the sixth century, the Turks of Central Asia had already adopted a method of writing of semitic origin. This Turkish runic alphabet was accepted by the Khazars and, through them, by the Magyars. The Hungarian runic alphabet, which survived among the Székelys of Transylvania until the eighteenth century, added the letters *f, h, l,* and *a,* taken from the Greek. This must have been done to facilitate the writing of ecclesiastic texts in Hungarian by Greek priests.

The "king" of the Hungarians invited Methodius in 882 to his residence on the Lower Danube. This does not mean, however, that Christianity had made inroads among the Hungarians. Before 1000 it frequently happened in Europe that the leadership of a given people accepted Christianity, Islam, or Judaism to prove that they were the equals of the rulers and nobles of the civilized empires. Religion was a political matter. The Hungarian people and their leaders followed the shamanistic cult of ancestor worship. The Hungarian word for God, *isten,* is derived from the name of Istemi, a western Turk kagan who lived in the sixth century and was either the real or fictitious ancestor of their chief.

The leaders of Hungarian society in the ninth and tenth centuries were not yet masters of the lower-ranking members of their clans but had to induce them to give "voluntary" service. They also recruited people belonging to other clans or tribes and those who had joined the Hungarians. The latter did not become adoptive members of the leader's clan, but were the personal attendants of the chief.

To recruit a retinue of foreign warriors was also a common practice among the Khazars, Moravians, and Avars and later among the Czechs, Poles, Croats, and Eastern Slavs. The military retinue had two functions: it forced the clan, tribe, or tribal alliance to pay taxes and supply soldiers to the leader, and it raided neighboring lands for booty. Taxes and booty enriched the master and supplied his followers with food, clothing, and weapons. The expensive and therefore small professional force was insufficient to prevent raids by the similarly organized neighbors. Therefore, military obligations of the common people and the personal and economic freedom tied to it had to be preserved. The leader and his followers also needed a permanent labor force, which could be acquired only by procuring slaves from abroad. International trade also demanded slaves, and Central and East European peoples were constantly decimated by the raids of slave hunters.

The Hungarian tribal alliance, consisting of seven tribes, grew to ten when it was joined by the "Kabars," who had revolted against Khazar rule. This alliance developed its own peculiar political organization. Its basic units were the clans led by their respective *bős* (derived from the Turkic *bey*), and organized into tribes. The "lords" commanded all those who performed military service, irrespective of their clans. These seven military commanders were members of related families, partly of Khazar origin, and their rank was proudly symbolized by the lions in the coats-of-arms of their descendants. The supreme command was exercised by a princely triumvirate, the *kende*, the *gyula*, and the *harka*, in descending order of rank. The triumvirate was not a Hungarian invention, existing also among the contemporary Khazars and Avars.

Booty-producing raids usually began when one neighbor turned to the Hungarians and asked them to attack another. In 893, Leo the Wise, emperor of Byzantium, concluded an alliance with the kende Kurszán and the gyula Árpád against the Bulgarians but failed to supply the promised military support for the campaign. The Bulgarian Tsar, who wanted to retaliate, concluded an alliance with the nomadic Pechenegs, who attacked the Hungarians in 895 and chased them out of their home near the Black Sea, forcing them to move to the Carpathian Basin.

The Conquest of Hungary

According to eleventh century traditions, the road taken by the Hungarians under the leadership of Prince Álmos took them first to Transylvania in 895. This tradition is supported by an eleventh-century Russian tradition stating that the Hungarians moved to the Carpathian Basin by way of Kiev. The Russian version was accepted by thirteenth century Hungarian chroniclers, nineteenth-century historians, and popular tradition, which holds that under the leadership of Árpád (d.907), the son of Álmos, the Hungarians crossed the Verecke pass in 896 and penetrated the valley of the Tisza. This contradiction in traditions could be resolved by accepting that the Eskil-Bulgars joined the advancing Hungarians, led by their gyula, Árpád, and covered the main move into Transylvania by taking the northern route leading to the Tisza. Political considerations support this explanation. The region south of the Maros (Mureş) River eastward to the Tisza was controlled by the Bulgarian tsar. West of the Danube, Slav dukes ruled under German overlordship. The region around Nyitra (Nitra) belonged to the Moravian state. Only the valleys of the Tisza and the Szamos (Someş) were open. They became the first home of the seven Hungarian and three "Kabar" tribes. It is not known where each of the tribes settled originally because tribal ties had already disappeared by the mid-tenth century. Tribal chiefs became local aristocrats, who tried to extend their power without regard for former tribal boundaries. In this struggle for power, the highest dignitaries had great advantages, notably the largest and strongest military retinues, which attracted the tribal warriors. This gave them mastery over the already conquered segments of the Carpathian Basin and the means to regain through raids the wealth lost to

the Pechenegs. The chaos that reigned in the Carolingian Empire and the precarious situation of Byzantium, under steady Bulgar and Arab pressure, invited
attack. Besides securing wealth, the raids served to intimidate possible foes and
to keep the military occupied. The conquest of Hungary and the raids are
inseparable events.

The Raids

There is no reason to believe that the conquering Hungarians considered the
Carpathian Basin their final home. On the contrary, it was to their advantage to
move as far as possible from their Bulgar and Pecheneg neighbors. Because the
military tactics of all three of these peoples were identical, the Hungarians could
not catch them by surprise or at a disadvantage. For this reason no raids were
directed against the Bulgars or the Pechenegs, and only once, in 967, did the
Hungarians attack the Bulgars, joining the Russian Sviatoslav in an unsuccessful
war. On the other hand, they frequently attacked the Carolingian and Byzantine
Empires. They discovered quickly that while they could not find a home suited
for their semi-nomadic way of life, outside the Carpathian Basin there were
lands offering them substantial plunder.

The first campaign undertaken from their new home took them to Italy, in
898, as the allies of the German emperor, Arnulf, where they destroyed the army
of the ruler of the Po valley, Berengar. On the way home, they discovered how
badly Pannonia was defended, and two years later they occupied the province.
The death of Arnulf made their task easier. The chief-prince, Kurszán, established his headquarters in one of the amphitheaters of Roman Aquincum. The
southern border was defended by the gyula, Árpád, who settled near the ruins of
Roman Sopianae (today's Pécs). The harka, Tétény, who selected as his home
another Roman ruin, Savaria (today's Szombathely), watched over the western
border. Pannonia and its Slav inhabitants were, thus, ruled by the three major
leaders.

In 902, the Hungarian hosts attacked the Moravian state. They crossed the
Carpathians, occupied the Viennese basin, and established new borders at the
Enns river, making the Hungarians the neighbors of the Bavarians. The prince of
Bavaria tried to parry the new danger by having the chief-prince of the Hungari-
ans, Kurszán, murdered at a banquet. Retribution was swift. Year after year,
Hungarian raiders devasted the Bavarian lands. In the decisive battle near
Breclavsburg (later Pozsony-Bratislava-Pressburg), in 907, the Bavarian prince
lost his life, and his successor concluded a lasting peace with the Hungarians.
The western border was secured, and for one hundred years Hungary was not
attacked from this direction.

The leadership went to the gyula, Árpád, after Kurszán's death, and he succeeded in making the position hereditary in the male line of his descendants. His
relative, Bogát, became gyula, and the next harka, Bulcsú, was his son. Thus the
three major dignitaries were acquired by Árpád's family and their close relatives.

Byzantine sources, as well as local tradition, identify the Székelys as the "kabars" who had revolted against the Khazars. This theory is hotly disputed, but should it be correct then the original three Székely groups were used as border guards in Pannonia near Pécs, west of Nyitra, and along the roads leading to Transylvania in the Bihar (Bihor) region. The second and third of these regions became, in the tenth century, duchies *(ducatus),* with dukes of the Árpád family, and the Pécs area became attached even more closely to the Árpád family itself. It is safe to assume that after 904, the raiding Hungarians were led either by the oldest duke of the House of Árpád or by the gyula or the harka to protect the chief-prince from further dangers.

After the western border had been secured, further raids ceased to be random and took on the features of planned foreign policy. Hungarian troops usually fought in the pay of foreign rulers. Once the rulers suffering from Hungarian incursions promised regular yearly tribute, the campaigns were directed elsewhere. The tribute belonged to the three main dignitaries who paid their armies with it.

At first the Hungarians were only rarely defeated. This was due in part to the support or at least neutrality of their allies, but mainly resulted from the fact that their way of fighting was unknown in the West. The armies, consisting mostly of light cavalry, moved very quickly, arrived unexpectedly, and were gone before an important force could be mobilized against them, taking with them booty, livestock, and prisoners. If the Hungarians encountered a well-organized army, the heavy cavalry attacked while the light units outflanked the enemy and covered them with a veritable rain of arrows. If this was not enough, they feigned flight, tempting the enemy to break rank in pursuit, then they turned against the pursuing enemy individually. It took quite some time before the German kings understood the Hungarians' tactics and found suitable countermeasures. Henry I, the Fowler, was the first to inflict a serious defeat on the Hungarians, in 933 at Merseburg. For a while, the Hungarians left Germany alone and limited their military actions to Byzantine territories. Then, in 948, the harka Bulcsú, known as "the man of blood," went to Constantinople in the company of an Árpád duke. He not only concluded peace, but even accepted Christianity to gain a free hand for further ventures into German lands. While small fast units had penetrated as far as Bremen in 915, to the Pyrenees in 924, and to Rome in 928, Bulcsú's large scale "lightning wars" surpassed everything which the Hungarians had tried earlier. In 937, he led his troops through Saxony and Lorraine to the mouth of the Loire and returned, passing through the Rhone valley and the French and Italian Riviera to Capua. In 942, his forces passed through Lombardy, crossed the St. Bernard Pass, and invaded Moorish Andalusia. They raided Italy as far south as Rome on their way home. In 947, Bulcsú was again in Italy, and in 954 his men followed the Danube, then the Rhine to the mouth of the Scheldt, then moved south to Verdun, crossed Burgundy and Switzerland before returning home through Lombardy. These campaigns meant rides of several thousand miles, interrupted by battles and raiding expeditions, and on the way home the carts loaded with booty had to be defended. The prayer, seldom heard since Merseburg, was again used in churches: "Our Lord save us from the arrows of the Hungarians." Bulcsú did not foresee that his raids would start political and military centralization in Germany. This trend paid off in 955, when, at the Lechfeld near Augsburg, the Hungarians suffered a crushing defeat. Otto I had Bulcsú and the Árpád Prince Lél hung as common criminals. With this defeat the raids came to an end.

III

THE FOUNDATION OF THE HUNGARIAN CHRISTIAN STATE, 950–1196

László Makkai

The Establishment of the Árpád Dynasty

The princes of the Árpád family understood the meaning of the defeat at Augsburg and promptly and drastically changed their domestic and foreign policies. They wanted to remake Hungary into a European-type monarchy, fitting into Christian Europe as an independent state. First, however, they had to overcome serious difficulties. The Árpáds were not masters of the country; their power did not reach east of the Tisza. From this river to the eastern borders of Transylvania, the second dignitary ruled as hereditary gyula, practically independently. The gyula Bogát had conquered Transylvania south of the Maros after 904.

The gyula Zombor visited Byzantium in 953 as an independent prince and there accepted Christianity. Zombor was probably Bogát's son, and his realm expanded steadily. He established a missionary bishop from Byzantium at Szávaszentdemeter (Mitrovica), and, according to Byzantine sources, remained Christian and loyal to Byzantium and even ransomed prisoners taken by the western Hungarians during their Balkan campaigns. All this proves that Transylvania's gyulas pursued a foreign policy that was different from if not contrary to that of Árpád's descendants.

After the defeat of Augsburg, Taksony, one of Árpád's grandsons, became chief-prince. He had a western orientation and in 961 asked the pope to send him a missionary bishop. Otto I, soon to become Holy Roman Emperor, prevented this mission because he hoped to convert and include Hungary in his realm. In spite of this, Taksony did not turn to Byzantium like his rival, the gyula. On the contrary, he sent Hungarian troops to support the Bulgarian Tsar's anti-Byzantine campaign in 965 and that of the Kievan prince Sviatoslav I in 970.

It was Taksony who introduced an economic system, based on the model of the Carolingian system still used in German lands, that thoroughly transformed Hungary's social structure. There were several court-run sites in the country whose function it was to supervise the production and storage of a great variety of goods, which were then consumed by the constantly traveling chief-prince and the dukes and their followers. Taksony transformed these sites into permanent settlements whose inhabitants performed specific productive functions, retaining these in their names to the present—vineyard-worker (Szőllős), plowman (Szántó), wainwright (Ács), furrier (Szűcs), hunter (Vadász), fisherman (Halász) and others. To protect them, he settled nearby the warriors from the tribes near the Tisza, who had become "unemployed" when the raids ceased. These soldiers kept alive the memory of the seven conquering tribes: Nyék, Megyer, Kürtgyarmat, Tarján, Jenő, Kér and Keszi. Fairs were also held at these reorganized court sites, and the so-called "böszörmény," Muslim merchants, also settled at them.

The new settlement policy advanced trade and made possible the amalgamation of the people into a single Hungarian ethnic unit. This occurred first in Pannonia where court sites were numerous. The policy also weakened tribal consciousness, the main obstacle to the centralization of power. The tribal warriors brought their tribal names and identities with them to the court sites, but soon forgot them; finally, even tribal organization ceased. This was the first step in transforming Hungarians from free members of a tribal alliance, loyal only to their tribes, into subjects of the prince.

The next step was taken by Géza, the son of Taksony, who sent his representatives to the Holy Roman Empire's Imperial Diet of 973 and requested missionary bishops. (He did not go in person so as to avoid swearing fealty to Otto I, like the Czech and Polish princes.) Otto sent a bishop, Bruno, who, in spite of Géza's support, achieved very little among the free and high-ranking Hungarians. For Géza, breaking the power of the shamans, whose ancestor worship strengthened tribalism, was more important than was the conversion of Hungarians. Although baptized, he continued to sacrifice to pagan gods, explaining that he was important enough to serve more than one god. His wife, Sharolt, the daughter of Transylvania's gyula, was an Eastern Christian and certainly did not favor the introduction of the western rite. Her faith was described by the missionary priests as "worse than a barbarianism because it was infected with paganism" (Eastern Christianity).

Christianization was a foreign policy measure for Géza, who also gave up the Vienna Basin to live at peace with the emperor. When the Czech prince began to expand his realm to the Morava River, Géza sought the help of the Polish prince, who had married an Árpád princess. Maintaining the family's anti-Byzantine policy, his brother married a Bulgar princess, and Géza's son Vajk, baptized István, secured an even better marriage in 996, to the Bavarian princess, Gisella.

On the domestic scene, Géza went beyond using Christianity to erode tribalism and continued his father's settlement policy. To strengthen himself militarily, he constructed earthwork forts and invited western knights and Russian warriors to join his bodyguard. The most difficult task, however, the unification of Hungary and its transformation into a European feudal monarchy, was to be accomplished by his son.

The Reign of István (Steven)

István received a Christian knightly education and took it very seriously. His older cousin, Koppány, claimed Géza's realm and widow in accordance with the Árpád family's succession rules and organized a revolt. István defeated him with the help of his German knights and had him executed as an incestuous pagan. In 1000, István asked for and received a crown from Pope Sylvester II and, as Hungary's Christian king, moved against his uncle, the Transylvanian gyula. In 1003 he captured the gyula and his family and incorporated Transylvania into his kingdom. Five years later, István attacked and executed his relative, Ajtony, who had continued to defend the rights of the gyula. Then, to parry the Bulgar, Byzantine, and nomad dangers, István settled the Székelys in Transylvania. The gyula's rule was ended once and for all, and the entire territory conquered some hundred years earlier became a unified Christian kingdom.

While the early Árpáds had lived around present-day Budapest and traveled from there to their numerous courts, Géza spent most of his time at Esztergom. István selected this castle as his first capital. Near his own residence, he installed Hungary's leading bishop, later to become the primate, and he established ten bishoprics in Hungary. Those of Veszprém, Pécs, Győr, Eger, and Vác fell within the jurisdiction of the primate at Esztergom, while those of Csanád (Cenad) and of Gyulafehérvár in Transylvania reported to the archbishop of Kalocsa, as did the bishop of Bihar. In the eleventh century, Nyitra also obtained a bishopric. All Hungarians were converted, often by force (however, no attempts were made to convert Muslim or Jewish merchants). In addition to several thousand churches, Benedictine monasteries were erected, subordinated to the Chief Abbot in Pannonhalma. The two Orthodox Basilite abbeys were allowed to continue their activities. After the Byzantines destroyed, in 1018, the Bulgar state, István opened a heavily traveled pilgrimage route leading to Jerusalem through Constantinople. The route did not pass Esztergom, however, so István had a royal basilica built on it at Székesfehérvár, which became the royal family's funeral city and the site of the king's legislative meetings.

Continuing and expanding Géza's construction of earthwork forts, István used them as the capitals of districts or counties (equivalent to English shires) headed by officials, called *ispáns,* recruited both from the tribal aristocracy and knights of foreign origin. By the eleventh century, the number of counties reached forty. Free Hungarians supplied the officer corps that ran the counties and were titled "servants of the castle" *(iobagiones castri).* The rest of the population, organized into units of ten or a hundred, was given military duties or required to raise cattle or supply agricultural products. The "castle people," supported by the local Slav populations, lived in villages and worked on communal land, which was reassigned yearly. The people lived in thatch-covered huts in winter and in tents during the summer, often moving within the village's extensive territory. In the eleventh century, laws prohibited moving too far from the church. Another law demanded that burial grounds be around churches, thus tying pagan ancestor-worship to Christian holy grounds. The nobles established monasteries to serve as the burial grounds for their clans.

István did not incorporate his ancestors' court sites into the county system but kept them as royal domains, including the villages that served them. From these lands he made gifts to bishops and monasteries. The local and foreign nobles who served as ispáns owned property amounting to about one-third of the county's land, but made up mainly of small, unconnected parcels. These lands, called *praediums*, were at first worked for their lay lords by slaves *(servi)*. By the eleventh century, these people were using plows with draft animals and worked the land on their own account, delivering one-half or one-third of the harvest to their lords. When slavery disappeared, those "liberated" became the equivalent of the western serf stratum. Hungarian society under István began to resemble western feudal society. Its upper class, later called nobles *(nobiles)*, consisted of ispáns, royal soldiers *(servientes regis)*, servants of the castles, holding the position of the western European aristocracy and knights. The rest of the population became peasants, irrespective of whom they served. This early Hungarian feudal structure had a special Hungarian feature: every individual was—directly or indirectly—the king's servant. Even the most exalted individuals derived their wealth not so much from their own lands, but from that part of the royal income which was assigned to them as compensation for their service as the administrators of counties or royal domains.

Disorders and Reconsolidation

After the premature death of his only son, Imre (later canonized), István selected as his successor Peter, the son of his sister and the Doge of Venice. His nephew, Vászoly, however, sympathized with the pagan conspiracy secretly being organized by the king's opponents. Vászoly, who claimed the throne for himself and encouraged revolt, was captured and blinded, and his sons sought refuge abroad. István died in 1038 (he too was canonized and became Saint Steven, Hungary's patron saint) and Peter ascended the throne. The Hungarian high dignitaries, who felt neglected, elected instead István's brother-in-law, the palatine Samuel Aba, as their king. Peter fled to the emperor Henry III and with his help retook the throne as the emperor's vassal. The Christian lords, whose number had diminished considerably due to this partisan warfare, could not prevent the outbreak of a pagan revolt. One of the tribal chiefs, Vata, led an armed uprising, killing Peter, foreign knights, and priests, among them the protomartyr of Hungarian Christianity, the bishop Gellért.

The country's leading figures, Christians and pagans alike, now asked Vászoly's sons to return from Poland and Russia. Andrew I and his brother Béla defeated the pagans with the help of their Slav relatives and reestablished the Christian Hungarian state. Béla then successfully defended the country against Henry III, and Hungary regained her independence. Andrew's son, Solomon, even married the emperor's daughter. However, Prince Béla now claimed the throne, and in the ensuing struggle King Andrew lost his life. After Béla I's short reign, Solomon became king. Béla's sons, Géza and Ladislas, received titles and entire provinces as compensation, but the dynastic struggle continued, and Géza and Ladislas forced Solomon to flee to his brother-in-law, the German king Henry IV. Pope Gregory VII offered the Hungarian throne to Prince Géza on condition that he recognize the pope's overlordship. Géza refused and had himself crowned with a crown he received from the Byzantine emperor. His brother and successor (another future saint), Ladislas I, took advantage of the investiture struggle and occupied Croatia when his brother-in-law, the pope's vassal, died. (Some Croatian magnates had invited him to come.) Byzantium and Venice were able to expel the Hungarian forces for a short period. Pope Urban II was ready to support Ladislas provided he accepted vassalage, but he refused. His successor, Coloman, convinced the papacy that a Hungarian alliance was worth more than a forced oath of fealty and became king of Croatia, Slavonia, and Dalmatia in 1102 with papal approval. He appointed viceroys with the title of *ban* to rule each of these lands. Coloman funded his rule with income from Dalmatia whose cities' flourishing trade was protected by the Hungarians.

For the next three hundred years, Hungary's foreign policy was based on her Adriatic interests, making her the enemy of Venice and Byzantium. When Hungary's kings began to extend their rule over Serb territory, the Byzantine emperor, Manuel I, tried to counter, first by finding a claimant who disputed Géza II's right to the throne, then by trying to revive partisan struggles, and finally by placing puppet kings on the thrones of provinces south of the Drava. Manuel conquered these provinces with Venetian help. In 1071, he broke with Venice and changed his tactics. He took Prince Béla, the heir presumptive to the Hungarian throne, to Constantinople and made him his heir, hoping to gain Hungary in this manner. When Manuel's son was born, he let Béla go to occupy the Hungarian throne, which had just become vacant.

The Mature Early Feudal Hungarian Kingdom

Béla III took advantage of the uprising which ended Byzantine rule and created a new Bulgarian state. In 1185 he reconquered the lands occupied by Manuel and began the conquest of the lands of the feuding Russian princes. For a short time, his younger son, Andrew, became king of Galicia. His action left a difficult heritage to his successors because Hungary was not strong enough to expand simultaneously in the north and the south.

It was under Béla III that the early feudal Hungarian monarchy reached both its fullest development and the limits of its possibilities. In 1185, his income amounted to more than 160,000 marks (roughly 70,500 pounds of silver), about equal to the revenue of the king of France. The differences in population density and economic development in the two countries were so great that the equality of royal incomes can only be explained by the inequality of social and political structures. The French ruler shared the various incomes of his state with a powerful aristocracy. The Hungarian king used the overwhelming part of his state's revenues as he saw fit because he owned more than half of the country's territory directly and had the monopolies of coinage, customs, castle construction, and the settling of foreign immigrants. The importance of these monopolies increased considerably by the end of the twelfth century. The majority of royal income had previously consisted of revenues in kind; Béla's income was half cash, coming from the profits from coinage and the obligatory currency exchange, the income of the customs and mines, and the taxes paid in cash by the foreign settlers known as guests (hospites). These settlers were the result of the Hungarian rulers' conscious and consistent policy of taking advantage of Western Europe's overpopulation to acquire people and the latest achievements of Western civilization.

At fairs and markets, traditional Muslim, Jewish, and Russian merchants were joined by Italian, Walloon, and German traders. They offered the textiles of Flanders, the enamels of Limoges, and the weapons of the Rhineland in exchange for furs, leather, and wax but especially for the silver and copper produced in great quantities by Hungarian mines. Near the royal capitals of Esztergom and Székesfehérvár, permanent Walloon settlements (vici latinorum) were established. The latter's rights of self-government, fair holding, and exemption from customs became the model for the privileges of future Hungarian cities. In Transylvania and in the northern Carpathians, German miners opened one new bullion mine after the other. Even more significant was the massive immigration of western peasants to Transylvania and northern Hungary's Szepesség. They came, mainly in the twelfth century, from the Rhine region and became known as Saxons. The number of Walloons (known as Italians) was smaller, but they produced large profits by planting the wine region around Tokaj. These peasant "guests" received privileges far exceeding those of the local peasantry, but introduced the heavy plow and the better utilization of arable land by the open field system. They established permanent villages and introduced the construction of multi-room dwellings. The new techniques were adopted in hilly regions, while on the plains the traditional moving agriculture and animal husbandry remained dominant. The forests of the Carpathians and the mountain pastures were settled by forest-clearing Slovaks, pastoral Romanians, and Ruthenians. Increased production stimulated trade. The best craftsmen left their villages and home industries and settled near the fair grounds beside royal castles. Together with the merchants already residing there, they provided a base for future cities.

The upper strata of society became "Europeanized" even faster. Foreign knights introduced the heavy cavalry, limited to the royal bodyguard and the most prominent office holders. The garrisons of the forts remained light cavalry units and became more and more obsolete. Military changes also brought changes in clothing. Prominent persons dressed like western knights, but the majority continued to wear clothes of hemp, leather, and among the wealthy, silk kaftans decorated with furs. The common people wore long, rough woolen coats. The belts, buttons, and saddles decorated in pagan fashion disappeared.

Architecture changed the most drastically. While even the most prominent continued to prefer wooden structures and even tents as their homes, stone construction began with the building of churches. The early churches imitated the Byzantine models, thanks to Lombard builders, and were followed by Western-type churches with Lombard embellishments. The largest churches and monasteries were rebuilt to satisfy the demands of the twelfth century and represent the influence of a newer Lombard style, incorporating certain features of French architecture. (The best example of this style is the cathedral at Pécs.) The early Gothic came directly from France, with its most impressive example being the partially preserved palace of Béla III at Esztergom and parts of the Pannonhalma monastery. The Cistercians and Premonstratensians, who joined the Benedictines in Hungary, also built in this style.

Besides church building, the monastic orders, and in particular the Benedictines, supported the expansion of literacy. The introduction of Church Latin led to the gradual elimination of the ancestral runic script. Only a few short texts written in this alphabet survived, among the Transylvanian Székelys. The earliest surviving Latin texts are King István's laws and his admonitions written for his son. In the middle of the eleventh century, the first historical work, the *Gesta Ungaronum* was written, but it has survived only in thirteenth century versions. The legends that grew up around István, his son Imre, the missionaries Gellért, Benedict and Zoerard, and Ladislas I were also written down. Literary activity, which had slackened after István's death, revived under Coloman I, known as "the Bibliophile." Most of this renewed activity was ecclesiastic. Lay literature, especially in Hungarian, began under the influence of French knightly culture at the court of Béla III. The most significant author of the time was a cleric who had studied in Paris and who modestly called himself "Master P." This historian, by profession a royal notary whom future generations knew as Anonymus [sic], utilized foreign and Hungarian sources as well as oral tradition in writing a Latin history of Hungary's conquest. His work dates from the early thirteenth century, and is curious in its approach. Remembering Béla III, he assumed that strong royal power had always existed. Accordingly, he stated that the leaders of the conquest had received their lands as gifts from Árpád. He portrays these leading conquerors as heroic, consciously laic aristocrats imbued with knightly ideals. Master P. is also credited with the Hungarian translations of French knightly literature's most beloved works, the *Legend of Troy* and the *Romance of Alexander the Great*. These writings have not survived, but they made popular in Hungarian aristocratic families the names of Achilles, Priam, Alexander, and Helen. The first known Hungarian language work, "The Funeral Oration," also dates from these years.

The transformation of values and life style was strongest at the royal court, where the finances needed for it were most abundant. Already in the early twelfth century, a hierarchically organized royal household, following Byzantine and Western models, surrounded the king. The highest ranking official, the palatine, previously the manager of the royal estates, became the king's deputy in legal and military affairs. The man who replaced him as estate manager, the

Judge of the Court *(comes curiae)* soon thereafter acquired the functions and title of Judge Royal. The other court dignitaries (described in detail in chapter 5) left their managerial functions to their followers and became the king's political advisors. These dignitaries, the voivod of Transylvania, the bans of the Balkan provinces, the ispáns of the counties, and the archbishops and bishops, formed the country's ruling elite. An archbishop or bishop was in charge of the royal chancellery supervising the clerks of the royal chapel. In 1181, Béla III replaced the system of oral administration and jurisdiction with one based on written documents. Four years later, he organized the permanent chancellery. The need to produce written records for all public affairs made the need for public notaries universal. This function was entrusted to larger monasteries and royal cathedrals, and to collegiate churches. The result was that the elite of the clergy neglected its priestly duties and was transformed into bureacratic legal experts. Hungarian clerics, who used to frequent the University of Paris, where the emphasis was on philosophy and theology, began to study at Bologna, famed for its law school. Consequently, Christianity failed to be truly understood and accepted by the masses; shamanism flourished, as did the veneration of the relics of saints, to whom magic powers were attributed. This trend was reinforced by the fact that the relics of the canonized kings were officially considered the transmitters of divine will in trials by ordeal *(ordilia)*.

As the royal court grew in size and pomp, the crude products of peasant craftsmen no longer suited it. The importation of foreign luxury goods made the peasant settlements which had supplied the court superfluous. The ablest among the inhabitants of these localities moved increasingly to existing or developing cities and became professional artisans. The armament and tactics of the military guarding the forts also became obsolete. To reorganize the court and the military, the kings needed resources which could not be obtained from the garrisons or the population supporting them. Since counties and royal domains were increasingly unable to satisfy the royal court's economic needs, the king began to turn his land over to the aristocrats, who were eager to become owners of large estates.

IV

TRANSFORMATION INTO A WESTERN-TYPE STATE, 1196–1301

László Makkai

The Beginnings of the Large Lay Estates and of the Feudal Monarchy

The economic, social, and political developments of the twelfth century laid the groundwork for the great transformation of the semi-barbaric Hungarian feudal system into one resembling the Western European model which had developed a century earlier. Late in the reign of Béla III, large segments of the counties and royal estates and incomes from customs and fairs were given away by the ruler. The great office-holders began to call themselves barons, but retained the expression *de genere* in their names, indicating that their privileges and lands were based on the right of conquerors.

The transformation began with the struggle of royal rivals throughout the short reign of King Imre who came to the throne in 1196. When his brother Andrew succeeded, in 1198, in having Croatia, Dalmatia, and other smaller Balkan territories declared a semi-independent principality, a second power center came into existence. The resulting tensions produced yearly internecine conflicts and swept away the two-hundred-year-old royal estate policy. To gain and retain followers, both sides generously granted estates, legal and taxation privileges, and immunities. The conflict became very sharp when several leading royal dignitaries, including the palatine and three bishops, went over to Prince Andrew's side, and he gained the throne in 1205.

The logical, internal forces of feudalism induced Andrew II to continue on the road he had chosen prior to becoming king. A royal charter of 1217 specifically refers to the "distribution of the income of castles, counties, lands and other income to barons and warriors" as the "new institution's" basic principle. To replace lost royal revenue, Andrew II reorganized the fiscal system, basing it on the minting of coins, mining, the collection of customs, and extraordinary taxes often farmed out to Muslims and Jews.

The acquisition of private estates and the introduction of a money-based state economy were new forces and produced new questions. To these King Andrew

II gave hasty and ill-considered answers. The main reason for his haste was the need to modernize the court. He imitated the Western courts in all details, including the employment of such famous and expensive personalities as the troubadour Peire Vidal, the meistersinger Tannhäuser, and the architect Villard d'Honnecourt. Andrew's daughter, Elisabeth, became the wife of the markgrave at the Wartburg in Thuringia, one of the most important centers of knightly life. One of the early Franciscan ascetics, she died young from tuberculosis while taking care of lepers and became one of Europe's most revered saints. Andrew's massive land grants were not handed out as fiefs, but as possessions in perpetuity. Unlike the West, where the recipients owed services to their lords, even if only in theory, in Andrew's kingdom they did not. The farming out of the treasury's functions (coining, tax collecting, etc.) in the hope of quick profits rapidly brought misuses. The worst were the debasing of the coins and their obligatory exchange more than once a year. Though this was sheer exploitation, it produced less revenue than expected.

Andrew's foreign policy was not fortunate and did not increase his prestige. Between 1208 and 1216 he conducted five campaigns to reconquer Galicia, although the human and financial sacrifices could not be justified. He forced the resisting Russian boyars to recognize his younger son, Coloman, as "King of Galicia," but the short Hungarian rule ended in 1219. In the southeastern corner of Transylvania, menaced by the Cumans, he settled, in 1211, the German knights who had fled from the Holy Land. (These knights later began to organize an independent state and were chased out in 1223, bringing a conflict with the pope.) Andrew's very expensive crusade in 1217 produced nothing, but forced him to hand over to Venice, as payment for the rented ships, the Dalmatian port of Zara. When he returned to Hungary, in 1218, he complained to the pope that he "found a miserable country devoid of royal income." The "new institution" and Andrew's unsuccessful enterprises created growing social unrest. The clergy, which had lost significant income due to the "new institution," was discontent, as were all whose "freedoms" or legal and social status were endangered by the new landholding pattern. Most important were the discontented free small-holders, the royal soldiers (servientes regis), and the garrisons of the counties' castles (iobagiones castri), the future petty nobility. All those who had suffered from fiscal irregularities and the debasing of the coinage were also unhappy. Xenophobia added to the problem. Public opinion first blamed certain foreigners at court for inspiring the new policy, and court conspirators murdered Queen Gertrude (who came from Meran-Merano) and her German followers in 1213. Subsequently hatred was directed against the Muslim and Jewish employees of the treasury, abetted by the European anti-"pagan" and anti-Jewish hysteria that followed the decisions of the Council of Toledo (1218). The discontented placed their hope in the king's elder son, prince Béla. Aristocratic conspirators forced Andrew to create first a Slavonian and then a Transylvanian principality for him, in 1220 and 1226 respectively, thus recreating the second power center.

The first open opposition movement was organized by some magnates and forced Andrew II to issue, in 1222, his Golden Bull, the East European document most resembling the Magna Carta. The king had to make several promises, ranging from "reforming the conditions in the country," to forbidding the holding of multiple offices, and interdicting grants of entire counties. Most of the document concerned the rights of the royal "servants" *(servientes)* (the majority of those who forced the king's hand), protecting them from the arbitrary powers of the new landed magnates. The concluding paragraph of this document, which bore a golden seal, gave the bishops and magnates the right to resist should the king fail to keep his promises.

Later generations saw in the Golden Bull the basic charter of the nobility's privileges. At the time it was simply a list of desiderata, and the Bull's decrees were mostly not heeded. In the end, the clergy turned out to be the most effective opposition. When a revised version of the Bull was issued at the urging of the high clergy in 1231, it dealt mainly with the "freedoms of the church." The situation became so tense that in 1232 the primate of Esztergom, Robert, following papal orders, placed the country, the king, and the officers of the treasury under an interdict. Andrew II had to make concessions because the papacy, at the height of its power, used all its strength to support the Hungarian malcontents. The clergy got some compensation for the income it had lost and even obtained the banishment of Muslim and Jewish merchants. These measures eliminated the last oriental feature of the Hungarian towns. The Muslims of Pest were replaced by Germans, who received western-type city privileges of self-government, the right to hold fairs, and an exemption from customs. The central role of county fairs was at an end, and only a few fair sites developed into cities. It was also in the clergy's interest that after 1228 the royal court, under Prince Béla's leadership, began to take back the "superfluous and useless grants made in perpetuity." This action presaged Béla's policy as the new ruler, Béla IV. His openly proclaimed policy, in contrast to that of Andrew II, sought "the restitution of royal rights that have practically ceased to exist," and "the restoration of the situation which existed in the country at the time of Béla III of blessed memory." Between 1235 and 1239, royal commissions traversed the country and retook the royal domains granted to lords since 1196. The young ruler was a sharp contrast to his spendthrift father. He had strong principles, was deeply religious, and tried very hard to restore the shaken power of the early Árpáds. To restore the majesty of the royal person, he had all chairs removed from the council chamber, forcing his lay magnates to stand while participating in counsel.

Béla IV had little use for the old monastic orders, now allies of the aristocracy and deeply involved in politics and bureaucracy. He favored the newly emerging mendicant orders, in particular the Dominicans. While still prince of Transylvania, he had cooperated with them in converting the Cumans living along the lower Danubian plain and in organizing a Cuman bishopric. He sent the Dominican Julian into what is today the land of the Bashkirs to find the Hungarians still living there and bring them to Hungary. Julian found them, but returned from the banks of the Volga bringing the news that the approaching Mongols had subjugated the Hungarians there and were approaching Hungary, driving the Cumans before them. In 1237 Béla admitted some forty thousand fleeing Cumans who, being pagan nomads, did not fit in well and irritated Hungarian Christian society. He accepted them because he needed obedient and reliable military support.

Young Béla IV's mistake was that he attempted to turn back the clock. Royal power had been eroded to the point where the restitution of lands proved to be an illusory remedy. It did, however, turn the aristocracy against royal power. Restitution "was the bitter pill; it was the sword which pierced the heart of the Hungarians," wrote the chronicler Rogerius, who left a clear picture of the hatred the magnates felt for their king on the eve of the Mongol invasion.

The Mongol Invasion and Its Lessons, 1241–1242

At the beginning of the thirteenth century, Genghis Khan began the conquests that formed the Mongol Empire. It expanded rapidly and by 1221 the Mongols ruled all of Central Asia. Two years later they destroyed the Cumans. Between 1236 and 1240, they conquered the Russian principalities, with the exception of Novgorod, and by the spring of 1241 appeared on the Polish and Hungarian borders. The Mongols, called Tatars in Europe, invaded the Carpathian Basin in three columns. The northern advanced through Silesia, the southern through Transylvania, and the main force, under the leadership of Batu Khan, Genghis Khan's grandson, entered through the pass of Verecke. The total invading force consisted of nearly 100,000 men. By the middle of March, the vanguard of the main column was nearing Pest, destroying everything in its way.

The political situation paralyzed Béla IV's defensive preparations and led to a fateful scandal. According to Rogerius, the magnates' position was "let the king, who brought the hated Cumans into the country, fight." Mass hysteria resulted from a rumor that the Cumans had called the Mongols into the country. In Pest the crazed mob murdered the Cuman prince Kötöny and his followers. The Cumans, seeking revenge, moved to the Balkans, killing and pillaging on the way. Thus, on the eve of the attack, the most efficient military force was lost. The army that moved eastward from Pest lacked spirit and was badly prepared. As Rogerius noted, the magnates leading the army "were discontented and, therefore, lacked the needed will and enthusiasm. They even hoped that the king would lose the battle, making them even more important." The crucial battle was fought on April 11, 1241 at Muhi at the Sajó River, a tributary of the Tisza. The Hungarian army was annihilated, and tens of thousands fell in battle. The king escaped, with great difficulty, to Dalmatia.

After the battle, Batu Khan's armies conquered all of Hungary east and north of the Danube, while those of Kadan (another grandson of Genghis Khan) put Transylvania to the sword. The conquest was accompanied by the ruthless extermination of the population. The county centers, lacking defenses, and the residences of bishops, protected at best by moats, fences, or wooden towers, were no obstacles. Using ballistas, the Mongols leveled the primitive forts, and they put settlements to the torch. Where possible, people sought refuge in the mountains or in swamps, but the wide stretches the Mongols moved through were totally depopulated. The mass exterminations of the first onslaught continued even after the Mongols established taxation districts. They lured the people out of hiding with the help of falsified royal decrees, put them to work and then killed them.

The fleeing Béla IV appealed to Pope Gregory IX and Emperor Frederick II in May 1241, asking for intervention. Unfortunately, these two leaders were just then in sharp conflict with each other. Even the army which the emperor's son, the German king Conrad IV, had assembled disbanded when it appeared that the Danube would halt the Mongol advance. In February 1242, the Mongols crossed the frozen river and after trying without success to take a few fortified cities, including Székesfehérvár and Esztergom, speedily moved to the shores of the Adriatic Sea, where they organized a manhunt for Béla IV.

The humiliated king sought refuge in the fortress of Trau, on an island, and was finally saved when news of the Great Khan's death reached the Mongol armies in Europe. The expected problems of succession induced Batu Khan to order a general retreat in March 1242. On their retreat, the Mongols behaved as mercilessly as during their advance.

Mongol depredations lasting nearly a year had produced devastation unparalleled in Europe for centuries. According to contemporary Austrian monks, "no country had suffered such a tragedy and misery since the birth of Christ." Damages caused by sword and fire were followed by famine and epidemics. A contemporary chronicler noted that "the calamity of bitter starvation decimated the Hungarian people as effectively as the Tatars' heartless butchery." Even at the end of the century, documents often mentioned the large "empty lands," unsettled since the Mongol invasion. In the plains between 50 and 80 percent of the settlements were destroyed. In forested areas, in the mountains and in Transdanubia the demographic loss is estimated at 25–30 percent.

The ruler who returned from Dalmatia in May 1242 had to face not only the general destruction but also the implications of this tragedy. The absolute success of the Mongol invasion made it obvious that the country's defensive organization had been outdated. The majority of the Hungarian forces consisted of light cavalry, who appeared "oriental" to Western observers. Yet this army had given up nomadic battle tactics and proved useless facing the masters of this style of warfare. Hungarian tactics were a mixture of Eastern and Western traditions, as were the ineffective walls of palisades reinforced by clay bricks. Two elements of the Hungarian defense had proved effective, however: close combat with massed armored knights and stone fortifications. At Muhi, Prince Coloman, the king's brother, and Ugrin, archbishop of Kalocsa, leading small armored units of the Knights Templar, successfully repulsed the first Mongol attack. A few well-fortified county seats, well-built forts defended mainly by citizens (Székesfehérvár and Esztergom), and even the well-fortified monastery of Pannonhalma successfully resisted the Mongol siege.

The inadequacy of defensive and military organization threw a harsh light on the hopelessness of young Béla IV's reform attempts. The military measures which had proved useless belonged to that institutional system the ruler had tried to reestablish. The creation of armored units and the building of stone castles required the utilization of resources which the large landed estates represented. The defeat also showed that the obsolete early feudal institutions, including the royal counties, could not mobilize the various social strata. The defense offered by the "Latin" (Walloon) citizens at well-fortified Székesfehérvár showed the importance of fortified cities.

Equally urgent was the need to recognize the political lessons of the tragedy. If nothing else the hostility of the aristocracy had to convince the king that it was impossible to govern the country. Béla IV could only reach one conclusion: his pre-invasion policy needed drastic revision.

The "Reformation" of the Country

The central concern of royal policy after the Mongol invasion was the reformation of the state. The goal was not rebuilding the old order, but true ordered reform of the country's military, economic, societal, and political structures.

The political preconditions for reform were created by the post-1242 stability of the government. The major offices were occupied for some two decades by about two dozen "loyal barons." No partisan struggles or revolts disturbed the work of the reformers, and the king gave the barons what they wanted. A document of 1248 states "it is the power of the king that demands that he increase, not minimize, his grants." Even counties and the royal domain were given away, although Béla IV tried to keep the alienation of the land within certain bounds. He preferred to grant estates lying in areas depopulated by the Mongols or equally neglected border areas, forcing landlords to find settlers for them. The organization of landownership began in 1254 in cooperation with the local nobility. What happened was the legalization of the existing situation, a programmatic division of the land between the king and the nobility.

Because the Mongols were expected to return, the modernization of the military was the most important task of the reformers. The king used a great variety of methods to achieve this aim. In 1247 he concluded a feudal agreement with the Knights of St. John, giving them the southeastern borderlands in exchange for supplying armored cavalry and building fortifications. The knights left Hungary after a time. To secure troops familiar with nomadic warfare, Béla IV called back several tens of thousands of Cumans and settled them on the depopulated Great Plain. The military potential of the aristocracy was increased when the members of the society's middle strata, thus far directly dependent on the king, were allowed to enter into the barons' service. Land-granting documents stated that the fighters living there were "to serve their master" on condition that he lead them properly equipped (in armor) to his majesty's army. Other documents stated that in principle "the nobles of our country can enter the military service" of bishops "in the same way in which they can serve other nobles." Free men entering service in this manner were known as *familiares*. The armies of barons and bishops composed of these men *(armata familia)* became the most important segments of the country's armored might. This personal dependence reminds one of Western vassalage but was less formal and only seldom involved the granting of fiefs (see chapter 5). To elevate the best fighters to the rank of armored knights, after 1250 the royal soldiers, free owners of small or middle-sized estates serving directly under the king's command, were included (with the barons) in the nobility. They were to be members of a country-wide collective *(collegium)*, and the king promoted many of them from the lower ranks into that of free landowners. Another new military formation also came into being; the new settlers in the north were given land and "conditional" nobility in exchange for the obligation to fight in armor at the king's request. Even cities received privileges in accordance with the number of armed men they were able to supply.

Military reform naturally involved social change. While the building of modern fortifications became primarily the duty of the king and the magnates, it involved the cities too. The example was set by the king, who had the old country forts modernized and new stone fortifications erected. The greatest barons and landowners competed with the king because grants were often tied to the building of stone fortifications. The new stone forts became the symbols of the prestige of the owners of large estates.

The castle and its attached villages, the castle domain, were an entirely new phenomenon in Hungary. Reforms introduced for the sake of defense served, in this manner, as a force which modernized the entire state structure. While at Béla IV's death 37 percent of the stone forts built were still royal castles, several of the reinforced country forts were populated by "guests": the merchants and artisans who moved into them for protection. Under Béla IV and his successors, they formed new communities, joining the few remaining original inhabitants. Thus was born the *civis (Bürger, polgár)* urban class, protected by privileges. Signs of its double origin survived in documents, which still referred to them as "*cives et hospites*." The soldiers were usually Hungarians and the merchants and artisans Germans; thus amalgamation did not take place easily. A new patrician group arose, their power based on ownership of land, in particular vineyards. Indeed, vineyards were the origin of such important cities as Esztergom, Székesfehérvár, Buda, Győr, Pozsony, Sopron and Kolozsvár (Cluj, Klausenburg). German settlements, as well as county forts, also developed into cities, including Pest and Nagyszombat, Kassa (Košice, Kaschau), Lőcse (Levoča), Nagyszeben (Sibiu, Hermannstadt), Brassó (Brașov), and many others. Besides the already established Radna (Rodna) and Selmecbánya (Bănska Štavnica), German companies built additional mining towns—Besztercebánya (Baňska Bistrica) and Gölmicbánya (Gelnica). The free royal towns, depending directly on the king and having privileges of self-government, faced such difficulties of urban development that their ranks diminished rather than grew. In any case, they made Western-style cities the dominant urban agglomerations in the country and be-

came the centers of commerce and the money economy of the country. Along
the main trade routes that carried the increasing commerce with the West, yearly
fairs were established in the third quarter of the thirteenth century. The fair at
Buda was the creation of Béla IV, who thought of this town as a potential
capital.

Besides the citizens of the rebuilt cities and the Cumans, Béla IV needed
additional supporters to withstand the mighty barons. He looked to ennobled
royal soldiers and to castle garrisons, whose interests both coincided and
conflicted with those of the magnates. He made these lesser nobles an organic
part of the new political order. The loyalist nobility, too, felt the need to
create its own independent organization because the royal counties were dis-
integrating, forcing the military to find means to counter the despotism of the
barons. In several counties they organized their own courts, consisting of four
sheriffs *(iudices servientium-szolgabirók),* but these lacked the power to enforce their decisions. In 1265 Béla IV remedied this situation. A petition from
the nobility, based on preceding laws, demanded the reconfirmation of the
nobility's privileges and the restitution of nobiliary land that had been assigned to forts. Béla IV responded by recognizing as free nobiliary lands the
possessions the royal soldiers and garrisons held as compensation for their
services. At the same time he regulated the legal process by unifying the judiciary powers of the *ispáns* and sheriffs and creating county courts with enforcing powers. This measure transformed the royal county into a nobiliary
county, which became an organ of the state apparatus, because in his royal
decree of 1265 Béla also stipulated that each county was obliged to send two
or three deputies to the royal legislative assembly. This decree created the
germ of the future estates-based monarchy by trying to balance the corporate
bodies of barons and lesser nobles and by giving them representation at the
royal diets. (It took another century before this new monarchic organization
was fully developed.) By fitting together the royal free cities, the nobiliary
counties, and the autonomous Székely, Saxon, Romanian, and Cuman districts, Béla created the structure of the estates-based monarchy. He was unable, however, to make these institutions immediately effective.

In foreign policy, success and failure alternated. The Mongols did not return.
The southern borders were secure in the hands of Béla's son-in-law, Prince
Ratislav, and in the north Béla achieved the same result by securing the alliance
of the Russian princes. This left him free to get involved in the succession
struggle in Austria, where the Babenberg family had died out. Béla concluded an
agreement with the Czech king, Ottokar II, thereby acquiring Styria. He appointed his son István as its prince. The Styrian barons, however, dissatisfied
with Hungarian rule, offered their throne to Ottokar, who took it, defeating the
Hungarians in 1260. After losing Styria, István demanded of his father a share in
the country's government. The barons, who hoped to gain offices and more
land, took his side, and an armed clash ensued. István, with the title of "junior
king," received the eastern half of the country, where he introduced his own
government. Not even Béla's saintly daughter, Margaret, a Dominican nun, was
able to reestablish the peace between her father and brother.

The Last Árpád Kings

During the short reign of István V, the barons began to fight openly among themselves. Royal power became the mere appanage of the strongest baronial faction at any given moment. While Ladislas IV, nicknamed "the Cuman," was a minor, two baronial factions ruled the country alternately. They kidnapped the young king and, using him as their emblem, fought for power. One party sought the support of Ottokar II, while the other concluded an alliance with Rudolf Habsburg. On the Marchfeld in 1278, Hungarian troops helped Rudolf to gain his victory and the emperorship, establishing the Habsburg dynasty.

Ladislas IV grew into an enterprising young man and tried to rid himself of the tutelage of the oligarchy with the help of the Cumans, his mother's relatives. (The Cumans, free herdsmen, had the right to bear arms.) Because the Hungarian landlords tried to force them into service, the Cumans sided with the king, who offered to protect their liberties and tolerated their pagan religion. The barons united against the king and the Cumans. Their leader, Lodomér, archbishop of Esztergom, secured the help of the papal legate and demanded that the king fight the Cumans and force them into accepting Christianity and the life of settled peasants. Ladislas refused to issue the required "Cuman law," and the papal legate excommunicated him. Ladislas retaliated by handing the legate over to the Cumans, breaking openly with the church, and repudiating his wife. He installed himself among the Cumans, lived in a tent, and married a Cuman woman in a pagan ceremony. Lodomér organized a crusade, but before a battle could be fought, Cumans hired by the barons killed the young king.

The barons now elected Andrew III (the grandson of Andrew II), who had lived in exile in Venice, but he was powerless to end the disorders. The country, in fact, broke up into independent districts ruled by groups of barons who considered the royal domain and the lands of the church and nobility theirs for the taking. The despoiled and homeless prelates turned to the king for protection, but he was helpless and lacked even the support of the papacy. When Ladislas IV had died, the Holy See declared Hungary a vacant papal fief and gave it to the minor Charles Robert, a descendant of the Árpáds through a female line. This young prince of the Neapolitan Angevine dynasty soon found some supporters among the Hungarian oligarchs. Andrew III tried to legitimatize his own rule by calling a diet, representing the nobiliary counties but excluding the barons. The king's lawyers even made this procedure legal, but could not enforce their ruling due to the resistance of the barons, who dominated most of the other nobles as their *familiares*. The death of Andrew III, the last Árpád, in 1301 transformed the anarchy into a struggle for the throne, which lasted for decades.

The Development of the Hungarian Peasantry

The thirteenth century's three great crises—the disappearance of the royal counties and domains, the Mongol invasion, and the partisan struggles—contributed to the emergence of a peasant-landowner system resembling that which had long ago developed in the West. Previously, however, the legal position and obligations of various groups of the peasantry had been tied to their status and varied greatly. The majority of those living under direct royal jurisdiction had been free or partially free men. The king did not directly manage his domain, and, therefore, he needed no slaves. The population of counties and royal domains was organized into groups performing hereditary duties as soldiers, artisans, agricultural workers, vineyard workers, fishermen, hunters, and so on. These hereditary obligations were also treated as privileges by the royal intendants until some professions became obsolete and new ones necessary. When this happened the population was reorganized into new professional groups without changing the system. The people continued to feel secure until lands were given away in the thirteenth century.

The lay landowners used freed slaves, tied to their persons and considered a saleable commodity, to work the land and tried to force the previously free inhabitants of the former royal lands to serve them under similar conditions. These people sometimes received permission to move when the land was given away, but the shrinking of the royal domains made this increasingly difficult. The peasants accepted the new owners' demands simply to retain their lands and homes.

The peasantry living on ecclesiastic lands had originally been treated like those on royal lands, and slaves under the jurisdiction of the clergy were few. Therefore, on estates managed by the church, free peasants worked the land and paid fixed dues in produce. The clergy tried to increase forced labor, resulting in several appeals to the king in the thirteenth century. However, the less land the king owned, the more difficult it became for him to influence the life of peasants. The traditional system disintegrated and was replaced by the arbitrary rule of the landlords. The peasants, unfortunately, had to defend their position not only against the lords but also against other peasants seeking to improve their situation at the expense of others. This dissension prevented unified action. The peasantry's main goals were to regain their security, to terminate the unlimited corvée obligation, which did not leave them enough time to work their own lands, and to fix other obligations on an acceptable level.

What the peasants wanted to achieve was the privileged status of royal "guests" *(hospites)*. These guests, irrespective of where and how they lived, had fixed rights and obligations. They elected their judges and priests, paid in cash a yearly amount in accordance with the size of their land, and either sent a fixed number of soldiers to the royal army or paid a fixed amount for not doing so. Military service was the indicator and precondition of freedom in Hungary. The people living in fortified places and other free men who accepted service under a baron paid a fine, the "free denarius," if they did not perform military duties. In the twelfth century, lay lords also were calling in guests under similar conditions, but part of these people's labor, either in the form of military service or cash, went to the king. Personal freedom was the most important privilege enjoyed by royal or other guests. They could change lords at will, something which even free Hungarians could not do. When the royal county disappeared, the "free denarius" was abolished and replaced by the *collecta,* which the non-military paid directly to the king. The royal guests continued to pay only the cash tax, in accordance with the size of their land.

This was the situation which the Hungarian peasantry saw as desirable, and the anarchy following the Mongol invasion made its attainment possible. Only some of the former inhabitants of fortified places returned, and many moved to the "open lands" of the large landowners, who settled them as guests and re-served their services for themselves. The best agricultural techniques known at the time had been learned by the Hungarian peasantry too. This made it possible to establish permanent settlements in which houses and outbuildings were erected side by side on plots of fixed size *(sessiones).* Beyond the village's bor-ders each plot had its assigned arable land and meadow, while the pastures and forests were used in common. These villages were established on royal domains and on the lands of lay lords (called *praedium*s) who granted guest rights to their people. When people left their praedium plots the large self-managed estate worked by forced labor ceased to exist, and it was replaced by smaller manorial cultivation based on wage labor.

The anarchy at the end of the thirteenth century made this transformation general. When competing oligarchs not only lured away each other's peasants, but often used force to acquire them, the earlier status differences disappeared, the required services became standardized, and a uniform peasant estate emerged. The peasantry paid its dues either in cash or produce and performed minimal labor services. In exchange they owned their hereditary village plots, were entitled to the hereditary use of the lands beyond the village borders, and, most importantly, acquired the most cherished privilege of the guests, the right of free migration. The peasantry now became known as *jobbágy.* The personal dependence of the peasantry on its lords did not become as loose as in the West, but their former subservience was ended. Thus the structure of Hungarian soci-ety began to parallel that of Western Europe.

V

THE AGE OF THE ANGEVINES, 1301–1382

Pál Engel

The Supremacy of the Oligarchy

Royal power became increasingly nominal under the last Árpáds. While the formal unity of the country was maintained as long as members of the ancient ruling family sat on the throne, it became more and more difficult, and finally impossible, to enforce compliance with central decisions in the provinces. Effective power there was exercised by a few lordly families, sometimes formally acting in the name of the ruler as his local representatives but sometimes also in open opposition to him. The rule of Andrew III, the last Árpád king, was spent in the hopeless endeavor to break by force of arms the growing power of local oligarchs and in attempts to bind them to him through alliances. After his death in 1301, the effective power relation appeared undisguised, and, in practical terms, the country dissolved into semi-autonomous provinces.

The power of the new oligarchy rested on a combination of family wealth and political offices. Its members belonged to the most prominent lordly clans from the Árpád period, and their wealth was based on the generous gifts they had received for royal service to Andrew II and Béla IV. In the chaotic second half of the thirteenth century, they ran the affairs of state as barons, and, as holders of the state's highest offices (palatine, vajda, ban, and ispán), they gradually acquired the various royal estates and those attached to royal castles. Consequently, they were able to exercise practically unlimited control over certain regions of the country, forcing the lesser landlords into their service or chasing them away if they resisted. Their military strength resided in the strong stone castles that had been built in great numbers since the middle of the thirteenth century. By 1300, practically every castle either belonged to or was controlled by an oligarch.

Máté Csák is still considered the archetypal oligarch, probably because he was the most successful in opposing royal power. While he was satisfied to call himself palatine (not claiming sovereignty), in fact he ruled king-like from his

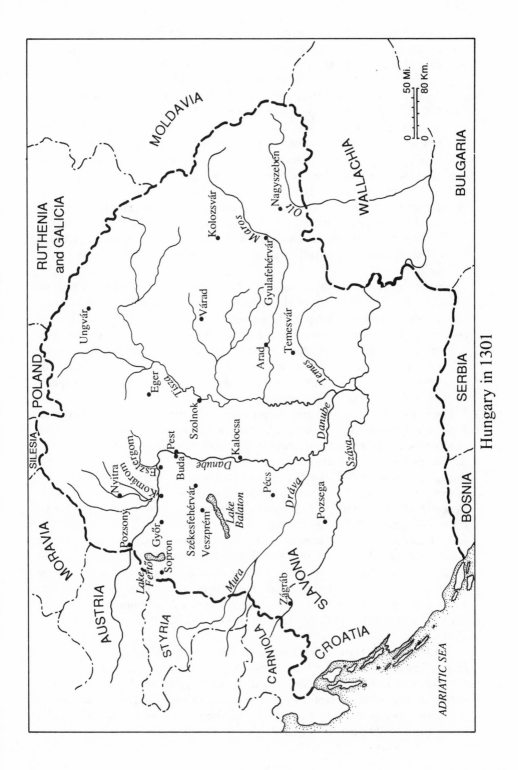

Hungary in 1301

castle in Trencsény (Trenčin) over a region stretching from Esztergom to the border of Moravia. In the northeast, in the area between the Zipps and Munkács (Mukachevo), the palatine Amadeus, a descendant of the Aba clan, occupied a similar position, with his capital at the castle of Gönc in the valley of the Hernád River. Transylvania and the Maros valley were ruled by the vajda László Kán, who had been appointed by Andrew III. The region between Transylvania and the Tisza River was in the hands of Kopasz Borsa and his brothers. The southern part of the country was controlled by another member of the Csák clan, Ugrin, the lord chief treasurer. The larger, southwestern part of Transdanubia was ruled by the masters of Kőszeg, the sons and grandsons of Béla IV's leading baron, Henrik Héder. For the overlordship in Slavonia, a bloody war was fought between the oligarchic families living south of the Sava River and Croat Babonićes. Besides these major provinces, there were several smaller ones. For example, at Diósgyőr, near Miskolc, was the court of István Ákos. This "palatine" was lordly enough to acquire a Bavarian princess as wife for one of his sons.

Yet the supremacy of the oligarchy did not signal the end of the kingdom. The three-hundred-year rule of the Árpáds had produced such a solid institutional framework that Hungary, as a political unit, proved to be viable. The continuity of the state was represented by the symbol of royal power, the Holy Crown, whose origin was already associated with the state-founding king, István I. It is certainly no accident that the crown acquired political significance for the first time in the critical years after 1301 and became the subject of a quasi-religious veneration lasting for centuries.

The respect for the crown and the prestige of the Árpáds were such that upon Andrew's death in 1301, no oligarch tried to acquire the throne. Instead, they proposed several foreign candidates for the kingship, each of them related to the Árpáds through the female line. The struggles between these candidates and their partisans produced anarchy, years of civil war, and the growth of the local power of a handful of oligarchs. A coalition of great families first brought Venceslas III, the son of the Bohemian king Venceslas II, to the throne. Though not yet of age, he was the descendant of Béla IV and the fiancé of Andrew III's only daughter. The new king considered the situation so hopeless that he quickly returned home and transferred his Hungarian claims, in 1305, to the Bavarian prince, Otto Wittelsbach, the grandson of Béla IV. Soon after being crowned, Otto was captured by László Kán, the master of Transylvania, and was lucky to reach Bavaria alive in 1306. His departure left only one candidate, the most persistent of them all, the Angevine Charles Robert (Charles I), a grandson of István V.

Charles was half French, half Hungarian. His great-grandfather, the brother of Louis IX of France, was Charles, Duke of Anjou, who, with papal help, acquired the throne of Sicily in the 1260s and with it the Kingdom of Naples. Since then, the family had ruled in Naples and could count on papal support for its foreign policy ventures, including the acquisition of the Hungarian throne. Because his family had already tried this in 1290, Charles Robert was an experienced claimant. He entered Hungary in 1301, and his partisans promptly crowned him king. Although the crown used was not the holy one, and the legality of the coronation was therefore disputable, he considered this event the beginning of his reign. At first he had relatively few followers, but as the other claimants disappeared, his camp grew, and the support of the Church, and especially that of the papal legate, proved decisive. Cardinal Gentilis, who came to Hungary in 1308, removed the last obstacles from Charles' path to the throne. With the entire ecclesiastic hierarchy and most barons having joined him, one oligarch after the other paid him homage. He was crowned a second time, with a makeshift crown, in 1309 and finally, on August 27, 1310, with the holy one after Cardinal Gentilis forced László Kán—who had had the crown since Otto's flight—to return it. Once again, the country had a legal king, and the interregnum came to an end.

The Reunification of the Country

The third coronation was only the beginning of the establishment of a new dynasty. Charles had to fight long and hard before the country had not only a king, but also a real master. His task was difficult: he had to end the anarchy that had prevailed for decades and liquidate the power structure of the dreaded oligarchy, which was in the process of becoming institutionalized. That he was ready to undertake this seemingly hopeless task is in itself deserving of respect. That he accomplished it makes him one of the most successful rulers of the Middle Ages. No chronicler found this struggle important enough to record it, and what we know rests on fragmentary documentary evidence.

The king's base of operations was the south, whose lord, Ugrin Csák, was one of his first and most determined followers. The new king made Temesvár (Timișoara) his temporary residence and base of military operations in 1315 and selected Visegrád, in the center of the country, as his capital only eight years later, after the end of the hostilities. From the southern counties, he directed campaigns in every direction, expanding his rule over the entire country. With great patience and tenacity he besieged one castle after another, restricting the movement of their masters. At first his army was small, but as time passed it grew as important nobles from all parts of the country, who had had more than enough of the oligarchs' arbitrariness, rallied behind him. Charles was also successful in isolating his enemies from possible help from abroad. He and the king of Poland were close friends; the sister of the king of Bohemia became his wife; and the Austrian Habsburgs, his maternal cousins, even gave him military assistance.

Charles was also aided considerably by his foes' behavior. Instead of uniting, they gave him the chance to deal with them individually. Only once, at the beginning of the struggle, did the oligarchs attempt joint action, but without success. The sons of the deceased Amadeus Aba turned to Máté Csák for help, but they were defeated on June 15, 1312 in the Battle of Rozgony (Rozhanovce) near Kassa. Several of the Aba castles fell into the hands of the king. After this first victory, Charles dislodged Máté Csák from Visegrád in 1315, the lords of Kőszeg from Transdanubia in 1316, and defeated the Borsa brothers near Debrecen in 1317. Later he conquered Komárom (Komárno), while his lieutenants liquidated the remnants of Aba power in the northeast. Between 1318 and 1321 came the conquest of Transylvania, and one year later Slavonia capitulated. Charles respected only Máté Csák's power. He waited until his death in 1321 before sending his troops into the newly lordless provinces. The reunification of the country was complete in 1323, when Pozsony opened its gates to the king. Only then could Charles claim to be the true master of the country. While the lords of Kőszeg half-heartedly tried to organize revolts, no one could any longer doubt the authority of the Angevine dynasty.

During the following years, Charles concentrated his energies on the consolidation of his power. Though during the hostilities he had proved to be a capable military leader, Charles was primarily a politician and not a soldier. He never risked what he had already gained and avoided irresponsible action.

Once the unity of the country was assured, the majority of the nobility hoped that the new dynasty would resume the Árpáds aggressive foreign policy, especially in the direction of the Balkans. They were certainly disappointed when they realized that the king had no intention of following his predecessors' example. Charles accepted without a fight Venice's overlordship in the Dalmatian cities that the Árpáds had claimed and did not even attempt the subjugation of the recalcitrant lords of Southern Croatia. He concluded an alliance with the ban of Bosnia and was satisfied with his nominal homage, leaving him in possession of the provinces of Sol and Ušora, which had come under Hungarian rule in the thirteenth century. He conducted only a few Balkan campaigns. One of these allowed him to reestablish the Banate of Macsó (Mačo) in northern Serbia (1319), while another almost resulted in a major defeat, justifying Charles' cautious policy. In 1330, he had decided to teach his southeastern neighbor, the Wallachian ruler, Basarab I, a lesson. After nominally submitting, Basarab entrapped the approaching Hungarian army in one of the passes of the southern Carpathians. Charles and the majority of his army were saved from destruction only by the self-sacrifice of one of his followers.

Whenever possible, Charles worked for peaceful relations with his northern and western neighbors. With the Polish kings Władisław I and his son Casimir III (the Great) he maintained a firm alliance, in which he tried very hard to include the Luxemburg rulers of Bohemia and Moravia. This was no easy task, because the Poles claimed Silesia, which was under Bohemian rule, and the Luxemburgs actually demanded the Polish throne. The outstanding issues were settled in 1335, when the three rulers met in Visegrád, with Charles acting as mediator. The meeting ended with the formal alliance of the kings. Although not specifically stated, it was obvious that the new alliance was directed mainly against the masters of Austria, with whom Charles' relations had become strained due to border disputes. The Czech-Polish-Hungarian political agreement was subsequently reinforced by dynastic ties. Charles, who had been married since 1320 to Casimir's sister, arranged the engagement of his son Louis to the daughter of the Czech crown prince.

Charles died on June 16, 1342, and was succeeded on the throne by one of his three sons, Louis I (the Great), born in 1326, who ruled until 1382. His second son, Prince Andrew, was supposed to inherit the throne of Naples and had lived since 1333 in the court of his great-great-uncle Robert, king of Naples, whose heir and granddaughter Johanna was his wife. In spite of the long struggle leading to mastery of the country, Charles had had less trouble in establishing a dynasty than in becoming popular. His contemporaries valued his son's martial spirit and ostentation more than Charles' determined and purposeful policy and thrift. They soon forgot that the passing glory of the son rested on the work of the father.

Louis the Great

What the Hungarian nobility wanted was not a wise statesman, but a warrior king who saw in war and not in peace the road to glory and divine grace. This attitude corresponded to the spirit of the time. In Louis I they got such a ruler. From him they got what they wanted: an aggressive foreign policy, yearly military action, and regular income in the form of loot. It is not surprising that he acquired the epithet "the Great" immediately after his death, and that for centuries his long reign lived in the nation's memory as the most glorious period of its past greatness, offering some solace for "the misery and the bad conscience of the present."

As far as can be established from the biased surviving sources, Louis had a commanding personality, reminiscent of Edward III of England, with the important difference that in his country Louis was much more dominant. In contrast to Edward, he did not have to struggle with Parliament and obstreperous barons, and he could base his policy solely on his dynastic interests. The foundations of Angevine power had been laid so solidly by Charles that nothing could shake them until Louis' death. As far as can be gleaned from the sources, Louis was also free of financial worries. There was certainly always enough money for military ventures. However, the military balance sheet produced more glory than profit; Louis was a glorious warrior but certainly not an efficient or circumspect ruler.

The difference between glory and success is well illustrated by Louis' Neapolitan adventures. These were prompted by the fate of his brother Andrew, who had been living at the court of his great-great-uncle, King Robert of Naples, since 1333. When King Robert died in 1343, his granddaughter Johanna, Andrew's wife, inherited the throne. Andrew had to be satisfied with the modest status of a prince consort. The Hungarian court spared no effort to see him crowned. The queen mother Elisabeth went to Italy and, according to contemporary sources, spent more than five tons of gold and even more silver in bribes and for propaganda. The sudden shower of Hungarian gold florins created a sensation on the gold-starved Western money market, but it failed to achieve its aim. By the time Louis succeeded in winning the pope, the overlord of Naples, to his cause, Andrew had been killed by his enemies. This occurred in 1345, and two years later Louis was on his way to Italy to punish his brother's murderers.

Hungarian historians have always dwelt with pleasure on Louis' two Neapolitan campaigns, during which the king repeatedly gave proof of his personal courage. The unvarnished truth is that these expeditions cost much blood and money without producing any concrete results. During the first campaign (1347–1348), the Hungarian king conquered all of southern Italy in a few weeks, entered Naples, and added "King of Jerusalem and Sicily" to his other titles. It was easier, however, to conquer a far-away land than to keep it. As soon as Louis departed, his garrisons found themselves in a desperate situation. The same problem arose following his expedition of 1350. Louis finally had to accept that the unification of Hungary and Naples was a pipe dream, and he withdrew his troops from southern Italy in 1352.

Louis' campaigns against his southern neighbors to gain their allegiance to Hungary brought similarly meager results. Since the twelfth and thirteenth centuries, the kings of Hungary had considered themselves—irrespective of the political reality of the moment—kings of Račka (Bosnia), Serbia, Bulgaria, and of "Cumania" (later known as Moldavia and Wallachia). Louis felt that his armies were strong enough to transform these nominal sovereignties into effective ones. The international situation was relatively favorable. The only great Balkan power, the realm of Tsar Stepan Dušan of Serbia, disintegrated in 1355. While the Ottomans had taken permanent possession of Gallipoli a year earlier, establishing themselves on the western shores of the Dardanelles, they were still far from the Hungarian zone of interest.

Louis spent much time and energy in attempts to force the Balkans to recognize Hungarian supremacy, in most cases leading his armies in person. Because the chronology of his southern campaigns is still unclear, their number is also uncertain. Undoubtedly he attacked Bosnia three times and Serbia on five occasions. He moved against Wallachia at least four times and invaded Moldavia probably seven times. Only once did Louis attempt permanent annexation: in 1365 he captured the Bulgarian tsar of Vidin and replaced him with a Hungarian governor, a "ban of Bulgaria." The experiment was not encouraging. Within a short time the position of the Hungarian garrisons became so precarious that Louis found it more advantageous to accept the homage of the tsar, and he reinstated him in 1369. These were not wars of conquest, and it is quite likely that the other Balkan campaigns had the same goal: to force the various rulers into accepting positions of vassalage. Looting was certainly an important consideration also. The number of campaigns attest that the political goals were not achieved. Hungary's military supremacy is evident from the fact that no one could contemplate, let alone mount, a counterattack. Nevertheless, some noteworthy Hungarian failures were recorded. During the 1363 Bosnian campaign, the situation was so confused that even the seal of state was lost, and a new one had to be carved. Before recognizing Louis as his overlord, the prince of Wallachia annihilated a Hungarian army including its leader, Transylvania's vajda. Because he subsequently submitted, the prince was not punished for this deed.

Only the Croatian and Dalmatian wars brought tangible results. The northern provinces of Croatia had been reunited with Hungary in 1322 by Charles, but he had left the lords of the south unconquered. Louis defeated them in 1345, and all of Croatia was ruled once more by a Hungarian ban, as had been the case under the Árpáds. It was more difficult to acquire the port cities of Dalmatia. Zara (Zadar), Trau (Trogir), Spalato (Split), and Sebenico (Šibenik) had been the prizes over which Venice and Hungary fought for centuries. As early as 1346 Louis and his army had besieged Zara but suffered a crushing defeat. The second Venetian war, however, brought success. In this war Louis was helped by allies from northern Italy. The Venetians were unable to fight successfully on several fronts, and in 1357 a number of Dalmatian cities submitted to Louis, including the crucial city of Zara, after a lengthy siege. The Hungarian king's conquests were legalized on February 18, 1358 in the Peace Treaty of Zara. Venice guaranteed free navigation of the Adriatic to the merchants of the Dalmatian cities and was even forced to accept Hungarian protection over Ragusa (Dubrovnik) in southern Dalmatia. These achievements were finalized as the result of Louis' third Venetian campaign (1372–81). In this war most of the fighting was done by Venice's great maritime rival, Genoa, but the results favored Louis. According to the Peace of Turin (1381), he not only kept Dalmatia and Ragusa, but Venice was also obliged to pay him a yearly tax of seven thousand gold florins.

Louis' aggressive foreign policy was directed mainly against Italy and the Balkans. In relations with his northern and western neighbors, he followed his father's policy and worked for peaceful relations. He had a very close and friendly relationship with his maternal uncle, Casimir of Poland, whom he supported repeatedly (1345, 1351, 1352, 1354) in his wars against the latter's dangerous eastern neighbors, the Lithuanians. Casimir had no children, and as early as 1339 he promised the Polish throne to the Hungarian Angevines. Louis had to wait patiently, but Casimir finally died, and on November 17, 1370 the Hungarian king was crowned in Poland as his successor. The short-lived Hungarian-Polish union (1370–1382) did not satisfy Hungarian hopes and brought Louis more troubles than glory. His rule was not popular in Poland. The Poles took offense when Louis placed Halich (Galicia) under Hungarian rule, and they resented even more the fact that he did not live among them but was represented in their country by a governor. Until 1376 this was his mother, Elisabeth, who, although Casimir's sister, surrounded herself in Kraków with Hungarians. This was at the root of growing irritation and dissatisfaction, culminating in 1376 in the massacre of the queen mother's Hungarian retainers.

During the last years of his life, Louis was more and more preoccupied by the question of succession. The once numerous Neapolitan Angevine dynasty was near extinction. Louis had no sons and only one distant male relative, Charles, the prince of Durazzo (Durrës), who had grown up in the Hungarian court. Charles was a possible successor, but Louis, although he liked him, had other plans. His second wife, Elisabeth of Bosnia, had borne three daughters, Catherine, Mary, and Hedviga. Louis hoped that one of them, together with her future husband, would succeed him on the Hungarian and Polish thrones.

The possibility of acquiring two thrones with the hand of one princess awoke great interest in most European courts, and especially in those of the French Valois and the Czech-German Luxemburgs. In the ensuing competition, the French took the lead in 1374 when the crown princess Catherine became engaged to Louis, Duke of Orleans, the brother of the French king, Charles V. Catherine, however, died before her father. As a consequence, Sigismund, markgrave of Brandenburg, the son of the emperor Charles IV and brother of the Czech king Venceslas IV, since 1375 the fiancé of Mary, now became the presumptive heir to the Hungarian and Polish thrones. In exchange for serious concessions, known as the Privileges of Kassa, Louis secured the agreement of the Polish magnates. He compensated Charles of Durazzo by lending him some Hungarian troops, with which he occupied Naples. Louis died on September 10, 1382, believing that the future of the Hungarian-Polish Empire he had created was secure.

Angevine Society and the Emergence of the Nobility as an Estate

Surveying the reigns of the first two Angevines, one gains the impression that their active foreign policy was made possible by domestic order and stability. Scholarship has confirmed this view. The sources do not mention violent social movements. On the contrary, they show that the Angevines assured a relatively secure existence for their country's population, although they constantly menaced the neighboring states. This period of stability was important for the development of Hungarian society. It witnessed the end of those violent transitory processes that, since the beginning of the thirteenth century, had destroyed the archaic societal structure of the Árpád period. With the end of this disintegrative process under the Angevines, two more or less homogeneous strata, which were to be the major components of Hungarian society for centuries, emerged: the serfs (iobagio) and the nobility. The development of serfdom, which occurred during the troubled decades around 1300, has already been discussed. The final shaping of nobiliary society took place under the first Angevine.

It must always be kept in mind that medieval Hungary was situated on the periphery of Christian Europe. This meant that the structure of her society and economy and her institutional organization remained archaic compared to those of the West, or, at best, that it continued to retain some outdated features. Among these, probably the most characteristic and peculiar were the dominant role in society and the specific structure of the nobility. Only in neighboring Poland was the situation comparable. In both countries power remained in the hands of the nobility for many centuries. The other two determinant elements of medieval European society, the Church and the cities, played only a very subordinate role in these two states. The concept of the nobility was very different here than in feudal Western Europe, although similarities did exist.

The major similarity between the Hungarian nobility and that elsewhere in Europe was its caste-like elite position; status was inherited and protected by specific privileges. One of the major differences was that, up to the sixteenth century, the position of the Hungarian noble rested on his ownership of land. If for any reason the noble lost his land, he also lost his nobility. Already in the fourteenth century, the noble *(nobilis)* was only a land-owning person *(homo possessionatus)*. In the general opinion of the time, a sharp distinction was made between him and the popular masses, who, because they did not own "noble land," were forced to live on somebody else's "in the manner of peasants." Because they were non-owners *(impossessionati)*, they were automatically also non-nobles *(ignobiles)*. Both city dwellers and serfs belonged to this category.

In Hungary, the nobility constituted a much larger proportion of the population than in Western Europe. The majority were people who, in fact, lived like peasants, though naturally they were still a small segment of the total population, not more than 3–5 percent according to fifteenth century estimates. Nevertheless, tens of thousands of families belonged to the nobility and became the guardians of a "noble mentality," which influenced society as a whole. The central feature of this attitude was pride of ownership. After all, it was land ownership and the privileges attached to it that raised even the most miserable poor noble above his fellow subjects and permitted him to feel superior to those from whom he differed neither in life-style nor moral values.

The large noble population resulted from the merging of three societal elements in the thirteenth and fourteenth centuries. The richest were the descendants of the ispáns, the ruling elite of the Árpád period. Some of these claimed that their forefathers had been the leaders of the migrating and conquering Hungarians, while others listed among their ancestors those knights who came from the West in the eleventh through thirteenth centuries and were rewarded with large estates. The bulk of the Hungarian nobility, however, was not made up of these relatively few, partly rich families, but of the descendants of those free Hungarian warriors who called themselves "royal servants" in the first half of the thirteenth century. After 1267 they are already mentioned in the sources as nobles. It was their massive action that forced King Andrew II to issue his Golden Bull in 1222, granting their privileges. In later centuries this document was considered to be the first and most important written guarantee of the nobles' rights and freedoms. The third segment of the nobility emerged when the royal castle system disintegrated, beginning with the end of the thirteenth century, and most of the fighters of this system, known as castle warriors, also became nobles. In the Angevine period their descendants were regularly listed as nobles. The noble estate also included the originally lower-ranked and less privileged nobles of Transylvania and Slavonia. This centuries-long development was finally legalized by the famous legal code of Louis I (1351). This document not only confirmed the Golden Bull of Andrew II but specified, once and for all, that all "true" nobles living in the country were entitled to the same freedoms *(sub una et eadem libertate gratulentur)*. As this law makes clear, not all nobles were "true" nobles. For example, those who lived on estates owned by the Church and were obligated to serve in perpetuity as soldiers had the status of nobles but were not among those who enjoyed all the rights and freedoms of the nobility.

The nobles did not pay taxes to the state, nor could troops be quartered on their property. After 1405 they were even exempted from paying the tithe. Only the noble's person, his family, his home *(curia)*, and the plot on which it stood were privileged. The people who lived under the seigneurial jurisdiction of the nobility were not included. These exemptions were, therefore, most important for the lesser nobles, who worked their land themselves, though only these privileges differentiated them from the peasantry. Another important prerogative enjoyed by the nobles was that in important legal cases they were subject only to the jurisdiction of the king or of the country's highest judges (palatine and judge royal). They remained free until a valid judgement was passed against them.

In the last analysis, all prerogatives rested on the fact that nobles owned land as freeholders, i.e., in the form of allodia. The feudal institutions of Western Europe were not transferred to Hungary. With very few exceptions, the principle of granting lands in exchange for feudal services remained unknown. The nobility claimed descent from the conquerors of Hungary and considered that its ancestral lands were its share of the occupied country. Consequently, this land was considered free and could not be encumbered. By the fourteenth century, most of the nobility's property consisted not of ancestral lands but of royal gifts, but by this time, the freehold concept was so deeply embedded in the thinking of the nation that these gifts too were considered allodial. The nobles got them in "perpetual ownership" from the king for services rendered and not conditionally for future services. Thus the nobility did not owe feudal military service and had to resort to arms only if the country was under attack and the king called for a "general levy" *(generalis exercitus)*.

The conservatism of the nobles prevented the introduction of feudal institutions and was firmly anchored in their attachment to patriarchal traditions. These became an integral part of the customary laws and gave the nobility its particular features. The most prominent of these were the lack of free disposition of land and the predominance of patriarchal custom. During the thirteenth century, especially in the troubled decades, the owners' rights of disposition were liberalized, and the ability of the individual to resist the claims of his relatives was greater than in later times. The Golden Bull of 1222 made free testatory dispositions possible, and we have indications that even the buying and selling of estates was possible. In the Angevine period, however, conservative tendencies gained the upper hand. The relevant paragraph of the Golden Bull was declared inoperative by Louis I in 1351, putting an end to a developmental trend. The new legal system, which remained in force for centuries, was based on the principle of entailment *(avicitas)*, meaning that the noble estate was the common property "in perpetuity" of the ancestor, i.e., of the original owner and his male descendants. This principle remained unchanged even if the heirs decided to split their possessions—also with eternal validity. In this case also, their right to inherit from each other remained unchanged. Should one branch of the family become extinct in the male line, the other branches were entitled to its possessions. In this system of inheritance, the individual's alternatives were very limited, and females could play only a minimal role. Boys inherited the land in equal measure, while the so-called "girls' quarter" *(quartalicium)* had to be paid in cash and movable property. The new system was somewhat favorable for the Crown also. Because the right of free testatory disposition was abolished, the lands of extinct clans reverted to the king.

The Angevine State

The immense energy expended by Charles I in the destruction of the oligarchy brought positive results. The conquered land was the king's, and he could create a new ruling system, one which proved more stable than either those that preceded or those that followed it. The power of the king was never greater than under the two Angevines. When, in their documents, they referred to the "plenitude of their power" *(plenitudo potestatis)* in the manner of their great Sicilian ancestor Frederick II, the claim rested on considerable fact.

Angevine power was based on the immense wealth that the confiscated lands of their enemies represented. During the struggle of Charles I with the oligarchy, practically every castle and estate acquired new owners, changing the distribution of landed property drastically. While the royal domain had diminished rapidly and constantly during the thirteenth century, now the process was reversed. The king retained the greater part of the reconquered lands, using the rest to reward his partisans. In this manner he created a wealthy landowning aristocracy, which remained the constant supporter of the dynasty. He also amassed a royal fortune, compared to which even the largest private wealth appeared insignificant. When Louis I died in 1382, the royal family owned 15 percent of the country's land. If this appears relatively modest, because the Church owned the same amount and the nobility the rest, it is important to remember that the king was the master of about half of the country's fortresses (he owned about 150 castles and the domains attached to them) and also owned most of the larger cities and markets. The royal domain had not only economic significance, as in the past, but was also important politically. The royal castles demonstrated the stability of royal power, and the income derived from the appurtenant estates was used to reward the most important royal officeholders. It served, therefore, to lure a part of the nobility into royal service, making the maintenance of royal power important for them. The result was the creation of a court aristocracy, which became differentiated from the nobility at large and served as the societal basis of the monarchy. This relatively small but influential group, imbued with an aristocratic mentality, was unreservedly loyal and the foundation on which Angevine power rested. They ran the affairs of state and profited materially from the prestige associated with wielding power. This group provided the chief lay and ecclesiastic dignitaries of the realm. More than any other element in Hungarian society, the court aristocracy could expect to receive estates and privileges. Consequently it did everything possible to increase the power of the dynasty.

The elite of the court aristocracy was formed by the highest lay and ecclesiastical officeholders. Sources refer to them as the prelates and barons of the realm (*praelati et barones regni*). Included in this group were the two archbishops and twelve bishops, the chief justices of the realm, the palatine (*palatinus regni*), the judge royal (*iudex curiae regni*), the lord chief treasurer (*magister tavarnicorum*) (who was the chief justice of the cities since the days of Charles I), the regent of Transylvania with the title *vajda* as well as those of the southern provinces, the bans of Slavonia, Croatia, and Dalmatia, Macsó, and Szörény, and, finally, the chief dignitaries of the royal household (*aula*)—the master of the horse (*magister agazonum*), the royal cup-bearer (*master pincernarum*), the warden of the king (*magister dapiferorum*), and the lord ostiary (*magister ianitorum*). In a wider sense, the officers of the queen's household and all those charged with the command of royal castles or the administration of counties were also considered to be barons. In fact, the government was run by the prelates and barons, who were the members of the king's permanent council, which decided all politcal issues and represented the country in foreign affairs.

Barons were recruited from among the wealthiest nobles, although they owed most of their wealth to the Angevines' generosity. In spite of this, their power and exceptional status in society did not rest on their noble descent and wealth but on their "honors" (offices) and on the usufruct of castle estates' incomes, which they were granted provisionally by the king. This primitive form of rule had been general in Western Europe too in the ninth through twelfth centuries, before it was replaced by feudalism. In Hungary it served as a substitute for the feudal system, and, while it probably had roots in earlier times, it flourished under the Angevines. In the fourteenth century the income of most royal castles was used to remunerate the barons, with only a few castles remaining under the direct management of the king's or queen's household. A baronial "honor" could sometimes comprise as much as eight or ten castles and was usually connected with the governance of a province. These domains, which the baron held "at the king's pleasure" were always much larger than his own inheritance. In a sense, the barons became a service aristocracy within the estate of the nobility. Their rank derived not from their wealth but from their offices and honors.

The court aristocracy included, besides the barons, all those who, in one or another form, belonged to the ruling institution and profited from it. Members of the king's, queen's, and the barons' retinues belonged in this group. The king's retinue, fairly disorganized under the Árpáds, became well organized under the Angevines and played an important role in the running of affairs. Under Charles I its permanent name became *aula regia* and corresponded to the Anglo-Norman royal household in composition and functions. The *aula* had a hierarchical organization and included knights, squires, and pages. They made up the king's immediate entourage and were always there to carry out his orders. The members of the *aula* were primarily responsible for putting into action the decisions of the king and his barons. The queen had her own *aula*, organized along identical lines. This institution too was very important politically during the reign of Louis I, because of the queen mother Elisabeth's great influence on him and thus on the country's affairs. In the widest sense, the retinues of the barons were also members of the ruling institution. They represented their masters by governing their castles and running their offices, sharing the accompanying incomes and power.

Naturally, everybody at court was a noble. In a society built on the strict differentiation between nobles and non-nobles, the latter could advance only in the church. Nevertheless, only a small segment of the nobility profited from Angevine rule—those who were either rich or lucky enough to enter royal, baronial, or possibly a prelate's service. This service took the institutionalized form of *familiaritas*. Occasionally this is mentioned as the Hungarian version of feudalism, but it resembled it as little as the income received as an honor resembled a fief. The noble who became the *familiaris* of the king or a great lord entered into his service only as a person. His possessions were not involved. By swearing fealty to his lord, he became a member of his household and his dependent. What tasks he performed depended on the position of his master. Occasionally a great lord's *familiaris* governed an entire province. His service consisted of work for which he was paid either in cash or in goods. If he owned noble land he remained its free master, irrespective of what duties he performed. The privileges which were his as a noble remained inviolate.

The honors of the barons and the institution of *familiaritas* were the pillars on which Angevine power rested. Honors attracted most of the aristocracy into royal service, while *familiaritas* gave lesser nobles a chance to rise in the service of either the ruler or his barons. Although not yet beyond dispute, it appears that the same twin pillars supported the Angevine army also. What is certain is that in the numerous wars of Louis the Great, the royal, baronial, and ecclesiastic units played the major role. It is also clear that those who fought in these units were *familiares*. It was the right and duty of prelates and barons to command troops under their own banner (*vexillum* or *banderium*) in battle. Hence the name of this type of army organization, the banderial system. The army was composed entirely of cavalry. Its core consisted of armored knights, but its major component was made up of lightly armed bowmen. Special units were furnished by the dreaded marauding units of free Székelys and the non-noble Cumans and Jazygians. In the hope of loot and rewards, numerous independent nobles also joined the royal army. More than once Louis I proclaimed the general levy arbitrarily for his external ventures.

In the fourteenth century, orders were mainly given orally, and soldiers played a greater role in running the state than did clerks. Literacy grew, nevertheless, by leaps and bounds in the Angevine period. In all aspects of life, government included, the role of writing increased significantly. From the Angevine period several tens of thousands of documents have survived in contrast to the mere ten thousand from all the previous centuries. The majority of these, as with most medieval records, are legal documents. They either fix privileges or are the products of court proceedings. The administration of justice was the branch of government in which literacy became practically universal in this period, making the legal procedure both more professional and more complicated. In 1342 Louis I transferred to his capital, Visegrád, those courts (the palatine's and the judge royal's) which had nationwide jurisdiction. In 1377 he created a third permanent court, which operated in the name of the king in his "special presence." In fact it worked under the supervision of the lord chancellor. Literacy, although to a lesser degree, increased in state administration too, bringing about the growth of the chancellor's office. Besides the traditional great seal of state in the safekeeping of the lord chancellor, Charles I began to use a secret seal also. With time this became the true symbol of the royal will. For a while, under Louis I, the royal signet ring was also used. Around the secret seal, a secret chancellery was organized in 1374. Those serving in the chancelleries and courts were recruited more and more, as the century progressed, from those lay people who, while not university graduates, were thoroughly familiar with the local customs, quite similar to the English Common Law. Louis even attempted to organize a Hungarian university on Czech, Polish, and Austrian models though the one established at Pécs in 1367 as well as that started at Óbuda in 1395 closed their doors after a few years.

The Economy and Royal Economic Policy

The picture that emerges of Angevine Hungary is that of a country that, in spite of developments, was archaic compared to feudal Europe, due both to the patriarchial nobiliary structure of her society and to the system of honors on which her government was founded. This relative backwardness characterized her economic structure also and was most obvious in the low density of the population and the low level of urbanization, resulting in the minimal economic and political role of the cities.

During the reign on Charles I, between 1332 and 1337, papal tax collectors traversed Hungary and produced, for each bishopric, lists of the papal tithe paid by each parish. Records are lacking for three sees, but nevertheless these documents give an idea of the population distribution of the early fourteenth century. They prove that the plains and the hill country had long been well settled, but there was still plenty of room for additional settlers in the forested border regions. We have no firm statistical data, but it is certain that the population density did not reach twenty-five people per square mile; overpopulation was not a danger. The European demographic crisis of the fourteenth century hardly affected Hungary. While the bubonic plague did not spare the country and killed, among many others, Louis' first wife in 1348 and several barons in 1360, it probably did not do much damage in the villages, and no indications of famines have survived.

The significant settling of Slovakia and Ruthenia began in earnest in the Angevine period. These counties were inundated by Ruthenian, Polish, and occasionally German settlers, creating numerous villages on newly cleared land. The royal, ecclesiastic, and baronial estates of Transylvania saw the arrival of masses of Romanian peasants who immigrated after the 1320s, mainly from Wallachia. These people were mainly sheep herders. This colonization lasted in certain regions until the seventeenth century and even later, significantly determining the ethnic composition of these regions. During the first Angevine migration, the settlements generally followed the pattern of the German *Ostsiedlungen* (eastern settlements). They were organized by rich German entrepreneurs who became the free hereditary headmen and judges of the new villages and were known either as *scultetus* or *advocatus*.

Although it did not change significantly the pattern of settlement, urbanization also advanced after Angevine rule was firmly established. Urbanization must be understood primarily in the legal sense. In the fourteenth century, the number of localities that acquired urban privileges grew by leaps and bounds. The sources mention them either as "free villages" *(liberae villae)* or as "cities" *(civitas)*. These urban rights included the right to elect the local judge, which meant local self-government and exclusion from the jurisdiction of the county's ispán. The latter stipulation excluded these localities from the honors of the barons, with taxes being paid directly to the royal treasury. These "cities" became economically important for the court, which explains why Charles I and Louis I were generous in granting letters of urban freedom. These documents alone could not transform the villages into cities, however. The economic preconditions for this transformation were missing, and not even Angevine power could create them. Cities in the Western European sense remained rare. If city walls are considered the symbol of the political autonomy of the European city, then Hungary had less than twenty, and these were small and relatively poor. The populations of even the largest—Buda, Pozsony, Kassa, Sopron, and Nagyszeben—were limited to a few thousand. A few patrician families were the masters of the cities. Most of these were German in origin and speech and, until the end of the fourteenth century, thought of themselves more as landowners than as merchants. While they maintained good relations with the nobility, they lived in aristocratic isolation amid their fellow citizens.

Foreigners were struck by the rarity of cities and their lack of people. An unknown traveler, who wrote a *Descriptio Europae Orientalis* in the early fourteenth century, spoke of Hungary as an "empty land." After Mantua's ambassador crossed Transdanubia in 1395 on his way from Dalmatia to Buda, he reported the impression of seeing practically nothing except forests. He certainly exaggerated, because this region was already the most densely populated in the country, where village followed village, but he was probably right to note the great difference between Hungary and Italy. What he noticed was economic underdevelopment.

It is easier to list the symptoms and indicators of backwardness than to explain its causes. Most of these were rooted in the centuries-old social structure. A geographic factor must also be stressed for Hungary had become a backwater of international trade by the fourteenth century. After the Mongol conquest of Kiev in 1240, the major international trade routes no longer passed through

Hungary. Transit trade and the profit derived from it became insignificant. The country became the terminus of trade routes leading into it mainly from Vienna and Dalmatia. Consequently, the staple rights of Buda had no international significance compared to Vienna's, and no administrative measures could alter this fact. Nevertheless, the Angevines tried. Together with the Czech and Polish rulers, Charles I attempted to divert the western trade from Vienna to Kraków and Brno, while Louis I gave Kassa staple rights in 1347. None of these measures could save the Hungarian economy from dependence on Western merchants. By the fourteenth century, Italian merchant houses were the most important in Hungary as elsewhere in Europe. While the Florentines were naturally in the lead, the role of Paduan capitalists was also noteworthy. After 1330 the number of German merchants, mainly citizens of Nürnberg and Köln, was on the increase, and within a short time Hungary became a hunting ground for German tradesmen. After 1344 Louis granted numerous customs privileges to German cities and trading companies.

Foreigners were drawn to Hungary mainly by bullion, especially gold. Prior to the discovery of America, Europe suffered from a chronic gold shortage and until Florence issued its famous florin in 1252, gold coins did not circulate. The spice trade with the Levant absorbed whatever gold was available, and only the black West African states could supply a meager replacement. Under these circumstances, gold mines were highly valued. In the fourteenth century, Hungary turned into a veritable El Dorado. Her silver production was already among the most significant in Europe, but gold had hardly been mentioned. After 1320, however, one rich mine after another was opened at Körmöcbánya (Kremnica), Nagybánya (Baia Mare), and in Transylvania, and silver production also increased. Contemporary estimates from the middle of the century placed the yearly yield of Hungarian mines at 4,500–5,000 pounds of gold and 22,000 pounds of silver. The majority of the mines were situated on the royal domain, and the miners, mostly Germans from Bohemia-Moravia, were enticed to move into the country by very generous privileges granted to them by Louis I.

Both the promotion of mining and the regulation of the country's monetary system were the work of Charles I. His monetary reform proved to be of lasting importance in two respects. First of all he ended, once and for all, the anarchy in minting practices that characterized the Árpád period. He abolished the practice of issuing new money yearly, which went hand-in-hand with a forced return of the old coins to the treasury, and beginning in 1323, and permanently after 1336, he issued silver coins with a constant value. The treasury's resulting loss was compensated by the introduction of a new tax aptly called "the chamber's profit" and it was collected from each serf household. The second measure was the introduction of a gold coin, the *florenus,* modeled on the Florentine florin and minted with a precision and weight that was unaltered for centuries.

While the flood of bullion made the king and court very rich, it proved to be of no value to the Hungarian economy. What happened is very similar to what occurred in Spain after the discovery of the New World. The gold did not reach the producers but the members of the ruling elite, who pursued a life-style of conspicuous consumption. They were interested in luxury items that the unpolished craftsmen of the few Hungarian cities could not produce. The Italian and German merchants supplied spices, arms, and high quality textiles in large quantities in exchange for large amounts of gold, which the Hungarian economy was unable to retain. The Hungarian gold florenus made the rich Western merchants even richer, while its influence on the Hungarian economy was minimal if not detrimental.

Cultural and Court Life

Since the days of Saint István Hungary had been a part of Christian Europe, and during the thirteenth and fourteenth centuries it became superficially more European in character. The traveling knight, merchant, or priest on an eastward journey could feel more or less at home in Hungary. He found cities built in the Western manner, knightly castles, and churches and monasteries. He could converse in Latin with well-educated clergymen and meet knights and burghers dressed in the Western manner. Nevertheless, the traveler encountered numerous signs in Hungary indicating that he had reached the borderland of Europe.

Two social groups were the main transmitters of European culture, due to their close contacts with the West—the mainly German inhabitants of the cities and the clergy, who belonged to the international organization of the church. The fourteenth century saw the rapid development of cities and in them the erection of numerous new buildings. The remnants of the earliest patrician homes and baronial mansions, found under the ruins of baroque buildings after the destruction wrought by World War II, date from this period. Most of these are in Buda and Sopron. The parish churches from these years also illustrate the wealth of cities; probably the most impressive of these was the St. Mary's Church (today's Matthias Church) of Buda's German burghers.

As elsewhere in Europe, the typical fourteenth century cityscape included the churches and monasteries of the mendicant orders. Helped by the protection of the royal court, these orders entered Hungary fairly early. At first the Dominicans were favored, and between 1221 and 1300 they established twenty-five monasteries; the most important was in Buda, where, around 1304, a theological school *(studium generale)* was established. (Its ruins are part of the Hilton Hotel today.) Not far from it, on Rabbit Island (today's Margaret Island), they also maintained a nunnery, which became famous as the refuge of Margaret, a daughter of Béla IV. Her father had contemplated a politically important wedding for Margaret, but with the help of the Dominicans she disobeyed him, living in the cloister on the island until her death in 1272. (Her tomb became a site of miracles and was visited by many pilgrims, and as early as 1276 the court made unsuccessful attempts to have her canonized. The partially surviving papal protocol dealing with this issue is the most interesting document of the cultural history of the period. (Margaret was finally canonized in 1943.) Because they supported Margaret, the Dominicans lost the court's favor.

The future belonged to their rivals, the Franciscans. They had had their own province in Hungary since 1238, and by the end of the Middle Ages the Franciscans established 115 monasteries in the country. The funds were supplied mainly by barons and magnates. The ruling elite favored, in general, the more traditional forms of monasticism. Other monastic orders also gained ground all through the thirteenth century, and up to 1270 one richly endowed monastery after another was built for the Cistercians and the Praemonstratensians. When their popularity ceased, their place was taken by the Pauline order (of Hungarian origin), which took its name from the hermit Saint Paul. The Paulines followed the rule of St. Augustine, which the papal legate approved in 1308. In 1367 the pope officially sanctioned the order's activities. While their reclusive form of monasticism was already on the wane elsewhere, in Hungary the number of Pauline monasteries reached ninety by the end of the fifteenth century. With the help of the Angevines, the order entered Poland, where its monastery at Częstochowa (established in 1382) is to the present day the favored place of pilgrimage of the faithful.

Not only did the tastes of the lay elite determine to a considerable extent the development of ecclesiastic institutions, but they also shaped worldly culture. In the thirteenth and fourteenth centuries, this ruling circle was made up almost entirely of members of the dynasty and the court aristocracy, in whose lives Western influences intermingled with the customs of the Hungarian nobility. While this amalgam gave the court culture of the later Árpáds and the Angevines a somewhat European complexion, the Hungarian element remained dominant. Western influences had a greater impact on outward appearances than on mentality. These external influences were visible in the fine arts, as, with some delay, Hungarian artists followed the general European trends. Buildings were erected mainly in the Romanesque style until roughly 1250, when the Gothic became dominant. The builders were certainly in part foreign masters, but the majority consisted of Hungarians who had studied abroad. The best of these served the court. Judging from the few structures that survived the massive destruction of the sixteenth and seventeenth centuries, these artists produced first-class work. This also is true of the other art forms. The highest European standards were equalled by the italianate royal castles of Zólyom (Zvolem) and Diósgyőr, the remnants of the well of the Angevine palace at Visegrád, and the remains of carvings from Louis the Great's funeral chapel at Székesfehérvár. The same can be said about the few remaining manuscripts of the royal library, especially of the *Illuminated Chronicle*, a summary of Hungarian history, famous for its splendid miniatures (*circa* 1360). The famous sculptors of Kolozsvár, Martin and George, were probably also of Hungarian origin. Most of their work has disappeared, but their mastery survives in their statue of St. George (1373), presently in the Narodní Gallery in Prague.

The court did adopt some of the customs of knightly life. In the thirteenth century the magnates donned knightly armor and to a limited extent began the use of coats-of-arms. Descriptions of knightly tournaments survive from the Angevine period. However, on the first page of the *Illuminated Chronicle*, a picture of Louis I's court, only some barons are dressed in the Western manner, wearing stockings, while the others wear long caftan-length coats. Clearly the Hungarian court never became a truly knightly establishment. What was absent, first of all, was the Western knightly culture and mentality. This is quite obvious in literature. Only the slightest indications exist that the most popular chivalric epics dealing with the Trojan war and Alexander were known in the royal court of Hungary in the thirteenth century. Lyric poetry was unknown. The place of poets of chivalry was taken by popular bards, whose major topic had to be unreserved praise of the barons and their ancestors. Probably the best known "knightly legend" in Hungary was that of Nicholas Toldi, one of Louis I's knights. It survived in a sixteenth century version and became popular thanks to János Arany's nineteenth century lyric trilogy.

The survival of archaic values from nomadic times fits into the already discussed origins and values of the Hungarian nobility. According to all indications, the nobility was very consciously cultivating its distinctive traditions, even in Christian surroundings. The only form of secular literature that flourished from earliest times, historical writing, proves this point. While most authors were clerics, in these works the pagan heritage received a much more detailed treatment than did the influence of Christianity. Around 1200, a priest—known today simply an Anonymus—who had studied in Paris and who referred to himself as the notary of a king, probably Béla III, used his imagination in recounting the conquest of Hungary. In his *Gesta Hungarorum,* he presented the Árpáds as the descendants of Attila the Hun. (His is the earliest surviving secular work although we know that earlier works existed.) Another cleric of noble origin, Magister Ákos, invented the theory of the common ethnicity of Huns and Hungarians. His theory not only gained general public acceptance but until quite recently influenced scholars too. Based on this work, Simon Kézai was able to produce a historical work around 1285 in which he reconciled the nobility's unique ideology with the most up-to-date political theories of the West. His work proved to be extremely influential in and after the fifteenth century. Among the historians of the Angevine period, by far the best was János Apród of Solymos (known as János Küküllei), who described in gesta form the deeds of Louis I.

Naturally, all these works were written in Latin and were available in very few copies. Because the culture of the secular elite was entirely oral, written Hungarian developed in the context of the Church. The earliest written remnant of the Hungarian language, dating from around 1200, is a one-page funeral oration. The first known poem, *Mary's Lament,* dates from about a century later. The refined style proves that Hungarian poetry had to be fairly common by this time. The earliest codex in Hungarian *(circa* 1370) also deals with a religious topic, the life of St. Francis. The surviving copy was produced around 1440.

VI

THE LATE MEDIEVAL PERIOD, 1382–1526

János Bak

Succession Struggles, 1381–1387

After the death of Louis of Anjou, the succession was anything but smooth. He had no son, but at first it seemed that his new, loyal aristocracy would have power enough to guarantee the succession, if not of his daughter, at least of her future husband. The older daughter, Mary, betrothed to Sigismund of Luxemburg, son of the emperor Charles IV, was indeed crowned soon after her father's death, having confirmed the privileges of the nobility (this became the accepted practice at every coronation). Sigismund had numerous followers in the country, but little power as margrave of Brandenburg to make his claims good, and the dowager queen Elisabeth had other marriage plans for Mary. Mary's rule, or rather that of her mother and her favorites, was challenged by the adherents of Charles of Durazzo, king of Naples, whom Louis had educated in Buda. Supported by the great lords of the southeast, above all by the Horváti clan, and by a great many lesser nobles who found the inheritance in the female line an anomaly, Charles landed in Dalmatia to assert his claims. He was crowned king of Hungary as Charles II on the last day of 1385, having forced the queens to acquiesce formally to his rule.

Years of civil strife followed. Charles was assassinated by the queens' agents only thirty-nine days after his coronation; the two royal ladies were taken captive; Palatine Miklós Garai was killed; and a few months later the queen mother was strangled by Garai's men. The death of Charles and the capture of Mary turned the tide in favor of Sigismund. A group of great lords who had appointed themselves guardians of the realm, acting in the name of the holy crown and swearing to defend the interests of the kingdom even against its ruler, offered the crown to the margrave. After signing an agreement with his followers assuring them a share of power in return for support, Sigismund was elected and crowned king. With the help of Venetian diplomacy, he soon secured the release of his wife and ruled "in concert" with her until her untimely death in an accident in 1395.

For almost two decades Sigismund's hold on the kingship was at best tenuous. During the early years of the reign, still fighting for the throne and his wife's life, he could hardly help giving away much of the royal domain. Through donations in perpetuity or mortgages (which were rarely redeemed), more than half of the castles and estates of the Angevines were in the hands of the barons by the end of the century. The royal domain, which in the fourteenth century was still sufficient to remunerate barons and supply the household, had virtually vanished. Out of 230 major castles and estates, only forty-seven were in the king's hands in 1407. By reversing his policy later, Sigismund recovered ten or so additional castles. Of the approximately twenty-two thousand villages of Hungary, of which some 3,350 (15 percent) were still the property of Angevine kings and queens, Sigismund could retain merely 1,100 (5 percent). Most of the Crown's losses became the gains of a handful of great landowners, who also enlarged their properties at the expense of lesser nobles.

Sigismund's Struggles with External and Internal Enemies

Sigismund was the first of the kings of Hungary who had to contemplate seriously the defense of the realm against Ottoman advances. After the Turkish occupation of the southern Balkans, the first skirmishes between Ottoman and Hungarian troops were fought under the Angevines, but the magnitude of the danger was not clear until the defeat of the Serbian and allied troops at Kosovo Polje in 1389. Following the traditions of Hungarian foreign policy and the mood in the country, Sigismund embarked on several offensive forays into the border areas in response to incursions by Ottoman detachments into Hungarian territory. In 1395, he called on the chivalry of Europe to confront the pagans. The crusading knights assembled in impressive numbers: "Their lances could have upheld the sky from falling," wrote Sigismund about the host of Burgundian, French, German, and Hungarian warriors. However, the days of the mounted knight were about to end. The international army lacked discipline and unified command, in contrast to the not much larger, but well-trained contingents of Sultan Bayazid, whom they encountered at the lower Danube. The defeat the crusaders suffered at Nicopolis (Nikopol) on September 28, 1396 cost the lives of many knights, and hundreds of thousands of ducats ended up in the Sultan's coffers as ransom for the notable captives. It had also shown that even a joint European chivalric action could no longer beat the Ottomans in open battle.

Although the defeat did not enhance the king's position at home, it gave him an occasion to propose serious reforms. At a diet in 1397 in Temesvár, to which the nobles sent legally empowered deputies from every county, a military reform was enacted. The obligations of prelates and barons to supply banderia for the defense of the realm was regulated in a more systematic fashion, and, as an innovation, it was decided to augment these feudal levies with a militia. This was to be supplied by every landowner, at the ratio of one light cavalryman for every twenty (later thirty-three) tenant holdings. Whether this *militia portalis* (so called from the tax units, *portae)* was to consist of peasants or of hired soldiers is unclear, but they were paid and equipped by the nobility according to their landed property.

At the same diet, Sigismund tried to build an alliance with the county nobles by confirming the privileges of 1222 and 1351 (without, however, the clause on the nobles' right of resistance!) and promised to dismiss his foreign counselors, whom they resented. Of course, their dislike was motivated less by national or ethnic motives than by the fact that these counselors owed their position to the king's pleasure and not to noble family connections. However, Sigismund did not keep his word, and a few years later he was openly attacked in Buda, and many of his Czech and German followers were killed. In 1401, the king's own party rebelled against Sigismund and took him captive, while a baronial council administered the realm in the name of the Holy Crown of Hungary. This device proved useful in giving the magnates a legal base of power and also indicates the progress made during the interregnum and under the weak king toward an abstract notion of a state distinct from the person of the ruler. However, before the "council of the realm" was able to agree to offer the crown to another prince, Sigismund negotiated his release by making an alliance with his captors and marrying Barbara Cillei, daughter of the powerful Slavonian lord, Count Hermann Cillei, thereby also becoming the brother-in-law of the leading Hungarian baron, Miklós Garai the younger.

The last major challenge to Sigismund's rule came from King Ladislas of Naples, the son of the hapless Charles of Durazzo, who in 1403 tried to renew his father's claim to Hungary. Supported by Rome (the pope disapproved of Sigismund's adherence to his rival in Avignon), he landed in Dalmatia, accompanied by a papal legate, and had himself crowned. He could count on a good number of dissatisfied Hungarian lords, who had sworn an oath on the relics of Saint Ladislas to abandon Sigismund, but the king's league proved to be more powerful and swiftly restored order. The king returned from Moravia, where he was pursuing Luxemburg family matters, appeared in the Castle Visegrád, and presented himself to the people under the "Crown of Saint István"—thus counterbalancing the symbolical power of the oath of his adversaries. The troops of his party took care of the rest. Ladislas returned to Naples, and most of his Hungarian followers were pardoned by the victorious king.

The papal support for the pretender offered Sigismund a good occasion to proclaim the king's supreme right of patronage in the Hungarian Church and to prohibit appeals to Rome. This so-called *placetum regium* (1404) was a major step toward gaining control of the wealthy Hungarian prelatures. A decade later, at the Council of Constance, Sigismund negotiated an agreement with the pope-elect about his rights in the Church. Although these were soon abrogated by the Holy See, future kings of Hungary wielded considerable power through *de facto* appointments of their favorites to lucrative and influential positions in the Hungarian Church.

Government and Reforms under Sigismund

Sigismund was now finally in a position to stabilize his rule. In 1408 he united his faithful barons in a formal league, the Order of the Dragon. This was based on the new aristocracy, the great landowners, whose power rested on extensive landed properties with several castles each and thousands of tenant peasants. They were now regularly called barons, not because they held "baronial offices" (as had their predecessors under the Angevines), but merely because of their status and wealth. They held some seventy or eighty castles, far more than the king.

In the subsequent decades, Sigismund issued a series of important laws on criminal jurisdiction, coinage, and trade and confirmed the right of peasant tenants to change lords. He attempted to strengthen the legal and economic position of the towns, whose deputies he had consulted on several occasions. However, the increasing conflicts in Bohemia and Germany tempted Sigismund all too often, and his interests turned more to the West. For years the country was in fact governed by the barons of his league, and, as far as one can ascertain, not badly. Sigismund's last decades were more devoted to European than to Hungarian matters. The impact on Hungary of the personal union with the Holy Roman Empire (1411–1439) needs more study than has hitherto been devoted to it. It certainly permitted many Hungarian barons, churchmen, and even lesser knights in the entourage of the king-emperor to acquaint themselves with ideas and institutions very different from those of Hungary. They accompanied the king to Italy and Germany, were present at the Council of Constance, and became familiar with the great issues of the age. The growing role of legally trained secretaries in the king's council and his secret chancellery, the attempt of Sigismund to centralize the administration of Hungary, and his reliance on councilors with burgher and lesser noble backgrounds surely received some impetus from Western models.

Cities and Market Towns

Sigismund's interest in the cities may have been influenced by his experiences in much more urbanized Bohemia and Germany but was essentially due to his need for regular income and also for fortified bases, once most royal castles had been lost. Continuing the development of the capital, started by Louis around 1350, Sigismund ordered the construction of a magnificent new palace in Buda and initiated extensive building works in Visegrád and Pozsony. Hungary had very few cities in the early fifteenth century: contemporary reports speak of twenty walled ones altogether. These were in fact that handful of urban settlements which enjoyed the same privileges as Buda, were directly subject to a judge royal (the *magister tavarnicarum),* were, as corporations, regarded as having equal standing with a nobleman, and were later to be called "royal free cities." They included, besides Buda, Pozsony, Sopron, Nagyszombat, Kassa, Bártfa (Bardjevo), and Eperjes (Prešov). A dozen more unwalled cities had approximately the same status. Sigismund encouraged the building of walls, as in the case of Kolozsvár, and the cities of the Saxon communities in Transylvania, headed by Nagyszeben and Brassó, did the same. The mining towns of northern and northwestern Hungary were under the jurisdiction of the Chamber, thus closer to royal liberties, but many of them were alientated in the fifteenth century. The location of these cities suggests that the limited urban development was motivated by external trade: cities of any importance grew up at the gates of trade routes toward Austria, Poland, and the Balkans. There was virtually no network of cities in the central areas of the country.

The economic boom that Hungary had experienced in the fourteenth century, when her gold and silver briefly dominated the European economy, did not become the basis of an economic flowering. The profits of mining precious metal enriched Italian and later South German entrepreneurs, either as their earnings for administering and managing the mines and mints or as the result of Hungary's continuous negative balance of trade. From the customs data of the mid-fifteenth century, we are able to estimate the order of magnitude (if not the exact size and proportions) of Hungarian foreign trade. It amounted to about 200,000 gold florins annually, of which 80 percent was import. Most of the imported goods were fine and medium quality textiles (79 percent), metalwares (12 percent), and some spices and sundry (9 percent). The export consisted almost exclusively of cattle and wine, with a minimal amount of textiles and metalware going south to the Balkans. In the course of the century, agricultural exports increased somewhat, but so did the need for better textiles and luxury goods. Wine exports to Austria and Poland also grew, but the transit trade towards the Ottoman areas probably declined. The 174,000 florin foreign trade deficit was paid with massive exports of silver, gold, and, later, increasingly of copper. As a student of the economic development of the period put it, Hungarians were "a poor nation in a rich country."

The close connection with external trade is also obvious from the internal structure of the cities. Their leadership came originally from German *Ritterbürger*—half-adventurers, half-traders—then was taken over by families of German long-distance traders and finally, occasionally, by mixed groups of merchants from Germany and Hungary. Under the Angevine kings, the Italian presence in Buda was conspicuous, but at the end of the century South German entrepreneurs began to take over. Although Sigismund attempted to inhibit trade "with foreigners," the trend to conduct business to the advantage of the South Germans remained unchecked. These merchants had the capital needed for the exploitation of the natural resources and the connections to export them. Thus they could skim off the profit from Hungary's main commodities and had little interest in developing domestic manufactures.

Royal support for urbanization was rather haphazard. Sigismund's "urban decree" of 1405 attempted to standardize weights and measures according to Buda's customs and to strengthen urban liberties by granting royal justice to walled cities and urban privileges to some developing market centers. Yet only a few years later Sigismund gave away Debrecen, one of the towns that had just received new liberties. The cities were not united among themselves, were economically too weak to count for much, and, under baronial rule, had little chance to become a political factor. Because the kings of the fifteenth century had to resort repeatedly to squeezing out additional revenues by taxing the cities (or requiring "loans" from them), the urban sector was essentially seen as a source of cash and as valuable military support, and were not the objects of conscious economic policies or of significant alliances with the crown.

The leadership of the rich merchants was occasionally challenged in the fifteenth century but nowhere broken. The craftsmen were too poor to bring about changes in city government comparable to those of the *Zunftrevolutionen* in German towns or of the communes of western and southern Europe. Most cities were rather small compared with those of the neighboring countries: Buda had some eight thousand inhabitants, two or three other cities three to five thousand and the rest far fewer. Urban unrest broke out in Buda in 1402, when members of the richer craft guilds attacked the old Council of Twelve and elected a popular assembly of thirty-six members (including members of some lesser guilds). The conflict was probably more an expression of Italian-German rivalry than of internal social confrontation. However, in 1439, the renewed conflict pitted Germans against Hungarians, the latter representing the up-and-coming skilled craftsmen. Henceforth, half of the council was to be elected from the Hungarian burghers, and the magistracy was to alternate between the two groups. Ultimately, though, the council remained in the hands of rich merchants, now joined by some successful Hungarians.

While the development of true cities lagged behind that in the countries west of Hungary, the size and number of market centers had grown ever since the fourteenth century. These were, in fact, overgrown villages, with weekly markets and occasionally even annual fairs. The market towns (in Hungarian *mezőváros;* in the sources mostly *oppidum* in contrast to *civitas*, city) developed from the free villages and the centers of estates of the preceding centuries. They were situated along trade routes, the meeting points of plains and highlands and in the specialized agrarian areas (such as livestock and wine-producing districts). By 1440 there were some three hundred of them, and by 1520 about eight hundred settlements were so classified, even though probably only three or four hundred of these were in any way genuine market centers. *Oppida* did not enjoy urban privileges, although some of them were granted certain autonomous rights by their seigneurs, and the tenant farmers living in them were often permitted to pay their *census* in a lump sum. The market or agrarian towns attracted many enterprising peasants and some craftsmen working for the less sophisticated internal market. While a typical peasant village comprised not more than twenty or thirty *portae* (tax units) (with perhaps twice as many families), *oppida* counted at least one hundred *portae,* some even as many as three to five hundred. They were much more evenly distributed over the entire territory of the realm than were cities. The role of these towns in Hungary's belated urbanization is a debated issue and one with implications lasting into our own time. Certainly, however, they secured greater personal liberty, some social privileges, and economic access to commodity production for many thousands of peasants and served as nuclei of exchange. They also furnished some cultural and administrative centricity. On the other hand, the many hundreds of small, semi-urban communities may have only decentralized the limited internal market and thus slowed down even further the growth of genuine cities. Owing to their dependence on ecclesiastic or secular lords, the market towns were at the mercy of their owners, few of whom realized the possible profits they might reap by supporting urban development. Even the king, as a landlord, was not consistent in protecting his *oppida*.

Hussitism and Rural Revolt

The inhabitants of the agrarian towns seem to have been more affected by reforming and revolutionary ideas than any other segment of the population. Hussitism, for example, which most Hungarians experienced merely as the plague of incursions from Moravia by Hussite armies, took root precisely in the *oppida* of the wine-producing country of Syrmium (Srem). It was here that Hussite preachers prepared the first Hungarian translation of the Bible (which has survived in several incomplete versions). Here, too, in 1436–37, the papal inquisitor, the Minorite Giacomo di Marca, found thousands of heretics to burn at the stake. The Hussite community of Kamanc (Kamenica) was forced to flee and ended up in Moldavia. As we shall see, in 1514, the market town population also played an important part in the greatest rural revolt of medieval Hungary, and *oppida* came to be significant centers of the Protestant Reformation as well.

It has been suggested that Hussitism had some influence on the first recorded major peasant revolt in Hungary, the uprising of Hungarian and Vlach (Romanian) tenants, settlers, urban poor, and petty freemen in Transylvania in 1437–38. Recent studies have dismissed any immediate connection between this uprising and Hussite teachings. The immediate cause of the rebellion was the demand of Bishop György Lépes that the tithe be paid in coin, and for several years of arrears, as well as that petty noblemen and Romanian settlers, exempt before, should also pay their due. A major issue was the increased restriction on the movement of peasants from one landlord to another, having once paid their dues. This matter came up at several Diets, and Sigismund repeatedly legislated in favor of peasant mobility. Apparently, however, the land to labor ratio developed unfavorably for the landowners, especially the lesser ones, and lords began to hinder the movement of their tenants. Under the leadership of a poor nobleman, Antal Budai Nagy, supported by the plebeian element in the city of Kolozsvár (Cluj), the armed revolt was initially successful. Apparently, the need to arm and train the peasants of Transylvania, exposed as it was to Ottoman attacks, meant that a broad segment of the rural population was familiar with the art of war. Having scored a victory over local noble troops at Bábolna (Bobêlna) on

June 6, 1437, the peasant leaders negotiated an agreement with the bishop and other landlords at the monastery of Kolozsmonostor. In this, the *universitas regnicolarum,* the community of inhabitants of the realm, was assured of a solution to the tithe dispute, guaranteed the right of free transfer to other lords, and freed of the seigneurial tithe (the *nona).* Other burdens were also lightened. Annual meetings were to be held, where complaints could be made against violators of the agreement. This document is significant, insofar as it opened up the possibility of corporate development (including peasants) in a way similar to, for example, Tyrol. However, the landowners, having been taken by surprise at the outset, prepared a counter-attack. In the fall, the "three nations of Transylvania," namely, Hungarian nobles, free Székely guards, and privileged German (Saxon) settlers, concluded a pact assuring mutual support against the Hungarian and Romanian peasants. (This Union of Kápolna was renewed in February 1438 as the Union of Torda and remained the constitutional cornerstone of Transylvania for centuries to come.) Strengthened by the united support, the lords forced the peasants to accept a less favorable agreement, which was to be submitted to King Sigismund for arbitration. Disarmed by the protracted negotiations, the peasants became easy prey to the landowners' troops. The last center of resistance, Kolozsvár, fell in January 1438.

Losses and Defense at the Southern Border

Although the very negative assessment of Sigismund's achievements that used to dominate textbooks has been revised in recent decades, it cannot be denied that the king's Western European orientation caused losses to Hungary. Among the country's neighbors, Venice was the first to use the king's many absences to reconquer the Dalmatian territories, claiming that Ladislas of Naples had sold them to the Signoria in 1409. In 1433 a truce was signed, in which Sigismund accepted what he could not or would not alter. After three hundred years, Hungary's Dalmatian presence ended. At the other end of the country, Sigismund lost territory to Poland: on one of the many occasions he found himself short of cash, he pawned thirteen towns of northern Hungary in the German-settled area called Szepesség. These were never redeemed and were returned to the realm only after the partition of Poland in 1772.

The greatest losses were sustained by Hungary outside of her borders. The Ottoman Empire, recovered from succession struggles, expanded its control in the Balkans to the confines of the "buffer states" that had protected Hungary from immediate Ottoman attack for decades. Hungary did not use the period of Turkish-Mongol wars and the years following the Ottoman defeat at Ankara to recover territory taken by the Muslims in the preceding years. The defeat at Nicopolis certainly suggested that offensive actions had little chance to succeed, and Sigismund learned that lesson well. His attempts at securing the loyalty of Balkan rulers during the time of Ottoman weakness were partially successful: the ruler of Serbia, Despot Stefan Lazarević, was a true ally for decades, and in

Bosnia, Hervoja was also won over for some years. But neither the Wallachian rulers nor the decentralized authorities in Bosnia could be drawn over to Hungary's side.

Faced with the decrease of Hungarian influence beyond the borders, Sigismund and his barons, above all his Florentine financial councilor and commander, Pipo Scolari, concentrated on building up the defenses along the kingdom's southern border. Scolari was given command over several counties and banats as well as the income of the salt monopoly (which he reformed) to rebuild and reorganize the fortresses of southeastern Hungary (with Temesvár at its center) and establish a system of defenses along the entire southern border. In the course of a decade, Scolari, in concert with a number of southern Slav princes and nobles who had fled their country and found refuge in Hungary (frequently with a good number of retainers), established two lines of border forts from the lower Danube to the Adriatic Sea. The mobile troops were frequently supplied by the light cavalry of the refugee South Slavs, experienced in anti-Turkish warfare and always a match for the pillaging expeditions of *sipahis*. The keystone of this system, the Castle Belgrade, was acquired by Sigismund in negotiations with Despot Stefan Lazarević. Scolari's successors, the Talóci brothers, Ragusans by origin, managed to unify the command of the entire southern defense. For its upkeep, they held two banats, forty-four castles, the income from the salt mines, the portal tax and several episcopal sees, as well as the estates of the Hospitalers. Under favorable circumstances, the fortresses and the mobile defense permitted even offensive actions. Even though the line of defense had to be pulled back close to the country's borders, Sigismund and his barons' achievements cannot be disregarded: it was in fact this system that protected Hungary for almost a century from being overrun by the Ottoman army.

Albert I (1437–1439) and the Double Coronation of 1440

The death of Sigismund in late 1437 presented a succession problem, for Sigismund was the last member of the house of Luxemburg. He left no son, but his daughter Elisabeth was married to Albert of Habsburg, duke of Austria. Following the example of Mary and Sigismund, Albert was "elected" king. Elisabeth and Albert were crowned on New Year's Day 1438. However, the administration of the queen and the Garai-Cillei clan while Albert was absent on imperial and Bohemian business brought about a reaction by the nobility. The *decretum* passed by the Diet of 1439 indicated the rise of a new power in the realm, that of the assembled county nobility. The promises Albert had made to the leading magnates, like his father-in-law half a century before, were formulated in the interest of the prelates and barons and aimed at dismantling whatever remained of Sigismund's reforms. In contrast, the law of 1439 included several clauses limiting the rights of the aristocrats, which strengthened the king's hand in granting offices and properties without the approval of the barons. As a matter of fact, Albert made use of this right and gave away most of the castles and estates that had been recovered by Sigismund. Thus the final dissolution of the Angevine domain may be dated from the years of his short reign. Barons received some twenty-five castles and the queen about fifteen.

In 1439 the Ottoman army attacked Serbia, Hungary's ally. The noble levy was called up, but too late to rescue the land of Djuradj Branković, Despot Stefan's successor. Serbia fell, the despot fled to Hungary, and Albert died of dysentery in his camp, hardly more than two years after his ascension to the throne. With the king's demise, the smoldering conflict between court and county nobility flared up. A few months after Albert's death, his widow bore him a child, Ladislas, called Posthumus. Elisabeth's adherents, the courtly or Habsburg party, led by Ulrich Cillei, were supporters of "legitimacy" (a Western orientation) and the succession of the infant to the throne. The queen managed to have the Crown of Saint István taken from its guardians, and her son was crowned on May 5, 1440 in Székesfehérvár. Their opponents, the party of the "soldier barons," and their supporters, the numerous nobility of the counties, were more interested in the southern orientation and favored the elective principle of kingship. They wanted to have a king on the throne who could actively lead the fight against the Ottomans. They turned to the king of Poland, the young and valiant Władysław II, called Jagiełłonczyk, and asked him to accept the crown. This was also a demonstration of the Diet's power to elect the monarch. The baronial electors made sure that Władysław I (Hungarian form, Ulászló) first signed election promises and upon his coronation swore an oath to uphold a set of ancient privileges presented to him by the noble assembly. These included not only the Golden Bull, but also a set of decrees issued in assemblies of the late thirteenth century, and apparently forgotten for 150 years, which reflected the far-reaching political program of the lesser nobility and clergy. Since the Crown of Saint István was in the hands of the queen and her party, Władisław had to be crowned with another insignia. The estates issued a charter in which they argued that the validity of coronation did not depend on the insignia but rather on the "will of the inhabitants of the realm" and declared the coronation of the infant null and void. Władysław was crowned on July 17, 1440, with a crown that had adorned a reliquary of Saint István.

The two coronations meant nothing less than civil war. When the majority of barons accepted Ulászló, and the commanders of his troops, Miklós Ujlaki and János Hunyadi, defeated those of the Habsburg barons, a stalemate developed. Most of northeastern Hungary remained in the hands of a Habsburg supporter, Jan Jiskra z Brandýsa, who ruled that rich territory for decades in the name, but hardly to the benefit of, the Habsburgs. Some western towns acknowledged the queen and after her untimely death were taken over by the head of the Habsburg dynasty, Duke Frederick of Austria, who also took young King Ladislas Posthumus as his ward.

Ulászló's decisive victory at Bátaszék (1441) was the first event of national significance connected with the name of János Hunyadi. He and his son, King Matthias I ("Corvinus"), were to determine to a great extent Hungary's fortunes for the half century that followed. Hunyadi was a descendant of a Vlach (Romanian) noble family that had moved to Hungary. His father received the estate of Hunyad (Hunedoara) from Sigismund in 1409. Hunyadi grew up as a servitor of Hungarian barons and prelates and learned the craft of war in Italy and in Sigismund's entourage as a "knight of the household." In cooperation with Frank Talóci, Hunyadi received commissions at the southern border, and by 1439 he was made ban of Severin. As a leading figure among the soldier barons, he came to be Albert's close associate and, by 1441, one of the greatest land-owners in Hungary. He obtained in grant or commission several castles, was in charge of Belgrade, administrator of the salt monopoly, and shared the voivod-ship of Transylvania with Ujlaki. After the confiscation of the estates of oppos-ing barons and his exchanges with Branković of Serbia (discussed below), Hunyadi held some twenty-five castles, thirty towns and over one thousand villages—much more than Albert's royal domain.

The Debacle of Varna

With the fall of Serbia, the Ottoman Empire reached the very border of Hungary. The defense system built up under Sigismund still protected the fron-tier, but the glacis in front of it shrank from year to year. In 1441–42, Hunyadi, well understanding the pugnacious mood of the country, led counterattacks against the bey of Smederevo and won several battles in Transylvania and Wal-lachia. After decades of defensive action, Hungarian troops were moving into enemy territory; Hunyadi became the idol of the nobility. Thus, when Pope Eugenius sent Cardinal Cesarini to negotiate peace between the Habsburg and Jagiełłonian parties in Hungary and prepare the field for a crusade against the Ottoman Empire, the auspices for an offensive campaign were good. In fact, during 1443–44, in the so-called "long campaign," Ulászló and Hunyadi led a Hungarian army, supported by allies from the Balkans, as far as the Rhodope Mountains and had to return only because winter had set in. The king, satisfied by having restored Branković to at least a part of his lost kingdom, agreed to negotiate a peace with Sultan Murad II. These peace talks, arranged by Branković (Murad's son-in-law) ended in the Peace of Szeged, later confirmed formally at Várad. Murad vacated Serbia and promised to pay one hundred thousand florins to Ulászló and to supply troops if Hungary needed help. Branković, who could return to his realm, handed over several cities and north-ern Hungarian estates to Hunyadi, in return for his support of the deal. Prepara-tions for a new attack were made immediately in Hungary, even though the king swore an oath on the peace, which was to last ten years. He was assured by the cardinal that promises to the infidel need not be kept. Barely more than a month after the treaty had been signed, counting on international cooperation arranged by the papacy, Hungarian troops crossed the Bulgarian border.

The Ottoman leaders, though temporarily lulled by the peace negotiations, acted swiftly. Murad, who had been engaged in internal struggles in Anatolia, brought his army across the Straits and marched north with surprising speed. On

November 10, 1444 the Ottoman army confronted the Hungarian-Polish camp on the Black Sea coast at Varna. The Christian side seemed to be winning the encounter, when the impetuous young king and his comrades, in true chivalrous manner, threw themselves into the melée, only to be cut down by Ottoman janissaries. The king and Cesarini fell with the greater part of the army; Hunyadi barely escaped with his life. The defeat once more demonstrated the futility of crusading plans and weakened the resistance in the Balkans against the Ottomans.

The Coming of Age of the Noble Diet

Given the strength of corporate politics at the election of Ulászló, it was logical that once he was gone power would devolve on the barons and nobles. The years that followed Varna witnessed the maturing of the idea of a noble-aristocratic polity and the establishment of a number of institutional frameworks that were to last, *mutatis mutandis,* until the end of Old Hungary in 1848. The underlying idea was that decisions, such as the election and corona-tion of a king, should be made by a gathering of all the propertied men of the realm. The meaning of the term "inhabitants" *(regnicolae),* which in 1437 (in Kolozsmonostor) could still mean nobles, freemen, peasants, and settlers, came to be limited to the *possessionati:* noble landowners, the Church, the privileged royal cities, and the foreign communities, such as the Germans (called Saxons). Similar gatherings, *congregationes generales* or Diets, had been called intermit-tently in the preceding decades and centuries, but now they came to be virtually annual meetings of the upper strata of the nobility, with secondary roles as-signed to the county delegates, the urban deputies, and churchmen. The dele-gates of the major counties, two or four noblemen from each, were frequently present at least for the opening; if the Diet lasted too long, they went home, having run out of expense money, leaving the decisions to the barons. Many of the nobles were, in any case, retainers *(familiares)* of the greater lords and acted more or less as their supporters. However, the nobles retained the right to appear personally *(viritim)* at the Diet, and did so not infrequently. When major decisions were taken, such as Hunyadi's election to the governorship in 1446, thousands of noblemen assembled in the fields of Rákos (presently the eastern side of Budapest). In the early sixteenth century, such tumultuous Diets were usual. The major cities sent representatives to the earlier Diets but soon realized that it was not worth the expense: their dozen votes against the (occasionally) hundreds of the nobles carried little weight. Many of the city dwellers were Germans and understood little of the negotiations in Magyar, and the usually xenophobic petty nobles were unlikely to listen to their counsel anyway. There is good evidence to show that urban delegates were occasionally consulted by the leading men, for example at the governor's election, but even so they were not legally counted as an "estate." They were too insignificant to constitute a third estate. In fact, the aristocracy and nobility counted, *pro forma,* as the only estate, one that regarded itself as the sole speaker for the nation, the representative of the "community of the realm." The prelates fitted in insofar as they, too, came from the aristocracy.

The ideas and forms of this corporate polity, resembling more the Polish republic of nobles than a representative assembly of Western Europe, were forged to a very great extent during the interregnum of 1444–53. Parts of its ideology were present in the *decreta* of 1291 and 1298 (renewed by Ulászló I in 1440), in the widely known thirteenth-century chronicle of Simon Kézai (which reflected the Pan-European notion of a Golden Age "popular sovereignty"), and in the theory and practice of royal councils acting "in the name of the Holy Crown." All these elements, which had their roots in contemporary European political thought and above all in canon law and conciliar ideas, came together in the documents of the noble Diets and prepared the way for a theory according to which the landowners, the free cities, and the major dependent territories were members of an organic whole, the "body" of the state.

The practical base that supported the corporate idea was the noble corporation of the counties. Since the first assemblies of royal servitors in the thirteenth century, ever more tasks of local administration, jurisdiction, peace-keeping, and authenticating of transactions were entrusted to these communities in the sixty-odd counties of Hungary and Slavonia. With, on the one hand, the regular calls on the county levies and the frequent commission to the counties of collecting the direct taxes and, on the other, the decline of the central authority and jurisdiction, the noble *universitates* in the counties were in fact managing the realm. That in times of civil war and anarchy, such as 1382–97 and 1440–45, some semblance of administration of justice and organized resistance to robber barons was upheld, seems to have been due to the nobles of the counties. Sigismund, counting on their strength on the local level, legalized emergency assemblies to restrict the violent actions of local potentates. While the head of the county was still a royal appointee, though usually a local magnate, his deputy, the *vice-comes (alispán),* tended to be as much a representative of the nobles as of his lord, whose retainer he was supposed to be. He and the elected noble magistrates *(iudices nobilium, szolgabiró)* were in fact the administrators of the smaller units. This organization was often all that could be called "government" in the entire realm. The county nobles' interest was in certain respects identical with the king's, or if you will, the country's: keeping the peace, limiting the lawlessness of the powerful, and holding together what was increasingly perceived as the "nation." In other respects, of course, they represented forces of inertia. Dominated by the middle nobility, the county was the institution that kept the poor nobles and especially the tenant farmers out of power. Increasingly interested in their properties, as landed gentry the county nobles tried to avoid as much military service as possible, leaving the problems of defense to the king. Xenophobic and particularistic as it was, the county nobility was opposed to the growth of towns, which endangered their hold on the labor force in the villages, and to urban participation in matters of the realm.

A far-sighted leader could build an alliance with this lesser noble mass, still a valuable military power and a vociferous political support against the selfish interests of great barons. Hunyadi did that in the first years of his regency and so did his son, Matthias. In return, the privileges of the lesser nobles were repeatedly confirmed, and under Matthias they acquired the right to elect the actual head of county administratrion, the *vice-comes.*

The Regency of János Hunyadi (1446–1453)

In the kingless years after Varna, the party struggles between Habsburg supporters and their opponents came into the open again. The Diet of 1445 worked out a compromise. Negotiators were sent to Frederick III, king of the Romans, to ask for the return of Ladislas Posthumus and the territories occupied by the Habsburgs. Awaiting his answer, a council of regency was nominated and seven captains, including members of both the Hunyadi and the Habsburg parties, were commissioned to restore the peace. The negotiations did not yield fruits for some years to come. Therefore the 1446 Diet decided to elect Hunyadi governor. He was given many royal rights but was limited in capital jurisdiction and major donations; these sovereign rights remained with the council. The following year's Diet proceeded, still in the absence of the young king, to establish formally what may be termed the model of a "corporate state." This time the Diet consisted of a fair number of county delegates (half of the counties were represented), the Slavonian delegates, thirty-six barons, and some ten prelates. They agreed that the Diet should meet every year at Pentecost and that every noble owning more than twenty *portae* should attend personally. The barons should place their offices at the disposal of the Diet and receive it from the assembly. The captainships were abolished and decisions were to be made by unanimous vote. This "constitution" looked good on paper, but regular parliamentary government did not develop for centuries. However, with the Diet's support, Hunyadi managed to restore peace in most of the country, courts resumed operation, and in the next year even a formal truce with Ulrich Cillei was established. Jiskra in northeastern Hungary maintained his title as chief captain and refused to yield to the Diet or to Hunyadi, who led several unsuccessful campaigns against his extensive territory. A truce was not arranged until 1452.

The governor's position changed considerably in the meantime. Hunyadi's defeat in another Crusade at the second Kosovo Polje disaster in October 1448 began to undermine his reputation among the warrior nobility. In 1450 Hunyadi and Ujlaki entered into a league with the Habsburg party: first with Palatine László Garai, then with Frederick III, who acknowledged Hunyadi's governorship. The alliance with the court faction made the support of the dietal nobility superfluous, and Hunyadi accordingly abandoned his former allies. He acquired new territories on the Moravian border and acted as the now legitimate regent for the young king.

Ladislas V Posthumus (1453–1457)

In 1452 the Austrian estates rebelled against Frederick III and, in concert with the Czech nobility and finally also with Cillei and Hunyadi, forced him to let his ward go. The Hungarian lords negotiated a settlement with Ladislas, and the Diet of 1453 approved it. A general amnesty was proclaimed, the donations of both King Władisław and Queen Elisabeth were annulled and the royal government was restored, though the council of barons retained. There was no talk about a new election or coronation; the corporate program of 1440 was buried without pomp and circumstance. Hunyadi was entrusted with the administration of the royal revenues and was granted, in place of his governorship, the title of chief captain and perpetual count of Beszterce. However, in the following years he lost his position as leader of the Hungarian noble party and began to work only for his own interests. Eventually, even his old friends, including the chief ideologue of the noble polity, his confidant and the tutor of his sons, János Vitéz of Zredna, abandoned him and supported the king in his attempts to restore royal influence in Hungary.

The return of Ladislas Posthumus to the throne started a struggle for the recovery of the royal income. A valuable document has survived containing information about the financial resources of the Hungarian crown in the mid-fifteenth century. Though it is a program for the reform of the revenues rather than a record of facts, it reflects in outline form the structure of the country's finances.

The most significant item, equal to all other sources of revenue put together, was the income from the royal salt mines; under Sigismund they allegedly yielded 100,000 gold florins. The second largest source of revenue was the direct tax paid by the peasants (*dica, lucrum camerae),* levied on every *porta.* The author of the reform proposal believed that from the 400,000 *portae* under Sigismund, only 200,000 had remained (he probably overlooked certain changes in the counting of tax units) and expected a forty thousand florin annual tax revenue. The third major source of income was mining and minting. An incomplete figure set its worth at twenty-four thousand florins, to which were added two thousand florins from the sale of copper. The cities' taxes added up to only seven thousand florins, partially because the income from Pozsony and northern Hungary (Jiskra's territory) could not be included "due to adverse conditions." Taxes and dues from Transylvania, including the lump sum paid by the Saxons, were listed at thirteen thousand florins, the tax of the Jews as four thousand florins, and the payments rendered by special groups (Slavonian marten pelt tax, dues of Cumans, etc.) as fourteen thousand florins, plus dues in kind. Customs duties (the so-called "thirtieth," i.e., three percent of the import and export value) were estimated at ten thousand florins, and minor items, such as the sturgeon catch on the Danube, at two thousand florins. The monetary items added up to "at least" 218,000 florins and were to be augmented by many thousands of oxen, hundreds of horses, and many thousands of bushels of foodstuffs from privileged Székely, Cuman, and Jász people. The impressive amount of dues in kind is a telling comment on the country's essentially agrarian character.

The revenues were contrasted with some major expenses. The largest sum, thirty-three thousand florins, went for the defense of the border from Belgrade to Severin, together with another eight thousand for the Danubian fleet. The 4,600 florin salary for the palatine and six thousand for Hunyadi were essentially also payments for keeping troops; the captains of Szeged and Temesvár received 1,400 florins. Ladislas received for his court no more than twenty-five thousand. To put these figures in some context, one should remember that the pay of an army of fifteen to twenty thousand men (cavalry and infantry)—the minimum force that might be of some use against the Turks—for three or four months would have been around 250,000 florins. Thus the regular revenue, even if rigorously collected and well administered, could only have covered the bare necessities of defense, to say nothing of expenses for the royal household, buildings, salaried office-holders, and official functions.

The Relief of Belgrade and Its Aftermath

Hungary had been preoccupied with internal power struggles, but the fall of Constantinople to the Turks in 1453 once more alerted all of Europe to the Ottoman threat. The imperial *Reichstage* decided to collect special taxes, and the Hungarian Diet called up extraordinary levies and approved of higher than usual war taxes, but little was accomplished, and in 1455 Serbia fell again under the sway of the sultan. However, when the Ottoman army besieged Belgrade in 1456, the response of Hunyadi and his followers was immediate. The castle, defended by Hunyadi's and Ujlaki's seven thousand men, was besieged by Mehmed II's army of about 100,000. Hunyadi mobilized some ten thousand soldiers from his estates and retinue, while Giovanni di Capestrano, preacher and inquisitor, called for a crusade in Austria and Hungary. From the southern parts of Hungary, some twenty-five to thirty thousand peasants and townsfolk took up the cross and marched toward Belgrade. The relief of the castle by the crusaders became a legend in its own time. The mass support enabled Hunyadi first to cut the supply lines of the Ottoman forces, then to help the garrison repel a major Turkish attack, and to relieve the besieged fortress on July 22, carried by the impetuous crusaders' unforeseen surge. The far larger Ottoman army left the field overnight. The crusaders, among whom seditious voices were heard denouncing the lords and professional soldiers (who seemed to be claiming the popular victory for themselves) were quickly sent home. There could be no thought of pursuing the enemy. Nevertheless, no major Ottoman attack threatened Hungary for several decades. The victory at Belgrade was the last deed of both Hunyadi and Capestrano. Hunyadi, the hero of his country, died two weeks later in an epidemic that broke out in the camp, and Capestrano—soon to be venerated a saint—followed him a few months afterward.

The events of the following months were as melodramatic as they were conse-
quential. In spite of promises to Hunyadi, the king named Ulrich Cillei chief
captain. László Hunyadi, the elder son of János, seemed to accept the new
commander, but on November 9, 1456 his men killed Cillei in Belgrade. The
king, virtually a prisoner of the Hunyadi party, promised amnesty. However, as
soon as he was able to act freely, he realized that his most influential allies (such
as Ujlaki) would not support the Hunyadis in the ensuing political struggle. In
March 1457 Ladislas had László Hunyadi and his brother Matthias arrested;
László was hurriedly tried and executed a few days later. Hunyadi's widow,
Erzsébet Szilágyi and her brother Mihály, using the enormous economic and
human resources of the family, rose against the king and his supporters. The
young king fled to his Prague residence, taking Matthias Hunyadi with him. On
November 23, 1457 Ladislas Posthumus died, not yet eighteen years old. Ac-
cording to rumors, he was poisoned.

Matthias I "Corvinus" (1458–1490)

With the news of King Ladislas' death, the Hunyadi party moved to prepare
the way to the throne for Hunyadi's surviving son. At the same time, the Bohemian estates decided to abandon the Habsburgs and elected the Czech counter-
part of János Hunyadi, Jiři Poděbrady, king of Bohemia. Elisabeth and Mihály
Szilágyi made an alliance with László Garai and his supporters, promising that
Szilágyi, as governor, would guarantee their role under the new king. Helped by
this aristocratic backing, the Hunyadi resources, and the popularity of the family's name, it was only a matter of form to have Matthias (later called Corvinus
from the raven on the family crest) elected king. On January 24, 1458 the assembled nobility acclaimed the son of the hero of Belgrade and the brother of the
"treacherously executed" László Hunyadi with great enthusiasm. The eighteen-
year-old king returned from Prague engaged to Poděbrady's daughter, with a
military escort given to him by his future father-in-law, and was enthroned at
Buda. He could not, of course, be crowned, since the Holy Crown was still in
the hands of Emperor Frederick III.

Matthias did not intend to keep his family's bargain. Almost immediately, he
rid himself of Szilágyi, and with the assistance of János Vitéz, soon to become
primate of Hungary, began to build an alliance with the lesser nobles, whom he
called to a Diet and to whom he promised some part in the central government.
One of the most urgent tasks was to make peace with Frederick III, who not
only could hinder Matthias' coronation, but in 1459 was in fact "elected" king
of Hungary by the barons of the Garai party, who felt cheated by the young
king's independent moves. Years of negotiation, threats of war, and finally eighty
thousand florins moved Frederick, in 1463, to accept a compromise: he adopted
Matthias as his son, retained the title of king of Hungary, and received the right
to inherit the throne should Matthias die heirless. As the king was some twenty
years the emperor's junior, it did not seem likely that this arrangement would

ever become significant. In fact, it was the first step toward the Habsburgs' acquisition of Hungary, which was to last for four hundred years. At the time, however, the "imperial kinship" promised to help the *homo novus* Matthias, whose grandfather was an unknown Vlach knight, to compete with the established dynasties of Habsburg and Jagiełło. On March 29, 1464 Matthias was crowned. Since in the meantime the leader of the opposition, Garai, had died, his reign was secure from any serious challenge.

While his diplomats haggled, Matthias followed in his father's footsteps and led a few successful campaigns against the Turks, securing the frontier and even gaining some new territory in Bosnia through a combination of force and bargaining. He had also learned from his father that the country's defense needed a more reliable basis than the outdated noble levy, occasionally augmented by hired troops. In order to remedy this situation and strengthen the power of the monarchy, Matthias embarked on a series of financial reforms. First, the regular (portal) tax was given a new name, allowing the cancelling of exceptions and immunities, and the treasury acquired considerable new income. Then the "thirtieth" customs duty was renamed *vectigal coronae* (duty of the Crown) and more rigorously collected. The administration of the royal revenues was placed in the hands of royal officials. Most significantly, from the 1470s onwards, Matthias managed to win the support of the noble Diet in collecting the "extraordinary" subsidy virtually every year, in return for confirming the nobility's privileges. Thus Matthias, who also had the tremendous family fortune of the Hunyadi at his disposal, easily doubled the income of the Crown. At the end of his reign, he may have had an annual income of close to a million gold florins, a sum not significantly lower than the revenues of France or Burgundy at that time. It is true, however, that most of it still came from the peasantry's taxes and only some 10–15 percent from urban sources and export-import duties, suggesting that little had been achieved in modernizing the country's economy.

The Wars of Matthias

With his income Matthias could attempt to build up a mercenary army, loyal only to him and trained in the art of war. This he began to do in 1462 by hiring the last remnants of the ex-Hussite Czechs who occupied castles in northern Hungary. He gradually expanded this force with domestic and foreign mercenaries. The commanders of the army came from Hungary, Bohemia, Austria, and Silesia, and it was a veritably multi-ethnic force. Reports from the 1470s maintain that at that time Matthias led an army that consisted of some twenty thousand mercenaries, besides the many thousands of banderial soldiers and auxiliaries from Hungary and vassal territories (Moldavia, Wallachia, etc.). The court historian, Antonio Bonfini, wrote that at the muster of 1486 the standing army of the king consisted of twenty-eight thousand trained men with nine thousand war-wagons and some artillery. However, the country's own resources, even if rigorously collected, could at best finance the upkeep of the extensive border fortifications.

Matthias maintained throughout his reign, especially in his diplomatic correspondence, that his final aim was to expel the Ottomans from Europe. In fact, he fought most of his wars in the north and the west, in order to secure his status among the royal dynasties of the neighboring countries and, perhaps in the long run, to acquire those additional financial and political resources that would have allowed a major campaign in the Balkans. The mercenary force was the means to expand Hungarian sovereignty, but it was also the major item in the budget and tended to swallow up the additional income. Furthermore, an army fighting abroad meant that the many thousands of florins paid to its soldiers were drained from the country.

Combining this mercenary force of heavy cavalry, infantry, and Hussite-type war-wagons with the royal banderia and the light cavalry supplied by the counties and banats, Matthias' generals successfully applied traditional Hungarian hit-and-run tactics. Just as the Ottoman irregulars and sipahis were wont to harrass Transylvania, Croatia, and Hungary by swift raids for booty and destruction, the troops of the southern defense, under their legendary commoner commander, Pál Kinizsi, conducted similar forays into Ottoman-held territory. In 1479, Kinizsi and the voivode of Transylvania won a spectacular victory over Ottoman raiders in Transylvania. The most significant military successes were scored in Silesia, Poland, and Austria. Matthias had severed contacts with the Hussite King George after the death of his first wife in 1464. Arguing that with George at his rear he could not fight the Ottomans, Matthias, with Rome's blessing, volunteered to lead a crusade against "heretical" Bohemia. Though Matthias was hailed by the Catholic barons in 1468, the war did not bring quick results, instead the constant military efforts in the north caused losses on the southern front.

Ostensibly provoked by these failures, several aristocratic rebellions broke out in Hungary and Transylvania. The instigators were in fact alarmed by Matthias' growing power, new policies, and counselors elevated from lesser noble and burgher families. In 1471 his closest supporters turned against him and, led by Archbishop Vitéz, offered the crown to Kasimir, the youngest of the Polish Jagiełło princes. The Poles marched into Hungary and received considerable support, but Matthias quickly returned from Bohemia and stifled the revolt by diplomacy and force. Vitéz managed to make peace with the king, but his nephew, the humanist poet and politician, Janus Pannonius, died while fleeing Matthias' wrath. The 1470 rebellion further induced Matthias to rely only on his favorites. The centralizing trends increased, and the royal offices, as well as the episcopal and archepiscopal sees, were ever more frequently filled by the king's foreign counselors.

After the death of King George in 1471, the fortunes of the Bohemian campaign took a turn for the better. The new king, Władisław Jagiełło, commanded much less loyalty than his predecessor, and the country was exhausted by decades of war. In the peace of Breslau (1474), confirmed in Olomouc in 1478, the two kings partitioned the lands of Saint Wenceslas: Matthias received Moravia,

Silesia, and Lusatia; Władisław retained Bohemia proper; and both were to be styled *rex Bohemiae*.

In the south, no major Ottoman attacks were launched for some time, but even in the years of minor skirmishes, the military balance slowly shifted to the advantage of the Ottoman Empire. In order to placate the anti-Ottoman mood of the nobility, Matthias led a campaign to the lower Danube, where his army captured Šabac, a newly built Ottoman fortress. The prospects for a major campaign in the Balkans were promising because the Ottoman Empire was shaken by struggles for succession, and the subject Balkan peoples were ready to rise in support of a liberator. Yet Matthias was still primarily committed to his western projects and in 1477 turned against Austria.

During the following decade, Matthias' armies, in alliance with the Archbishop of Salzburg, occupied most of Styria. In 1485 Vienna was besieged and captured, and two years later all of lower Austria was in Hungarian hands. Matthias now ruled a veritable empire that was able to finance both a Renaissance court and an army of nearly thirty thousand men, larger than any other fighting force of the age, except that of the sultan. However, anxious to secure the future of his achievements, Matthias was engaged almost exclusively in preparing the succession of his natural son, János Corvin. He did this by planning for him a marriage with Bianca Sforza of Milan, committing the Hungarian lords to his support, and waging war in Poland to augment the prince's heritage. Amid all these plans, at the height of his victories, Matthias Hunyadi died in Vienna on April 6, 1490, not yet fifty years old.

"Matthias the Just"

Matthias' reforms in the administration of revenues were carried further by strengthening the royal power vis-à-vis the powerful magnates of the royal council. The king replaced aristocratic office-holders with men from his own following, lesser nobles or burghers from the great reservoir of Hunyadi retainers, and with foreigners. Of the thirty-one major office-holders during Matthias' reign, twenty were *homines novi* (new men), who held their posts not by family tradition but by the king's grace alone. Nonethless economic and military, hence also political, power rested still with the old baronial families, and the newly risen men succeeded only if they managed to be accepted and assimilated. The king was aware of the strength of the aristocracy, whose troops he still needed for defense. Since he could not well afford to face their united opposition, he never openly challenged the council's jurisdiction, but rather undermined it by establishing offices that co-opted the traditional office-holders' jurisdiction.

In the last decades of Matthias' reign, the treasurer (a new office) and the minor or secret chancellery were much more active in government than the council-controlled greater chancellery. The king used the newly established court of the "personal presence" to take over the administration of justice from the baronial courts. The trend of professionalization of the judicial system had began before Matthias and was to continue under his successors, but it received a definite boost under him. Judges at the royal courts were usually retainers of the barons who became high justices (palatine, judge royal, etc.). These lesser nobles, and occasionally even commoners, received their posts after proving their abilities in local administration, in lower courts, or as "apprentices" (scribes, notaries) of a practicing lawyer. They were rarely trained at universities, but rather learned in the practice of law, through handbooks and formularies, and in everyday business. Yet it was they who interpreted the customary and statute law of the realm. Hundreds of them are known by name from the mid-fifteenth century onward. They constituted the first significant stratum of a secular intelligentsia in Hungary. Some of them wrote history, such as the pro-tonotary of Matthias' court, János Thúróczy, whose *Chronica Hungarorum* (1488) was the first printed Hungarian history. Others became active politicians, such as István Werbőczy, a central figure in the turbulent years of dietal politics in the early sixteenth century. With increasing frequency, these experts in the administration of justice retained their posts even when their baronial superiors were transferred or lost their positions. Matthias made extensive use of their abilities and their loyalty to the crown. The central courts of law were gradually transformed into institutions actually run by trained professionals, even though, *pro forma,* their presidents continued to be aristocrats untrained in law. It was certainly due to the influence of these lawyers that Matthias attempted to re-vamp the country's judicial system by granting new rights to the county magis-trates and by issuing a law (the *Decretum Majus* of 1486) that was to have "eternal validity." The replacement of the many contradictory medieval decrees with a systematic law code was a typical feature of the "new monarchies." Though not all of these reforms were successful, Matthias' attempts to establish uniform laws and his personal efforts to curb corruption and overbearing local potentates (he allegedly traveled incognito among his subjects) resulted in his posthumous fame as the "just" king. The proverb, "dead is Matthias, lost is justice" originated only a few years after his death.

Renaissance Humanism

Besides his military and administrative reforms, Matthias Corvinus is best remembered for his patronage of the arts and learning. Humanism had reached Hungary quite early in the fifteenth century. The royal chancellery of Sigismund was a center for refined Latin style. Although the civil wars and interregna did not favor learning, the churchmen who grew up in those decades, above all the former chancellery clerk, János Vitéz, came to be admirers and supporters of the new learning. Vitéz's episcopal court was one of the first centers of Italian humanism north of the Alps, and his pupil, King Matthias, turned the royal court into an impressive gathering of visiting Italian authors and artists. Matthias was well aware of the political value of his image as a magnanimous Renaissance sponsor of the arts, which went well with his background as the son of a self-made man, similar to many Italian princes of the time. He spent enormous sums on artists and architects to glorify his patronage. The ruins of his buildings in Buda and Visegrád and lesser castles—unfortunately lost during the centuries of Ottoman occupation and wars—bear witness to the splendid court he kept. Especially after his marriage, in 1476, to Beatrix, daughter of Ferdinand of Aragon, king of Naples, Buda became a regular stopping point for humanist scholars.

Though Vitéz did not have the chance to acquire the new education himself, his nephew, Janus Pannonius, was among the many whom he had sent to study in Italy. When the young poet, already well known in Ferrara and Florence, returned home, he immediately received high posts in Matthias' government and later served as envoy to Rome, where he tried to gain papal support for an anti-Ottoman crusade. The humanist rhetoric he and others were able to infuse into the chancellery was an integral part of Matthias' diplomacy. It was only logical that Matthias and Vitéz would try to establish a university, actually the third or fourth attempt in Hungary. King Louis' foundation in Pécs (1367) had followed closely on the heels of the Central European universities of Prague (1348), Kraków (1364), and Vienna (1365), but does not seem to have functioned for longer than a decade. Sigismund's university in Óbuda, founded in 1395 and refounded in 1410, hardly survived him. The *Academia Istropolitana*, Vitéz's university in Pozsony, started under excellent auspices but folded after the political fall and death of its sponsor. Hungarian students had to continue studying abroad, which they did in great numbers. Vienna and Kraków had special Hungarian colleges *(bursae)*, with sizable memberships, well into the sixteenth century.

Though the university did not endure and the printing press in Buda (started in 1472) was also short-lived, Matthias was able to establish a cultural monument unique for its time, the *Bibliotheca Corviniana*. For decades, tens of thousands of ducats were spent on books copied and illuminated in Italy and later also on the book-producing workshops of Buda. Counseled by his humanist companions, Matthias selected a wide variety of titles for his library, which counted over two thousand manuscripts and incunabulae at his death. Visitors in the late fifteenth century, who often generously helped themselves to the holdings, spoke of unparalleled riches in Hebrew, Greek, and Latin books. Many authors in Italy dedicated works to Matthias. Although barely a tenth of the library survived, the Corvina volumes, now spread all over the world, are tangible proof of the taste and knowledge of its sponsor. The library project succeeded because it needed much less support than a university or a printing press. Janus Pannonius complained bitterly about the "barbarian" conditions of his country. This was partly literary convention, but even among the churchmen and magnates learning and the arts did not develop until after Matthias' death. In the last decades of medieval Hungary, amid political turmoil and growing external danger, the seeds of humanism sown in the times of Corvinus germinated in many episcopal courts and even noble castles. Tamás Bakócz, a commoner who rose in the church hierarchy under Matthias to become primate of

Hungary in 1498, had the archepiscopal palace rebuilt, and several of his fellow prelates spent a fair amount of their impressive revenues on art, architecture, and the sponsorship of learning. Around 1500 even vernacular literature, an important part of Renaissance civilization, experienced a major upswing.

While the wisdom of Matthias' foreign policy continues to be debated, his governmental reforms were leading toward the establishment of a strong kingship, reminiscent of the "new monarchies" of contemporary Western Europe. His extensive financial and judicial legislation contained measures that could have led to more equitable taxation and administration of justice, but the power of the great landowning families was too well entrenched to be seriously limited by a handful of non-aristocratic royal officials or a set of laws. The collapse of Matthias' "Renaissance state" a few months after his death proved the weakness of the entire political edifice. Ironically, it was his cultural achievements, for which the king needed only wise counsel and good taste, that survived. Even the book-illuminating workshop managed to continue for quite a few years after the king's death. The royal court of his successors, however poor it may have been, remained for decades a cultivated center of humanism, and Hungarian clerics and scholars were in touch with all of early modern Europe's learned circles.

The Age of the Jagiełło Kings (1490–1526)

Although King Matthias had done everything he could to secure the succession of János Corvin to the throne, he died without a loyal palatine to rule in the interim. The Diet that had gathered for the election of a new king had to choose between a number of claimants: Corvin, who was initially supported by a number of lords from his father's closest entourage; Maximilian of Habsburg, who based his rights on the Peace of Wiener Neustadt between Frederick III and Matthias; Władisław of Bohemia, with whom Matthias had shared that kingdom and whom many of the great lords preferred; and the latter's brother, Jan Olbracht Jagiełło, heir to the throne of Poland. Additionally, Matthias' widow, Queen Beatrix, did her best to bar Corvin from the throne and to secure her own influence. The intrigues and cabals are too complex to be followed in detail. The powerful lords decided to elect a king "whose braids they can hold in their hands" and who would guarantee that the centralizing reforms of Matthias would be reversed. They gave their support to the Bohemian Jagiełło, who signed a detailed document of election promises, including the abolition of extraordinary taxes and other "harmful innovations." He was elected and crowned as Ulászló II. Corvin was at first pacified with rich properties and titles but then rose in arms against the Diet. His supporters, however, abandoned him, and he was defeated by Matthias' famous general, Pál Kinizsi. The queen was placated by the promise that the new king would marry her; although this was never taken seriously, it took many years to sort things out. The younger Jagiełło soon gave up his claims; although a sizable group of lesser nobles tried to place him on the throne by acclamation, they were silenced by the barons.

Maximilian was the least conciliatory: he marched with his army into western Hungary and had to be repulsed by armed force. For this purpose, ironically, the extraordinary subsidy was levied, only months after its eternal abolition. In late 1491 Maximilian and Ulászló made peace and signed an inheritance treaty. This was followed in 1505 (and confirmed in 1515) by the double betrothal of Ulászló's son Louis to Mary, granddaughter of Maximilian, and of Ferdinand of Habsburg to Anna of Hungary, which in 1526 brought the Crown of Saint István to the Habsburgs.

Ulászló was seen by contemporaries as a yes-man. He was called King Dobže ("very well"). While many of Matthias' reforms, such as the central courts and treasury offices, were retained, they now served not the crown but the magnates, who held the actual power. The Jagiełło kings had, of course, no property of their own in Hungary. Therefore, Ulászló could hardly help but use up the last remnants of the royal domain, which under Matthias had still yielded some 500,000 florins annually. According to Venetian observers, royal income fell to some 200,000 florins and under Ulászló's son, Louis II, even lower. Matthias' mercenary army, unpaid for many months, disintegrated into robber bands, which were dispersed in a bloody battle in 1492 by Kinizsi himself. At the same time, the pay of the garrisons at the Ottoman frontier alone amounted to some 170,000 florins annually. No wonder that, as an often quoted contemporary source reported, the king's cooks sometimes had to borrow food to serve their lord's dinner.

The history of the last three or four decades of medieval Hungary is highly complicated by the almost continuous struggle of different factions of the nobility among themselves and with the central authority. The three major forces in these political contests, court, aristocracy, and Diet, tended to change positions and alliances frequently for purely pragmatic reasons. Tumultuous Diets were held nearly every year; in some years there were more than one and sometimes different ones were summoned by the king and by the "opposition." Meanwhile, the country's defenses deteriorated, the power of the Ottoman Empire grew, and ever-increasing areas of the kingdom were devastated by Ottoman raids. The strategic position of Hungary gradually worsened to the point of no return. The debates in the Diets, however, resounded with patriotic phrases about Scythian valor and Hungarian national greatness. The particular interests of noble factions, especially the lesser nobility and their occasional leader, János Zápolyai, vajda of Transylvania and the greatest landowner of the country, were frequently couched in nationalistic terms. (In 1505, for example, it was decreed that no foreigner could be elected king in the future.) Yet the patriotism of the assembled nobility was rarely apparent in their actions.

The attempts made to update the country's defense had greater significance for internal development than for the military situation. In the first years of Ulászló II's reign, the distribution of the extraordinary war tax changed drastically. While Matthias' practice of regularly levying these subsidies was upheld, the income did not now flow into the king's coffers but was partially collected by the barons for the upkeep of their banderia, and partially by the counties to hire mercenaries. The counties, however, often used this money to hire troops not for defense but to press their particularist demands at Diets. In 1498–1500 laws were passed regulating banderial duties: they spelled out the names of the few dozen great landowners who were obligated to show up with their private armies in the king's camp. This list became the basis of a definite political and legal demarcation between the aristocracy proper and those middle noble families who, although not barons, had risen to considerable power in the preceding generations. In compensation some of the demoted magnates were elected to represent the lesser nobles on royal councils, but these reforms did not last long. Once they had lost the right and duty to keep their own banderia, the upwardly mobile families, mediatized as they were by the counties, tended to vanish from the political scene. Thus, while the legal fiction of a single, undifferentiated nobility survived into modern times, the dividing line between "banderial lords" and the rest of the nobility came to be a hard and fast one. The magnates had always held separate meetings at the Diet, but with the defintion of their special status, their consultations became the nucleus of the "upper house" in the formally bicameral system that developed in the subsequent centuries.

Rural Revolt and the Laws of 1514

In the last years of the reign of the ever more melancholic King Ulászló, Hungary experienced the most bloody and ferocious rural revolt of her history. The economic and social situation of the peasants had begun to deteriorate in the late fifteenth century, when Hungarian landlords, like their fellows in Poland and Bohemia, started to impose restrictions on their tenants. One of the reasons was that the lords, wanting to profit from the rise of food prices on the European markets, wished to enter the marketplace with foodstuffs extracted from their serfs. Seigneurial dues in kind, together with the tithe (mostly rented by the landlords from the church), and different traditional taxes gave the seigneurs control over a considerable amount of marketable produce. Laws of the late fifteenth century confirmed their right to trade in these commodities free of taxes and customs duty. Some landowners began to return to farming their immediate holdings and forced their tenants to perform more *corvée* labor than had been usual for many generations. While one day a week of *robot* counted as a quite heavy obligation in the preceding century, three days weekly was not rare by 1520. The growth of the market towns, with their limited but promising liberties, seemed also to have threatened seigneurial interests, and beginning in 1492 Diets revoked the right of peasants to transfer from one lord to another or from village to market town. The "new" restrictions, based on obligations that had long ago become obsolete, hurt the peasant burghers of the market towns most: they feared that the upward mobility which they had experienced and enjoyed would be curtailed.

These seem to have been some of the fundamental causes of the rural revolt that developed from a call for a crusade against the Ottomans. In the spring of

1514, Archbishop Bakócz returned from Rome (where he had hoped to be elected pope) with a bull calling for a crusade and naming him papal legate for all of Eastern Europe. The preaching of the cross was entrusted to the highly popular Observant Franciscan friars, whose Hungarian province was one of the largest of the whole order. By mid-April, many thousands of peasants and townsmen had gathered around the capital, Buda, and a warrior from the border fortifications, a certain György Székely (in later sources called Dózsa) was entrusted with the command of the crusaders. In early May the crusaders, some twenty thousand men, moved toward the southern border, gathering strength while passing through the great market towns of the Hungarian Plain. Hardly had the crusading army left Buda, when rumors reached the archbishop that "rebellion and revolt" were rampant among the rustics. The campaign was immediately cancelled and the friars ordered to stop preaching the cross and make the peasants return to their villages. The crusaders, in turn, encountered resistance from lords who hindered their serfs from joining the army. Thus, when Archbishop Bakócz's orders reached Dózsa's camp in southeastern Hungary around May 23, the leaders of the peasants refused to disperse but rather attacked and defeated a seigneurial force that stood in their way. For two months, the Hungarian Plain was aflame with burning manor houses and pillaged castles. Besides the main force operating along the river Maros in a well-organized military campaign, there were other centers of uprising close to the capital, in northern and northeastern Hungary, around Várad, and in the south.

The few documents surviving from the revolt suggest that a complex set of ideas moved the peasants. The idea of a crusade was central to their program, but it came to be radicalized. The peasants turned against those lords who were seen as unwilling to defend the realm, actually hindering the "holy host of the Cross" from fighting against the infidel, and were therefore worse than the Ottomans. Thus the mixed rural and market town peasantry saw themselves as true crusaders fighting against the infidel within and without; they declared their loyalty to the king and the archbishop but not to the lords, and they imposed the punishment for treason on those not willing to follow their call to arms. Similar sentiments had been heard in 1456 after the relief of Belgrade, and peasants revolting in neighboring Austrian provinces had also accused their lords of treachery.

Alarmed, the king and the nobility called for outside help, mobilized the levy, and sent word to Zápolyai, vajda of Transylvania, to return and disperse the rebellious rustics. The lesser centers of rebellion were soon pacified, while Dózsa's army got bogged down in its siege of Castle Temesvár. In mid-July Zápolyai attacked and easily dispersed the peasant army. Dózsa and his followers were taken prisoner and, around July 25, 1514, horribly executed. Dózsa accused of wanting to be king, was "enthroned" on a stake, and his companions, starved for days, forced to bite into his burning flesh. The quartered body of the peasant leader was exhibited on the gates of towns across the Plain.

The Diet called for in the fall of the same year enacted what came to be the legal basis for hundreds of years of servile status for Hungarian peasants. The rebellious peasants were to be subject to "eternal servitude," deprived of arms, and forced to pay extensive damages. Most of these decrees, like so many others, were not enforced and were even formally suspended in subsequent decades, just as peasants were again called to arms when Ottoman danger demanded it. However, when the economic developments of the later sixteenth century made the increased exploitation of serfs appear useful, the laws of 1514 offered the legal basis for these arrangements and continued to do so until 1848.

Coincidentally, the same Diet was presented with that great collection of customary law, which, never formally promulgated, but printed in Vienna in the following year, became the actual law of the land for centuries: the *Tripartitum* of István Werbőczy. Werbőczy, a practical jurist mentioned earlier, a leading partisan of Zápolyai and of the lesser noble party in the Diet, compiled the customary laws of the country that had evolved in the course of the medieval centuries, utilizing certain elements of Roman legal thinking, especially in systematizing them. His lawbook reflects the interests of the great number of lesser nobles. This was probably the main reason why this work was not sent out to the counties by the aristocratic royal council. Still, as the actual administration of justice rested primarily with the local courts of the noble county, Werbőczy's printed compilation became the basis of legal practice and, beginning in the seventeenth century, was seen as a constitutive part of the "body of law," the *Corpus Iuris Hungarici*. The *Tripartitum* entrenched the privileges of the nobility vis-à-vis both the crown and the disenfranchised commoners for centuries to come. In stating that the community of nobles constituted the abstract sovereign "crown," as maintained by the noble Diets ever since the mid-fifteenth century, Werbőczy formulated the legal basis for a republic of nobles, very similar to that which developed in Poland. There was not time to apply this constitutional theory to reality, for barely more than a decade later, the medieval kingdom of Hungary collapsed under the Ottoman attack. Werbőczy died as magistrate of the Hungarians in Ottoman-occupied Buda; the partitioned country had fallen under the domination of the great empires west and south of it.

The Road to Mohács

The system established by King Sigismund, composed of border fortresses and the mobile troops of the magnates in the southern regions, together with Serb and Croat peasants and their lords, was able for almost a century to keep the Ottoman forces from pillaging Hungarian territory unpunished. The system was not, however, sufficient to stop these forays nor the gradual deterioration of the Hungarian positions in the northern Balkans. The considerable expenses for the upkeep of the fortifications far surpassed the means of the impoverished royal treasury, while due to incessant warfare in the south, tax revenues also declined. Between 1494 and 1516, the taxable units in southern Hungary and Slavonia fell by some 18 percent. Even the reformed system of aristocratic and county banderia was too slow, too cumbersome, and too unreliable to resist an attack by major Ottoman forces. In the first decades of the sixteenth century, with the sultans engaged in expansion in North Africa, in the Near East, and in the Mediterranean, Hungary was not the target of any major campaign. The truce between Buda and Istanbul could be repeatedly renewed, but peace did not mean any serious break in annual pillaging and slave-taking expeditions by lesser Ottoman commanders and their auxiliaries along the border. The considerable financial and military burden that had to be borne even in "peace time" may have been one of the reasons for Hungary's otherwise unexplainable refusal to renew the truce with the Sublime Porte after the death of Sultan Selim I in 1520. Although no international support was forthcoming, and the Hungarian army was in no way prepared for a major defensive effort, the envoy of Sultan Süleyman I was mistreated, rather than sent home with the usual truce agreement.

When, in the following year, Belgrade was besieged by Ottoman imperial troops, the Hungarian royal army called for its relief was not even nearby. On August 29, 1521, the castle, after several weeks of valiant resistance, fell into Ottoman hands. The Ottomans had also taken Šabac and Zimony (Zemun) and now devastated all of Syrmium before they had to return home. These events, together with the loss of minor positions during the preceding decades, made the southern defense system virtually worthless. The castles that remained in Hungarian hands were in poor repair and had to be supplied with all necessities, as they stood unsupported in deserted land. Hungary was open to Ottoman attacks and essentially at the mercy of the sultan.

In the subsequent years, the breach was widened by the campaigns of local Ottoman commanders. As far as the deliberations of the divan can be reconstructed, this was also the time when the "continental party," (arguing from the well-known saying, "God gave the seas to the infidel and the land to Islam") convinced the young sultan to concentrate on the expansion toward Hungary and Austria. It was merely a question of when the next attack would come.

In these last years of medieval Hungary, the king, the queen, and their court tried to strengthen once more the central authority and to counterbalance the financial disaster aggravated by inflation and overall changes in the European economy. However, the repeated changes of government and the haphazard decisions (such as the cancelling and renewing of the contracts with the Fugger-Thurzó bankers, who farmed Hungary's most important copper and silver mines) only worsened the unstable political and economic situation. Worldwide economic changes, international price developments, and the redrawing of trade routes were also detrimental for Hungary. Further problems were created by the appearance in the country of the followers of the Protestant Reformation.

The fact is that the king tried to muster outside help against the growing danger. Hungarian envoys spoke at German Imperial Diets, and innumerable alarmed and alarming letters were sent to Rome and Western Europe, with little result. The southern command was entrusted to Pál Tomori, a former favorite at court who had retired into a Franciscan convent but was called to serve as Archbishop of Kalocsa. When the Ottoman attack came, in 1526, he was as prepared as he could be, but his fortifications could not delay the sultan's advance long enough to enable the very slowly gathering Hungarian army to intercept the Ottomans at the fords of the Drava. On August 28, 1526 the two armies, very unequal in size and quality, met near Mohács. Tomori's troops and the light cavalry attacked the Turks, unaware of their hidden artillery. Within two hours the battle was over and the Hungarian army annihilated. At least ten thousand foot soldiers, virtually the entire cavalry, many barons, and almost all the bishops were killed. The fleeing king fell from his horse and drowned in a rivulet. The Ottoman army marched without resistance to the capital, pillaged the city, and retreated to the Balkans, only occasionally opposed by local bands of peasants and soldiers.

This event is traditionally taken as the end of the medieval history of Hungary. But while the death of the young king and of the leading men of Hungary was shocking, it was by no means clear that Hungary was lost to the Ottomans. Only the ensuing conflict between two kings, well utilized by the sultan, and the inability to reorganize the realm, in spite of Zápolyai's serious efforts, sealed unequivocally the fate of the kingdom. Still, long-term developments had undermined Hungary's position relative to the Ottoman Empire for decades before the Battle of Mohács.

VII

THE EARLY OTTOMAN PERIOD, INCLUDING ROYAL HUNGARY, 1526–1606

Ferenc Szakály

The Tripartite Division of the Country

Because the Hungarian estates elected two kings simultaneously after the death of Louis II on the battlefield of Mohács, the internal consolidation of the country became very difficult. The majority of the nobility elected János Zápolyai, the vajda of Transylvania, while a small group of magnates grouped around Queen Mary recognized the claims to the throne of the Habsburg archduke and Bohemian king, Ferdinand I. Under the circumstances, Zápolyai had not the slightest chance to assure the country's independence, fighting on two fronts against the empires of the Habsburgs and the Ottomans. It became rapidly obvious that the Habsburgs considered the acquisition of the Hungarian throne the keystone of their eastern policy. They would have been unwilling to recognize the election of Zápolyai even if as Louis II had done, he had given proof of his willingness to subordinate his foreign policy to that of the Habsburgs in exchange for imperial help against Istanbul. At first Zápolyai was the dominant force in Hungary. The Italian wars of the Holy Roman Emperor, Charles V, the brother of Ferdinand, prevented the latter for more than a year from asserting his claim. After the fall of Rome in May 1527, Ferdinand was able to send armies into Hungary, and by the end of the summer the situation began to change. The well-trained German mercenaries had no difficulty defeating Zápolyai's rag-tag armies. He first retreated to Transylvania and in 1528 sought refuge in Poland. His choices were abdication or seeking Ottoman aid. His ambassador was received with open arms in Istanbul, from whence he had already received encouragement.

During their advance through the Balkans, the Ottomans had worked out a three step method of conquest. First, with small-scale conflicts and marauding expeditions, they weakened the economic and military establishments of the region they intended to conquer. They then left garrisons in key fortresses and withdrew the rest of their troops, leaving pro-Ottoman governments in power. Finally, when the inhabitants had become used to the military and political presence of the Ottomans and even begun to think of them as true allies, the Ottomans attacked again and incorporated the country into their empire. Süleyman I apparently intended to use the same method in Hungary. After the battle of Mohács, he left garrisons in the forts of the Srem region, anticipating that Zápolyai, given his position, would prevent the reestablishment of unity in Hungary. This policy explains why Süleyman, early in 1528, recognized Zápolyai as the legitimate king of Hungary and, in the Treaty of Istanbul, promised him military assistance without requiring the usual tribute.

The Ottoman armies reappeared in Hungary in the summer of 1529 and had little difficulty in pushing Ferdinand's troops into western and northern Hungary. Buda was occupied for a second time. Because the sultan had about a month and a half left before the end of October, the traditional conclusion of the Ottoman campaign season, he attempted to take Vienna. After a siege of a month, the attempt had to be given up. That the attack on Vienna was not a momentary whim, however, is proven by Süleyman's second attempt to take this city in 1532. This time an army of thirty thousand had been assembled to defend Vienna, and Süleyman changed his plans. He wasted a month trying to conquer Kőszeg, a not too important fort in Transdanubia, and then returned home. Had he succeeded in conquering and retaining Vienna, he would have paralyzed the Habsburgs and could have done with Hungary whatever he wanted.

After the 1532 failure, the Porte became more careful and systematic. It paid more attention to the control of the territory under Zápolyai's jurisdiction and to the organization and expansion of Ottoman-held areas. Explaining that Zápolyai needed support, the sultan left Ottoman units at Buda. With the help of these troops, the real master of Hungary between 1529 and 1534 was Aloise Gritti, the Venetian banker, merchant, and tax farmer, who enjoyed the favors of the sultan and the grand vizier Ibrahim. Zápolyai appointed him treasurer, commander-in-chief, and even regent, although the country had never had one simultaneously with a king who was of age. Gritti's baffling manipulations contributed significantly to the growing internal confusion in Hungary. Because Buda could be reached in a few days from the Srem region, the Ottomans were able to make certain that no developments unfavorable to them occurred. Thus this relatively small but strategically important region assured Ottoman influence in the country. In 1536 the Ottomans expanded their sway by moving into the eastern regions of Slavonia, which they held successfully when the Habsburgs counterattacked a year later.

Historians refer to the fifteen years between the Battle of Mohács and the final loss of Buda in 1541 as the period of civil war. The frequent clashes of the kings' partisans and their steadily changing loyalties altered the borders separating the rulers' domains. In spite of these events, the major trend was determined by the not too frequent Habsburg-Ottoman clashes. During these years Hungary became the battleground on which the fate of two empires was to be decided, while Hungarian troops were degraded to serve as auxiliaries of either the Habsburgs or the Ottomans. The future territorial division of a country already trisected since 1526 depended entirely on the outcome of the political and military conflicts between Vienna and Istanbul. Much of the country was under Zápolyai's jurisdiction for most of these years.

The Hungarian estates, who were not ready then or later to accept the dismemberment of the country, tried to settle problems themselves during the "years of peace" that followed 1532. Their numerous meetings, at which they attempted to solve the question of unity by deposing one, the other, or both kings, could not succeed because the decisive influences came from abroad. The civil war, from which only the Ottomans profited, finally forced the two kings to begin direct negotiations to reunify the country. After lengthy preparations, the Treaty of Várad was concluded on February 24, 1538. Ferdinand was to inherit Zápolyai's lands but was obligated to defend the country with imperial forces against the resulting Ottoman attack. The Zápolyais were to retain their immense wealth.

This treaty did not assure the reunification of the two non-Ottoman parts of the country. King János Zápolyai married Isabella, the daughter of King Sigismund I Jagiełło, in 1539, and she gave birth to a son shortly before his death in 1540. When he died in July, his all-powerful treasurer György Martinuzzi, bishop of Várad, not only refused to hand the country over to Ferdinand, but had the infant elected King János II and the election confirmed by Istanbul. He must have figured that the maintenance of the Hungarian buffer state was in the interest of the Ottomans, giving him time to get a better settlement from the Habsburgs for his new master. Ferdinand, as repeatedly in the past, did not have enough troops to occupy János' kingdom. In both 1540 and 1541, his armies were unsuccessful in their attempts to take Buda.

In August 1541, Sultan Süleyman and his armies reached Hungary's capital. He came, said the sultan, to protect the infant's rights against Ferdinand. While he gave a dinner for János' followers, his troops discreetly occupied the city's most strategic points. For the next 125 years, the country's capital became a garrison town, the seat of the governor of Ottoman Hungary. The sultan assigned to Isabella and János II the lands east of the Tisza River and Transylvania, thus creating a new state, the Principality of Transylvania.

The Institutions, Economy, and Society of Ottoman Hungary

After the dismal failure of the "imperial effort" of 1542 to retake Hungary, the Ottomans dominated Hungarian battlefields until the end of the century. One year after Buda had fallen, Joachim, markgrave of Brandenburg and his army of fifty-five thousand tried to retake the capital but could not even enter Pest. In 1543 Süleyman appeared once more in person. The conquest of Valpó, Siklós, Székesfehérvár, and Esztergom secured the region between the heartland of the Ottoman-occupied zone and the important military road running from

Buda to Esztergom on the right bank of the Danube. By conquering several smaller but strategically important cities and forts during the next two years, the pasha of Buda created a ring of strong points around Buda, the heart of Ottoman Hungary. In the south of the plains, Szeged became the major stronghold of the Ottomans after the pasha of Buda conquered it early in 1543.

On June 19, 1547 the envoys of Emperor Charles V concluded a five-year armistice with Süleyman at Edirne. Ferdinand had to pay thirty thousand gold florins yearly to the Porte as "taxes" for those parts of the country he controlled. Until the end of the century, this tax was regularly paid. However, the armistice lasted only four years. When royal Hungary and Transylvania were reunited (see chapter 9), Mehmed Sokollu, then *beylerbey* (governor) or Rumeli, began the conquest of those forts in the southern plains that protected Transylvania. In 1551 he had little difficulty in occupying strong points along the lower Tisza and Maros rivers, including the important fortress of Lippa (Lipova), but did not succeed in securing the most important fortification, Temesvár. He had to end his campaign, as usual, in the fall, and the counterattack launched jointly by the bishop of Várad and governor of Transylvania, György Martinuzzi, and the imperial general, Gianbattista Castaldo, retook these forts in the beylerbey's absence.

The following year Kara Ahmed, a high-ranking pasha, commanded the Ottoman armies. After a hard month-long siege, he conquered Temesvár on July 27, after a heroic defense by the ispán of Temes county, István Losonczy. Simultaneously, the pasha of Buda increased Ottoman-held territory by conquering first Veszprém and then several smaller places north of the Danube. During his campaign, he destroyed a Hungarian-German army that was supposed to defend the mining towns in northern Hungary. The two armies converged on just-built Szolnok and occupied it on September 4 after a two-week siege. The Ottoman advance was halted at Eger where, under the command of István Dobó, 2,500 men withstood a five-week battering until the end of the campaign season forced the Ottomans to leave on October 18. The defenders of Eger were the first to prove that not even the Ottomans were invincible.

The conquests of 1552 established an Ottoman-held zone in the center of the country. Roughly triangular, its borders ran from Lake Balaton northward to the Danube, then east to the Tisza and the Transylvanian border. Ferdinand's ambassadors were unable to conclude a new armistice in Istanbul, but for nearly fifteen years no major new Ottoman campaign was conducted in Hungary, although local garrisons continued to enlarge the occupied zone. In 1566 Süleyman ordered János II Sigismund, Prince of Transylvania, to attack northern Hungary, while his own armies launched a two-pronged attack. Pertev pasha and his thirty thousand men needed almost two months to force László Kerecsényi to surrender the important fort Gyula in the southeastern corner of the plains. The sultan in person moved against Szigetvár, an important strong-point on the road to Vienna that the pasha of Buda had failed to take in 1556 and in 1566. The defenders, under the commander of the Transdanubian district, Count Miklós Zrinyi, held out for over a month, but the situation became hopeless when a relief army failed to move. They sallied forth from the castle on September 8 and died fighting. Because Süleyman had died while the siege was in progress, the Ottomans returned home after acquiring only a few additional minor positions. The conquests of 1566 pushed the corners of the base of the Ottoman triangle further to both east and west.

The second Peace of Edirne (February 17, 1568) ended the war. It confirmed, more or less, the first peace concluded in that city in 1547. For the next twenty-five years, Ottoman armies did not fight in Hungary. The local garrisons alone were responsible for the defense of their ruler's lands and for possible new acquisitions. Formal peace between the Ottomans and Habsburgs never meant real peace. Marauding expeditions, raids, local conflicts, and the capture of prisoners were not considered violations of the peace treaty, and the loss of smaller border strongholds by either side did not disturb this equilibrium.

The Porte transformed the Hungarian lands it ruled into imperial provinces and placed these under military rule on the model employed earlier in the Balkans. The pasha of Buda was the governor of the Hungarian province *(vilayet)*. Militarily, he could order the armies of the vilayets of Bosnia and also Temesvár into action. The occupiers were not interested in the administrative divisions which had evolved in Hungary. They replaced the counties with *sandjaks,* basic administrative units, in accordance with their military interests. A bey headed each sandjak. The pasha of Buda was also the master of the most extensive sandjak, comprising most of the area between the Danube and Tisza rivers as well as the lands on the Danube's right bank. Pashas and beys were responsibile for military, administrative, legal, and police matters relating to their vilayets and sandjaks. They were helped by a council *(divan)* composed of the main military dignitaries and the leaders of the judicial and police establishments.

Localities yielding the richest revenues, the larger prairie towns, customs stations, and ferries, were declared imperial properties *(haas)* and were placed under separate jurisdiction. Pashas and sandjak beys were assigned the usufructs of estates yielding revenues of several tens of thousands of *akches* yearly. (At the time of the second Peace of Edirne, the akche contained 1.7 grams of silver and was considered to be worth fifty Hungarian florins. Its value declined seriously during the next century.) The usufruct of the remaining revenue-yielding places (villages, parts of estates, prairies) was assigned in accordance with military rank to deserving soldiers as *ziamets* or *timars* (timars yielded the least income). As time went on, less and less income could be assigned to individuals, and the yield of more and more timars was used to pay the wages of the regular troops stationed in the border fortifications. Paying the ten thousand (later fifteen thousand) regular soldiers and supplying them with food and arms became a heavy load, which the Ottoman treasury could not carry easily. According to some sources, it was the yearly equivalent of the income collected from the empire's richest province, Egypt.

The peasantry living in the Ottoman-held lands was still mainly Hungarian, with significant Serbian elements in the southern plains. It owed more or less the same services to its new lords as it had performed previously for Hungarian landlords, the state, or the Church. The Ottomans issued their regulations based on a study of Hungarian laws and customs. Taxes included a fixed amount in cash, called the house tax, and a tithe on income derived from agriculture, wine-producing, beekeeping, and livestock. Various dues and legal fines added to the lords' income. Only a few localities, mainly the most significant prairie towns situated on imperial haas land, gained the privilege in the sixteenth century to transform all their obligations into one yearly cash payment, which the Otto-mans called *maktu*. The poll tax, *cizye*, was first collected from only those heads of households who either owned moveable property or stocks of goods valued at three hundred akches, but after 1570 everyone had to pay this tax. The corvée obligations in connection with the building and maintenance of forts and with transportation were retained by the new masters. The duties relating to trans-portation developed into the most onerous of all service obligations. While all these payments and services were almost identical with those of the pre-Ottoman days, the Ottoman tax system became more oppressive and less condu-cive to progress because of the continual changing of the lords and the often arbitrary actions of the authorities.

While campaigns and sieges involved serious destruction and population losses, the medieval settlement pattern remained unchanged until the end of the sixteenth century. In the seventeenth century the cities of Kecskemét and Nagykörös were surrounded on all sides by prairies, whereas in the sixteenth they had been surrounded by dozens of villages. On the other hand, the eco-nomic and social structures began to regress rapidly during the first fifty years of Ottoman rule. With local artisans able to satisfy only the most basic needs, textiles and metal goods became the major imports. The Hungarian nobility and the Hungarian and German inhabitants of free royal cities left for either royal Hungary or Transylvania. The majority of the wealthier citizens of the prairie towns soon followed their example. The focus of the all-important agricultural sector of the economy began to shift from intensive to extensive production. During these first fifty years pastoral cattle-raising became the backbone of the economy, with more than one hundred thousand cattle driven westward every year and sold on Austrian, Moravian, Italian, and South German markets. The cattle merchants of the prairie towns became the elite of Hungarian society under Ottoman rule. They acted as middlemen along the commercial route leading from Istanbul to Venice and Nürnberg. Some of them became truly rich in terms of Hungarian values and the conditions of the time.

In spite of appearances, Ottoman mastery of Hungary was anything but com-plete. The Ottoman military, already in the sixteenth century recruited among Southern Slavs to a considerable extent, could not prevent the incursion into and even some control of Ottoman lands by troops garrisoned in the Hungarian border forts. In a sense, the occupiers became almost prisoners in their fortifica-tions. They moved between forts only in well-guarded convoys. The lords who collected income from the land did not settle these, and outside of the cities the network of Ottoman judicial offices, so effective in controlling the life of people elsewhere, was not established. Turks did not settle in Hungary. The Hungarian forces constantly penetrated the occupied lands and even managed to force the peasantry to pay dues and taxes not only to the Ottomans, but also to their landlords, the Hungarian state, and the Church, beginning around 1550. This system of "double taxation" developed into something like an Ottoman-Hungarian codominium. The occupying authorities had to accept it, and it remained in force to the end of the occupation. On the other hand, there were regions within the defensive lines of royal Hungary and Transylvania whose inhabitants also paid taxes to both their own authorities and to the Ottomans. As time passed, the amount of nonoccupied land taxed by the Ottomans increased. Yet while the Ottomans were satisfied to collect ever higher taxes in regions they did not officially hold, the Hungarians were able to add to taxation administrative and judicial functions that began to replace the Ottoman institutions.

The Institutions, Economy, and Society of Royal Hungary

Hungary was not prepared to defend herself against the Ottomans in a drawn-out war. Except for on the plains, the country had enough fortifications, but few of these had strong enough walls to resist artillery fire for more than a few days. This explains the feverish fortifying that took place in the 1540s and 1550s in royal Hungary under Habsburg rule. Military leaders and administrators of large estates vied with each other to fortify the palaces of lords, monasteries, watchtowers, and manor houses in the "Hungarian manner" by building walls of compressed earth between rows of heavy logs. By 1555 Transdanubia alone had forty-three strong-points arranged in four lines across the land. Vienna entered the fortification construction activity somewhat later, during the second half of the century. Nevertheless, the treasury could afford only the reconstruction and modernization of key strong-points. This work was done by Italian military engineers.

The new border-fort system erected in the heart of the country began at the borders of Transylvania. It was anchored first at Temesvár, then Gyula, and, after the loss of these strongholds, at Kassa. The line of forts ran northwestward, skirting the line of Ottoman fortresses. Eger and the major mining towns were the important bases. The line moved south of the Danube at Komárom and ran southward along the northern shores of Lake Balaton, with Győr, Pápa, and Nagykanizsa as its fortresses. It bisected Croatia, reaching the Adriatic at Zengg (Senj). Even disregarding the numerous twists and turns of the line, it ran for some 370 miles from Kassa (five hundred miles from Temesvár). Seven (later only six) commanders were in charge of several border forts each along this line. These commanders, usually members of the Hungarian and Croatian aristocracy, had jurisdiction only over those royal mercenaries who were stationed in their districts. In 1556 about fifty forts were manned by the king's soldiers.

Before the battle of Mohács, Hungarian military commanders had settled Serb peasant-soldiers, who had escaped from Ottoman-held territory, on the lands situated between the border strongholds. When popular levies were proclaimed in the sixteenth century, the task of defending these open regions fell mainly on the major landlords and to some extent on the county nobility. The important land-owners maintained sizable armies in the border forts and military settlements on their estates. They paid these soldiers partly out of royal revenues placed at their disposal and partly out of their own income. Because the South Slav element, which had played a major role in border defenses, had largely been killed in battle and could not be replaced, the soldiers serving in the royal or magnate forces were overwhelmingly Hungarians and Croatians in the southwest. It was during this period that the lightly armed hussar cavalry became the Hungarian military forma-tion preferred to all others. Slowly even the infantry became more and more a Hungarian branch of the military. It was recruited mainly from among the home-less but armed peasant refugées, known as the free *hajdu*.

In the so-called "peaceful years" of the sixteenth century, between thirteen and sixteen thousand soldiers were paid by the treasury. This totalled around 800,000 florins per year by the middle of the century, and reached one million by its end. Several hundred thousand more were needed to supply weapons and munitions and to maintain the forts. The income the treasury collected in Hun-gary (taxes, customs, royal revenues, etc.) amounted to only 30 percent of this amount. The remaining 70 percent had to be supplied by sources outside the country. In times of war, the country could pay for an even smaller proportion of the military expenditures. Those mobilized had to be paid, while income declined due to their absence and the destruction wrought by war.

Fortunately for Hungary, those provinces of the Habsburg domain with which their common ruler brought them in contact were able to produce the needed amounts in most instances. The largest amount was contributed by the imperial estates, but relatively the largest sacrifices were made by the Habs-burgs' hereditary provinces, which usually agreed to pay the expenses of those border forts that protected the lands nearest to them. If all these sources of revenue proved insufficient, as happened repeatedly, the credit of the House of Habsburg and its ability to use diplomacy to raise money came to the rescue. Still, the aid reached Hungary only sporadically, and the entire amount was never made available. The border forts often lacked supplies, and the soldiers went unpaid for long periods. In spite of these irregularities, it was due only to this foreign aid that the Habsburgs made available that Hungary did not share the fate of the Balkan states and fall entirely into the hands of the Ottomans.

The Hungarian estates had to pay for this support by relinquishing some important aspects of the country's sovereignty. The military pressure alone justi-fied the centralization of military, financial, and foreign affairs. The direction of military affairs became the function of the Military Court Council *(Hofkriegsrat)* established in 1556. The Hungarian Treasury and the Hungarian Chancellery became subordinate organs of the Court Treasury *(Hofkammer)* and the Court Chancellery *(Hofkanzlei)*. While these developments could be interpreted as the natural consequences of the needed centralization, the same cannot be said of the fact that at the court, residing outside Hungary, the country's leading figures lost practically all influence in determining their master's policies in Hungary.

While the legislatures dutifully elected first Maximilian I (Maximilian II in Austria) and then Rudolf, they did not give up the principle of free royal elections and required that the new ruler swear to uphold the constitution and the common law. The approving of taxes was a strong weapon in the hands of the estates, and they also retained the supervisory functions in judicial and administrative matters. The latter were especially important because only the nobiliary counties could put into force the decisions of the central authorities. Thus a certain kind of dual power developed because the Hungarian estates, too, had means to make their influence count. They gave up only those of their prerogatives which, under the circumstances, had to be sacrificed.

In a curious manner, the main strength of the estates rested on privileges that they stubbornly refused to give up, although in practice they did not enjoy them any longer. The legislature's meetings were always voicing more or less justifiable complaints about abuses of power by the ruler, government, or military command and threatening to withhold taxes. With the help of this legislative weapon, the estates forced Vienna to recognize that Hungary was a special segment of the dynasty's domains and had to be ruled in accordance with her own special laws. Naturally, the estates too knew what the limits of their power were. Until the beginning of the seventeenth century, everybody recognized that without the help of the Habsburgs, Hungary would become an integral part of the Ottoman Empire.

The power balance that determined the political life of royal Hungary in the sixteenth century rested on a compromise between the Viennese court and the main landowning aristocracy. This system took root between 1526 and 1541, when the borders of the two kings' realms coincided with those of the estates of their followers, mainly the major landowners. For this reason both Ferdinand and János (see chapters 8 and 9) tried to gain by numerous grants of lands and honors the favor of the new aristocracy that made its appearance during their struggle. Out of the hugh estates amassed in this manner by families like the Batthyánys, Nádasdys, Zrinyis, Erdődys, Révays, Báthoris, and others developed little kingdoms. These landowners rapidly extended their sway over the lesser landowning nobility living near them, who began to serve their mighty neighbors as soldiers, managers of estates, or administrators of the political districts under their jurisdiction. The lower nobility became dependent on the large landowners and followed their lead, and thus the nobiliary county played a smaller role in the sixteenth than it did later in the seventeenth century. The major offices of the kingdom were filled by members of these few landowning aristocratic families. The court left the post of palatine unfilled for forty-six years after the death of Tamás Nádasdy. These families also filled the positions of high ispán in the counties. While most of them were followers of the Habsburgs, they took the side of the Hungarian estates in day-to-day political questions. When the royal court, now on foreign soil, ceased to play a leading role in the social and cultural life of the country, it was replaced by those smaller courts that developed around a few dozen major landowning families. United, they represented a formidable opposition to the royal court.

In the sixteenth century, the large estates got involved in local and export trades and in supplying the military. For this reason, the landlords steadily increased, with the help of paid labor, those parts of their holding which they managed themselves. These areas were called *allodia*. Yet, the lion's share of the landowners' income, just as with the middle-sized and small domains, was still supplied by the serfs' obligations. In theory, the sixteenth-century serf had the same obligations as his ancestors: he had to pay a tax in cash *(census),* turn over one-tenth of his cereal and wine harvest *(nona),* and perform a fixed amount of corvée. The manpower loss resulting from the wars made it impossible for the lords to increase the serfs' obligations or change the tax system. Because the serfs still retained the right to move at will, the lords could not prevent the transforming of *nona* and corvée obligations into cash payments. They even had to tolerate that entire villages pay in cash *(summa)* for all the obligations of all their inhabitants. In spite of constant wars, these developments were favorable to the serfs. In villages and prairie towns, the better-off serfs began to play a considerable role in the producing and selling of goods.

The most important social change in the sixteenth century was the emergence of the soldiers of the border forts as a separate social group. Although those serving in these forts were increasingly of peasant origin, due to the heavy losses suffered by the nobility in the wars, they acted as nobles and, as a group, tried to increase their privileges, hoping to equal those of the nobility. This attitude was made possible by two circumstances. By granting land and noble titles to deserving soldiers, the king fostered their social rise. Furthermore, it was this military element that enforced the Hungarian feudal system in the Ottoman-held lands and sometimes even in royal Hungary. (As time passed, hostility developed between these border warriors and the peasantry because the former, often unpaid and short of supplies, had to plunder to survive.) However, this was only the beginning of a trend. While these soldiers were already potential upholders of the noble estates' aspirations, they became a decisive force only in the next century.

The development of cities was cut short in the occupied center of the country, but those on the western fringes continued to develop. Royal and other free towns were always represented when the legislature met, but their political influence was minimal. Nonetheless their role was significant in organizing domestic and foreign trade. German and Hungarian merchants of Kassa, Nagyszombat, Pozsony, and other towns exported cattle, hides, and wine and imported textiles and metal goods. Hungary's foreign trade balance was favorable in the sixteenth century, and some capital did accumulate in these areas. Yet these merchants had no part in the trading of one of the country's most important export commodities, raw copper. This became the monopoly of the Fuggers of Augsburg, cooperating with one of the newly powerful magnate families, the Thurzós. Throughout the century, the burghers made their money as merchants but invested most of their profits either in buying vineyards and arable land or in buying titles of nobility.

The Reformation and Cultural Life

The spread of religious reform was the major intellectual event in sixteenth-century Hungary. The reformers found their first followers among the German-speaking city dwellers and among the clergy of some large estates. Beginning in the late 1530s the Reformation began to affect the Hungarian peasantry and burghers, but it spread at first only very slowly. Then, in the late 1540s and early 1550s, the new creeds gained momentum and conquered the country with amazing speed. Only traces were left of the once dominant Catholic Church, and a considerable number of priests and monks converted. Ex-Franciscans, for example, were among the most successful Lutheran preachers. Chapters disintegrated and monasteries stood empty, and the lower and middle levels of the Catholic hierarchy were practically wiped out. While in accordance with the principle *cuius regio eius religio,* the conversion of landlords played a large role in spreading the Reformation among the lower social classes, the majority of the population converted voluntarily and out of conviction, often making serious economic sacrifices to back and spread the new creeds.

The momentum of the Reformation was not slowed by the split within the movement or by the acrimonious debates between sects, which on occasion degenerated into violence. Even before a Lutheran church organization (of the Augustan Confession) had time to emerge, this creed lost most of its followers to Calvinism, whose major spokesman was Péter Méliusz Juhász, a priest in Debrecen. While Calvinism became the religion of the people living east of the Tisza, and then of those on both sides of the Danube, this faith too was seriously challenged by the Antitrinitarian (later Unitarian) followers of Michael Servetus, who had been executed on the orders of John Calvin (see chapter 9). All segments of society followed with lively interest the religious debates conducted all over the country. The Catholic-Lutheran debates had hardly ended when the Calvinist-Antitrinitarian ones began. In the end, the Calvinists were able to prevent the spread of the Antitrinitarian doctrine in Hungary, where the latter creed also split into two factions. By the late 1570s and 1580s, the religious map of the country had stabilized somewhat. Only Calvinist dioceses led by bishops (superintendents) independent of each other could be found in Transdanubia, on the plains between the Danube and the Tisza, east of the Tisza and in the southern foothills of the Carpathians. In this Calvinist sea, some Antitrinitarian and Catholic islands survived. In the mountainous counties of northern Hungary, Lutheran dioceses predominated, but here too some Catholic strongholds remained. Although Maximilian I sympathized with Protestantism, the Habsburgs became the most important supporters of Catholicism and, following the decisions of the Council of Trent, introduced the Counterreformation in Hungary. The results were meager. At the end of the sixteenth century,

90 percent of the population followed one or the other of the Protestant creeds. Yet the Roman Catholic Church organization survived. Even bishoprics and other benefices in Ottoman-held territory were regularly filled; the members of the hierarchy continued to hold important administrative positions, such as palatine and chancellor; and the Church continued to collect the tithe, even from Protestants.

The Protestants owed their rapid expansion and continued popularity not only to theological arguments but also to their ability to give satisfactory answers to questions that bothered Hungarian society. The Turkish conquest forced Hungarian society to reassess its values and self-image in the most serious manner. Some of the answers worked out by Protestant preachers became commonplace but nevertheless helpful explanations. God, they preached, sent his scourge, the sultan, to punish the Hungarians for their idolatry. This explanation implied that by turning to the true faith, God's grace would be regained and everything would turn in the Hungarians' favor. God, went another explanation, always punished His chosen people the hardest. Just as He had liberated the Jews from their Babylonian and Egyptian captivities, He would certainly free the Hungarians from the Turkish yoke. The simple people were attracted not only by reassuring messages, but, very importantly, by the fact that these were presented in their native languages.

Following the Lutheran emphasis on the native idioms, Gáspár Károlyi succeeded, after a few false starts, in publishing the entire Bible in Hungarian in 1590. The use of the native tongues gave a great impetus to the improvement of education, especially on the elementary level. These lower schools supplied students to first rate institutes of higher learning (Pápa, Tolna, Sárospatak, Debrecen), whose graduates continued their studies at foreign universities, mainly at Wittenberg. It was due to the Protestant students who had studied abroad that royal Hungary, and for a while even the occupied zone, was kept up-to-date on the major cultural trends and movements of the West. Occasionally, Hungarian theologians even contributed significant works. For example, a theological systematization written by a preacher operating in the Ottoman region, István Kis of Szeged, was published in Basel in 1585 and used as a textbook in German lands.

It was the Reformation that was mainly responsible for the new models of expression that the burgeoning Hungarian-language literature began to use. Works began to appear in a steady stream, including the translations of the Psalms that, together with Károlyi's Bible translation, influenced the development of Hungarian literary language for centuries. Other works that appeared were biblical romances, songs containing moral messages, and even some morality plays. The first Hungarian printing presses—disregarding the short-lived official one of the previous century—also were established during these years, serving mainly the cause of the Reformation. These were originally established in the courts of magnates but soon became business ventures, first of the preachers and then of private citizens, in such major towns as Pápa, Kolozsvár, and Debrecen.

The humanistic endeavors that had begun prior to the Battle of Mohács gained ground together with the Reformation. The Reformation was to some extent inspired by humanism and carried its traditions further, while the Hungarian Catholic intelligentsia continued to build on its ideals. Collections of the antiques (Roman stones, coins, inscriptions) found everywhere, but especially in Transylvania, became very fashionable. It was, therefore, not a mere accident that the *Monumentum Ancyranum,* containing the political testament of the emperor Augustus, was discovered and copied in 1555 near Ankara by members of a Hungarian embassy. Following the philological rules of Erasmus of Rotterdam, the by-products of earlier unsuccessful Bible translations yielded the first Hungarian grammars (1539, 1549) and a Hungarian-Latin dictionary (1538). Suddenly several people felt the need to inform Europe about the land, natural resources, and peoples of Hungary. The first work of this kind, *De conflictu Hungarorum cum Turcis ad Mohatz,* was published in Kraków in 1527. This work, written by the bishop István Bordarich, was followed by others in the same vein, whose authors included the secretary of the queen, Miklós Oláh (1536) and an employee of the treasury, Georg Wernher (1551).

The writing of history first took mainly the form of historical songs, relating current events in Hungarian. The twenty-five rhymed narratives of the scribe Sebestyén Tinódi give a practically uninterrupted narrative of events in Hungary between 1541 and 1552. His *Cronica* was printed in Kolozsvár in 1554. Later chroniclers turned to classical models. Bishop Ferenc Forgách and the deputy palatine Miklós Istvánffy wrote in Latin prose about the history of the country between 1540 and 1572, and 1490 and 1607 respectively. The bishop Antal Verancsics secured his place in Hungarian historiography as a collector and systematizer of primary source materials.

The first poets who tried to write in Hungarian about nonreligious subjects imitated Western European humanistic models. The first, and for a long time the best, of these poets, Bálint Balassi, the scion of a magnate family, soon found his own language and style. His poems, still enjoyed by Hungarians today, give a clear picture of his contemporaries' perceptions of love, nature, and God. His works dealing with the life of the soldiers serving in border fortifications are the most effective. He even tried his hand at drama by translating an Italian pastorale. Much more interesting and successful was the translation and adaptation to Hungarian conditions, *Hungarian Electra,* published in 1558 by the Lutheran preacher, Péter Bornemissza.

The cultural life of the sixteenth century, just like the political life, was concentrated in the hands of the major landowners. The most prominent built Renaissance palaces for themselves, acquired sizeable and valuable libraries, sent their sons abroad to study, and tried to surround themselves with the leading intellectuals of the time. They spent considerable amounts on fostering the country's cultural life and consciously tried to take over the functions of the royal court, now residing abroad. It is worth noting that in Vienna, at the court of Ferdinand I, an important Hungarian cultural center was also established. Smaller but very important cultural centers emerged at the residences of bishops, in the colleges established by the Protestants, and among the followers of the most influential Protestant preachers. While their means were considerably more modest, the Hungarian and German inhabitants of cities and prairie towns also supported the publication of books and financed local schools. Several burghers even tried their hands at poetry and history.

The Fifteen Years War ("The Long War") and Bocskai's War of Independence

After the Peace of Edirne (1567), as before it, local conflicts had been commonplace along the entire border separating the Ottoman zone from Transylvania and royal Hungary. At the end of the sixteenth century, open war broke out again. Although Emperor Rudolf and Sultan Murad III agreed to prolong the armistice in 1590, the pasha of Bosnia, Hassan, attacked Croatia repeatedly in 1591–1592. In the summer of 1593, he besieged Sziszek, but was badly defeated at the end of June by Croatian and Austrian troops that had arrived on the scene. The sultan answered by declaring war, and his armies, led by the aged Sinan pasha, began to destroy the border defenses of royal Hungary, occupying, among other places, Veszprém and Várpalota.

The Habsburg supreme command and the Hungarian estates had discussed repeatedly during the previous two decades the possibility of war against the Ottomans and debated the means most likely to bring success. The Hungarians argued for an offensive action during the winter months because they knew from long experience that the Ottomans withdrew their armies from the country, moving them into winter quarters around the end of October and leaving only garrison troops behind. This way of thinking proved to be the correct one. In November and December royal troops were able to reconquer several forts, including some just north of the Danube, thus weakening the defensive perimeter protecting Buda.

Royal armies under the command of the archduke Mathias tried to build on the previous winter's successes and in 1594 attempted to reduce the defenses around Buda even further. Banderial units were active simultaneously to the south and succeeded in conquering some strong points in southern Transdanubia. The attack on Buda was stalled, as had been the case more than once in earlier years, at Esztergom, which withstood a two-month siege during the summer. The fortunes of war favored the Ottomans. At the end of September, Sinan's troops occupied the fortress of Győr, considered the key to Vienna and therefore carefully fortified for years.

As soon as the war began, the Habsburg government made serious diplomatic efforts to organize the often discussed anti-Ottoman Christian alliance. While the Christian League they managed to organize contributed considerably in men and finances to the war raging in Hungary, the defection of Transylvania and the Romanian principalities from the Ottoman camp was even more significant. After lengthy discussions at its Gyulafehérvár session, the Transylvanian legislature decided, in April 1595, to adhere to the League, forcing the Ottomans to conduct a two-front war in the Hungarian battle zone. Because the Ottomans had to divide their forces, the royal army under Karl Mansfeld was able to take the important fortress of Esztergom in September. Transylvanian armies occupied numerous fortifications along the Maros river, and, on October 29, they and their Wallachian allies won a great victory over Sinan's forces at Djurdjevo.

However, the advance of the Christian forces was stopped, and the next year witnessed important Ottoman successes. This time Sultan Mehmed III commanded his troops in person. His aim was the conquest of Eger, which fell in mid-October. The armies commanded by the archduke Maximilian and the Transylvanian prince Zsigmond Báthori were able to engage the enemy, but they suffered a crushing defeat after a battle that raged for three days.

This battle of Mezőkeresztes was the greatest of the Fifteen Years War, but it did not prove decisive. In 1597, the forces of the League failed to retake Győr, and the Transylvanians were equally unsuccessful at Temesvár. However, the Christian forces made new advances in 1598. The unexpected attack led by Miklós Pálffy and Adolf Schwarzenberg brought the surrender of Győr on March 19, followed by those of several north Transdanubian garrisons. The royal army even attempted to reconquer Buda but had to retreat after a siege lasting some thirty days. The Ottomans had to return home without any major victories. They failed to take the crucial fortification of Nagyvárad (Oradea), occupied by Habsburg troops since the abdication of Zsigmond Báthori (see chapter 9).

By this time, both the Ottomans and the League were seriously hampered in their efforts by internal dissension. The Ottomans faced a revolt in Anatolia, while the Habsburgs had to pay attention to the massive disorders that followed the abdication of Zsigmond Báthori in Transylvania, which detached not only this, but also the two Romanian principalities from the anti-Ottoman alliance (see chapter 9). The Ottomans recovered first. In October of 1600, the grand vizier Ibrahim occupied Nagykanizsa, which became the seat of the fourth vilayet established by the Ottomans on Hungarian territory. During the following year, the attempt to retake this very important fortress, which had protected the hereditary provinces of the Habsburgs, failed. While two sandjak capitals, Székesfehérvár and Simontornya, had to surrender, the Ottomans retook these also in 1602. In both 1602 and 1603, imperial troops under general Hermann Russwurm tried unsuccessfully to attack Buda.

The seemingly endless war brought immense suffering for all elements of the population. It demanded huge sacrifices in blood and brought great physical destruction. The resulting internal bitterness destroyed the consensus that up to then had united the Hungarian estates and the court circles. What bothered the Hungarians was that the main dignitaries who ran the affairs of state in the name of Rudolf (who lived in the castle of Prague and paid attention to nothing) disregarded the rules of the game that had slowly developed since 1526. They instituted legal proceedings against several magnates hoping to acquire their fortunes to bolster the rapidly diminishing resources of the treasury. The greatest interest centered around the treason trial in which István Illésházy, a great magnate who had found refuge in Poland, was condemned to loss of life and property.

The Catholic prelates who held important administrative positions now felt that the time was propitious to institute against the Hungarian Protestants the same measures they had applied earlier in Lower Austria. Protestant churches were occupied by armed forces. After the 1604 legislature had finished its work, the court added to the laws that had been passed the stipulation that in the future religious issues could not be discussed at the legislature.

When, in October 1604, the imperial forces stationed in Kassa began to occupy the castles in Bihar belonging to the Calvinist magnate, István Bocskai, a considerable segment of the Hungarian estates also ceased to observe the rules of the game. For the first time, they took to arms to protect themselves, their privileges, and their position. Bocskai found strong allies in the by this time rather numerous and mainly Calvinist *hajdu*. They were considered the reserve units of the imperial forces, but because they were never paid regularly, lived rather miserably on the margins of society. It was with the arms of the hajdu that Bocskai defended himself against the imperial forces stationed in the region, and he owed it primarily to them that, in spite of two defeats in battle, by the end of the year he was the effective master of all of northern Hungary (see also chapter 11).

On February 21, 1605, the Transylvanians elected Bocskai as their prince. Not satisfied, he continued to fight the Habsburgs with Ottoman help to secure, he declared, the constitutional rights of the Hungarian people and religious freedom. During the spring and summer, his troops controlled the northern regions of royal Hungary, raided the hereditary provinces, Moravia and Silesia, and even had some temporary successes in Transdanubia. The estates of royal Hungary, who had joined the war, elected Bocskai prince of Hungary on April 20, 1605. The Ottomans were ready to recognize him, but he accepted the crown Istanbul sent him only as a personal gift.

While the Habsburgs were concentrating on Bocskai, the Ottomans reoccupied Esztergom. This made the estates realize that the Ottoman alliance was not without serious drawbacks and dangers. In Bocskai's camp too, the number was steadily growing of those who, under the leadership of István Illésházy, advocated that the war be brought to an end as soon as the noble estates' "liberties" were once again secured. This approach had partisans in Vienna too because the archduke Matthias needed the help of the Hungarian estates to depose his brother Rudolf and take over his throne. The negotiations between the archduke and the estates in revolt, which began in November 1605, lasted for months and culminated in the Peace of Vienna on June 23, 1606. Bocskai was confirmed for his lifetime as prince of Transylvania (the position was to revert to the Habsburgs at his death). The court accepted the noble estates' requests; after a long interval the estates were again allowed to elect a palatine; the major Hungarian offices were to go only to Hungarians in the future, irrespective of their religion; all royal regulations that contradicted Hungarian law were withdrawn, and freedom of religion was granted to the nobility, to the inhabitants of cities and towns, and to soldiers serving in the border fortifications. In practice this meant complete freedom of religion.

The Peace of Vienna also stipulated that peace had to be concluded with the Ottomans. Bocskai served as mediator between the Habsburg and Ottoman negotiators. The so-called Peace of Zsitvatorok, signed on November 11, 1606, brought important changes regulating the relations of the two empires. By paying a lump sum of 200,000 florins for the Hungarian lands under his rule, the Habsburg ruler was relieved from the yearly taxes he had paid to Istanbul. With this concession, the sultan recognized the emperor as his equal. The peace was based on the status quo of 1606. This meant that the Ottomans retained Eger and Nagykanizsa, while the Habsburgs kept those forts north of Buda that they had taken early in the war. The rest of the border was very similar to what it had been in 1593.

While the long war hardly changed the borders between the two empires, it produced immense changes in the settlement pattern, population density, and ethnic composition of the country. Because the Ottomans, breaking with their previous habits, kept parts of their army—including Tatar auxiliaries—permanently in the country during the war, Hungary had become practically a wasteland by the end of the sixteenth century. There had been years during the war when only a few prairie towns were able to maintain a precarious existence in the face of numerous dangers and calamities. The settlement pattern, which had suffered only minor changes in the previous years, was totally altered. The destroyed villages were never rebuilt. Their lands were taken over by their neighbors, mainly the larger prairie towns. The destruction was considerable even in regions not under direct Ottoman rule. These, too, suffered practically irreparable damages due to the direct and indirect effects of the war. Because the Fifteen Years War was fought mainly in the central, Hungarian-inhabited regions of the land, the ethnic composition changed everywhere in favor of other nationalities: Slovaks in the north, Romanians in the east, Serbs in the south. The ethnic changes of this period had a tremendous influence on political developments of Hungary in subsequent centuries, and, finally, became crucial in determining her fate.

VIII

THE LATER OTTOMAN PERIOD AND ROYAL HUNGARY, 1606–1711

Katalin Péter

Demography and Living Standards

During the Fifteen Years War (1592–1606), Hungary suffered not only from military action but also from repeated epidemics and natural catastrophes. The resulting shortages and astronomic prices brought famine and other woes to the entire country, though the magnitude of devastation varied greatly from region to region. The hardest hit was Transylvania, where a great proportion of the national wealth and about 50 percent of the population disappeared. Similar disasters occurred in two regions of the country under Ottoman rule: on the right bank of the Danube, where the Ottoman armies regularly marched on their numerous campaigns; and north of this river between the Austrian border and the point where the river turns southward. The latter area suffered more than any other part of royal Hungary. The end of hostilities left the country in dire straits, and the rest of the century brought only further epidemics and wars.

The plague appeared about once every decade and usually lasted several years or longer, with epidemics in 1620–1627, 1632–1634, 1643–1645 and 1660–1665. The other great killer was smallpox, which decimated the wealthy. These people had the means to flee plague-stricken regions, but smallpox, with its long incubation period, could not be escaped.

In the first half of the seventeenth century, most wars were fought in royal Hungary; Transylvania and the Ottoman zone became battlefields in the second half. The Hungarian stages of the Thirty Years War (1618–1648) were fought mainly in royal Hungary, primarily by Transylvanians and their allies, the Ottomans, who moved through the occupied lands. Between 1657 and 1664, the country suffered from the last demonstration of Ottoman military might. Marching through the occupied regions, the Ottomans first directed their attack against their former ally, Transylvania, then against royal Hungary. Only southwestern Transdanubia was spared somewhat from the effects of this campaign.

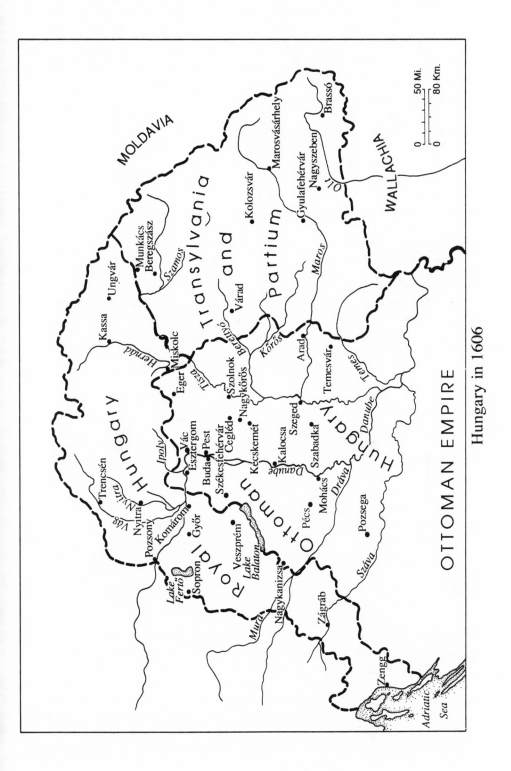

Hungary in 1606

The last series of wars began with anti-Habsburg operations in the 1670s, continued with the anti-Ottoman wars of liberation, and closed, once again, with military actions against the Habsburgs. All of Hungary, including Transylvania, became a battlefield in these years.

The three parts of the country reacted differently to the numerous dangers. In the occupied lands, the population moved in increasing numbers into those cities in the hands of local Hungarian administrators. For example, in Halas two-thirds of the 106 heads of households were immigrants by the end of the century, and Debrecen's nearly twenty thousand inhabitants were mainly ex-peasants who had moved in from the surrounding villages. It was during these years that these cities acquired their peculiar structure. The houses stood closely bunched in the center of four concentric rings of land. The first was occupied by barns, orchards, and vegetable gardens. Then followed an inner zone of pastures; then came plough-lands; finally, a zone of outlying pastures merged into the surrounding lowland plains. From the cities roads led in every direction. This structure favored animal husbandry, but with its rings also offered protection against attacks.

The concentration of the population in towns had mixed results. While the towns offered protection in times of war, the flight of the country folk left large areas uninhabited. These regions turned into swamps and marshes. While offering good refuge in times of need, they also became the breeding ground of epidemics, and insect swarms moved from them into the inhabited regions. The boggy regions of the middle Danube and along practically the entire length of the Tisza remained the lasting, unhealthy reminders of the Ottoman occupation well into the nineteenth century. In sharp contrast, around Győr and Komárom, in a region of royal Hungary hard hit by the Fifteen Years War, the regulation of the Danube and Rába began around 1620. Here, the population reacted to hardships with measures that not only reestablished but improved its living standards.

The best indication of this civilizing trend was the growing number of doctors, pharmacists, and barbers. (Early in the century a barber of Vágújhely, [Nové Mešto nad Váhom], became so famous that he was actually called to Vienna for consultation.) During the sixteenth century, infirmaries had been rare even in cities; in the seventeenth, they appeared even in villages, and serfs were exempted from services on the various estates to work in them. Health care brought with it a growing awareness of the importance of cleanliness; the number of public baths increased, and the regular changing of underwear became general.

Increased understanding of health matters spread primarily among the upper classes, but it affected all segments of society to some extent. Documents reveal that an understanding of the importance of a balanced diet resulted in the growing of more fruits and vegetables and in efforts to preserve them. Beds might have existed earlier, even in peasant homes, but it was during these years that their use became general, and barons, nobles, and burghers began to use sheets and wear night clothes.

The composition of the population also changed in the seventeenth century. Tax records, which list only heads of households and other male members of families, are the sole source of data from this period but nevertheless present a vague outline of the most important changes.

While the number of births in the seventeenth century did not increase, infant mortality seems to have decreased. Those families whose genealogies have survived were larger than they had been before the Fifteen Years War. While burgher families, on the average, lasted only for three generations in the male line in earlier centuries, they survived longer in the seventeenth. Based on tax records, peasant families also appear to have become larger. It is likely that a population explosion followed the Fifteen Years War. Needing heirs, people married at an earlier age and took good care of their children.

In the Ottoman-ruled regions, immigration accounted for the fact that cities maintained or even slightly increased their size. In the villages, the steady shrinkage of the native population accelerated the influx of Serbs, which had begun earlier. Some of the Serbs were settled in Hungary by the Ottomans, but most migrated voluntarily because living conditions were even worse in the Balkans than in Hungary. In certain regions, half of the villages were inhabited by Serbs. The cohabitation of Serbs and Hungarians reached its apogée when the mixed demographic region reached the Debrecen-Pest line. During the anti-Ottoman wars of liberation, the Serbs began to withdraw, and Rákóczi's war of independence pushed them back to the southern regions.

In the two parts of the country free from Ottoman rule, following the decimation of the war, the growth of the resident population was augmented by immigrants. In Transylvania and attached lands, the newcomers were mainly Romanians. In northeastern royal Hungary, the immigrants were mainly Ruthenians, and Vlachs began to move to the north from the southeast. These people had either lived in the country before or entered it as wandering shepherds. In the seventeenth century, they were settled by the authorities or moved voluntarily into the agricultural areas. It appears certain that their place was taken by others from the neighboring countries, but information is not available to establish their exact number in the country at any given moment.

Our knowledge of seventeenth century demographics remains hazy. While data concerning migrations and settlements have survived, it is difficult to evaluate them. The improvement of living standards, the population explosion, and the appearance of immigrants in the two free sectors of the country are facts, but how these influenced the fluctuation of the total population remains unclear. It is known that on the eve of the Fifteen Years War, the population of Hungary was around three to three and a half million, but for the later years of the seventeenth century, no figures are available. For the future the important period was the one which followed the wars of liberation when the government and the landlords introduced a systematic, and large scale settlement policy. By the 1740s, after the departure of the plague and the arrival of settlers in the millions, Hungary, no longer threatened by demographic collapse, was ready to face the future with a population of about five million.

Economy and Society

Even our sketchy demographic knowledge suggests that no important changes could occur in the economic structure of the country in the seventeenth century. At the beginning of the century, the population density per square mile was 32.5 in royal Hungary, twenty-two in Transylvania and eighteen in the occupied lands. These figures did not change much, and under these circumstances, the domestic consumer demand was insufficient to trigger major economic development. International factors were also unfavorable to economic growth. In the first half of the century, Europe's economy stagnated and even regressed (England and the Netherlands excepted), and this was the case in Hungary too.

Foreign trade data are scarce, but the records of one important customs station suggest that international commerce declined significantly from the previous century. While prices had increased sharply earlier, they remained unchanged after the turn of the century. The price of wheat, the most important export item, shows this clearly. The devaluation of the currency was an even more serious problem. It became almost impossible to exchange the masses of small copper coins for real money anywhere in the country and even more hopeless abroad. Both the Hungarian and Transylvanian legislatures repeatedly protested against the debasement of the currency.

Symptoms of pan-European economic trends were also observable in Hungary. It became obvious that the division of labor that had developed during the previous century, had acquired permanence for the foreseeable future. Hungary and its neighbors, taking advantage of the general demand for agricultural products, had become specialists in exporting these goods, and southern Germany and Italy had become the most important buyers of cattle. This demand fell off in the seventeenth century, first in Italy, then in Germany, as general economic decline caused people to eat cereals rather than beef, at least for a while. Given the difficulties of transportation, wheat could not be shipped to faraway markets. Manufactured goods would probably still have been exportable, but the capital that had accumulated in Hungary at the end of the previous century had not been utilized to create an industrial base. Except for agricultural products, the country had nothing to sell. After a temporary decline, the West was able to stabilize its economy by industrialization, but Hungary could react only by changing the composition of its agricultural marketbasket. While animal husbandry declined, wine became the leading export item.

By the middle of the century, it became clear that Hungary's position in Europe's economy was unfavorable. The prosperity of the earlier periods placed it for a long time in the ranks of agricultural suppliers on the international market, and the country took a different road than the industrializing West.

The three parts of the country were affected in different degrees. Despite its loss of population, Transylvania was the least affected economically. While the shift of the major trade routes deprived it of the Levantine trade, the country remained the major transit station between Europe and the Ottoman Empire. American gold and silver diminished the demand for the principality's mineral wealth in general, but its mercury trade continued to prosper. Mercury was shipped to Venice and Istanbul, in exchange for luxury goods, carpets, expensive textiles, spices, and rare foods. Because Transylvania was self-sufficient, it did not import consumer goods. Another advantage Transylvania enjoyed was the demand for agricultural and industrial goods from the countries on its southern and eastern borders. This ensured a secure market, and until the 1680s, the existence of the Ottoman Empire ensured Transylvania's economic life.

The Romanian principalities bought everything Transylvania could produce. While these lands served as the larder of the Ottoman Empire, this function made industrialization impossible, forcing them to buy everything from wooden nails to medical instruments from their western neighbor. Wheat could be transported eastward into the occupied lands. The trip was short, because the Transylvanians had to go only as far as Temesvár.

The special economic situation of Transylvania was reflected in prices and wages. In western Hungary, as everywhere else in Europe, artisans' wages lagged behind agricultural and industrial prices. In Transylvania, this was not the case in the seventeenth century. Wages there increased slightly more than did prices. This relative economic strength made Transylvania able to bear an incredible economic burden at the time of the wars of liberation. According to the treaty of 1685 between the emperor and the Transylvanian prince, in one particular year Transylvania was asked to supply 420,000 imperial florins, 1,650,000 bushels of either wheat or flour, and more than fifteen thousand oxen and cows, as well as vast quantities of wine, oats, hay, and straw. Two years later, when even these figures were further raised, no mention was made of arrears. The total tribute Transylvania had paid to the sultan during 150 years was less than what she had to pay for the wars of liberation. The country was economically exhausted when these wars ended.

While it is not possible to measure the relative damage caused by internal decay and the declining European economy, the occupied lands suffered the most. The Danube ceased to be a major commercial route by the seventeenth century, but it is not known whether this was due to decreased demand or to the insecurity brought by the destruction in the region. Contact between the occupied lands and royal Hungary decreased considerably. Prior to the Fifteen Years War, travel through Ottoman lands was common, and for certain persons it was quite natural to spend part of their lives in Ottoman and part in royal Hungary. In the seventeenth century, it took courage to traverse the Ottoman zone. Foreigners avoided it altogether, and Hungarians organized caravans or arranged military escorts if they had to pass through these lands. The regular routes between Hungary and Transylvania skirted the Ottoman-held regions. As a result, the contact between the occupied zone and the outside world became limited to the collection of a great variety of taxes and to the cattle trade.

During this period, herds of cattle numbering in the tens of thousands were still driven to market, but the drop in foreign demand naturally had its repercussions in Ottoman Hungary also. By the middle of the century, it was not uncommon for some of the cattle that had been driven to Vienna at great risk to be driven back again because buyers were lacking.

The landlords with holdings in the occupied zone, whose claims the Ottomans recognized, did not diminish their demands on the peasantry. They began to require payments from the peasantry not in cash, but in cattle. They shipped large amounts of valueless money to their serfs living in Ottoman-held land, asking them to buy either cattle for it or to exchange it—with the help of usurers—for good money. The same landlords profited also from the change in the agricultural pattern that resulted from changed demands. In the Ottoman-held regions too, viniculture began to replace the growing of cereals. Landlords began to collect their taxes and dues in wine and then forced the local innkeepers to sell only this wine and to remit the proceeds to them in good money.

In a sense, the economic situation of the occupied lands did not change in the seventeenth century. Lords living in royal Hungary continued to garner more income here than the occupiers. Significantly, however, whereas in earlier days the royal and princely treasuries collected most of the revenue coming from the occupied lands, in the seventeenth century, the lion's share of the profits went to the landlords. In the sixteenth century, it was occasionally possible for those living under Ottoman rule to amass fortunes. In the seventeenth, this was no longer true. The central part of Hungary, paying taxes to two masters, was stripped bare by the time the wars of liberation began. Even the richest town, Debrecen, went bankrupt as a result of the senseless tributes exacted by the imperial forces. Passive suffering was all these people could contribute to the wars of liberation. Yet when the new struggle began in 1703, directed against the developing new Habsburg order, they were among the most active resisters and fighters.

In royal Hungary, the seventeenth century's economic developments appear contradictory. While the demand for agricultural products declined, the landlords appropriated ever greater amounts of serf lands for cultivation under their own management. These new production units acquired the name of farm (majorság) and were worked by the serfs' forced labor. The record books show that cash income declined because those who had previously paid their dues in cash were now paying with labor. These notations show clearly the gradual development of the phenomenon known as second serfdom, which became characteristic of Europe east of the Elbe river.

The trend towards demanding payment in corvée instead of cash from serfs had actually been started earlier by the lords with the largest estates, but by the middle of the century, owners of middle-size estates also followed the practice. This development is not contrary to the mentioned decline of agricultural prosperity, for these new farms produced not cereals but wine. One example will illustrate this trend. On the Fraknó estate of the Esterházy family, the majority of farms produced cereals in 1610, but by 1630, 64 percent of the cash income of the entire large estate was derived from the sale of wines. The same was true in Northeast Hungary too where, for example, fifty-two of the eighty-six farms on the lands of the Rákoczis produced wines. When, in the 1670s, the lands of numerous nobles were confiscated, the authorities discovered that wine producing was the major activity on most of them.

Wine had a good market during the entire century. Exact figures have survived only for exports to Poland, but even these show that sales were steadily increasing. Only years of bad harvest broke the otherwise steadily mounting curve. When, for various reasons, export difficulties occurred, the lords simply forced their innkeepers to dispose of their stock.

There can be no doubt that the lords profited from the new servitude of their people, yet the entire economy was trapped in a vicious circle. The introduction of corvée was the direct result of the devaluation of the currency. The few *denars* the serfs delivered to their lords added up to sacks of worthless metal, which could be transformed into real money only with the greatest difficulty. It was simpler for landowners to produce something saleable on self-managed farms, even if this was not always easy. The result was that the landlords' cash income shrunk at exactly the moment when Europe went through a price revolution. The shortage of cash forced even the richest lord to borrow even small amounts at usurious rates or to raise cash by pawning some of his possessions.

The cash shortage among the landowners determined the structure of the entire economy. To begin with, not only agricultural products but everything the estates needed was produced by those who served with their labor. Serfs made furniture, clothing, arms, even jewelry. Only rare items were bought abroad, usually on credit. The lords were not alone in lacking cash. The cities were the hardest hit by the emerging second serfdom. The more the estates strove to be self-sufficient, the smaller the market for the artisans in the cities became. While the rest of Europe was rapidly urbanizing, Hungary's cities stagnated. Several cities had tried, in earlier decades, to become free royal towns; none had the money now to buy these privileges. When, in the last third of the century, the government was ready to sell privileges to raise money, no cities applied. Whatever money Vienna was able to extort from the cities by hook or by crook had been earned by the citizenry's agricultural activities.

Already, in the years of agrarian prosperity, the cities had sought to increase their income by adding agriculture to their other activities. When even their domestic markets collapsed, they had no choice but to make a living from agriculture. As corporations or as individuals, city dwellers rented land from landlords, attempting to make their towns self-sufficient or to make profits from the sale of wine. Thus, while those living from agriculture withdrew from the cities' markets, the burghers became increasingly independent from the agrarian sector. As a result, the country's economy stagnated during the entire second half of the century.

During the Renaissance, the rich citizens of towns had constructed homes and churches, depicted their professions and their way of life on altarpieces, and, in general, developed an urban civilization. Now, the lifestyle of the burghers began to change. Considerably poorer than their ancestors, they began to imitate the nobility.

Nevertheless, the social structure of royal Hungary remained unchanged. Imitating nobles was simple affectation; social mobility was practically nonexistent. Sebestyén Thököly, a rich cattle merchant, ennobled by the king in 1598 had no successors. Not only was the bourgeoisie not gaining ground in Hungary, but, on the contrary, the nobility were penetrating all spheres of society. The nobility acquired the right to buy homes in cities and hold offices there. Yet while the 1646–1647 legislature freed even the lowest-ranking nobles from the magnates' right to pass death sentences on them, even within the nobility upward mobility was blocked. Very early in the century, those who married daughters of magnates could still move up. Of those who became lords in this manner, Zsigmond Rákóczi, Miklós Esterházy, and István Illésházy soon became important political figures. After 1620, however, a new baron was a great rarity.

Unlike those elsewhere on the continent, Hungary's magnates remained a closed ruling elite. In 1680, the same seventy or eighty families made up this circle of aristocrats as a hundred years earlier. Their social prestige was even greater than during the previous century because they were the ones able to extricate themselves first from the general economic decline. The distance between them and the rest of society grew steadily. They also increased their influence on ruler and court: it was typical that in royal Hungary all anti-Habsburg movements were organized by mighty magnates. The leaders of the great war of liberation were members of the Zrinyi family, prominent since the Middle Ages, and of the Rákóczi family that gave three princes to Transylvania. It was not until after 1680 that the royal court tried to weaken the power of the old aristocracy by again raising new families to their ranks.

Civilization and Culture

The economic decline and social stagnation were reflected in intellectual pursuits as well. While Bálint Balassi, the greatest poet of the previous century, had glorified ladies and women of easy virtue alike in his love songs, the only lyric poem expressing personal feelings written by the greatest poet of the seventeenth century, Miklós Zrinyi, lamented the death of his son. Zrinyi devoted most of his efforts to politics and war, allowing István Gyöngyösi to rule the literary field with his endless poems glorifying carefully arranged marriages.

The decline of learning is dramatically illustrated by the number and nature of publications. The growth of published works dealing with secular topics was arrested. Prior to 1571, 40 percent of the books published were nonreligious in content, reaching 58 percent during the last thirty years of that century. In the first third of the next, this figure did not change. Subsequently, the total number of new books increased, but theological works and publications for ecclesiastic use regained their dominance. Although the number of works in Hungarian grew somewhat, those in other languages—except German—disappeared entirely. While 107 literary volumes were published in Hungarian in the last three decades of the sixteenth century, only thirty appeared in the next thirty-five years. Those whose education did not include Latin had practically nothing to read.

The Hungarian version of baroque culture differed from that of the West. Schematically, we can distinguish three major differences. First, the most important intellectual trend of the century, the emergence of modern scientific thinking, did not lead in Hungary to lively debates among scientists, but was limited to the lonely activities of a few remarkable individuals. Second, in contrast with the West, religious conflicts did not come to a close at the end of the sixteenth century in Hungary. In the Counterreformation, Catholicism regained its dominant position in royal Hungary, and both there and in Transylvania, the struggle with Protestantism revived. Third, it was a Hungarian peculiarity that the courts of the magnates became not only the incarnations of the baroque way of life, but also the organizers of the cultural life of the country. Even the Ottoman zone was influenced by these trends to a limited extent.

In the realm of science and philosophy, the important men can easily be listed. The imperial mathematician, Dávid Frölich, published a heliocentric treatise in 1632, mentioning the work of Copernicus. In 1653 appeared in Amsterdam the *Encyclopedia* of the Transylvanian preacher and professor János Csere Apácai, based on Cartesian philosophy and including the results of Descartes' work. Bacon's first follower in Hungary was the professor János Bayer. At Sárospatak, János Pósaházi created his own modern eclectic natural philosophy, in which he paid some attention to the experimental method. Márton Tönkö Szilágyi, who worked in Debrecen, expressed his regrets that demonstrations were not possible because the equipment needed for experiments was not available due to "bad times and general indifference." István Simándi was already able to import the needed equipment from Leyden to Sárospatak.

While these men did not adopt Newton's worldview, they recognized the importance of observation and experimentation. They approached Newton as closely as their work permitted. The Enlightenment of the next century was to take Hungarian science further, but in the seventeenth century, Aristotelian scholasticism remained dominant. In the better Protestant schools, due mainly to the work of Puritan professors, the philosophy of Descartes gained ground, but among the orthodox Protestants and the Catholics, Aristotle remained supreme. In Hungary and neighboring countries, the old and new theories lived peacefully side-by-side without provoking theoretical debates. The followers of the "new philosophy" were often received with hostility, their lives were often unpleasant, but in Hungary science was not yet sufficiently developed to prompt serious debates.

While intellectual life evoked little interest, everybody was deeply affected by and interested in the complicated chain of events tied closely to the Counterreformation. Around the 1620s, the majority of the aristocrats returned to the faith of their ancestors. By the 1660s, numerous nobles of all levels had followed the example of the magnates. No exact data are available, but the legislature of 1638 already had a Catholic majority of deputies representing the counties, while the cities were still solidly Protestant.

Religious persecution was undertaken by Catholic landlords who put serious pressure on people living on their domains. More important was the violence used against Protestants in the name of the ruler. Ferenc Nádasdy, a Catholic magnate who had used violence against his own serfs, could also lead resistance movements in the 1660s, fighting, among other things, for religious freedom. The failure of this movement revived religious persecution by the Catholic authorities, which had ceased following Bocskai's revolt (see chapter 7). The violence which began in 1671 knew few if any bounds during the following "decade of Protestant bereavement." Atrocities occurred mostly in the cities, and the nadir was reached when, in 1674, numerous Protestant ministers and professors were sent to the imperial galleys on trumped up charges. Dutch diplomacy was able to gain the release of the survivors a year later.

Not only did Catholicism not gain from this violence, but it even hurt the state by reinforcing the determination of the Protestants. Violence created Protestant martyrs and converts to Catholicism were now considered traitors. It is, therefore, not difficult to understand why the great anti-Habsburg war that marks the end of this period was fought, among other things, for the Protestants' religious freedom, although the leaders were Catholics.

The religious debates of the Counterreformation are well-documented because both sides published numerous books and pamphlets. Noteworthy is the fact that while the clashes of theologians attracted great interest—just as they had a century earlier—theology had practically nothing to do with conversions. Mysticism appears to be the main reason that brought people back to Catholicism.

During the Counterreformation, all the organized churches were regenerated. The first church to reform itself was the Catholic. Left practically without followers, it gave up its superior attitude and embarked on missionary work. Instead of concentrating on the clergy, this church addressed the people, whom it sought to win over with the help of mysticism and sermons tailored to their understanding. The master of these sermons was Péter Pázmány, the cardinal of Esztergom. He addressed his listeners in magnificent Hungarian, using examples and similes that made perfect sense even to the least educated. It was primarily he who made the seventeenth one of the great centuries of the Hungarian language. The archetypal mystical missionary was Mátyás Hajnal, who described allegorically the mystic union of Jesus with the souls of believers. Following his example, the number of written works published by the Catholics in which sentiment and not reason was stressed increased. Appealing celebrations such as processions and saint's day festivities also multiplied. The Jesuits established congregations everywhere to honor the Virgin Mary but made certain that these served not only religious, but also social functions.

The Protestants reacted almost at once. The orthodox were unable to counter the dangerous new challenge, but among those, both Lutheran and Calvinist, who were not church dignitaries, there were some who turned to new methods. Among the Calvinists, the Puritans who had studied in England and the Netherlands favored congregational meetings in and out of church and stressed the importance of mystical experiences. Pál Medgyesi, court chaplain in Transylvania, was a leading organizer of congregations. His sermons show clearly how Protestant mysticism worked without statues and pictures.

The Lutherans imported Pietism slightly later from Germany. Its leading Hungarian exponent was not a clergyman, but a woman, Sidonia Kata Petröczi, who found solace in Pietism after a sad and tragic life. Her writings had personal, emotional appeal similar to that of the mysticism of the Catholics.

Cultural life in this era took distinctly different turns in the occupied lands and in Transylvania than in royal Hungary. While the lords collected money in Ottoman-held lands, they paid no attention to the spiritual or cultural life of the inhabitants, and what cultural life existed was due to the activity of the clergy. The circumstances were most unfavorable. The well-known schools of Tolna and Ráczkeve left these places only temporarily during the Fifteen Years War, but never regained their former excellence. The Ottoman-held lands produced nobody of real cultural or intellectual significance in the seventeenth century. A few individuals born there found their way to good schools elsewhere, but those who taught in the occupied regions were usually individuals whose education had ended with the trivium. Even the education of the clergy was deficient. Catholic congregations often had to be satisfied with so-called license-holders who had no theological training and were not ordained.

In Transylvania, the princely court led cultural activities (see chapter 9). It reached its high point under Gábor Bethlen, but the decline that followed the death of his successor affected cultural activities too. Transylvania's importance in the history of Hungarian civilization became negligible for a while, and its nobility was excluded from running the affairs of state. In royal Hungary the situation was similar. Already during the anti-Turkish wars of liberation, Hungarian politicians were not consulted, and after 1711 their role was curtailed even further.

In royal Hungary, leadership in cultural life evolved as a direct result of the relationship between Hungary's king and its aristocracy. The ruler paid practically no attention to the internal affairs of the state. One cannot speak of a royal cultural policy, except perhaps the Counterreformation. Leopold I built his power, often described as absolutist, without help from any social stratum in Hungary. Except for a few priests, whose vision was limited to the problem of the Counterreformation, the king had few supporters within his country.

In the absence of social or cultural leadership from the royal court, this role devolved upon a few intelligent magnates, who became the patrons of art and education. Regardless of their motives, these activities affected the living conditions and standards of everybody who worked on their estates, from the highest official to the lowliest serf.

Patrons had to make greater sacrifices in the seventeenth century than in earlier times. The Reformation, for example, had not required the building of new churches and had no use for abbeys and monasteries. The return to Catholicism, on the other hand, demanded expensive and luxurious churches, imposing monasteries, and shrines that were not only holy, but also spectacular. All were built in great numbers. It was the palatine, Miklós Esterházy, who built the first baroque church modeled on Rome's *il Gesu*. This church, at Nagyszombat, was followed by several others which he and his son Pál, also a palatine, founded. These two men alone probably were responsible for more churches and other religious structures than were all the patrons together during the Reformation. Entire generations of North Italian and Austrian architects were employed in building the religious and worldly edifices ordered by the magnates. They were followed by excellent painters, who produced in Hungary not only altarpieces and calvaries, but also gigantic murals. Symbolic historical murals became the fashion.

The immense buildings symbolized the practically limitless power of those who had them erected. Yet they are also significant as signs of how diverse the knowledge of the serfs had become. While the planning and possibly the decorating of the various structures was left to famous foreigners, the great monuments of the baroque were the handiwork of the serfs. While both the economic dependence of the serfs and the corvée demanded of them increased, as a group and as individuals these people became incredibly versatile. This development had favorable consequences for the country's cultural development. The lives of lord and serf became inextricably interwoven. As a result, people belonging to the lowest social stratum acquired professions requiring extensive intellectual or practical training. Serfs became musicians, tailors, dressmakers, and landscape gardeners. This acquisition of skills influenced the economic possibilities of the masses. For those who had special talents or knew how to manage their affairs, it opened numerous doors. The situation was not different from what had prevailed earlier at the royal court. There, those members of the lower nobility who attracted the ruler's attention found chances for advancement. Now serfs found similar opportunities in the service of the magnates.

The seventeenth century brought contradictory changes in the lot of the serf in royal Hungary. On the one hand, it saw the final ossification of a serfdom more onerous than ever before. Indeed, the landowners lived in fear of a peasant uprising, and the danger of one was a constant refrain in legislative assemblies. On the other, a growing number of serfs mastered sophisticated professions and became free individuals who discharged their obligations through cash payments or skilled services.

Politics

In the days of the economic and social supremacy of the major landowners, politics also reflected their dominance. This is clearly seen from the behavior of the Transylvanian legislature, which, following Bocskai's death, elected its own candidate as prince, in opposition to both Vienna and Istanbul (see chapter 7). The Hungarian legislature showed similar independence. When it met in January 1608, it modified the clauses of the Peace of Vienna in the landlords' favor (see chapter 7). While this peace had left the relationship between lord and serf somewhat vague, the legislature stipulated that the king had no right to regulate it. Furthermore, those present ensured their political supremacy by passing laws specifying whom the ruler had to invite to future sessions of the legislature. It was this legislature that elected Matthias II to replace Rudolf, who had abdicated, on the throne.

The events between the two anti-Habsburg wars of liberation (Bocskai's and Rákóczi's) cannot be explained as a simple clash between absolutism and the interests of the estates. In Hungary absolutism was not a fact, only a possible danger. The two major conflicts of these years resulted from the actions of the Transylvanian princes Gábor Bethlen and György I Rákóczi (see chapter 9). The events which followed the liberation of Ottoman-held Hungary in 1686 fit the standard pattern even less because they had practically nothing to do with the country's internal affairs.

The political events of the seventeenth century can nevertheless be arranged in three phases. The first ends around mid-century, when the Thirty Years War came to a close. The second lasted to about 1684, when it became clear that the wars against the Ottomans would be concluded successfully. The final phase includes the anti-Ottoman wars and Ferenc II Rákóczi's war of independence.

The politicians of the first period lived with the memories of the Fifteen Years War. The Peace of Zsitvatorok in 1606 forced them to admit that a large part of the country would be ruled by Istanbul for a long time. The great effort of the country, supported by foreign aid, had not been successful, and the Ottomans could not be expelled. Leading politicians somberly hoped for a miracle. "The country reached the moment of perdition," repeatedly observed documents of the time. Under the circumstances, the major political goal, the expulsion of the Ottomans, faded into the background. Among those who thought responsibly about the country's future, two groups began to emerge. Both were dissatisfied with the policy of the Habsburgs. One faction hoped to solve the problem by governmental reform, while the other believed that what was needed was the end of foreign rule.

The reform party began to advocate the establishment of a standing army, even before the Long War came to a close. Miklós Esterházy, the leading spokesman of this faction, expanded the reform concept considerably. Between 1627 and 1642, he produced numerous proposals. In his view, two major weaknesses had led to the country's decline: the neglect of the military and the misguided disbursement of the national income. What was needed, according to Esterházy, were thorough reforms, changing the military establishment and the tax system. These tasks had to be tackled by the leading nobles until the ruler found time to deal with Hungarian issues. Esterházy and those who thought like him believed that Habsburg neglect of Hungary was only temporary because the rulers were concentrating on problems in their western lands, and that as soon as the war, which broke out in 1618, had ended, the liberation of Hungary from the Ottoman yoke would follow.

The other party was not willing to wait. It sided with the numerous enemies of the Habsburgs, believing that the Thirty Years War, which had begun following the revolt in Prague on May 23, 1618, offered a chance to reestablish a national kingdom. Early in the hostilities, this way of thinking was dominant, and Gábor Bethlen had enthusiastic support when he opened his first campaign (see chapter 9). On August 25, 1620, the Hungarians deposed the House of Habsburg and elected Bethlen as their king. It became obvious very quickly that should he prove victorious, Bethlen would rule without consulting the estates, just as he did in Transylvania. His partisans' aims were just the opposite. Thus Bethlen lost his Hungarian supporters at about the same time that his major allies were defeated at the White Mountain. The Hungarian estates were frightened equally by the prospects of the revenge of the Habsburgs (which they were observing in the neighboring Czech lands) and of the absolutism of Bethlen. They were glad to get full amnesty from Ferdinand II when the Peace of Nikolsburg was concluded (see chapter 9).

Those who had advocated the reestablishment of a national monarchy lost ground and became a minority among the country's politicians. They did not support the subsequent efforts of Bethlen nor those of György I Rákóczi, which came later. Rákóczi's efforts nevertheless brought one important change. The Peace of Linz (December 16, 1645) included a clause guaranteeing the serfs' religious freedom. The legislature of 1645–1646 passed a law confirming this decision. Because most landlords were Catholics, the Protestants seemingly had gained a major victory. Yet the law was disregarded even by Protestant landlords.

A new situation was created by the Peace of Westphalia in 1648 ending the Thirty Years War. The liquidation of Ottoman rule became, once again, the major desideratum of Hungarian politicians. Hungarians had followed the ups and downs of the just-concluded war with great interest in the expectation that its conclusion would mean the opening of war with the Ottomans. The Habsburgs had been promising to drive out the Turks since 1526, and in 1648, everybody was certain that hostilities would begin at once. The leading figure of the younger politicians, Miklós Zrinyi, wrote the greatest epic of Hungarian literature, *The Peril of Sziget,* to commemorate the death of his ancestor, also called Miklós, who had defended the fortress of Szigetvár. This epic served as an emotional manifesto, preparing the country for war. Even György II Rákóczi, prince of Transylvania, whose father had only recently fought against Ferdinand III, offered his cooperation to the Habsburg ruler. Vienna had other plans. The troops which had been withdrawn from German lands were sent home. It became obvious that the government did not plan a new war.

The disappointment in Hungary was boundless. Both court and country subsequently followed policies that were increasingly illogical. Quite unexpectedly, these policies finally led to the great war of liberation. By that time, however, feelings had become so bitter that even the long-hoped-for success could not diminish the tension.

When, after thirty years of fighting, the Habsburgs were not willing to embark on new hostilities promptly, the disappointment in Hungary was boundless, and even the loyal Esterházy faction turned against the ruler. They plotted to elect

Zsigmond Rákóczi, the brother of the Transylvanian prince, king of Hungary. When he died at a young age in 1652, they shifted their attention to the prince himself, György II Rákóczi. As will be seen in Chapter 9, this prince was a bad politician, and his Polish policy, together with his incorrect assessment of events in Istanbul, destroyed him. Rákóczi's tragedy provoked the second violent reaction of the royal Hungarian opposition.

Rákóczi's senseless behavior provoked an Ottoman attack. First Transylvania was ravaged, then, after the fall of Nagyvárad, a sizeable additional part of the country was annexed by the Ottomans. In 1663, the second Köprülü grand vizier, Ahmed, turned against royal Hungary. He faced practically no opposition because the high command, in spite of the obvious imminence of hostilities, had made no defensive plans. The Hungarian armies were badly supplied and could not take advantage of the help that came from the empire and France. Even Miklós Zrinyi's victories were due to the absence of Ahmed during the winter months. Ottoman supremacy became obvious.

When, on August 1, 1664, the allied forces won the Battle of Szentgotthard, Leopold I seized the chance to make peace. Not only the opposition, but the entire country reacted unfavorably. By this time, Zrinyi was already negotiating a pact with the Rhinish Confederation, but his death ended the talks, and his well-conceived plans degenerated into a magnate conspiracy. In 1666, Ferenc Wesselényi, the palatine, reached an understanding with the high chief justice, Ferenc Nádasdy, and the ban of Croatia, Péter Zrinyi. They began to look to France and Venice for foreign help and even sent a delegation to the grand vizier, who was conducting a campaign in Crete. Their offer, the submission of royal Hungary, was rejected by Ahmed Köprülü.

The court had been well apprised of every development ever since the Zsigmond Rákóczi plan and had its agents among the conspirators. Yet nothing happened until March 1670, when a sudden decision brought savage reprisals. These began with the arrest of the leaders, who were executed amid general national and international indignation. The occupation of the country by numerous foreign mercenaries had begun about nine months earlier. They occupied Protestant churches and spent their time pillaging. On trumped up charges, numerous lesser nobles and burghers were tried as coconspirators. The repressive measures included new, unpayable taxes and the cashiering of two-thirds of the border fortifications' garrisons. The government could not have chosen a more effective means of creating a social stratum of discontented individuals with no means of support. Forced into hiding, these ex-soldiers, members of the lower nobility, and outlaws, first referred to themselves as "the hidden," and later used the expression "*kuruc*" for their group. The imprudent measures taken by the government created this element, which had no choice but revolt. They found the Ottomans ready to support them. Out of the general indignation evoked by the Habsburgs' unwillingness to fight the Ottomans grew an Ottoman-supported revolt. This revolt, whose original successes misled the Porte, culminated in the anti-Ottoman wars of liberation.

The Transylvanians placed Imre Thököly in command of those kuruc who sought refuge on their territory. He was well-suited for leadership. He was young, ambitious, a good soldier, and the scion of a new magnate family. Beginning in 1677, his troops won victory after victory. Five years later, he was in position to conclude a very favorable armistice with Leopold I. This gave Istanbul the impression that the time was ripe for a new attack on Vienna. Sultan Mehmed IV accompanied the Ottoman army from Istanbul as far as Edirne, where the grand vizier took command. The well-known third siege of Vienna began on July 14, 1683.

Had the Ottomans not overestimated the successes of Thököly, inducing them to attack Vienna and thus frightening all of Europe, the war would probably not have begun for several more years. But the Ottoman action made it possible for Pope Innocent IX, in the spring of 1683, to organize the Holy Alliance which included the papacy, the empire, Venice, and Poland. (Mihály Apafi, the prince of Transylvania, was also invited, but being entirely in Ottoman hands he could not move. See chapter 9.) The forces of the Alliance moved to defend Vienna, and the siege ended on September 12, with heavy Ottoman losses.

The Polish king, Jan III Sobieski, won several battles with the Ottomans in Hungary on his way home from the siege of Vienna, but the war there exploded in earnest the following year. The attack on the Ottomans began simultaneously from the north and south. Visegrád capitulated on June 13, and Verőce (Vitrovica) on July 22. The next year saw action mainly against Thököly's forces.

Thököly had cleverly avoided getting involved in the siege of Vienna, and the Ottoman defeat there had indicated that his alliance with Istanbul had outlived its usefulness. (The changed situation in royal Hungary also indicated this. The general resistance had forced the ruler to agree, in 1681, to revoke the senseless taxes and end religious persecution.) Yet while keeping his troops on the Ottoman side made little sense, Thököly and many of his followers were unwilling to terminate their anti-Habsburg war. Some of his soldiers did switch sides and distinguished themselves in the war against the Ottomans. Yet in this fratricidal conflict, the royal and allied armies, in their struggle to expel the Ottomans, were also opposed by Thököly and his followers, who were to fight against them to the end.

In June 1686, the preparation for the crucial battle began. Charles of Lorraine appeared at Buda with an army of sixty-five thousand men, composed of the soldiers of the Alliance and numerous volunteers from all over Europe. This was the moment for Transylvania to act. On June 28, the principality declared itself independent from Ottoman overlordship. Two days later, the first attempt was made to retake Hungary's capital. The final attack began early in the morning of September 2. By five in the afternoon, the victory was certain, and two hours later Buda was delivered from 145 years of Ottoman occupation. All of Europe celebrated.

During the remaining months of the year, most of the lands under Ottoman rule were liberated, but the war continued for another thirteen years. In 1690, it appeared that the Ottomans would regroup, but in the end they were only able to prevent the allied invasion of the Balkans. Both Belgrade and Temesvár remained in Ottoman hands. The Peace of Karlowitz, signed on January 26, 1699, confirmed that the Holy Alliance was victorious and liberated Hungary to the Sava-Maros line, as well as all of Transylvania. Yet even before the end of the war it had become clear that the long-sought victory would not lead to the calming of spirits, but would create instead new political and social problems.

The expulsion of the Ottomans is one of the most important events in Hungarian history, ending the physical and spiritual destruction of the country and liberating hundreds of thousands from a life of daily humiliation. But it was not the Ottoman presence that had been responsible for the unfavorable economic developments and the dominance of the wealthy landowners. Liberation could not suddenly restore the country. Contemporaries often stated that the country's future would have been better assured if the liberator had not been a foreign ruler, but the major problem was not that the Habsburgs were foreigners. They did not play favorites and did not exploit Hungary to the advantage of their other provinces. Their policy was dynastic, not imperial, and consequently their rule in the hereditary provinces did not differ from that in the Czech lands or Hungary. What aggravated the situation during the second half of the seventeenth century was the personality of the ruler, Leopold I. He was a decent individual, but a very bad politician and a worse military leader.

The Hungarian politicians had taken the first inevitable step when the legislature met at Pozsony on October 18, 1687. As proof of their gratitude "for his majesty's successful action against the Turks," they recognized the House of Habsburg's hereditary right to the Hungarian throne and also gave up the right of resistance, which the nobility had had since the Golden Bull was issued in 1222 by Andrew II. Under the circumstances, these concessions were formalities, but they also indicated a willingness to cooperate. Unfortunately, the court was not prepared to take advantage of this clear and generally supported intention. The logical step would have been to let the estates and important landowners return to their holdings, over which they had retained jurisdiction during the long years of Ottoman occupation. Vienna did not permit this solution. While several plans were drafted, describing what institutions should be introduced into the liberated areas, the final solution was designed simply to maximize the financial exploitation of the region. Not even Leopold Kollonich, then Bishop of Győr, the most loyal of all those who cooperated with the court, could make Vienna listen to the plan he summarized in his work, *The Organization of Hungary*.

Rather than introducing economic measures that could have improved the country's well-being, new and heavy taxes were levied. The liberated lands were rented by auction to the aristocrats of the empire, while those of Hungary were required to pay reparations for the damages of the war. Trumped-up charges of cooperation with Thököly led to numerous trials ending with the confiscation of property. Sixteen people were executed in the spring of 1687, and many died in the torture chambers. An endless stream of regulations, which lacked legislative sanction, were executed by officials who had no connections with the estates. After 1690, the organization of these estates and the cities was placed under the supervision of royal commissioners. Nevertheless, there was a great difference between the actions of absolutist rulers elsewhere and the rule of Vienna in Hungary. Absolute monarchs usually cooperated with some segments of society or at least tried to enrich their lands. In liberated Hungary, this was not the case. The consequence was that, following the liberation of the country, a popular uprising, although now without Ottoman support, blossomed into another war of independence involving all segments of society.

The first disturbances occurred during the summer of 1697 in the wine-producing regions around Tokaj where in spite of the difficult situation certain economic possiblities still existed. The new taxes ruined a once fairly well-to-do population. Under the leadership of one of Thököly's former officers and the judge of a prairie town, the population rose in revolt. These people invited the young Ferenc II Rákóczi to lead them. He was the grandson of György II Rákóczi, Imre Thököly had been his stepfather, and his name alone represented anti-Habsburg sentiments. This was not the first time simple people had asked one of the country's richest aristocrats to lead them. Bocskai, too, had been the leader of society's outcasts, the hajdu, when he began his fight (see chapter 7). Rákóczi, however, could not then see himself in Bocskai's role and sought refuge in Vienna. The Tokaj uprising was put down.

In less than six years, Rákóczi's views underwent a drastic change. Far from Hungary, an important event had occurred during his absence. In February 1699, the heir apparent to the childless Charles II, the last Habsburg ruler of Spain, died. A great new international conflict seemed imminent. Leopold I now claimed the Spanish throne for his family, but it was obvious that the growing power of Louis XIV's France would block his way. Rákóczi could not let such an opportunity pass without trying to profit from it. His letter of November 1, 1700 to Louis XIV led to a chain of events that resembled fiction. His courier betrayed him, he was arrested, then escaped, and finally sought refuge in Poland. When the War of the Spanish Succession erupted in 1702, Rákóczi had no foreign friends or contacts and had to turn to the Hungarian people.

On May 6, 1703, he concluded an alliance with those who had kept alive the memory of the Tokaj uprising, to free Hungary from its "illegal and intolerable yoke." He himself joined the peasant armies in June. The fighters again referred to themselves as kuruc. From this moment on, support for the war of independence spread like wildfire. Prudently, Rákóczi began by occupying his own estates, where the nobles were his *familiares* and the serfs had to obey his commands. By the end of 1704, he was master of practically the entire country. One of his units even entered Lower Austria. When the Transylvanian assembly elected him prince, on July 8, 1704, Leopold held only the westernmost border regions and some Saxon districts.

Yet despite these successes, the Habsburg victory over the allies of France in the Battle of Höchstädt (August 13, 1704) made the defeat of Leopold impossible. This was a great disappointment, for Rákóczi had succeeded in establishing good foreign contacts. A close ally of Louis XIV, Maximilian Emanuel, the elector of Bavaria and one of the heroes of the anti-Ottoman wars, had been Rákóczi's candidate for the Hungarian throne from the beginning. After Höchstädt, Rákóczi's foreign policy became confused. He made contradictory decisions in great haste. In the fall of 1707, he concluded, practically simultaneously, two agreements. One offered the Hungarian throne, this time officially, to the Bavarian elector. The other concerned Rákóczi's possible selection as king of Poland. By this time, only the Polish plan had some remote chance of success, because it brought Rákóczi in contact with the great eastern power, Peter the Great's Russia. But to get himself elected by the Poles, the international relations of most of Europe would have had to undergo drastic changes. This needed much preparation and time. When Rákóczi finally encountered the tsar for the first time, on May 12, 1711, only a few days were left before Joseph I's widow, the queen-regent, ratified the peace treaty his followers had concluded in his absence.

Hungary's internal problems grew out of originally favorable developments. A large number of great landowners and the majority of the nobility had joined the war for independence. The lords, quite naturally, had taken over the military and political leadership of what had been a popular movement. (It was, of course, inconceivable that a serf officer should give orders to a gentleman.) The original leaders of the movement and the masses of the military felt more and more left out. More important, the peasant masses had fought in the hope that victory would free them from their feudal obligations, while nothing could have been further from the aims of the landlords who had joined the war. Rákóczi, who had promised freedom to the serfs in arms and their descendants, was obliged by the lords to reverse himself. Nevertheless, when the legislature met at Sárospatak in 1708, he forced through a law freeing those serfs who continued to fight, along with their children who were minors. By that time it was too late, however, for the masses were tired of war.

The growing war weariness had not only social, but also economic causes. The war of independence had originated in regions that had been devastated by the Long War. No economic measures could suddenly make these areas flourish again. Rákóczi and his staff tried in vain. A permanent Economic Council was created in January, 1705, but it spent its time almost exclusively trying to find ways to collect the heavy war taxes. Ironically, the leaders of a war provoked by heavy taxes had to increase this load beyond what the Habsburg government had collected in the 1690s. The economic situation deteriorated further when the leaders, following the dominant economic theory of the times, attempted to solve their economic problems by debasing the currency. As usual, the measure failed, and the war chest was bankrupt.

Such were conditions in Rákóczi's Hungary after 1704. It fought for nearly seven more years, while its territory and the number of its supporters shrank steadily. From time to time glorious military feats revived the spirits. For example, János Bottyán, one of the greatest military figures of the war of independence, conquered Transdanubia in the fall of 1705 by brilliant action and was even able to hold it for a long time. Rákóczi's personality was a major factor in keeping the struggle going. He was a born leader, able to fascinate his followers, although he never forgot his social superiority and did not mix with his soldiers.

The legislature deliberated repeatedly in various cities in 1704, 1705, 1706, and 1708. It established, early in 1704, a court council based on the Transylvania model and the next year created a senate to work with the prince based on the Polish model of the estates' confederation. In 1705, the legislature also elected Rákóczi commanding prince. Still, the thought of electing him king was never entertained, although in June of 1706 the legislature deprived the House of Habsburg of its rights to Hungary's throne. The majority of those who voted for this drastic measure probably did not know that their leaders had in mind a foreign candidate for the throne. This knowledge would probably have brought to an earlier end a war kept going only by the bitterness of anti-Habsburg feelings.

Finally, the price of the war became too high. Not even the prospect of a native dynasty could justify it. More and more people defected, and while Rákóczi was abroad, his remaining followers quickly made peace on April 30, 1711. In this treaty, not a word was said about the serfs. What mattered to those who negotiated it was the reestablishment of the rights of the nobility and a general amnesty for those who returned to the Habsburg fold. The treaty stipulated that those who swore the required loyalty oath within three years would retain or recover their estates. The war of independence, which had begun as a popular uprising, ended by securing the rights of the landowners.

IX

THE PRINCIPALITY OF TRANSYLVANIA

Peter F. Sugar

Historical Background

Transylvania proper consists of a triangular plateau situated in the eastern part of historic Hungary. The Carpathians form its eastern and the Transylvanian Alps (Southern Carpathians) its southern borders. The third side of the triangle consists of several lower ranges stretching from the end of the Transylvanian Alps back to the Carpathians roughly in the direction of the source of the Tisza River. While an independent principality, Transylvania's borders also included areas to the west, known as the Partium, including the important towns and fortresses of Arad, Temesvár, Lippa, Jenő (Ineu), and Nagyvárad, as well as Ruthenia and parts of northeastern Hungary (today Slovakia). These borders, however, changed often and drastically.

As has been seen in chapter 3, the conquering Hungarians established their rule firmly in Transylvania around 1003, when Saint István installed an ispán in the old Roman Apulium, Gyulafehérvár. From that moment on, the administrative, political, and social developments paralleled those of Hungary with some important differences. The most significant of these resulted from Transylvania's geographic location; it was the borderland most often attacked by the later waves of migrants coming from the east. It therefore needed a special defensive organization. A high official, the vajda, was placed in charge of the entire region. For all practical purposes, he became a viceroy (just like the ban of Croatia), had the right to appoint the ispáns of the counties after the middle of the thirteenth century, and even could call local assemblies to pass special laws for Transylvania as long as they conformed to general Hungarian law and received the king's approbation.

This right gave the Hungarian nobility a special status and transformed those who had political rights into the territory's first *natio*. Those who acquired full political and legal freedoms subsequently were absorbed into it. While the Latin word *natio* is the root of *nation*, the two are not identical. *Natio* denotes only those people who are politically and legally free, either because they inherited their freedoms or because they had newly acquired them.

The second *natio* was that of the Székelys. While clearly related ethnically to the Hungarians, whose language they shared, their origin is still subject to dispute (see chapter 2). As professional border guards, they elected their own leaders and enjoyed several privileges. As a free people, they formed the second *natio*. The third was composed of German-speakers, known as Saxons, who were first invited into Transylvania during the reign of Géza II as border guards. Later immigrants swelled their numbers and their activities diversified, as will be seen shortly. They too were free, had their privileges and organizations, and formed the third *natio*.

While Hungary—apart from the citizens of free towns and a few other exceptions—had only one *natio* (the nobility), Transylvania had three. This is the second important difference (the position of the vajda being the first) that made Transylvania a special part of pre-Mohács Hungary.

Demography and Society

When Transylvania became an independent principality in 1540, four major ethnic groups lived within its borders, although their exact ratio cannot be established clearly. Hungarians lived in all parts of the country (except in the solidly Székely and Saxon regions), and while they occupied all the social classes, from nobles down to serfs, they were the dominant group politically. The nobility was Hungarian or Hungarianized, and the vajdas and other high office-holders always came from this group and continued to be recruited from its midst when Transylvania was independent. The Hungarian lower nobility supplied administrative and judicial personnel and the commanders of the army. All magnates and the wealthiest people were Hungarians, and Hungarian was the only language used—besides Latin—in the deliberations of the legislature, at court, and in legal and other documents.

The first Saxons had settled in and around Nagyszeben (Sibiu), and later arrivals established themselves around Beszterce (Bistriţa), but most grouped around their original home between the Olt and Nagyküküllő (Tărnava Mare) rivers. They became active in mining and farming, and the very important eastern trade (see chapter 8) was mainly in their hands. Andrew II codified their rights in 1224 in the *Andreanum,* whereby they were given a fixed territory, could elect their own *comes,* mayor, judges, and priests. This document, which also determined their taxes and military obligations, transformed them into the third *natio*. Attempts to violate their rights occurred repeatedly, both prior to and during Transylvania's independence, often leading to conflict, but in general they were able to maintain their position.

Living in southeastern Transylvania, the Székelys, as free soldiers, were considered lesser nobles. Under their elected *comes,* they were self-governing. Their society was organized on communal lines, making the amassing of wealth and titles very difficult. They owed loyalty to the king and vajda but paid no taxes, and their military duties were fixed. Several attempts were made to abrogate their privileges as a *natio* too.

The fourth and probably the largest ethnic group was the Romanians, who claimed to be the original inhabitants of Transylvania, the descendants of the Dacians who gave the name to the Roman province of Dacia. That some of these could have survived the repeated waves of invaders from the east is possible, but most must have been destroyed, with the remnants seeking refuge in the Carpathians and beyond. When they acquired their later Latin language is subject to dispute. During the Hungarian conquest, everyone in Transylvania was subjugated without rights or privileges. The Romanians, who, beginning in the twelfth and thirteenth centuries, entered Transylvania repeatedly, mainly as shepherds, originally joined the enserfed population. This was not the result of a "nationalistic" policy, but corresponded to the values of the time. Those who had no personal, regional, or group privileges were serfs automatically. The few Romanians who rose in the social scale were absorbed by the *natio*s. This was difficult because it involved conversion (the Romanians were Orthodox Christians) and, therefore, a total break with their past. When the Romanians revolted in the fifteenth century, they did so as serfs, not as Romanians.

Although this revolt was discussed in chapter 6, a short summary of the events is warranted because of their importance for Transylvania. Among the numerous reasons for the uprising, the most important were the steady increase of illegal obligations demanded by the landlords, the deterioration of the currency (making it more difficult to meet these obligations), and the Transylvanian legislature's law that tripled the peasantry's military obligations in face of the growing Ottoman danger. Unrest began around 1429 and grew into a mass revolt, due to the senseless behavior of the archbishop of Transylvania, György Lépes, who in 1436 not only demanded that the Orthodox peasantry pay a tithe to his church but proclaimed them heretics, invited the Inquisition, and started forced conversion. At first the peasantry was victorious, and the settlement of 1438 forced Lépes to withdraw all his measures and demands, abolish serfdom, and reinstitute free migration. The peasants even gained the right to a yearly armed assembly with the power to punish unjust lords. These concessions could conceivably have led to the emergence of a free peasantry or even to a fourth, Romanian-dominated *natio*. Obviously, this was not what the wielders of power wanted. The leaders of the three *natio*s got together, and on September 16, 1437, formally established the Union of Three Nations. Hostilities were renewed, the peasantry was defeated, and its newly gained rights were lost. The system established on September 16, 1437 became ossified, and those who were not included in the Union could not gain rights in Transylvania. This was one of the features the future principality inherited.

The problems of Székely society were of a different nature, but played an even more important role than the peasant revolts in the development of Transylvania. In Székely territory, the problem was demographic pressure as the population outgrew its land. Some notables, consequently, tried to grab the land and enserf the people. The details of the struggle are unimportant; suffice it to say that with royal help the Székelys retained their status. The problems, however, were not eliminated. István Báthori, who from 1491 to 1493 was both vajda and comes of the Székelys, treated them as his serfs. Thus began the Székelys' hostility to the Báthori family, which became most important in the independent state. The Székelys became the devoted followers of János Zápolyai (who took the side of the lesser nobility in its struggle with the magnates) and became his partisans when in 1510 he became vajda of Transylvania. This friendship did not last long. During the chaotic conditions prevailing during the reigns of the two Jagiełłonian kings, Ulászló II and Louis II, Zápolyai became the self-appointed guardian of law and order. He played a crucial role in defeating the peasant revolt led by György Dózsa in 1514 (see chapter 6) and then turned against the still dissatisfied Székelys five years later. The man with whom the history of independent Transylvania began turned out to be as hostile to this people as his brother-in-law, István Báthori.

The Establishment of the Principality of Transylvania

Transylvania did not secede from Hungary; her three *natio*s had no reason or wish to move in this direction. János Zápolyai, his wife Isabella, and his son, János-Zsigmond, considered themselves Hungary's royalty. Only after János-Zsigmond ratified the Peace of Speyer a few days before he died, on March 10, 1571, accepting the title of hereditary prince of Transylvania, did a new state come into being. Legally, it was still a part of Hungary because at Speyer János-Zsigmond recognized Maximilian I, who since 1564 also claimed the kingship of Hungary, as his overlord. Because his father had previously acknowledged the Ottoman sultan as his overlord, the new state's ruler had two masters.

The separation of Transylvania from the rest of Hungary began with the battle of Mohács and the subsequent events discussed in chapter 7. While the two kings elected in 1526 and their successors struggled for some fifty years to assert themselves, Ottoman power in Hungary grew. It became the decisive factor making the unification of the country impossible, creating instead royal Hungary in the west and Transylvania in the east, with the Ottomans masters of the center.

In the long and complicated struggle, the partisans of the two kings switched sides repeatedly, depending on whom they considered more likely to succeed, but neither side had enough power to achieve reunification. Zápolyai and his son were weak, vacillating individuals, and while Isabella had a strong, determined personality, she lacked political sense and was more interested in ostentatious living than politics. When Zápolyai died, Isabella became the head of a regency, but real power was in the hands of one of the regents, George Martinuzzi, the bishop of Várad and lord high treasurer. A very able diplomat, he maneuvered with great skill between the Habsburgs, the sultans, Isabella, and the various parties and factions. He believed that only the Habsburgs were strong enough to reunify Hungary. After several attempts, he had reached an agreement with Vienna that satisfied even Isabella, who abdicated in 1551, when an imperial army, under Giambattista Castaldo, entered eastern Hungary. Natually, Ottoman reaction was strong. Castaldo's ability left much to be desired, and when Martinuzzi tried to deflect the Turks with clever diplomacy, the general had the cardinal assassinated. The struggle continued, and was not concluded until the Peace of Speyer. János-Zsigmond's reign was uneventful except for the events connected with the Reformation, which will be discussed separately.

János-Zsigmond died childless. All subsequent princes were formally elected by the legislature and were members of established magnate families, with very few exceptions. (For example, István Báthori, who succeeded János-Zsigmond and later became king of Poland, was Isabella's brother-in-law.) Princely power, which rested mainly on personal wealth and free disposition of state revenues, was practically absolute, and no institution, not even the legislature, could significantly influence the prince's decisions. Little love was lost between the three *natio*s, which made it easier for the princes to establish this primitive form of absolutism. Military and foreign affairs were entirely in their hands, following the Hungarian model.

The prince's closest advisors were the members of a council modeled on the royal council of Hungary. The first Transylvanian laws stipulated an elective council, acting as the prince's executive organ, but these laws were disregarded. The members of this body, never more than twelve, were princely appointees and had neither legislative nor executive power. They studied problems at the request of the prince, and gave advice, but the prince was still free to act as he pleased.

The main executive organ of Transylvania was the Princely Chancellery headed by the chancellor and manned by secretaries and scribes. It was not a large office (one to three secretaries, and up to thirty-five scribes), but it was the land's most important institution, whose instructions put into effect the orders and decisions of the prince. While tax collection was the duty of a Small Chancellery, the main chancellery had fiscal power and also handled military and foreign affairs, local administration, and so forth, acting both as government and supervisor of internal affairs.

The treasury was in charge of princely domains, mining revenues, and the tithe but operated under the supervision of the chancellery. While the chief general of the army was appointed by the prince, the chancellery was in charge of mobilization, supplies, wages, and the maintenance of border fortifications.

The Supreme Court, over which, in theory, the prince presided, also showed some similarity to Hungarian institutions. Just as the Hungarian palatine was the chief judicial office-holder and president of the legislature's upper house, the Transylvanian High Court's president was also the president of the one-house legislature.

Although the laws were basically Hungarian, the Transylvanian legislature differed more from the Hungarian model than any other institution of the principality. Not only was it a one-house legislature, but it legislated practically nothing, beyond approving the propositions submitted to it by the prince. It included the members of the council, supreme court, and other major dignitaries—as many individuals as the prince invited personally to a given session. Also included were the deputies of the local authorities, including the chief dignitaries of the *natio*s. Attendance was obligatory, and the legislature assembled at least once a year. Compared to the power of the prince, that of the legislature was insignificant.

Reformation and Civilization

The first patron of the Reformation in Hungary was Queen Mary, the wife of Louis II. Her unpopularity made the diffusion of the new creed difficult among the Hungarians, but it spread among the German settlers of northern Hungary and Transylvania. In the latter region, the leading Lutheran reformer was Johannes Honterus of Brassó, whose influence spread first to the other German settlements and then to the other nations. János Zápolyai, who remained Roman Catholic, did not interfere because the pope had excommunicated him as an ally of the Ottomans. By the time Isabella resumed her rule, Transylvania's non-Orthodox were mostly Lutherans, although most magnates remained Catholic.

Isabella found not only Lutherans in her realm, but also Calvinists. Márton Kálmáncsehi was the first major apostle of the creed of Geneva, and the city of Debrecen became the "Calvinist Rome." He had little if any success in Transylvania proper, but his successor, Péter Mélius-Juhász, converted Kolozsvár in 1559. Within five years, most Hungarians followed his religion. Transylvania by then had three non-Orthodox churches, Calvinist, Lutheran, and Catholic, each with its own clergy and bishops. The 1564 legislature recognized this fact, giving the three churches equal rights and privileges, although the tithe and estates lost by the Catholics did not fall into the hands of the Protestants but were appropriated by the ruler. For those who followed one of the three "accepted" religions, religious freedom went beyond the limits established by the Peace of Augsburg (1555) or even by the Peace of Westphalia, which ended the Thirty Years War in 1648. The Transylvanian law did not extend to Muslims, Jews, Armenians, nor most importantly, the Orthodox. There was a sharp difference between "accepted" and "tolerated" creeds. The adherants of the latter could practice their religions, but their clergy had no official positions, rights, or privileges.

János-Zsigmond, under the influence of his chief advisor, Mihály Csáki, a Protestant, and his personal physician, George Blandrata, favored these developments. Blandrata was primarily responsible for the emergence of the fourth "accepted" religion. He had left his native Italy because of his Antitrinitarian views, going to Poland, where he joined Isabella's circle. He then moved with her to Hungary. Under his influence, Ferenc Dávid, a Calvinist bishop of Kolozsvár with a magnetic personality, began to preach a new creed, later called Unitarianism, in this city in 1564. Four years later, the legislature, meeting at Torda, gave partial recognition to the religion. When the legislature assembled in Marosvásárhely (Târgu Mureş) three years later (under István Báthori), it gave Unitarianism full "accepted" status.

Dávid went even further and became a leading advocate of the Sabbatarians. This was too much for István Báthori, who called the Jesuits into his land and started the Counterreformation. Dávid was tried and imprisoned as a heretic. Nevertheless, some of the Unitarian Székelys continued to follow his more extreme teachings. With the partial success of the Counterreformation, the various religions began to follow ethnic lines, aggravating the divisions between the three *natios*. The Hungarians were either Calvinists or Catholics, the Saxons followed Lutheranism, and the Székelys were mainly Unitarians.

The situation of the Orthodox Romanians is also of interest. The reformers, naturally, wanted to convert them too. First the Lutheran Saxons, followed by the Calvinist Hungarians, began to translate the scriptures into Romanian. An attempt was even made by the clergy to replace Church Slavonic with Romanian in Orthodox churches. This interesting development, which could have given the Romanians of Transylvania a new literary language and diminished the cleavage between them and the rest of the population, was cut short by István Báthori, who established the first Orthodox archbishopric in Transylvania in 1572. The archbishops rapidly led their flock back to traditional Orthodoxy.

The major figures of the Reformation and Counterreformation were highly educated individuals whose importance extended beyond the purely religious issues. Yet they were neither the only nor the most important figures of the cultural and intellectual life of the principality. While the main cultural center of Hungary had always been the royal court, the various artistic and cultural trends coming from the West penetrated the easternmost regions of the country too, as the numerous Romanesque and Gothic churches situated here prove. As mentioned in chapter 3, two of the most talented artists of the fourteenth century, the sculptors Márton and György, were natives of Kolozsvár.

While those who had studied abroad were mainly clergymen, scions of wealthy families, including Transylvanians, also found their way to the great universities of Western Europe. After the fifteenth century, Padua became their favorite school. From here they returned imbued with the humanistic spirit of the Renaissance. After 1540, in eastern Hungary, or Transylvania, numerous high officials were graduates of Padua. The princely court, where they served, became the cultural center of the country, while the royal court, now situated in Vienna, lost this function. Transylvania became the home of Hungarian intellectual life, and court-centered culture reached its apogée under Gábor Bethlen. Even in times of war, Gábor Bethlen spent at least 40 percent of the state's revenue on his court. From Italy he imported silk stockings in every color of the rainbow, masques, exotic cakes, and jewelry, and spent hugh sums on balls, theatrical performances, orchestras, dancing masters, and all other forms of entertainment and luxury. Bethlen paid attention to other aspects of culture too. He established in 1622 an academy at Gyulafehérvár, supported education in general, and revived the custom of sending young Transylvanians to study at the famous institutions of Western Europe. His mercantilist policy assured, by the end of his rule, a yearly state revenue nearing a million florins. He used some of this money for education, increasing the upward social mobility of his subjects.

In the sixteenth century, most of the leading intellectual figures were high officials, including five chancellors: Ferenc Forgách, Farkas Kovacsóczy, Simon Pécsi, János Bethlen, and Pál Gyulai. They mainly wrote historical works in Latin, which were read by their fellow intellectuals. Simon Pécsi, who became a Sabbatarian, translated parts of the Bible and the Talmud, as well as numerous psalms into Hungarian, while also writing some original church songs. Among the other reformers, Gáspár Heltai, translator of the Bible, poet, and historian was the most important writer in Hungarian. Honterus, among the Saxons, was not only a religious leader but also a poet, geographer, and lawyer, who established many schools, began the codification of Saxon law, and was among the first to stress that he was a German, not a Hungarian. (While the two languages gained much by the activities of these men and many others, their use of the vernaculars at the expense of Latin made the divisions between the nations even clearer.) The Hungarian Protestants too, were patrons of schools. When, under István Báthori, a Jesuit higher school was established in Kolozsvár in 1581, the Protestants already had four, and the Unitarians one.

In the seventeenth century, travel to Western centers of learning became more difficult, and, although good, the local schools were not of the same caliber. Times were also more agitated and life less secure. Literary activity declined somewhat, and memoirs written by the magnates became the dominant literary form. Some of these do have real literary value in addition to their historical interest.

The economic and demographic trends of these centuries, so important in the development of cultural life, have been dealt with in chapter 8. It is, nevertheless, worth stressing that Transylvania's natural riches and trading with the east made her the wealthiest of the three parts into which Hungary was divided. It was this relative opulence that allowed the princes to follow their ambitious policies and often made them financially careless.

The Political Position and Importance of Transylvania

The kingdom of the Zápolyais, later the principality of Transylvania, was about the size of New Jersey when János-Zsigmond died. This small state and its princes played a much larger role not only in Hungarian, but also in European events than its size would seem to have warranted. Several circumstances explain Transylvania's importance.

It should be remembered, first of all, that Transylvania's nobility and all the important public figures including the rulers, as well as the population of the various regions attached to it for longer or shorter periods, were Hungarians. While they were unable to influence events in the Ottoman-ruled lands, they repeatedly got involved in the affairs of royal Hungary, and sometimes determined the actions of the Habsburgs, with lasting results. The reverse is also true; the Habsburgs never gave up their claims to Transylvania and expended much energy in asserting themselves there. Furthermore, the strategic location of the country made it of great interest also to the Ottomans, the Poles, and the rulers of Moldavia and Wallachia. On occasion even the Swedes and the French showed a lively interest in Transylvanian events.

In the period between the dismemberment of Hungary and the end of Transylvania's independence (circa 1690), religious issues cannot be separated from political considerations. After the success of the Counterreformation in Austria, royal Hungary, the Czech lands, and Poland, Transylvania became the bastion of Protestantism in East-Central Europe. Even her Catholic princes championed religious freedom, especially in royal Hungary, with the same zeal with which the violent exponents of the Counterreformation tried to extend their activities into Transylvania. This involved the principality in the religious clashes of the period, in particular the Thirty Years War. The Protestant and anti-Habsburg forces (mainly France) hoped that the Transylvanians would open a second front against their enemies. For the Hungarians of the principality, these wars represented opportunities to fight not only for religious freedom, but for their national goals, and therefore they usually joined them, becoming actors, occasionally important ones, on the international scene.

Finally, but very importantly, the policy of Transylvania's princes has to be understood. As has been seen, these men were practically absolute masters, especially in military and foreign affairs. Situated between Habsburg and Ottoman power, their position was precarious. Nominally vassals of the emperor and the sultan, they looked at both as their enemies, but, as a rule, they had to side with one against the other. In most cases they preferred the Ottomans to the Habsburgs. That they could make these choices indicates that they considered themselves independent rulers with the right to formulate their own policies; they declared wars and concluded alliances and peace treaties without consulting their "overlords." It is not easy to determine what considerations dictated the actions of the princes. Their interest in the developments in royal Hungary was certainly often a motivating factor, as was the security of Transylvania and the issue of religious freedom. It is less certain, even in the cases of careful and talented princes, to what extent these were determining considerations. In the sixteenth and seventeenth centuries, dynastic interests were every European ruler's primary concern: their aim was to secure the future of their families, to extend their domain, and to increase their power. The princes of Transylvania were no exceptions; gaining full sovereignty over their domain, establishing dynasties, acquiring the crowns of Hungary and Poland, and forcing the rulers of Moldavia and Wallachia to recognize them as overlords were at least as important for them as their Hungarian nationality and their religious ideas. In hindsight, it is easy to see that their lasting achievement was to save Hungarian Protestantism and to save the country as a whole from becoming one of the hereditary provinces of the Habsburgs. For this the country owed them a great debt, regardless of their motives.

The Báthori Period

The first successor of the Zápolyais, István Báthori, related to the family of his predecessors and to the kings of Poland, was one of Transylvania's ablest and most successful rulers. His family connections and immense wealth assured his selection as prince in 1571, when he was thirty-eight years old. He brought prosperity to his country, ensured religious freedom, successfully foiled Habsburg intrigues and revolts, kept the Ottomans away, established a dynasty, and gained the throne of Poland. Highly educated, a good judge of people and circumstances, and strong willed, he was a born ruler.

Báthori began his rule by paying homage to the sultan and allowing the Habsburgs to appoint him vajda of Transylvania, but at once showed that he was his own master. The Habsburgs reacted by turning to Gáspár Békés, to whom they offered the office of vajda. Békés turned to the enemies of the Báthori family, the Székelys, and twice in 1571 and 1575, led them in revolt. István defeated them on both occasions and after his second victory took bloody vengeance and suspended the Székelys' privileges. It is typical of the first Báthori that he recognized the talents of Békés and later, as king of Poland, used him as commander of his cavalry in his wars against Ivan the Terrible. While he organized and consolidated his country between the two revolts, Báthori got more and more deeply involved in Polish affairs. In 1572 Sigismund-Augustus, the last Jagiełło king of Poland, died. Maximilian II (Maximilian I in Hungary), who had some Jagiełłonian ancestors on his mother's side, claimed the throne. Naturally, his two major adversaries, the French and the Ottomans, were opposed. The only other logical candidate was Báthori, who had a Jagiełłonian wife. The Poles surprised everybody by electing Henri de Valois as their ruler, but two years later he left them to claim the French throne as Henri III. This time the Poles selected Báthori, who moved to Kraków early in 1576 to become one of Poland's greatest rulers. He retained the throne of Transylvania with the help of his older brother, Kristóf, who acted as vajda until his death in 1581. Kristóf too was very well educated and had political ability, and he was unreservedly loyal to his brother. Unfortunately, he died while his replacement, Báthori's son, Zsigmond, was still a minor. A regency council governed in the names of the young vajda and the absent prince. After the death of István Báthori in 1586, the partisan struggles of the regents became intolerable, and two years later, in 1588, the legislature proclaimed the majority of sixteen-year-old Zsigmond and elected him prince.

One of Báthori's few mistakes was the selection of Zsigmond as his heir in Transylvania. Inexperienced and psychologically unstable, but very ambitious, he was unfit to rule. Although the 1588 legislature banished the Jesuits from Transylvania, he retained as his chief advisor his tutor, the Spaniard Alphonse Carillo, who like many other Jesuits remained in the country in the garb of a simple priest. Carillo was staunchly anti-Ottoman and therefore pro-Habsburg and greatly influenced his young charge. Zsigmond's other preoccupation stemmed from his jealousy. He hated his cousins Boldizsár, István, and especially András whose rank of cardinal he envied. On the European scene, efforts initiated by the papacy to form a Holy League against the Ottomans were slowly maturing. In Transylvania, Carillo and István Bocskai, an able soldier and relative of the Báthoris, were in favor of joining the League, while another party, headed by Boldizsár, counseled neutrality. Zsigmond sent Carillo to the emperor Rudolf in Prague to negotiate Transylvania's joining the alliance. The Ottomans contacted Zsigmond and asked for his support. Not knowing what to do, the prince resigned in favor of his hated cousin Boldizsár. He quickly changed his mind, reclaimed the throne, ordered the execution of Boldizsár and several of his friends, and decided to fight the Ottomans. Thus started the Fifteen Years or Long War, which lasted until 1606.

Now Bocskai went to Prague to discuss details. The people under Ottoman rule were ready to follow Transylvania, and Sinan pasha's advancing armies were attacked and defeated by the prince of Wallachia, Michael the Brave. Instead of joining him, Zsigmond enraged him by demanding that Michael become his vassal. This gave Sinan pasha time to regroup. Bocskai organized the Transylvanian army. The Székelys regained their rights in exchange for their participation. They were still discontent and Bocskai had to fight them first. Nevertheless, at first the Ottomans were unsuccessful, but then they took the initiative and at Mezőkeresztes, on October 26, 1596, smashed the united Habsburg-Transylvanian forces. This was the decisive battle, although the war dragged on for another ten years. Meanwhile, Zsigmond married an Austrian archduchess, but the marriage was a total failure. This turn of events pushed Zsigmond over the brink. He now wanted only two things: the dissolution of his marriage and a cardinal's hat. Because Rudolf promised him both, together with some rich estates, he resigned in his favor in 1597. This was not to be revealed until Rudolf's governor reached the principality. However, the secret leaked out, the country was indignant, and Bocskai, fired by the Habsburgs, engineered a coup and brought back Zsigmond, who remounted the throne for the third time. The country, in turmoil, could not resist the Ottoman attacks. Zsigmond resigned for the last time in 1599 and left for Poland. Bocskai retired to his lands, where he began to organize an army of hajdu—free, professional soldiers who did not own property. The cardinal, András Báthori, now became prince for a few months but had no forces left to defend himself against the Habsburg armies, advancing under General George Basta and his ally, Michael the Brave of Wallachia. Michael arrived first and was joined by the anti-Báthori Székelys. András lost his life in flight. While another Báthori ascended the Transylvanian throne a few years later, the Báthori period, which began with glory and prosperity, ended in defeat and misery.

The Michael-Basta Interlude

For the next four years, Transylvania paid a heavy price for Zsigmond's folly. Although some of Michael's troops were paid by the Habsburgs, he had no desire to hand the country over to them. General Basta arrived to take possession of the principality for his master. Michael, who could not pay some of his troops because Prague stopped his subsidies, lost control over part of his army and the unpaid soldiers looted and burned, killing many. Because the Poles moved against him, Michael had to lead his best troops into Moldavia to face them. Those whom he left behind, unpaid and leaderless, ran wild. Basta's troops now attacked their ally, who had lost all local support except that of the Székelys. Basta was victorious and the Székelys once again lost their privileges. Basta's mercenaries did not behave any better than Michael's forces had. To make things worse, Zsigmond, with Polish help, tried to return in 1601, but Basta defeated him and for the next two years instituted a reign of terror. He got rid of his rival, Michael, by arranging his murder. With the large scale physical destruction of the country producing famine and epidemics, the situation was intolerable. It was inevitable that someone attempt to oust Basta. This was tried by Moses Székely, with the help of Ottoman and Tatar troops. After his first successes, the Transylvanian legislature elected him prince, but a few weeks later Basta defeated him, and Székely lost his life in battle. A few of his followers escaped into Ottoman-held territory, including Gábor Bethlen, who planned to use the Ottomans to get rid of Basta.

The Habsburgs, now temporarily in full control, made a mistake. István Bocskai, who had always leaned towards them when the Transylvanians had to choose between Vienna and Istanbul, was stripped of his offices and lands. Bocskai, to defend himself, turned to the hajdu. He promised them only one thing: land on which they could settle after victory. From these modest beginnings grew Bocskai's war of liberation, which was discussed in detail in chapter 7. Not only the Transylvanians, but most Hungarians joined him after his first successes, and he received Ottoman support thanks to the efforts of Gábor Bethlen. He pacified Transylvania, returned the freedoms of the Székelys, and settled the hajdu around Debrecen, giving them rights equal to those of the nobles. He refused the Hungarian crown because he felt that accepting it would tie him too closely to the Ottomans and make a long struggle with the Habsburgs inevitable. Instead of the royal title, he wanted peace. First he concluded the Peace of Vienna with the Habsburgs on June 23, 1606. Although Transylvania gained some territory as a consequence, the Peace was mainly important because it extended religious freedom to royal Hungary and ensured that the country would be governed by Hungarians through Hungarian institutions. Bocskai then mediated the Peace of Zsitvatorok (November 15, 1606) ending the Fifteen Years War. Unfortunately, he died the same year, and the reconstruction of Transylvania had to be undertaken by his successors.

Gábor Bethlen and the Rákóczis

With Bocskai's death, new tensions arose. Vienna claimed that the lands attached to Transylvania in June 1606 were ceded to Bocskai, not to the principality. The disputed territory included the lands on which the hajdu, whose rights to land and privileges Vienna did not recognize, had been settled. The man the Transylvanians elected as their prince upon Bocskai's death, Zsigmond Rákóczi, was not ready to face the growing problems around him and resigned. Rákóczi, fairly wealthy and a good soldier, came from northern Hungary, where the nobility hoped to see the Bocskai days continue, permitting them to live under the same master as their Transylvanian friends. Their candidate was the last Báthori, Gábor.

Gábor Báthori's rule started well. He reached an understanding with Vienna, settled the hajdu problem, and maintained peace for a short while. However, the promise of the first months was not fulfilled. The young prince lived for pleasure and paid little attention to anything else. His mental balance was precarious, and when he faced difficulties, he reacted in an irrational manner.

Some fanatic Catholics living in royal Hungary hoped to get rid of him and place someone on the throne who would be their partisan. An attempt on Gábor's life failed, but turned him into a violent anti-Catholic. The next conspiracy against him was organized by the Poles and Wallachians, and while he led his armies against them, the Ottomans attacked and the Saxons revolted. He had to return home and, with Bethlen's help, mastered the situation. Something like a persecution mania began to dictate the young Báthori's actions now, and even Bethlen was dismissed. Late in 1613, Gábor was murdered by the hajdu.

Fortunately, his five years in power did not seriously hamper the country's recovery, which had begun under Bocskai and continued during the short reign of Zsigmond Rákóczi. It was a solid base on which the new prince, Gábor Bethlen, could build, bringing Transylvania back to prominence and prosperity. A few words have already been said about his court and its cultural life, and chapter 8 discussed his very successful economic policies (when he died, Transylvania's treasury was full and her people were prosperous). His political and military role remains to be surveyed.

Bethlen had to be very careful when he began his rule. His close ties with Istanbul and with Gábor Báthori were viewed by many with great suspicion, and both Vienna and Istanbul put pressure on him. Fortunately Bethlen, a first-rate diplomat, was up to the task he faced. Six years after he became prince, the legislature noted with satisfaction that law and order had returned and the economy was flourishing. The most critical problems he faced were caused by the situation in royal Hungary, where Catholics continued to intrigue against him, the Counterreformation entered a violent phase (see chapter 8), and the Peace of Vienna was disregarded. Bethlen saw clearly that these events were parts of a much larger European crisis. The Habsburgs faced growing opposition not only in their own lands, but outside of them, where a coalition hostile to them also began to take shape. Bethlen felt obliged to defend the Peace of Vienna and also saw in the gathering storm a chance to force the Habsburgs out of Hungary. When, in 1618, the fanatic Ferdinand II ascended his forefathers' throne and the Czechs revolted, the Thirty Years War broke out. Of all the European princes, Bethlen moved first. In 1618 his troops conquered northern Hungary, crossed the Austrian and Moravian borders, and besieged Vienna.

Hostilities continued until 1620, when Bethlen and Ferdinand concluded an armistice, leaving northern Hungary in Bethlen's hands. Bethlen then concluded an alliance with the Czechs and attacked again but unfortunately did not reach the battlefield soon enough to get involved in the crucial Battle on the White Mountain, which concluded the Bohemian phase of the Thirty Years War. Prior to the defeat of the Czechs, Bethlen had been elected king of Hungary by the Hungarians but had refused to be crowned, indicating that this move would be premature. The Battle on the White Mountain proved him right.

Bethlen continued the war for another year, until on the last day of 1621 he concluded the Peace of Nikolsburg with Ferdinand. Bethlen gave up his royal title in exchange for full sovereignty for Transylvania (ending the theoretical double vassalage). Religious freedom in Hungary was again reconfirmed, and northern Hungary remained part of the Transylvanian state. The focus of the war shifted to Germany, but Bethlen continued to be involved both diplomatically and militarily, attacking the Habsburgs twice more in 1623 and 1626, when the Peace of Pozsony simply reconfirmed the clauses of Nikolsburg. By this time he was respected enough all over Europe to obtain the hand of Catherine of Brandenburg, the sister of the elector, in marriage.

Unfortunately for his flourishing, united country, he died three years later. A year of instability followed. Bethlen had named his wife his successor, with his brother István as her main advisor. The two hated and intrigued against each other, and both rapidly lost whatever popularity they had had. In 1630 the Transylvanians put an end to this squabble by electing György I Rákóczi as their prince.

György I married the very wealthy Zsuzsana Lorántffy and by the time he became prince, he was immensely wealthy. He had numerous talents but no real strength in any field; fortunately, he knew himself and his limitations well and became a very careful and cautious ruler. Under him the land continued to prosper and the "second golden age" that had begun under Bethlen continued. He followed his predecessor's example closely and was an absolutist in politics and a mercantilist in his economic policy. Puritanical and deeply religious, he proved to be a very able prince. He reentered the Thirty Years War in 1644 to regain those parts of northern Hungary that had reverted to the Habsburgs at Bethlen's death. The Peace of Linz in 1645 returned these lands to him and once again reconfirmed religious freedom in Habsburg Hungary. He maintained the international prestige Bethlen had acquired, and Transylvania became one of the signatories of the Peace of Westphalia. Although György I died a few weeks after this, no crisis in leadership ensued because his son's succession had been arranged six years earlier.

György II Rákóczi destroyed Bethlen's and his father's work. He was very well educated but had no knowledge of public life when he assumed power. Where his father was careful, he was rash, but just as obstinate, once he had made up his mind, as György I had been. He was married to the last of the Báthoris, Zsófia. His first move of importance was sending his armies, under the command of his father's general, János Kemény into the Romanian principalities to counter Polish intrigues and Cossack penetration. This venture was successful, and the two neighboring princes recognized him as their overlord.

It was György's next move that destroyed him and his country. Several factors, besides his obstinacy, contributed to a series of errors with tragic consequences. His faulty political judgement resulted in misunderstanding the struggle that was developing between Charles-Gustave's Sweden and Jan-Casimir's Poland. At the same time, he did not recognize the drastic changes occurring in the Ottoman Empire, where the first of the Köprülü grand viziers, Mehmed, began his reforming activities in 1656. He was also influenced by his religious convictions, which were as strong as his father's had been, and by boundless personal ambition. By intervening in the Swedish-Polish conflict, György hoped to conduct a Protestant crusade and gain the throne in Kraków. In solidly Catholic Poland, these were contradictory aims. His mother and wife headed the antiwar party, but nobody could influence the prince.

At first, he was caught on the horns of a dilemma. The Protestant Swedes, convinced that they could handle Poland without help, refused his advances, while the Catholic Poles, who needed help badly, offered the throne of their country to his young son, provided that he convert. György was saved from this quandary by the unexpected initial Polish victories. He now became involved in the first plan to partition Poland between Sweden, some ambitious Polish princes, Brandenburg, the Cossacks, and himself. Most of Poland and her crown would have become his had the plan succeeded.

In January 1657, György and his general, Kemény, entered Poland. At first, everything went according to plan, but by spring his luck began to fail. For once the Polish nobility united behind its king and put up stiff resistance. Sweden, attacked by the Danes, withdrew her armies. In spite of these events, György persisted, though the Ottomans ordered him to desist. He was first defeated by the Poles, and then his retreating army was totally destroyed by the Tatars on Ottoman orders. György and a few men got home, but most including Kemény, became prisoners of the Tatars. Ottoman armies also began to move ominously. The defeat dealt a heavy blow to the prince's prestige, and he alienated most of his followers by refusing to dip into his own pockets to ransom the prisoners. It was under these circumstances that the Transylvanians received an order from the sultan to depose his much too independent vassal. The legislature hoped to escape from this situation with a compromise. They elected Ferenc Rhédey, with the understanding that should the sultan relent, Rhédey would hand the throne back to György. Rákóczi refused to accept this solution, decided not to bow to Ottoman pressure, and attacked Rhédey, whom he defeated. This was too much for the grand vizier, who in 1658 attacked Transylvania from the south and ordered his Tatar and Cossack allies to move in simultaneously from the north. Weakened Transylvania could not fight a war on two fronts. The attacking armies within a few short weeks destroyed the principality as thoroughly as had the forces of Basta and Michael the Brave some sixty years earlier. The "Second Golden Age" was over. As master of the country, Köprülü appointed Ákos Barcsay prince, and the legislature reacted to this usurpation of its rights by stripping the new prince of practically all power. György II continued to fight until he lost his life in the battle of Gyula two years later.

The Last Year of the Principality

The death of György II did not end Transylvania's agony. The Ottomans continued to move (see chapter 8) and Kemény, finally back home and elected prince, could do nothing to stop the devastation. The Ottomans could have transformed Transylvania into one of their provinces, but finding indirect rule cheaper, decided instead to appoint Michael I Apafi as their puppet prince. At the Peace of Vasvár (1664), the Habsburgs had to recognize the new Ottoman conquests and the new situation created in Transylvania.

Apafi was a tragic figure. A withdrawn scholar and art collector, he never had any interest in politics, for which he had not the slightest talent. Being prince affected him deeply: he became an alcoholic and totally ineffective and by the time of his death suffered from a serious persecution complex. He had no policy, never took the initiative, and left the affairs of state to others.

Transylvania had suffered serious manpower and economic losses before, but men like Bocskai and Bethlen were able to reverse its fortunes. After the catastrophe caused by György Rákóczi's Polish venture, such a recovery was impossible. The weakness of the current prince was not the major reason for this. Indeed Mihály Teleki, Apafi's chancellor, was a high-minded, able man, but he faced a hopeless situation. Transylvania's fate was closely tied to events in royal Hungary, to the Habsburg-Bourbon struggle centered around the question of the Spanish succession, and to the last resurgence of Ottoman power under the leadership of a series of Köprülü grand viziers. All these affairs were discussed in detail in chapter 8, but a few developments of special importance for Transylvania deserve brief mention.

Because of continual Ottoman raids and incursions, the principality never had the chance to recover from demographic and economic losses or to rebuild its armed forces. Consequently, Mihály Teleki could not formulate policy independently and constantly had to seek help outside Transylvania. He got involved in the disastrous Zrinyi-Frangepán conspiracy (see chapter 8) and could not take advantage of his French alliance because of his country's weakness. He also faced a new political force he could not control.

After the executions that followed the crushing of the Zrinyi-Frangepán conspiracy, Leopold I instituted a veritable reign of terror in royal Hungary, and a steady stream of refugées entered Transylvania. Usually well-armed, these men conspired constantly to mount a campaign against the emperor. Leopold, naturally, tried to neutralize them and put heavy pressure on Transylvania to extradite them, creating new difficulties for the Apafi-Teleki regime. Irrespective of how the Transylvanian leadership felt, it lacked the power to act against the fugitives. At the same time, allowing imperial forces into the country to get them would have turned the population against the prince and would have incurred further Ottoman intervention.

The refugées and all those in Transylvania who had had more than enough of Leopold's repression found an able leader in Imre Thököly. The anti-Habsburg war of liberation that he unleashed at the head of his "kuruc" troops gathered momentum, and his successes indicated to the grand vizier, Kara Mustafa Köprülü, that the time was ripe for a second major attack on the Habsburgs. Many of the subsequent events have been recounted in chapter 8, but two had a profound impact on Transylvania.

The steady advance of the imperial troops, ably commanded, for a change, by the princes Charles of Lorraine and Eugene of Savoy, made the submission of Transylvania to Vienna inevitable. In 1686, the year in which Buda was reconquered by the Christian forces, along with towns as far south as Szeged, the Transylvanians had to sign a treaty with Leopold at Balázsfalva (Blaj) on October 27. The treaty kept Apafi on the throne and reconfirmed the privileges of the various nations and orders, but placed the entire principality under Leopold's protection and forced it to admit his garrisons into the country's forts and fortifications. For all practical purposes, this treaty ended Transylvania's independence. The tribute Vienna exacted from its "protectorate" was heavier than the one the Ottomans had collected previously. The commander of the imperial troops, General Anton Caraffa, a cruel and hard man, became the country's real master after he was installed as Transylvania's royal commissioner in 1688.

The death of the unfortunate Apafi in 1690 allowed Leopold to take the logical final step. Though the legislature, using its recently reconfirmed rights, elected Apafi's son, Michael II Apafi, as their prince, Leopold did not recognize the election and prevented him from taking office. Instead, on December 4, 1691, he issued an edict that became known as the *Diploma Leopoldinum,* which essentially settled Transylvania's fate until 1867. In this document, Leopold took the title of prince of Transylvania, "reconfirming her independence." He recognized the rights of the nobility, the three *natio*s, and the four religions. Transylvania retained her legislature, which had the right to elect the principality's officials. Imperial troops were stationed in the country, whose yearly taxes were fixed at one hundred thousand florins. Most of these seemingly generous provisions were almost totally meaningless: for centuries all important decisions affecting Transylvania were made in Vienna.

From the time of the Battle of Mohács (1526), Habsburg rulers, Transylvanian princes, and most Hungarian patriots had dreamed of the reunification of pre–1526 Hungary. Yet even after the Peace of Passarowitz (Požarevac) (1718) forced the Ottomans to evacuate their last Hungarian possessions, total reunification was prevented for another one hundred fifty years by the *Diploma Leopoldinum.*

X

COOPERATION AND CONFRONTATION BETWEEN RULERS AND THE NOBLE ESTATES, 1711–1790

Horst Haselsteiner

The Rule of Charles III, 1711–1740

The Compromise of Szatmár

The Peace of Szatmár, which safeguarded the nobility's privileges, also reestablished the self-government of the nobiliary counties and the nobles' tax exemption. In conformity with the principle of estate-based dualism, the Diet retained its role in the legislative process, and the ruler had to legislate with its cooperation. The ruler was, once again, obligated to swear to respect the laws and customs of the country in accordance with its constitution. The treaty indicated that the Habsburgs were ready to give up the absolutism and centralism of Leopold I, which would have meant the incorporation of Hungary into a unified empire. The religious freedom assured to the Protestants in 1681 was reaffirmed, as were the concessions of 1687, designed to safeguard the Habsburgs' dynastic interests.

Ferenc II Rákóczi rejected the peace as well as the amnesty (which would have included even him) and moved, in 1713, from Poland to France and, four years later, to the Ottoman Empire. In 1717 this state was at war with the Habsburgs, and Rákóczi hoped to renew his struggle also. He died, in April 1735, in Rodosto (Tekirdağ) on the Asiatic shores of the Sea of Marmara.

Charles III returned to Vienna from Spain after the death of Joseph I and gave his approval to the Peace of Szatmár in March 1712. With this move he sanctioned the ruling house's compromise with the Hungarian estates and regained the position his family had enjoyed in Hungary prior to 1687, considerably strengthening his position as ruler. His reorganization of the Hungarian administration also solidified the empire's central administration.

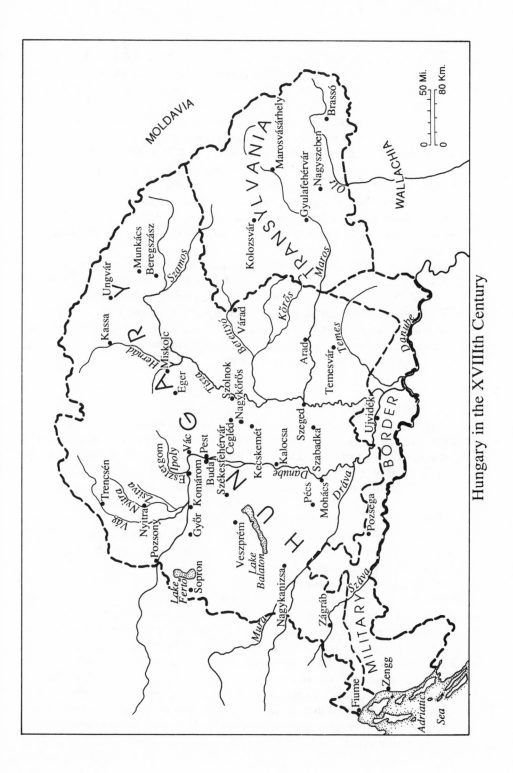

Hungary in the XVIIIth Century

The Hungarians had reasons to be dissatisfied, and not only with the consolidation of the emperor's power which was not in the interest of the nobility. Their demand that the unity of the Lands of the Crown of Saint István be reestablished was not accepted by Charles III or his successors, Maria Theresa and Joseph II. Transylvania and the Partium (see chapter 9) retained their separate administration. Maria Theresa proclaimed Transylvania a grand duchy, thus underlining its independence. The regions known as the Military Border were subordinated directly to the Imperial Council of War in Vienna. The Banat of Temesvár, reconquered from the Ottomans in 1718, was first kept under military jurisdiction and then ruled, in essence, by the Imperial Treasury (Hofkammer) up to 1779. Even the thirteen cities in northern Hungary that had been leased to Poland many years earlier were not reunited with Hungary until 1771. The noble estates protested repeatedly against these violations of Hungary's integrity.

The Peace of Szatmár did create favorable conditions for a compromise between the emperor and the Hungarian nobiliary estates and for the reconstruction and consolidation of the country after centuries of Ottoman rule and the difficult years of the kuruc wars. It was, nevertheless, not certain that these conditions were sufficient to overcome the contradictions between the existence of a state based on the nobiliary estates on the one hand and the centralizing tendencies of Habsburg power on the other.

Administrative Reforms

Ten years after he ascended the throne, Charles III undertook the reorganization of the Hungarian administration, beginning with measures submitted to the estates at the Diet of 1722–23. As the highest organ of the Hungarian administration, the Hungarian Court Chancellery was reorganized. It was headed by the court chancellor and his second in command, the court vice-chancellor. The chancellery had twelve counselors, who were supposed to work as a collective. All these officials were nominated by the ruler and were, without exception, members of his inner circle. The chancellery was situated in Vienna, and moved the few miles to Pozsony, the seat of the Diet, only while this assembly was in session. The highest financial organ, the Hungarian Court Treasury (Hofkammer) resided there permanently.

Charles also created a new chief administrative office, the Lord Lieutenancy (Consilium Regium Locumtenentiale Hungaricum), headed by the palatine. In the not-too-rare cases when the office of the palatine was left open, the Lieutenancy was headed by a lord lieutenant. The Lord Lieutenancy, like the Chancellery, was a collegial body of twenty-two counselors. Decisions had to be approved by simple majority, and for valid votes the presence of at least thirteen counselors was required. Although it was not an office of the Court, the Lieutenancy was subordinated directly to the ruler. It had to submit its decisions and propositions to him through the Chancellery. Its members were nominated by the ruler from among the high episcopacy, the magnates, and the middle-ranking nobility. At the outset the Lieutenancy was organized into five departments dealing with religious affairs, education, military taxation, economics, and all other issues. The lieutenancy was empowered to deal with all administrative problems of the Hungarian kingdom but not with those of territories that had not been reunited with it. The only issues not under its jurisdiction—military and financial affairs—were the domains of the Imperial Council of War and the Hungarian Imperial Treasury.

The Diet of 1722–23 also reformed and reorganized the highest judicial offices of the country. These and other measures introduced by Charles III separated administration and judiciary, but legal decision-making remained as slow as always.

These reforms and innovations give the impression that Charles III, in cooperation with the estates, created a Hungarian administrative system that conformed to Hungarian concepts. Yet it should be noted that these reorganized or newly created offices were not national institutions and that they were subordinated directly to the ruler, who nominated those who served in them. More important, it must be remembered that questions concerning Hungary were not decided by these Hungarian authorities. The Hungarian Court Chancellery, the lieutenancy, and the county administrations were limited to executing the decisions taken by the central administration in Vienna. Consequently, the position of the monarch and the centralizing tendencies were strengthened and, in the final analysis, the compromise reached at Szatmár worked against the interests of the Hungarian estates.

Reforms touching on education, economics, and agriculture are more appropriately discussed with the reigns of Maria Theresa and Joseph II, but military reforms, like administrative ones, began with Charles III. In 1711 several problems made military reform in Hungary necessary. The Ottoman and kuruc wars of the second half of the seventeenth and the early eighteenth centuries had shown how inadequate the medieval banderial army organization was. The general levy of the nobility (see chapter 5) could not satisfy the requirements of modern warfare. Yet the tax exemption of the nobility rested on its obligation to serve in the military and was, therefore, the cornerstone of the nobility's special status. At the 1715 Diet, the ruler and the estates were ready to face this complicated issue since all agreed on the need to reconquer the Hungarian lands still in Ottoman hands.

The jointly worked-out reforms of 1715 established a permanent army *(regulata militia)*, charging the emperor with organizing a number of regiments to be determined. Soldiers for these units were to be recruited both in and outside Hungary. The expenses were to be covered by the country, but the Diet retained the right to determine their magnitude. This measure represented a heavy new obligation for the peasantry, which had both to pay the taxes required for the new army and to supply the needed recruits. The nobility's obligation to obey the ruler's call for a general levy was retained. In calling the nobility to arms, he had to follow long-established laws, thus preserving the Diet's role in raising these troops. It appeared that a solution to the military problem had been found, whereby the nobility justified its tax exemption and retained its legislative prerogatives.

Demography and New Settlements

The repeated wars and insecurity of the late seventeenth and early eighteenth centuries produced a serious decline in Hungary's population. There were an estimated 3.5 million inhabitants in 1720 compared to about four million during the rule of King Matthias I (Corvinus) 250 years earlier. (During the same time period, the population of Europe as a whole increased from eighty to 130 million.) More than two-thirds of the population lived in the western and northern counties, in Transdanubia and northern Hungary, and less than one-third in the southeast, in the lands bordered by the Danube, Tisza, and Maros rivers. In the regions reconquered from the Ottomans, low population density was matched by low levels of economic and cultural activity. The two-field system dominated, and pastoral pursuits played a leading role in the economy. The task the landlords and authorities faced was to find settlers and workers for the newly reconquered lands. Consequently both the court and noble landlords followed a repopulation and colonization policy.

After Rákóczi's war, the circle of landlords underwent drastic change as the old, established Hungarian families lost their dominant position. Leopold I and his two successors gave large areas in the southeastern regions to the numerous followers of the House of Habsburg, to their officers, and to nobles from the family's other lands and kingdoms. Because of the long, complicated, and often hopeless procedure involved in proving the established titles of ownership required by a new commission (the *comissio neoadquisita)*, numerous Hungarian landowners lost their lands, which were taken over by the state or the Imperial Treasury. Most of these estates were either handed out as rewards or sold by the treasury, though several remained state or treasury domains.

Regardless of how or when they had acquired their land, all the landlords had to find new inhabitants and colonists for their estates. Large numbers came from the western and northern counties, motivated by the generous promises made by the landlords. The colonists were promised more land for cultivation than they had had before, together with tax and delivery concessions, lower corvée obligations, and animals. Most of these migrants had been serfs in northern Hungary, where the land was poor. In certain counties, 50 percent of the inhabitants left for the southeast. Most were Slovaks, Ruthenians, and Germans.

At the same time, the Imperial Treasury recruited colonists among the peasantry of the other Habsburg lands and in the Holy Roman Empire, promising them land, tax exemptions, and agricultural implements. The authorities were mainly interested in repopulating the Banat reconquered in 1718. These diverse settlers were transported down the Danube by boat until they reached Buda or Pest, and from there they were taken by cart to their destinations. They became known as the "Danubeswabians" and came from Frankonia, Swabia, the Pfalz, Bohemia, from German and French-speaking Lorraine, and from the Habsburg-ruled parts of Italy. Private landowners also recruited colonists from these lands, and a total of 400,000 immigrants reached Hungary as a consequence.

The third source for new inhabitants was the southern and southeastern border regions still under Ottoman rule. The most spectacular of the migrations from these regions had already occurred under Leopold I, when the Orthodox patriarch of Peć, Arsenije III Crnojević, led thirty thousand Serb families across the Danube into southern Hungary in 1690. Serbs continued to immigrate and, along with Romanians from the Danubian principalities, settled mainly in the Banat and in Transylvania.

These migrations and colonizing efforts increased the population of Hungary to more than nine million in 1787. (Especially impressive was the population increase in Hungary's southern counties. For example, in the county of Bács the population grew from thirty-one thousand to 227,000 during the eighteenth century.) The new inhabitants succeeded in drying up marshy regions and made cultivatable the south-Hungarian regions. In carefully planned, unified settlements, modern agricultural methods and technology made their appearance. Furthermore, mining in the Transylvanian Ore Mountains was revived.

From the point of view of the Hungarian nobility and Magyardom in general, two additional points must be noted. First, in these revived regions, separate administration remained in force for some time, well into the nineteenth century in the case of the Military Border. More important, the new settlers drastically changed the ethnic composition of the country's population. The immigration of non-Hungarians transformed Hungary into a multi-ethnic state in which the Hungarians lost their absolute majority. The resulting problems were to emerge in full force in the second half of the nineteenth century.

The Solution of the Royal Inheritance Question: The Pragmatic Sanction

In the early years of the eighteenth century, the question of succession in the Habsburg lands acquired great significance not only for Hungary but for all of Europe. Family law, based on Spanish law, aiming to prevent the dispersal of the family's possessions, stipulated undivided inheritance in the male line based on primogeniture. When the War of the Spanish Succession began, Leopold I was forced by Great Britain and the Netherlands to give up the right of his two sons to inherit each other's domains. Charles was to rule in Spain and the family's Italian possessions, and Joseph in the other lands of the Habsburgs. Nevertheless, a secret family agreement of 1703 proclaimed that the descendants of these two archdukes could inherit each other's lands according to the principle of primogeniture. In anticipation of a lack of male heirs, the agreement extended the principle to females too, giving Joseph's daughters a vaguely defined preference. In his testament, in 1705, Leopold confirmed this arrangement.

When Joseph I died without male heirs, Charles became the ruler of the

Habsburg domain. After 1711 the new ruler began to work on changes in the family law to assure the succession of his own rather than Joseph's daughters, should he die without a male heir. The first moves were made in Croatia. The Croatian legislature (Sabor) accepted the proposal of the bishop of Zágráb (Zagreb), Count Imre Esterházy, and voted that Croatia would be ruled in the future by that member of the Habsburg family who also ruled Austria, Styria, and Carinthia. The law included the right of inheritance in the female line. The Hungarian estates were not pleased with this Croatian initiative, which they considered to be beyond the Sabor's power and therefore not legally binding. Even Charles received this Croatian decision of 1712 with reservations.

Nevertheless, during this same year, Charles III felt obliged to begin negotiating the succession question with the Hungarian Diet. These talks failed because he was not ready to make the constitutional concessions the Hungarians demanded in exchange for recognizing the right of the female line to the throne.

On April 19, 1713 Charles, who was still childless, assembled his counselors and ministers in Vienna. He acquainted them with the family agreement of 1703 and added two elaborations. First, he declared all Habsburg-ruled lands an indivisible and inseparable unit, the inheritance of which was based on primogeniture, including the female line, should the male die out. Second, he strictly defined this inheritance of the throne by the female line. Charles' daughters had the first claim, followed by those of Joseph, and finally those of Leopold. Other Habsburg daughters could be considered only if these died childless. The changed family law was accepted and notarized.

This new law, the "Pragmatic Sanction," had to be accepted by the European powers, and the various lands and kingdoms of the Habsburgs, including Hungary. This became Charles' next task and an issue of primary importance when his infant son died in 1716, leaving Charles with only two daughters, Maria Theresa and Anna. The agreement of the great powers was eventually secured (greatly facilitated by the two daughters of Joseph, who renounced their claims), and in 1720, the hereditary provinces of the Habsburgs, except for the Tyrol, accepted the Pragmatic Sanction without resistance.

Hungary remained the major problem for Charles III. When the Diet of 1715 assembled, Charles, still hoping for a son, confirmed the right of the nobiliary estates to elect a king, should there be no male heir. Two regions, separately administered, accepted the Pragmatic Sanction: Croatia in 1721 and Transylvania in 1722. When the Diet of 1722 began its deliberations, the chances for its accepting the Pragmatic Sanction were poor. The majority of the county nobility was opposed to the extension of the right of succession to the female line. It felt that the concessions made in 1687 and 1711 already went too far, and it was not willing to give up the right to free royal election. Charles III conducted several informal discussions, handed out numerous estates and other preferments, used the support of the magnates (primarily Count Sándor Károlyi, the Esterházys, and the Pálffys), and succeeded in having the needed proposals submitted to the Lower House of the Diet. Following a rousing speech by the county notary of

Pozsony, Ferenc Szluha, the Lower House, followed by the House of Magnates, accepted the Pragmatic Sanction. Succession in the female line was accepted but limited to the daughters of Charles III, Joseph I and Leopold I. Free royal election was retained in case the House of Habsburg died out entirely in the lines of the descendants of these three rulers. It was also recognized that Hungary and the other Habsburg lands were indivisible and inseparable, and the need for common action was stressed, especially in case of attack from other powers. (These decisions became crucial some 140 years later when the Compromise of 1867 was negotiated. See chapters 13 and 14.) In exchange for this decision, Charles solemnly reconfirmed Hungary's estates-based constitution and the rights of its nobility (Law III/1723).

Wars Against the Ottomans and Limited Expansion

Of Charles III's wars, the two conflicts with the Ottomans were the most important for Hungary. The situation in 1716 was not promising. The War of the Spanish Succession had just ended and involved some loss of territory for the Habsburgs. Charles' finances were shaky, and the people had had enough of wars. In spite of these problems, the ruler and his advisors, primarily Prince Eugene of Savoy, decided to attack the Ottoman Empire. There were several reasons for this decision, of which the least important was concern about Ottoman moves. (Istanbul repeatedly reaffirmed its peaceful intentions and stressed that it would respect the Hungarian borders.) In fact, Charles wanted to gain territory to compensate for that just lost, though he proclaimed that he wanted to secure Hungary's borders and regain the Hungarian lands still held by the Turks.

Troops from other Habsburg lands joined forces with the new standing army and the general levy. Prince Eugene commanded the forces and Field Marshal János Pálffy commanded the cavalry, playing a prominent role in Eugene's victory at Pétervárad (Petrovaradin) in 1716. In 1717 Eugene besieged Belgrade. In spite of advancing Ottoman reinforcements, Eugene ordered an attack on the fortress and occupied it in July. The Peace of Passarowitz the following year brought considerable gains, with the Ottomans ceding Belgrade, the Banat of Temesvár, Little Wallachia, and parts of Bosnia and of Serbia. To the Hungarians' great regret, these lands, to which their country had historical claims, were not incorporated into Hungary but were placed under military jurisdiction. The Hungarian estates felt that they were not compensated for their sacrifices.

Charles III had concluded an alliance with Russia in 1726 and supported that country during the Wars of Polish Succession. Thus, as Russia's ally, he participated in the Tsarist empire's war against the Ottoman in 1736–1739, aided by Hungarian troops. Prince Eugene had died and neither the Duke of Lorraine, nor George Oliver Wallis, nor Friedrich Seckendorff were able to replace the great general. Their mistakes brought defeats on the battlefields. When the French mediated the Peace of Belgrade in 1739, most of the gains of 1718 had to be given up. Only the Banat of Temesvár was retained, though, in spite of the demands of the Hungarian estates, it remained first under military jurisdiction, then under the jurisdiction of the Imperial Treasury. Disillusionment was great. The nobility felt that their loyalty and cooperation were not appreciated and that their efforts had not advanced Hungarian unity.

The Reign of Maria Theresa, 1740–1780

For the political, economic, social, and religious development of Hungary, the five decades of the reigns of Maria Theresa and Joseph II were crucial. Such reform concepts as mercantilism and cameralism, the Enlightenment, and the influence of the physiocrats and early romanticism deeply affected the country and its inhabitants, although many of these concepts remained only ideas and several reforms had to be revoked by Joseph II. Meanwhile, the relations between Hungarians and their rulers underwent drastic fluctuations, culminating in dangerous confrontation.

Hungary and the Wars of Succession

When Charles III died in 1740, his elder daughter, Maria Theresa, succeeded him. Twenty-four years of age, she had been married since 1736 to Franz Stephan of Lorraine. Despite the recognition of the Pragmatic Sanction by the European powers, she began her rule under difficult circumstances, due to her father's second, unsuccessful war against the Ottomans. Her subjects were tired of wars, and Hungary, which had carried most of the war's burden, was complaining that the quartering of troops was too onerous. To this was added in Hungary a deep dissatisfaction with Habsburg policy, which placed great burdens on the country without bringing the expected results and compensations. An even greater problem for the young queen was the financial situation. When her rule began the treasury had only 90,000 gulden in its coffers.

Europe's sovereigns quickly showed that the Pragmatic Sanction offered no protection for Maria Theresa's throne. Frederick II (the Great) of Prussia was the first to attack, invading Silesia. The circular letter Maria Theresa sent to the rulers of Europe, reminding them of their guarantees, brought no results. Even Charles Albert, elector of Bavaria, the husband of Joseph I's younger daughter, proclaimed that he was not bound by his wife's renunciation of the Habsburg throne. Claiming Austria and Bohemia, he invaded these lands with French help. A European front, excluding only Hannover and Great Britain, menaced the future of the Habsburg-Lorraine dynasty, their aim the division of the Habsburgs' domain.

The estates in Austria beyond the Enns and those of Bohemia rapidly submitted to Charles Albert. In this catastrophic situation, Hungary and the position of its nobility became crucial. At Pozsony, Maria Theresa appeared in person before a meeting of the Diet in May 1741. She and her advisors were faced with a long list of demands aimed at altering decisions taken by her father. These included changing the coronation oath in conformity with the nobility's wishes, reorganizing the

Lord Lieutenancy, excluding the Hungarian military from the jurisdiction of the Imperial War Council, granting full independence to the Hungarian Court Treasury, easing the state monopolies' competence, and lowering custom tariffs in the interests of Hungary's economy and trade. Maria Theresa refused to change the coronation oath but promised to regulate the other issues in cooperation with the estates. She was crowned queen of Hungary on June 25, then proceeded to reject most of the estates' requests. The estates considered cancelling the Diet but decided to resubmit their demands. The situation remained tense.

While these events took place, the international situation deteriorated further. After lengthy reflection, Maria Theresa decided to appeal to the estates and request their full support. The members of both houses were asked to visit her in the fortress of Pozsony on September 11, 1741. Count Lajos Batthyány, the royal Hungarian chancellor, explained the situation to the assembled nobles and asked them to support their crowned sovereign. This speech was followed by a personal appeal from the young queen. She placed the country, the Holy Crown of Saint István, herself, and her children under the protection of "the famous Hungarian arms." The estates reacted with great enthusiasm, offering their blood and lives to their queen, the crown, and their fatherland. They offered four million gulden in war taxes, sixty thousand recruits, the nobility's general levy, and food and forage for the army. Several great lords also promised additional sums for the war.

In exchange for this generous support, Maria Theresa announced several concessions and made additional promises. She declared that in the future she would consult only Hungarians in matters dealing with Hungary and would appoint only Hungarians to ecclesiastical positions in the country. She confirmed the independence of the Hungarian court administrative organs and promised that revenues collected in Hungary would be handled exclusively by the Hungarian Court Treasury. She also indicated that those territories to which Hungary had historical claims would be reunited with the country. Finally, she promised to build a castle in Hungary in which she would reside for certain periods. Only some of these promises were kept.

In spite of the stipulations of the Hungarian constitution, Maria Theresa called the Diet into session only twice more, in 1751 and 1764. In this respect her rule did not differ from her father's, who also assembled the Diet only three times, in 1712, 1722, and 1728. The Hungarian nobility was also somewhat remiss in fulfilling its promises. Neither the volunteer cavalry commanded by Count János Pálffy, nor the general levies of 1741 and 1744 produced the number of troops promised.

Nonetheless the memory of the queen-petitioner and the Diet's enthusiastic response had lasting effects. In her subsequent Hungarian policies, the queen tried, as much as possible, to satisfy Hungarian requests. She introduced reforms with great circumspection, always keeping in mind the laws of the country and its estates-based constitution. The estates and the entire population—including the burghers and especially the peasantry—retained their sympathy for the queen and appreciated her wise policies.

The war against Frederick II and his allies was for the most part unsuccessful. The Hungarian troops and leaders fought with distinction, taking part in the campaign against Bavaria that ended with the capture of Munich. Count Ferenc Nádasdy and his hussars crossed the Rhine in 1743 and occupied Lorraine, and later, during the Seven Years War, his cavalry played a vital role in the victory of the Habsburg armies at Kolin in 1757. During the same year, the cavalry of Count András Hadik entered Berlin. The first confrontation between Maria Theresa and Frederick II had ended unfavorably for the queen, who was forced in 1742 to cede Upper and Lower Silesia and the county of Glatz to the Prussian king. This meant the loss of her richest provinces, and for the rest of her rule she never gave up trying to regain them. Nonetheless, in the Peace of Aachen, concluded with the maritime powers and France in 1748 the Habsburgs accepted the definitive loss of most of Silesia and some Italian provinces. The treaty recognized, however, all other borders and possessions as well as the validity of the Pragmatic Sanction (and thus the domain of Maria Theresa).

The lessons learned from the War of Succession determined the future foreign policy and internal reform efforts of Maria Theresa. Her hostility towards Prussia and her wish to regain the lost territories were the cornerstones of her foreign policy. At the same time, the military failure and the loss of her most valuable provinces influenced the queen's domestic policies as well. Her reform plans were inspired by advisors who were influenced by the concepts of the Enlightenment and the doctrines of mercantilism. The administrative reforms introduced in the hereditary provinces and Bohemia by Count Friedrich Wilhelm Haugwitz were designed to increase the Habsburg empire's position as a European power. A reorganized military, based on improved economic policies, would ensure a successful foreign policy. Haugwitz and his master saw as the major obstacle to efficient administration and economic policy the self-centered attitude of the various lands of the realm and their administration by their respective estates. Therefore they attempted to diminish the influence of the nobility and to limit the independence of the various lands, moving in the direction of absolutism and centralization. This attempt also required restructuring the relations between church and state. The deeply religious Maria Theresa moved very carefully, but already under her rule certain steps presaged those of Joseph II and indicated the state's dominance over the church. The final consideration that influenced the queen was her clearly announced desire to improve her subjects' economic, cultural, and social position, especially that of the burghers and peasants. This was consonant with the wish to build a powerful state, which could function only if the burden of revenue was distributed equitably between the various lands and social strata.

Haugwitz's administrative reform in the hereditary provinces and Bohemia considerably diminished the authority of local estates and assemblies and created a modern, centralized, and uniform administrative system. In Hungary, the old administrative system, in particular the strong position of the counties, remained unchanged. Here, as already mentioned, Maria Theresa moved carefully, trying to respect established privileges and constitutional forms. Thus, beginning in the 1750s, something like a dualistic regime began to develop in the lands of the Habsburgs. It consisted of a centralized and highly bureaucratized Austia and Bohemia and of a constitutional, estates-based Hungary.

Economic and Tax Reforms

Even in the broad and complex issues of economic policy, Maria Theresa was influenced by the lessons learned from, and the consequences of, the War of Succession. She saw in an ineffective economy the major weakness of her realm. Her economic program aimed to invigorate all sectors of the economy, to ease the shortage of capital, to find a substitute for Silesia, and to distribute equitably the financial obligations of her subjects. Inspired by her advisors, her economic measures were protectionist, based on mercantilist, cameralist, and early physiocratic principles.

As far as Hungary was concerned, Maria Theresa continued the settlement policies of her father. Keeping the principle of equalization of financial obligations in mind, she found the tax exemption of the nobility intolerable. Pressed by her counselors, she tried to equalize Hungary's contributions by formulating new economic priorities, altering customs regulations, and instituting protectionist measures at Hungary's expense. The crafts, manufacture, and trade of the hereditary provinces, Bohemia-Moravia, and the remnants of Silesia were supported by state funds. The lands of the Bohemian Crown received heavy support, for they were supposed to take the place of Silesia as the realm's industrial heartland. Agriculture was to be modernized and production increased throughout the Habsburg realm, with Hungary to be the major supplier of agricultural products. By supplying cheap food and raw materials to the industrial regions, Hungary was to contribute to the relatively low prices of finished manufactured items. The overall economic plan was anything but favorable to Hungary and had to have a retarding influence on its crafts and trade. Furthermore, Hungary's contribution to the common finances of the monarchy, the nobility's tax exemption, and the "compensating" measures of Maria Theresa had long lasting consequences.

In all other Habsburg lands, the nobility had lost its tax exemption considerably earlier. The Hungarian nobles' privilege rested on their obligation to serve in the army at the ruler's request. To ease the realm's financial difficulties following the War of Succession, Maria Theresa tried, at the 1751 Diet, to get the war tax raised. The amount approved in 1728 had amounted to 2.8 million gulden. Charles III had tried, without success, to raise this tax. His daughter now asked for an increase of 1.2 million arguing that this would create parity between Hungary's contributions and those of other lands, primarily Bohemia. The deputies refused, pointing to the still-felt shortages resulting from the anti-Ottoman and Succession wars, the already heavy burden borne by the peasantry, and the disadvantages under which the Hungarian economy labored due to the prevailing customs regulations. At the same Diet, the queen also proposed ending the general levy in exchange for a fixed cash payment. This would have amounted to taxing the nobility and was, therefore, rejected out of hand. Maria Theresa was extremely disappointed.

She reacted with customs reforms that were to the disadvantage of Hungary. In 1754 an "internal customs barrier" was erected, separating Hungary from the rest of the Habsburg lands. Deliveries, mostly manufactured goods, from the hereditary provinces and Bohemia to Hungary received preferential treatment and were subject to a duty of between 5 and 15 percent. All other imports (coming mainly from the Holy Roman Empire) had to be shipped through Austria and were subject to a considerably higher duty. A very high tariff was placed on all Hungarian exports to non-Habsburg lands and on Hungarian manufactured goods sold in Austria and Bohemia. Those agricultural and raw material exports needed by the industries of the various Habsburg lands received preferential treatment, but the rest were so highly taxed when exported that their prices became excessive. Goods which were needed in Austria or Bohemia could not be exported. Maria Theresa took these measures on the recommendation of her Court Commercial Council, which predicted they would force the Hungarian estates to make concessions on the tax issue. As events ten years later showed, they were mistaken.

The Seven Years War, which ended with the Peace of Hubertusburg in 1763 and left Silesia in the hands of Frederick the Great, once again ruined the empire's finances. Once again, Maria Theresa tried to have the war tax raised and the general levy abolished in exchange for cash payments. This time her move was preceded by a propaganda campaign.

Before the Diet assembled, a booklet by Ferenc Ádám Kollár was published in Vienna. Kollár, of Slovak origin, was an ex-Jesuit and the protege of Maria Theresa's close collaborator, Gerhard van Swieten. His work, *A Special Booklet about the Origins and Perpetual Use of the Legislative Power of Hungary's Holy Apostolic King,* prepared with the help of the Court, was based on the principles of centralization and absolutism and argued in favor of the unified state and against the privileges and influence of the estates. Kollár was thoroughly familiar with Hungarian law and tried to support his arguments with references to it. His main goal was to show that it was in the ruler's competence to force even ecclesiastic dignitaries to pay taxes and to produce recruits and goods for the military. Cleverly, the first attack was directed against the clergy. Kollár also attacked the privileges of the nobility and depicted the heavy burden borne by the peasantry. By stressing the ineffectiveness of the "general levy" Kollár became an advocate of the taxation of the nobility.

With the help of Kollár's historical and legal arguments, Maria Theresa presented the Diet of 1764 with two demands: a drastic increase of the war tax and the abolition of the general levy in favor of cash payments. The nobles were furious. Even the upper house and dignitaries like the bishop of Esztergom and the palatine were opposed. The Diet pointed out that the increase of the war tax approved in 1751 had been granted for only three years but had already been collected for thirteen. The estates also claimed that the Austrian taxes were paid with Hungarian money collected through the protectionist customs duties. After long and arduous negotiations, the Diet agreed to the previously approved 700,000 gulden addition to the war tax.

Vienna again reacted by increasing the customs and economic measures directed against Hungary and cancelling plans for the support of Hungarian manufactures. The customs regulation of 1775 increased the protectionist measures in favor of Austrian and Bohemian enterprises and of non-Hungarian agricultural production. The new tariffs hurt the country very much because the same duties were levied on its agricultural products as on items imported from other countries and because the import tariff for Austrian and Bohemian products was limited to a uniform 5 percent.

The queen never again called the Diet into session. As her son continued to rule in this manner, unconstitutionally, for nearly thirty years the Hungarian legislature did not function.

The Habsburgs' severe economic policies were not the only factor inhibiting economic development in Hungary in the eighteenth century. Although some pro-Habsburg magnates had invested their own funds in the 1720s and 1730s in cloth manufacture, they were unsuccessful for several reasons: Hungary lacked the needed capital, a problem aggravated by the backward credit structure of the country. It also lacked technical expertise. The nobility did not understand the principles of mercantilism, and without a strong, enterprising bourgeoisie, the country had no entrepreneurs. Furthermore, roads and other transport facilities were poor; weights and measures were not uniform; the home market was limited; there were neither large cities nor a burgher element with buying power; most of the magnates lived outside Hungary; and neither the Court nor the military was ready to place important orders in Hungary.

Thus the "internal customs barrier" aggravated an already difficult situation. It deprived Hungary of her traditional markets, including the fairs in Leipzig and Breslau (Wrocław) and the Polish and Silesian markets. Most damaging were the losses of the cattle exports to Venice, wine exports to Poland and Great Britain, and grain exports to other non-Habsburg lands. Hungarian merchants who had enjoyed considerable credit in the German lands did not receive it from their Austrian and Bohemian suppliers and were ruined. Hungarian trade became entirely dependent on Austria and Bohemia, with 87 percent of its traditional exports (cattle, wool, grain, copper, wine, tobacco, raw skins, and potash) going to Austria and Bohemia between 1760 and 1790. Imports from these lands amounted to 85 percent of the total. Hungary became an economic dependency of the other Habsburg lands.

The restrictions on Hungary's economy hurt the other Habsburg lands too, since Hungary's economic weakness made it impossible for the Austrians and Bohemians to exploit her market potential. A better economic balance would have helped both halves of the monarchy and increased state revenues. There can be no doubt that the Hungarian nobility's tax exemption did produce disparities and cause the introduction of restrictive measures. Yet Vienna's Hungarian economic policy appears unjustified. Its claim that Hungary did not carry its share of the empire's financial burdens cannot be supported. The income derived from the salt monopoly, from the state and treasury estates, the mines, the minting of coins, and most importantly from the deliveries in kind to the military at low fixed prices more than compensated for the low war tax. Furthermore, the expenses of local administration in Hungary were paid by the nobility. Taking all this into account, Hungary's contribution to the total state budget amounted to between 26 and 29 percent.

Agrarian Policy and the Peasant Question

Hungary's economy was predominantly agrarian. In this respect the eighteenth century brought no changes, although advances were made in agriculture. Not only in the southeast but everywhere in the country, landlords made strenuous efforts to bring new lands under cultivation. Root crop cultivation was expanded, and potatoes, corn, and tobacco were especially favored. Animal breeds were improved, thanks in part to the efforts of state-owned estates and stud-farms supplying the military. The increased stabling of animals and the growing of clover and alfalfa also contributed to the improvement of animal husbandry.

Nevertheless, compared to Western European agriculture, Hungary remained backward. Only a few new settlements and large latifundia were able to approach European standards. In other regions the two-field system remained dominant, and Vlachs, Serbs, and even Hungarians continued to follow unproductive pastoral methods of raising animals. Animal husbandry and wine production remained more important than the production of crops. Agricultural technology was dated, manure was in short supply, and modern tools were practically non-existent.

In addition, the medieval, feudal agricultural structure of the country has to be considered. In the first half of the century, the nobility was not satisfied simply with retaining its rights. It tried systematically to withdraw the concessions made to the peasantry during the last years of the anti-Ottoman wars and the Rákóczi period, as well as the promises made to the new settlers. The nobility tried, in particular, to expand its allodial possessions and to expropriate the lands of the serfs. Since this would have diminished state revenues due to the nobility's tax exemption, the rulers and the state authorities were opposed.

The peasantry's situation was grave. They suffered the most during the numerous wars, had to pay the war tax, and supplied the recruits. Because Hungary had no barracks prior to the reign of Joseph II, the troops stationed in Hungary were quartered in the homes of the peasants, who had to feed the soldiers living with them. The expenses of housing and feeding the troops were deducted from the war tax, but when products rather than cash served as the basis for calculations, the peasants lost heavily because the prices were not based on market prices. When cash was involved, the peasants had to take care of the troops before the corresponding amount was deducted from the next tax payment. The peasants also had to provide transportation for the army and perform free labor on fortifications. With the landlords making similar demands the peasants spent long periods away from work and home.

Due to the wars, agricultural prices rose steeply in 1740–48 and 1756–63, encouraging the nobility to increase production on their own farms. The nobles decided that three days of corvée per week were not sufficient and forced the peasantry, illegally, to do more. Quite understandably, Hungary's peasants became restless. Several riots occurred, including those of 1735 and 1753 in the "storm corner" along the upper Tisza Valley. Peasant discontent and the still-remembered kuruc tradition contributed to an uprising in 1735 in the region around the Maros and Körös (Kriş) rivers. Several thousand peasants and herdsmen, led by Pero Szegedinac, András Pásztor and Mihály Vértesi, destroyed the possessions of the Duke of Modena and the Haruckern family. The leaders were executed, and several thousand were condemned to forced labor. Popular uprisings also occurred in 1755 in Croatia, in 1764 in the Székely region, and in 1765 in Transdanubia.

Motivated by both humanitarian and economic considerations, Maria Theresa tried to convince the nobility to resolve the peasant problem at the Diet of 1764–65 (using, once again, materials prepared for her by Kollár). The estates refused even to discuss the reform proposals, and Maria Theresa, angered by this attitude and the failure of her tax reform proposals, addressed the peasant question without their cooperation. Her Urbarial Patent of 1767 defined the normative size of peasant holdings and regulated peasant obligations. (The size of holdings depended on local circumstances, primarily the productivity of the land.) Lands to which each peasant family was entitled were fixed as follows: for home and outbuildings, 1.4 acres; for agricultural pursuits, between 22.5 and 70 acres; for pasture, between 5.7 and 21 acres. The peasants were also given free use of forests to gather building materials and fuel. Peasant obligations to landlords included rent for their lands in cash and one-ninth (with certain fixed additions) of their products. Corvée obligations were fixed at fifty-two days per year if animals were to be used and otherwise at one hundred four days per year. Furthermore, the first steps were taken to reestablish the peasantry's right of free migration; for example, children of peasants could decide what profession they wished to follow and what education they were to receive without obtaining the lord's permission. The measures taken to protect the peasants against misuses of the lords' patrimonial jurisdiction were mainly theoretical. The attorney general of each county was ordered to represent the peasants, but because these individuals were also members of the county nobility, this brought meager results.

The nobility unanimously opposed these changes in the country's agrarian order. It took ten years to break their resistance and enforce these reforms with the help of specially delegated royal commissioners. Even so the regulations did not extend to Transylvania, nor did they constitute the liberation of the peasantry.

Maria Theresa's son, Joseph II, continued her policies regarding the peasants, in conformity with his absolutistic and physiocratic principles, but the freeing of the peasant was something he could not achieve. The new ruler did issue numerous regulations and ordinances in 1783 and 1784, regulating the relationship between lords and their peasants. He also extended the peasants' right to free migration, ordered the free selection of professions for the peasants and forbade the use of the expression "serf," and the expropriation of peasant lands without adequate compensation. These decrees were valid in Transylvania also, where a massive peasant revolt occurred in 1784. It was led by the Romanian peasants Vasile Horia, Ion Cloşca, and Gheorghe Crişan and was centered in Hunyad county and parts of the Transylvanian Ore Mountains. Between twenty and thirty thousand peasants were involved, and the homes of the nobility along the Maros were burned down. The insurgents demanded religious freedom and the abolition of serfdom and also voiced some national demands. Joseph II hesitated but finally used military force. In 1785, the leaders of the revolt were executed, showing clearly the limits of the ruler's willingness to help the peasant. Nonetheless, the reforms of Maria Theresa and Joseph II were generally favorable for the peasantry.

Schools and Education

Prior to Maria Theresa's reign, the Hungarian educational establishment left much to be desired. As late as the 1760s, the country had only 7.5 schools for each ten thousand inhabitants (far below the European average) and the vast majority of these schools had only a single teacher. The educational concepts of the Enlightenment greatly influenced Maria Theresa, who held that everyone should have equal access to education, that instruction had to be improved qualitatively, and that it was the duty of the state to encourage the population to learn. She did not consider education a means to the betterment of a selected few, but rather as something fundamental for the improvement of society and state.

The school reforms were based on guidelines worked out by the Abbot of Sagan in Silesia, Johann Felbiger, in his 1774 work, *The General Regulations of German Higher, Middle, and Elementary Schools.* He argued for obligatory schooling of all male inhabitants, for the separation of schools from the church and their subordination to the state (this trend was later helped by the dissolution of the Jesuit order), and for an education that prepared graduates for state service. To achieve these goals, he advocated the establishment of a uniform school system. Viewed from his position, Hungary was worse off than Austria or Bohemia. The country's school system was characterized by regionalism and estates-based considerations, making upward mobility for graduates very difficult. Schools were still closely tied to the Church, and, except for elementary schools, Catholic schools were almost exclusively in the hands of the Jesuits and Piarists. In addition Hungary's administration was still carried out in Latin, further limiting access to middle and higher education.

Maria Theresa wanted to introduce in Hungary too, a school system under state supervision, uniform and accessible to the majority of the population. In 1777, she promulgated her *Ratio educationis* prepared by Kollár and based on Felbiger's guidelines. A new branch of the lieutenancy, the Education Commission, became the highest educational organ of Hungary. The country was divided into nine school districts, each under the supervision of a director of education. Schools were separated from the church, whose rights of supervision and inspection were transferred to the state. The second section of the *Ratio* fixed the curriculum of elementary schools for the entire country. In accordance with the principles of the Enlightenment, "practical" subjects were favored, mainly mathematics, history, and geography.

The queen also established in Vienna the Oriental Academy and the Theresian Academy for training statesmen, administrators, and diplomats. These two schools, especially the latter, had numerous Hungarian students, and specialized schools were established in Hungary also. A mining academy was opened in Selmecbánya in northern Hungary, and Pozsony, Győr, Nagyvárad, and Zágráb became the seats of law schools.

Agriculture profited from the efforts of individual initiatives, such as that of Samuel Tessedik, a Lutheran minister, pedagogue and writer. After attending schools in Hungary, he continued his studies at several German universities where he became familiar with the ideas of the Enlightenment and the philanthropic approach to education. In 1767, he returned to Hungary and became minister at Szarvas. He tried, first of all, to improve the lot of the peasantry. In 1780, he established a training school for young peasants and equipped it with a library, workshops, and a model farm. He taught such subjects as crop rotation, the growing of forage plants, and modern fruit orchard management. He was responsible for numerous innovations, and his influence was felt all across the great Hungarian plain. In a similar vein, one of the great magnates, György Festetics, established the Georgicon in Keszthely, devoted to agrarian experimentation and innovation.

Maria Theresa also transferred Hungary's university from the north-Hungarian Nagyszombat to Buda and then to Pest. In accordance with her promise of 1741, Maria Theresa had a royal castle erected in Buda, and although she never resided there, she allowed the university to use it.

In the cultural and literary renaissance of Hungary, another of Maria Theresa's institutions played a considerable role. In 1760, she created the Hungarian Bodyguard in Vienna. To establish contact with the middle-ranking nobility of the counties and show her close relations with Hungary, she invited two young nobles from each county to serve in this unit. In Vienna the young men became familiar with the culture of the Italian and German late Baroque and with the French and German concepts of the Enlightenment. From the stimulating salons of the imperial city, they returned to their homes as advocates of new ideas and literary activities. Many played a significant role in the history of Hungarian literature, among them György Bessenyei, one of the major figures of the early Hungarian literary renaissance (see chapter 9). He joined the guard in Vienna in 1765 and studied French, German, and

Italian literature. He began his literary work by producing translations and in the process became conscious of the value and beauty of his own language. Francis Ádám Kollár brought him to Maria Theresa's attention, and Bessenyei dedicated his work, *The Tragedy of Agis,* to the queen. He lost royal favor under Joseph II and returned to Hungary.

The Reign of Joseph II, 1780–1790

The Basic Concepts of Josephinism

The ten years of Joseph II's reign were stirring times in Hungary. With a plethora of reforms, edicts, decrees, and regulations, the ruler tried to transform Hungary in conformity with his concepts of enlightened absolutism. Joseph's political, economic, cultural, and social programs were based on the works of theorists who published their works in France, Great Britain, and in the German lands. He wished to transform theory into practice, and was a levelheaded, pragmatic wielder of power.

His basic concepts formed an integrated whole and did not represent a break with his mother's policy. The major difference between his policies and his mother's was that Joseph's were clearer, more systematic, and more radical. He was also less tactful and more impatient than Maria Theresa.

The major aim of Josephinism was the creation of an internally and internationally secure modern state, a great power. He wanted a state organization based on "reason," uniform in its administrative organization, administered by a centralized bureaucracy, and run for the good of every inhabitant. In this state the ruler was to be the highest ranking civil servant, following the principle announced in Prussia by Frederick II. The concerns of the community and the state took precedence over individual or local interests.

Joseph was a firm believer in the absolute power of monarchs and was, therefore, vehemently opposed to the nobility's privileges and all regional rights and institutions. To avoid the coronation oath and the resulting obligation to recognize the special position of the kingdom, he refused to be crowned king of Hungary and never even considered working with the Hungarian Diet. Symbols of the old regime, including the Crown of Saint István, meant nothing to him. In April 1784, he had the crown and all other royal insignia transferred to the treasury vaults in Vienna over the vehement protests of the Hungarian court authorities and the counties. The crown and Hungary's special status had no place in Joseph's ideal state. It was not to be an empire made up of numerous heterogenous parts, but one built organically on the principles dictated by reason, ruled by one ruler with the help of a centralized government and army.

Following the example of England, Russia, and the Protestant states, Joseph subordinated the various churches to the state and drastically reduced their influence. He dealt with educational issues without consulting the clergy and, in spite of its protest, liberalized censorship. He even controlled the correspondence of the Catholic clergy with Rome.

Culture and Civilization: Late Baroque, Rococo, Enlightenment

The feverish building activity that had begun under Leopold I intensified after the Peace of Szatmár, thanks to the solid financial position of the Hungarian magnates and episcopacy. Indeed, the most prominent Hungarian lords were among the richest people of the Habsburg realm. The richest among these, Prince Esterházy, had a yearly income estimated at 700,000 gulden. The Catholic hierarchy also controlled considerable wealth: the primate-archbishop of Esztergom had a yearly income of 360,000 gulden, the bishop of Eger 80,000, and the bishop of Nagyvárad 70,000.

The construction of the magnificent baroque castle of Prince Esterházy at Kismárton (Eisenstadt) began as early in 1683. Work on the Esterházy palace at Cseklész started in 1714, and soon afterwards builders appeared at Fertőd to erect another Esterházy palace, the crowning glory of the Hungarian baroque. Other great families followed the Esterházys example, building baroque palaces: the Károlyis at Erdőd (Ardud), the Pálffys at Nagygurab and Királyfalva, the Festetics at Keszthely, as well as the Batthyánys. During this first phase of building, architects and artists from Italy, Austria, and Bohemia-Moravia were active in Hungary. Two of them in particular had a great influence on Hungarian architects and artists, Domenico Martinelli and Johann Lucas Hildebrandt.

The visible signs of the success of the Counterreformation during the reigns of Charles III and Maria Theresa were the magnificent baroque buildings erected by the Catholic Church. At the episcopal sees of the Vác, Szombathely, Veszprém, Kalocsa, and Eger, new baroque churches were built. Around churches and the palaces of bishops, the architects erected squares designed to impress. The various religious orders (in Csorna the Praemonstratensians, in Eger the Minorites, in Győr the Carmelites, the Benedictines in Győr and Pápa, and in Sopron and Kalocsa the Jesuits) built new churches and had the houses of their orders reconstructed. The frescoes, statues, bas reliefs, and stuccos were the work of Austrian and Italian artists, but in numerous city and some village churches native architects and artists proved their artistic talents. The baroque was not the exclusive domain of the nobility and the Catholic clergy. The Lutheran and even the Calvinist nobility also followed the prevailing trend in building their residences and manor houses. Even the buildings erected by the Serbs, who entered Hungary after the Ottomans had left, were baroque not only in southern Hungary but also in Buda, Pest, Szentendre and Komárom.

After the 1740s the rococo style, with its rich ornamentation, made its entry into Hungary. By the end of the 1760s the typically Hungarian variant of the late baroque, with its classical features, known as the Zopfstil, made its appearance and became dominant until the end of the century. It was followed by the neoclassic of the pre-March period. Out of the originally foreign artistic influences grew a Hungarian artistic style in architecture, sculpture, and painting.

In philosophy and literature, foreign influences were possibly even stronger than in architecture and the visual arts, due in part to the memoirs and letters written by Hungarians in exile in France and the Ottoman Empire. Ferenc

Rákóczi's autobiographical works, written between 1716 and 1719, were strongly influenced by French authors, primarily Rabelais and Fénelon. Rákóczi wrote in French and Latin, openly criticizing the ignorance and egotism of the Hungarian nobility. His private secretary in Turkey was Kelemen Mikes, who in 1758 completed the 270 fictitious *Turkish Letters,* following French models and expressing his views about life in exile and the situation in Hungary.

In Hungary proper, literature was mainly the domain of the nobility. Magnates and members of the middle-ranking nobility were active as writers, poets, and literary patrons, occupying themselves primarily with the literary, political, and social ideas of the Enlightenment. This was especially the case in Transylvania, where traditional contacts with France were continued. Quite early, a circle of aristocrats formed there, devoted to spreading French ideas and French literature. (In 1755, Count László Haller translated Fénelon's *Telemaque.)* In Hungary, Count Mihály Sztáray, whose mother was French, combined his francophile position with anticlericalism and anti-Habsburg attitudes. The poetry of Count János Fekete owed much to the French enlightenment, and he was a constant correspondent of Voltaire. Among the factors that broadened the horizons of the Hungarian nobility were their "gentleman's trips" to France, the Netherlands, and Great Britain; their studies at Protestant German universities; and their contacts with French and British officers during the Seven Years War. In spite of the strict censorship still in force under Maria Theresa, the magnates (less strictly handled by customs officials when they returned from abroad) were able to bring the literature of the West into the country. Count István Csáky owned five thousand volumes, mostly French, including first editions of Voltaire and Rousseau, and Count Sztáray, and the Széchenyis, and the Orczys had libraries not much smaller. These contained not only the classics of the Enlightenment but also volumes by radical, materialist, and early socialist authors, including Guillaume Raynal, Baron Paul Holbach, Gabriel de Mably, and others.

The writers and poets inspired and supported by these magnates will be discussed in the next chapter. Suffice it to note that these literary figures, who followed the styles of the rococo, classical, or early romantic movements, saw as their primary duty the cultivation of their native Hungarian language. They redoubled their efforts after Joseph II issued his edict introducing German as the official language.

Freemasonry, relatively widespread in Hungary, also contributed to the dissemination of modernizing thought. Freemasonry also was an aristocratic import from Vienna. Lodge meetings brought together aristocrats and representatives of the bourgeois intelligentsia, advocates of humanism, tolerance, interconfessional cooperation, and the ideas of the Enlightenment. During the last years of Maria Theresa's reign and especially during Joseph's the freemasons played an important role in Hungary. The two highest-ranking Hungarian dignitaries, the royal Hungarian court chancellor, Count Károly Pálffy, and the president of the Lord Lieutenancy, Count Károly Zichy were freemasons, as were the leading officeholders in the most important Hungarian offices in Vienna and Buda. In something like twenty lodges, holders of high offices, leading figures of the counties, and the county nobility mingled with magnates, members of the middle and lower nobility, and teachers, clergymen, military officers, and others.

Joseph II's edict of 1785 regulated freemasonry, placing it under state supervision. The number of lodges was limited, and these secret societies had to report their membership to the authorities. The five sanctioned lodges, and several illegal ones, continued their activities. Hungarian freemasons were originally favorably disposed to Joseph, and several of his reforms in Hungary followed principles with which the masons agreed. However, his attempts to regulate freemasonry changed the position of the lodge brothers. This resentment was soon coupled with the need to defend Hungary's estates-based constitution, and concepts of the radical Enlightenment turned them against the ruler and his centralistic tendencies.

During the last years of Joseph's rule, the county nobility accepted the constitutional and political principles of the French Enlightenment, primarily in matters of public law. Montesquieu, Voltaire, and Rousseau were the sources of the arguments the estates used against the ruler's centralizing efforts and in defense of their positions and privileges. While the nobility appropriated the concepts of natural law and the social contract, the ideas of the Enlightenment were consciously or unconsciously adapted to suit the nobility's desires and goals. This was particularly evident after the French revolution, whose slogans were used with enthusiasm. To the Hungarian nobility, liberty meant the freedoms reserved for themselves by the Hungarian constitution; fraternity meant cooperation with nobles of other religious persuasions; and equality meant equal privileges for all nobles. The overwhelming majority of the Hungarian nobility, even the freemasons among them, were not willing to extend fraternity and equality to the burghers and peasants.

Josephinian Reforms in Hungary

Joseph II introduced numerous reforms in Hungary, all of them based on the assumption that royalty could legislate without the cooperation of the Diet. These reforms were especially significant in the realms of ecclesiastic policy, the language question, the reorganization of the administration, and recruitment for the military.

In Hungary the Catholic Church enjoyed a privileged position, and the episcopacy was among the richest of the country's landlords. To a considerable extent, the Church regulated the spiritual life of Hungary. It controlled all schools from the elementary to the university level, and by strictly enforcing the regulations of censorship, it controlled the publication of books and thus everything the public was able to read. During the late phases of the Counterreformation under Maria Theresa, the Church showed no inclination to practice tolerance of other religions, though non-Catholics were numerous in Hungary. (Besides the Orthodox Serbs and Romanians, over 7 percent of the inhabitants were Lutherans and nearly 12 percent Calvinists.)

New political tendencies began under Maria Theresa which, however, became fundamental principles of ecclesiastic policy under Joseph II. The power of the Catholic Church was significantly curtailed and that of the state in all religious matters was greatly expanded. Joseph II's approach was not dictated by hostility towards religion or the Catholic Church. He was religious himself but was determined to prevent the Church from becoming a state within the state.

The best known of Joseph's religious edicts was his Patent of Toleration, promulgated in 1781. This edict extended the "free practice" of religions to all confessions, though some restrictions remained. Non-Catholics could not ring church bells or erect steeples; the entrances of their churches could not open on main streets; and non-Catholic missionary activities were forbidden. Nonetheless, non-Catholics received full rights as citizens. In the professions, they could become guild masters, and in education they could earn university diplomas within Hungary (previously they had had to go abroad). They were also admitted to service in state offices.

Reaction to the Patent took various forms in Hungary: the Catholic episcopacy submitted a petition to the ruler demanding its revocation, and some of the Catholic-dominated counties refused to follow Joseph's orders. Two years later, however, Joseph went further. In a new patent, he fixed the status of Hungarian Jews, granting them the right to practice their religion freely. While they did not receive full citizenship rights, as had other non-Catholics two years earlier, special regulations dealing with them were ended, and they became subject to the general laws of the country.

Joseph also closed the monasteries and abbeys of the contemplative orders. In Hungary, this meant the closure of one hundred thirty-four monasteries and six nunneries. Their possessions became the property of a newly created "religion fund." Joseph used some of these assets to finance the establishment of new parishes considered necessary by civil authorities. Most of the money, however, was used to open new elementary schools. With the remaining funds, Joseph established a General Seminary in Pozsony for the training of priests and closed the old ones run by the bishoprics. In the new seminary, the future priests were trained in the spirit of the Josephinian state church. The episcopate's freedom to correspond with Rome was restricted, and the ruler's permission was required for the public reading of papal bulls and encyclicals. Not satisfied with these measures, Joseph regulated the details of the church's internal affairs. He limited the number of processions and pilgrimages, forbade music during services, specified the number of candles and church ornaments that could be used during services, and so on. Though his reasons were pragmatic—the reduction of ostentatious spending—Joseph's regulations met with hostility, not only from ecclesiastics but from the great majority of the Catholic laity.

In July 1781, Joseph eased censorship and removed it from church control. As a result, a flood of books, journals, newspapers, and pamphlets began to appear. These publications disseminated the ideas of the Enlightenment, of the estates-based constitutionalists, and of the Hungarian language reformers, as well as those of early classicism and romanticism.

To advance the creation of a unified and centralized empire and to make administration easier, Joseph made German the official language in Hungary and Transylvania also. Describing Latin, which the Hungarian nobility knew and used, as a dead language, in April 1784 he gave all state employees and county administrators three years to prove that they could carry out their functions in German. Subsequently, Joseph issued a supplementary directive, making German the language of instruction in all schools. (Only religion could be taught in the students' native languages.) The General Seminary was to admit only candidates who could prove that they could speak and write German.

The reaction in Hungary was violent. At county assemblies, the nobility demanded the revocation of the language regulations and the reintroduction of Latin. A few counties argued that if Latin was to be replaced by a living language, that language should be Hungarian. Officials declared that they were incapable of learning German in three years, and indeed, as late as 1790, several Royal Commissioners were forced to translate the ruler's German edicts into Hungarian for the estates and county officials. Clearly, the language edict did not make administration easier.

A further result was that numerous Hungarians, particularly the nobility, began systematically to work on reforming the Hungarian language and to patronize Hungarian literature. Hungarians, including the members of the high aristocracy, began to wear ostentatiously Hungarian clothing and generally cultivated native traditions. Ironically, Joseph's measures contributed to the Hungarian literary revival and gave impetus to the movement to make Hungarian the official language (though this was not to happen until 1844).

When the king ordered a census to establish the exact number of Hungary's inhabitants and simultaneously ordered that the land be measured and surveyed, he once again brought into question the tax exemption of the Hungarian nobility. In his rescript, addressed to the Hungarian Court Chancellery, of May 1, 1784, Joseph indicated that the census would take the form of conscription (including members of the nobility) and that "German military units" would carry it out, using "German conscription forms." Despite Joseph's protestations to the contrary, the proceedings had a decidedly foreign and militaristic flavor. Hungarian authorities warned the ruler of the consequences of this method, which the Hungarians would consider a new slight to their special position. The Court Chancellery refused to use the German forms and indicated that local authorities were quite capable of carrying out the required counting and measuring. They stressed that serious disorders might result from the involvement of the military.

As usual, Joseph was not worried by the warnings of the Hungarian civil authorities. He stuck to his original instructions, which were transmitted, on August 16, through the lieutenancy to the counties. The resistance was even stronger than the Hungarian authorities had feared. A general meeting of the counties protested unanimously against the conscription and pointed out that it violated the Hungarian constitution. Joseph remained unimpressed. Repeatedly he insisted in rescripts addressed to the counties that his orders be carried out. They were carried out in the following years, but in many cases military intervention became necessary, first with the conscription and then, after 1786, with the survey of the land. Though Joseph appeared victorious, an unbreachable barrier was created between the ruler and the counties. Infuriated by the occasional armed resistance, Joseph began to think about restructuring the administrative apparatus of the country.

In March 1785, Joseph sent a circular to the various main Hungarian authorities. In it he objected to the counties' repeated protests and resistance and especially to their ineffectiveness in carrying out his orders. For these reasons he announced that the old administrative structure of Hungary was abolished. Henceforth Hungary and Croatia-Slavonia were to be organized into ten districts, each of which subsumed four to five counties.

Joseph also eliminated the old administrative offices and functions of the local bureaucracy. The office of high ispán was abolished, as was that of the vice-ispán. The high ispáns were replaced by a royal commissioner for each new district, aided by other functionaries also nominated by the emperor. Joseph appointed as royal commissioners men who had his full confidence and whom he expected to carry out their duties resolutely and unmercifully.

What this restructuring of the administration was supposed to achieve was spelled out by Joseph in the instructions he gave in 1785 and 1786 to his newly appointed commissioners. First and foremost, he wanted to curtail the county nobility's freedom of action. They could no longer elect from among their own ranks officials and bureaucrats nor hold general county assemblies. Furthermore, they were forbidden to correspond with each other, as representatives of counties, making it impossible for the estates to formulate actions on a national scale. Joseph also clearly defined the position and duties of the commissioners. They were simply chief executives whose role was to execute the ruler's orders and make certain that his intentions were widely explained and understood.

Joseph hoped to create an administrative structure in Hungary entirely dependent on the royal will, one that would respond to orders quickly, efficiently and without opposition. Yet traditional, organic, and firmly rooted institutions are resilient, and the new order, vehemently attacked by the Hungarian nobility, had yet to prove its effectiveness in time of crisis. The new Hungarian system faced this crisis with the outbreak of a new war with the Ottoman Empire.

The Ottoman War and the Collapse of Josephinism

To create an effective counterweight to Prussia, Joseph and the imperial chancellor, Prince Wenzel Kaunitz, had already tried to reach an agreement with Russia during the reign of Maria Theresa. The queen was opposed to any arrangement with Catherine II, whom she did not like or trust; nevertheless, Joseph traveled to Mogilev during the lifetime of his mother, met the Tsarina, and laid the groundwork for a rapprochement with Russia. The lively correspondence that followed resulted in an agreement in 1781, in which Joseph promised to join in any wars against the Ottomans and not to conclude a separate peace. This agreement placed Joseph, the weaker of the two partners, at the mercy of

Catherine II and made it almost impossible for him to formulate his own eastern policy.

Having been harassed and pressured repeatedly by the Russians, the Ottomans imprisoned the Russian ambassador in the Yedi Kule fortress in Istanbul and declared war on Russia in August 1787. Unexpectedly and unwillingly, Joseph II found himself at war with the Ottomans. From the fall of 1787 to his death in 1790, Joseph enlisted recruits and collected the needed supplies for the army in Hungary by issuing decrees in disregard of the constitutionally required cooperation of the estates. To get soldiers and supplies, he was forced to reactivate the county assemblies he had recently abolished. In 1787 and 1788, the county assemblies cooperated, and it appeared that the Josephinian system in Hungary was functioning.

When the ruler asked for new recruits twice in 1789, however, resistance began to mount, becoming almost universal by October. The change was due in part to military reverses. It took until September 1789 for Marshal Laudon's forces to conquer Beograd, and further advances into the Balkans did not follow. By this time the human and material resources of the country were exhausted, and the severe drought of 1789 resulted in an extremely poor harvest. There were also other influences at work, notably the revolt of the estates in the Austrian Netherlands (today's Belgium) and the French Revolution, whose effects in Hungary cannot be overestimated.

The opposition to Joseph II united the disparate elements of Hungarian society. The nobles of the estates were joined by the peasants in opposition to recruitment, and the intelligentsia joined them, following its pacifist and radical principles. Practically all the counties wrote letters of protest to Joseph in 1789, refusing to send new soldiers and supplies to the army. They demanded the reestablishment of constitutional rule, the revocation of the unconstitutional Josephinian edicts, and the proper coronation of a king of Hungary.

The county assemblies began to correspond with each other again, developing a unified, anti-Josephinian position, and armed resistance was used to oppose the demands of the ruler. Certain segments of the discontented nobility began to seek foreign help, and Prussia appeared willing to support the dissatisfied nobles. Should the insurrection prove successful, the plan was to declare the throne of the Habsburgs vacant. Carl August of Weimar (the patron of Goethe) was selected as the future king of Hungary and the country was on the brink of armed rebellion.

By the end of 1789, Joseph's leading Hungarian and Austrian advisers held that yielding had become unavoidable. Even his brother and future successor, the grand duke of Tuscany, Leopold, argued for the appeasement of Hungary. The situation was made worse by the steadily deteriorating international situation, the unsuccessful war, and the growing pressure exercised by Prussia. These circumstances, combined with his rapidly deteriorating health, made Joseph pessimistic and resigned to his fate.

On January 28, 1790, Joseph II addressed a letter to the lieutenancy and all Hungarian counties wherein he revoked all his reforms. Hungarian laws and institutions were to revert to what they had been on the eve of his accession to power. Only three of his measures remained valid: the Patent of Toleration and the decrees regulating the situation of the peasants and that of the parishes. Joseph also promised that he would convoke the Diet in 1791, after ending the war and reestablishing peace and order. The potential crisis in Hungary had led to a practically complete failure of the Josephinian system there.

Joseph II was disappointed by the Hungarian reaction to the revocation of his reforms and edicts, for the emperor's concessions did not prevent the Hungarian estates from renewing their demand for the immediate convocation of the legislature. In addition, Joseph's expectation that the nobility would now offer recruits and supplies for the army as a quid pro quo proved to be illusory. The policy of appeasement in Hungary, which the ruler had accepted with great reluctance, proved to be a failure. The concessions Joseph made served only to strengthen the solidarity of the estates and their demands became sharper and more insistent. The danger posed by the newly unified Hungarian estates became the most urgent problem facing Joseph's successor, Leopold II.

Reliquary bust of Saint Ladislas, cathedral of Győr. Work of the Kolozsvári brothers, 14th century.

Matthias Corvinus. Contemporary bas–relief by Giulio Romano.

The cathedral of Kassa (Košice).
14th–15th century.

The Esterházy Palace at Fertőd.

Buda in the time of Matthias Corvinus. From the Schedel Chronicle, 1493.

GABRIEL BATORI RELIGIONE CATHOLICVS.

Gábor Báthori.

Gábor Bethlen. By Matheus Marian (1593–1650).

GABRIEL BETHLEN D. G. PRINCEPS TRANS
SYLVANIÆ, PART. REGNI HVNGARIÆ DOMINVS
ET SICVLORVM COMES, ETC.

Ferenc II Rákóczi. By Adam Mányoki (1673–1757).

Lajos Kossuth, 1843. By Eybl.

István Széchenyi.

Sándor Petőfi, 1845. By Miklós Barabás
(1810–1898).

Francis Joseph. By Fülöp László.

Queen Elizabeth.
By Gyula Benczur.

The destroyed and temporary bridges, Budapest, 1945.

View of contemporary Budapest with Elizabeth Bridge in foreground.

XI

THE AGE OF ROYAL ABSOLUTISM, 1790–1848

George Barany

The sixty-eight years that separate the death of Joseph II from the collapse of the "Metternich-System" in March 1848 constitute a period of dramatic change in Hungarian history. At the end of the decade that saw this most consistent of enlightened despots as the sole ruler of the realm of the Habsburgs, Hungary was under threat of losing its distinct political separateness and of becoming but one of the many provinces of a multinational empire governed from Vienna. When they succeeded in reasserting Hungary's status as an independent king-dom vis-à-vis a Germanized central administration in the imperial capital, the Hungarian estates seemingly restored the authority of a medieval feudal consti-tution ridiculed by the just deceased "hat-wearing king." In less than seven decades, however, Hungarian feudalism was challenged by autochthonous forces echoing the ideas of Western liberalism. This led to the proclamation of Hungary's first independent government, appointed by a Habsburg monarch, but responsible to a popularly elected parliament.

Economic grievances directed largely against Maria Theresa's discriminatory tariff policies formed an important part of the wave of protest that fueled Hun-garian resistance to Joseph II's central bureaucracy. Articulated vigorously at the feudal Diets of the 1790s, these protests were first presented in a systematic fashion in the writings of the progressive economist-publicist Gergely Berzeviczy. Only later, after the fall of Napoleon, when the industrial revolution began to spread from the northern and western sections of the continent toward the southeast, were questions regarding the economic integration of the Habs-burg lands and Hungary's role in this process reexamined, with far-reaching practical consequences.

Frustrated challenges to the prevailing spirit of immobilism in the political arena and subtle but disquieting structural changes in the economy were charac-teristic of the era between 1790 and 1848. The transformation of literary and cultural life was more conspicuous and radical. When Joseph II died, the ruling Hungarian aristocracy was about to confirm the Magyar vernacular, one of many spoken in the kingdom, as an official language. This nationalistic reaction to the emperor's attempts to Germanize the central administration permeated politics and cultural life alike. The birthpangs of a Magyarizing nation-state threatened to disrupt the age-old structure of the Habsburg realm: by the *Vormärz,* European diplomatic chanceries started to speculate that there might be a Hungarian question in Central Europe demanding their attention.

Josephinism and the Impact of the French Revolution, 1790–1795

In January 1790, the mortally ill Joseph II cancelled all rescripts and enactments issued for Hungary and Transylvania during his reign. This concession to the Hungarian noble opposition excluded only his Toleration Patent (1781), edicts relating to the new church, and those benefitting the unfree population. With a stroke of the pen, the emperor thus intended to restore, by and large, conditions as they existed at the time of Maria Theresa's death. Joseph hoped that this conciliatory gesture would enable his younger brother and successor, Leopold II, to resume the work of enlightened reform at a more auspicious time. In the same month, however, he also consented to a further tightening of the censorship of books and newspapers under the auspices of a newly established Ministry of Police. (Although the restored autonomy of Hungarian counties limited the police system controlled by Vienna, secret agents and spies provided ample information to the Austrian authorities until the beginning of the constitutional era in 1867.) This measure marked the culmination of the increasing concern of the monarch's last years caused by the dangers inherent in the French Revolution, a war with Turkey, an uprising in the Austrian Netherlands, Prussian pressure, and the feudal nobility's brewing revolt in Hungary. Taken together, the actions taken by Joseph II on his deathbed opened the door for reconciliation, reform, and repression alike. His successors pursued one or another of these policies as circumstances warranted.

Leopold II, who had successfully implemented a series of enlightened reforms as grand duke of Tuscany, called the Hungarian Diet into session with the intention of getting himself crowned king of Hungary with all the traditional pomp and ceremony. The Diet, the first to convene since 1765, enacted a number of laws, which were regarded as guarantees of constitutional freedom and socio-economic progress by two generations of patriotic reformers. These stipulated that: Hungary was a free and independent kingdom to be governed in accordance with her own laws and customs; legislative power was vested jointly in the king and the Diet, and the former would not govern by patents and ordinances; following the monarch's death a coronation Diet had to be convened within three months; the Holy Crown had to be preserved in Buda; Diets had to be held every three years; the lieutenancy could remonstrate against unlawful decrees; taxes could be approved only by the Diet; Magyar should be taught in secondary schools and institutions of higher learning (although, for the time being, the central government agencies should continue to use Latin in their official correspondence); and Protestants should be permitted to exercise their religious rights freely and be given equal consideration in appointments for public office. The Diet also renewed Maria Theresa's urbarial patent of 1767, which regulated the mutual obligations of lord and peasant and secured the serfs' right to freedom of movement. It also voted six thousand recruits for the army and elected nine committees to draw up a blueprint for systematic reform in a broad spectrum of fields.

The legislation passed by the Diet of 1790–1791 reflected a compromise acceptable to the court and imposed on the Hungarian feudal opposition after a protracted political tug-of-war. It reflected the ideas of the American and French revolutions as well as those of the frustrated supporters of Josephinian reform. Prior to and during the Diet, radical noblemen argued that by his refusal to be crowned, Joseph II had forfeited the Habsburgs' right of succession to the throne. They held that the sovereign noble nation should negotiate a new contract with a king who would not be allowed to veto any law more than once. Representatives of the opposition offered the Hungarian crown to King Frederick William II of Prussia, in return for Prussian help against the Habsburg dynasty.

Meanwhile, critics of Hungarian feudalism who were not nobles, including the scholar József Hajnóczy, the university professor Károly Koppi, and the abbot and scientist Ignác Martinovics, advocated popular sovereignty, religious equality, the taxation of the nobility, the rights of the underprivileged classes, the promotion of commerce and trade, educational reforms, and the contractual regulation of the landlord's relationship with his serfs.

In order to weaken the potentially dangerous noble malcontents, Leopold II initially supported, in secret, these non-noble opponents of the feudal order. He continued to do this even after reaching an agreement with Prussia in mid-1790, thereby outmaneuvering his domestic opposition. At the end of 1791, he encouraged Martinovics to organize a petition drive for better legislative representation of burghers and peasants.

Demography supplies a partial explanation for the peculiarities of the court's policies toward the Hungarian ruling elite and the latter's ultimate acceptance of a political compromise in 1791. The population of Hungry, estimated at about 4.1 million in 1720, more than doubled in the eighteenth century. Of the country's over 8.5 million inhabitants in 1787 (excluding the Military Frontier with about 700,000), less than 5 percent belonged to the nobility, the majority of whom were opposed to sharing their privileges with the rest of the people. The country was still underdeveloped, with fewer than a half million inhabitants in sixty-one chartered royal cities. With a few exceptions, Hungarian cities were large villages with hardly any stone or brick buildings. The resettlement of the country after the Ottoman withdrawal had also changed Hungary's ethnic composition in favor of the non-Magyars, who probably constituted well over half of the population.

The beginnings of the Hungarian national movement coincided with the incipient political awakening of the kingdom's non-Magyar nationalities. This was in part because these too reacted to the Germanizing, centralizing, and secularizing tendencies of the Josephinian state system, and in part because they too drew inspiration from the Enlightenment and the American and French revolutionary legacy. Since religious and ethnic consciousness tended to merge among the intellectual leaders of Hungary's Orthodox population, religious equality served as a vehicle for broader ethnic rights. These rights were essentially incompatible with the idea of a Magyarizing Hungarian feudal state, if not with Habsburg absolutism. Thus Leopold II agreed to invite the Serbian Orthodox metropolitan and seven bishops to the Diet of 1790 and also to the first Serbian National Congress in Temesvár in the autumn of that year, although he rejected the latter's request for Serbian territorial autonomy. After consulting the Transylvanian Diet, which had convened in the meantime, he also refused to grant the *Supplex Libellus Valachorum,* a petition of the Romanian bishops of Transylvania, which advocated the recognition of the Transylvanian Romanians as a fourth *natio* of that principality. At the same time, however, Leopold II ordered the establishment of a new Illyrian Court Chancery in addition to reseparating the Hungarian and Transylvanian Court Chanceries in Vienna (previously united by his predecessor). This careful balancing of the conflicting ambitions of different ethnic and religious groups was aimed at keeping them all under Vienna's control.

The overwhelming majority of both Magyars and non-Magyars were peasants. In the absence of large urban centers and a significant middle class as a counterbalance to the nobility, enlightened absolutism in Hungary focused on the peasantry. This pro-peasant policy, rather than constitutional grievances and national resentment, catalyzed the feudal revolt that gathered momentum toward the end of Joseph II's reign. The feudal revolt was also supported by an increasing number of Protestant noblemen, originally favorably disposed to the emperor, who had abolished religious discrimination and admitted them to the civil service. In fact, opposition to the Habsburgs seems to have been centered in the northern and eastern counties of Hungary and Transylvania, where the overwhelmingly Protestant masses of the gentry and lesser nobility felt threatened economically. Fear of losing their tax exemption was particularly acute among the impoverished members of the privileged classes, while the upper strata, often educated in Western countries and familiar with enlightened ideas of government, also resented the growing arbitrariness of the Josephinian state.

Many aspects of the Austrian version of enlightened absolutism were initially far from unpopular in Hungary. Progressive members of the nobility, the intelligentsia, and the embryonic middle classes favored the secularization and modernization of the country's administration and educational system, religious tolerance, the lessening of the peasants' burden, and greater opportunities for non-nobles in the state service. Some young aristocrats, too, were influenced by Josephinian legal theories, which stated, among other principles, that the state had the right not only to change outdated feudal institutions, but also to control the Church.

While national feeling ran high in the Diets of the early 1790s, segments of the

Hungarian nobility kept pressing for reforms. Resentful of the authoritarian trends of Josephinism, they were nevertheless its spiritual children, imbued with enlightened ideas. Aside from this, the feudal classes were forced into a compromise that stabilized political conditions in Hungary for the lifetime of the next generation. The essence of the compromise was the retreat of enlightened absolutism to the status quo of pre-Josephine days and the reaffirmation of the domination of Hungary's internal affairs by the nobility.

Among the factors motivating the acceptance of the compromise with the dynasty, fear of a peasant revolution loomed very large. With memories of the violent peasant outbursts of the eighties in Hungary and Transylvania still fresh, the enthusiasm of the Hungarian estates for French revolutionary ideas diminished. Hungarian nobles were mindful of the radical pamphlets circulating among their serfs. Some pamphlets were written with the approval of Leopold II, who intended to use the controlled unrest of the lower classes as a counterbalance to the unruly nobility and also to continue subtly his older brother's work of enlightened reform. Finally, the discovery of the so-called Martinovics conspiracy and its cruel suppression in 1794–1795 ended all plans for reform and silenced all political opposition in Hungary.

The Hungarian Jacobin movement was directed by Ignác Martinovics, a highly educated but utterly ambitious and unstable man. A member of the Franciscan order (which he abandoned under Joseph II to become professor of physics at the University of Lemberg), he was widely traveled and familiar with the English and French philosophical and political literature of his time. An enthusiastic supporter of the reforms of Joseph II, he hoped to implement his own anticlerical and democratic political ideas under Leopold II, whom he regularly informed about the activities of the secret societies, Jesuits, and patriots in Hungary. Spurred by a combination of wounded vanity and resentment against court reaction under Leopold's son and successor, Francis, and perhaps also by a sincere desire for social progress, the former police agent decided to organize two societies. One of them, the Association of Reformers, was destined for the nobility, the other, the Association of Liberty and Equality, for the radical intelligentsia. The noble reformers were kept ignorant of the existence of the more radical society, which was to use members of the first group as its tools, and to eliminate them after the success of the first phase of the planned insurrection. Thus Martinovics attempted to exploit both the radicals' longing for social reform and the Hungarian national party's constitutional opposition to the court.

The conspirators, however, were unknown to the masses and had no public support. The police watched their organization for a few weeks, then suppressed it in mid-1794. During the next spring, a series of trials resulted in severe punishment that included seven death sentences. Among those arrested were many noblemen from "good families." Especially important, from the point of view of the further development of the Enlightenment in Hungary, was the long imprisonment of many of the leading literati, including Ferenc Kazinczy and the revolutionary poet János Bacsányi. In an atmosphere of suspicion and intimidation, the slightest connection with the Martinovics circle, such as the reading of a declaration or the translation of a revolutionary poem or pamphlet, was sufficient cause for detention. A generation of Hungarian literati was silenced for many years.

Hungarian Cultural Life from the French Wars to the Age of Reform

The accession of Francis I to the throne as king of Hungary coincided with the French declaration of war against Austria, Catherine II's intervention in Poland, the proclamation of the French Republic, and the repeated victories of the French revolutionary armies over the joint Austro-Prussian forces in the autumn of 1792. The execution of Louis XVI and of Marie Antoinette, Francis II's aunt, the following January and the Jacobin takeover in France further widened the conflict in Western Europe. In the East, the defeat of the anti-Russian uprising led by Thadeus Kosciuszko resulted in the disappearance of Poland from the map of Europe simultaneously with the crackdown on the Hungarian Jacobins.

The danger of a social revolution advancing with the French armies frightened the overwhelming majority of Hungary's nobility into expanding very considerably the assistance voted for the war against France. At the coronation Diet of 1792, they approved an additional fifty thousand recruits. Further financial help was approved by the Diet of 1796. The feudal assemblies held in the years 1802, 1807, 1808, and 1811–1812 also proved to be loyal to the Habsburgs and continued to support the war against Napoleon. The cause of reform, still debated in the dietal committees in 1792, was taken off the agenda for a generation.

Yet Hungary's incipient cultural life showed remarkable resilience during the first half of the reign of Francis I, a period of war, political reaction, harsh censorship, and a suffocating intellectual atmosphere. This is all the more noteworthy since there was hardly any organized cultural activity. Writers, artists, and composers needed wealthy aristocratic patrons to survive. Several of the first Hungarian newspapers and magazines were published in Vienna and in predominantly German-speaking cities in Western or Northern Hungary. The first Hungarian theatrical troupe was established in Buda in 1790, though it was rather short-lived. The pioneers of the eighteenth-century Magyar literary and cultural revival were mainly members of Maria Theresa's Hungarian Bodyguard, whose activities were discussed in chapter 10.

The more conservative Magyar school tried to elevate literature to the level of that of Western Europe. The most popular author of the group, András Dugonics, was politically motivated. Out of resentment of Germanization, he published his novel *Etelka,* the first bestseller in the Magyar tongue, in 1788. The book dealt with Árpád's conquest of Hungary. Dugonics revealed his xenophobia by contrasting the virtues of the "truly" Magyar leading characters in the book with the reprehensible unscrupulousness of a number of evil and intriguing advisors, all of whom were Slavs, that is, foreigners. Another work, *The Journey of the Village Notary to Buda (Egy falusi nótáriusnak budai utazása),* written by József Gvadányi in 1790, was a violent satire of Joseph II's regime and reflected the author's shock that the ancient Magyar capital was full of foreigners. His strong opposition to the cosmopolitan culture of the Hungarian aristocracy was tellingly expressed in the slogan, *Extra Hungariam non est vita, si est vita, non est ita* (there is no life outside Hungary, but if there is, it is not the same). Thus, during the incipient period of modern Magyar nationalism, political, linguistic, and cultural issues were closely interrelated.

In the wake of European Romanticism, the Hungarians were also looking for their "historical roots." However unrealistic the poetic image of past glory might have seemed to the critical observer, the past still seemed preferable to the present or the future. After all, did not the father of romantic folk nationalism, Johann Gottfried Herder, predict the disappearance of the Magyars from the community of nations? This prophecy was to haunt generations of writers and political leaders.

Herder's prediction that the Slavs, Germans, Romanians, and other surrounding peoples would absorb the Magyars had a traumatic effect on Hungarian nationalists. It partly explains their attempts to make Magyar the universally accepted language in multinational Hungary and to Magyarize the non-Magyar inhabitants of the kingdom. Herder asserted that a man could realize his full potentialities only through his national group and that a people could fulfill their God-given mission only by using their native tongue. This became a strong argument for championing the supremacy of the Magyars in all of Hungary, even though this was a far cry from the humanitarian and enlightened roots of Herder's ideas.

Hungarian literary historians used to take special pride in arguing that Hungarian literature is the record of Hungarian patriotism. This type of national pride, manifested in the conscious linking of literature and national aims, went far beyond the old-fashioned estates nationalism, even though the two were not incompatible. Whereas the joint symbols of sword and lute may possibly be regarded as reflections of an unbroken and tradition-bound fighting spirit, they were not always wielded in a chivalrous mood.

The appearance of a modern Magyar national self-consciousness coincided with the awakening of the non-Magyar peoples in Hungary. Yet on account of their aristocratic superiority complex, the Magyar nobility, and later the rising intelligentsia and middle classes, refused to see any similarity between the defying of "despotic" Vienna by Hungarian nationalists and the demands of the Croatians, Romanians, and Slovaks. Actually, the increasing awareness of national differences suggested to Magyar leaders that something should be done to repair the numerical inferiority of the ruling people. Samuel Decsy raised the question in 1790 of whether the schools and churches could be used to "Magyarize imperceptibly." "Imperceptible Magyarization," deeply resented by the non-Magyars, was not quite innocent in actual practice. While the Roman Catholic clergy and the aristocracy were, on the whole, more cosmopolitan and

Habsburgtreu (loyal to the Habsburgs), members of the lower nobility were rather narrowly Magyar-minded. Furthermore, the letter and spirit of various laws enacted by the Diets and sanctioned by the monarch were frequently "adjusted" on the local level by the semi-autonomous counties. They often interpreted the laws in an extremely nationalistic sense, perverting the spirit of the measures actually approved by the Diet.

As early as the last decade of the eighteenth century, the endeavors of Hungarian nationalists to promote the use of Magyar rather than German or Latin in public life was strongly seconded by a forceful Magyarization campaign waged in the contemporary press, in numerous pamphlets, and in the official correspondence of the counties. Whereas Article IV of 1805 only permitted that Magyar, along with the Latin text, be used in official correspondence with the court and the Hungarian chancery, the county assembly of Pest decided to keep its protocols and correspondence with other counties exclusively in Magyar. In a similar manner, thirteen other counties, which were inhabited mostly by Slovaks, Germans, Romanians, and Serbs, resolved to press the Magyarization of the subject nationalities. Pest County instructed all communities in which there were no Magyar schoolmasters to employ teachers who spoke Magyar. Similarly, in 1806, Békés County, which had a large Slovak population, made the teaching of Magyar compulsory in the kindergartens and elementary schools. These practices were considerably expanded in the 1830s, when tension increased between the Magyar and non-Magyar nationalities.

More farsighted Hungarians were less obsessed with linguistic nationalism and gave preference to social reform. Martinovics rejected the concept of a Magyar "political nation" and was willing to give equal treatment to all the nationalities of Hungary. Hajnóczy, a former secretary and protégé of Count Ferenc Széchenyi, executed with Martinovics, presented the most systematic challenge to the Hungarian feudal constitution prior to 1848. He started out as a Josephinian but was inspired by British, American, and, above all, French political thought.

There were other Hungarian patriots who respected the cultural value of the different peoples living in the kingdom. One of the many Hungarian protestant youths who had studied at the University of Göttingen was Mátyás Rát. Editor and publisher of the first Magyar language newspaper, the *Magyar Hirmondó* of Pozsony, he wished to introduce unbiased investigation based on primary sources and also put emphasis on commerce and agriculture. Rát sympathized with the Americans in their war of independence against the British. His paper was one of the early focuses of Hungarian cultural life, propagating literature and scholarship in Magyar. Yet he belonged to that small minority of Hungarians who rejected linguistic intolerance and hoped that "none of the nations living in the two fatherlands [Hungary and Transylvania] will make its idiom common [universal] here . . . " The economic reformer Gergely Berzeviczy wrote and published in Latin and German. He was one of the few members of the gentry who understood the economic, social, and moral implications of serfdom. Like the two Széchenyis, Ferenc and his son István, Berzeviczy was deeply impressed by England's commerce and industry. He was particularly delighted to see the well-being of "that lower class of inhabitants whom we call peasants." Convinced that the modification of the feudal system in England and Western Europe benefited society as a whole, Berzeviczy anticipated István Széchenyi by proposing that the abolition of feudalism was the foremost task of reform in Hungary. Cognizant of Hungary's multi-religious composition, he claimed that Hungarians of different creeds ought to be human beings and citizens of one fatherland first. Perhaps reflecting on the Magyarizing tendencies of his compatriots in a multi-ethnic country, he wrote in a letter of 1808, "actually, we here in Hungary are not a nation . . . " Berzeviczy's attitude was shared by others, including those who, in the eighteenth century, planned to create an academy and scholarly association for the promotion of the sciences, arts, and letters. It was first proposed by György Bessenyei. The novelty of his proposal was that it visualized the Hungarian scholarly association as an agency whose exclusive task would be to cultivate the Magyar idiom, the assumption being that the development of the Magyar tongue would stimulate the evolution of all branches of scholarship. Yet even at a time when Magyar national sentiment was on the rise as a reaction to Joseph II's policies, the historian Márton Kovachich ignored the demands of Magyar linguistic predominance in his proposals for a Hungarian Historical Association and Institute in 1787–1792.

Eventually, the less cosmopolitan and more nationalistic plans for the academy prevailed. They focused on the humanities rather than on the natural sciences. The reasons for this are complex. There is some justification for the allegation that it was in the realm of literature that the "rich program of the Enlightenment" was able to survive. Literature, after all, was the medium capable of articulating Magyardom's right to its idiom, a right formulated in the Age of Enlightenment. Kazinczy described literature as a nation-sustaining force, but at the same time, this "father of Hungarian literary criticism" also indicated to a friend that in his struggle against darkness and superstition he would use as a shield the ideas of Voltaire, Rousseau, Helvetius, and freemasonry.

Still, Kazinczy's example serves as an important caveat. A supporter of the Josephinian school reforms (he was one of two newly appointed Protestant school inspectors in northern Hungary), he was not afraid of using German in teaching to help the progress of civilization. Yet he promoted Magyar as the "first and common" idiom, which German, Slovak, Serb, and Romanian children ought to learn. The identification of language with nationality and the predominance of Magyardom in spreading civilization in Hungary, however, implied that the triumph of Kazinczy's movement (an apolitical one aimed at renovating the language) ultimately led to the prevalence of Magyar nationalistic trends over the more comprehensive Hungarian, essentially multilingual patriotism of a Berzeviczy or a Kovachich. Enlightened ideas were ingredients of both trends, but the literary and cultural struggle won by Kazinczy for those who identified the cause of national literature with that of the fatherland tended to narrow down literature to the Magyar tongue alone. Although replacement of Latin by the vernacular was one way of making Hungarian cultural life more democratic, a byproduct of the process was an ethnocentric provincialism characteristic of Magyardom's outlook until very recently.

This change in emphasis greatly contributed to the transformation of an essentially pluralistic Hungarian patriotism into modern, or exclusively Magyar nationalism. It should be noted again, however, that enlightened cosmopolitanism and national pride coexisted in the minds of most Hungrian pioneers of the Enlightenment.

The possibilities of a newly born literary language reflecting the dynamic forces of the Enlightenment were first suggested in the poetry of Mihály Vitéz Csokonai. The work of this creative genius suggests an impressive expansion of the Hungarian intellectual horizon in the Age of Enlightenment. Csokonai has rightly been called the truest Hungarian rococo poet. Of humble birth, he studied at the Calvinist College in Debrecen, where he was later entrusted with the teaching of undergraduates. Expelled from the college, he went to Pest to find a publisher for his poems, and on that occasion he witnessed the execution of the ringleaders of the Hungarian Jacobin conspiracy. Unable to get a permanent job, he toured the country looking for support, visiting with friends and noble patrons. He died at the age of thirty-one.

Enamored of the beauties of the Magyar idiom as spoken by the common folk, Csokonai was the first to include, in his play *Tempefői* (1793), the text of a true Hungarian folk tale. In accordance with the program of the enlightened literati, he strove consciously to enrich the vernacular with translations, mainly from German and Italian but also from English, French, Latin, and Greek. His translations were often "adjusted" to the Hungarian milieu. In a note to one of his own poems, he justified the incorporation of a metaphor from Voltaire's *Henriade* by saying that it had been "dressed in new clothes and Magyarized." Local color and present-mindedness, however, did not imply provincialism, as can be judged by the sophistication and cosmopolitan aspects of Csokonai's poetry. Italian songs, French minuets, Polish mazurkas, German and Hungarian dances, Arab and Persian meters were rendered marvelously by his rhythms.

In the preface to his comic epos *Dorottya*, Csokonai held that poetry must not only entertain but also edify. Consequently, he ridiculed "national luxury and degeneration" and condemned the "mischievous revelry" of the youth in the poem. Stressing that he preferred a mediocre but original work to a first-rate translation, he dissented from most contemporary literati, who thought the reverse. (The great organizer of Hungarian literary life, Ferenc Kazinczy, regarded it as the main task of his life to transplant the flowers of European literature to Hungarian soil.) At a time when writers had low status even in the German lands, Csokonai dreamed of living by his pen alone.

The promise inherent in Csokonai's poetry remained unfulfilled because of adverse circumstances and his untimely death. Still, the gentle poet's work is suggestive of many intellectual crosscurrents in a period of change and stress, at once enlightened, crude, and romantic. The intermingling of diverse trends in the repressive political atmosphere of backward Hungary was a telling phenomenon in the era of Francis I. The career of Count György Festetich, brother-in-law of Ferenc Széchenyi, is a good example of how the spirit of the Enlightenment combined with nationalism to move Hungarian patriots. As a lieutenant colonel in 1790, he supported the negotiations of the "Party of Liberty" with the Prussians and signed a petition "to the honorable estates of the sublime fatherland," demanding Hungarian officers and Magyar as the language of command for Hungarian army corps. After the failure of the feudal revolt and his retirement from the army, he founded the Georgicon, the first agricultural institute of the monarchy, on one of his estates on Lake Balaton. At the end of his life, he organized annual cultural festivals, known as the Helicons of Keszthely, to honor eminent writers and artists. Turning to other writers, the case of the historian György A. Belnay is illustrative of the mood of the times. In 1790, he published a Latin pamphlet that opposed "the noble autocracy" reminding it of the lessons of the American Revolution. He contrasted with the "monstrous" feudal system the equal rights of every member of a society based on natural law. Nine years later, in a work dedicated to Francis I, the same author listed István Bocskai and Gábor Bethlen, both champions of Protestantism and of Transylvania's independence from the Habsburgs, among the "outstanding patrons" of art and literature in seventeenth-century Hungary. Belnay's essay, published in Vienna, suggested by implication the political neutrality of art and literature, and this may have pleased the censors of the Franciscan system. It was perhaps this vision of a neutral and apolitical literature that permitted literature to again become the rallying point of Hungarian cultural life in the early nineteenth century.

Literature did indeed become that "nation-sustaining" force that Kazinczy intended it to be after the turn of the century. After spending "2,387 days" in jail, as he put it in his memoirs, Kazinczy became the literary dictator of Hungary, thanks to his ability to channel the latent energies of his educated compatriots into literature while steering clear of overt political involvements. Only one year after Csokonai's death, the first Hungarian newspaper of the new century, *Hazai Tudósitások (Reports from the Homeland)*, began publication in Pest in 1806. Its editor, István Kulcsár, who was not allowed to publish political news from abroad during the first two years, concentrated on the promotion of the Magyar language, literature, and theater. The paper ushered in a new era, after a decade of repression, because it shifted the center of Hungarian journalism from Vienna and Pozsony to Pest, contributing to Pest's emergence as Hungary's cultural capital at a time when the literary revival was handicapped by fragmentation and lack of communication among writers.

Kulcsár's program was summed up in a passage that appeared in 1823: "The foremost ornament of every nation is scientific learning. We must strive for this not only because thereby we can raise our human dignity and enrich our domestic conditions but . . . even more because through the diffusion of the sciences in the nation we can make the country's strength more potent, the nation's glory more radiant." This formulation of the creed of Hungarian enlightened patriotism could have been and indeed was set forth by István Széchenyi in *Hitel (On Credit)*. *Hitel* appeared only in 1830. In 1823, Széchenyi was still trying to find his identity, and in 1809, in a letter to his father, Ferenc, the founder of Hungary's National Museum, he high-handedly repudiated "the bluffs of cunning illuminati" because of their presumed hostility to the ideals of Christianity.

The immense value of the enlightened and patriotic propaganda of men like Kazinczy or Kulcsár in the early nineteenth century and the inner tensions that they had to overcome cannot be overstated. Aside from a few aristocratic patrons, the Hungarian cultural milieu was almost hopelessly provincial. With the exception of those who were in the military service, stationed in Vienna, or perhaps studying at foreign universities, few Hungarians had an opportunity to go abroad. Domestic travel, too, was inconvenient if not impossible during certain parts of the year. There were no literary salons and theaters, and private library facilities and manuscript collections were too far away for many writers and scholars. The fine arts were practically non-existent; it was only in the western corner of Hungary that serious music could be heard in the chateaux of the Esterházys and a few other magnates. For many years, Joseph Haydn was conductor and composer-in-residence in the Esterházy castles of Kismárton and Eszterház (now Fertőd). The last-mentioned palace, built by Prince Miklós Esterházy, "the Magnificent," was called by the French ambassador the "Hungarian Versailles." A show piece of baroque and rococo architecture decorated by Austrian, French, German, and Italian artists, Eszterház was famous for its opera, ballet, and theater performances, which were often attended by the imperial court and the diplomatic corps. While Eszterház remained one of Europe's significant cultural centers for about two decades, the best poets of the period had never attended a symphonic concert or seen an opera. It is against the background of this isolation from the mainstream of European civilization that their achievements must be measured.

Even in the field of literature, change came slowly. In 1815, ten years after Csokonai's death, the erudite Mihály Fazekas published a comic epic poem, *Ludas Matyi (Matthew the Gooseherd)*. His hero, a peasant lad, succeeds in getting even three times with the lord who once had whipped him. Because of "our nation's insensitivity toward [writers]," Fazekas had to publish his poem anonymously.

Frustration and the elusiveness of artistic success were also the experience of one of Hungary's greatest playwrights, József Katona. His masterpiece, *Banus Bánk*, revolving around the assassination of the German-born queen of the thirteenth-century king, Andrew II, by his lieutenant Bánk, concentrates on Hungarian resentment of foreign oppression. Along with the main theme, the tragedy has another focus, expressed in the bitter complaints of Tiborc, an old serf, about the reckless exploitation of the common people by their lords. Thus the anti-German national tendency was interwoven with the menace social revolution. The drama was never performed during the author's lifetime but was put on stage on the first night of the victorious Pest revolution in March 1848.

Another great talent, Dániel Berzsenyi, became well known for his patriotic odes to the idealized virtues of the Hungarian nobility and the dynasty during the anti-Napoleonic campaigns. The pathos and imagery expressed in classic meters by this "Hungarian Horace" were aimed at the moral regeneration of a noble class fallen into decay. The same intent also permeated the poems of a younger contemporary, Ferenc Kölcsey. Ironically, it was an appreciative but critical review by Kölcsey that forced the introverted Berzsenyi to all but cease writing poetry in the last two decades of his life. Kölcsey, himself an accomplished poet, was perhaps his generation's most ethical thinker. At times biased and overly demanding, Kölcsey's severe critical standards led to temporary unpopularity; yet in the final analysis, Hungarian literature benefited from the application of more rigorous esthetic values in the evaluation of artistic work. Kölcsey's great political and philosophical poems, such as the "Hymnus," which subsequently became Hungary's national anthem, are profound and even tormented analyses of national life and the human condition. Kölcsey, in his later years, became the admired master of Hungarian parliamentary oratory and one of the leaders of the liberal opposition.

Popular success was achieved by the brothers Sándor and Károly Kisfaludy. Sándor's two-part *The Loves of Himfy,* which exuded a nostalgia for the idyllic but endangered way of life of the nobility, developed a Hungarian-style sonorous rhythm, the Himfy-stanza, which appealed to his noble readers. His romantic verses, which combined love stories with the heroic deeds of the anti-Turkish wars, were also very popular, especially among the widening circle of female readers.

Károly Kisfaludy was a bohemian by nature and abandoned the lifestyle of a noble landowner. He excelled as a writer of patriotic and romantic dramas. His best plays, however, were comedies, whose characters, atmosphere, and lively dialogue pioneered the way for the new Hungarian theater. His excellent short stories and much of his poetry appeared in the literary almanac *Aurora,* first published by him in 1821. *Aurora* opened its pages to both the older generation of writers and a younger one such as the poet Vörösmarty or the literary critic József Bajza. Published in Pest, *Aurora* marked the beginning of a new period in Hungarian literature because it gradually made Pest the true capital of Hungary's literary life.

None of the literary figures mentioned so far were revolutionaries in the strict sense of the term. All of them were children of the Enlightenment in one respect or another. One major writer, however, János Bacsányi, turned his eyes toward revolutionary Paris and summoned his compatriots to do likewise as early as 1789. Together with Kazinczy, Bacsányi was one of the co-founders of the first Hungarian literary periodical, the *Magyar Museum* of Kassa. A supporter of the national resistance to Joseph II's Germanization, this political poet and talented editor turned even more radical after the nobility's compromise with the dynasty. His sharp attacks on king and clergy, his sympathies with the serfs, and his Jacobin ideas led to his imprisonment. While in prison, Bacsányi wrote his beautiful elegies. Upon his release, he continued to fight for complete national independence from the Habsburgs. When the French occupied Vienna in 1809, Bacsányi translated and may even have drafted parts of Napoleon's proclamation to the Hungarians, summoning them to secede from the Austrian Empire and elect their own ruler according to ancient customs. When the French withdrew from Vienna, Bacsányi went with them and lived in Paris, where he was arrested by the Austrian authorities in 1815, imprisoned again, and ultimately interned in Austria until the end of his life.

Bacsányi was one of those rare Hungarian intellectuals to whom the overdue social revolution was more important than the reassertion of the nobility's power and privileges. He was willing to work for his country's independence by supporting Napoleon, who in his eyes symbolized the French revolution. He erred no less than the overwhelming majority of his noble countrymen, who lent their support to Vienna for exactly the same reason. Unlike Napoleon's creation of the Grand Duchy of Warsaw, which was popular among the Poles, his appeal to the Hungarians found no favorable response among noblemen in dread of a peasant uprising. In fact, Napoleon's imperial policy of opting for an Austrian marriage alliance proved the futility both of the worries of those who feared him and of the hopes of those who trusted him. The revolutionary vein introduced by Bacsányi's poetry, which heralded radical political and social change, was doomed to failure until the appearance of the works of Baron József Eötvös and Sándor Petőfi in the 1840s.

In two decades, Hungary's feudal nobility provided Vienna with about one million soldiers and thirty million florins for the wars against France. The burden of the military campaigns fell almost exclusively on the taxpaying serf. Only once, in 1809, did an ill-equipped and inexperienced noble levy try to take a stand against Napoleon. (They were routed by the French at Győr.) Although each of the five Diets between 1796 and 1811 repeated Hungarian grievances concerning unfair tariffs and requested the increased use of Magyar as an official language, the court made only minimal concessions, accepting bilingual, (i.e., Latin and Magyar) dietal petitions to the throne, the use of Magyar by lower courts, and Magyar replies by the Lieutenancy to petitions submitted in that tongue. The temporary improvement of Austro-French relations following Napoleon's marriage to Marie Louise, the daughter of Francis I, stiffened Vienna's attitude towards Hungary. The complicated currency reform of 1811 was put into effect without consultation with the Hungarian Diet, although Hungary was expected to shoulder almost one half of the state's debt and to double her contribution in taxes. When the Diet refused to agree to the extension of the imperial patent to Hungary, Francis dissolved the Diet in May 1812. He imposed the patent "provisionally," that is, until the convocation of a new Diet, which he failed to call into session for thirteen years. Thus the country fell under absolutist rule, following the pattern in the dynasty's hereditary provinces. Although the counties' autonomy was left untouched in theory, in practice Vienna's will was fiat because it was enforced by royal commissioners when there was the slightest resistance.

Resentment of Vienna's absolutism gained additional momentum after Austria's involvement in the last anti-French coalition, which led to the ultimate defeat of Napoleon. To finance the war, the Austrian government was forced to float a number of undersubscribed loans and to issue increasingly worthless paper money, in spite of previous promises not to do so. A new devaluation of the currency in 1816 further undermined the credit system and confidence in the government. Moreover, Austrian preparations for new military conflicts necessitated additional revenues. As a member of the Holy Alliance initiated by Tsar Alexander I at the Congress of Vienna in 1815, Austria, with Russia and Prussia, undertook to maintain the status quo on the European continent in the post-Napoleonic period. Chancellor Klemens Lothar von Metternich-Winneburg, who conducted Austrian foreign policy between 1809 and 1848, intervened in Italy on behalf of the Holy Alliance, quelling the popular uprisings in Piedmont and Naples in 1820 and 1821. Vienna demanded thirty-five thousand Hungarian recruits and ordered the collection of taxes voted by the Diet a decade earlier in silver coins, which meant a de facto increase of 250 percent. The counties protested and asked for the convocation of a new Diet. Fifteen of them refused to execute the royal decrees but were forced to back down when royal commissioners resorted to military force. Groups of particularly recalcitrant noblemen were ordered to Vienna, where an indignant Francis I told them in person that even "if the entire world went crazy and desired a constitution" he would have none of it.

However, the "craze for a constitution," so manifest in the revolutionary upheavals on the Italian and Spanish peninsulas during the early 1820s, suggested caution. The king's younger brother, the archduke Joseph who, as palatine of Hungary, controlled the country's administration for half a century, recommended concessions in the area of foreign trade as well as in the observation of the feudal constitution. Since Metternich also preferred compromise to confrontation, a reluctant Francis I convoked the Diet for 1825.

Opening the Age of Reform, 1825–1840

The Diet of 1825–27 began with the deputies emphasizing the need to secure the integrity of the feudal constitution. This implied the limitation of royal absolutism. Despite the lengthy debates, the legislation enacted could hardly be considered a great achievement. Francis I did sanction several laws, in which he recognized his obligation to abide by the constitution, not to make changes in conscription or taxation without the consent of the Diet, and to call it into session every three years. These laws, however, only reconfirmed royal obligations enacted by the Diet of 1790–91, and the necessity of their confirmation was in itself proof that the real relationship between crown and estates was not in accordance with constitutional provisions. Undefined procedures in legislative matters made it difficult to deal in an efficient way with the great number of far-reaching problems accumulated during the thirteen-year interruption of legislative activity.

The initiative for new legislation lay with the king. He summoned the Diet, to which he submitted the royal suggestions for new laws. The two chambers of the Diet had to agree on the text of the law. It was sometimes a matter of several months before such an agreement could be reached, if at all, for neither of the chambers could force its will on the other, and the correspondence between them could drag on indefinitely. In case of an agreement between the two chambers, the king might still refuse to give his consent to any piece of legislation he disliked. In effect, he had veto power. On the other hand, governing by royal decrees was considered unconstitutional in Hungary and could be resisted in extreme cases (as under Joseph II or Francis I in 1823) by civil disobedience. In the Diet, there were no political parties in the modern sense of the word. Motions were decided not by direct voting but by giving preference to the "sounder" and more influential group, whose votes had to be pondered and evaluated rather than just counted. This practice, and the frequent necessity of mediating between the two chambers and between the Diet and the throne, gave significant power to the personalis and the palatine, the two presidents of the chambers, who were, however, nominees of the king. The personalis and palatine, respectively, were also presidents of the King's Bench *(Tabula Regis)* and the Septemviral Bench *(Tabula Septemviralis)*, the two highest courts of the realm, together called the Royal Curia *(Curia Regis)*. During the sessions of the Diet, the courts remained closed; in fact, the justices of the King's Bench had the right to sit in the chamber of deputies.

Deputies of the "lower" chamber were representatives of privileged classes or corporate bodies, the nobility, the clergy, and the chartered or free royal cities. Unlike their Anglo-Saxon counterparts in Parliament, they had to abide by the instructions of their constituents or be forced to resign. Most members of the "upper" chamber, or "table," attended the Diet because of their high ecclesiastic or secular position or high birth, and at royal invitation. According to the tradition going back to Werbőczi (see chapter 8), members of the two chambers constituted one single legislative body. Sitting separately most of the time since the seventeenth century, they would nonetheless be called into "mixed" sessions chaired by the palatine on certain solemn occasions or when differences of the two chambers had to be straightened out. In these cases, the procedures for decision-making were rather ill-defined. If there was no lawful basis for voting by estates *(curiatim)* in the Hungarian feudal tradition, there was no precedent for yielding automatically to a numerical majority either, especially since the chamber of magnates was not based on representation. Furthermore, the presidents of both chambers had various means of persuasion, from intimidation to the dangling of royal favor or promotion to a desired office. This made it difficult to organize, let alone maintain, even a simple majority opposing the administration.

The Hungarian Diet was a mixture of people representing either themselves or their constituents; some were independent, while others had to stick to the directives drawn up by those in whose name they claimed to speak. The order of procedure, the discussion and work in the plenary and circular sessions, which developed from private conferences, depended largely on precedent and the maneuvering skill of the presiding officer. Agreements, once reached, were frequently disputed, because of the unreliability of the protocols. The evaluation of the votes cast, and even the decision of when to put a question to the vote, were not exempt from subjective judgment or conflicting interpretations. Not until the 1830s did the principle of following the will of the majority rather than evaluating the votes cast begin to prevail.

The timidity the feudal Diet showed in introducing democratic voting practices into its undemocratic procedures was but one of the obstacles in the path of Hungary's modernization. If the long overdue social and economic reforms were not thrust on Hungary by an unwilling Diet, neither was the administration made happy by the postponement of measures that could conceivably have simplified the governing of the traditionally reluctant Magyars. Legislatively, the Diet ended in a stalemate. The return to the constitutional status quo of 1790–91 was a reflection of the inertia of both court and Diet; it also suggested the great difficulties of creating a modern nation with a feudal Diet.

The symbolic breakthrough leading to a modern Hungarian national state came with the founding of the Academy. Nationwide public opinion was led by poets, writers, and the educated members of the nobility, who demanded and prepared an academy for the promotion of national culture. That the Magyar idiom was capable of becoming the unifying literary language of the educated and the vehicle of Hungary's cultural life was proved again by Vörösmarty's *Zalán futása (Zalán's Flight)*. The publication of this romantic epic about the conquest of the country by Árpád coincided with the opening of the Diet and the foundation of the Academy. Vörösmarty's poetry initiated an era of "national romanticism" in literature, which became a unifying spiritual force helping to eliminate sectional and religious differences among the literati.

The program for the cultural emancipation of the Magyar language was well on its way when the Diet began to consider again the role of Magyar in education, administration, and public life. After listening to one of the heated debates in early November 1825, a Captain of Hussars stepped forward and offered one year's income from his estates, estimated later at sixty thousand florins, to establish an insitution "to propagate the national idiom and to raise sons worthy of a fatherland like ours." The army officer was thirty-four-year-old Count István Széchenyi, third and youngest son of Ferenc, founder of the National Museum, and a member by birth of the Diet's Upper Chamber. His initiative, followed by other landowners, high officials, and patriotic donors, set in motion the legislative machinery for the creation of the Hungarian Academy of Sciences, of which he became the first vice president in 1830.

For the second time in a quarter of a century, poets wrote odes to a Széchenyi, and patriots praised a leading aristocrat for having embraced the cause of national culture. Still, there were important differences. During the last two decades of his life, the former Josephinist and enlightened reformer, Ferenc Széchenyi, became a sponsor of the Viennese romantic Catholic circle, spending many hours a day on his knees in prayer. István underwent another kind of metamorphosis in the same period. Thanks to his family connections, the younger Széchenyi was attached to the headquarters of Prince Charles Philipp Schwarzenberg, allied commander-in-chief in the last phase of the war against

Napoleon. Well-liked and courageous, he gave a good account of himself and was decorated with Austrian, Prussian, and Russian medals, largely because of the courier service he performed in the Battle of Nations at Leipzig. A charmer and womanizer, he was a European dandy at the Congress of Vienna, where he took the measure of the powerful. Yet István was tranformed by voracious reading and travels in England, Western Europe, Italy, and the Balkans, as well as by his friendship with the leader of the Transylvanian liberal opposition, the Baron Miklós Wesselényi. The talented but eccentric dilettante became a hard-working disciple of Benjamin Franklin and a man of affairs anxious to lift his country from its appalling backwardness, of which he was reminded again and again during his foreign trips. A loyal Roman Catholic, he preached and prac-ticed tolerance toward Protestants and even Muslims and Jews, although his Christian humanism was marred, especially in his later years, by racial prejudice. The scion of a leading Hungarian magnate family intermarried with the Austrian, Bohemian, Croatian, and Italian aristocracies, Széchenyi imbibed the liberal po-litical philosophy that spread in the wake of the American and French revolutions.

In a series of exchanges with Metternich, Széchenyi, co-founder of a club of young liberal magnates attending the Diet at Pozsony, pointed out to the chan-cellor the shortcomings of absolutist government and the superiority of consti-tutional monarchy and representative government. Siding openly with the liberal, "new" opposition as Metternich saw it, Széchenyi nevertheless stressed his abhorrence of violence and his anti-revolutionary feelings, an attitude char-acteristic of his entire public career. However, his offer to mediate between throne and nation was brushed aside as presumptuous and naive by the chancel-lor, who underestimated Széchenyi's talents.

Diet, feudal constitution, and the views of most of his compatriots, as well as the regime of Francis I, were hopelessly out of step with the times, and Széchenyi knew this by 1825. His first book, *Lovakrul (On Horses)*, was pub-lished in Hungarian in 1828 to popularize his mother tongue and issues of social, economic, and cultural reform. "While I am talking about the horse, the sheep or the cow," he wrote to a friend in 1829, "I keep on rasping, step by step and very gently, the prejudices of our compatriots." In the same year, Széchenyi noted in his diary the significance of the Prussian-led *Zollverein* as a means to German unification, revealing his awareness of the interdependence of economic matters and national and international politics.

This was a new tone on the Hungarian scene. Also new was the application of European standards and statistics to illustrate the backwardness of Hungarian conditions, a method he used with vigor in his major work *Hitel (On Credit)*, which appeared in 1830. The book's message was primarily economic, and can be summed up as follows: The Hungarian landowner was condemned to starva-tion despite his herds, grain stores, fertile lands, and tax exemption. He was sunk in debt though he carried none of the burdens of the country while many hands worked for him without being paid. The cause of this sad situation was the lack of credit. The lack of capital and credit was due to the antiquated legal system, which gave no security to the creditor. Outmoded farming methods and feudal institutions prevented the landowner from modernizing his farm and laying the foundation for his spiritual and material well-being. Bad roads and underdeveloped trade also were additional causes of backwardness. Unlike those who blamed the country's geographic situation or Austrian tariff policy, Széchenyi pointed rather to bureaucratic interference with commerce, production, lack of communication, low domestic consumption, uncertainty of export tariffs, and dishonest commerical practices as the basic causes of economic misery. As a cure, he suggested education, publicity, and discussion, a national bank, improvement of the quantity and quality of production, export premiums, and "above all, the sanctity of credit." Széchenyi went far beyond the sphere of political economy in a chapter called "What to Do and Where to Start." He drew a line between "credit in the strict sense" and "credit in a broader sense." This issue involved a series of other legal and political problems closely connected with the nobility's prerogatives and with the law of aviticity, or entail. Széchenyi openly advocated the rights of the creditor, the financier, and the merchant in a country where tradition, law, and national pride had always been on the side of the debtor of noble blood. Stressing the importance of a money-based rather than a subsistence economy, his work prepared the way for capitalism in feudal Hungary.

On Credit proves that Széchenyi the nationalist cannot be separated from Széchenyi the reformer. In his book, he tried to convince the reader that feudalism was morally wrong, made no sense in the modern world, and hurt even those who were supposed to benefit from it. To argue against the injustice done by the 400,000 privileged to the "ten million not even mentioned in the Diet," meant to ignore the constitution and the social patterns of a country in which the nobility *was* the nation. By presenting the law of entail as a primary cause of the country's poverty and by interpreting the privileges of the nobility as moral and economic wrongs, Széchenyi took an axe to the roots of Hungarian feudalism. He exposed the inefficient forced labor of the serf not only as unfair to the peasant, useless to the privileged, and a farce as a domestic public works system, but also as a national disaster which criminally wasted the country's valuable resources.

To realize his vision of a nation where all parts of the population would have their rights and duties, Széchenyi proposed to heighten considerably domestic consumption as a prerequisite of economic welfare. To achieve this goal, he demanded the improvement of the lot of the tiller of the land by asking the landowning classes to help shoulder the burdens of the country. As an ulitmate aim, he launched the idea of "emancipating all our compatriots through participation in civil rights."

On Credit was a challenge to friend and foe alike. In the closing part of the work, Széchenyi himself anticipated these questions: "How can a born Hungarian magnate say such things and how can he expose his compeers to mockery, hatred, and ridicule all over the fatherland? What is his intention? To overthrow the good old order with his dangerous principles and to cause general confusion?" In reply he pointed out that sincere patriotism does not refrain from attacking backwardness, prejudice, and ignorance; that devotion to the fatherland is not equivalent to blindness; and that truth is preferable to self-deception. Instead of an uncritical admiration of past glory, Széchenyi reminded his nation: "The *Past* has slipped from our grasp forever, but we are masters of the *Future*. Let us not bother, then, with futile reminiscences but let us awaken our dear fatherland through purposeful patriotism and loyal unity to a brighter dawn. Many think: 'Hungary *has been*'; I like to believe: she *will be!*" There can be no doubt that *On Credit* provoked sharp antagonism among the public. Henceforth, national life was to center on political questions rather than literary debates, as it had in previous decades.

With his next polemical work *Világ (Light,* 1831), Széchenyi intended "to show the public Hungary's backwardness in everything" because this realization was the prerequisite of all progress. He endeavored to prove that "Hungarians were a youthful people full of vigorous energy and . . . capable of achieving anything if they would develop their Public Intelligence and Nationality." He wanted to convince his readers that the intellectual and political good of the country depended greatly on the unification of Buda and Pest into one capital city, where the creative forces of the nation could be concentrated. After illustrating how feudal social conditions prevented investors from establishing factories and able foreign craftsmen from settling in Hungary, Széchenyi concluded that "either . . . noble privileges must be restricted or else the same privileges must be extended in a modified form to all inhabitants of our fatherland . . . " Asking "Where is the Hungarian Nation today?" he answered that it could not be found anywhere in Hungary, because the term *nation* had no meaning.

Ironically, even before Széchenyi, deputies in the Diet often came to the defense of the "wretched taxpayer" against exaggerated demands of the crown, and county congregations sent many petitions asking for the reduction of the serfs' tax burdens. Throughout the early decades of the nineteenth century, deputies and counties competed with each other in describing the unbearable burdens of the peasantry every time the administration wanted to raise the amount of the military contribution (the tax paid to the treasury). These accounts, however, kept a remarkable silence about the questions of the lord-peasant relationship.

The rapid progress of the West and the spread of individualism and humanitarian ideals had hardly any impact on this relationship in Hungary. Prominent literary figures such as Kazinczy, Berzsenyi, and Sándor Kisfaludy sharply condemned the economist Berzeviczy for having exposed, to the alleged detriment of the nation, the conditions of peasant life. Even Berzeviczy stopped short of demanding the abolition of serfdom. Articulate public opinion, reflecting the convictions of the privileged, thus refused to see that the life of the serf had been steadily deteriorating.

The causes of deteriorating conditions for peasants were not confined to the feudal mentality and influence of the ruling classes. The basic socio-economic changes had begun to develop with the establishment of a permanent army, which, from the point of view of the lord, became an important consumer.

Aside from the horrors of forcible recruitment for life, the whole peasantry suffered from the military contribution, the direct tax paid exclusively by the peasant for the maintenance of the army. The increasingly heavy military contribution was one of the main economic considerations that motivated Maria Theresa to impose the urbarial legislation on her reluctant Magyar estates. In the last half of the eighteenth century, the enlightened self-interest of the Habsburg monarchy made the protection of the serfs' ability to produce and pay taxes mandatory even in Hungary.

The basic measures of the urbarial legislation (see chapter 10) remained in force until the revolution of 1848. Urbarial land was the basis for taxation by the state, whereas the demesne or allodial domain of the lord continued to be tax exempt. Protection of the "tax base,"—the peasant—was less determined under Francis I than under his predecessors in the previous century. The change in Vienna's attitude has been attributed to the impact of the French Revolution and to the need for order and noble support during the Napoleonic wars. The worsening conditions of peasant life, however, cannot be ascribed exclusively to political factors or the increasing clumsiness of the bureaucracy. Though all of these played an important role, the process was complicated by economic trends unfavorable to the peasant.

In addition to his customary right to a certain amount of land in permanent tenure, the hereditary serf also had the right to pasture his cattle on common meadowland or mast his hogs in the common woods. For these rights, as in other parts of feudal Europe, the Hungarian serf owed the landlord a certain rent made up of labor, produce, and, to a much lesser extent, money. Conditions were slowly improving, thanks in part to Széchenyi and to the spread of liberal ideas. Yet, the improvement was more in the atmosphere than in the economic and legal realities.

The "great patriot," as Széchenyi became known by the 1830s, advocated and anticipated a spiritual rejuvenation of the aristocracy, a hope that, on the whole, failed to materialize. With few exceptions, the foremost representatives of "Széchenyi's Age," who promoted the liberal ideology imbibed by reading Széchenyi's as well as foreign works, came from the upper layer of the landed gentry, the *bene possessionati*. It was the liberal, relatively well-to-do gentry led by Ferenc Deák that began to dominate the political scene with the Diet of 1832–36, achieving both numerical superiority in the Chamber of Deputies and moral authority among the intellectuals, many of whom were of non-noble and non-Magyar background. The liberal gentry, together with the educated segments of the poorer and landless nobility, constituted the core of those Hungarian "historic" middle classes that played a central role in the country's administration for the next hundred or so years.

The initial momentum of the trend toward the formation of a liberal Hungarian nation-state under Magyar leadership unfolded in the second quarter of the nineteenth century. The gradual social and economic if not legal or political emancipation of the peasant masses was part of this trend. So was the desire to eliminate, step by step, the considerable remaining religious discrimination against Protestants, the Orthodox, and, above all, the Jews. In the Diet of 1839–1841, Count Lajos Batthyány, a member of one of Hungary's wealthiest families, replaced Wesselényi (accused of high treason because of his public attacks on the administration) as the new leader of the liberal opposition. This small but articulate group included, in addition to Széchenyi, Baron Joseph Eötvös, a sensitive poet, fine novelist and perhaps the noblest of all in Hungary's great generation of reform. In two political essays published in 1840, Eötvös simultaneously argued the need to alleviate human sufferings in Ireland, caused by century-long oppression, and the emancipation of the Jews, persecuted through the ages. By 1839, even the new leader of the young conservatives in the Upper Chamber, Count Aurél Dessewffy, embraced the idea of overdue government directed administrative reforms.

The slowly organizing liberal opposition in the Diets of the 1830s was effectively helped by a substantial number of law students attending the sessions. This so-called "Dietal Youth" (some 1,500 of them in 1832–36) wanted to get acquainted with Dietal proceedings. In most cases, they were hired by the counties or, less often, by members of the Upper Chamber to copy official documents and to prepare the records of the proceedings. Often, they represented absent magnates or their widows and had a right to sit in the Chamber of Deputies. Although such a substitute could not vote and would very seldom take the floor, he still was a member of the Diet and enjoyed certain privileges. Moreover, the Dietal Youth constituted a Magyar audience in German-speaking Pozsony.

Patriotic and noisy, the Dietal Youth often interfered with dietal proceedings by booing "reactionary" members of the Diet and by encouraging progressive deputies. Imbued with liberal ideas, the law students drafted programs for a modern parliamentarian democracy with a responsible government and popular representation, thus going well beyond Széchenyi. The behavior of the law students, who would occasionally hamper rather than promote legislation, left much to be desired. At the same time, many talented leaders of the Hungarian liberal era came from their ranks and were sincerely devoted to the causes of Magyardom and social progress.

Some liberal counties sent as many as forty scribes with their deputies to further the cause of reform at the Diet and to inform the public at home. Some of the students were well educated and came from or had close connections with leading noble families in the counties. They became powerful opinion-shapers at a time when the publication of Dietal records was slow and incomplete and when politics were unconstitutionally banned from the country's only newspaper.

Besides Széchenyi, the Dietal Youth had other sources of inspiration. The leaders of the *Jugend-Verein,* several times reorganized but under constant police surveillance, formed an association for human rights, supporting the cause of the oppressed and the outcast of society, such as Poles and Jews. One brilliant young patriot, László Lovassy, was the first to come out openly for the emancipation of Jews at a meeting of the law students' casino during the Diet of 1832–36. Lovassy and other leaders of the young liberals gave active assistance to

Polish refugees, supporting the fight for a free and democratic Poland. Inspired by Polish revolutionaries, these radical republicans condemned the Holy Alliance, the Austrian administration's failure to help the Poles, and even the conservative wing of the Polish leadership. No wonder the secret police and Metternich associated them with Young Italy and French and Swiss revolutionaries, suspecting the existence of an international conspiracy to overthrow legitimate rule, such as that of the Habsburg monarchy.

Popular sovereignty and the liberation of the peasants were also among the goals of these young liberals. Admiring personal courage and enthusiastic about constitutional rights, they lionized Wesselényi. When their idol was prosecuted, they organized nationwide protests and demonstrations of sympathy in his support.

The younger generation of the county nobility served, in a broader sense, as the social basis for the Dietal Youth. Closely affiliated with this core of "Young Hungary" were the college students, Hungary's budding intelligentsia, who were often of non-noble background. The youth of Pest was a particularly important segment of this nationalistic and socially progressive part of the politically active populace. Under Joseph II, Buda became the seat of many government offices including the lieutenancy. At the same time, the Hungarian University was transferred to Pest; in subsequent decades, the foundation of the National Museum, National Academy, and National Theater all contributed to making Pest the literary and cultural center of the country, while the casino and Széchenyi's other enterprises tended to stimulate the city's economic development.

The radicalism of the Dietal Youth actually became an important factor in Hungarian politics. Young Lajos Kossuth contributed to its influence. Himself a representative of two absent magnates, he became the editor of the *Országgyülési tudósitások (Dietal Reports)*. The reports, dictated by Kossuth to a number of law students, who also took care of their distribution, made history in Hungary. Out of the reports, Kossuth forged a mighty weapon, which he masterfully wielded for the advancement of the reform movement. Besides Széchenyi's books, Kossuth's dietal reports were probably the most efficient formers of public opinion. They were read in casinos, the country houses of the nobility, and offices of county administration and influenced even the supplemental instructions sent to the deputies during the Diet. After the Diet, the dietal reports were in fact continued under the title of *Törvényhatósági Tudósitások (Municipal Reports)*. Assisted by a well-organized group of local correspondents, Kossuth informed the public about the county congregations following the Diet, thus keeping alive interest in the cause of progress and reform.

The mood of the politically articulate public and the authorities' reaction to it were greatly influenced by the violent events that took place abroad as well as at home during the early 1830s. The July Revolution in France and the Polish anti-Russian uprising of 1830–31 convinced many, including Széchenyi, of the need to make concessions to the lower classes. Fears of an alliance between a restive peasantry and the lesser nobility were borne out in the summer of 1831 by Hungary's most furious peasant insurrection since the Dózsa rebellion of 1514.

The jacquerie came on the heels of the Poles' defeat and the massive influx of Polish refugees into northern Hungary and Transylvania, where they were cordially received by a sympathetic landed nobility. Unfortunately, along with the Poles came cholera, which attacked over half a million people in northern Hungary. Half of these died. Some forty-five thousand terrified and destitute Slovak, Romanian, and Ruthenian peasants, joined in many places by the poverty-stricken "sandal" nobility, blamed lords, doctors, Jews, and Catholic priests for allegedly poisoning the wells. The outburst of mob violence against the well-to-do, the clergy, and the nobility was quelled by the military. Opponents of reform urged beheadings and hangings to put an end to the spread of "Széchenyi's plague." Thus the cholera uprising tended to polarize public opinion, which in the long run helped the administration.

Vienna also benefited from developments in the Near East during the 1830s. Russia's increased influence in Istanbul, viewed with suspicion in London, gave Metternich a certain maneuverability between England and Russia and strengthened Austrian positions in the Balkans. At the same time, the alliance of the three absolute monarchies was confirmed in the Treaties of Münchengrätz and Berlin in 1833. By granting the right of mutual intervention to the sovereigns of the three powers against any internal or external enemy, the treaties bolstered the conservative order internationally as well as domestically. The close cooperation between Austria, Prussia, and Russia in Ottoman, Polish, and indeed all potentially subversive affairs could not but be directed at Hungarian malcontents. Increased Austrian confidence was a factor in the crackdown on the leaders of the Dietal Youth (Lovassy was sentenced to twenty years in prison, where he went mad) and of the renewed attempt to intimidate the Hungarian opposition in the late 1830s.

This attempt, made by Hungarian chancellor Count Fidel Pálffy (nephew of Count Franz Anton Kolowrat-Liebsteinsky, the all-powerful director of Austria's internal affairs), failed because of the strength of the Hungarian opposition at the Diet of 1839–41. Another international crisis related to the Eastern question also forced Vienna to avoid a confrontation with Hungary. Pálffy had to resign, and a political amnesty inaugurated a short period of good feelings between the court and moderate liberals such as Deák, who was instrumental in working out a compromise between the administration and the Hungarian opposition.

Few understood Hungary's vulnerability to contending international forces better or was more aware of her backward economy's fragility than Széchenyi. Insisting on the indissolubility of his country's "mixed marriage" with Habsburg Austria, he yearned for domestic tranquillity as a guarantee of the success of his economic enterprises. Economic progress, in his view, was a precondition for political advancement and a greater measure of independence. The construction of a permanent suspension bridge over the Danube connecting Buda and Pest, a project which was to preoccupy Széchenyi for over two decades, was to make the future Hungarian capital the commercial center of the country and the hub of its transportation system. The bridge also became a symbol of the abolition of the nobility's tax exemption, since noblemen were also supposed to pay the toll for using it. For this, and other major enterprises, Széchenyi needed Austrian and foreign capital, technological know-how, machinery, engineers, skilled technicians, and craftsmen and, above all, the government's cooperation. Fortunately he had warm personal relations with the Archduke Joseph, Hungary's respected and well-liked palatine, and good contacts in Vienna, primarily with Prince Metternich's circle. In 1833, Széchenyi was appointed royal commissioner in charge of improving Danubian navigation.

While the planning and construction of the Chain Bridge was directed by two English engineers, Adam and William Tierney Clark, (not related), Széchenyi's assistants in implementing his gigantic plans for the regulation of the Danube and later the Tisza rivers were the Hungarian engineers József Beszédes and Pál Vásárhelyi. The flood control plans for Hungary's two main rivers laid the foundation for the expansion of agricultural production in generations to come.

The technology of England, home of the industrial revolution, had fascinated Széchenyi ever since his first trip to the island country. When he managed to smuggle a "gaslight machine" out of England, he thought he had got hold of "the soul of the [English] nation, an engine" for a bribe of two pounds. Many years later, as promoter of the Danubian Steamship Company, he remarked, on seeing the vessels being pulled upstream by humans, that "the steam engine cannot stand the stench of feudalism." Incompatible as the two may have been in theory, without a social revolution, feudalism and capitalism were bound to coexist in Hungary for a long time. The Diets of 1832–36 and 1839–40 did enact new commercial and exchange laws as well as legislation for the construction of the Chain Bridge and the first railroads in Hungary (enterprises in which Viennese capital was also interested). However, only watered down versions of reforms liberalizing the relationship between lord and peasant were permitted to pass, due to the veto power of the conservative Upper Chamber and the court. Similarly, the overrepresented Catholic hierarchy in the Upper Chamber managed to frustrate in both Diets all efforts to grant religious equality to Protestants. Hence, discriminatory practices and rivalries between the two major branches of Western Christendom continued to hamper the otherwise growing momentum of modern Magyar nationalism. This nationalism was manifest in the 1840 law that replaced Latin with Magyar as the official language of all legislative and administrative activities in Hungary proper, exempting only Croatia.

Among the positive steps taken by the Diet of 1839–40 was the new urbarial law permitting individual serfs, as well as entire communities, to pay a fixed sum as manumission compensation, thus opening the way for serfs to become free landowners. The Diet also acted to safeguard the free development of industrial enterprises and to limit child labor and decided to prepare a new penal code on the basis of the best available foreign sources, including American. It also passed the first legislation favoring the Jews since 1791, permitting Jewish citizens legally resident in the country to choose their domicile (except in the mining centers), to own real estate, and to pursue freely any trade, craft, or profession.

In the euphoria following the political amnesty ending the Diet in the spring of 1840, cooperation between moderate liberals, under the leadership of Deák, and the aging members of the *Staatskonferenz,* which took over the direction of affairs upon the accession to the throne of Ferdinand V in 1835, did not seem impossible. Many liberals hesitated to abolish the constitutional privileges of the nobility even while resisting the wave of terror initiated by the *Staatskonferenz* after the Diet of 1832–36. Yet the idea of maintaining feudalism politically while introducing elements of capitalistic free enterprise piecemeal—to foster modern liberal nationalism based on Magyar supremacy and simultaneously challenge Austrian leadership in the empire—proved problematic.

Reform or Revolution, 1841–1848

Kossuth was one of those released from prison as a result of the amnesty that led to the happy ending of the Diet of 1839–1840. In a spirit of reconciliation and with the connivance of Matternich, he was even permitted to become editor of a newspaper, *Pesti Hirlap (Gazette of Pest).* This was perhaps because the government thought he would now be easier to control or in the hope that Kossuth's pen would split the opposition.

First published in January 1841, *Pesti Hirlap* appeared twice a week and opened a new era in Hungarian political journalism. Its editor intended it to be the true mirror of the nation's life and introduced a new genre, the editorial, to focus public attention on the great issues of the day. In a lively, at times emotional style, Kossuth's editorials, along with other articles, discussed both domestic and international issues, and reported on local events and conditions, thanks to a well-organized network of correspondents. In six months, the number of the paper's subscribers increased to five thousand; its readership constituted about one-fourth of the estimated 200,000 Hungarians who read newspapers at the time. Thus Kossuth's paper became a powerful opinion-shaping force.

Even though limited by censorship, Kossuth and other contributors to *Pesti Hirlap* managed to discuss domestic issues in the context of the achievements of the French Revolution and West European and American experiences of capitalism and political liberalism. These included the right of non-nobles to own land, taxation of the nobility, representation of non-nobles in county assemblies and of cities at the Diet, as well as questions of tariffs, railroads, industrial development, and opening foreign markets for Hungarian agricultural products. In addition to critical analyses of French and English constitutional models, Kossuth also expressed an interest in the institutions of the United States. Aside from the analogous tasks of abolishing slavery and serfdom or facing the problems of the industrial revolution, Hungarian liberals turned their attention to the progressive American prison system praised by Sándor Bölöni Farkas in his popular *Journey in North America.* Indeed, the reform of the penal code considered by the Diet of 1839–40 was discussed by Kossuth in the first issues of *Pesti Hirlap.* The subject was taken up again by the Diets of the 1840s as well as in an essay by Eötvös on *Prison Reform* (1838) and in his social novel, *Village Notary* (1845). Kossuth's paper also stimulated debates on the role of the press, trial by jury, primary education, municipal self-government, and representative parliament, all issues which preoccupied the increasingly well-informed and liberal political elite of the pre-March.

With its egalitarian overtones and emphasis on human rights, Kossuth's ideology, as expressed on the pages of *Pesti Hirlap,* reflected the frustrations and ambitions of a younger generation of lesser noblemen open to Western ideas, eager to challenge an ossified absolutist system, and, above all, ready to take over the government of a country. A new, activist band of reformers organized by Kossuth emerged, dubbed the "Party of *Pesti Hirlap,*" by opponents. This group seemed to aim at a radical transformation of Hungarian society at a time when, as Széchenyi believed and conservatives argued, the Vienna government had dropped its anti-constitutional tendencies and even seemed willing to accept the Magyarization of public life, a common goal of all Hungarian nationalists.

While insisting that he still shared Kossuth's liberal principles, Széchenyi attacked the editor of *Pesti Hirlap* in a book-length diatribe entitled *A Kelet Népe (People of the Orient,* 1841). Apprehensive of another confrontation with the government (whose support he needed for his projects) and also jealous of the young new leader, Széchenyi accused Kossuth of promoting revolutionary anarchy by pitting the poor against the rich, the lesser nobles against the magnates, and one nationality against the other. Warning that with his agitation, the editor of *Pesti Hirlap* might "assassinate the Magyar" and strengthen Viennese despotism, the "father of Hungarian reform" nevertheless avoided a position similar to those who followed an anti-liberal line and were subsevient to the imperial administration.

In the protracted public debate provoked by *People of the Orient,* liberals and even such moderates as Deák and Eötvös sided with Kossuth in deploring the divisiveness of the book. Conservatives did not fully trust the "great patriot" either. Indeed the "Westernizer" Széchenyi's romantic nationalism was not without racist ambiguities (the title refers to Magyardom's alleged unique Asiatic qualities). Still, Széchenyi was more conciliatory toward other ethnic groups and more critical of Magyar chauvinism than were most of his liberal fellow Magyars.

It was Aurél Dessewffy who formulated the doctrine of modern Hungarian conservatives. In contrasting the views of Széchenyi and Kossuth, he found that Kossuth's political creed rested on the crucial role of the autonomous county in Hungary's administrative system and on reliance on a free press as an opinion-forming centralizing factor. Széchenyi, he observed, was less concerned with the constitutional aspects of administration than with pursuing cultural and economic goals.

Dessewffy's new conservative program advocated close cooperation with the imperial administration in the interest of all the heterogeneous nations of the empire and effective central control of local government under firm conservative leadership at the county level. In favor of improved education and transportation and a moderate on the religious question, he challenged the "party of reform," as the liberals liked to be called, with his concept of "deliberate progress" or conservative reform. Supporters of the Viennese government often used deceptively liberal slogans to take the wind out of the sails of the opposition. This in itself was a sign of changing times. Another was the heightened spirit of Magyar nationalism that motivated the younger generation of both liberals and conservatives. When they joined forces, they were able to obtain occasional concessions from Vienna. For example, the Diet of 1843–44 made Magyar the official language of all authorities, courts, and schools within the confines of the kingdom. (This was done over the protest of the Croats, who in turn replaced Latin with their own vernacular as the official language in the autonomous "associate country" of Croatia-Slavonia at a Croatian Diet three years later.)

Alternately resisting and yielding to the pressures of clashing linguistic nationalisms, the Austrian authorities were less willing to make concessions in the economic sphere. Both chambers of the Diet of 1843–1844 jointly requested the modification of internal tariffs separating Hungary from the rest of the Habsburg lands. This plea, of concern to liberals and conservatives alike, received only an evasive answer. Indignantly, the predominantly liberal Chamber of Deputies passed a resolution supporting the recently founded National Protective Association *(Országos Védegylet)*. This group sought to exclude Austrian manufactures from Hungary under the slogan "Buy Hungarian!" Led by distinguished liberal aristocrats and patronized by their ladies, the new association elected as its director Kossuth, who had recently been forced out of the editorship of *Pesti Hirlap*. Yet even Kossuth's energy and organizational ability could not overcome the absence of a domestic industrial base. Politically, the association strengthened separatist trends and was regarded as a threat by Metternich, who exaggerated its significance for his own reasons.

The attempt coincided with a shift in Vienna's economic policies. Faced with the challenge of the Prussian-led *Zollverein* in the German lands and British competition in all foreign markets, Metternich and the head of Austrian finances, Baron Karl Friedrich Kübeck, resolved to modernize Austria's tariff system. This required the incorporation of Hungary and Transylvania into the imperial market, and the elimination of the internal tariff. To compensate the treasury for this loss of revenue, Vienna contemplated doing away with the Hungarian nobility's tax exemption and extending to Hungary the imperial tobacco monopoly. To put into effect these far-reaching and clandestine plans, Hungarian economic nationalism had to be overcome and feudal sensitivities considered. Therefore the neo-conservative program of strengthening the Hungarian central administration and breaking the liberal grip over the majority of the counties appeared a feasible alternative.

The often frustrating discussions of the nineteen-month Diet of 1843–44 failed to justify the hopes of either liberals or neo-conservatives and exasperated the Court. Aside from the language law, extolled by Magyars but resented by other ethnic groups, only a few pieces of new legislation passed. These included the enactment of the right of Christian non-nobles to hold any office (but not to vote in the elections) and to own noble land (not exempt, however, from the law of entail). Also limited, yet nevertheless important, was the liberalization of the law covering mixed marriages and conversions among Catholics and Protestants. Still, the Diet, which was preceded by a corrupt and unusually violent election campaign, revealed a further polarization. This prevented overdue action on issues including a new civil code, city representation in the Diet, the redemption of peasants from serfdom, general taxation, and establishment of a land bank. Though the debates on granting equal rights to Protestants were exceptionally acrimonious, both Catholic and Protestant leaders closed their eyes to the needs of the country's substantial Orthodox population, mainly Serbs, Romanians, and Ruthenians. While half of the counties eloquently advocated the enfranchisement of Jews to advance the liberal cause in the cities, the other half objected, using blatantly racist arguments and even suggesting the revocation of the concessions made by the previous Diet. There could be no doubt that social tensions were on the rise, and politically articulate Hungarians were divided on most of the important issues.

Particularly galling, from Metternich's point of view, was the fact the the Diet concerned itself with the legal and constitutional status of cities, the system of public education, and the development of trade and industry. In his opinion, these were the domain of royal prerogative. In a set of memoranda circulated among high officials while the Diet was still in session, he claimed that Hungary was not governed at all, that the country was on the road to hell and revolution, and that immediate steps had to be taken to prepare a new Diet with the assistance of the conservative party.

Metternich and a special secret committee on Hungarian affairs thus accepted the neo-conservatives' argument for a strong executive as a guarantee of effective administration and economic modernization. It would also serve as a shield against the inefficiency of local administration and public anarchy. The designation of Count György Apponyi as head of the Hungarian Chancery in Vienna in late 1844 was followed by the dispatch of centrally appointed and highly paid administrators to recalcitrant Hungarian counties. They were to take firm control, if necessary by force, and secure the election of reliable officials. Through bribery, intimidation, and reliance on the military, Apponyi's system began to produce results. In local elections and in the bitterly fought elections to the Diet of 1847, liberals were replaced by conservatives. Some traditionally liberal counties sent conservative deputies to what turned out to be Hungary's last feudal legislative assembly. Others provided their dietal representatives with anti-liberal instructions or connived in their deputies' behind-the-scene deals in the hope of receiving government favors.

The initial successes of Apponyi's aggressive policies were due in part to the lack of unity in the leadership of the opposition. Besides personal rivalries, such as that between Kossuth and Lajos Batthyány, there were disagreements on principles, manifest in the takeover of the editorship of *Pesti Hirlap* in mid-1844 by László Szalay, a historian and legal scholar who represented the city of

Korpona (Krupina) in the Diet. Szalay, along with Eötvös and another major writer and politician, Zsigmond Kemény, belonged to a small intellectual elite highly critical of county autonomy. Unlike Kossuth, they regarded it as an obstacle to rather than a prerequisite of liberal reform. Advocates of a strong central government responsible to parliament, these "centralists" favored an independent judiciary and a Western-type parliamentary system. The partisans of municipalities and centralists closed ranks in the wake of the introduction of the new system of administrators, which was seen as a threat not only to municipal autonomy but also to the constitution.

Széchenyi's prestige added momentum to the conservative cause. Despite his attack on Kossuth, Metternich still believed in early 1842 that Széchenyi was not ripe for reward from the government. Yet the "greatest Magyar's" ideas about building railroads paralleled those of the administration, and he feared a social revolution no less than the conservatives. Trusting that he would receive greater government assistance for his plan to organize a unified Hungarian transportation system, Széchenyi accepted the chairmanship of the Transportation Commission of the Hungarian lieutenancy. With Metternich's and the archduke-palatine Joseph's support, Széchenyi thus entered Apponyi's government, which needed him to enhance the credibility of its reforms.

Without delay, Széchenyi undertook the most important economic project of the pre-March period, aimed at the prevention of the recurrent floods of the Tisza River valley. Relying on his experience as royal commissioner of Danubian navigation, he was also determined to make the country's second largest river navigable and to reclaim over 1,840 square miles of swampland. Széchenyi organized a Tisza River Valley Association of riparian landowners. As starting capital, Viennese banking houses opened a credit account in the amount of 400,000 gulden, the Royal Treasury pledged fifty thousand gulden for the first two years, and the Hungarian Salt Fund one hundred thousand annually for the duration of the work. During the complicated negotiations with the Austrian financiers and a reluctant Baron Kübeck, Apponyi vigorously supported Széchenyi. Széchenyi stressed again and again in his tireless public relations campaign that the Tisza region was the "most Magyar" part of the fatherland, whose welfare should be promoted by every patriot. In fact, he and Apponyi also knew that several of the counties in the affected area were strongholds of the opposition. Winning them over to the government-sponsored project appeared the best way of generating a climate favorable to conservative reform on the eve of the elections for the 1847 Diet.

The Tisza River project proved that conservative reform could be imaginative and workable in the hands of a Széchenyi. It is also clear that his cooperation with Apponyi was not confined to pragmatic considerations. In early 1847, in his *Politikai Programm-Töredékek (Fragments of a Political Program)*, Széchenyi launched another sharp attack against Kossuth and his followers, whom he considered revolutionary hotheads. He again accused Kossuth, who in the meantime had become the editor of the *Hetilap (Weekly Journal)*, of exciting the non-Magyar ethnic groups and goading the peasants to rebel against their lords.

He also asked that Kossuth desist playing the role of a leader, for which he was not qualified, adding that the government itself championed the cause of reform and that to oppose it was tantamount to treason. Széchenyi sent the first two copies of his pamphlet to Apponyi and the archduke Stephan, who was to succeed his own deceased father as palatine of Hungary.

Széchenyi had put his finger on the two most crucial issues then facing Hungarian society: the state of the peasantry and the relations among Hungary's ethnic groups. In 1846, peasants in neighboring Galicia had risen against their Polish landlords. The revolt spread into the northeastern counties of Hungary in a year of famine, instilling in the nobility the fear of a jacquerie.

Second in importance only to the agrarian situation was the question of the nationalities. Of multi-ethnic Hungary's 12.9 million inhabitants (including Transylvania and Croatia), less than 40 percent, 4.8 million, were ethnic Magyars around 1840. The balance comprised Romanians (2.2 million), Slovaks (1.6 million), Croats (1.3 million), Germans (1.2 million), Serbs (800 thousand) and Ruthenians (400 thousand). Save for the Croats and the German Saxons of Transylvania, none of these national minorities were recognized by the Hungarian constitutional tradition as having corporate autonomy. Magyar nationalists, even though resentful of Vienna's presumed or real Germanizing tendencies under Joseph II and his successors, failed to see why the linguistic claims of non-Magyars should be permitted to prevail in the public domain, or even locally at the village level. Croatia, whose separate constitutional status under the Crown of Saint István was recognized, had the right to send deputies to the Hungarian Diet but during the 1840s, pressure on them increased to make them use Magyar in their speeches. In the Croatian provincial Diet at Zágráb, conflict deepened between the minority pro-Magyar party and the majority "Illyrian" Croat national party. In Transylvania, the ruling Magyar elite was hesitant to give up its autonomous status and accept the Hungarian urbarial legislation, from which the grand-duchy was exempt. Yet they grew more susceptible to the liberals' agitation for the unification of the "two Magyar fatherlands" as fears of the overwhelmingly Orthodox Romanian population's demands for religious and ethnic equality increased.

Characteristically, the liberal "Opposition Manifesto," initially drafted by Kossuth but put in final form by the more cautious Deák in June 1847, did not mention non-Magyars' ethnic rights, although it stressed the claims of Magyar nationality, the inviolability of the Hungarian constitution, and the civil rights of all including non-Magyars. It also took a firm stand against Vienna's absolutist government and demanded constitutional institutions for all the provinces of the Habsburg monarchy. The manifesto recognized the Pragmatic Sanction and Hungary's interest in maintaining the unity of the Habsburg monarchy but only on the basis of equity and without violating its territorial integrity, its administrative structure, and the religious liberties embedded in the constitution. Requesting the reunification of Transylvania with Hungary, it also insisted on the government's accountability to Parliament, and on freedom of association, openness in public life, a free press, and the lifting of censorship. The manifesto defined as urgent tasks of the upcoming Diet general taxation under parliamentary control, the establishment of non-noble citizens' civil rights and their representation in local, municipal, and national legislative bodies, equality before the law, mandatory abolition of serfdom with state-guaranteed compensation, and the elimination of the law of entail to make access to credit and the purchasing of land easier.

Conciliatory in tone, the program announced in the manifesto was flexible enough to be put into effect step by step. Instead, it became the platform for the sweeping reforms introduced in March and April of 1848, when a sudden change in the international and domestic situation demanded rapid action. In this sense, the Manifesto worked out painstakingly between 1845 and 1847 prepared the liberal leadership for a lawful response to unexpected revolutionary events which had little to do with Kossuth's agitation or Széchenyi's predictions. Its ideas, though occasionally vague (making it acceptable to all factions of the opposition), reappeared in Deák's negotiations leading to the Compromise of 1867.

The neo-conservative program, published seven months before the Opposition Manifesto was formulated, also stressed Magyar nationality and professed to strive for a constitutional majority in the pursuit of its goals. Prudent concern for the unity of the Habsburg realm and support of those government policies deemed constitutional were other themes of the platform, which preferred reforms initiated by the government to what it described as the blind imitations of foreign examples and excesses of the previous Diet's opposition majority. Respect for the sanctity of property and for the moderating influence of landowning did characterize conservative attitudes, but even the conservatives advocated important reforms. These included alleviating urbarial burdens, safeguarding freedom of speech in public meetings, completing new civil and penal codes, improving county administration, reorganizing cities and establishing their voting rights, and arranging easy credit for landowners. Both these demands and those concerning commerce and tariffs were on the deceptively similar agendas of both liberals and conservatives. However, the conservatives put greater emphasis on regular party meetings and in fact stole a march on the opposition in introducing modern party organization into Hungarian politics.

The royal propositions for the Diet of 1847–48 seemed to bear out the conservative contention that the government wished to promote progress and reform and even recognized the need to govern by relying on a parliamentary majority. They listed all the important measures considered in recent years, from prison reform, tariffs, and transportation to manumission compensation. Liberal and conservative forces appeared to be in a tense balance at Pozsony when Emperor Ferdinand opened the Diet in November. Kossuth, the opposition leader in the Lower Chamber, was a deputy of Pest County and coordinated the anti-governmental actions of other liberal administrative units. To counter Kossuth's influence, Széchenyi gave up his seat in the Upper Chamber and had himself elected deputy in anticipation of a tough contest of wills.

The spirit of liberalism that forced the government to offer concessions in the legislative agenda, despite its wish to uphold the feudal power structure, also manifested itself in the traditionally ultra-conservative Upper Chamber, where the number of liberal aristocrats increased. Their leader, Lajos Batthyány, and Count László Teleki, the most radical among the magnates, were also permanent members of the liberal caucus of the Lower Chamber. It is noteworthy that in the dietal debates, leaders of the opposition repeatedly raised not only the question of Hungary's trade and political relations with Austria and all other hereditary provinces but also with other countries such as Russia. Although some speeches tended to reflect a lack of realism (as shown by exaggerated fears of the Panslav danger), they were signals of a new national leadership's ambition to be heard in the arena of independent nations.

Instead of discussing the administration's proposals, the Lower Chamber first took up national grievances. In early February 1848, Kossuth was defeated by a single vote (cast by the Croatian deputies) on the critical issue of immediately ending the system of administrators. The defeat, brought about by a clandestine deal worked out by Apponyi, Széchenyi, and several leaders of the opposition resentful of Kossuth, was only temporary, and Kossuth soon regained the upper hand. The Lower Chamber remained evenly divided until the news of the February Revolution in Paris undermined both Metternich's position in Vienna and the feudal order in Hungary.

For a few weeks, the initiative was to pass to the youthful revolutionaries of Pest, the city selected by both liberals and conservatives as the seat of Hungary's next National Assembly. Devastated by a flood in 1838, Pest, within the following decade, became the country's commercial and industrial center, as well as its main railroad terminal. Together with Buda, Hungary's largest city had more than 150,000 inhabitants, numerous public buildings (such as the National Museum and National Theater), and Széchenyi's Chain Bridge, nearing completion. Although the first banks founded in the 1840s were dependent on foreign (chiefly Austrian) capital, the development of Danubian shipping and the plan to connect the future Hungarian capital with the Adriatic port of Fiume (Rijeka) by railroad held out the hope of linking the country with the world at large.

Above all, Pest attracted the best intellectual talent of the country. The period of Romanticism, reflected in the works of Vörösmarty and the two Kisfaludys, was followed by more realistic trends in literature, as represented by the critical social and historical novels of Eötvös and Baron Zsigmond Kemény, the "Hungarian Balzac." But it was Sándor Petőfi, son of a Southern Slav butcher-innkeeper and a Slovak mother, whose appearance in Pest marked the beginning of national classicism in Hungarian literature. Through the poetry and writings of Petőfi and his close friend, János Arany, the language spoken by the common people became the vehicle for artistic expression, setting the norms of modern Hungarian literature. One of the greatest lyricists who ever wrote in the Magyar tongue and the first to achieve international acclaim through translations, Petőfi was also an ardent nationalist and revolutionary.

Around Petőfi formed a circle of radical intellectuals who held regular meetings in the Pilvax coffee house. Labelled "Young Hungary" (a reference to Giuseppe Mazzini's Young Italy movement), the circle grew increasingly critical of the inconsistencies of the opposition, especially after the "lessons" of the Galician peasant revolt. Mainly of noble background, these young radicals shared the way of life of their non-noble peers. Teachers, lawyers, office workers, publicists, or writers, they had no interest in maintaining a feudal society and stood for the full emancipation of the popular masses. Admirers of the French Revolution, the members of this politically articulate new intelligentsia included the leaders of the more than one thousand university students at Pest. By the end of 1847, the "Pilvax Club" began to hold meetings twice a week. Burghers were invited to its political debates, which were occasionally attended even by interested persons of the middle or working classes.

There was a rather heterogeneous mass of lower class people in Pest, somewhat loosely tied to the tradition-bound feudal structure. This group, in the country's most urbanized and rapidly changing economic center, is estimated at some twenty thousand people, half of whom were journeymen exploited by their guild masters and by "bunglers," many of them Jews, who were not admitted to the guilds but whose competition was real and often encouraged. There were also thousands of factory workers, artisans, peddlers, small shopkeepers, apprentices, domestic servants, and day-laborers, forced from the countryside into the city by a series of bad harvests in the mid-1840s. Their precarious economic existence made them restive and susceptible to appeals holding out the hope for a better life.

The more farsighted among the liberal reformers, such as Eötvös (or in his younger years Széchenyi), not to mention Kossuth, were well aware of the potential social dynamite in both the rural and urbanizing areas. In his second masterpiece, *Hungary in 1514,* Eötvös placed the social turmoil and horrors of Hungary's greatest peasant revolution in the center of his novel, one year after the uprising in Galicia. In the same year, 1847, Petőfi struck a different note, stating with confidence that "if the people dominate poetry, they will be close to dominating politics as well." In his poem on "The Poets of the Nineteenth Century," he sounded a warning:

> When from the cornucopia of plenty
> All can equally partake,
> When all can equally sit
> At the table of justice,
> When the sunshine of the spirit
> Sparkles on the windows of every home:
> Only then shall we say,
> Let's stop now, Canaan has come!

Like his contemporary, the great Polish poet Adam Mickiewicz, Petőfi shared the romantic idea that poets were leaders of their nations and had a prophetic mission to fulfill. No less romantic, and even more utopian, were the communistic dreams of a new social order set forth by the self-taught scion of serfs, Mihály Táncsics, and propagated in his pamphlet *The Word of the People Is*

God's Word (a paraphrase of *Vox populi, vox Dei*). The pamphlet resulted in his arrest.

To be sure, there were indications that the golden age of Hungarian literature might be transformed into a real "Springtime of Peoples." The feudal Diet accepted in December 1847 the principle of mandatory redemption of serfs on the basis of state-sponsored compensation of landlords. The Jews, often protected by the owners of large estates and local administrations, made considerable advances in business, the professions, and their adoptive Magyar culture, hoping for full emancipation. Many literati, teachers, scholars, engineers, state officials, clerks, and clergymen were assimilated Germans or Slavs. It is also true that increased grain and wool production and the gradual but steady improvement of transportation (especially steamship navigation on the Danube and Tisza rivers and on Lake Balaton) generated a new momentum of urbanization. As a result, by the 1840s 13 to 14 percent of the population (some two million people) lived in urban areas, liberated *de facto* from the jurisdiction of feudal landlords.

Still, education remained a royal prerogative. At the elementary level, it hardly went beyond the three Rs. Geography and history stressed loyalty to the dynasty, and schools were under strict church control. Although the second *Ratio Educationis* (1806) stipulated compulsory education of all children between six and twelve years of age, it was only the ordinance of the lieutenancy in 1845 that obliged village communities, landlords, and ecclesiastic authorities to maintain two-year elementary schools, with three additional grades added in the larger villages. The roots of feudalism and racial hatred lay deep and the resilience of the European conservative reaction was strong. Petőfi and Hungary's glorious "Youth of March" were to learn some bitter lessons—and so were subsequent generations of Magyars and non-Magyars.

XII

THE REVOLUTION AND THE WAR OF INDEPENDENCE, 1848–1849

István Deák

The revolution of 1848 was one of the greatest moments in Hungary's history. There had been violent social and political upheavals before, and even a national revolution under Prince Ferenc II Rákóczi early in the eighteenth century, but none matched 1848–49 in the international attention it received, the domestic passions it aroused, and the wealth of reform legislation it produced. Although revolutionary Hungary lost the military conflict with Austria that followed the bloodless revolution of March 1848, the triumphant Habsburg state left unchanged, and in fact gradually extended, the liberal economic and social reforms adopted by the Hungarian Diet in March and April 1848. After the war, the Habsburg authorities revoked the virtual political sovereignty the Hungarians had achieved in the spring of 1848, yet, less than twenty years later, Hungary recovered it. The Compromise Agreement concluded with Emperor Francis Joseph I in 1867 made Hungary an equal partner with the Austrian half of the Habsburg monarchy, something that would have been far more difficult to achieve without the supreme national effort of 1848–49. The compromise was a direct if belated consequence of the revolution and war of 1848–49.

The revolution, especially in its first bloodless phase, represented Hungary's greatest spontaneous effort to achieve modernization. During these months, the Hungarian leaders attempted to adapt the country's official ideology, as well as its government, society, and economy, to the most enlightened Western standards. The great leap forward was not unsuccessful. No less important, at least from the point of view of a small and hitherto little-known nation, the events of 1848 brought the Hungarians widespread recognition. For a few decades after the revolution and the war, the Hungarians stood, in the eyes of liberal world opinion, as a shining example of humanity's unquenchable thirst for individual rights and national freedom. In 1848–49, the Hungarians fought longer than any other group for the right to national self-determination; they defied what for liberals were the world's two worst tyrannies: the Austrian Habsburg and the Russian Romanov empires. The Hungarians had embraced—in the view of the liberals and democrats of mid-century Europe and the United States—the most progressive ideas of their age.

Because Hungary lost the War of Independence but won the peace that followed, the revolution and the war of 1848–49 are the most celebrated and, simultaneously, the most hotly debated events in the country's history. Immediately following the War of Independence, the politically conscious part of Hungarian society became divided in its evaluation of what had actually happened and why. This division has continued to our day. For the last century and a half, the Hungarian public and historians have been questioning when and how the mistakes were made that led to military defeat by Austria: whether at the beginning of the revolution, when Hungary went too far, or perhaps not far enough, in her drive for self-determination; or in September 1848, when an initially peaceful revolution turned into a bloody conflict; or in April 1849, when the Hungarians proclaimed that the Habsburg dynasty had forfeited its claim to the Hungarian Crown. Or perhaps the revolutionaries had made no mistakes at all, and Hungary was simply the victim of aggression. Nationalist spokesmen have hinted darkly at anti-Hungarian machinations by the Vienna court, the liberal Austrian government, the Czechs, the South Slavs, the Romanians, the Russian Tsar, and even Great Britain; radicals have accused the reactionary and treacherous Hungarian aristocracy and high clergy; orthodox Marxists, who identify the Hungarian national cause with that of the international proletariat, have complained of betrayal by the exploiting classes; and finally, conservatives have blamed the rabble, as well as individual rabble-rousers, for ruining what could have become a peaceful and gradual evolution. Even the more moderate Hungarian historians have tended to assign praise or blame on the basis of purely national considerations. The critics of Hungary, especially among its neighbors, have used the same approach to arrive at exactly the opposite conclusions. Every generation has judged the events of 1848–49 according to its own *Weltanschauung*, and only in recent years have some Hungarian historians come up with a more balanced judgment. They now see the Hungarian events of 1848–49 as part and parcel of a great ecumenical European upheaval, which put an end to one of the longest periods of relative European peace. The 1848 revolutions, Hungary's among them, clearly demonstrated the decline of the great conservative alliance that had controlled Europe in the preceding decades, but it also demonstrated the mutual incompatibility of the various European liberal-nationalist movements. The Springtime of Peoples, as 1848 has come to be called, opened the way to a century or more of national and social conflicts. It led also to one of the most dramatic developments of modern European history, the drives for the creation of aggressive and expansionist national states in Germany, Italy, Hungary, Poland, and the Balkans in the second half of the nineteenth century. On one thing alone all Hungarian historians agree, namely that 1848–49 was a truly great historical event of which the nation has good reason to be proud, and there is no reason to disagree with their assessment.

Because the word "revolution" has and will be bandied about in this chapter, it should be defined. If by revolution we understand the sudden and violent overthrow, by an armed multitude, of an established political order, then the events of March 1848 do not qualify as a revolution. Hungary was, before 1848, a kingdom under the Habsburg scepter, governed, more or less constitutionally, by a curious combination of centralistic bureaucracy and powerful provincial nobility. The events of March 1848 did not change these facts. Despite, or perhaps because of, what happened in March, the monarchy continued to exist under the same king; the ancient liberties of the nation were reaffirmed and codified into law; the provincial nobility actually increased its influence and power; and the bureaucrats remained in office (although they were now supposed to take their orders from Budapest, rather than from Vienna, through the intermediary of the Budapest Viceroyalty). Furthermore, the very politicians who had created and led the dramatic events of March 1848 insisted then and forever after that they had always acted legally. In their opinion, they had done nothing in March 1848 except restore the historic privileges of the nation, which a callous and reactionary Viennese administration, the evil "Camarilla," had violated.

Yet the March events can be considered a revolution if we are prepared to extend the meaning of the term to include sudden and dramatic concessions wrung from an intimidated central authority by a number of determined politicians, using the threat of political violence and supported by a widespread political movement. This is what happened in Hungary, and it seems reason enough to accept the Hungarian custom of referring to the events of March 1848 as a revolution. Perhaps it would be better to call it a "lawful revolution!" The events of March were something akin to what had taken place in France in the summer of 1789, when the Estates General upheld the authority of the king but also wrung enormous concessions from him and legislated the abolition of a whole series of local and caste privileges.

As the storming of the Bastille on July 14, 1789 is considered the beginning of the great French Revolution, so the events in Hungary of March 15, 1848 are usually designated as the start of Hungary's revolution. Yet even before that memorable day, momentous events had taken place in Vienna, Pozsony, and Budapest.

The Lawful Revolution, March–April 1848

In 1848, Paris was the undisputed cultural capital of Europe and the city to which all political innovators looked for inspiration. On February 22, Paris rose in revolt against the regime of King Louis Philippe and, within three days, drove him into exile, proclaimed a republic, and established a provisional revolutionary government. Explanations for this extraordinary event include dissatisfaction with a dull, "bourgeois" king, frustration over the loss of French world power vis-à-vis Great Britain, the clamor of the newly rich bourgeoisie for political influence, popular infatuation with the French revolutionary tradition, an equally romantic infatuation with the idea of a socialist utopia, and the discontent of the urban poor over unemployment, high prices, and slum living conditions. News of the successful Parisian uprising spread with the speed of the new railroad to Central Europe, where the revolutionary fervor was heightened by news coming from Italy. Southern Italy had been in ferment since January, and new disturbances had spread to Austrian-occupied Northern Italy as well.

Grievances in the Habsburg domains were similar to those in France, though complicated by a host of other, local ones. The urban poor in Vienna and the other cities of the monarchy were suffering the consequences of several bad harvests, which had made bread very expensive, and from unemployment resulting from a crisis in production. Craftsmen in Central Europe hated and feared the new machines, which seemed to threaten their traditional crafts; businessmen and factory owners criticized the restrictions designed to protect the traditional crafts; peasants complained of the corvée and other obligations to the landowners; the Austrian nobility resented the loss of their political power to the omnipresent state bureaucracy; intellectuals chafed under censorship; German nationalist students wanted Austria to participate in the all-German national renewal; and Hungarians, Czechs, Serbs, Croats, Slovaks, Romanians, and Poles (or rather, their self-appointed political spokesmen) yearned for national autonomy and territorial expansion. Everywhere nationalists clamored for the creation of unitary national provinces or states. It would take a separate chapter to list the many reasons why there was so much agitation for change at this particular moment.

As usual in the history of the Habsburg monarchy, the treasury was empty, making the public uneasy about the government's ability to honor its promissory notes. There was a rush on the state exchange counters to convert banknotes into silver. News of the Paris revolt reached Vienna on February 29; a day later the Hungarian Diet at Pozsony learned of the event. Prompted by the growing public unease over the financial situation, Lajos Kossuth, a deputy in the Lower House, assumed unofficial leadership of the Diet and, by extension, the country. He was not to relinquish this command position until August 1849. Four weeks earlier, Kossuth had suffered a serious setback in the Lower House, when one of his proposals was voted down by the combined votes of the conservatives, other deputies loyal to the Viennese administration, and the delegates of Croatia-Slavonia opposed to Kossuth's Magyar nationalism. Now, on March 3, in a great speech to an unofficial meeting of the Lower House, Kossuth insisted that, instead of fussing over monetary matters, the deputies should discuss all the major issues confronting Hungary. Kossuth's speech can be considered the inaugural address of the revolution. The next day, it was translated into German by sympathizers and distributed in Vienna, creating immense excitement. During the next few days, the great cities of the monarchy were infecting each other with news of their own revolutionary agitation. The impetus had come from France and Italy; the movement had now become self-generating.

In his address, Kossuth voiced most of the demands that were to become laws a few weeks later. When the Upper House of the Diet engaged in its usual delaying tactics to soften the radical demands of the Lower House, Kossuth easily persuaded the deputies to send an Address to the Throne directly to Vienna. A delegation was selected that included Kossuth and the other greats of Hungarian politics. However, by the time the delegation reached Vienna, on March 15, the old order had virtually collapsed. Two days earlier, revolution had broken out in the imperial capital: mass delegations marched on the imperial palace to present their non-negotiable demands; workers in the suburbs set fire to factories and demolished the hated machines; and bloody encounters took place in the city between demonstrators and soldiers. Reacting to all this, the court dismissed Chancellor Metternich, as well as the police minister and the Hungarian chancellor. The attempt to turn these men into scapegoats did not help much, nor did the emperor's promise to grant a constitution. Meanwhile, news of disturbances was coming in from Milan, Prague, and Berlin.

While the Viennese public celebrated their new hero, Kossuth, and his compatriots, revolt broke out in Budapest, Hungary's unofficial capital (the administrative capital was still Pozsony). Led by a few radical intellectuals, with Sándor Petőfi, Hungary's greatest poet, foremost among them, a large crowd made up of students and the hitherto peaceful burghers seized the university and City Hall. The crowd then marched on the building of the Viceregal Council demanding the abolition of censorship, the release of political prisoners, the recognition of a revolutionary Committee of Public Safety as the sole authority in the city, and the neutrality of the imperial-royal military garrison. The Viceregal Council, thoroughly cowed, granted everything. The great day concluded with the release of Hungary's only political prisoner, a radical journalist.

Hungarians tend to overestimate the importance of the events of March 15 in Budapest. In reality, their significance was mainly symbolic: the people had taken matters into their own hands. The Budapest Committee of Public Safety, composed of radical intellectuals, burghers, and two of Kossuth's representatives, did not even control Budapest, and the committee gradually became less and less radical. Developments continued to be guided by the Pozsony Diet, especially by Kossuth, who used the Budapest disturbances as a card to play in negotiations in Vienna. He himself never submitted to the authority of the radicals.

On April 16, the Hungarian delegation in Vienna and the archdukes Louis and Francis Charles, who acted in the name of the emperor-king, began to bargain for a compromise. This was very much in the tradition of Hungary's relations with her Habsburg rulers, except that this time the Hungarians had the upper hand. Everything seemed to militate in their favor: the total bewilderment of the simple-minded, epileptic ruler, Ferdinand V; the limited intelligence of the two archdukes; the confusion and conflicting opinions of the court officials; the popularity of the Hungarians in Vienna; the bad news from all parts of the monarchy; and the fact that troops had been withdrawn from the capital to avoid further bloodshed. On the other side, the Hungarians mustered a seasoned political leadership, now in temporary unity, ranging from the suddenly optimistic Count István Széchenyi to the daring Kossuth. The latter knew better than anyone how to mix threats with declarations of undying loyalty and gratitude to the throne.

On March 18, the State Conference in Vienna approved the appointment of Count Lajos Batthyány, a progressive member of the Upper House, as Prime Minister of Hungary and entrusted him with the task of forming a cabinet. At the same time, Palatine Archduke Stephen was made the king's plenipotentiary in Hungary. Subsequently, this Hungarian-born Habsburg prince did his best to serve both his family and the Hungarians. For his pains, he would later be called a traitor by both sides.

Only in one respect was the court able to counteract Hungarian pressure. On March 23, the king appointed Colonel Josip Jelačić as ban of so-called civil Croatia-Slavonia. Subsequently, Jelačić was made a two-star general and put in charge of the Croatian-Slavonian section of the Military Border. By promoting this Austrian officer, who was supremely loyal to the ruler but also a Croatian patriot, the court hoped to secure the loyalty of the Croats. This was absolutely essential, for the Croatian border guards, the famous *Grenzer*, were among the monarchy's best soldiers. Without the Croatian units now serving under Field Marshal Count Joseph Radetzky, the Italian provinces of the Habsburg Monarchy would have been lost. As far as Habsburg-Hungarian relations were concerned, Jelačić's appointment was the beginning of a great tragedy. Jelačić hated the Hungarian "radical lawyers" of the Kossuth type, and five months later he would invade Hungary with his Croatian troops, initiating the Austro-Hungarian war.

Aside from the Jelačić affair, there were to be no more contretemps for Kossuth and his friends. The unfortunate king, wishing to be left alone, signed almost everything that was put before him. Kossuth and Batthyány drafted the text of royal decrees, which the king or Palatine Stephen would then sign.

In the second half of March, the Diet in Pozsony worked feverishly to pass new laws. Bills were generally drafted by Kossuth, but Deák, Batthyány, or Széchenyi were scarcely less active in proposing legislation, promoting it, and smoothing out differences. There was occasional trouble with the reluctant archdukes and the Austrian government in Vienna, but by early April, the work was done. On April 11, the king solemnly closed the most fruitful Diet in Hungarian history. Soon thereafter, the deputies went home with printed copies of the thirty-one "April Laws" in their baggage.

The new constitution, which is what the thirty-one new laws really were, attempted to provide for the basic needs of a nation bent on modernization. The constitution made clear that Hungary was a constitutional hereditary monarchy with a king whose extensive rights were curtailed by a government responsible to an annually convened parliament. The monarch continued to be responsible for war and foreign policy; he alone could make the important appointments, but none of his decisions was to be valid without the signature of a minister. Hungary continued in union with the other kingdoms and provinces of his majesty, but only as long as the king upheld the rights and liberties of his loyal Hungarian subjects. Parliament was to consist of an upper house, which included the titled nobility and the high dignitaries of the realm, and of a lower house made up of deputies popularly elected for three-year terms. Hungary was to have her own army, militia, administration, and judiciary. All citizens were equal before the law, as were all religious denominations (hitherto the Catholic church alone had enjoyed full privileges), except for the Mosaic (Jewish) faith. Taxation was made general and proportional (previously the nobility had paid no taxes); all estates, churches, nations, and corporations lost their special privileges; and the franchise was given to all who, by virtue of their profession, position, or income, had a stake in the stability of society. All peasants were given their personal freedom, and former urbarial peasants were granted full ownership of the lands they held; patrimonial jurisdiction, labor services (corvée), tithes to the church and the landowners, and all payments in kind and cash on former servile lands were abolished; entailment and other traditional restrictions on the free flow of goods and labor were suppressed; and citizens could live where they wished and engage in any profession. The hitherto church-controlled university was placed under state supervision; provisions were made for the rapid development of the economy and transportation network; arbitrary arrest and detention were forbidden; trial by jury for political crimes was introduced; and the inviolability of person and property was guaranteed.

Naturally, not everyone was satisfied with these "April Laws." Nor were the laws perfect from the point of view of contemporary liberalism. Still, they were better than other contemporary Central European constitutions. For instance, the restricted Hungarian suffrage was more generous than the one that the reputedly quite radical Prussian revolutionary assembly adopted in the same year. The constitution did not grant full equality to the Jews, but this had been withheld only out of fear of anti-Semitic excesses. (In reality, the Hungarian government would treat the Jews most fairly, which they repaid by being among the most ardent followers of Kossuth.) Nor did the constitution grant absolute freedom of the press. This, however, did not prevent the flourishing of periodical literature, some of which advocated the most extreme views and wildly attacked the government. The constitution did not fully abolish peasant obligations. Those considered to stem from property relations, rather than feudal rights, were left unchanged. Thus, hundreds of thousands of peasants who held parts of their lord's demesne in private contract were not given full ownership of their plots. This was understandable: one would not expect a group of landowners legislating in the Diet in the name of free enterprise to give up what, according to the same principle, was their own property. The purpose of the economic and social reform was to free both labor and goods from the chains of feudalism, not to encroach on property rights. It was astonishing enough to see these landowning nobles freely surrender their historic privileges in exchange for the state's vague promise of financial compensation sometime in the future.

The constitution had other shortcomings of a more practical than an ideological nature, though this did not make them less grave. The king's privileges were threatened by the special status granted the palatine, who might one day be a Hungarian rather than a Habsburg archduke. The competencies of the "minister near his majesty" were not specified; the Hungarians would regard him as their foreign representative, dealing with Austria and even foreign powers. Since Austria now also had a foreign minister, this meant that the Habsburg monarchy would have two foreign ministers, two foreign services, and, conceivably, two different foreign policies. Nor did the April Laws make clear what the job of the Hungarian minister of finance would be, or how much of the traditional royal revenues would actually reach the court. In any case, the Hungarians refused outright to contribute a single penny toward the astronomical Austrian state debt, which was, after all, also their debt. Finally, there was to be a Hungarian minister of war and a Hungarian army, but no one had the slightest idea how this minister would coordinate his activities with the newly created Austrian minister of war. What troops would belong to the Hungarian army? How would it be recruited? Would it defend only Hungary's frontiers or also those of Austria? Would it be willing to march against the Italian enemy, with whom the Hungarian liberals and radicals ostensibly sympathized?

A monarchy consisting of two foreign services, two financial administrations, and two armed forces was ungovernable. Therefore, it was only a question of time before the Hungarians would either make some concessions to sanity, secede from the monarchy, or go to war against Austria.

The trouble was that the Hungarian leaders themselves could not decide whether Hungary should or could stay in the monarchy. Their fear of Russia, the Pan-Slav movement, and peasant or national minority revolts drove them toward a close alliance with the ruler and the Austrian half of the monarchy. Their nationalist ambitions, on the other hand, and their fear that the monarchy might collapse any day, prompted the Hungarian politicians to prepare for complete independence.

The result was confusion, which satisfied neither the Austrians nor the Hungarian nationalists. The best solution, from the Hungarian point of view, would have been for the king to move to Budapest and for the center of the monarchy to shift to Hungary, its most powerful member state. The Hungarians requested this insistently, but the emperor-king's advisors would not hear of it.

There were two more problems, perhaps the gravest of all. The first was that of Hungary's relations with her subordinate state, the Kingdom of Croatia-Slavonia, where Croatian nationalists strove for exactly the same rights and privileges that Hungary had wrested from the king. But whereas Hungary had to negotiate directly with the king and his Austrian advisors, the Croats could eventually go over the head of the Hungarian government to find allies in Vienna. For the time being, the Hungarians, not the Croats, controlled the king, but this situation could easily change.

The second intractable problem was that of Hungary's national minorities, the Germans, Slovaks, Ruthenes, Romanians, and Serbs. Together, these groups would make up an absolute majority of the population, following Transylvania's anticipated union with Hungary. The constitution had nothing to say about the national minorities, except to confirm that Magyar would be the language of legislation and administration throughout the country. This was understandable in view of the prevailing conviction that granting special rights to the minorities would help restore the despicable feudal system of local or corporate privilege. Furthermore, contemporary liberals were unable to distinguish between state and nation. They were inspired by the French revolutionary principle of one nation in one state and could not understand that Central Europe was quite different from France. The old conservative practice knew only subjects who were free to use their vernacular and live according to their tradition as long as they were loyal to the monarch. The new, centralized, liberal state demanded that its citizens swear loyalty to the tri-colored national flag. Unfortunately for the Hungarians, the national minorities in the country had also experienced their own liberal-national ferment, inspired partly by the Hungarian example. Soon they would clamor for their own constitutions and their own national liberty. The Croats, for instance, would go as far as to demand their own national army and their own foreign service. To have granted such demands would only have multiplied these institutions within the monarchy. At the same time, the national minorities were perfectly ready to disregard the national claims of other minorities living in their own midst. The situation was becoming untenable. The only question was whether these problems could be solved without recourse to arms. For several months, a peaceful resolution of this crisis still seemed possible.

Revolutions Against the Revolution, April–August 1848

In the spring and summer of 1848, the Habsburg monarchy had no real government. In May, the emperor and the court fled to Innsbruck in Tyrol to escape the Viennese revolutionaries, many of whom demanded that Austria meld with the united German national state now forming at Frankfurt. The Austrian government, revolutionary in origin but not in spirit, remained in Vienna, but it was overshadowed by the local student organizations and other democratic committees. In Prague, a National Committee claimed authority over the Czech lands. In Hungary and Transylvania, several national committees sprang up in defiance of the new Hungarian government. Northern Italy was in a turmoil, and so, to a lesser extent, were the Polish and Ruthenian inhabitants of Galicia. Unconditional loyalty to the Habsburg cause seemed to be concentrated in the army, but its troops were dispersed all over the empire. Meanwhile, the Hungarian government demanded that all regular army units stationed in Hungary, Transylvania, and Croatia take their oath to the Hungarian constitution, irrespective of their nationality or territorial origin. Only momentarily stunned, the officer corps or, rather, a handful of generals, began to think of the restoration (better to say "creation," for such a thing had never existed) of a unitary monarchy. The generals were determined to do this in defiance, if necessary, of the written orders of his majesty.

It boded ill for the revolutionary movements everywhere that Field Marshal Radetzky, the best of the army commanders, was able to keep his troops well in hand. His so-called "Italian Army," made up of Austro-Germans, Croats, Hungarians, and members of the rest of the monarchy's many nationalities, did not waver in its loyalty to the imperial cause. (Only some of the Italian troops defected, as did most of the Austrian fleet, which went over to Daniele Manin's revolutionary Venetian republic.) Attacked by both the Italian revolutionaries and the regular forces of the Kingdom of Sardinia-Piedmont, Radetzky withdrew his army from Northern Italy into the Quadrilateral, a system of mighty fortresses south of the Alps. There he ignored urgent requests from the Austrian government to make concessions to the Italian revolutionaries. Instead, he prepared for a counter-offensive. Radetzky's triumphant campaign in the summer of 1848 would be a signal to other Austrian generals to begin the elimination of local revolutionary forces everywhere.

Radetzky and the other generals counted on the mutually conflicting claims of the mostly aristocratic or middle-class revolutionaries and on the relative unpopularity of the latter among the lower classes. The peasants, who constituted perhaps 80 percent of the population of the monarchy, had their own grievances, but they were generally not against the dynasty. Rather, they expected the redress of their complaints from the near-mythical figure of the Father-Emperor. This had always been the peasants' tradition when subjected to the exactions of the local bureaucracy or landowners. Back in 1846, when Polish revolutionary nobles and intellectuals mounted a revolt in Galicia against Habsburg authority, the local Polish peasants busily cut down the nobles or brought them to the Austrian officials. When questioned, the peasants quietly insisted that they themselves were not Poles but "imperial peasants." The Poles, they explained, were the gentlemen. Now, in the spring of 1848, when reforms were introduced everywhere to improve the condition of the peasants, the rural population understood the reforms to come, not from the revolutionary assemblies, but from the emperor. He was, in their eyes, the only solid point in a world gone mad; he would—they claimed—defend their newly won rights. The peasant masses—with the possible exception of the Magyar peasantry—rallied behind the throne. The generals would certainly not have been able to act without the dedication of the peasant soldiers in their army.

This confrontation occurred later, in the summer of 1848. For the time being, all the various authorities and committees distributed conflicting orders and exhortations in the name of the emperor or the king. Few bothered to obey, partly because many people were unaware that the emperor and the king were one and the same person.

In the spring of 1848, the new Hungarian government faced a multitude of problems. As early as April 12, news came of restiveness in Croatia and among the Serbs, of revolutionary agitation on Hungary's southern and eastern borders, and of anti-Semitic disturbances in Hungary proper. It was absolutely necessary to set up the new administrative machinery and organize the police force, but the funds for this were nonexistent. The Hungarian treasury was empty and to expect to collect much in taxes and duties under the chaotic circumstances was unrealistic. Kossuth, as minister of finance, undertook to create something out of nothing, and while he accomplished near-miracles, ultimately, he was forced to resort to the time-honored practice of destitute governments: simply to print money. This in turn, led to grave trouble with the Austrian government, which denied the Hungarians' right to issue their own currency. The revolution in March had started with a panic over banknotes; the war with Austria was likewise to begin in September with a dispute over money.

Defense forces had to be organized. The new Hungarian minister of war, Colonel Lázár Mészáros, was still with Radetzky's army in Italy. It was Prime Minister Batthyány who took steps to ensure the return of the regular troops originating from Hungary and for the creation of a new, national army. Eventually, the Austrian minister of war sent back several so-called Hungarian regiments, even though Hungary gave up none of the troops stationed in the country. This was only one of several developments testifying to the Austrian government's earnest desire to get along with the Hungarians.

The regulars, however, were few in number. Nor were they always reliable, especially because their officers showed little sympathy for the Hungarian "separate way." Batthyány found a solution in setting up a special force within the National Guards, a civilian militia that had come into existence in the spring of 1848 in order to defend life and property. The National Guards were a characteristic creation of the Springtime of the Peoples, but as a national defense force they were virtually useless. Batthyány assembled the best and youngest among them into a Permanent National Guard, soon to be called *honvéd*, or Defenders of the Fatherland. The call for the creation of ten honvéd battalions went out on May 16. Their officers were recruited from among regular army officers who had retired or resigned from service. This small force was the nucleus of the national honvéd army that was to fight against Austria together with regular army units loyal to the Hungarian government.

There was trouble enough to justify the creation of an armed force. On April 19, for example, apprentices in Budapest looted Jewish-owned shops and brutalized the city's Jewish population. The mob was dispersed by army regulars and the National Guard. Then, on April 21, the religious leader of the Serbian minority in southern Hungary, Metropolitan Josef Rajačić, called a Serbian national congress in his metropolitan city without prior consultation with the Hungarian government. On the same day, the Saxon national *Universitas*, the organization of the Saxon-German inhabitants of Transylvania, sent a memorandum to Ferdinand protesting the planned unification of Transylvania with Hungary. Four days later, Ban Jelačić ordered the Croatian authorities to break all contacts with the Hungarian government, their constitutional superior. On May 10, Budapest radicals organized a demonstration against the imperial-royal military commander of central Hungary, whom they accused of hiding arms from civilians. Regular troops attacked the demonstrators, resulting in one death and several other casualties. The Budapest radical press was enraged and virtually declared war on "perfidious Austria." On the same day, a Slovak National Congress in northern Hungary demanded wide-ranging national autonomy for the Slovaks. A few days later, the Serbian National Congress under Rajačić demanded even greater autonomy and acclaimed a Habsburg army lieutenant as commander of the Serbian national forces. On May 15–17, a Romanian National Assembly in Transylvania demanded extensive social reforms on behalf of the peasantry and, not surprisingly, national autonomy for the Romanian minority. On June 2, an international Slavic Congress opened in Prague, where orators branded the Germans and the Hungarians as the mortal enemies of Pan-Slav unity.

Caught up in a turmoil that began to resemble that facing the Austrian government since early March, the Hungarian government did not panic, thereby proving that Hungarian sovereignty was no fashionable invention but part of an old tradition. The men in charge of Hungarian affairs had had long practice in running their own estates as well as county administrations. Batthyány, who in these early months was more in control than Kossuth, understood clearly that the problem lay in the South, with the Serbs, who had a long tradition of religious autonomy, and with the Croats, who had their own state. The worst problem was presented by the armed border guards in Serbian and Croatian territories. Because Hungarian influence still prevailed at court, Batthyány obtained the signature of the king, first to condemn Jelačić and then, on June 10, to deprive him of all of his offices. Jelačić, who also had friends at court, ignored the royal decrees.

Worse was to come. On June 12, the Serbs of southern Hungary rose in armed revolt against the revolutionary Hungarian regime. Palatine Stephen ordered regular army units and the National Guard under a Habsburg general against the Serbs, who were led by a lieutenant of the same army. In the first encounters, the general suffered ignominious defeat. The Serbian rebels, who had been joined by regulars and freebooters from the neighboring Serbian principality, looted and burned the non-Serbian villages of southern Hungary. The Habsburg army officers had had no compunction about leading imperial-royal regulars against such "bandits," but the officers were in for a surprise because the best troops among the "bandits" turned out to be imperial-royal Border Guards led by Habsburg army officers. The Serbs flew the flag of the emperor-king alongside the Serbian national flag. Thus began the most curious of all wars, in which troops on both sides flew the same flag, claimed loyalty to the same ruler, and treated their opponents as traitors and rebels. Battlefield promotions and decorations for bravery were handed out in both camps in the name of Ferdinand and, incredibly, he subsequently confirmed some of them. Many officers believed sincerely that his majesty was on their side; others were Magyar or Serbian nationalists; the majority were desperate and confused. Officer after officer begged the Austrian and Hungarian ministers of war for permission to remain neutral in the conflict or to be transferred to Radetzky's Italian army where the issues were clear. The two ministers simply instructed the officers to do their duty, whatever that might have been.

The mutual reluctance of many combatants did not prevent the war in the South from deteriorating into general brutality. In the extraordinary ethnic mosaic of the banat (present-day Vojvodina in northern Yugoslavia), where Serbian, Hungarian, Romanian, German, Slovak, and Bulgarian settlers of the Catholic, Orthodox, and Protestant faiths had lived in peace for centuries, people were massacring one another in the name of nationality. The primary responsibility for this bloodbath lay with Serbian and Hungarian radical politicians, who recklessly incited the peasants against each other. The war in the South dragged on until the fall, when it melted into the general war.

Meanwhile, the Hungarian government had moved to Budapest and there organized the parliamentary elections provided for by the constitution. The elections were held in June under the new suffrage, but, of course, voting stations could not be set up everywhere. The elections brought no surprises. The Hungarian noble deputies were returned en masse; the peasantry and the national minorities received only a handful of seats. The chief losers were the unconditionally pro-Habsburg conservatives, who lost all their seats. During the same period, the union of Transylvania with Hungary was proclaimed in Kolozsvár, over the protests of the Transylvanian Saxon and Romanian representatives.

Most Hungarians were convinced, quite wrongly, that the Serbian national revolt was due to the machinations of the imperial court. This feeling provided all the more reason for indignation when the king requested military assistance from the newly opened Hungarian parliament against the Italian revolutionaries. His appeal caused an uproar. The moderate deputies argued that Hungary could not expect any assistance from his majesty against the Serbs and the Croats unless the country gave him assistance against the Italians. The radicals claimed that the Italians were fellow freedom-fighters and that, in any case, no Hungarian soldiers could be spared. The result was a compromise resolution that satisfied neither the king nor the Hungarian radicals. In the controversy, most members of the cabinet supported the moderates, but it was Kossuth who had the ear of the deputies, and he refused to say either yes or no to the Austrian request. Instead, he delivered a flaming address, on July 11, on the danger to the fatherland and persuaded the deputies to vote a high credit for the creation of a great national army.

The country was rushing headlong toward a break with the court and the Austrian government. These two had not always been in agreement in the past, but now they began to act in unison against the Hungarians, whom they accused of fatally endangering the unity of the monarchy. Unfortunately for the Hungarians, European developments had turned against them. The French government proved peaceful despite its internationalist revolutionary slogans. In any case, it was busy exterminating its own radical opposition. The Polish revolutionary effort had come to naught. The radical uprising in Prague had been suppressed in mid-June by General Prince Alfred Windisch-Graetz, one of the most conservative aristocrats in the monarchy. Windisch-Graetz now clamored for the right to deal first with the Vienna radicals and then with the Hungarians. In Vienna itself, the burghers began to tire of the turmoil, which was bad for business, and they begged the emperor to return to his capital.

On July 25, at Custozza in northern Italy, Field Marshal Radetzky smashed the Piedmontese army. Two weeks later, King Charles Albert signed a humiliating armistice. The Hungarians found themselves almost alone on the international scene. They now made the great mistake of declaring, on August 3, that if there was a war between Austria and the Frankfurt assembly (which represented the dream but not the reality of a united, liberal Germany), Hungary would not help the king. This was an outright denial of Hungary's constitutional obligations and should have been followed by Hungary's secession from the monarchy. Kossuth, however, wanted no such thing; instead, he again urged the king to set up his residence in Budapest.

The government received its reply on August 31, when the king transmitted a memorandum of the Austrian government, along with one of his own. In those memoranda the Austrians argued that the Hungarians had violated the Pragmatic Sanction (see chapter 10) by setting up their own ministries of finance and war. The Austrians and the king now demanded their dissolution.

The Austrian government, born in a revolution, cut a rather poor figure in accusing the Hungarians of being revolutionary, and the king himself had signed the articles of the new Hungarian constitution. Nonetheless, the Austrians were correct in arguing that the situation had become untenable. The Hungarians should have taken one course or the other; instead, they offered almost complete sovereignty to Croatia. This was a generous move, but it changed nothing in Austro-Hungarian relations. Batthyány and Minister of Justice Ferenc Deák now went to Vienna, where the court had returned in August, but as they brought no offer of submission, they achieved nothing.

Under the pressure of events, Széchenyi suffered a nervous breakdown and was taken to a mental asylum near Vienna. Prince Pál Esterházy, Hungary's foreign minister and the country's greatest landowner, had long ago broken away from the government. Now other ministers, among them Baron József Eötvös and Ferenc Deák, began to retire from governmental functions. Batthyány remained at his post, still hoping for a compromise, while Kossuth was determined to lead the nation whatever happened.

On September 11, events took a fatal turn when Baron Jelačić crossed the Hungarian border with thirty to thirty-five thousand rather ill-equipped Croatian troops, heading for Budapest to put an end to what he called "the rebellion in Hungary." The Hungarian government proclaimed Jelačić a rebel and ordered imperial-royal forces stationed in Hungary, as well as honvéd battalions, against him. Once again, Habsburg army officers were expected to lead troops against each other in the name of his majesty. Yet even in this extreme situation, a compromise was not impossible, since, even though Jelačić had received some encouragement from Vienna, not all the court and Austrian governmental leaders were behind him. Unfortunately, however, mutual distrust dictated that instead of a new compromise there would be a war.

Austria Defied, September–October 1848

The news of the Croatian invasion prompted Prime Minister Batthyány to resign, but, at the request of the palatine, he agreed to form a new government. For the next few weeks, he would hesitate between his desire to escape the burden of the growing crisis and his deep personal commitment to the nation. Kossuth alone remained calm, and under his guidance Parliament passed a series of emergency measures. These included authorizing the printing of banknotes; directing all new recruits into the honvéd battalions rather than the regular army; abolishing the tithe on vineyards (thus currying the favor of a large number of peasants); appointing Palatine Stephen commander of the army sent against Jelačić (which meant that an Austrian archduke now was facing an Austrian general); appointing an itinerant parliamentary commission to supervise the archduke and the army; and, finally, on September 21, delegating six parliamentary deputies to supervise their own government. The delegates, who called themselves the National Defense Committee and were headed by Kossuth, gradually came to replace the government. In its origins and function, the committee was very similar to the Committee of Public Safety set up by the French National Convention in 1793 to deal with the emergency of war. Both meant the seizure of executive power by the legislative branch. The National Defense Committee was slated to remain in office, under Kossuth, until April 1849, when Hungary's independence would be formally established and a new regular cabinet formed.

Palatine Stephen attempted to negotiate with Jelačić, but his efforts came to naught. He then resigned from all his offices and left the country, pursued by the curses of the Hungarian radical press. The Hungarian army, a motley little force of regulars, honvéd, and National Guards, saw itself abandoned by one commander after another and was in continual retreat. Finally, on September 29, it made a stand under the command of General János Móga. The battle of Pákozd, fought some thirty miles southwest of Budapest, was little more than a major skirmish. Nonetheless, it became a milestone in Hungarian history. Historians rightly characterize it as Hungary's Valmy (after the artillery duel in eastern France in September 1792, where the French revolutionary army stopped the invading Austrians and Prussians). At Pákozd, the Hungarian forces stopped Jelačić, proving that the new national army was able and willing to fight. There followed a temporary armistice between the "Royal Hungarian" and the "Imperial-Royal Croatian" armies, which Jelačić used to beat a hasty retreat in the direction of Vienna to join forces with Prince Windisch-Graetz.

The Croatian invasion might simply have gone down in history as a ludicrous incident in the ludicrous circumstances that marked the monarchy at that time, but for the catastrophic events that took place about the same time in Budapest. On September 25, the king withdrew his confidence from Batthyány and appointed a Habsburg general of Hungarian origin, Count Franz Philipp Lamberg, commander-in-chief of all the Habsburg armed forces in Hungary. Lamberg's appointment was illegal because it lacked the signature of a Hungarian minister, yet it was meant to put an end to the internecine struggle in the country. Lamberg was not unsympathetic to the Hungarian cause; as commander-in-chief he might have been able to separate the two hostile camps. Batthyány himself was eager to talk to the general, but because of a series of misunderstandings, the two were unable to make contact.

When the appointment of Lamberg was made known, Kossuth returned immediately from a recruiting trip in the countryside and, on September 27, caused

Parliament to issue an inflammatory declaration denouncing Lamberg as an intruder and a traitor. On the following day, while Lamberg, alone and in civilian dress, was searching for Batthyány in Budapest, he was recognized by the mob and hacked to death. Although Parliament subsequently decried the event, while attempting to place most of the blame on Lamberg and the Vienna "Camarilla," the die had been cast. The liberal Austrian government, which had grown increasingly worried about the intentions of Jelačić and other conservative generals, now bowed to the wishes of the military, who alone seemed able to preserve the monarchy. On October 3, the king issued a later famous manifesto, dismissing the Hungarian parliament, subjecting Hungary to military rule, and appointing Jelačić supreme commander there. Whoever found himself on the Hungarian side after that date risked treatment as a rebel against his majesty. The Hungarian parliament ignored the order of dissolution and enlarged the National Defense Committee. Now only force of arms could decide the conflict between Austria and Hungary.

The second Hungarian revolution, for there is no better term to describe the events of September, led to a new revolution in Vienna—a clear repetition of the events of March. At the news of Jelačić's defeat and the murder of Lamberg, the Austrian minister of war, General Count Theodor Baillet von Latour, decided to send regular troops from Vienna to support the Croatian ban. The Viennese students and other radicals who idolized the Hungarian revolutionaries agitated among the troops to prevent their departure, and on October 6, the Richter Grenadier Battalion defied orders to march in the direction of the Hungarian border. A bloody clash followed between the grenadiers and the demonstrators on one side and troops loyal to the minister of war on the other, the only time in the upheaval of 1848–49 when men of the Habsburg army fired on one another without orders from their officers.

The new Vienna revolt succeeded immediately. Within hours, the fourteen thousand imperial troops were driven out of Vienna, and on the same night (October 6), Latour was hanged from a lamppost. The emperor, the court, and almost the entire Austrian government fled to Olmütz (Olomouc) in Moravia. The Austrian parliament, or Reichstag, remained behind, but power in the city passed into the hands of democratic revolutionary committees. Now both Windisch-Graetz from the north and the Hungarian army from the east began marching toward Vienna, but while the prince managed to assemble seventy thousand well-trained soldiers for the campaign and acted swiftly, the little Hungarian force dragged its feet. In fact, it stopped at the Austro-Hungarian border because General Móga and his officers were reluctant to pursue Jelačić on Austrian soil. Móga still hoped that the nightmare of Habsburg generals fighting each other would somehow come to an end. Kossuth himself gave contradictory orders, for even he felt that it was one thing to defend the fatherland against Croatian rebels and quite another to make war on the king. The Vienna revolutionaries were no more decisive; with a few exceptions, they were reluctant to call in the Hungarian rebels. With the name of the ruler still working magic among his reluctant enemies, precious weeks were lost, and when the

Hungarians finally decided to march into Austria, they were met by the formidable united forces of Jelačić and Windisch-Graetz. At the battle of Schwechat (the site of present-day Vienna's airport), on October 30, the Hungarians were easily put to flight; the Hungarian irregulars, in particular, did not stop until they reached their homeland. A day later, Windisch-Graetz's Czech, Moravian, Galician, and Croatian forces captured and looted Vienna. A few revolutionary leaders were executed, others imprisoned; the city was never to see another revolution.

Immediately after Schwechat, General Móga resigned his command. Kossuth appointed Arthur Görgey general and entrusted this former Habsburg first lieutenant with the task of recreating the by-then almost non-existent Hungarian army. A new and feverish period began in preparation for a regular war between Austria and Hungary.

Withdrawal and Near Defeat, November 1848–January 1849

Arthur Gorgey was barely thirty when Kossuth made him commander of the army facing Windisch-Graetz. Both Kossuth and Görgey came from impoverished Lutheran noble families in northern Hungary, and their mothers were German burghers. There, however, the similarities ended. Kossuth's family eked out a living in the local county administration and as estate managers; Görgey's family had no compunction about serving the emperor-king as officers or officials. Görgey had been trained in a military technical school and began his career in a regiment of Hungarian hussars but quit in 1845 because he could no longer afford his elegant but underpaid vocation. He then tried his luck, in vain, as a professor of chemistry and as an estate manager. The creation of a permanent National Guard in the spring of 1848 came as a blessing to him. He joined up immediately and rose quickly through the ranks as befitted his vigor and military expertise in an armed force woefully short of professionals. Kossuth and Görgey had exactly opposite characters, cause enough for the two to admire and hate each other. They were the two stars in the firmament of the war of independence, yet their personal enmity speeded Hungary's military defeat. The controversy over their wartime politics has split Hungarian society as much as the controversy over the pre-revolutionary politics of Kossuth and Széchenyi. Kossuth was warm, passionate, elegant, and flamboyant; Görgey was cold, sarcastic, puritanical, and contemptuous. In many ways, Kossuth was a typical lawyer, Görgey a soldier through and through.

Unfortunately for Görgey and probably for the country, he also dabbled in politics. In the fall of 1848, he had attracted Kossuth's attention by ordering the execution of a Hungarian aristocrat caught with Jelačić's manifesto in his luggage. By making this supposed revolutionary a general, Kossuth made a wise military choice; Görgey proved himself a brilliant strategist. As a political choice, the appointment was a disaster because Görgey detested Kossuth's supposed radicalism, as he detested all civilians. Kossuth hoped for total military victory;

Görgey was aiming at an honorable peace. The two political goals virtually neutralized one another. Kossuth thought to win the war with an army composed of well-trained regular honvéd and enthusiastic irregulars; Görgey believed that to give arms to amateurs was a waste of money and weapons. The two men therefore clashed on every conceivable aspect of tactics and strategy.

It was only a matter of time before the Austrian army would invade Hungary. Incursions by minor Austrian commanders had begun almost immediately. In the east, the local Austrian commander, General Baron Anton Puchner, took Kolozsvár, the capital of Transylvania, on November 17. In a brilliant move, Kossuth now appointed General József Bem, a hero of the Polish revolutionary movement, as Hungarian commander in Transylvania. Next to Görgey, the Polish Bem proved Hungary's most talented military leader. He fought his war in Transylvania almost independently, and although he was never able to clear that province completely of the Austrian army, he did succeed in protecting the rear of Hungary's beleaguered regime. Without Bem, the war of independence would most likely have been lost as early as the fall of 1848.

The task of organizing the Hungarian war effort fell to Kossuth and Görgey. The two accomplished what foreign observers believed impossible: within a few months, Hungary had an armed force of about 170,000 men, which by the spring of 1849, surpassed the local Austrian forces in numbers and equipment. While Görgey instituted iron discipline in his Army of the Upper Danube and taught his raw recruits the elements of warfare, Kossuth, along with the rest of the National Committee of Defense, the War Ministry under Colonel (now General) Mészáros, and the itinerant governmental commissioners recruited officers and volunteers, enforced military conscription, created a war industry where there had been none, set up military hospitals, organized logistical support, and infused the new national army with enthusiasm. Eventually some fifty thousand old army regulars, including almost one thousand five hundred career officers, found themselves on the Hungarian side. They were complemented by dozens of honvéd battalions, most of them consisting of Hungarian peasants. Interestingly, there were many Poles and Germans among the officers, and some of the honvéd battalions consisted of Polish revolutionaries, Slovak miners, Viennese students, Ruthenes, and even Romanian peasants. (However, the crack honvéd battalions were made up primarily of urban intellectuals and artisans.)

All this took several months. In the meantime, on December 13, Windisch-Graetz's main army crossed the Hungarian border from the west. The Austrian invasion was well-prepared militarily as well as politically. Earlier, on November 21, the liberal Austrian government had been replaced by a new cabinet headed by General Prince Felix zu Schwarzenberg, who brought with him a new political orientation of extreme centralism and absolutism. Schwarzenberg detested not only the Hungarian rebels and the revolutionary intellectuals but also his unruly fellow nobility. He sought to govern with the help of the army, the bureaucracy, and the loyal peasantry, and his ultimate goal was the creation of a great German reich under Habsburg hegemony. His first move was to dispose of Emperor Ferdinand, who had made his own position impossible by granting constitutions to all comers. On December 2, 1848, Ferdinand's nephew, Francis Joseph, took the throne. Only eighteen, this son of Archduke Francis Charles and Archduchess Sophia was under the influence of the generals and the high-ranking bureaucrats. Characteristically, the main roles in the ceremony were played by four soldiers—Schwarzenberg, Radetzky, Windisch-Graetz, and Jelačić; the president of the Austrian parliament was not even invited. The Hungarian parliament rejected the change of rulers and insisted that Ferdinand was still that country's king.

The concerted attack of the Austrian armies from the west, the south, and the north proceeded smoothly, and the Hungarian troops continued to withdraw. (Only Bem, in the east, in Transylvania still had the upper hand.) On December 30, one of the major Hungarian armies suffered defeat at Mór, west of Budapest, and on New Year's Eve, the National Committee of Defense, Parliament, the ministries, and the workers of the banknote and newspaper presses, the arsenal and the armaments factories began to evacuate the capital. Kossuth and most of the offices moved to Debrecen in eastern Hungary, but few doubted that this would be only a temporary asylum. Görgey, who faced double superiority in numbers and whose own officers were deserting en masse, withdrew his forces to the north to recuperate in the mountains there. Before disappearing from sight—because this is what his army actually did—he issued a manifesto at Vác on the Danube on January 4, challenging the right of the National Defense Committee to govern and asserting the loyalty of his army to the king, his army's enemy. Central and eastern Hungary, and with them the Hungarian revolutionary government, were left virtually defenseless.

Windisch-Graetz established himself at Budapest, where he received the rather abject submission of many Hungarian authorities, including those of once-revolutionary Budapest. He even received a peace mission sent by the Hungarian parliament, but since the prince demanded unconditional surrender, these peace efforts came to naught. The delegation included Deák and former Prime Minister Batthyány. Deák was allowed to return to his estate, but Batthyány was placed under Austrian arrest. The war appeared to be over, which is what Windisch-Graetz reported to Vienna. The Austrians, however, had underestimated the energy and undaunted optimism of Kossuth, as well as the ability of the Hungarian army to regain the initiative.

Military Success and Political Derring-Do, January–May 1849

Having established itself in great discomfort at Debrecen, a large peasant town in the northeast of the Great Hungarian Plain, the National Defense Committee struggled to rekindle whatever enthusiasm was left in the country. Incredibly, even though the great majority of civil servants had remained in Budapest and submitted to Windisch-Graetz, the ministries were working again within a few weeks, and so was the transplanted war industry. The heart and soul of the effort was Kossuth, who commanded, cajoled, and begged his followers not to

abandon the struggle. Parliament was in session, even though the majority of the
deputies had submitted to the Austrians or sat at home waiting to see which way
the wind would blow.

Historians have speculated on whether or not during this period Hungary was
a dictatorship. Formally, given the fact that Kossuth and the rest of the committee governed by decree, there was a dictatorship. Yet parliamentary debates
remained acrimonious, and the newspapers felt free to criticize the political
leadership. With the Upper House gradually fading into unimportance (most of
its members had not made the trek to Debrecen), the Lower House made clear
to the National Committee of Defense that the latter governed only by the grace
of the deputies. Only Kossuth's position was unassailable: all understood that
his popularity and prestige were the guarantee of continued struggle.

Parliament was divided, roughly, into three groups: a radical left; a non-
descript center, composed of those who obediently followed the dictates of
Kossuth; and a so-called Peace Party. Socially, there was no appreciable difference among the deputies: they were Hungarian nobles, with a sprinkling of titled
aristocrats and commoners among them. Nor were the social programs of these
groups very different. Almost all deputies felt that further social reforms had to
wait until after the war. The radicals, whose best known and most strongly
criticized leader was László Madarász, the head of the postal service and the
police, clamored for complete Hungarian political independence, the extension
of suffrage, and revolutionary terror. The Peace Party, one of whose leaders was
Pál Nyáry, a former radical and now a colleague of Kossuth in the National
Defense Committee, insisted on dynastic loyalty and opposed revolutionary justice (which, as they understood all too well, would be directed mainly against
them). Kossuth played one group against the other and in general succeeded in
keeping above the melée. His problem was not Parliament but the army, in
which a series of momentous events were taking place.

At the end of January, Görgey's army materialized seemingly from nowhere
and, breaking through the Austrian ring in northern Hungary, joined the forces
that Kossuth had put together in the northeastern part of the country. This was
Görgey's most brilliant campaign, one which earned the admiration of, among
others, Friedrich Engels. During the same period, Hungarian forces were withdrawn from southern Hungary to join the main army, which was preparing for a
general counter-offensive. Surprisingly, Kossuth now appointed a Polish general,
Count Henryk Dembiński, commander-in-chief of the army. Bem's appointment
in Transylvania had been a stroke of genius on Kossuth's part; Dembiński's
appointment was a mistake. Not only was he incompetent, but one more Polish
officer at the head of the Hungarian forces made it easier for the Austrians to
propagate the myth of the Hungarian war of independence as an international
radical, even communist, conspiracy.

Dembiński's appointment was a slap in the face for Görgey, who accepted the
humiliation, though only temporarily. On February 26 and 27, at Kápolna,
northeast of Budapest, the main Hungarian army clashed with the Austrians and
was defeated. The battle, even though lost, served notice to the world that the

Hungarian war was far from over. In fact, Windisch-Graetz had made a capital error by virtually abandoning the campaign after his capture of Budapest and devoting himself instead to the administrative reorganization of the country. It is interesting to contemplate how things might have developed had this prince had his way in Hungary. Windisch-Graetz was an arch-conservative, which meant that he was willing to respect the pre-war liberties of the Hungarian estates. He distrusted the liberal and radical leaders of the national minorities as much as he distrusted Kossuth. Nor did he support the kind of administrative centralization and modernization favored by Schwarzenberg and the latter's colleague, Alexander Bach, a former Vienna revolutionary lawyer.

Görgey used the Kápolna defeat to discredit Dembiński and depose him in an officers' putsch. It had become clear that most officers trusted only Görgey because he was a Habsburg army professional who opposed the "radical lawyers' clique" in Debrecen, represented the illusion of legality, and was a true leader. For the first, but certainly not the last, time, Kossuth had to bow to the will of the officers. He took petty revenge by withholding the title of commander-in-chief from Görgey, but this only served to envenom relations between the two men.

Early in April, the honvéd army began a major counter-offensive under the effective, if not formal, command of Görgey, and within a few weeks it had liberated a large part of the country. A series of brilliantly fought battles brought the Hungarian army into the eastern part of Budapest. Unfortunately for the Hungarians, the Austrian flag continued to fly from Castle Hill in Buda, the western part of the capital. On April 22, the honvéd came to the rescue of the beleaguered garrison of Komárom, a mighty fortress on the Danube northwest of Budapest. Soon the imperials began fortifying Vienna in expectation of a Hungarian attack.

Could the Hungarians have won the war at this point? It is not very likely. The Austrian forces in Hungary had only been weakened, not annihilated, and Austria still disposed of large manpower reserves. In fact, by late April, the Austrians scarcely had any other opponents than the Hungarians. On March 23, Radetzky had again defeated the army of Piedmont-Sardinia at Novara in northern Italy. King Charles Albert signed a second and final armistice and then abdicated. Now only the Venetian Republic was left in the field, and it was barely able to hold onto the city of Venice itself. A part of Radetzky's victorious army was now hurrying toward the Hungarian border to join other forces being set up by the Austrian high command. There was little chance that Hungary could have imposed her will on Austria, given the latter's greater industrial might, larger army, and the popular support of the empire's Germans and Slavs. In any case, the war was not being decided on the battlefield alone. During the Hungarians' splendid spring campaign, important political events were taking place in both Austria and Hungary that were to determine the outcome of the war, as well as the course of Austro-Hungarian relations for decades to come.

On March 4, Francis Joseph dissolved the Austrian Reichstag, then sitting at Kremsier (Kroměříž) in Moravia, and promulgated a new constitution, known as the Stadion or "octroyed" constitution. It was a mixed piece of legislation, remarkably liberal with respect to civil rights, municipal self-government, and national equality, but also highly centralist and absolutist. To the Hungarians, the Stadion constitution was totally unacceptable, since it detached Transylvania, Croatia-Slavonia, the Military Border, and the Vojvodina from Hungary proper and treated the Hungarians as just one of the many subject peoples of the monarchy. The Hungarians would have done far better had they accepted the Austrian plan of late August 1848 for the reorganization of Austro-Hungarian relations, but now it was too late. Kossuth replied to the Stadion constitution on April 14, when he had the Hungarian parliament in Debrecen proclaim the independence of Hungary and acclaim him its governor-president. "The perfidious House of Habsburg-Lorraine" was dethroned, but it was not decided whether Hungary would remain a monarchy or become a republic.

The Hungarian Declaration of Independence, which clearly took its cue from the American Declaration of Independence, was directed primarily to foreign powers, in the hope that they would come to the aid of Hungary or at least grant her recognition. Nothing of the sort happened. The French president Louis Napoleon (later Napoleon III) was preoccupied with domestic and Italian affairs, and Great Britain, Prussia, and Russia, for diverse reasons, favored the preservation of the Habsburg monarchy. In Hungary, the declaration was universally acclaimed because both the Peace Party and Görgey had been so outraged by the Stadion constitution that they now vied with Kossuth in abominating Austria. Unfortunately national unity lasted only as long as the Hungarian army continued to be victorious, which is to say another six or seven weeks. All in all, the Declaration of Independence made little difference, except to serve as an excuse for Russia to intervene militarily on behalf of Austria. Russia would have intervened in any case; she was only waiting for an Austrian request. The Austrians had hesitated for a long time before taking such a humiliating step. Curiously, it was the panicky generals who finally forced the politicians' hand, even though there was little military reason for the Austrians to deprive themselves of the satisfaction of defeating the Hungarian rebellion on their own.

Back in the winter of 1848–49, General Puchner, the Austrian commander in Transylvania, had solicited the assistance of the Russian forces in the neighboring Danubian Principalities (the core of present-day Romania). The Russians did actually march into Transylvania, only to beat a shameful retreat before General Bem's tiny but heroic army. Thereafter, Tsar Nicholas I, an ultra-conservative believer in the Holy Alliance, made clear to his young "cousin," Francis Joseph, that the Russian forces were ready to march at a moment's notice, but would do so only if there was a direct Austrian appeal and only if the Russians were able to offer massive and decisive aid. Nicholas feared revolution as much as did the House of Austria, especially a Hungarian revolution in which Polish patriots played such a conspicuous role.

On May 1, when Francis Joseph was finally able to bring himself to appeal to the tsar for armed help in "the holy struggle against anarchy," the military situation was the following: in April, as noted above, the honvéd army had liberated the beleaguered garrison of Komárom; the Austrian forces were retreating toward the border, and the road to Vienna seemed to lie open before Görgey's army. Yet, instead of sending his troops in pursuit of the Austrians, Görgey now turned his forces southward in the direction of Budapest, where the Austrians on Castle Hill were still holding on. The siege of Castle Hill lasted three weeks because General Heinrich Hentzi's few thousand Austrians fought very bravely and because Görgey had only a few siege guns. Castle Hill fell, finally, on May 21, but by then it was too late for the Hungarians to do much else except delay the inevitable defeat. On May 9, Tsar Nicholas had solemnly promised aid to Austria, and at the end of the month the reorganized Austrian forces in Hungary got an energetic new commander-in-chief in the person of General Baron Julius Haynau, who had earned a reputation in Italy for brutality and military talent. It was now only a question of time before the combined Austrian and Russian armies would roll over Hungary.

The question has been raised a thousand times why Görgey did not march on Vienna at the end of April to force negotiations on Austria. Görgey later blamed Kossuth for wanting to make a triumphal entry into Budapest and also pleaded the exhaustion of his troops. Kossuth, in turn, blamed Görgey for having played a political double game. Görgey's excuses seem lame, since he had always been only too happy to disobey Kossuth in the past, and the Austrian forces in Hungary were not less exhausted than the Hungarians. In all likelihood, Görgey simply made a great tactical error in turning against Castle Hill. It was his sole mistake in the war, but it was a very bad one indeed. Yet one can also argue that no matter what Görgey had done, the war of independence would have been lost.

Toward Final Defeat, June–October 1849

Following the capture of Castle Hill on May 21, Kossuth made his triumphal entry into Budapest. He was now a true constitutional president. Much of his former quasi-dictatorial power had passed into the hands of the government under Bertalan Szemere, former minister of the interior in Count Batthyány's cabinet. In its social composition and political beliefs, Szemere's ministry was not dissimilar from Batthyány's, except that this cabinet was committed to the complete independence of Hungary. Convinced that the war had been won, the govenment set out to consolidate its power and to restore law and order. This meant, among other things, the abolition of almost all of the recently established revolutionary courts. There was, however, no time to reap the fruits of victory. In mid-June, Field Marshal Prince Ivan Paskievich's Russian forces, some 200,000 strong, began crossing into Hungary from neighboring Poland and the Danubian Principalities. At the same time, Haynau opened his offensive with 175,000 well-equipped Austrians. Against these two armies, the Hungarians could muster only 170,000 troops and one-third as many field guns as their opponents.

The Russian army was still scarcely in contact with the Hungarians when Haynau defeated Görgey in a series of well-planned battles in the vicinity of Komárom. Now it was Görgey's turn to beat a retreat. Once again, he made himself virtually independent of the government, which led to renewed controversies with Kossuth. On July 8, the governor-president, the parliament, and the administration left Budapest again, moving first to Szeged and finally to Arad in southeastern Hungary. The rest of the story is marked by a series of Hungarian defeats at the hands of the Austrians and, more rarely, the Russians. The honvéd forces were simply unable to cope with the overwhelming superiority of their two enemies, especially because the rank-and-file now began to show signs of discouragement. Nor did it help matters that the political and military leadership displayed less and less unanimity. Kossuth's appeal for a national crusade against the invaders fell on deaf ears; military conscription was increasingly evaded; and the population in occupied areas submitted to the enemy. True, Görgey again showed his mettle by his brilliant maneuvering behind the backs of the rather incompetent Russian generals, but all he could achieve was the preservation of his forces intact for the final surrender. The other Hungarian armies, including that of Bem in Transylvania, were defeated one by one.

In the midst of defeat, the governor-president and the government demonstrated indomitable optimism and astonishing energy, registering a number of political successes that offered proof of their truly progressive spirit. On July 14, at Szeged, Kossuth and two liberal Romanian revolutionary leaders signed a *Projet de pacification*, which gave the Romanians in Hungary and Transylvania significant ethnic rights. In exchange, the Romanian politicians promised to set up a Romanian legion to fight on the side of the honvéd army. Things had indeed changed for the national minorities in Hungary. The Romanians, for instance, began to understand that the Russians were at least as grave a threat to them as the Hungarians. Even the Serbs, hitherto unequivocal opponents of the Hungarian cause, came to sense that the new absolutist and centralist Austrian state was no more willing to honor Serbian claims to national autonomy than was the liberal and centralist Hungarian state. On July 28, the Hungarian parliament at Szeged adopted a bill granting hitherto unheard-of ethnic rights to all the national minorities. On the same day, "citizens of the Mosaic faith" were granted equal rights with the other denominations in Hungary. All this came too late to change anything, yet these noble Hungarian gestures were reminders of what the peoples and the religious groups in East Central Europe could achieve if they finally chose to cooperate.

Early in August 1849, all the Hungarian field armies found themselves in, or moving rapidly toward, southeast Hungary. Bewilderingly, Kossuth again made Dembiński commander-in-chief, which led to renewed setbacks and a final and catastrophic defeat, on August 9, at Temesvár, not far from Arad. True, on that day Bem was in charge of the honvéd, but Dembiński was responsible for the army's miserable position. At the Battle of Temesvár, Hungarian losses included several hundred dead and six thousand prisoners; the rest of the honvéd simply headed for home. Only a few dozen of Haynau's Austrians were killed. Now there was only one major Hungarian force left, that of Görgey. It set up camp near Arad, where Kossuth, the parliament, and the government had also found a final refuge.

On August 11, Kossuth resigned his position and appointed Görgey dictator of Hungary. On the same day, Kossuth left Arad for the southern border with a disguise and a false passport. Now it was up to Görgey to put an end to the fighting. On August 13, at Világos (Şiria) near Arad, he surrendered to the Russians eleven generals, 1,426 officers, 32,569 troops, 144 guns and sixty battle flags. The act of surrender took place according to traditional military decorum; still, it was a controversial move that divided Hungarian public opinion for decades to come. By surrendering to the Russians and not to Haynau, Görgey showed his contempt for the Austrians. He and his generals also hoped that the tsar would protect them against the Austrians and might even take them into Russian service. Nothing of the sort happened; Nicholas was able to secure an amnesty only for Görgey. The rest were left to the tender mercies of Haynau and his superiors.

Görgey's surrender must be seen as inevitable. A continued guerrilla struggle, as recommended by Bem, was inconceivable to these former Habsburg regulars and would have only prolonged the general suffering. Nevertheless, Görgey's unconditional surrender had tragic consequences. Unfortunately for future Austro-Hungarian relations and for the monarchy as a whole, Francis Joseph, Schwarzenberg, and Haynau lacked the wisdom and foresight displayed by Emperor Joseph I and his advisors following the collapse of the Rákóczi rebellion in 1711. Instead of attempting an immediate reconciliation on the model of 1711, the Austrian leaders mercilessly punished the Hungarian commanders, as well as a number of civilians. As for Görgey, he had to bear the odium of having handed over his lieutenants to the hangman and the firing squad. He bore the blame, of which he was largely innocent, in dignified silence for the remaining sixty-seven years of his life.

On August 17, Kossuth crossed the Ottoman border at Orsova on the Danube, together with a few thousand Hungarian soldiers, the entire Polish legion, and a number of civilians. As soon as he was on Ottoman territory, he again assumed the title of governor-president, demanded unconditional loyalty from all Hungarians, and denounced Görgey as a renegade and a traitor. The result was the division of the Hungarian public into those unalterably opposed to the House of Austria and those willing to compromise.

Curiously, the catastrophic defeat at Temesvár and Görgey's surrender at Világos did not end the war. A number of fortresses remained in Hungarian hands, and even though most of them surrendered rapidly at Görgey's request, the mightiest of all, Komárom, continued to resist for another six weeks. Its commander, György Klapka, one of Görgey's most able fellow generals and a former Habsburg army lieutenant, fought on, while continuing to negotiate. He ended by achieving an honorable surrender and amnesty for the entire garrison. When Komárom pulled down the Hungarian flag on October 5, the Springtime of the Peoples and the Hungarian War of Independence had come to an end. The following day the execution of the Hungarian revolutionary leaders began.

There can be little doubt that the end of the war came as a relief to the peoples of the monarchy, including most Hungarians. The internal problems of the monarchy, however, had not been resolved. The conflict over its government and Hungary's government, as well as the other nations' right to autonomy continued, if only in the political sphere.

War losses were significant, although not devastating. About fifty thousand Hungarian soldiers and an equal number of Austrians died. The Russian expeditionary forces lost only 543 in battle. On the other hand, Paskievich's army buried 11,028 cholera victims. In fact, Russia derived little benefit from the war. She had neither asked nor received the slightest compensation for her sacrifices and effort. Worse than that, five years later, during the Crimean War, Francis Joseph would repay the tsar's generosity with signal ingratitude.

Material destruction in Hungary was heavy but not irreparable. The damaged localities were reconstructed within a few years. The most pathetic loss was the violent death of thousands of peasants of all nationalities in the worst ethnic conflict in the history of the Danube Basin.

We shall never know whether the war could have been avoided or whether it was worth fighting. One thing is certain, however: the victorious Austrian government would never think of revoking the most noble achievement of the revolution, the emancipation of the peasants and all other unfree persons in the vast lands of the Habsburg monarchy. If only in this, Kossuth and his compatriots had achieved praiseworthy results.

XIII

THE AGE OF NEOABSOLUTISM, 1849–1867

Éva Somogyi

The Establishment of Absolutism in Hungary

The great powers suggested to the Habsburgs, whose victory had been assured by foreign arms, that they seek a negotiated settlement. Tsar Nicholas I warned the young emperor with paternal concern, "Your Majesty has been deceived . . . the instigators must be handled in accordance with their deserts." Nevertheless, the young emperor "rushed into the bloody orgies perpetrated by the weak people who had assumed power." In the months following the Hungarian surrender at Világos, more than a hundred people were condemned to death and more than a thousand to twenty years of prison or forced labor. The official data only give information on those who belonged to the nobiliary estates, whose sentences appeared in the papers of the time. It is not known how many fugitives were executed by the military tribunals, who simply listed them as highwaymen or bandits. However, some forty to fifty thousand officers and soldiers were forcibly inducted into the imperial army and stationed in Austrian provinces, and the leaders and simple soldiers of the revolution fled the country in large groups, creating a massive core of emigres. The horror culminated on October 6, 1849, the anniversary of the uprising in Vienna, when thirteen honvéd generals were executed at Arad. Count Lajos Batthyány, Hungary's first prime minister, shared their fate in Pest.

The sentences produced sharp indignation all over Europe. The British foreign minister, Lord Henry John Palmerston, remarked resignedly that the Austrians knew only one argument, violence. The tsar tried diplomatic intervention to save the life of the generals and took it as a personal affront when his démarche was ignored.

Subsequent generations have been repulsed by the morbid violence of Prince Felix Schwarzenberg, Austrian prime minister, and by the horrifying boast of General Julius von Haynau, commander of the armies in defeated Hungary: "I will hang the revolutionary leaders and will shoot every imperial and royal officer who served the revolution . . . I will shoot hundreds with a clean conscience because it is my firm conviction that this is the only way to set a deterrent example for all future revolutions." But the convergence of character and situation in the Habsburgs' revenge campaign is not enough to explain what happened.

The Hungarian revolution of 1848–49 had shaken the foundations of the Habsburg Empire. The Italian provinces acquired during the Napoleonic wars, Lombardy and Venice, could be given up, and Galicia's desire for autonomy did not distress Austrian politicians. Hungary, however, was different. Hungary was not just a province of the empire; it was half of it. Given the size of its territory, the number of its inhabitants, and its economic, military, and political significance, a great Habsburg power simply could not exist without Hungary. Consequently the Habsburg counterrevolution tried to hold onto Hungary at all costs and sought to rebuild a centralized empire, of which Hungary was to become an integral part.

None of the Habsburg rulers of the late feudal period had ever attempted to abolish the estates-based constitution (Leopold I only suspended it in 1670). Constitutional rule had always been the traditional protection of national rights in a Hungary governed by a foreign ruler.

Now, however, explained Schwarzenberg, the Austrian prime minister, to Francis Joseph, having resorted to arms in their struggle with their king, the Hungarians had "forfeited" their historic rights, their centuries-old constitution, and their special status. This gave the ruler a free hand to erect a unified German state centered at Vienna. The theory of forfeited rights became the ideological justification for the absorption of Hungary into the empire. In accordance with this tenet of the Schwarzenberg-Bach government, absolutist rule in Hungary in the 1850s became less restrained than ever before.

The associated lands, Croatia-Slavonia and Transylvania, were detached and placed under the direct control of Vienna. The central administration also ruled the Serb voivodeship and the Banat of Temesvár, both created to satisfy Serb demands, as well as the military frontier districts that had their own administration. The remaining Hungarian lands were divided into five military districts, which, with some alterations, became the framework for the emerging civil administration also. These districts were headed first by high ispáns, later vice presidents of regencies, who were directly subordinated to the central government. The government expected that, given time, these new administrative units would, on the model of the hereditary provinces, become integral parts of a unified empire.

Schwarzenberg believed that the Habsburg Empire, strengthened by a central administration, would be able to regain its European position. Indifferent to the nationalist trends of the age, he planned to create a Central European economic entity, including the entire Habsburg domain, with its Italian provinces, Galicia, and Hungary. His primary goal was to increase the power of the dynasty, but he also hoped his plan would attract not only the German speakers in the Habsburg state but also those living beyond its borders. After all, his plan offered the

Germans, the strongest nation of the region, political power and economic possibilities.

This plan came to naught. This was partly because Schwarzenberg, who planned for the distant future, died prematurely, but mainly because the other German states and the great powers, England, France, and Russia, were opposed to the increased power and prestige of the Habsburg state. Only the centralized empire became a reality: a bureaucratic-military state based on informers, spies, and a police system that concerned itself with the smallest details of everyday life.

Austrian policy of the 1850s (known as the Bach period, after Alexander Bach, the all-powerful minister of the interior) was characterized by unrestrained absolutism and empire-wide centralization, by a legal system governing civic, economic, and social affairs, and by reaction and reform attempts. The legislature was never called into session, and the self-governing institutions of counties and municipalities were abolished. In this manner the country lost not only its political power, but also all possibilities for making its views known in any legal manner.

The centralizing, Germanizing new Austria was, at the same time, a civic state, which retained the basic achievements of the bourgeois revolution: the freeing of the serfs, the legal equality of citizens, and proportional taxation. The government placed middle-class specialists into offices previously occupied by elected officials and attempted to separate consistently administrative and judicial functions. A series of regulations served to strengthen civil, economic, and social institutions. In 1852, *avicitas* (see chapter 5) was abolished, eliminating the biggest obstacle to the introduction of equality into proprietary law. The introduction, in 1853, of the Austrian Civil Law Code promoted the free disposition of personal property, making the introduction of the cadastral register system (in 1855) necessary to ensure the security of real estate transactions.

These certainly progressive measures, because they were introduced in the interest of the unified monarchy, were disliked in Hungary. It is hard to determine to what extent the resistance was directed against the progressive reforms themselves and to what extent it was a reaction to the absolutist government that introduced them.

Economic and Social Conditions

The freeing of the serfs from their feudal obligations was, without doubt, the greatest achievement of the revolution. Not only was their economic and social status changed, but they became free citizens of the state. The transformation of the entire economy became possible with the freeing of the serfs, who were now able to work for wages. Land became private property and could be bought and sold, thus making possible capitalist developments. Though the serfs were officially liberated in April 1848, the detailed regulations of this very complicated matter had to wait until 1853, when the so-called Labor Statute Patent was issued.

The freeing of the serfs involved the freeing of 14.4 million acres held as fiefs, and the state was to pay compensation for these to the lords. The peasantry also held other lands, whose legal status varied greatly. These included the so-called residual lands (two million acres), consisting of clearings later transformed into arable land, pastures subsequently put to the plow, and so forth. These were not included in Maria Theresa's urbarial registers (see chapter 10), but they had been in the hands of the peasants, who paid feudal dues for them to their landlords. (There were regions where lands of this kind amounted to 20–50 percent of the peasantry's possessions.) According to the patent, the peasants could redeem these lands but had to pay for them. The peasants also worked about 700,000 acres of manorial fields and vineyards (see chapter 8). The patent stiffened the 1848 regulations relating to these lands and left it to the landlords to decide their fate. In fact, it was not easy to determine which lands originated in fiefs and which in manors, although this was crucial in determining the manner of freeing the serfs. The urbaria of Maria Theresa, which served as the basis for determining the status of the land, were not exact, and not every village had one. In Transylvania, where the queen's urbarial regulations had not applied, even these basic documents were missing. Furthermore, the situation had changed drastically during the last century; families had died out, estates had new owners, and so on. What made the distinction between fief and manorial lands even more important was that the division of forests and pastures used by landlords and the serfs alike was based on the size of fief lands. Thus, the determination of the land's type became the basic problem connected with the freeing of the serfs. Only after this issue was settled could it be determined which segments of the estate would be handed over to the peasantry (and only then, often, did they realize how little they had received). The legal suits that arose over land distribution began in the late 1850s and lasted for decades.

According to more-or-less accurate calculations, 1,366,749 peasant families tied to landlords lived in Hungary at the time of the revolution. Almost half of these became free owners of their lands. The remaining 800,000 or so families had been either cotters or servants and did not even own a fraction of a serf-holding or a home. Although, according to rough calculations, the average size of the plots that liberated serfs got out of fief lands was 16.4 acres, this average hides an important fact, for the cotters, who made up more than half of the peasantry, received only a few acres when the serfs were set free. About 1.4–2.8 acres of arable land per family, usually converted pastures or vineyards, allowed them to eke out a living and gave them the illusion that they were their own masters. The poverty-stricken peasant masses were tied by a few miserable acres to the village and its way of life. Escape from this life was very difficult because of the economy of the village and, indeed, the structure of the entire Hungarian economy. Urban industry could not offer an alternative to the poor of the countryside until after the end of the capitalist period.

Throughout the centuries, no socio-economic change in Hungary had affected a larger segment of the population than did the freeing of the serfs and the redistribution of property in the 1850s and 1860s. Yet their liberation did not

alter the balance of the Hungarian landowning system. The large estates remained dominant, with 75 percent of the total population owning only 46
percent of the land.

The freeing of the serfs made the transformation of agriculture possible, but
this did not occur automatically. The peasantry retained the traditional three-
field system, leaving one-third of the land fallow each year, which made only the
growing of cereals possible. Root crops, commercial plants like tobacco or
hemp, and fodder-crops could not be grown in this way because they had to be
harvested at different times. The peasants could grow new crops only in their
small garden plots.

On the lands still owned by the nobility, the liberation of the serfs had caused
problems of a different nature. With the abolishment of corvée, the landlords
had lost most of their labor force, and, even more important, the draught animals, without which the land could not be worked. Corvée had supplied these in
the past. They had to replace these animals and hire permanent farmhands. A
modern agricultural system, based on wage labor was needed. The lords were to
receive the money for this from the state, in compensation for the services of the
serfs. However, there were delays in issuing indemnification debentures and at
first the state paid only interest on them. It took decades for them to be redeemed. When the landlord was unable to find the capital for large-scale
market-oriented production, he either rented his lands out or experimented with
share-cropping. Because of the lack of capital, even the large estates faced difficulties in modernizing, and the uncertainty created by absolutism in Hungary
made the situation even more complicated. Nevertheless, there were some favorable developments. In the 1850s, a cereal boom occurred all over Europe; cereals fetched a high price, and sales were helped by the elimination of the customs
barrier that had separated Austria from Hungary. It should be remembered,
however, that the disappearance of customs barriers was favorable to the country only in the short run. In the long run, it helped to maintain the dominance of
agriculture, primarily extensive cereal production.

Not all nobles owned big estates. Nobles made up an amazingly large segment, 5.2 percent, of the country's population, and of the 130,000 noble families, at most thirty thousand could have owned large or middle-sized estates.
Even before 1848, it was only their privileges that differentiated the remaining
one hundred thousand from the peasantry. They lived like peasants or made a
living as artisans in the villages or as civil servants. When privileges were abolished, a considerable segment of these people became either peasants or members of the petty bourgeoisie.

Of the landowning nobility, about six hundred mostly aristocratic families
had estates of over 8,500 acres; two to three thousand owned at least fourteen
hundred acres; and the great majority, whose wealth varied greatly, owned anything down to sixty acres. The modernization of agriculture was the least difficult for those who possessed around fourteen hundred acres, some of whom
had switched to wage labor in working their lands even before 1848. In the
period of absolutism, they were the first to receive indemnification debentures,

had the least problems in receiving credit, and were in a position to switch to capitalist ways of market production.

The liberal economic policy of the absolutist regime went hand-in-hand with the attempt to create an economically united empire. Hungary became the supplier of raw materials to the more developed western regions of that empire for several reasons. The internal forces of economic development, especially the differing regional economic roles that had developed within the empire throughout the centuries, were reinforced by such measures as the removal of restrictions on entering the various trades, the abolition of internal tariffs, and the introduction of unified monetary and tax systems, all of which were part of a fairly clear economic policy. This division of labor within the empire became even more pronounced later, during the decades of free economic competition.

The most spectacular economic development in Hungary during the years of absolutism was the growth of the railroad network; between 1848 and 1866, it grew from 110 to 1,340 miles. The lines connected the cereal-growing regions of the plains and the livestock-breeding areas east of the Tisza with the capital and, through it, with the European markets. The construction of railroads led to the beginnings of industrialization by attracting much-needed foreign capital and boosting the production of coal and iron in Hungary. Machine industry tried to supply the equipment needed by agriculture and the rapidly growing food processing industry but (in the years under discussion) remained less significant than mining and metallurgy.

Food processing was the leading industry in the first two decades after the revolution. The profits of the cereal boom of the 1850s accumulated in the hands of grain dealers, and the numerous flour mills built in Pest and in the countryside in the 1860s were financed with this money. By 1867, Pest had fourteen large mills, but the smaller localities too had several large enough to work for the export market. The flour export of the monarchy, originating mainly in Hungary, grew from an average of 20,500 tons between 1840–50, to 97,000 tons by 1862 and 440,000 tons by 1869. The number of distilleries also increased significantly. It was also during these decades that sugar refineries switched from sugar cane to the home-grown sugar beet. Although sugar consumption tripled, and the production of the refineries increased tenfold, the importance of the industry declined as a percentage of the monarchy's output. The Hungarian sugar industry faced raw material and capital shortages and was hampered by the imperial tax structure, which was unfavorable to it.

The unified customs area was most detrimental for the textile industry. The peculiar division of labor of the region had been well established prior to 1848. The majority of Hungary's wool harvest found its way to Bohemian and Moravian clothmakers and factories. It was during these decades that cheap cotton goods became popular in Hungary and that factories replaced cottage industry. The new cotton goods factories were either in the Czech lands or in Austria.

In spite of the significant industrial development during the years of absolutism, machines remained a rarity in Hungary. The entire industrial complex used only 480 steam engines, with a total capacity of 8,100 horsepower. The disproportionate development of a single industry—food processing—is another sign of the country's economic backwardness. Of the 480 steam engines, 380 were in food processing plants, with only fifty-three in the iron and metal industry and seventeen in the machine industry. The rest of the trades used none.

The Opponents of Absolutism

The ruthless persecutions in the aftermath of the failed War of Independence left Hungarians hostile to the new order. The situation was exacerbated by the total absence of self-government and free expression, the government's unwillingness to summon the legislature, the abolition of the counties' autonomy, the keeping of records in German by foreign officials, and a police system previously unknown in Central Europe. Furthermore, the military-police state was extremely expensive for the taxpayers.

All of Hungarian society was opposed to the new state structure. Even the conservative aristocracy, which had distanced itself from the revolution and accepted only those laws that Vienna recognized now opposed centralization, Germanization, and the territorial division of the country.

To oppose the new system, the political leaders of the country, the liberal nobility, took their stand in support of the 1848 laws and preached passive resistance. This program was the idea of Francis Deák, who in the 1850s, became the undisputed leader of the Hungarian nobility. Deák was the only remaining liberal leader from the reform and revolutionary periods. Kossuth had emigrated; Batthyány had been executed; and self-accusation had driven Széchenyi into madness. "After the calamitous events of the recent past . . . it would be a mistake to participate in public life even if this were possible," Deák declared. The only duty was "to maintain enthusiastic support for the principle of constitutional rule," meaning adherence to the laws of 1848, and to wait until circumstances became more favorable. Passive resistance became the political program and way of life of the 1850s.

> The rich magnates and the well-to-do nobles, the intellectuals and the citizens have decided that they will not pay their taxes until the executor knocks at their doors. Only those supplies that cannot be hidden will be handed over to the military. People will deny understanding German and will everywhere demand answers and verdicts in Hungarian. Nobody will truthfully report the status of his wealth and income. If anybody is asked a question, the answer has to be—I do not know; if information is sought about a person, the answer has to be—I do not know him; if events have to be verified, the answer has to be—I have seen nothing. The slogan is: detest absolutism and ignore its servants as if they were not living amongst us.

The peasantry awaited the return of Kossuth. For them, his name stood not only for national liberty, but also for the distribution of land. Kossuth took on, in these decades, a mythical status as the protector of the peasantry.

The Hungarian exiles, of whom Kossuth was the undisputed leader, worked on the assumption that a new war of independence could be launched. It was a matter of seeking allies among the Habsburgs' enemies as soon as the Habsburg Empire became involved in a new European conflict. The decade-long exile provided the time to reassess the events of the past. Kossuth and his fellows realized that the outcome of a new war of independence would depend on their ability to gain the collaboration of the other nations in Hungary, who made up slightly more than half of its population. Such was the goal of the draft constitution published in Kütahya, Turkey in 1851. In this draft, Kossuth proposed the free use of languages on the county level and that the nationalities be allowed to establish country-wide national organizations and to elect their national leaders. For Croatia, he envisioned total political autonomy, and he hoped that once the minority rights he proposed were established, the Romanians of Transylvania would demand union with Hungary. "All those living in the country should be free, equal, and brothers," he proclaimed. In accordance with the liberal views of his time, Kossuth believed that a democratic Hungary, whose state structure rested on universal suffrage and extended local autonomy, would attract the nations living on its territory. He also believed that a Hungary organized along these lines would be more equitable to all than one composed of politically autonomous regions, whose population would, inevitably, be mixed.

While several exiled Hungarian leaders, including Count László Teleki, General György Klapka, and Dániel Irányi, had concepts that went far beyond Kossuth's, they were ready for united action when the right moment came, in May 1859, with the outbreak of the anti-Habsburg French-Italian war. Klapka's negotiations with the Romanian prince, Alexander Cuza, were successful. In the agreement, which they reached in May 1859, Klapka promised that if the war were successful, the Transylvanian Romanians would have rights in accordance with the Kütahya constitution and that the people of Transylvania would be allowed to decide by plebiscite the question of union with Hungary. Cuza, in turn, promised to urge the Romanians of Hungary to support the Hungarian uprising. Kossuth negotiated along the same lines in London with the crown prince of Serbia.

Finally, the exiles appeared to have achieved success. Napoleon III, receiving Kossuth in the Tuileries as the recognized leader of the Hungarian nation, promised to send French troops to Hungary. Backed by a Hungarian uprising and the Hungarian Legion, recruited abroad, the French were to fight until the total independence of the country was assured. The next day, the Hungarian National Directory (the Hungarian government in exile) was established in Paris. It included Teleki, Klapka, and naturally, Kossuth. The directory called upon the Hungarian people not to revolt until the call to arms was given and to try to reach agreements with the various nationalities based on the draft constitution.

The backing of a great power was essential to the success of an anti-Habsburg campaign, and Kossuth had prepared the French alliance with great care. Yet just when, after a decade of preparations, it seemed possible to tie the issue of Hungarian independence to a European war, the chance evaporated in an instant. The Austrian forces suffered a decisive defeat at Solferino, and Napoleon III had no further need for the eventual military support of the Hungarians. The French emperor quickly concluded an armistice with the Austrians, disregarding the promises he had made to his Italian and Hungarian allies.

The Liquidation of Absolutism in the Empire

At Solferino, the monarchy lost more than a battle and a province. The battle proved that the system erected with great care since 1849 was not viable. In a military-bureaucratic state, the military had been defeated, and the high-ranking bureaucrats were incapable and financially unreliable. The vacillating Francis Joseph promised rather vague "improvements" to pacify his people and began a series of experiments to transform his empire. These experiments lasted until 1867.

The moderation of the centralized absolutism of the 1850s was not the result of a clearly established policy. The first steps were determined by the extremely difficult financial position of the monarchy, whose credit had to be reestablished. On the urging of his finance minister, the emperor called the Reinforced Imperial Council into session in the spring of 1860. The Imperial Council had been called because the pressure exerted by the bourgeoisie was too strong to resist. Nonetheless, in the council the aristocrats were in the majority. The Hungarian aristocrats, supported by like-minded German and Czech colleagues, became the council's most vocal members, and criticized most vehemently the centralist-bureaucratic system, which had pushed them into the background. The October Diploma, the first "constitutional" experiment in the Habsburg empire since 1849, reflected their concepts.

The diploma restored the local legislative bodies throughout the empire—the *Landtage* in the hereditary provinces and the legislature in Hungary—though their authority was restricted. The imperial budget and legislative measures dealing with military affairs remained in the hands of the Imperial Council, which as before, was not an elected body. Foreign and military affairs remained the unrestricted domains of the emperor.

Although the restriction of the ruler's power and the abolition of centralism began slowly, the October Diploma was, nevertheless, an attempt to pacify Hungary. In reestablishing the autonomy of the legislature and the county administrations and in reintroducing the pre-1848 Hungarian governmental offices, it tacitly recognized the historical separate status of Hungary. Yet the diploma eliminated only those features of absolutism and centralism necessary to pacify the imperial aristocracy and the court circles. It did not go far enough to satisfy those in both halves of the empire who represented the demands of the masses—the liberal nobility in Hungary and the liberal bourgeoisie in the rest of the empire.

Within government circles, the diploma faced serious opposition from the beginning, even from the more or less liberal bureaucratic-centralist group. The minister of finance, Ignaz von Plener, proclaimed: "Without a firmly established unified empire and without an imperial constitution, the financial problems of Austria cannot be solved." After the issuing of the diploma, Plener used every opportunity to frighten the emperor with the spectre of a bankrupt state. Plener and the new minister of state, who had been appointed on his recommendation, Anton Ritter von Schmerling, finally convinced the ruler that the diploma was a mistake. They prevailed upon the emperor to take a new political step, the proclamation of the February Patent of 1861.

Although Schmerling owed his popularity in liberal circles to the fact that, in 1851, he left the government in protest of Schwarzenberg's absolutism, his views paralleled those of his former chief with regard to the European role of the Habsburg Empire. He wanted a centralized Austria under German leadership to play a leading role among the German states. He tried to reconcile this "Greater Austria" concept with his moderately liberal constitutional beliefs.

His constitution, the February Patent, was an attempt to create, for the first time since 1849, an imperial parliament. Each province of the empire, including Hungary, was to send a specified number of delegates to a new 343 member Imperial Council. The February Patent made constitutional government possible because a central legislature is better suited to limit the power of the crown than provincial assemblies dealing only with local issues. Yet at the same time, the patent strengthened the position of an imperial centralized government in its dealing with the provinces. Thus the 1861 patent brought constitutionalism to the empire in a manner that contradicted the principles of Hungarian constitutional theory and historical tradition. This attempt to force representation in the Imperial Parliament on Hungary finally endangered the very concept of constitutionalism.

Hungary in 1860–1861

In convincing his imperial master that the October Diploma had been a mistake, Schmerling had pointed to the bad reception it had received in Hungary. In Hungarian cities, mass protest demonstrations were held in front of governmental offices. Deák and his followers rejected the diploma and continued to demand the reintroduction of the laws of 1848. Yet they also felt that the institutions reintroduced by the diploma—the county assemblies and the legislature—should be utilized to force the reinstatement of those laws. Therefore they gave up passive resistance and became extremely active politically in the counties. Numerous counties proclaimed that taxes introduced by the absolutist government without the legislature's approval were illegal and urged the population not to pay them. In the following months, something like war broke out between the localities that refused to pay their taxes and the military sent to collect them, though the outcome was never in doubt.

In January 1861, the council of ministers had decided to call the Hungarian legislature into session in accordance with the still valid October Diploma. Yet other winds were blowing in Vienna: the Plener-Schmerling concept was gaining ground. The Austrian liberal-bureaucratic ministers were not in the least interested in a compromise with the Hungarians. In thinking back to the spring of 1861, Schmerling later remarked: "My soul was roused to indignation by the numerous concessions that were made to this rebellious nation, which had brought so many troubles to Austria." The situation of Hungarian politicians was very difficult in the spring of 1861. They had a chance to discuss, during the session of the legislature, the conservative constitutional law projects of the October Diploma, yet in Vienna it had already been put aside. It was, therefore, quite obvious that the work of the legislature would lead nowhere. When the Hungarian liberals began to work on their party's platform, they understood that it could not address itself to the problems of the day, but had to be a declaration of principles, serving as guidelines for a future beset by social and political difficulties.

When this important legislature met, Deák took the only possible constitutional position. He rejected the October Diploma, demanded the reintroduction of the laws of 1848 and the reunification of the country, and suggested that the legislature demand the nomination of a responsible Hungarian government. He made it clear that in accordance with the Pragmatic Sanction (see chapter 10), a correlation existed between the joint rule over Hungary and the hereditary provinces on the one hand and the constitutional governing of Hungary on the other. To put it more simply, Deák made it clear that since the eighteenth century, the precondition of Habsburg rule in Hungary, as stated by law, was respect for the constitutional rights of the country. Deák's address to the crown, a masterpiece of logic and composition, was a firm stand on the principle of constitutionality. The major remaining problem before the legislature was to find the means to unite Hungary's various social strata and nationalities; without unity the demand for the laws of 1848 could not be enforced.

In 1860–61 the peasant unrest related to the distribution of feudal lands reached serious proportions. Representatives at the legislative session explained the shortcomings of the relevant laws and urged that the problem be settled as soon as possible. As a whole, however, the legislature was unwilling to listen to the peasantry's demands. When various localities turned to the legislature, asking for redress for unjust court verdicts, the legislature refused to act, pointing out that it was not competent to do so.

During the months following the issue of the October Diploma, several signs indicated that Hungarians and non-Hungarians recognized that they had to cooperate in their struggle against absolutism. In spite of this rapprochement, the Serb Congress of Karlóca in April 1861 demanded the erection of a Serb voivodate with full internal autonomy, and the Slovak Congress in June 1861 at Turócszentmárton (Martin) demanded the establishment of a Slovak district in Hungary. These requests raised the frightening prospect of the country's dismemberment. The nationalities subcommittee of the legislature proclaimed that "all citizens of Hungary, irrespective of their native language, comprise in the political sense only one nation, the Hungarian nation, which is one and indivisible in accordance with the historical concept of the Hungarian state." Thus the *nation* was conceived of as a political collective formed by history and uniting peoples of different languages. What the nationalities wanted was the recognition of their existence as independent nations and the acceptance of the fact that the common fatherland was inhabited by several nations. The nationalities subcommittee made it clear that the various nationalities of the country had equal rights and could freely satisfy their national demands within the limits of the political unity of the country. This principle reflected the liberal position of the times. It was, nevertheless, a great mistake that the legislature refused to discuss those demands of the nationalities that went beyond these limits.

The Road to Compromise

In August 1861, the emperor dissolved the legislature, suspended the counties' autonomy, and introduced a "provisional" administration that resembled that of the 1850s. Yet, neither the oppression nor the determined resistance of the 1850s was reestablished. The voices which counseled reason became more numerous, especially in Hungary.

Hungary's leaders including Kossuth, held that the cause of Hungary's independence must be evaluated in the context of international power shifts. International relations did not then favor Hungary, and the war of 1859 had proved that the great powers would aid the Hungarian liberation movement only for their own gain and only as long as it served their purposes. After 1862 the Italian struggle for liberation was temporarily halted, and in 1863–64, the Russians, with Bismarck's support, suppressed the Polish uprising, in which many Hungarian volunteers participated. Events indicated that national resistance movements had practically no chance to succeed.

In 1862 Kossuth's plan for a Danubian Confederation became public knowledge. It was to consist of Hungary, Transylvania, the Romanian Principalities, Croatia, and possibly even Serbia. The common affairs of the members, including defense, foreign affairs, customs, commerce, and so forth, were to be handled by a federal council, whereas the legislatures, legal systems, and internal administrations of the member states were to remain fully independent of one another. The confederates were to be equal in every respect, with the capital shifting from Pest to Bucharest, Zagreb, and Beograd. The plan included the regulation of the nationality problem of Hungary. Kossuth not only recognized Croatia's right to autonomy but even that of the Transylvanians to decide the question of union with Hungary by plebiscite. He even toyed with the idea of an autonomous Serb region in Hungary. In the rest of Hungary, every county and locality would have decided the question of its official language by voting.

Promoting his plan, Kossuth argued: "It is not a concession, but a mutual and freely accepted alliance. Even if every nation living on the banks of the lower Danube could succeed in uniting all its co-nationals living outside its territory, the resulting states would be second-rate powers with their independence in constant danger, inevitably subject to foreign influences. Should the Hungarians, Southern Slavs, and Romanians accept the plan, they would create a first-rate, rich, and powerful state of thirty million inhabitants, whose influence in Europe would be great." Kossuth's Danubian Confederation plan was an attempt to block a compromise with the Habsburgs. However, it had the opposite effect. A liberal politician explained that if even Kossuth believed that the Hungarians could not stand alone then it was "better to move to Vienna and live with Germans than it is to go to Beograd and associate with Serbs." Another expression of the same sentiment stated that "the price of peace with Austria and the ruling house is not as steep as the one demanded by the nationalities, which some clumsy revolutionaries appear to be willing to pay." The landowners had another reason to advocate a compromise with Vienna. They were afraid of the peasant movement all over the country that resulted from the land distribution problem. They hoped, furthermore, that the regulation of the political situation would bring economic opportunities too. The voice became louder and louder of those who had had enough of patient suffering and who dreamed of position, prestige, and well-paid employment.

The Austrians also began slowly to change their position concerning a compromise. Schmerling wanted to build a centralized constitutional monarchy under German leadership. The Germans of Austria were at first in favor of a policy that would have brought them constitutional rule and an absolute majority in Parliament. They hoped that as time passed, constitutional provisions would be expanded and that a truly liberal constitutional state would evolve, including a responsible ministry and regulation of the churches. As the years rolled by, it became clearer and clearer that a liberal centralized monarchy could not be realized. The Hungarians continued to reject the idea of a centralized state, the 1861 legislature refused to send deputies to the sessions of the central parliament, and while the German deputies in Vienna discussed the ways and means to develop constitutionalism further, absolutism reappeared in Hungary. Schmerling even revived the almost forgotten theory that Hungary had lost her rights in 1848–49. In 1863, the Czechs and, a little later, the Poles left the Vienna parliament in protest against the conditions in Hungary and numerous other grievances. The central parliament planned by Schmerling had failed. It became obvious that while it was possible to centralize the empire by disregarding the history, traditions, and national aspirations of all provinces, this could not be done with the cooperation of the elected deputies of the various peoples. It could only be done, as in the 1850s, with the help of arbitrary justice, military might, and informers. Even the Austro-German bourgeoisie was disappointed. Its hope that an imperial constitution could solve the empire's problems had proven unjustified. The Austro-German liberals began to understand that the conditions prevailing in the other half of the empire were of importance for them too. They realized that, as the Hungarians had understood since 1848, constitutionalism had a chance only if it was introduced in Austria and Hungary at the same time.

In spite of its internal contradictions, Schmerling's policy remained the first attempt to introduce constitutionalism into Francis Joseph's empire. The emperor disliked it and only efficient rule could have compensated the ruler for the curbs placed on his absolute rights. When Schmerling's attempt was unsuccessful, Francis Joseph began to look for new means to solve his realm's internal problems. In Austria, he attempted to return to the conservative-aristocratic solution, based on the rights of the provinces, envisaged by the October Diploma. In Hungary, however, he turned, for the first time, to the representative of the liberal nobility, Deák. Around Christmas of 1864, the emperor tried to find out, with the help of intermediaries, what Deák's conditions for a compromise were.

On April 16, 1865 (Easter Sunday), Deák published an important article in the newspaper *Pesti Napló*, in which, for the first time, he wrote about possible modification of the laws of 1848. Deák did not—as was believed for a long time—initiate negotiations. He only made public that the issue of a compromise had reached a turning point. His article was an answer to the willingness of Vienna to reach a solution. In this article Deák wrote: "One of the aims is to assure the continued existence of a strong empire. We do not wish to subordinate this consideration to any other concern. The other goal is to maintain the constitutional existence of Hungary, her rights and her laws . . . of which it would neither be just nor expedient to relinquish more than is absolutely required to assure the secure future existence of the empire."

The Easter article was only the first step on the road leading to compromise. In the Hungarian legislature that assembled at the end of 1865, it was apparent not only that the compromise faced difficult obstacles, but also that Vienna, in spite of its rigid position, did not wish to break off talks. A conciliatory attitude became especially necessary when war broke out between Austria and Prussia in the summer of 1866. Since coming to power in 1862, Otto von Bismarck, the chancellor of Prussia, had found joint Austro-Prussian leadership in the German Confederation unacceptable. He wanted to reorganize the alliance of the German states and create a unified Germany with the exclusion of Austria. He had no doubt that without a war against Austria, his plans could not be realized. During the spring of 1866, he concluded an alliance with Italy to force Austria into a two-front war and in June provoked an armed conflict. Austria's defeat in the Battle of Königgrätz (Hradec Králové) was unexpectedly swift and decisive. It was with great consternation that Germany received the news that it took only a few days to destroy an army that had been the pillar of Austrian power. All of Europe was surprised by Austria's weakness.

Hungarian policy did not change as a result of the military debacle. The Hungarian liberals expected and hoped for an Austrian victory in the Austro-Prussian war. They assumed that once Austria, with her western provinces, became a member of a strengthened German Confederation, she would be forced to give Hungary greater independence. Unexpectedly, however, Austria lost the war and was excluded from the German Confederation. According to the calculations of the Deák party, this did not increase the chances that Austria was ready to make concessions to Hungary. Still, Hungarian liberals were unwilling to take advantage of Austria's plight. They believed they needed the protection of the Habsburg Empire because they were threatened by the nationalities and the Russians. Hungary's liberal leaders did not wish to endanger the empire, but their motive was self-interest rather than loyalty.

Königgrätz was a setback for the Austro-Germans who, in a monarchy without a foot in Germany, suddenly became only one of the various nations. Although some liberal Austro-German groups had understood even before Königgrätz that true constitutionalism had to be established simultaneously in both halves of the empire, they had not been heeded. Now, however, the attempt to establish contacts with the Hungarians received a strong new impetus from the lost war. The Austro-Germans believed that their national position needed strengthening and that this could be done by transforming the western half of the empire into a unified state under one nation's leadership, into a state like Hungary. The German-Hungarian rapprochement was not dictated by liberal politics but by the mutual need for support of two leading nations.

Königgrätz was also a setback for the Habsburg dynasty. The emperor Francis Joseph, who had been the most powerful German ruler, had to accept that he would no longer play a role in the German Confederation and that Germany would become a unified state without Austria's participation. Yet Austria was not totally humiliated. Bismarck himself wanted to end the war without annexing Austrian territory, and Central Europe's multi-national empire remained a great power. In addition, quiet reigned within the empire, and none of its nations tried to join the advancing enemy. Thus while the dynasty was forced to conclude peace and introduce internal changes, it still had alternatives.

Francis Joseph never took important decisions in a hurry. His options included the continuation of the centralized state (the choice of the court as well as the leading military and bourgeois bureaucratic circles), the federation of the empire (as demanded by conservative governmental circles, including Prime Minister Count Richard Belcredi and the Slav national politicians), and the establishment of constitutional dualism (proposed by Deák and supported by the Austro-German liberals).

In October 1866, the emperor appointed Friedrich Ferdinand Beust to handle his foreign affairs. Beust, who knew very well that without internal peace, the new international plans of the empire could not be realized, convinced him to opt for the third alternative. He argued: "We must stand, first of all, on solid ground . . . This solid ground, as things stand at present, is the cooperation of the German and Hungarian elements in opposition to panslavism."

Finally, in January 1867, negotiations began in Vienna, based on the compromise proposal of the Hungarian legislature. (The Hungarian negotiator was not Deák but Count Gyula Andrássy. He was recommended to the ruler by Deák, who made it quite clear that he would not become a member of the Hungarian government that was to be established.) The essence of the legislature's proposal was the recognition that the two halves of the empire had some "common affairs," namely national defense and foreign policy. Given this, the legislature would allow the partial modification of the often vague laws of 1848–49. (In fact, it left the ruler practically absolute power to deal with them.) The proposal demanded the reestablishment of the popularly elected parliament of 1848, a ministry responsible to Parliament, and the total independence of Hungary as far as internal affairs were concerned. An important precondition of the compromise was constitutional government in both Austria and Hungary. The acrimonious debate lasted for days, but all those concerned—the Vienna government, the court, and the Hungarian delegation—were ready to reach an agreement. The discussions ended with the appointment of Andrássy as Hungarian prime minister. He agreed to obtain the needed modifications of the 1848 laws from the Hungarian legislature. The compromise was debated by the Hungarian legislature in the spring of 1867. While the discussion was dominated by the partisans of the compromise, serious objections were also voiced. Once again, Kossuth asserted his conviction that Hungary's interests and the rule of the House of Habsburg could not be reconciled. The well-being of all nations living in Hungary depended on the country's total independence, which could only be assured through armed struggle. Kossuth also objected to the acceptance of "common affairs," in which he saw the voluntary relinquishing of the country's rights and the most important elements of its independence. Common defense might involve the country in international disputes not in its interests and might endanger those friendly relations with neighboring peoples essential for the well-being of Hungary. The common army was seen by Kossuth as the same efficient tool of absolutism, reaction, and oppression it had been in the past. According to him, "the compromise represented an alliance of the ostensibly liberal conservative-reactionary Hungarians with those Austro-Germans who were opposed to liberty, and it was aimed at the suppression of the other nations and nationalities."

When Deák supported the compromise in his speech before the legislature, he answered, consciously or unconsciously, the arguments presented by Kossuth. He tried to prove that "common affairs" had existed since the eighteenth century between Austria and Hungary, and that common defense had existed since the signing of the Pragmatic Sanction. In the laws establishing the compromise, the novelty was not the recognition of the existence of "common affairs" but rather the manner in which they were to be administered. Deák refuted the argument that the compromise destroyed Hungary's constitutional independence. "The compromise is a better guarantor of our survival than are speculations based on unforeseeable events," he said. Deák rejected not only the revolutionary solution to the country's problems but also the argument that Hungarians should wait for favorable turns in international relations to gain their independence. Deák and most of those of his class believed that Hungary was not strong enough to exist as a fully independent state. The years that had passed since the revolution had convinced him that Hungary, situated between two great powers—Germany and Russia—and faced by the increasing demands of the nationalities, needed the protection offered by the Habsburg monarchy. Deák did not attempt to present the compromise as a victory. He only stated that a better solution could not be found.

When the final vote was taken, on May 29, 209 deputies voted for the acceptance of "common affairs," eighty-nine opposed it, and eighty-three abstained. After this vote, political struggle gave way for a short time to festive peace. On June 8, eighteen years after his dethronement, Emperor Francis Joseph was crowned King of Hungary in a brilliant ceremony. The festive mood was dampened by rumors that the reviewing stand would be blown up and by Kossuth's somber warnings.

The historical experience, in particular the power relations of the previous two decades, had convinced most of those concerned that concessions had to be made. This was true of the emperor-king, whose supporters were the army and the bureaucracy; of the Austro-German bourgeoisie; and of Hungary's major landowners, who represented the views of the middle class as well. The ruling elements of both halves of the empire demanded national hegemony, civic institutions, and constitutional rule, and the compromise gave this to them. National hegemony was not absolute, however, because, in accordance with the tenets of liberalism, the other nationalities were assured of basic national rights. Liberal constitutionalism too was restricted because it was limited in matters of defense and foreign affairs.

The compromise of 1867 was the result of bargaining during which everybody had to give up something. As with all compromises, each side felt it had given up more than the other. Contemporary Hungarians (and subsequent generations) objected to "common affairs" because they limited national self-determination. The Austro-Germans felt cheated because the idea of the centralized monarchy—which in fact had never existed, but of which they always dreamed—had to be given up. The voices of the other nationalities were hardly even heard in an empire based on the supremacy of the two leading nations.

XIV

HUNGARY AND THE DUAL
MONARCHY, 1867–1890

Tibor Frank

The Mechanism of the Dualist State System

The Compromise *(Ausgleich)* of 1867 became the basic law of a new country, Austria-Hungary. It divided the realm of the Habsburgs into two legally equal parts whose relations with each other were based on parity. (A similar law was passed in the other half of the new state, also.) In their internal affairs, the two halves were sovereign, with their own legislative, legal, and law enforcing organs. Their relationship was regulated in part by the person of the common ruler and in part by the joint management of the so-called "common affairs." Some of these common affairs were deduced from the Pragmatic Sanction ("pragmatic affairs"), while the communality of others was dictated by practical considerations ("non-pragmatic affairs").

The most important common affairs based on the Pragmatic Sanction were foreign policy, defense, and the finances needed for these. The management of common affairs was entrusted to the common ministers appointed by the emperor. These ministers were responsible to both the ruler and the "delegations" (see below).

The highest administrative and executive organ of the dual monarchy was the Common Council of Ministers. When the ruler presided, it was called the Crown Council, but in most cases the common minister of foreign affairs presided with the other common ministers and the prime ministers of Austria and Hungary in attendance. The role of the common minister of foreign affairs was of paramount importance. Not only did he conduct foreign affairs, but, in collaboration with the ruler, he worked out the main outlines of the empire's political policy. Of the ten ministers who served in this office during the fifty years of the Dual Monarchy's existence, three were either Hungarians or Hungarian subjects. Of the eleven common ministers of finance, four were Hungarians. None of the common ministers of defense was Hungarian.

The political decisions that determined the fate of the empire were not taken by the Common Council of Ministers but by the ruler and his informal advisors. Frequently the Common Council of Ministers served only to legalize the previously established decisions of the emperor-king. Francis Joseph's Cabinet Bureau and Military Bureau had an influence equal to that of the ministries, especially as far as personnel affairs were concerned.

That the policies of the Dual Monarchy were in the best interests of the dynasty was assured by the power of these hand picked unofficial advisors and by the nature of those who worked in the various offices of the central government. Serving the Habsburg dynasty was a centuries-old tradition among the court aristocracy, the bureaucracy, and, most important, the highest ranking officers of the loyal officer corps. The ruler had the right of appointment and did all he could to safeguard the influence of these loyal elements in the new state system. For example, diplomatic posts were filled according to lineage and wealth. While higher offices were slowly made available to people of different ethnic origins, in certain areas differences remained visible to the end. For example, the number of Hungarians serving in the diplomatic corps reached 30 percent by the turn of the century, but only 5–6 percent in the leadership of the common armed forces.

There was no common Austro-Hungarian parliament. The Austrian and Hungarian parliaments elected from among their members sixty "delegates." These "delegations" were supposed to assure the constitutionality of foreign and military affairs, and they had to approve the expenses needed for running them. However, their cumbersome organization soon proved that they were incapable of fulfilling their "parliamentary" functions. This made the maintenance of the ruler's broad powers possible and allowed the common ministries to function practically without constitutional checks. As far as foreign affairs were concerned, the Compromise assured the right "of the ministries of both halves" to be consulted before decisions relating to them were taken. This gave the Hungarian government, and through it the Hungarian parliament, the possibility of influencing foreign affairs.

Besides "common affairs," the common currency and customs barriers also strengthened the unity of the Austro-Hungarian monarchy. Furthermore, there were other "affairs to be decided in common," dealing with a whole series of important questions that touched on issues of interest to both halves. As far as these were concerned, the two halves were to reach agreements every ten years. Issues that had to be regulated in this manner included the percentage of common expenses that each half had to contribute. Originally, Hungary had to pay 30 percent, and her contribution was gradually raised subsequently. Customs and trade agreements, the monetary system, the national bank, excise taxes, and common railroads were also common affairs.

There can be no doubt that dualism functioned well in the internal affairs of the two halves. The personal power of the ruler, however, remained strong enough to influence significantly the development of domestic affairs in both states. In political, economic, and military affairs, Austria-Hungary remained a centralized state retaining some absolutist features.

The reaction to the Compromise among the various major nations living in the empire differed. In Austria there were some serious reservations that left their mark in the wording of the Austrian Compromise law, which differed in several details from the Hungarian. The Austrian law did not stipulate that the common government had no right to interfere in the affairs of the two separate governments; it gave legislative power to the delegations, expressing the hope that in time they would develop into a common parliament; and, finally, it did not mention in connection with some common affairs that they were subject to renegotiation.

While Austrian politicians had reservations, the Czechs were opposed to the dualist transformation of the empire. The transfer to Prague of the insignia of Czech royalty and Francis Joseph's visit to Prague were insufficient to placate Czech nationalists and to calm public opinion. Czech politicians based their demands on the historic rights of the Czech crown and demanded a reorganization of the relationship between ruler and nation. They also refused to recognize the constitutional settlement Vienna had reached with Hungary. The Poles of Galicia also voiced their demands, requesting full administrative, judicial, and educational autonomy. The government refused this autonomy out of deference to Russian sensitivities, although the Croat settlement had established a precedent for regulating Polish affairs.

Croatia had maintained commonwealth relations with Hungary for some 750 years but retained numerous rights of self-government. This relationship came to an end in 1848. When the Compromise was concluded, the relationship between the two states had to be renewed in accordance with new concepts of statehood. The agreement with the Croats, known as the *Nagodba,* was concluded a year after the Austro-Hungarian compromise. The Croats had to give up their demands of national autonomy. They finally agreed that Croatia and Hungary "were part of the same state complex," which was a part of the reorganized monarchy. Within this complex, the Croats were a political nation with its own territory, which would be ruled by its own legislature and government. The Croatian ban was appointed by the ruler on the recommendation of the Hungarian prime minister, and he was to be responsible to the Croatian legislature. Croatian became the country's official language. The numerous affairs Croatia and Hungary had to handle in common were to be administered in a way similar to that stipulated in the freshly concluded Compromise between Austria and Hungary. The *Nagodba* assured important autonomous rights to Croatia, which it retained until the dissolution of the monarchy, although subsequent Hungarian governments tried repeatedly to gain greater influence in Croatia than was constitutionally allowed.

The Compromise had made Transylvania an integral part of Hungary again, a decision that displeased the Romanian inhabitants of the region.

The Nationality Problem

Before the Compromise, Hungarian political leaders had repeatedly promised the other nationalities that their rights would be legally guaranteed. Yet the Compromise ended the nationalities' hope of a federative reorganization of the empire and left them defenseless in the face of Hungarian hegemonist ambitions. For this reason, Hungary's non-Magyar nationalities were unanimously opposed to the Compromise. While the Compromise was being negotiated, the representatives of the other nationalities in the legislature demanded equal rights for the six "nations of the state" (Hungarians, Romanians, Serbs, Slovaks, Ruthenians, and Germans), but Hungarian public opinion rejected this solution. As soon as the Hungarian government was formed, the nationalities subcommittee of Parliament promptly worked out a nationalities law, but the Hungarian public found that it gave the minority nationalities too many rights, while the non-Hungarian representatives and press attacked the proposal for not going far enough.

At the end of 1868, a version of the proposed law reached the floor of Parliament, where a heated discussion developed. In his speech in the lower house, Ferenc Deák insisted that Hungarian as the official state language be legislated as part of the proposed law. The representatives of the nationalities stuck to their own bill; to show their dissatisfaction with the government's proposal they walked out.

The law that was finally accepted (1868/XLIV) did not recognize the existence of separate nationalities and did not grant them collective national rights or political institutions. The law was liberal only as far as the usage of languages was concerned. Although the non-recognition of the nationalities finally led to tragic results, Hungary was, as least, the only country besides Switzerland to try to solve the nationality problem by legislation at the time.

The Hungarian liberal leadership believed in the creation of a unitary Hungarian national state. They could not reconcile with this the territorial autonomy, collective national rights, and independent political institutions demanded by the minority nationalities. The conflict between the unity of the state and the demands of a multinational population was a problem the liberal Hungarian nationalists tried to eliminate by equating the concepts of state and nation. The ideals of the liberal thinkers were not reflected in the actions of the Hungarian political leadership, which tried to transform the "common homeland" into a Hungarian national state.

The Hungarian leadership attempted to ensure its domination in legislative action and administration, although, until the 1880s, its efforts to enforce the "notion of the Hungarian state" did not involve forced Magyarization or linguistic and ethnic assimilation. At first, official government policy concentrated on supporting voluntary Magyarization in place of a process called "grammatical Magyarization," compulsory learning of the languages. The Hungarian school system in the villages and especially in the high schools was designed to turn the intellectuals of the nationalities into Hungarians. The Hungarian leadership even took some societal measures in regions inhabited by the nationalities to ensure Magyarization with the "help of all legally permissible means." During the second half of Kálmán Tisza's premiership, Magyarization was pursued much more openly and forcefully, and Hungarian nationalism emerged clearly in its forceful impatience.

The Development of the Modern State

The government that came to power when the Compromise was concluded represented Deák's party, led by the older Count Gyula Andrássy. It promptly began to build a modern bourgeois-liberal state. During the long period of absolutism that had followed the War of Independence, an entire generation had grown to maturity. This generation did not even remember that the first responsible Hungarian government had already taken steps in this direction in the spring of 1848. Thus the Andrássy government had to renew some of the laws of 1848 and to formulate new legislation that fundamentally altered a social-political system that still retained numerous feudal features. As it turned out, however, the reforms introduced by the Andrássy government were less radical than those of 1848 had been.

One of the first duties of the government was to address the issues of freedoms of the press, of assembly, and of association. The government modified the press law of 1848 by lowering the amount of money that had to be deposited by those who wished to start publishing a newspaper or magazine. Yet the government also increased its ability to intervene in libel suits by making press-related issues subject to jury trials. The press law shows clearly how the government, calling itself liberal, restricted basic freedoms when these could have been used to challenge Hungarian supremacy. The same tendency induced the government and its successors not to define the rights of assembly and association by passing relevant laws, but to regulate them by decrees. By not regulating these rights in legal form, the leading elements tried to restrict the rights of assembly and association of peasants, workers, and the nationalities.

The transformation of the legal system began with the codification of new rules of procedure. This included the abolition of nobiliary privileges and proclaimed the citizens' equality before the law. A law passed the following year established the basis for modern bourgeois legal services and procedures. It separated judicature from administration and dealt with the conditions of the judges' independence. Judges could not be removed, once appointed, but they had to refrain from political activities. While this law was debated in Parliament, it became obvious that those who had drafted it also hoped to curtail the power of the counties. They proposed that the judges of the lower courts, the county judges, be appointed and not elected. This case well illustrates the struggle that began at that time and continued to the end of the dualist system, pitting the modern centralized government against those who defended the power of the traditional and often feudal counties.

Numerous other laws dealt with the modernization and organization of the judicial system, and the legislative process that followed the Compromise placed the bourgeois-liberal judiciary system on a solid basis in Hungary. The liberal wing of the Deák party planned to promulgate a new criminal code and to make the jury system universal. Their plan, however, was defeated by the conservative opposition, which made it possible to use the authorities to suppress political activities not in the interests of the ruling element.

The government considered the transformation of administration one of its most important tasks. Familiar with the strong tradition of local authorities and of the traditional political rights of the counties, the Andrássy government submitted a reform bill that took into account the interests of local authorities. The state system created by the Compromise was further developed and strengthened by "the compromise between state and county" dealing with the "reordering of public authorities." The major feature of this law was that it designated the county and municipal assemblies as the only legal constitutional bodies of political discussion outside Parliament. The law also stipulated that local executive authority would be exercised by the government through the locally elected self-governing office-holders. The government assured its power, however, by making a large number of local ordinances subject to preliminary sanction by the Ministry of the Interior. Furthermore, most of the local power was placed into the hands of a high ispán in each county. This dignitary, who was appointed and could be removed only by the government, had broad authority in controlling the activities of local authorities, in making new appointments, and in disciplinary cases. Through these officials the government effectively controlled the activities of self-governing authorities. To be able to act against recalcitrant local authorities, the law also endowed these new dignitaries with extraordinary powers, which represented the remnants of absolutism in a liberalized and partially decentralized public administration.

The same law regulated the political role of the so-called *virilists,* those citizens who paid most of the direct taxes due to the state. These men joined the elected members of local legislative bodies. Thus the *virilists* became hereditary local legislators, ensuring the political supremacy of the wealthier landowners in the counties and that of the high bourgeoisie in the cities. The legally guaranteed political power of the richest element in society became one of the characteristic features of post-Compromise Hungary. The opposition repeatedly stressed in parliamentary debates the dangers of this anti-democratic arrangement. An interesting feature of the *virilist* debate in Parliament was that Deák opposed this law, while the prime minister of his choice threatened to resign if it did not pass.

One of the laws passed during the same legislative session in 1873 united Pest, Buda, and Óbuda, thus legally creating a new municipality, the capital of Hungary, Budapest. The new city was headed by the chief mayor whom the municipal council elected from among candidates selected by the ruler. The government could not remove him from office. In addition, the citizens of the capital and, in general, those of all cities received extended rights from the legislature.

The administrative system introduced during the first years of the dualist period was basically bourgeois in character. Nevertheless, it differed in important respects from those in force in the more developed Western European states. The new administrative system of Hungary was in many respects conservative and anti-democratic. Besides the *virilist* law, a good example of this conservative tendency is the subordination of villages to the jurisdiction of the counties. Hungary's vast peasant population was thereby prevented from participating in the country's political life. This created serious trouble, especially in the large agricultural regions inhabited by the non-Hungarian nationalities, and contributed to the growing dissatisfaction in dualist Hungary.

Educational reform, together with the judicial and administrative reforms, became one of the new state's cornerstones. In 1867, only 41 percent of the male and 24 percent of the female population over the age of six knew how to read and write. It was impossible to organize a modern bourgeois state economically and socially while public education remained on this low level.

Parliament attempted to change the situation by passing the elementary school law. The bill was submitted to Parliament by Baron József Eötvös, minister of religious affairs and education, one of the most highly educated persons of his time, whose vision was broadly European. He had held the same office during the 1848 revolution. Eötvös' proposal in 1868 was less drastic and more circumspect than that of twenty years earlier. He did not, this time, require that all teaching be done in Hungarian. He proposed to build the elementary school network on the existing confessional schools, which were to be supplemented by state-owned village and municipal schools. The bill produced stormy debates in Parliament and was sharply attacked by the Catholic clergy. The law, which finally passed in 1868, represented a major step in raising the general educational and cultural level of the country. All schools were placed under state supervision, obligatory subjects were introduced into the curriculum, an inspection system was established, and teacher-training institutes were founded.

The reform of religious affairs was less drastic. The most important measure, also passed in 1867, gave equal citizenship and political rights to Jews. At that time this was a significant measure, in spite of the fact that a law of the following year limited to members of "accepted" Christian religions, the freedom of changing creeds and concluding mixed marriages.

The Development of a Capitalist Economy

"The period of creation and construction . . . of intellectual development and material prosperity began for us in 1867." These words of Finance Minister Count Menyhért Lonyay clearly reflect the optimism with which those who had negotiated the Compromise viewed the country's economic possibilities. The great expectations were justified. Around 1867, Hungary was economically backward, and only a small segment of the population was employed in industry. Agriculture accounted for two-thirds of the national product. The Compromise supplied the political preconditions for further developments.

With large-scale industrialization not yet a possiblity, emphasis was first placed on the capitalistic transformation of agriculture, on the creation of modern credit and transportation networks, and on the increased production of the more important industrial raw materials. Furthermore, great attention was also paid to increasing the quality of products. The most important task facing the would-be developers and modernizers of the economy was to end the shortages of capital and of specialists. It was relatively easy to attract foreign capital and specialists after the Compromise, and both were welcomed without restrictions. French, German, and Austrian capital was dominant, but British, Belgian, Dutch, and Swiss capital also played a role in the development of the Hungarian economy. Foreign investments diminished following the economic crisis of 1873, but after 1880 they played an important part in the construction of the railroad network, the modernization of urban services, the mechanization of agriculture, the creation of the machine industry, and in the establishment of the major banks of Budapest.

The importation of capital often took the form of deliveries of complicated machinery, which Hungary's under-educated population was incapable of using. Consequently, engineers, skilled workers, and entrepreneurs moved into Hungary from abroad. In the 1870s about 25 percent of the industrial labor force in Budapest was made up of foreigners, though later their numbers gradually diminished. Hungarian specialists began to appear by the end of the century, due to improved general and special education.

It was a characteristic feature of the economic life of the Compromise period that industrial enterprises and corporations sprang up like mushrooms after a spring rain. The record cereal production further encouraged the influx of foreign capital. In 1867–68, 170 new industrial corporations and 552 credit institutions were established, and 2,500 miles of new rail lines were built.

The panic that swept the Vienna stock exchange on May 9, 1873 condemned most Hungarian capitalist enterprises to death. Foreign capital was withdrawn from the country, and the financially weak, newly established enterprises went bankrupt. The economic crisis that began on the Vienna stock exchange grew into the most serious depression of pre–1914 Europe. While it affected the entire continent, it probably hit Austria-Hungary the hardest.

A few years later, Hungary was again hard hit by difficulties affecting cereal exports. Lower overseas prices and the growing protectionist policies of most states closed the foreign markets to Hungarian exports. While production costs steadily rose, the falling prices seriously diminished the income of cereal producers. By the end of the 1870s, the agrarian crisis made it obvious that the state's active support was needed not only for industrialization, but also for making agriculture competitive. In the 1880s, the state began to play its part in the technical modernization of agriculture. State intervention did not limit private enterprise; on the contrary, it encouraged it.

For decades after the Compromise, the most important sector of the economy remained cereal growing. Between 1867 and 1890, the areas devoted to grain production were increased and yields were improved. The additional areas devoted to cereal production consisted partly of previously fallow lands and partly of land once used for other agricultural products. Intensive, market-oriented agricultural management also made its appearance. Hungary became one of the period's leading grain exporters, but at the cost of a decline in animal husbandry.

Hungarian industry was closely connected with agriculture, and not surprisingly, the most important sector of large-scale industry was milling. The number of steam-driven mills grew from 146 in 1863 to 1,843 in 1895, and in the 1860s, Hungary exported as much flour as all other European states combined. In the 1870s, the capital's mills ground not only domestic wheat but also the cheap grains of the Balkans which they subsequently exported. Hungarian mills, especially in Budapest, were among Europe's best as far as their technical equipment and the quality of their products were concerned.

Agriculture was also the determining factor in the growing importance of coal and iron mines. The railroads and steam engines used in agriculture and industry required more and more coal, and the iron and machine industries demanded iron. The machine industry, which had its golden age in the 1880s, was able, with the help of foreign capital, to produce not only milling equipment but locomotives and threshing machines. The most modern light industry was printing. In the 1880s, Hungarian newspapers were appearing in tens of thousands of copies, coming off the most modern American rotary presses.

The Origins of the Labor Movement

The capitalist development of Hungary will be discussed in chapter 16. Nevertheless, one of its aspects, the growth of a labor movement, must be treated within the framework of this chapter.

The domestic labor market was incapable of satisfying the demands of the country's many-faceted industrialization. The main source of labor was the agrarian proletariat and the poor peasantry, but these uneducated people could not satisfy the need for trained labor. Therefore, surplus agricultural labor sought employment instead in railroad construction, in river regulation, in construction, and in construction materials production. More and more of these people sought to improve their lot by emigration overseas. Most of the country's industrial labor force was concentrated in Budapest, which in 1890 housed 80,000 workers, a high figure for a city of about 500,000. Skilled labor was relatively well paid. Becoming a worker meant an improved living standard and a higher social status, in contrast to the mass misery the industrial revolution had produced earlier in the West.

When the Hungarian workers' movement began, it followed the tenets of Ferdinand Lassalle, the father of the first German socialist movement. The Comprehensive Association of Workers, established in 1868, worked for the recognition of the political and economic equality of the working class. The workers of the capital were especially active, but a united labor movement could not be formed out of the various organizations.

The Paris commune made a great impression on the Hungarian workers, whose movement rapidly became more radical. After the defeat of the commune in June 1871, the Hungarian workers held a meeting and expressed enthusiastic support for their French comrades' struggle. The leaders of Hungarian socialism were arrested on the day following the meeting and accused of disloyalty. The disloyalty trial paralyzed the activities of socialists for a long time, and the authorities issued a series of ordinances in the early 1870s aimed at making socialist agitation impossible. New activities began only toward the end of the decade, due mainly to the activities of Leo Frankel.

Frankel had been one of the leaders of the Paris commune and later became a close associate of Marx and Engels in London in the Chief Council of the International. His Hungarian activities began in 1876 when he began to develop a party press and to organize a workers' congress for 1878. He was an experienced, world-wise politician, who wished to end the socialists' isolation by establishing contact with the left wing of the most radical bourgeois party. He corresponded regularly with Marx, Engels, and several leaders of the French and German labor movements.

By the end of the 1870s, the labor movement had split into two parties, but this division was ended in May 1880 with the establishment of the United Workers' Party of Hungary. The constituent meeting of the new party promised to mark the beginning of a renewed labor movement, but the organization soon lost its revolutionary appeal as the leadership tried to improve the position of labor "by peaceful and legal means." By giving up some of the basic principles of social democracy, the party tried to win the support of the petty bourgeoisie. In 1889, the radicalization of the party resulted in the first congress of the Social-Democratic Workers' Party of Hungary in 1890.

The Kálmán Tisza Government

The years following the Compromise saw the beginning of political consolidation in Hungary. After having served as prime minister for a few years, Andrássy was appointed common minister of foreign affairs by Francis Joseph, proving to even the most skeptical that Hungary had gained parity with Austria.

In 1875 the Deák party, which had concluded the Compromise, united with the most important opposition group, bringing into one camp the Liberal Party, the majority of the important landowners and most of the leading industrial capitalists. For the next thirty years, the heterogeneous Liberal Party remained the ruling party. It was a typically nineteenth-century "club," without permanent membership or central organization. An excellent parliamentary tactician capable of reconciling diverse interests, Kálmán Tisza, who had spent many years in opposition, became the party's leader after Deák's death in 1876. For fifteen years, 1875–90, he was Hungary's prime minister.

In the years following the Compromise the "left center" under Tisza's leadership was able to divide the opponents of the Compromise. These people wanted some modifications of the 1867 Basic Law and detached some voters from the followers of Kossuth who were strenuously opposed to the Compromise even after it became law. After his party united with that of Deák, Tisza tried to push the erstwhile Deákist into the background, securing the leading roles for his "left center" followers. Very quickly the party gained the respect of the country and had an overwhelming majority in Parliament. Tisza achieved these results by retaining the semblance of anti-Austrianism and by beginning to threaten the nationalities with an iron fist.

First the Tisza government turned to solving the serious financial problems resulting from the 1873 economic crisis. The budgetary deficit had reached sixty million florins in 1874, and the national debt amounted to a half billion. To large foreign investors, Hungary appeared to be losing her credit-worthiness. External affairs also made it necessary to settle the financial problems. The political reorganization of the Balkans appeared to be imminent, and Austria-Hungary had to be strong and economically influential to play her part. Hungary had her own interests to consider and had to be strong within the Dual Monarchy to defend them.

To cover the deficit and to diminish the national debt, the government, at first, contracted new debts. It replaced the former short-term loans with long-term bonds. Furthermore, it introduced strict economic measures into the budget, imposed new direct taxes, and increased the excise taxes. The results were disappointing. Therefore, in the summer of 1875, the government began negotiations with the Austrian government, aiming to modify the commercial and customs unions and the proportional distribution of the revenue of certain excise taxes. After three years of discussions, only compromises could be achieved, which were included in the new commercial and customs union agreement, the new customs duties, and the law regulating the percentages of common expenses. In the end, the new customs agreement, which included light protective tariffs, served to ensure the dominance of Austrian industry in Hungary.

The concessions to Austria created dissention in the Liberal Party. In protest, two groups of deputies, about one hundred in all, left the party. The situation was worsened by the struggle to create an independent Hungarian National Bank to end the Austrian National Bank's monopoly on issuing currency. The prime minister knew very well that foreign policy and economic considerations required compromise on this issue. The Austrian National Bank was transformed into the Austro-Hungarian National Bank with alternating Austrian and Hungarian governors and vice-governors.

His various concessions weakened Tisza's position as prime minister. Those who had hoped that this former leader of the opposition would modify the Compromise in keeping with national demands were disappointed. In three years, he practically lost his parliamentary majority and came near to being voted out of office. Yet there was no opposition party capable of assuming power, and his opponents within the party had no leader of equal stature. The emperor too supported the Tisza government because he saw in it the defender of common affairs. Tisza remained in office and his position, after some difficulties, became stronger again. In the second, longer period of Tisza's leadership, the dualist system acquired its final, stable form.

The prime minister was, above all, a master of political detail. Step by step, he built up his party's prestige, then, gradually, the entire governmental system. He remained minister of the interior, thus retaining direct control over the entire administration and political system. He was in charge of the period's most controversial institution, the electoral system, tied to extremely high property qualifications for voters. Elections were characterized by corruption and, on occasion, by the government's hardly disguised intervention. Thus the overwhelming majority of the 413 deputies supported the government in Parliament in exchange for the numerous political and non-political advantages they enjoyed.

During Tisza's stay in office, several social problems emerged as the direct or indirect consequences of the country's capitalist development. The transformation of estates into modern enterprises considerably decreased the large landowners' income, while that of bankers and other investors increased. This development sharpened the conflict between landowners and capitalists, and forced the landowners to organize to protect their political power and economic position. The resulting political movement demanded better planned social development and a new economic policy. The conservative critics of capitalism declared that they were fighting not only for the rights of large estates, but for those of all husbandmen. Thus they gained the support of some of the richer peasants. This approach seemed important to the conservatives, who feared the spread of socialism in city and village alike. The true goal of the "agrarian" movement was to protect the large estates and the gentry with outdated, even feudal, means if necessary.

The emergence of the Jewish bourgeoisie and its rapid Magyarization was another consequence of capitalist development. In Hungary, where the role of the urban population was played for a long time by nobles who owned middle-sized estates, the urban bourgeoisie developed very late, mostly from non-Hungarian ethnic groups. The segregation and legal disability of the Jews ended when the legal equality of all citizens was proclaimed after 1867. The rich among them, who owned considerable capital but no land, could now invest all their assets in credit institutions and commerce, and thus they became at once important in the new capitalist economy. The capital earned in the grain, wood, and wool trades earned interest in the new credit institutions or was transformed into industrial assets by the purchase of stocks. Jewish grain merchants became within one or two generations key members of the financial world. The richest either received or bought noble titles from the ruler, and the well-to-do sent their children to universities. Many of these students chose the free intellectual professions, becoming physicians, lawyers, or newspapermen.

The landowning middle nobility, the erstwhile bourgeoisie, and the gentry forced to sell its land looked with jaundiced eyes at the growing importance of this "foreign" bourgeois element. Soon the gentry too made its appearance in the political arena of the Tisza period with a neo-conservative and anti-capitalist program; joining the "agrarians," they became the first spokesmen of Hungarian anti-Semitism.

In 1882 the anti-Semitic groups tried to make political capital out of the death of a servant girl in the village of Tiszaeszlár. They accused the Jews of the village of having killed her for ritualistic reasons. A massive propaganda campaign started in the press and in Parliament, and Tisza's enemies hoped that it would lead to the formation of a large anti-governmental coalition. Newspaper readers all over Europe followed the great political battle between the anti-Semites and their liberal opponents. In 1883 at the height of the anti-Semitic wave, a National Anti-Semitic Party was established, but during the elections a year later it achieved little, and its representatives were received with disdain in Parliament. The liberals finally gained a great political and moral victory at the highly publicized trial that lasted for two months in the city of Nyiregyháza. Though this was followed by anti-Semitic riots in Budapest and in the countryside, the government took stern measures and reestablished order. From his lonely exile, even Kossuth voiced his influential opinion in support of the government: "As a man of the nineteenth century, I am ashamed by this anti-Semitic agitation, as a Hungarian it embarrasses me, as a patriot I condemn it." The end of Kálmán Tisza's rule in 1890 marked the end of an era in the history of Austria-Hungary. The bourgeois state had been erected, and the modern Western European legal system had been introduced. Further transformation was possible only at the expense of the political and economic power of the owners of large estates.

Austro-Hungarian Foreign Policy in the Decades Following the Compromise

After the Compromise, Hungary participated in the international power struggle within the framework of Austria-Hungary. With the Peace of Prague (1866), which closed the Austro-Prussian war, the Habsburgs had to accept that Germany would be unified under Prussian leadership. In the following years, the main aim of Austro-Hungarian foreign policy was to regain, if possible, Austria's position in Germany. In the Franco-Prussian war of 1870, the Austrian political leaders would have gladly supported France, but the clumsiness of French diplomacy made this impossible. The expectations of the French army's ability were soon proven erroneous, and an anti-Prussian foreign policy rapidly became dated. Austria-Hungary had no choice but to seek good relations with Europe's newest and most powerful state, Germany.

To work out the new foreign policy, Count Andrássy was asked to take over foreign affairs. The new foreign minister's nationalist and liberal orientation was the exact opposite of the dynastic and conservative traditional Austrian foreign policy. He wished to use the monarchy to stem Russia's expansion, but European developments forced him to follow a policy contrary to his personal convictions. It was he who concluded the Three Emperors' League in 1873, tying the monarchy to Germany and Russia.

From 1875 to 1879, the "Eastern question" occupied the attention of European diplomacy. Freeing the region from Ottoman rule became the most important problem for both the population of the Balkans and the great powers. The anti-Ottoman uprising began in Hercegovina but soon spread all through the peninsula. Austria-Hungary and Russia were equally interested in settling the region's problems. The originally preferred solution, the maintaining of the status quo, soon proved impracticable. The two great powers conducted a series of negotiations carefully defining and separating their respective interests. When, in the end, Russia declared war on the Ottoman Empire, she could count on Austria-Hungary's neutrality. The war ended in 1878 with the Treaty of San Stefano, which practically ended Ottoman rule in the Balkans but also disregarded the interests of the other great powers, including those of the Dual Monarchy and Great Britain. It was Count Andrássy who demanded the international revision of the treaty. This occurred during the summer of 1878 at the Congress of Berlin, where Russia was forced to make serious concessions, and Austria-Hungary, breaking with the policy of the Three Emperors' League, gained important diplomatic advantages. The monarchy was entrusted by the congress with the occupation of Bosnia-Hercegovina and took over this Ottoman province after overcoming stiff resistance. The occupation was badly received everywhere in the Dual Monarchy. Some people were afraid of adding even more Slavs to the state's population; others feared that the problems of ruling the province would destroy the dualist system; and, finally, there were those who were not satisfied with occupation and demanded annexation. The occupation produced political crises in both halves of the monarchy.

After the Congress of Berlin, Germany feared an Austro-Hungarian–Russian rapprochement and to prevent it proposed an alliance to the Dual Monarchy. The Dual Alliance of 1879 promised mutual military assistance in case of a Russian attack and was to remain valid for five years. Andrássy, who signed the treaty just before he resigned from office, was certainly not aware that he had just determined the main direction of the country's foreign policy for the next forty years.

Yet Russia's good will was also needed for Austria-Hungary's pursuit of her interests in the Balkans. Baron Heinrich Haymerle, who replaced Andrássy, concluded, in 1881, the Three Emperors' Agreement to safeguard the monarchy's position in the Balkans. It gave Austria-Hungary a free hand in Bosnia-Hercegovina and transformed the western Balkans into her zone of influence. Gustav Kálnoky succeeded Haymerle. He was in charge of foreign affairs when the Dual Alliance was transformed into the Triple Alliance in 1882 with the inclusion of Italy and when the anti-Russian alliance was signed between Austria-Hungary and Romania. Kálnoky's foreign policy sought Austro-Hungarian expansion in the Balkans, and this policy soon led to a total break with Russia between 1887 and 1890. While in the early 1880s Austro-Hungarian statesmen had tried to secure the monarchy's position in the Balkans through agreements with Russia, by the end of the decade they pursued the same aim through an anti-Russian policy.

Culture and Science

The economic development that followed the Compromise stimulated the growth of the sciences and technology. Hungarian scientists who had studied at

German or Austrian establishments of higher education became the reorganizers of Hungarian scientific life. Significant changes were introduced at the universities in the 1870s and 1880s. Numerous new teaching positions and departments were established, especially in the natural sciences and medicine. It soon became obvious that Hungary's only university, at Budapest, could not satisfy the country's needs, and a second one was established in 1872 at Kolozsvár. The Politechnicum was transformed into the Technical University in 1871, and by the early 1890s it was among the best engineering schools in Europe.

By the 1870s and 1880s, Budapest became a significant center of learning, thanks to the National Széchenyi Library with more than 500,000 volumes, supported by the collections housed in the Libraries of Parliament, the Academy of Sciences, the Statistical Office, and the Technical University. Economic interests brought about the establishment of the Geological Institute in 1869 and the Institute of Meteorology in 1870. A whole series of scientific and professional associations sprang up to link specialists working in different parts of the country. In almost all cases Budapest was the center of this scientific activity. Consequently, in the sciences as in practically all other manifestations of communal life, this heavy concentration led to an unbalanced development.

The arts also acquired their institutions of higher learning. The Academy of Music, under the presidency of Franz Liszt, was established in 1875 and soon achieved international stature. The Academy of Fine Arts, founded in 1872, was also highly successful.

On the whole, however, while science grew dynamically in these decades, the artistic trends that had begun to flourish before 1848 lost momentum. The various arts, which had made great progress since the Reform Period, and especially literature, found it very hard to give a satisfactory picture of the new socio-economic order or to depict the problems of modern man. In this sense, the cultural development that began with the process of "embourgeoisement" in the Reform Period came to a halt. Music was characterized by strong German influences and the late manifestations of post-romanticism. In the fine arts academism and in architecture historical eclecticism were dominant.

The rapid transformation of Hungary into an urban bourgeois society was better reflected in plays about peasants, popular music, and the growing popular literature. The rural proletariat and poor peasants began to migrate or emigrate, and the masses living under new conditions were no longer satisfied with traditional peasant culture. At the same time, the presses were transmitting information in quantities previously impossible. These phenomena totally transformed traditional mass culture.

XV

HUNGARY THROUGH WORLD WAR I AND THE END OF THE DUAL MONARCHY

Géza Jeszenszky

The End of Stability

The relative stability that had reigned in Hungary after 1867 came to an end toward the end of the century. Free trade gave ground to protectionism and attempts to monopolize the world market, and state intervention became more prevalent. In addition, the values and economic system introduced by the dominant liberals came under attack from two directions. First, the growing mass workers movement, although without agreement on the means to be employed, worked for the introduction of a new social and economic order. Second, a new conservative movement had appeared that wanted a regime based on prestige, elitism, and strength and was unwilling to tolerate the free play of conflicting forces.

Uneven economic development ended international stability too by the 1890s. Germany, rapidly becoming Europe's strongest state, demanded her rightful place in the sun and her naval and colonial interests brought her into conflict with the established colonial powers. The United States and Japan also became important actors on the international stage. The European powers tried to reestablish the vanished balance by diplomatic means and alliances. This attempt led, between 1891 and 1907, to the establishment of the British-French-Russian Triple Entente which faced the Triple Alliance of Austria-Hungary, Germany, and Italy. Nationalism produced power struggles that resulted in an armaments race. The stimulus of the national ideal that drove the great powers was absent in Austria-Hungary. At the same time, the wish to expand was growing in the small neighboring states, Romania and Serbia, and even in allied Italy. The increasing economic and social strength of all ethnic groups within the monarchy increased the expansionist appetite of their conationals in neighboring states. In the absence of aid from the great powers, however, these tendencies did not endanger the monarchy or the integrity of historical Hungary.

The optimism that had produced an economic boom after the Compromise did not revive after the economic crisis of 1873. Though everyone realized that free competition on a capitalist market involved problems, the workers and peasants, who carried most of the load, were relatively quiet. Dissatisfaction was voiced primarily by the steadily poorer East Hungarian nobility, who could not adjust to the new economy, and by the small entrepreneurs unable to compete. Their worries took the form of a new, neo-conservative anti-capitalism. They also found a ready-made scapegoat in the "foreign" (German and Jewish) entrepreneurs, who were annoyingly successful. Finally, all ills could be blamed on dualism, Vienna, and the real or imaginary political and economic influences of the common institutions and court circles. The discontented did not see total independence and democratization as a panacea for economic and social ills but sought it in the "further development" of dualism, i.e., in improving Hungary's position in relation to Austria. This attitude brought the two opposition parties closer in politics: the originally more democratic Independence Party, to the liberals' left, and, to their right, the conservative National Party. Democratic-socialist criticism also became more vocal in larger industrial centers, on the street, and among the rural poor.

The Liberals' Search for a Solution, 1890–1895

Kálmán Tisza left it to his successor to see some liberal reform bills through Parliament. The new premier, Count Gyula Szapáry, achieved some economic results through the activities of his talented ministers, Gábor Baross and Sándor Wekerle. Because protective tariffs were lacking, two laws were passed that encouraged industry, and the 1892 fiscal reform introduced in the entire monarchy a new stable currency, the crown, backed by gold. Labor got permission to celebrate May Day; Sunday became an obligatory day of rest; and obligatory health insurance was introduced. Despite these concessions, however, the government used force to suppress the rural proletariat in the eastern "storm corner" of the Great Plains in 1891.

The Szapáry government failed in its attempt to modernize public administration and the 1892 elections weakened the strength of the "dualists." Both the Independence Party and the National Party, led by Count Albert Apponyi, gained ground. The main planks of the National Party's platform were the solving of the agrarian problem by the "further development" of the Compromise and the expanding of "national achievement," meaning the presence of the court in Budapest on an extended basis, the more frequent display of Hungary's coat-of-arms, and the use of Hungarian in the training of officers.

Under these circumstances, the government was glad to take advantage of the renewed political activity of the papacy and the growing religious intolerance of the lower Catholic clergy. The clergy's anti-governmental agitation made it necessary to discuss in Parliament reforms affecting Church-state and inter-confessional relations. These issues were tailor-made to split party ranks and relieve the pressure exercised by the enemies of the Compromise. The post-1867 governments had been unable to settle the relations of the state with the very rich and traditionally very influential Catholic church. The registration of births, deaths, marriages, and divorces remained in the hands of the Church. In deciding the religion of children born in mixed marriages, the Protestants had difficulties enforcing their legal rights, and even after the emancipation of the Jews in 1868, the Church forbade their marriage with Christians. Szapáry and some members of his party were against radical reform and the emperor Francis Joseph supported them. However, the majority in Parliament and in the country, supported by Kossuth in exile, were in favor of reform. The ruler finally agreed that it was a political necessity that he strengthen the government's position in its defense of the existing public order, and allowed the new prime minister, the commoner Sándor Wekerle, to submit the bill separating church and state. In spite of the opposition of the Catholic clergy, supported by court circles, Parliament voted in 1894–95 for obligatory civil marriages, for a state-kept birth-death register, for freedom of religious choice, and for making Judaism an "accepted" religion. Even the London *Times* congratulated the Hungarian government.

Behind the behavior of the parliamentary majority stood the growing nationalistic spirit of public opinion. This was considerably strengthened by the universal mourning that followed Kossuth's death after forty-five years in exile and his funeral in Budapest. Francis Joseph was disappointed because the reforms did not end the nation's discontent. For this he blamed the prime minister, who, having lost royal favor, had to resign just after his great victory. Having regained some of its vitality during the state-church debates, the Liberal Party was not willing to accept the ruler's choice for a replacement, and he was forced to turn to the party's backbenchers to have a new government formed by the Transylvania Calvinist, Baron Dezső Bánffy. From this iron-fisted former high ispán the ruler expected, first of all, the curbing of the independent national spirit, but he was to struggle also with the alarming growth of social unrest.

The Transformation of Hungarian Nationalism and the Millenary Celebration

At the time of Kossuth's funeral, Vienna was afraid of the rebirth of the revolutionary spirit of 1848. Yet most Hungarians had made their peace with the Habsburgs and with the essence of dualism. They had given up the ideal of a fully independent Hungary and, instead, were chasing the chimera of a "unified Hungarian national state." Hungarian nationalism of the mid-century had pursued the most complete independence possible with maximum freedom for all, and the nationality law of 1868, exemplary for its time in spite of its flaws, had been based on this concept. Twenty-five years later, both the government and the opposition overestimated the strength of the Hungarian nationals, and neither side was ready to give political equality to the lower classes, which would have increased Magyardom's real power. The supporters of the Compromise stressed the advantage of being a great power and hoped that, given the country's geographic position and the relative homogeneity they hoped to achieve, Hungary would in time become the dominant partner in the monarchy. To reach this goal, the Hungarians had to gain the ruler's confidence and strong positions in the common government. Andrássy, and the long-serving common minister of finance, Benjámin Kállay, took this position as did the politicians of the Independence Party. Magyarization and economic progress, predicted the publicists, would lead to the rebirth of the empire of Matthias Corvinus, which, with its thirty million Hungarians, would dominate the Balkans.

These dreams, however deluded, did not sit well with the non-Hungarian inhabitants of the country, about half of the population. Since Deák and Eötvös, no one had tried to gain their loyalty and much was done to alienate them. Their peasants refused to become Hungarians, and their priests and intellectual leaders renewed their demands for national recognition and territorial autonomy. These ambitions were expressed by the Memorandum of the Romanian National Party, submitted to the court in 1892, and by the Nationalities' Congress of Romanian, Serb, and Slovak politicians held in Budapest in 1895. The Hungarian prime minister declared that under the circumstances the state could not afford to observe the niceties of the law, and several hundred activists of the various nationalities were subjected to libel suits, police surveillance, and shows of strength by the authorities.

The emphasis on and gradual extension of Hungarian lessons in schools brought meager results. (In 1910 only 1.8 million of Hungary's 8.3 million non-Hungarians knew Hungarian.) It was a great disadvantage for the non-Hungarians that very few were public employees, members of the intelligentsia, or in Parliament. In the economy, they advanced mainly within the lesser professions and occupations. Yet they developed a flourishing banking network, which guaranteed the financial independence of their political leaders and allowed them to purchase some of the land sold by the impoverished nobility.

Hungarian chauvinism became painfully visible when the Bánffy government passed a law, in 1898, Magyarizing the names of localities. This went hand-in-hand with pressure to Magyarize people's names also. Most of the press and public opinion not only agreed with these measures, but found them insufficient.

In 1898 the country celebrated with great pomp the millennium of the Hungarians' conquest of the Carpathian Basin. The non-Hungarians rightfully abstained from participating in the festivities, which neglected the venerable tradition of a multi-national Hungary and stressed the myth of the "lordly Scythians." This impatient nationalism was not a specifically Hungarian characteristic at the turn of the century. Most nations believed themselves politically chosen, with special talents and a "manifest destiny." Nevertheless, it was a foolish luxury for the Hungarians, in their politically and geographically exposed position, to alienate the people with whom they had lived for centuries in pursuit of illusory national goals. This attitude distorted political thinking, diminished the nation's prestige abroad, and, in the long run, proved very detrimental.

The Crisis at the End of the Century and Its Provisional Solution

The attention paid to the crucial issue of relations with Austria could not hide the fact that the solving of social problems and the political emancipation of the lower classes was one of the key problems Hungary faced. Industry, mostly big industry, concentrated in Budapest and some rural centers, raised the number of those whose breadwinners were workers to about 1.2 million. As has been noted, the first Hungarian workers' party had been established in 1880. It became a significant force only in 1890, when, following the establishment of the Second International, it changed its name to the Social-Democratic Party and accepted a Marxist program aiming to nationalize the means of production. In the following years, a struggle developed within the party between the radicals preaching class war and the moderates advocating the education and organization of workers and the gaining of the majority in Parliament. With the help of the relatively well-off skilled workers, the moderate wing gained the upper hand by the end of the 1890s, though the organization of unions and strike movements continued. The party's legality helped to parry the growing pressure that began in the days of the Bánffy government and to propagate Marxist ideas. For the sake of legality, the party practically gave up agitation among agricultural workers and poor peasants after 1897.

Serious agrarian unrest first made its appearance in the eastern regions of the Great Plain. The agrarian proletariat, squeezed between large estates and rich peasants, found it increasingly difficult after the 1880s to find work. Their movement first centered around wage disputes but after 1892 took on a clearly socialist direction. In the backward areas, illusory goals dominated from the beginning, including communistic ideas, equal distribution of wealth, and, finally, anarchism. István Várkonyi, who had left the Social-Democrats to establish the Independent Socialist Party, was the first to recognize that before land could be nationalized, it was necessary to give land to the poor peasants. The discontent and misery of the peasantry produced a general harvesters' strike in 1897 and, during the winter of 1898, a veritable riot and spontaneous distribution of land, especially in the northeast of the Great Plain. The government reacted with arrests, law suits, the expulsion of "agitators," and forceful intervention. That same year, Parliament passed a law that regulated agricultural wages and legislated against the most provocative abuses but also introduced severe penalities in the case of strikes. The waves of strikes came to an end.

A more important concern for the government than the socialist movement was the weakening of its own support and of the entire political structure. Within the Liberal Party, the mercantilist wing, in which Kálmán Tisza's son, István, became prominent, supported capitalist development, industralization, and close cooperation with finance capital. They were at odds with the party's agrarian wing, mostly the owners of large and middle-sized estates, who demanded protectionism for the agrarian market, the introduction of marketing and credit cooperatives, and the repression or at least control of the "foreign" and "mobile" capitalist interests. They tried to protect their privileges by presenting them as values affecting the entire nation. They accused the ruling liberals of protecting the weak and even flirted with a mild form of anti-Semitism. These agrarians, somewhat resembling neo-conservatives elsewhere in Europe, held prominent positions both in the governmental party and in the opposition and became an important pressure group. The cooperative movement, led by Count Sándor Károlyi, had a strong agrarian tinge. In 1896, an independent Hungarian Husbandsmen Association was also established.

Clearly neo-conservative was the People's Party, established in 1895 by Count Ferdinánd Zichy, which demanded the revision of the laws regulating State-Church relations. It proposed a social policy protecting the little man as the focus of its anti-capitalist platform and even promised "full considerations" to the nationalities. However, the People's Party was too closely tied to Catholicism and too aristocratic in leadership to become truly popular. Liberalism was still too strong to allow its opponents a majority position in parliament, so a conservative-liberal two party system could not develop.

Because it rejected the Compromise, the Independence Party could not form a government. It owed its popularity to an 1848–style ideology drawing on a mixture of empty slogans, legends, and intolerance and thus found itself in an awkward situation when its nationalism made it necessary to support the existing imperial connection with Austria. In spite of its mass support, the party's leadership refused to speak out in favor of popular and democratic reforms.

The Bánffy government produced some positive legislation. Following the work of the erstwhile minister of justice, Dezső Szilágyi, the judicial transformation of the state was concluded in a liberal spirit. An administrative court was established to judge cases in which citizens and the state were the litigants. Criminal law was codified and a limited jury system was introduced. To calm the national spirit, the training of Hungarian officers was made easier.

The renegotiation of the Compromise's economic clauses ended in failure in 1897, not because Austro-Hungarian relations had worsened, but because political conditions in both halves of the monarchy had reached a critical point. In the Austrian half, the power relations between the various nationalities and parties had changed greatly. The economic and political influence of the Slavs, especially of the Czechs, had grown considerably. Among the Austro-Germans, new anti-liberal parties had become popular among the masses, and the Greater Germany movement openly advocated union with the German Empire. Those peasants and petty bourgeois loyal to the Habsburgs adopted Christian Socialism, whose anti-capitalist program had an openly anti-Semitic plank, turning it against Hungary whose capital they called "Juda-Pest." At the same time, international Social Democracy became a strong force among the middle class and the intelligentsia. These people, like the dynasty, were deeply concerned with the struggles among nationalities, which they tried to solve with their "Program of Brünn" adopted in 1899. It tried to combine the territorial and extra-territorial cultural autonomy of nationalities and individuals.

After the fall of the conservative Taaffe government in 1893, governments based on rapidly changing party coalitions followed each other, and debates in the lower house became more and more raucous and scandalous. The Badeni government introduced two measures in 1897 trying to solve the nationalities problem. In April it made both Czech and German official languages in the Czech provinces, and in November it changed the rules of the House in a move whose constitutionality was questionable. These actions produced protests of such magnitude that constitutional government became impossible in Austria and was replaced by government by decree.

In April 1898, the Bánffy and Thun governments agreed on a new economic compromise. Among its concessions to Hungary were the increase of customs on agricultural products, a more advantageous distribution of the income from excise taxes, and full parity in the Austro-Hungarian Bank. The new agreements, however, raised Hungary's share of common expenses, and this produced protests and parliamentary obstruction by the Independents. The two governments finally agreed in August that they would keep in force the economic agreement of 1887 until the international trade agreements expired in 1903 or even longer, if necessary. The opposition accused the government of giving up the nation's right to settle its economic problems, and the National and People's parties joined the Independence Party in obstructing the workings of Parliament. Not even the budget could be passed.

Critically important principles appeared to be at stake, worth rejecting a favorable economic agreement, diminishing the prestige of Parliament by obstructionary tactics, and pushing the country into an "ex-lex" position by forcing the government to rule unconstitutionally in the absence of a budget. This was not the case as events proved.

Once the hard-pressed Bánffy government gave way in January 1899 to that of Kálmán Széll, Deák's son-in-law, who was on good terms with everybody, obstruction was terminated within a few hours, an agreement was reached on the budget and on recruitment for the army, and the National Party dissolved itself, with its members joining the Liberal Party. Széll paid very little for these concessions. He promised that the Supreme Court would handle cases dealing with electoral abuses and produced a meaningless legal formula that stated that because the commercial agreement could not be prolonged in a constitutional fashion, Hungary was henceforth legally an independent customs territory. This sounded so good that the opposition accepted the prolongation of the old agreement until 1903.

In presenting his program to Parliament, Széll promised to govern according to the requirements of "law, justice and equity," and as far as the minorities represented in Parliament were concerned, he kept his word. Thus in the 1901 election, the forces of independence repressed five years earlier by Bánffy made respectable gains. Against popular movements, Bánffy's methods remained more or less in force, but as far as the non-Hungarians were concerned, Széll was much more tactful than his predecessor had been. Yet he succeeded in gaining only a few years of relative tranquillity.

The crisis that hit both halves of the monarchy at the end of the century lowered its prestige on the international scene. Yet predictions of its dissolution in favor of national units were unfounded. The citizens of Austria-Hungary wanted not to destroy it but to reorganize it. While nationality problems in both halves were clearly worsening, the growing conflicts between the two ruling nations, the Austro-Germans and Hungarians, were the most important problem. The contradictions of the dualist system could have been solved either by separation or by the federalization of the state. The great majority of those who had political influence opposed both solutions. The result was growing chaos, rigidity, and repression.

The Transformation of Society

Hungary's population (Croatia included) grew from 15.5 million in 1869 to 20.9 million in 1910. (The European population explosion of the early nineteenth century began in Hungary only in the 1880s.) Growth was slowed, however, by massive emigration; within four decades, more than two million Hungarian citizens left the country, and 90 percent of these went to the United States. About a half million of the latter came back and about three to four hundred thousand returned from the Monarchy's eastern provinces. Thus, the country lost about 1.2 million inhabitants.

Internal migration also changed the country's demographic structure. People moved from the border regions and the less developed eastern provinces towards the center, especially Budapest, the other industrial centers, and the Great Plain. The population of urban settlements doubled within three decades, reaching 23.5 percent of the total population by 1910. Especially important was the growth of the capital. On the eve of World War I, Budapest had nearly one million inhabitants (considerably more counting suburbs) and was Europe's sixth largest city.

Hungary's various nationalities grew at different rates as a result of differing rates of both reproduction and emigration. The high Hungarian growth rate was due, first of all, to assimilation. Contemporaries and later historians explained this phenomenon by forced Magyarization, but documents and social history offer a different explanation. Assimilation was basically a spontaneous process due to economic transformation, urbanization and "embourgeoisement," the last speeded up by Magyarization. Assimilation resulted from the demands of society, the interests of the individual, and internal migration. Between 1880 and 1910, about a half million Germans, some 300,000 Slovaks, and tens of thousands of southern Slavs, Romanians, and Ruthenians became Hungarian in speech and culture, although not always in family names.

A special case was the assimilation of Jews. Their number doubled, partly by immigration, during the Dual Monarchy and reached one million by 1910. Jews, considered a religious rather than an ethnic group, played a prominent role in the development of Hungarian capitalism and urbanization. A few statistics will illustrate this point. In 1910 about 5 percent of Hungary's population was Jewish. Among the 250,000 Jews in commerce, 283 were bankers and 8,237 were bank employees. Twenty percent of Jews earned their living as clerks or in the professions, 38 percent were merchants or craftsmen, and 34 percent were workers. Twelve and a half percent of the country's industrialists, 54 percent of the merchants, and 43 percent of the employees of credit institutions were Jewish. Of those working in the free professions, 42 percent of the newspaper-men, 45 percent of the lawyers, and 49 percent of the doctors were Jews. The country certainly needed their talent, entrepreneurial spirit, and cooperation, while their assimilation tilted the ethnic balance in favor of the Magyar. What they got in exchange was full legal and economic emancipation as well as a national identity and culture. As one prominent Jew declared: "Those who had been homeless for millenia found a home on Hungarian soil." About 75 percent of the Yiddish-speaking immigrants who had entered Hungary by the turn of the century became Hungarians in speech, culture, and mentality.

Ethnic Hungarians were pleased with the growth of Magyardom, and the government tried to encourage it in pursuit of a unified Hungarian state. Yet despite the government's repressive measures, there was no legal discrimination, resettlement, or political pressure to justify the references in historical literature to "ruthless Magyarization." Detailed census figures show that Magyarization did not touch the great majority of agrarian people.

The capitalistic economic development, which accelerated after the 1880s, changed the country's social structure considerably. Within four decades it lost its Eastern European agrarian character, moving closer to the Western European industrial pattern. Between 1869 and 1910, the portion of the population living from industry rose from 12 to 26 percent. This meant that about two million people changed their occupation, and with it their place of domicile, social stratum, and way of living.

The two thousand or so landowners who had estates of over 2,850 acres owned 23 percent of the land. Of these owners, twelve hundred were magnates. The ninety-two large estates they owned, 35 percent of their land, were inalienable and indivisible entailed estates. During the years of dualism, the direct political power of the magnates diminished slightly, but their economic power and social prestige remained practically unchanged. Most of the major landowners successfully participated in the capitalist economy and wielded great influence. By their very existence, importance, and behavior, the owners of large estates represented a remnant of feudalism and adjusted to the new industrial society only to the degree to which they could profit from it. The new titles and decorations bestowed by the ruler created a new parvenu nobility, and something like nine hundred nobles formerly of middle rank acquired large estates of up to fifteen hundred acres. Finally, about 20 percent of all large estates belonged to members of the industrial middle class who had bought land. While these people adopted the trappings of aristocratic life, they continued to concentrate on their industrial and business activities.

Next in the social hierarchy came the haute bourgeoisie; the wholesale merchants, industrialists, builders, and bankers who understood the new economy.

Below these came the rich middle-class families. These two groups, together about four or five thousand families, included numerous Jews, the most successful of whom were actually ennobled. Their double mentality was interesting, for though they adopted the role of nobility, they retained their traditional middle-class virtues, worked hard, lived simply, were thrifty, and supported cultural establishments and charities. The most prominent among them retained their old family names, writing before them their new Hungarian titles.

In the middle of the social scale were the so-called "gentry" and the mostly assimilated middle class. The "gentry" families, erstwhile owners of smaller estates, had found it difficult to adjust to the new economic system. Between the ending of serfdom and 1867 the number of these smaller landowners fell by half, and in the next fifty years it fell by half again. About seven thousand families belonged to this group by 1910. Because of their extensive connections, they retained their social importance and their political influence in the counties. Those who had lost their lands were absorbed into the state bureaucracy, where their colleagues were mainly descendants of small landlords or landless nobles. Together they formed, after the 1880s, the "Hungarian gentry." Wickham Steed, the Austro-Hungarian correspondent of the London *Times,* estimated in 1905 that about 800,000 people belonged to the Hungarian gentry. While he may have overestimated, they amounted to something like 4.7 percent of the population. Steed described them as in "some regards . . . the backbone and in others the bane of Hungary." The middle class, of heterogeneous background, consisted of owners of small enterprises, shopkeepers, and owners of apartment houses and numbered around ten thousand.

Financially less advantageous was the position of the ever-growing bureaucracy and intelligentsia. Nearly 750,000 strong, they made up 4.2 percent of the population. To this group belonged the public employees and those working in the private sector as clerks and members of the free professions: doctors, engineers, lawyers, and professors. People of Hungarian origin or those who had been assimilated made up 82 percent of this middle class, and of these, about a quarter were Jewish. The mentality, lifestyle, and behavior of this mixed group was determined by the traditional values and "gentry mentality" of the nobility. Its main features at the turn of the century were conservatism in politics, agrarianism in economics, and gentlemanly behavior and exclusiveness in social life.

On the next lower rung of the social scale came the lesser artisans, owners of small shops, the office attendants, postmen, non-commissioned officers, foremen, apartment house superintendents, and so forth, about 2.3 million people (1.5 million of them Hungarians). This group was economically weak, disunited, with few exceptions not upwardly mobile, and not inclined to espouse radical or socialist alternatives.

Of Hungary's population, 62 percent lived from agriculture in 1910. Of these, seven million were landowning peasants, including about 2.8 million Hungarians. The best off were those of Transdanubia, who had introduced intensive farming. They were followed by those living in the middle and southern districts of the Great Plain. The peasantry's holdings and equipment differed greatly.

About sixty-five to seventy thousand rich peasants and about 250,000 moderately situated peasants (mostly non-Hungarians) successfully adopted capitalistic production methods, increased their holdings, and employed others. While in western Transdanubia and on the Little Plain profit-oriented modern agriculture gained prominence, on the Great Plain more primitive methods and thinking remained dominant. The 3.5 million peasants who owned between seventy and one hundred acres had a much harder life, but ownership and attitudes made them also part of the "husbandsman's society." The peasantry, as a class, in spite of its own sharp internal differences, had a totally different outlook from that of the landowning and bourgeois elements. Upward mobility was effectively blocked by the shortage of land and the pressure of the large estates. Because there was no thought of land reform, only emigration offered an alternative way of life.

The agrarian proletariat, about one quarter of the population, occupied the bottom of the social pyramid. This group included the servants of the estates, tied for life to their place; harvest hands, who had only seasonal work; and, migrant harvest workers, many of whom did not own a permanent home. If the 2.5 million peasants struggling to make a living from less than five acres are classed with this group then it was true, as a foreign historian observed, that materially "nearly half of the population of Hungary was living at a sub-human level." The Ottoman occupation, "second serfdom," and absolutism, had all contributed to the creation of these conditions, but it must be acknowledged that the regime spent far more effort on preventing the peasantry from revolting against their condition, than on trying to improve it.

After the 1890s, the most rapidly growing social group was the working class. In 1910 its 2.5 million members accounted for a good 13 percent of the population. Of them, 63 percent were Hungarian, 15.5 percent German, 10 percent Slovak, and 5 percent Romanian. The backbone of the labor force was the relatively well-paid group of skilled laborers, most of whom worked in the large factories of Budapest. After the turn of the century, their salaries stagnated while the amount of work increased and the housing situation deteriorated.

Hungary's emergence as a modern society was not accompanied by changes in power relations. The aristocrats and the gentry retained their hegemony and the supremacy of the Hungarians became more pronounced.

The Great Crisis of 1903–1906

The Dual Monarchy's international position weakened around 1900. Her rival in the Balkans, Russia, was strengthened by an alliance with France, while Great Britain, facing colonial problems, gave up its traditional pro-Austrian policy. Nationalism shaped the foreign policies of the great powers, but could not in Austria-Hungary, where fourteen nationalities lived together. Foreign Minister Count Agenor Gołuchowski, Jr. recognized that under the circumstances, the empire's foreign policy had to be defensive, and, although a Pole, he sought a rapprochement with Russia. Preoccupied with her Far Eastern policy, Russia was receptive. When the two emperors met in April 1897 in St. Petersburg, they agreed to maintain the status quo in the Balkans. The relationship between the two conservative powers improved, and when the Balkan people became restless again, Tsar Nicholas II did not support them, but agreed with Francis Joseph, whom he encountered in 1903 at Mürzsteg, to undertake a two-power démarche at Istanbul, asking the Ottoman government to settle the Macedonian question. When, in February 1904, the Russo-Japanese war began, Austria-Hungary aided Russia with her benevolent neutrality.

Although the Triple Alliance was renewed in 1902, Italy continued to distance herself from her partners. Italian irredentism centered on the half million Italians in the Southern Tyrol, and the country's growing interest in the Balkans cooled her relations with Austria-Hungary. Austria-Hungary's ties with Germany weakened also, mainly because Berlin did not support Vienna's ambitions in the Balkans.

While the parliamentary peace was still in force in Hungary, Baron Géza Fejérváry, Hungarian minister of defense, submitted a bill raising the yearly recruitment quota. Francis Joseph, the leaders of the army, and the partisans of dualism led by István Tisza, wanted to strengthen the army in preparation for any possible conflict. The opposition, mainly the Independence Party, had no objections, but saw the bill as a chance to demand the introduction of Hungarian as the service and command language for units recruited in Hungary. This involved the Magyarization of some ninety German expressions and commands. According to the Compromise, the ruler had the right to make decisions of this kind, and he was opposed to giving up the "unity" of the armed forces.

More was involved than simply ninety words. The "common" army was very unpopular in Hungary because it had retained a pro-Habsburg mentality that dated back to 1848–49, and it often behaved in a provocative manner. This last remnant of royal absolutism contradicted the spirit of dualism and the independence of Hungary and appeared to be a denial of the country's "Hungarian character." The opposition chose the debate over the recruitment bill as an occasion to fight for the full sovereignty of Parliament. They were thinking not only of the problems posed by the nationalities, but also of their future king. The heir presumptive, Francis Joseph's nephew, the archduke Francis Ferdinand, had made little effort to hide his anti-Hungarian feelings. His ideal was a unified and centralized monarchy in which Hungarians would have little to say, even about their own affairs.

Széll hoped that the new economic compromise, concluded on the last day of 1902 and favorable to Hungarian agrarian interests, would help to get the recruitment bill through Parliament, but the opposition paralyzed the session by its obstructionist tactics. Széll tried, unsuccessfully, to wait out the opposition, and Count Károly Khuen-Héderváry, the iron-fisted former ban of Croatia, who replaced him in June 1903 could not master the opposition either. The king then turned to István Tisza. Tisza was convinced that given the nationality problem and the international situation, the dualist system was politically the best solution for Hungarians. The dualist state had to be supported for economic reasons as well. Thus, Tisza believed, it was not wise to fight even for justified demands at that moment. Finally, the new prime minister was convinced that the recruitment bill had to pass to help to maintain the country's status as a great power and that parliamentary obstruction had to be prevented in the future to ensure the smooth working of the legislature.

Tisza's political thinking was logical. In character, honesty, and firmness, he was head and shoulders above his fellow politicians. He abhorred petty political tactics and cheap popularity, though these admirable attitudes were not designed to bring political success. Since the disappearance of those who had concluded the Compromise, the traditional Hungarian leadership did not have a man of his stature. The trouble was that his "traditionalism," with its paternalistic, aristocratic liberalism based on the supremacy of the "historical classes" (the unpopular large estates, the disappearing middle nobility, and the "national intelligentsia") had become anachronistic at a time of growing social stress and demands for democratization. In only one respect was Tisza truly a man of his time. He understood that industrialization and the introduction of capitalism in general was necessary and advantageous. However, his "mercantilism" turned the conservative agrarians of his own class against him, and at the same time he was not able to understand that he had to satisfy some of the demands voiced by the lower classes in order to strengthen his own liberal program.

To end obstruction once and for all, Tisza introduced provisional modifications into the rules of the House in an illegal fashion on November 18, 1904. He gained a pyrrhic victory. In protest, Gyula Andrássy, Jr., together with numerous others, left the Liberal Party and joined the coalition of independents, agrarians, and clericals, aiming to reach a common platform based on the "further development" of dualism and the toning down of radical demands. The election of January 1905, which was supposed to solve the crisis, brought the first defeat of the Liberals, ending their rule of thirty years. They gained only 159 mandates while the new coalition elected 235 deputies. The system established in 1867 faced its most serious crisis.

The Independence Party declared itself ready to assume power and lead a government based on respect for the Compromise, and Francis Joseph was willing to appoint Lajos Kossuth's son, Ferenc, as prime minister. The problem was that the king refused to act in accordance with the platform of the victors and "make national concessions" in cases which involved his "constitutional sovereign rights." On the surface the crisis hinged on constitutional issues. It became political due to the coalition's unwillingness to compromise. The real issue was in fact simply systemic. The crisis indicated clearly that there were several contradictions in the Compromise laws of 1867, that they placed limits on constitutionalism and parliamentary sovereignty, and that independence had been curtailed.

The failure of secret negotiations, which lasted for months, coupled with the example of revolutionary events in Russia encouraged a series of strikes. Tens of thousands were involved, and the movement of the iron workers of Budapest and the harvesters in Transdanubia even brought some results. The spirit of independence grew in the country, and some people in Vienna feared that the Hungarians would follow the example of the Norwegians (who had recently seceded from Denmark). Not even the most extreme politicans of the Independence Party had this in mind.

In June, Francis Joseph appointed a non-parliamentary caretaker government, with Baron Géza Fejérváry as prime minister to mediate between him and what he hoped was a weakening coalition. The lower house, in which the coalition had a majority, protested by calling for nationwide passive resistance including the non-payment of taxes and the refusal to send recruits to the army.

For most inhabitants of the country, the real issue was not that of German command words or even the rights of Parliament. The early 1900s witnessed a small-scale economic crisis followed by stagnation. This led to wage disputes, which strengthened the influence of the Social Democrats. The party's congress in 1903 retained as final goals the nationalization of the means of production and the "conquest of political power," but also stressed more immediate and popular demands, including universal secret suffrage. This program failed because it remained wedded to the doctrines of the Second International and did not come to grips with specifically Hungarian, that is Central European, problems. It continued to distance itself from the idea of land reform and from peasant problems in general. Establishing this linkage would not have been easy either in theory or practice. Nevertheless, it was unfortunate that the party not only accepted, but proudly proclaimed that it was "unpatriotic"; this lessened the possiblity of cooperation with other democratic forces. Yet the political crisis offered a good opportunity to express, through strikes and other means, the economic demands, political desiderata, and other requests and to tie these to a political resistance loaded with national implications. The socialist leaders first hoped that the coalition would introduce universal suffrage, but when József Kristóffy, the minister of the interior in the Fejérváry government, proclaimed that the government was ready to support universal suffrage instead of backing "the movement centered around the exaggerated issue of command words" the socialists began to back him.

The Crown Council of August 22 at Ischl under Francis Joseph's presidency discussed three alternatives: come to an agreement with the coalition by making military concessions; proclaim universal suffrage and create a new loyal majority with a broad reform program satisfying the social and national demands of large masses; or occupy Hungary by military force. The third alternative seemed indicated by a general strike and demonstration by some one hundred thousand workers in Budapest on September 15, but the leaders were satisfied with submitting a petition to Parliament and with the request of the president of the lower house for patience and confidence. Armed intervention was rejected at Ischl because requests for universal suffrage were coming from all over the empire and because of the attitude of the nationalities living in Hungary. Most of these took a wait-and-see attitude in observing the struggle between the crown and the coalition. The Croats, traditionally loyal to the dynasty, even decided to unite with the Serbs living among them and to cooperate with the Hungarian coalition. This is what their "Resolution of Fiume" of October 3 expressed clearly. In the end, Francis Joseph had no choice but to opt for the reform program of the Fejérváry government.

Threatened by reforms from above, even the remnants of the Liberal Party joined the coalition's "national resistance." On February 19, 1906, the army, violating the constitution, occupied Parliament, and a royal commissioner read a rescript dissolving the legislature without setting the date for new elections. The Fejérváry government also began to act energetically against those counties who had joined the national resistance movement. Faced with these actions, the coalition did nothing but search for a way of graceful retreat. On April 6, 1906, Ferenc Kossuth and Andrássy Jr. accepted the agreement offered to them by the ruler in secret: the coalition would be asked to form a government but would raise no military issues, would accept the international trade agreements that had been signed during the crisis, would not hold the Fejérváry government financially or legally responsible for its actions, and would introduce the electoral reform promised by Kristóffy.

The "national struggle" against absolutism lacked both power and the backing of society. The Socialists' belief that the dynasty would cooperate with them against its traditional allies also proved to be an illusion. Yet, the crisis did have lasting significance. The old order could not be reestablished, the prestige of the constitution was irreparably damaged, and the worker and peasant masses had learned that mass movements represented a real force. The non-Hungarian peoples had worked out new tactics and programs during the crisis and pursued with increased confidence their struggle for democratic rights. It was also significant that Europe lost confidence in the Hungarian political leadership and its liberalism and in the stabilizing role of the Dual Monarchy. Thus the crisis had lasting effects on the dualist system and the future of both Hungary and Austria-Hungary.

The Failure of the Coalition Government

The public did not know that the coalition had come to power through an agreement with Francis Joseph, and the coalition tried to present its capitulation as a victory. The "ministry of all the talents" headed by Wekerle and including Andrássy Jr., Apponyi, Ferenc Kossuth, Géza Polonyi, and Count Ferdinánd Zichy, was expected to bring drastic changes after forty years of one-party rule. After Tisza dissolved the Liberal Party, the Independence Party had no difficulty in gaining an absolute majority in the May election. For all practical purposes, the party had adopted a program based on the Compromise. The opposition consisted mainly of sixteen Romanian, nine Slovak, two Serb, and three Agrarian Socialist deputies.

The government took the reestablishment of public order seriously. It calmed the renewed strike movement and the discontented workers and agricultural population with a combination of restrictive measures and social reforms. The reforms included workman's compensation, higher salaries for railroad workers, the construction of apartments for workers, and the legal regulation of the rights of servants. In introducing these reforms, the government was anything but impartial, and this became especially obvious when the rights of servants were settled (although the general verdict that it "tied them to the soil once more" was exaggerated).

From a parliament dominated by the independents, public opinion expected, first of all, the satisfying of nationalistic aims and goals. Yet, as far as this issue was concerned, the government's hands were tied by the Compromise itself, the position taken by the Austrian parties, and last but not least, by the ruler. Francis Joseph's attitude became more inflexible due to the influence of the heir presumptive, Francis Ferdinand, who complained that the monarchy was "entirely in the hands of Jews, freemasons, socialists, and Hungarians." Francis Ferdinand created his own cabinet at the Belvedere Palace, where he worked with his advisors to reestablish a centralized and unified monarchy. It was typical that it took months before Andrássy Jr. succeeded in having Francis Joseph accept a watered-down version of the jurisdiction of administrative courts and the laws extending the self-government of counties and cities, considered to be the guarantees of constitutionalism. Popular but unrealizable were the demands that coupled an independent economy with an independent customs region, and in fact Hungary's contribution to common expenses was raised to 36.4 percent. Nevertheless, a law that considerably helped domestic industries passed in 1907.

Only in its attitude towards the nationalities could the government give free rein to its nationalistic proclivities. The growing strength of the nationalities, the increased activities of their by now bourgeois and professional leadership, and their increased representation in Parliament bothered the coalition and heightened its chauvinism. The school laws, known as the "Lex Apponyi," increased the level of education and made elementary education free, but the higher salaries mandated for teachers could not be paid by schools maintained by nationality communities and churches without state subsidy. This subsidy was tied to the number of hours devoted to teaching Hungarian, to the use of officially approved textbooks, and to programs inculcating an "exemplary patriotic attitude." Protests were launched, mainly by the affected ecclesiastic organizations, and the law was severely criticized in Western Europe also. Lajós Mocsáry and other radical intellectuals attacked it as undemocratic and nearsighted.

Within a short period the coalition also lost the sympathy of the Croats. The railroad regulations worked out by Ferenc Kossuth in 1907 made knowledge of Hungarian obligatory for all employees of the state railroads. The only concession made to the Croats was that knowledge of Croatian was required of those employees who were in contact with travelers. The coalition of Croats and Serbs considered this regulation a violation of the *Nagodba* and instructed its forty representatives in the lower house in Budapest to begin obstruction in Croatian. They had a right to use this language, but this was the first time that they had spoken it in Parliament. When the railroad regulations were introduced, order broke down in Croatia. The Croatian legislature *(Sabor)* had to be adjourned and absolutist rule introduced.

The government also took a "firm" stand in dealing with the nationalities' presses and their more outspoken politicians. "For incitement against the nation," that is, for criticizing the government's nationality policy, numerous law suits were instituted. In Slovak Csernova (Černová), after the consecration of a new church was prevented, protesters were fired upon by the gendarmery. Fifteen people died and fifty-nine others were sent to jail for "revolting." The news of the massacre reached all of Europe and was one of the reasons inducing the young British historian, Robert W. Seton-Watson, to write his indictment of Hungary's nationality policy, a work that convinced the entire English-speaking world.

Before it assumed power, the coalition had begun to negotiate with Serbia, but this approach died when it took over the government. Supporting protectionism in all its forms, the coalition agreed to customs wars "to teach Serbia a lesson," suggested by the Common Ministry of Foreign Affairs. Both Vienna and Budapest feared that Serbia would play the role of Piedmont in the Balkans. Franz Conrad von Hötzendorf, the chief-of-staff, demanded a "preventive" war against Serbia. The politicians were nearsighted enough to see only "foreign agitation" in the birth of the Croat-Serb Coalition and the growing popularity of the Yugoslav movement. They even "discovered" illegal contacts with Belgrade and instituted a process in Zágráb against fifty-three Serb politicians, accusing them of treason. News of the heavy punishments was received with great indignation all over Europe, especially after Professor Thomáš G. Masaryk, a Czech deputy in the Viennese parliament, proved that most of the documents submitted as evidence were forgeries. The accused had to be declared innocent.

Independently from domestic difficulties, the monarchy's international situation also deteriorated. Germany, using her economic strength, had embarked on an active world-wide policy that provoked the establishment of the Triple Entente. Russia, one of its members, tried to regain the prestige it had lost in the war against Japan through a reactivated Balkan policy and support for Slavs everywhere. Count Alois Lexa Aehrenthal, who became common minister of foreign affairs in the fall of 1906, rejected the defensive policy of his predecessor and believed that the country had to pursue an active policy in the Balkans, to reestablish its influence in the peninsula's western half. He reached an agreement with the Russian foreign minister, Alexander Isvolskii, according to which the monarchy could annex occupied Bosnia-Hercegovina in exchange for not opposing a revision of the convention limiting Russia's freedom to use the Turkish Straits. He proclaimed the annexation on October 6, 1908 before Russia had time to convince the other powers that new rules of navigation should be put in force in the straits. This action produced sharp protests from the Entente powers, the Ottoman Empire, and Serbia, which hoped to gain the annexed provinces itself. For the first time, Germany supported its ally openly, but this stance only deepened the chasm between the alliance systems. The Hungarian coalition government, in contradiction of its traditional policy, cooperated with the foreign minister, whose move it approved ahead of time. The coalition hoped that, given Hungary's medieval claims, Bosnia-Hercegovina would be placed under Hungarian jurisdiction. This did not occur. Bosnia-Hercegovina became an imperial province.

It was not foreign affairs that caused the country's dissatisfaction with the coalition's rule. The greatest disappointment was the electoral reform bill Andrássy Jr. submitted to parliament in 1908. "To avoid the dangers which the immediate introduction of a fully democratic franchise would entail," he proposed the introduction of a weighted electoral system. Depending on their wealth and education, men over the age of twenty-four were given one, two, or three votes, while the illiterates received one vote only for every twelve men. It was not so much an attempt to retain the supremacy of the upper classes as a measure directed against the nationalities. Nevertheless, the bill was badly received by practially everybody.

The supporters and some leaders of the Independence Party were disillusioned, first of all, by the government's failure to produce "national achievements" and by its loyal cooperation with the court. In 1908, the party's unity began to weaken, leading to a break following a dispute centered around the Austro-Hungarian Bank. Those who agitated for an independent Hungarian National Bank did so not because they expected important economic gains but because they saw in this bank a symbol of the country's full independence. In April 1909, Francis Joseph ended the debate by rejecting the idea of a syndicated bank. This produced the government's demission. After a transition period, the ruler's old advisor, Count Károly Khuen-Héderváry, formed a new government based on the support of the National Society established by Tisza. This group was transformed, a month later, into the Party of National Work.

The Democratic Challenge

The constitutional crisis and the rule of the coalition destroyed some old illusions, and the age of classical liberalism was over. Therefore, some hopes that earlier had not appeared immediately realizable were reawakened. It became obvious that the opposition was not interested in thorough reform, democracy, or social change. When given the chance to govern, it was even less satisfactory than earlier governments had been. The reform attempts of Fejérváry and Kristóffy placed on the political agenda alternatives which had been considered truly radical. Furthermore, social developments, economic progress, and a higher educational level increased the number of groups and individuals who wanted a share of profits and a larger voice in deciding affairs. Those who had been born in the late 1870s were partisans of reform and were often active as well in newly flourishing cultural activities.

In spite of errors, the early years of this century were an active period for Hungarian Social Democracy, which produced a group of very able leaders, including Ernő Garami, an ideal modern party leader, Jakab Weltner, who ably represented the working masses, and the more radical Dezső Bokányi, who proved to be a convincing public speaker. Zsigmond Kunfi represented those members of the intelligentsia who turned toward socialism. Finally, Ervin Szabó was an original theoretician of universal stature who turned, disillusioned, to syndicalism. A left wing, opposing this leadership, also made its appearance. Its members were among the founders of the future Communist movement.

The peasantry, true to the tradition of Kossuth, supported the Independence Party, but its interests and hunger for land made it dissatisfied with the party's activities. Because of their agrarian plank, the socialists could satisfy the agrarian proletariat, but only if they included nationalistic issues in their program. This was what Vilmos Mezőfi's Reorganized Social Democratic Party tried to do. After 1908, this party tried to gain the support of the small landowners too and changed its name to the 48er Social Democratic Party. Based entirely on the peasantry, and representing its special interests was the radical peasant movement organized east of the Tisza by the well-to-do farmer, András Achim. Even after he became a member of Parliament, he remained true to this program, which in 1906 demanded the nationalization of estates over fourteen thousand acres, the renting of these lands to peasants, and the legal recognition of agricultural strikes. Being of Slovak origin, he was free of nationalism and capable of establishing contact with Kristóffy. For a while he believed in the dynasty's reform program. The Independent Peasant Union of Hungary, which he founded in 1908, reduced the size of estates to be distributed to fourteen hundred acres. When, for reasons not merely political, his enemies murdered him in 1911, Achim's movement was already declining. The peasantry turned again to the Independence Party, now led by Gyula Justh.

During the years of the coalition's rule, a peasant movement with socialist leanings, the National Agrarian Party, made its appearance in the northeast of the Great Plain. More durable was the movement of the landowning peasantry of Transdanubia, established in 1909 by István Szabó Nagyatádi. This 48er Independent National Farmer's Party demanded land reform at the state's expense, universal suffrage, graduated taxes, and school reforms. It was opposed to revolutionary agitations and maintained contact with the independents.

Bourgeois radicalism was the best prepared and strongest democratic challenger of the regime. The magazine *Huszadik Század (Twentieth Century)*, which began publication in 1900, and the Social Science Association established a year later educated the new generation of Hungarian intelligentsia. This association, many of its members Jewish, became a political force during the crisis, when it backed the Fejérváry government, but its true ideology became clear while the coalition was in power, as it became the coalition's extra-parliamentary opponent. These men rejected the dated liberalism of their fathers, condemned the chauvinism and romantic bombast of the "national" ideal, and sought in modern social sciences the answer to Hungary's internal problems. At first their activity was not so much political as scientific and literary. Their program was made public by their multi-talented and brilliant leader, Oszkár Jászi, in his 1907 article, "Toward a New

Hungary." The program demanded an independent customs area, the dissolution of large estates, a cooperative network for peasants (who were educated in the methods of intensive agriculture), democratic local self-government, educational reform, graduated taxes, general health and social insurance, and the enforcement of the nationalities' law. The goal was to bring into one program, in a compatible fashion, the ideals of independence and democratic progress. As one of Jászi's friends put it, the aim was to harmonize "free thought with Hungarian thinking." Philosophically, these men were students of Spencer, social Darwinism, and Marxist historical materialism; they might have been the last followers of "scientific evolutionism." Their publicistic efforts centered around the economic and political emancipation of the peasantry, but their sociographic activity encompassed all of society.

Both theoretically and practically, their most important achievement was the support they gave to the nationalities and their cause. In his large volume devoted to this problem, Jászi explained that the birth of national conscience was not, as many Hungarians believed, the result of the work of hostile agitators, "but an unavoidable side effect of a universally observable historical development." He believed that "good schools, good public administration and good courts" would assure that all nationalities would be able to safeguard and develop their languages and culture and thus become satisfied and coequal citizens of Hungary. He advocated full independence for Hungary because he viewed it as the first step leading to the free cooperation of the peoples living in the Carpathian Basin in the creation of a truly federative state. The introduction of universal suffrage was, according to Jászi, the precondition for the emergence of a new way of thinking without which the other changes were unimaginable.

These bourgeois radicals, who included, besides Jászi, Robert Braun, Pál Szende, Bódog Somló, Arnold Daniel, and many others, did not advocate either revolution or the dissolution of Austria-Hungary. They felt that granting the nationalities their rights was fully compatible with the integrity of historical Hungary. They accepted socialism as a goal for the distant future and considered the Social Democrats their close allies. They found strong support in the Galilei Circle established in 1908 by university students, and after that year they approached the left wing of the independents and other movements with democratic leanings, including the Freemasons. They also had close contacts with the century's outstanding Hungarian poet, Endre Ady, whose work, in many respects, was the artistic voice of bourgeois radicalism.

The Twentieth Century group firmly believed in reason and in the force of a well-presented argument, yet they were on occasion intellectually stubborn and nearsighted. They attacked their fathers' dated liberalism unmercifully but did not see the difference between their political and their intellectual enemies. They were both typically Hungarian and also members of that universal movement which sought to find a way leading away from capitalism, imperialism, and the all-powerful and dictatorial state through unreserved faith in civil liberties and democracy. Their views gained credence after 1914 and especially after the Second World War.

In its aims and influence, the artistic renaissance of the early twentieth century paralleled the reform movement. Its leader and embodiment was Ady, who filled "the new age with new songs," asking the Danube region's oppressed nations to revolt jointly against "the outdated county hall," symbolizing the old order.

The old national art forms were still well-represented by Mór Jókai in literature, Victor Madarász, Bertalan Székely, and Gyula Benczúr in painting, and in architecture by Alajos Hauszmann and Imre Steindl. A new more civic spirit was represented by the writers Sándor Bródy and the somewhat archaic favorite of the middle class, Ferenc Herczeg together with the Comic Theater (Vigszinház), the eclectic architect Ignác Alpár, and the sculptors György Zala and Alajos Strobl. Theater, comedy, and operetta also became popular.

The secessionists differed from both the old and new trends, turning consciously to the *Art nouveau* of the Western bourgeois world, which it took as its model. Even the title of the magazine *Nyugat (The West)* expressed this trend. In its pages Mihály Babits, Árpád Tóth, Gyula Juhász, and Dezső Kosztolányi published their poetry while Margit Kaffka, Zsigmond Móricz, Frigyes Karinthy, and Dezső Szabó contributed prose. The outstanding figure of this new trend was Gyula Krúdy. In the theater the Thalia Company represented the same trend after 1904. In painting, the impressionist school working at Nagybánya, included Károly Ferenczy and János Thorma, broke new ground, together with József Rippl-Ronai and the outstanding Tivadar Csontváry-Kosztka. Hungarian folk art was the inspiration, in both form and motives, for Béla Bartók's and Zoltán Kodály's music, of Aladár Kőrösfői-Krisch's paintings, and of the artist colony of Gödöllő. Ödön Lechner and later Béla Lajta tried to create a Hungarian architectural style.

The early years of the century brought important cultural changes, and not only among the practitioners of literature and art. Hungarian society at large now began to support artistic self-expression, resulting in the divergence of high and popular culture. This differentiation of tastes had political overtones too, separating the innovators from the traditionalists. In spite of its modernity, the cultural renaissance rejected the idea of art for art's sake.

The best schools gave excellent scientific training and taught their pupils to think for themselves. University education was outstanding, especially in the natural sciences, medicine, and technical subjects. Among those emerging from Hungarian universities at this time were the internationally known physicists Loránd Eötvös and his pupil Győző Zemplén; Gyula König, who started a new school in mathematics; the master of the theory of functions, Lipót Fejér; and Frigyes Riesz, one of the pioneers of set theory.

A considerable medical network had been developed by the turn of the century. Frigyes Korányi and his son Sándor achieved notable results in clinical medicine, as did József Fodor in organizing public health services. Endre Hőgyes' physiological research was also widely acclaimed. The Technical University of Budapest successfully combined research and application. Among its students, Károly Zipernowsky, Miksa Déri, Otto Titusz Bláthy, and Kálmán

Kandó did excellent work in electrical engineering and Donát Bánki and János Csonka were among the pioneers working with the internal combustion engine.

The Last Years of Peace

Disappointed in the rule of the coalition, the country expected much from Khuen-Héderváry, who promised electoral reforms, liberal changes, and tolerance for the non-Hungarians. In the elections of June, the Party of National Labor gained the absolute majority, defeating the demoralized and faction-ridden Independents, the strongly reduced People's Party, and the deputies of the nationalities. The new majority agreed on maintaining the relationship with Austria, but while one of its wings believed that cautious reform was needed, the other defended stubbornly the old system, especially as far as suffrage was concerned. They also agreed that the international situation required domestic consolidation and the strengthening of the empire's power.

The tension between the alliance systems entered a new phase marked by a naval armaments race. In this respect Austria-Hungary was far behind, and her status and value as an ally were in danger. In response, the Hungarian government submitted a bill to Parliament in May 1911 considerably raising the number of recruits and military expenditures. The Second Moroccan Crisis and the Ottoman-Italian war of 1911 appeared to justify these measures.

Even the opposition agreed in principle with the new bill. They refrained from tying it to national demands, which had proven unrealizable, but asked for electoral reforms. The issue was raised by the Justh wing of the Independents, which began to see in the legalization of the new military measures the party's and country's true interest and started to cooperate with the Social Democrats and radicals in 1911. Khuen-Héderváry, who wanted to avoid a repetition of the failure of 1905 and feared the radicalization of the country, tried to wait out the storm and sought to gain the support of some parliamentary factions. László Lukács (who replaced him in April 1912) and the real leader of the party, Tisza, were convinced that this would produce no results and decided to end obstruction by force. In order "to reestablish order in Parliament and ensure its functioning," Tisza was elected speaker of the lower house on May 23.

While the majority in Parliament supported Tisza's selection, massive demonstrations opposing it took place in Budapest. The Social Democrats proclaimed a general strike and asked for peaceful demonstrations. The police were unable to keep the crowds away from the center of the city, and the demonstration degenerated into a street fight in which six people lost their lives. The party's leaders, fearing a revolution which could not succeed, ordered its followers off the streets. On June 4, the new speaker illegally ended debate in parliament. His followers passed the defense bill while the protesting members of the opposition were removed from the building by the police. The Immunity Committee of the House subsequently barred them from several sessions. Undaunted by an attempt on his life, Tisza—in the absence of the opposition, which boycotted the sessions—had the House accept several laws which were to become effective should a danger of war threaten the Monarchy. Finally he had the lower house accept a resolution restricting its rules, in force since 1848. The "Bloody Thursday" of May 23 and Tisza's parliamentary victories polarized the country, but the forces of progress did not gain by the support of counts and parliamentary speakers who joined their ranks protesting Tisza's actions.

The Balkans presented the next problem. Serbia, Montenegro, Bulgaria, and Greece temporarily forgot their differences and in the spring of 1912 jointly attacked the exhausted Ottoman Empire. Within a short time they gained a decisive victory, and Austria-Hungary had to accept the significant territorial gains that her by now unreliable small neighbors had made in a region formerly under her influence. The Dual Monarchy was able to keep Serbia away from the Adriatic by advocating the creation of an independent Albania, and her army forced Montenegro to evacuate Scutari (Shkodēr), turning the Southern Slavs even more markedly against her. When the dispute over the division of Macedonia produced the Second Balkan War in 1913, Austria-Hungary could not effectively support Serbia's enemy, Bulgaria, because Romania, an ally had also attacked that country. Bulgaria's defeat and the resulting Peace of Bucharest not only marked a serious loss of Austro-Hungarian prestige but also showed how isolated the monarchy was on the international scene. Austria-Hungary could not count on the Ottoman Empire, which ceased to be a European power; after Italy, Romania too proved to be an unreliable ally; Bulgaria was exhausted; the relationship with Russia, supported by its Entente partners, had deteriorated; and not even Germany supported Austria-Hungary diplomatically during the long negotiations connected with the two Balkan wars. The Hungarian public, previously not interested in foreign affairs, understood how serious the situation had become. Serbia's victories and considerable territorial gains greatly influenced the attitude of the Southern Slavs living in Hungary. The creation of a united Southern Slav state at the expense of Austria-Hungary became a possibility, provided Serbia could win the support of some of Europe's great powers. Under these circumstances, the makers of Austria-Hungary's foreign policy believed it imperative to break the hostile ring surrounding it. Bulgaria had to be won and strengthened, Romania's neutrality assured, and Serbia's ambitions dampened. The attitude of the Entente made any other policy impossible.

Unlike his fellow politicians, Tisza understood even before the first Balkan war how dangerous the foreign situation had become. He wanted to prepare Hungary for war. This is why he eliminated obstruction in Parliament and defended the traditional ruling elements' political power. The electoral reform bill presented in Parliament at the end of 1912 tied voting rights to qualifications of education and wealth so high that it only raised the number of those who could vote from 6 to 10 percent of the population. At the time, 25–30 percent of the population in Western Europe voted. Protests started anew. A strike of previously unheard magnitude was planned for the day Parliament was to begin debate on the bill, but at the last minute it was called off by the Social Democratic leaders who feared confrontation.

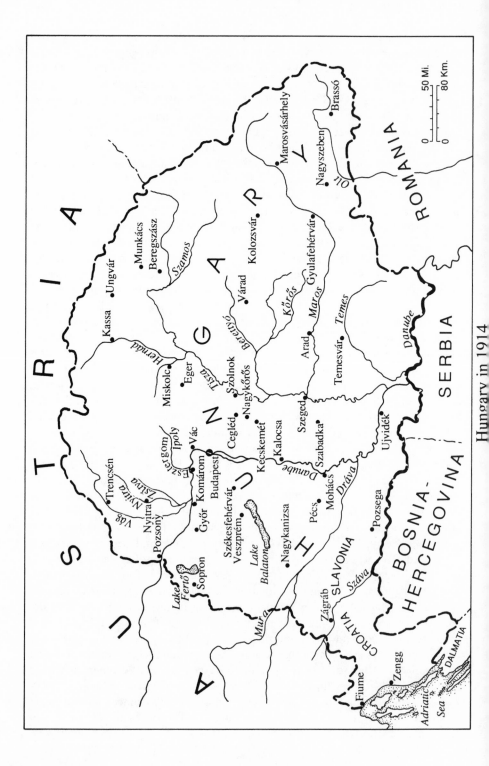

Hungary in 1914

Tisza replaced Lukács, accused of financial irregularities, in June 1913. He continued the "consolidation" of public life by having the legislature pass laws against activities he considered dangerous. Cases to be judged by juries were limited; press and libel laws were strengthened; and local authorities were given more power to restrict public meetings and associations. These measures dealt only with the symptoms of domestic discontent, but Tisza also made every effort to convince the upper and middle strata of society that he was pursuing the correct line. The establishment of the magazine *Magyar Figyelő (Hungarian Observer),* which attacked radical and socialist views mercilessly, served this purpose as did the strengthening of the role played in society by social organizations supported by the various churches. Attempts to come to an understanding with the nationalities were also part of Tisza's efforts to gain support. In 1913 he reached an understanding with the Croat-Serb coalition, and constitutional rule was reestablished in Croatia. Tisza even tried to satisfy the Romanians. He failed because Romanian leaders, encouraged by Romania's success in 1913 and by the advice of Francis Ferdinand, made demands that chauvinistic Hungarian public opinion considered unacceptable. By that time the leaders of the nationalities hoped that the imminent change of rulers and the reorganization of the state structure planned by Francis Ferdinand would satisfy their demands, and they did not expect serious concessions from the Hungarian government. This unrealistic hope was crushed when Gavrilo Princip, a Bosnian student, murdered the heir presumptive on June 28, 1914 in Sarajevo.

World War I and the End of the Dual Monarchy

The murder of the unpopular crown prince led to the outbreak of World War I. Political and military circles in Vienna were unanimous in their belief that the crime created a unique opportunity to settle the Serbian question and reestablish Austria-Hungary's prestige. This time even Germany's support was assured; the Germans were in favor of a military solution because William II and his generals believed that a confrontation between the two alliance systems was inevitable, and the power balance was beginning to tilt in the Entente's favor. The Hungarian prime minister did not agree. He was afraid of a Romanian attack on Transylvania and hoped to settle the Balkan situation by diplomatic means in cooperation with Russia. He made his position clear in two memoranda submitted to the ruler and also during a meeting of the two governments held on July 7, but he never made his views public. Encouraged by Germany, Francis Joseph and the other leading politicians decided to address the strongest possible ultimatum to Serbia, risking war. On July 14, assured that, at least for the moment, Romania would not attack, Tisza finally agreed, convinced by the ruler's resolute stance and warlike public opinion. He only demanded guarantees that Serbia would not be annexed and that no additional Slavs would be added to the monarchy's population.

The Serbs accepted the ultimatum, but with certain reservations. Austria-

Hungary declared war on her neighbor, and the military clauses of the alliances were invoked, leading to a general conflagration. Tisza was convinced that the monarchy could win the war only if he remained at his post. This is why he refused the offer of the opposition, which enthusiastically supported the war, to form a coalition government since he would have been forced to give up his office.

In Hungary, as everywhere else in Europe, enthusiastic crowds cheered the troops departing to fight what all believed would be a short and easy war. The defeats of the badly equipped and badly led army and the heavy losses suffered in Galicia soon changed public attitudes. Nevertheless, the forces of the multinational empire proved to be more reliable and capable than expected, and, with the help of the Germans, achieved considerable results beginning in 1915. They occupied Russian Poland and withstood the attack of their old ally, Italy, which had changed sides in May 1915. In 1917, at Caporetto, they beat the Italian army decisively. After Bulgaria had joined the war in 1915, the monarchy's forces occupied all of Serbia and in 1917 defeated Romania, which had attacked Transylvania a year earlier. Hungary carried a heavy load. It supplied proportionally more soldiers than the other half of the monarchy and, therefore, suffered heavier losses in dead, wounded, and prisoners. The economic resources of the home front were fully mobilized, but Tisza prevented the displacement of civilian authority by the military (which had occurred in Austria), and the Hungarian parliament continued to deliberate all through the war.

The signs of exhaustion began to multiply in 1916. Charles IV, who succeeded Francis Joseph upon his death, at the age of 86, in 1916, tried to calm the discontented through concessions and reforms. To save his throne and the dualist system, the new ruler began to negotiate in secret for peace, but to get it he would have had to break with Germany, which this weak man could not and would not do. In Hungary, internal unity broke down. In 1916, some deputies, led by Count Mihály Károlyi, left the Independence Party. Károlyi, who gradually moved away from his conservative-aristocratic position and became a radical supporter of reform, wanted peace. He and his colleagues began their own secret negotiations (with the new ruler's blessing) with the Entente. However, even had they had the power to conclude a separate peace, the attempt would have been doomed by the secret agreements the Entente had concluded with Serbia and Romania and with the Czech and Croat politicians who had left the monarchy. These secret arrangements had already decided the fate of historical Hungary during the first months of the war. Guessing that this was the case, Tisza and the majority of those in opposition did their utmost to assure Germany's victory. Those pacifists, radicals, and Social Democrats who wanted peace but were not represented in Parliament hoped that "peace without victory" would end the war in accordance with the views of President Woodrow Wilson or believed that the anti-war movements that grew everywhere after the two Russian revolutions of 1917 would lead to radical changes and a just peace.

In May 1917, Charles IV forced Tisza to abdicate because the prime minister refused to consider electoral reform. The new government, made up of members of the moderate opposition under Count Móric Esterházy's leadership, promised to be more receptive to reform. By August, this hope was shattered, and Wekerle again became premier. He was opposed to reform and supported the alliance with Germany.

Hungarian society began to disintegrate early in 1917 under the pressure of the heavy load imposed by the war, rising prices, and growing shortages. One strike followed another. After the October Revolution in Russia, the number of those who thought about ending hostilities and experimentation with major political and social reforms increased. Demonstrations expressing sympathy with Russia or asking for peace went hand-in-hand with increasing desertion from the army. In 1918, a military revolt actually occurred at Pécs.

The attitude of the country's non-Hungarians also began to change. When the war began, their leaders issued declarations of loyalty and the masses—except for a few Croats and Romanians, who emigrated—followed the ruler into war and fought bravely. The more doubtful the outcome of the conflict became, however, the more cautious was the position the nationalities took. At first the Entente spoke of the dissolution of the monarchy only because it was a good propaganda ploy. When it began to see immediate and longterm advantages in the empire's disappearance, it began to back seriously the secessionist tendencies of the Southern Slavs and Romanians. Consequently, the ideals of Romanian, Czechoslovak, and Southern Slav unity became more and more realizable and more and more a popular goal for the nationalities of Hungary. Therefore, when the monarchy was militarily defeated, it was natural for them (including their Social Democrats) to opt for independence and the victorious side. By this time, they considered their previous goal of a federated and democratic monarchy a dated concept.

Total economic and military exhaustion made the Joint Council of Ministers decide, on October 2, 1918, to ask for an armistice and peace negotiations based on President Wilson's fourteen points, which did not touch the integrity of the monarchy. Wilson informed Austria-Hungary that he had recognized Czechoslovakia as a belligerent state and agreed to the national unification of the Southern Slavs. He could, therefore, not negotiate on the basis of granting these people autonomy within the empire. When Bulgaria and the Ottoman Empire capitulated practically at the moment Wilson's answer was received, the monarchy's collapse became inevitable. Even Tisza had to acknowledge the fact. On October 27, Andrássy Jr., who had assumed the position of common foreign minister two days earlier, accepted all of Wilson's conditions, meaning the dissolution of the dualist system that his father had helped to create. In rapid succession, the nationalities proclaimed their independence. Between the 28th and the 31st, the Czechs, Croats, Slovaks, and Ruthenians seceded. An armistice was no longer important for the victors. It was signed on November 3 at Padova only after the Italians had taken bloody revenge for Custozza and Caporetto, attacking the dissolving Austro-Hungarian army.

External forces had decided the struggle between the centripetal and centrifugal forces within Austria-Hungary. The Dual Alliance of 1879 with Germany, the changes in international politics in the early years of the twentieth century, the new role of the monarchy in international affairs, the collapse of Russia in 1917, and the military defeat sealed the fate of the Central European monarchy, to which Hungary's fate had been tied since the Compromise of 1867. During the five decades of dualism, Hungarian society had changed drastically, and social forces made their appearance which made further democratic development of the country possible. Yet a continuing obstacle to such a development was the economic backwardness that lingered in spite of important growth. The future of the Hungarian people was not determined by the defeat of 1918, but by the question of what new beginning was possible given the domestic and international circumstances facing the nation. The possibility of a democratic transformation was present, but the international situation would determine whether the opportunity was seized or neglected.

XVI

REVOLUTION, COUNTERREVOLUTION, CONSOLIDATION

Tibor Hajdú and Zsuzsa L. Nagy

Part I. Revolution, 1918–1919

The End of World War I and the Road to Revolution

On October 16, 1918, Count Mihály Károlyi, the leader of the democratic and anti-German opposition in Parliament, declared: "We have lost the war, what is important now is to make certain that we do not lose the peace." What was at stake was the territorial integrity of the state. This realization was not new, but it had never been expressed in Parliament. The next day the former prime minister, István Tisza, stated in the lower house: "I agree with what Károlyi said yesterday. We have lost the war." With these words, which were received with frightened silence all over the country, the death knell of old Hungary began to toll.

The ruling circles admitted their defeat and, in fact, declared that they were giving up the struggle. The logical step, and this is what Károlyi had in mind, would have been to hand power over to an acceptable regime capable of saving the country from total dissolution and anarchy. The king considered the appointment of Károlyi, but in the end neither he nor his advisors had the courage to take this step. They plotted long enough to make the revolution, which not even Károlyi and his followers wanted, inevitable.

A revolution whose leaders attempted to the very end to reach an agreement with the last Habsburg ruler had to be a belated one. Had the forces of democracy been successful in 1905, 1912, or before the declaration of war in 1914, distancing themselves from Vienna, a proud and hopeful revolution could have laid the groundwork for a new Hungary. At the end of the lost war, the possibility existed that the victory of democracy might, in the short run, be detrimental for Hungary since victory could have entailed the secession of the Slav and Romanian population. Even the class composition of the tardy revolution was questionable. In the first decade of the twentieth century, the capitalists could still sympathize with a revolution that, if victorious, could have liberated them from the tutelage of Austrian capital and the Hungarian aristocracy. A new compromise would have forced the ruling circles to share power with the middle classes, improving their position and the chances for speedy economic and social growth. By backing the war, the capitalist circles renewed their old relationship with those in power, shared responsibility for the war, and had every reason to fear a Russian-type revolution. There can be no doubt that the radicalization of the Russian revolution greatly influenced the Democratic Party and its leader Vilmos Vázsonyi in its decisions in 1918. This party, whose members were recruited mainly from the well-to-do, mostly Jewish middle class of Budapest, destroyed the Electoral Reform Block, the last attempt at democratic cooperation in January of 1918, and declared in the fall that it would not join the new democratic alliance, the Hungarian National Council, organized by Károlyi on October 25. The Christian urban middle class, whose most prominent spokesman was Ferenc Harrer, and the democratic wing of the Christian Socialists, led by Father Sándor Giesswein, also refused to join the council. These people were not the ones mainly responsible for the delay in establishing the council. This was caused by the unsuccessful negotiations between Károlyi and Oscar Jászi, on the one hand, and the leaders of the Slav and Romanian national parties, on the other. The final establishment of the Hungarian National Council without the participation of these men foreshadowed the dissolution of old Hungary.

The only parliamentary party that backed the Hungarian National Council, Károlyi's Party of Independence, did not represent the majority of any social class. It was backed by some aristocrats, some of the lesser noble landlords, the traditional intellectuals, and some members of the democratic petty bourgeoisie. Jászi's Radical Party, backed by the more modern intellectuals and the radical bourgeoisie, represented formidable mental ability, but only insignificant popular support. Thus the strongest party in the new coalition became that of the Social Democrats. It represented mainly the class interests of the not too numerous skilled workers, and could rely on the disciplined organization of the unions. The Social Democrats ruled the streets of Budapest, and this gave them the determining role in the development of the revolution. Yet it was by no means certain, should the party be able to form a government, that it would not be forced by the workers to put into practice those basic tenets of Marxism which made up its platform up to then.

When the king finally decided not to appoint Károlyi prime minister, although he was called to Vienna for this explicit purpose, and turned, instead, to Count János Hadik on October 27, he only gave testimony of his irresolution. Hadik, a follower of the younger Count Andrássy, was a popular person but had neither a party nor a program. He counted on the anti-Károlyi feelings of most parliamentary parties and on the military units that had been concentrated in Budapest to prevent a revolution. By this time, the officer corps consisted mainly of reservists, young middle-class intellectuals, who were just as much fed up with the war as were their troops. As soon as the National Council had been established, they promptly organized a Soldiers' Council and made it very difficult for the king's loyal general, the Croatian Baron Géza Lukachich, whom his soldiers considered to be a second Jelašić, to take action.

The trial of strength came on the evening of October 30 when, in spite of the National Council's wishes, members of the Soldiers' Council and left wing Socialists provoked several brawls. Confidently, Lukachich sent his troops out of the strategically secure royal castle against the Hotel Astoria, where the more courageous members of the National Council headed by Károlyi awaited the outcome. The hotel was not well defended, but most of the troops deserted en route and those who arrived tore the royal emblems from their caps and, with arms in hand, swore to support the revolution. They replaced the discarded emblems with red and white asters, on sale everywhere to celebrate All Souls' Day, giving the revolution its name—the Aster Revolution. It is not clear to what extent the leaders of the revolution were indeed leaders during that crucial night. It is not likely that they were better informed about the events that occurred all through the night than were Lukachich, Hadik, or the archduke Joseph, who was the king's representative in the country *(homo regius)* and did not dare to leave the castle. The ruler was in the neighborhood of Vienna. Those who were still at the Astoria at dawn received their reward. In the early hours, Hadik phoned Károlyi and asked him to come to the castle and take over the government. Károlyi took his time. When he set out for the castle, he was followed by workers coming from the various suburbs who had gathered before the hotel.

The Károlyi Regime

The revolutionary government was composed of parties that belonged to the National Council. Károlyi's party was represented by two counts, a member of the lower nobility, and two attorneys from provincial cities. The military, which played the crucial role all through the revolutionary period, provided a pacifist artillery colonel, and the Social Democrats and Radicals several intellectuals, mostly Jewish. The peasantry, the non-Hungarian nationalities, and the lower middle class supplied no cabinet members, although the government's democratic platform made their participation desirable. Károlyi and his government have been repeatedly accused of lacking a sense of reality. This is true only to the extent that the leading personalities, including the Social Democrats, were imbued with the ideals of the liberalism of the turn of the century and could have made better use of their talents during a long, peaceful situation like the one that had prevailed then than under the circumstances prevailing when they became cabinet members. The main problem was that due to the omissions and failures of preceeding governments, they faced such a multitude of unsolved problems that even a more dictatorial regime would have had great difficulties mastering them. It should be kept in mind that after the war Hungary was one of the losers in a part of Europe where it was very difficult to satisfy even the victors.

The most pressing tasks of the revolution were to establish an independent Hungary, to clarify its international situation, and to get ready for the peace conference. Already, on November 1, the day after the revolution, Károlyi asked to be released from his oath of allegiance to the king and proclaimed Hungary's unconditional independence. Because the democratic principles of the leaders would have been satisfied fully only by a plebiscite or at least by a vote in Parliament, they hesitated for a while before they called a revolutionary mass meeting, which, on November 16, proclaimed the Hungarian People's Republic.

The government pressed the High Command to accept the armistice negotiated at Padova and accepted it as far as Hungary was concerned. When it was learned that it would be advisable to conclude a separate armistice on the Balkan front, Károlyi and the leaders of the National Council took a boat to Beograd, where, on November 7, they met General Louis Felix Franchet d'Esperey, the commander of the French Armée d'Orient. They did not sign at once the conditions he offered because these were harsher than the ones which had been proposed at Padova, demanding, among other things, the immediate military evacuation of the region south of the Drava-Maros line. It must have been at least a week before they learned that in the near future they would be ordered to give up even more territory.

Károlyi also attempted to establish diplomatic relations with the victors, who, on principle, refused to do this prior to the signing of a peace treaty. Thus, regular diplomatic contacts were established only with Austria and Switzerland. Ironically, relations of all kinds were the very best from the beginning with the former "oppressor," Austria.

The minister for nationality affairs, Oscar Jászi, planned to induce the leaders of the various peoples, mainly the Romanians, Slovaks, and Ruthenians, to keep their people within the borders of Hungary by offering them maximum autonomy. He was successful only in his talks with the Ruthenians (Carpatho-Ukrainians) because the chances of uniting all Ukrainian lands were very questionable. The Ukrainians of Hungary received their autonomy, and their representative joined the government.

After even the U.S.A. had recognized Romania as a co-belligerent, the leaders of the Transylvanian Romanians unanimously decided to join the Kingdom of Romania, hoping for an autonomous regime. Their hope proved to be in vain. On November 12, Jászi went to Arad to hold discussions with the leaders of the Hungarian and Transylvanian Romanians' National Council. The Romanian leaders rejected the offer of autonomy and on November 20 proclaimed their wish to secede from Hungary. At the end of the month, the Romanian army crossed into Transylvania, but, for the moment at least, stopped at the Maros line specified by the armistice agreement. After this military move, further negotiations became pointless. Where the Hungarian army was in control, Romanian movements were suppressed, while in the regions under Romanian control, Hungarian adminstrative organs, political organizations, the press, and so forth suffered the same fate.

The chances were somewhat better when Jászi, late in November, began discussions with Milan Hodža, who represented the Slovak National Council in Budapest. Hodža was ready to accept autonomy provisionally for the period preceding the conclusion of peace, but the attempt of these men to reach a compromise produced violent simultaneous reactions among the nationalists represented in both the Prague and Budapest governments. The attempt failed, and Jászi was saved from dismissal only by the support of Károlyi and the Social Democrats. While these events took place, hostilities had already commenced on the Slovak border between weak Czech and somewhat stronger Hungarian units.

The diplomatic and military confrontations ended when Edvard Beneš, the Czechoslovak minister of foreign affairs, succeeded in Paris in having the Entente issue a demand for the immediate evacuation of Slovakia by Hungarian forces. By January 20, 1919, the withdrawal was complete. In the meantime, based on the decision of the Romanian National Assembly of December 1, 1918 at Alba Iulia, but even more on the support of the French military command, the Romanian army crossed the Maros River, entered Transylvania's capital Cluj, and by January had reached the Sighetul Marmației-Baia Mare-Zalău-Ciucea-Vașcău (Máramarossziget-Nagybánya-Zilah-Csucsa-Vaskoh) line. They would have marched even further but for several developments: the Hungarian troops facing them, who had been recruited mainly among refugées from Transylvania, stiffened their resistance; the Hungarian government informed the French mission in Budapest that it would oppose further advances prior to the signing of peace; and the Romanian-Yugoslav controversy required the establishment of a French occupation zone. These were the major factors that ended the Romanian advance.

Since 1919, the question has been repeatedly raised: would it not have been better if the Károlyi government had offered more determined military resistance even before the Romanians reached Cluj? This question can easily be answered in the negative. First, Hungary's manpower losses had been much heavier during the war than were Romania's, and the chances of successful resistance were minimal. The lines of demarcation played no role in the decision of the peacemakers. Both Romania and Yugoslavia had to evacuate territory which they had occupied, but which was awarded to Hungary. Finally, the policy of the Károlyi government was based on "Wilsonism," and "friendship with the Entente" and it could not risk alienating whatever sympathies it enjoyed in Paris.

By January 1919, Hungary had lost more than half of her former territory and population. While it was still not clear to what extent the peace-makers would honor the by then generally known secret wartime agreements, the realists already felt that the peace conference that began in January would draw borders even less favorable than the lines of demarcation. Not since the battle of Mohács in 1526 had the country faced a tragedy of this dimension. Public opinion, at first optimistic, became gloomy, and more and more people began to place the blame not only on the lost war, but also on the Károlyi government's pacificism.

The most critical were the members of the old ruling classes. During the early weeks of its existence, these people saw in the revolutionary government the guarantor of order, private property, and "territorial integrity." This explains why Parliament declared its own dissolution without the slightest resistance and why the dignitaries of the country put pressure on the king to resign. The abdication proclamation was not without ambiguities. In these same circles, the original popularity of Károlyi was enhanced by the rather peaceful nature of the revolution. In the cities and in Transdanubia, practically no blood had been spilled. István Tisza, who had refused to flee and awaited his fate with Calvinist belief in predestination, was murdered in his home on October 31 by revolutionary soldiers. His death, received with great consternation, should have sufficed to satisfy the desire of the war veterans for revenge.

In the countryside, primarily in the eastern regions and in lands inhabited by non-Hungarians, the first wave of the revolution was less peaceful. A veritable peasant revolt raged throughout the country during the first half of November. This movement was totally unorganized but followed a traditional pattern. Gendarmes, notaries, and, in many places, landlords were chased away, and stores and castles were pillaged. The revolution, centered in the capital, had no rural base and had to use force to quell the peasantry. The blood of hundreds of peasants only deepened the cleavage between the urban and rural revolutions, although the villages, at least in Hungarian-inhabited areas, calmed down temporarily by the end of November.

The discontent of the peasantry and the difficult economic situation forced the government to introduce more radical social reforms than it had planned. The radicalization of the labor movement also played its part. In the first weeks of November, it seemed as if the participation of the Social Democrats in the government had calmed the workers down. Yet just the opposite happened. Because the Social Democratic ministers too advocated patience, the reestablishment of order, and "the suspension of the class struggle," they lost their influence among the working masses. When Béla Kun, who had recently returned from Russian captivity, established the Communist Party of Hungary, on November 24, 1918, a crucial change in the workers' movement occurred. Kun began his career as one of the young leaders of the Social Democrats in Kolozsvár. As a reserve officer, he was captured by the Russians and became the most outspoken of those leftist officers and soldiers who, while prisoners, had observed the Russian revolution and believed it the model that the Hungarian socialist movement had to follow. Only a small segment of the strong left wing of the Social Democrats joined the Communist Party, but they retained a growing influence on those leftists who were opposed to forming a new party and stayed with the old.

A typical representative of the left-wing Socialists was József Pogány, who, as the governmental commissioner of the Military Council, vied with the Communists for popularity and who, on December 12, organized a military demonstration that forced the new minister of defense, Lieutenant Colonel Albert Bartha, to resign because he was more militaristic than his predecessor. Bartha's resignation marked the beginning of a series of governmental crises. After Bartha, those old-fashioned liberals who could not agree with the radical turns taken by the revolution left the Károlyi cabinet. Early in January, the Military Council forced the resignation of Count Sándor Festetics, who had been in office for only three weeks. These changes, in themselves important, were followed by the drastic reorganization of the entire government on January 19, 1919.

Károlyi as President of the Republic

Because most of the country was under foreign occupation, elections had to be postponed. This left the two-month-old republic without a president. The National Council elected Károlyi provisional president, and he appointed Dezső Berinkey, an expert on international law, as prime minister. Berinkey's views were close to those of the radicals, but he lacked the ability to take the initiative. Thus Károlyi in fact continued to manage the affairs of government, especially foreign affairs. Before the new government could be formed, a violent debate took place in the Workers' Council of Budapest, dominated by the Social Democrats. The majority of the workers demanded the appointment of a socialist government. The more moderate Socialist leaders were opposed because they feared that the embittered and revolutionary public would force a socialist government to take radical steps and nationalize private property. Several of these leaders preferred a middle-class government which would leave the Social Democrats free to concentrate their efforts on regaining the streets and workers councils, where the influence of the Communists was steadily growing.

In the end, a compromise was reached. The number of Social Democratic ministers was increased, and one of them became minister of defense. This helped the government at least to the extent that Pogány ceased to attack all holders of this post. For the moment, the government's position was secure, but its support rested on a narrower social base. The majority of the old ruling elements ceased to support a government that had not produced any success in foreign affairs and threatened to introduce more and more radical reforms. To introduce reforms would have been very difficult under the existing circumstances, but the workers clamored for them more and more vehemently. They were conscious of their own strength, which all other groups lacked, and they became increasingly inclined to demand that the revolution follow the Russian model. The left wing of the Social Democrats acted as the internal opposition of the government. Its members did not accept cabinet posts; they served in lower governmental positions unwillingly and used these to pursue their own goals. The Radical Party's position moved closer to that of the Socialists, but Jászi, who had realized that his plan to federate the country had failed, left the cabinet. To broaden the social base of the government, István Szabó Nagyatádi, the leader of the Smallholders' Party, was invited to join it. He was the first peasant ever to hold the post of cabinet minister. Szabó's party, like the peasantry in general, was not organized. His membership in the government would have been of great importance if elections could have been held.

Fate gave the new government about a month and a half of relative peace, which it used to take three important steps to stabilize its position. These had foreign policy implications too, because the military missions that represented the peace-makers in Vienna and Budapest became more and more convinced that Hungary was rapidly becoming a hotbed of bolshevism and anarchy. The government decided to destroy the Communist Party, to hold elections in the unoccupied regions based on universal secret suffrage, and to distribute the large estates among the peasants. These measures would have brought Hungary closer to the East-Central European peasant democracies, to the model used elsewhere to combat revolution and bolshevism. What Hungary lacked and what the neighboring countries, which pursued identical goals, had enough power to ensure, was the victory of national goals to neutralize the partisans of class war.

Because it lacked this strength, the government could not realize its aims. On February 21, it was able to arrest Béla Kun and about a hundred other Communists, but the hoped-for results were not achieved. Kun's place was taken by men like the friend of Nikolai I. Bukharin, the experienced revolutionary Tibor Szamuely, and the already well-known philosopher György Lukács. The government had misjudged the workers' movement. Organized labor was interested in united action because it could exploit its strength and was not very much interested in ideological differences. They were angry with the Communists, who had destroyed the unity of labor, but they were also mad at those who had ordered their arrest, transforming into a police matter what they considered to be an internal quarrel. Such eclectic leaders of the Socialist left like Pogány and the economist Jenő Varga had other reasons too to oppose the government. They knew that the Social Democrats, who had a dominant role in government between January and March, could not emerge as the majority party from the planned elections. They were also certain that land distribution would further weaken the already minimal socialist influence in the villages. Therefore, Varga and his friends began to advocate the establishment of agricultural cooperatives as an alternative to economically unsound land distribution. The Communists watched the growing independence of the left wing Socialists with understanding and began secret talks with them to ensure future collaboration. In vain did Károlyi distribute his own estate, amid great celebration; the other landowners preferred to support the reborn rightist parties and associations getting ready for the election. The government now was forced to move against the radical right opposition too. The spokesman of the "white" officers, Captain Gyula Gömbös, fled to Vienna. It did not help the government that its pacifist foreign policy was, just at this moment, put to a severe test.

The head of the French military mission in Budapest, Lieutenant-Colonel Fernand Vix, handed Károlyi a note on March 20, 1919. Signed by General Paul-Joseph de Lobit on the previous day, it demanded that, in accordance with a decision reached in Paris on February 26, all Hungarian forces evacuate the region between the Tisza River and the mountains on the eastern edge of the Hungarian plain. This demand would have moved Hungarian forces some sixty miles further to the west, a considerable distance given what was left of Hungary. Erroneously, but understandably, the Hungarians assumed that the line to which they were asked to retreat represented the country's new borders. Their belief was based on the fact that the secret Treaty of Bucharest (1916) mentioned practically the same line as Romania's postwar border. This alone cannot explain the mass hysteria that engulfed everybody from Károlyi to the lowliest private when the note became known. Such mass feelings are the stuff from which revolutions and wars are made. Everybody realized that the Károlyi regime's pro-Entente stand was not appreciated and that his government would not be given more favorable peace conditions than the wartime government had it still been in power. The Russian Red Army made excellent progress during just these critical days in the Ukraine and was approaching the Carpathians. Hungarian political thinking, used to chasing illusion during the years of dualism, acquired a belief in miracles. Now that the illusion of "Wilsonism" was shattered, the possibility of a Russian alliance became the new miracle.

The timing of the Vix note was unfortunate for another reason. It was handed to Károlyi just as a new governmental crisis was developing. The idea had gained ground that a socialist government had to be formed to secure order in the country on the eve of elections and possibly to ensure the election of a workable majority. The government decided hastily to reject the Vix note and to hand power over to the Socialists, leaving to them the glorious obligation of conducting a war of national defense. In the Social Democratic Party, the decision depended on the left wing which, in accordance with the workers' mood, refused to take power without the collaboration of the Communists. It became clear that they had contacted Kun a few days earlier and asked him under what conditions he would agree to reestablish the unity of the movements. From his prison Kun sent a clear answer: only the dictatorship of the proletariat was acceptable to him. The bourgeois ministers were so eager to get out that they did not even inquire why the leader of the right wing Socialists, Ernő Garami, resigned from the party. On March 21 Károlyi still believed that he would continue to serve as president and appointed the centrist Zsigmond Kunfi prime minister. In the evening, he learned by accident that the Workers' and Soldiers' Councils of Budapest had proclaimed the dictatorship of the proletariat and that a Soviet government had been established with the stonemason Sándor Garbai as its formal president, but with Béla Kun as its real head. The workers celebrated with enthusiasm, and, for a short time, the entire patriotic public accepted as its visionary emblem the red proletarian fist—so well-known from numerous posters—smashing the peace table in Paris.

The Hungarian Soviet Republic

This optimistic mood, the honeymoon of the revolution, lasted only for a month. The Soviet Republic naturally did not evacuate the regions specified in the Vix note, and the unexpected results of the memorandum created momentary confusion in Paris. It gave the British peace delegation a chance to approach the French prime minister, George Clemenceau, and blame the overbearing behavior of his generals for the situation. On April 4, General Jan Christiaan

Smuts, prime minister of South Africa and a member of the British peace delegation, arrived in Budapest. He was interested in embarrassing the French generals,
but he came mainly to get a clear picture because the contradictory reports
coming from Hungary had created total confusion in Paris. Smuts offered several
concessions, including the moving of the Vix line sixteen miles further to the
east. The visit was considered to be a great success in Budapest and with good
reason. A politician of Smuts' stature did not visit the Soviet Union for another
fifteen years. Emboldened by this success, Kun answered by submitting his coun-
terproposals. He demanded that a meeting be called in either Vienna or Paris at
which the representatives of Hungary, Germany, Austria, Czechoslovakia, Yugoslavia, and Romania were to discuss the problems of borders and economic
relations, with General Smuts presiding. Smuts refused even to discuss the matter and left Budapest the following day.

In his report, Smuts supported the idea of the meeting proposed by Kun and
also suggested that once the Hungarians had accepted the demarcation line he
had proposed the wartime economic blockade be lifted. Paris was not too interested in his propositions but paid close attention to his conclusion: Hungary
truly had an essentially Bolshevik government. The peace-makers were still
hopeful that the Soviet Russian system was on the verge of collapse and were
not willing to tolerate the existence of another Bolshevik system in the center of
Europe practically next to Germany. The initiative shifted back to the French
military. The generals did not even consult the peace conference any longer but
quietly assured the Romanian government of their full support, allowing the
Romanian forces to move to the new line of demarcation.

On April 16, the Romanian army attacked along the entire front. The days
preceding belonged to Kun, who tried to take advantage of them. He issued
dozens of decrees aiming at nothing less than the introduction of socialism, the
establishment of equality, and public ownership of industry, agriculture, trade,
and finances. Although an amazing number of changes were introduced in a few
weeks, the results did not come close to what had been planned. The most
important means of production, banks, the wholesale trade, and so on were
nationalized and practically the entire economy was placed under state supervision. The state also assumed control over apartment houses, the bank deposits
and jewelry of individuals, courts, newspapers, the entire cultural life of the
country, and private schools.

The policy of nationalizing the entire economy (except small agricultural
holdings and most small workshops and retail stores) was not part of the Soviet
model but a conscious attempt to transcend it. Given the economic situation,
especially the shortage of raw materials and fuels resulting from the dismemberment of the country, these measures did not make much sense. Under the courageous and expert leadership of Jenő Varga, the economic policy was geared to
satisfy political goals. Domestically, it tried to prove that the republic was rapidly approaching the socialist promised land. This was supposed to calm the
workers, whose living standard could not be raised. Wages and other benefits
had been raised so drastically already after the first revolution, that the politi-

cally unavoidable further increases inevitably increased the rate of inflation. As far as foreign affairs were concerned, the measures were designed to encourage the population of the neighboring countries and Central Europe in general to follow the Hungarian example; they were, in this sense, propagandistic actions.

The transition to socialist economics went fairly smoothly. The contributing factors were the patriotic mood, the unity of the working class, and the ability of the Soviet Republic to open the doors to the young, progressive intellectuals the old regime had neglected. For the first and last time in his life, Béla Bartók accepted a governmental position. The new system could count on talents as diverse as that of the physicist Todor von Kármán and the movie director Sándor Korda. The psychologist Sándor Ferenczi and the sociologist Károly Mannheim became university professors as did many other lesser lights. The conservative union leaders ceased to play political roles but were crucial in organizing production and the military forces. In general, life in Budapest and other cities was more peaceful and calm than that of revolutionary Moscow or, earlier, revolutionary Paris. Yet there were problems too. The shortages of foodstuffs and raw materials could not be alleviated as long as the blockade was in force. The measures taken to produce equality and calm the workers, for example the utilization of larger private apartments, began to alienate the originally sympathetic urban lower middle class, and strict regulations transformed a lively press into a uniform and drab one.

For the revolution, the real problem was the village. The duality of Hungarian society became even clearer than in the days of the Aster Revolution. The urban revolutionaries did not know how to handle the villages. They produced endless radical but unworkable decrees ordering, for example, the creation of large collective farms without machinery. They harassed the priests, made inventories of churches' valuables, and in general irritated the religious peasants. The distribution of church-owned land would have had a different and politically important effect, but this was not done because land distribution was the one Soviet example the Hungarians did not follow. They looked too far into the future, forgetting the paramount goal of a revolution: the destruction of the outmoded social system against which it is fighting. Local Soviets, elected on April 7, saw the situation more clearly, but their suggestions were neglected by the central leadership. Thus, while they continued to voice their theoretical belief that the soviet system was better than the parliamentary, the village soviets worked much better with the central authorities. The "Soviet of five hundred" in Budapest became the true parliament of the revolution.

Béla Kun saw in the Hungarian revolution the vanguard of Central European revolution. He understood that without German, Austrian, or Czech socialist revolutions occurring, the Hungarian would not long survive. He did all he could to gain the Austrian Social Democrats for his cause, but while they showed neighborly good will and understanding, they refused to follow Kun's example. Kun even tried to establish contact with the Entente powers and to moderate his actions somewhat to please them. His efforts remained fruitless, but they created a left-wing opposition under Szamuely's leadership within the party. The importance of this wing remained limited because the expected Russian military help was not forthcoming.

All these issues became secondary after the Romanian attack. The very survival of the revolution was at stake. The organization of the Hungarian Red Army had begun at the end of March and was managed correctly. The Soldiers' Councils were abolished, Pogány was forced to give up the position of Commissar for Defense and Vilmos Bőhm, who enjoyed the confidence of the officer corps, was appointed Commander-in-Chief. When the Romanians attacked, Bőhm had some fifty-five thousand mostly unorganized men under arms.

The major thrust of the superior Romanian army was directed against the northern sector of the eastern front, which was defended by the Székely Division, recruited among refugees from Transylvania. This was the strongest division, but its leaders had shown anti-revolutionary tendencies while serving Károlyi. The commander, Colonel Károly Kratochvil, withdrew carefully for a few days, but when he realized that the southern wing of the front could not even do this, he opened negotiation with the enemy. After the loss of Nagyvárad, Arad, and Debrecen, he capitulated on April 26, having secured for his soldiers the right to return to their homes. That his treason did not have even more dire consequences was due to the fact that the government expected it and had lined up a new division, composed mainly of workers who volunteered, behind the Székely Division's positions. Some of the Székely soldiers rejoined the Red Army, but the entire region east of the Tisza had to be evacuated. On April 26, the Czechoslovak army also began its attack in the north, involving, among other things, the loss of Ruthenia.

While the workers of Budapest celebrated May Day with mass demonstrations and long-remembered festivity, the government was considering resignation. It seemed as if the Romanian forces, already far past the demarcation line, would cross the Tisza and endanger Budapest; the Czechoslovak army had occupied the industrial region around Miskolc and was approaching Salgótarján; and in the south, the French forces concentrated around Szeged began to move. During the preceding successful weeks, Communists and Social Democrats had cooperated fairly smoothly in the reunited party. Now the right wing and the center group openly proposed resignation. They hoped that the formation of a government based on the trade unions could safeguard the already introduced social reforms by accepting the Entente's political demands. Yet Kun still had forces in reserve. The avant-garde of the revolution, the "Soviet of 500," in a joint session with the shop stewards, decided to continue the struggle and asked the proletarians to take up arms. Within a few days, forty-four thousand workers were under arms, completely changing the political composition of the Red Army.

Kun was very confident that the planned attack of the Ukrainian Red Army directed against both the forces of Simon Petlura and the Romanians, would succeed, but the revolt of the Cossack Hetman Nikolai A. Grigoriev produced failure. Nevertheless, the Ukrainian attack, combined with the peace-makers' notification that they had gone far enough, arrested the Romanian advance at the Tisza. In Paris, the politicians expected the immediate collapse of the Soviet Republic and issued an invitation to the representatives of the next regime to join the peace conference. It became clear that the Yugoslav army would not join the fighting, and the government in Budapest decided to launch a counterattack against the Czechoslovak army. They took this decision for two reasons. Salgótarján is only fifty miles from Budapest, and the presence of the enemy there represented a direct threat. They had also discovered during the heroic defense of Salgótarján by weak army units supported by armed miners and workers that it was easier to oppose the Czechoslovaks than the Romanians.

By the middle of May, Salgótarján was relieved, and on the 21st, Miskolc, where the workers revolted, was also in the hands of the Red Army. Led by its very talented Chief-of-Staff, Colonel Aurél Stromfeld, the northern campaign of the Red Army began on May 30. Within a few days most of central and northwestern Slovakia was occupied, and it appeared that the Czechoslovaks would even have to evacuate Pozsony. Kun's agents were planning a revolt in Vienna for June 15, when the wheels of fortune took another turn.

The coup d'état in Vienna ended in failure, and in Russia the offensive launched by General Anton I. Denikin began. The Slovak troops of the Czechoslovak army were somewhat demoralized and a Slovak Soviet Republic was proclaimed in eastern Slovakia, but the position of the Czechoslovak government remained stable, and, by the middle of June, the retreat of its forces ended. The subsequent actions by the Hungarian and Czechoslovak armies brought no results. The Czechoslovaks received help at this time from Paris. On June 7, Clemenceau sent a note to the Hungarian Soviet Republic, threatening general intervention by those represented at the peace conference. Without consulting or negotiating with the Hungarians, he dispatched a second note, on June 13, in which he informed the Hungarians that their future borders with Czechoslovakia and Romania had been settled and requested that the Red Army draw back to these frontiers within five days. In practical terms, this demand concerned Slovakia, because the Romanians were not only in possession of those territories which had been assigned to them, but also held about one-third of the territory that was to compose the future Hungary.

In Budapest, the Congress of the Party and National Congress of the Soviets were in session. The message received from Paris contributed decisively to their discussions and the political situation in general. The two social elements which had been the strongest supporters of the revolutions reacted differently to the situation. One of these groups consisted of urban workers and members of the intellectual professions, the other of the officer corps and the refugees. The workers had had enough of war. Those among them who were not fully committed simply had enough of fighting, while the committed ones pointed out that after the world revolution, administrative borders would be meaningless. Given this attitude and the military situation, the moderate Social Democrats were able to take the initiative, even at the Party Congress, and began to negotiate with the representatives of the Entente in Vienna and Budapest.

The officers and refugees were ready to fight on, provided that the revolution adopt a national policy and reject the new borders. This was impossible, and under the circumstances even the majority of the Communists accepted the inevitable. For a week or two the government postponed the retreat, but when its army, exhausted and less and less well-supplied due to the blockade, was unable to produce any significant success, it ordered the evacuation of Slovakia, leaving the Slovak Soviet Republic in the lurch. The retreat detached the officer corps and nationalists from the revolution. Even Stromfeld resigned. While these events unfolded, a "white" government was organized, first at Arad, then in Szeged under French protection. The Szeged government, headed by count Gyula Károlyi, then by Dezső Ábrahám, spent its time squabbling and reorganizing itself. It not only had no standing in Paris, but even in Szeged nobody took it seriously. The "National Army" which Vice-Admiral Miklós Horthy organized under this government's sponsorship consisted only of officers and non-commissioned officers. Nevertheless, it represented a new alternative for the nationalists.

Of all the revolutionary months, June 1919 was filled with the greatest number of contradictions. The Party Congress ended, after some quarreling, by maintaining party unity and accepting a Leninist program. The Congress of the Soviets agreed on a Socialist Constitution for Hungary. While they were in session and soon afterwards several unsuccessful counterrevolutionary uprisings occurred. The most serious was the movement initiated by the professors and students of the Military Academy, but the rest of the army did not join them. It became obvious that the counterrevolution had no real strength because it lacked a unified, national program. However, it also became clear that the soviets and the party organization had also lost much of their prestige since March. In many cases "terror units" or "Szamuely's trains" hurriedly dispatched to trouble spots could reestablish order only at the price of bloodshed.

The weeks that followed the retreat in the north and the action against the counterrevolutionaries were relatively peaceful, but this calm was intolerable even for those in power. The blockade became more and more effective, and the villages quietly deserted the revolution. Working women standing in endless lines for supplies repeated the slogans of "white" pamphlets and cursed the "Jewish commissars." About half of the commissars, including Kun, Böhm, and Szamuely, were of Jewish origin. The result of the composition of the socialist intellectual circles, this situation was the same in Russia. The peasantry was especially upset by this phenomenon, and counterrevolutionary propaganda took advantage of it.

The Communists and the more moderate Socialists were more or less in agreement as far as the situation in Budapest was concerned. The Communists, however, wanted to fight to the last man for the world revolution irrespective of the hopelessness of the situation, while the Socialists would have liked to reestablish the pre-March 21 conditions with help from Vienna. Neither was realistic or feasible under the circumstances.

European trade unions organized protest strikes for July 20–21 in support of the Russian and Hungarian Soviet Republics. The strikes in Austria, Italy, numerous Yugoslav and Romanian cities, and elsewhere, while successful did not develop into the massive demonstrations which could have had some effect in determining European power relations. On the first day of the strike, the Hungarian Red Army crossed the Tisza with the explanation that while it had evacuated Slovakia, the Romanians had not retreated from Hungarian territory.

The attack along the Tisza made no military or diplomatic sense. The Red Army attacked a much stronger force that had enjoyed a rest of two-and-a-half months. Neither the situation in the country nor the organization of reserves and supplies justified the attack. This was simply a move born of desperation to prevent the collapse of the regime and disrupt the intervention plans of the Entente under the supervision of Marshal Ferdinand Foch. The Red Army advanced until July 23, when the Romanian reserve began to encircle the attacking spearhead, forcing it to beat a hasty retreat, which rapidly developed into a rout. On the 29th, the first Romanian units crossed the Tisza. Though the Council of the Trade Unions demanded its resignation on July 31, the government decided to counterattack and retake Szolnok. Before noon the next day, Szolnok was occupied, but this was a totally useless gesture. What was left of the Red Army was easily encircled and forced to capitulate.

On the morning of August 1, the Soviet government, after violent debates, decided that given the hopelessness of the situation it would resign in favor of a more moderate trade unionist government. The Social Democratic commissar Zoltán Rónai and Kun made this decision public the same afternoon during the last session of the "Soviet of five hundred." Kun and some of his followers were given refuge in Austria. Szamuely, who was recognized while in flight, shot himself. The unionist government was established on August 2 under the leadership of Gyula Peidl, the leader of the typographers' union. Two days later the Romanian army marched into Budapest.

Part II. Counterrevolution and Consolidation, 1919–1921

The Post-Revolutionary Period

The events of the summer of 1919 left open to question the form Hungary would take as it emerged from the ruins of the Dual Monarchy. How would the country find its place in Europe and in the Danubian basin? A further question remained unanswered: what form would the emerging bourgeois system take after the liquidation of the dictatorship of the proletariat?

The establishment and consolidation of the regime that followed the Soviet Republic went hand-in-hand with the organization of life in a country within new borders and with the establishment of an independent Hungarian state, foreign policy, and national economy. Because the country was no longer a partner in an empire, international considerations played a greater role in its economy and foreign policy than before and even influenced her domestic policies.

The new system owed its position not to its own achievements, but to foreign intervention, just as its end would be decisively influenced by those power relationships that decided the outcome of the Second World War. Like the rest of Europe in the 1920s, the country's institutions bore the stamp of the great Western democratic powers who had dictated the peace treaties. (This was to inhibit extremist, dictatorial tendencies until the international successes of the Right in the 1930s.) The new system rejected the revolution but was influenced by the revolution's impact and achievements. The peculiar character of the new order was determined by the fact that while rightists and even extreme rightists came to power, they did not ban democratic tendencies from public life. To accept being a member of a small state, with everything this implied, proved to be a difficult task for every Hungarian.

The Victory of the Counterrevolution

The abdication of the Revolutionary Governing Council was followed by chaotic conditions. Budapest and most of the country was occupied by the Romanian army. In spite of the new unionist government, a counter-government continued to function at Szeged. In the still unoccupied regions, workers' councils and red armed units fought rearguard actions facing those who wielded power prior to 1918 and were now reemerging.

The unionist government lacked armed might and was supported by neither the delegates at the peace conference nor, because of its unclear program, the Hungarian people. A coup d'état, supported by the Romanian army, put an end to it on August 6, 1919. The Habsburg Archduke Joseph, in his quality as *homo regius* (the king's representative), asked István Friedrich to form the first openly counterrevolutionary government. Friedrich had a university degree, owned a factory, and had entered politics in the fall of 1918 as a follower of Mihály Károlyi. He was loyal to the House of Habsburg, and his right-leaning conservatism was tinged with liberal ideas.

The national army and its high command transferred their headquarters from Szeged to Transdanubia in the middle of August. It acted independently from the government, and within a short time became the deciding factor determining the course of events.

The new regime brought naked terror. The government ordered numerous arrests and prosecutions and one execution followed another. Thousands were sent to internment camps without trial. In the occupied regions, the Romanian army instituted punitive actions against the revolutionaries. The white terror was, first and foremost, the result of action taken by the officers of the national army, who organized ruthless pogroms without regard for civil authorities. During the first three months of the counterrevolution, about five thousand people were executed and more than seventy thousand wound up in jail or internment camps.

The terror and the seemingly hopeless economic and political situation forced thousands to emigrate, including workers, politicians, and intellectuals and caused irreparable harm to the Hungarian left. Prominent communists—Béla

Kun, Jenő Ländler, György Lukács, Jenő Varga—and Social Democrats—Vilmos Bőhm, Zsigmond Kunfi, Ernő Garami, and others—were forced to leave. So was also the majority of the bourgeois democrats and radicals, including Mihály Károlyi, Oscar Jászi, Pál Szende, and others. The sociologist Károly Mannheim, the physicist Károly Polányi, the film director Sándor Korda, and the multitalented artist László Nagy Moholy were among the many who became famous abroad.

The fate of the Friedrich government was decided by the non-recognition of the peace-makers, by the absence of armed might, by the inability to gain popular support, and by the Romanian army's control and limitation of its actions.

The Clerk Mission

By the fall of 1919, the consolidation of the Hungarian situation was of international significance because without it the peace conference could not finish its work. The basic preconditions included the withdrawal of the Romanian troops and the formation of a coalition government which the peace-makers would accept as negotiating partners.

Romania was unwilling to call its army back without a guarantee that its border with Hungary would be that established in the 1916 Bucharest Agreement. For a long time it refused to sign the Austrian and Hungarian treaties because these contained paragraphs guaranteeing minority rights. Romania found these unacceptable as a limitation of its sovereignty. The Romanian high command expropriated and shipped out machinery, transportation equipment, food, and so on for months, disregarding the protests of the Hungarian government and the prohibition of the peace-makers.

The political scene was still in flux. The various conservative factions and the majority of the pro-Habsburg royalists joined the Christian National Unity Party. The Independent Smallholder Party, led by István Szabó Nagyatádi, had a broad base but was mainly the party of the peasantry. Under unfavorable circumstances the Hungarian Social Democratic Party was reestablished. The leftist middle class was represented only by the National Democratic Party under the leadership of the lawyer Vilmos Vázsonyi.

A new coalition government was formed with the help of the British diplomat, Sir George Russel Clerk, who was sent to Budapest by the peace-makers in October. While most of the successor states enjoyed the support of France, it was Great Britain that played the leading role in settling the Hungarian situation.

To begin with, Clerk intended to give a major role to the Social Democrats and the bourgeois liberals, but finally he had to accept the dominant role of the Christian National Unity Party (CNUP). The military high command and Miklós Horthy influenced this development decisively. Horthy commanded the only troops capable of maintaining law and order in the absence of Romanian units. His forces had previously interfered significantly in the country's activities, keeping a sharp eye on what the Friedrich government did, firing civilian commissioners, preventing the activity of political parties, and requisitioning and collecting taxes in Transdanubia.

On November 5, 1919, Clerk succeeded in bringing the various interested parties to an agreement. The role of the national army as the guarantor of law and order was accepted by all parties, and Horthy promised to subordinate his forces to the government. In the middle of November, the Romanian troops left Budapest, and the national army, led by Horthy, entered the capital. A government made up of members of the CNUP was established, with Károly Huszár as prime minister. The Social Democrats and the liberals received one ministry each. On December 1, the statesmen assembled in Paris recognized the government, which called for new elections.

In Budapest, Horthy demanded a settlement of accounts. The national army's terror was extended to the capital and later to the rest of the country. Industrial production was placed under its supervision, and its units dispersed the electoral meetings of the Smallholders, Social Democrats, and liberals. There was nothing the government could do. As a protest the Social Democrats left the government, boycotted the elections, and, until June 1922, refrained from participation in politics.

In accordance with the principles of the peace-makers and with the agreement signed with Clerk, a multi-party parliamentary system had to be introduced. Social democracy and several liberal tendencies were legalized; civil rights were guaranteed. The framework of the new regime was established, but Hungarian internal developments were to determine the workings of the system.

National Elections and the Election of the Regent, 1920

The two-chamber Parliament of the prewar period could not be reestablished. On January 25–26, 1920, the population elected deputies who were to sit in a one-chamber National Assembly. Following the wishes of the great powers, universal secret balloting was established, giving more than three million people the right to vote. East of the Tisza River, the elections had to be postponed until June, following the evacuation of the entire country by the Romanians in March. In spite of the efforts of the high command, the strongest party in the 218–member assembly was that of the Smallholders, with ninety-one mandates. CNUP had fifty-nine deputies, while the left was represented only by six NDP deputies elected in Budapest.

The most difficult tasks the assembly faced were to decide the form of government and to select a head of state. Public opinion was strongly in favor of retaining the monarchy. Law I of 1920 stipulated that Hungary was a kingdom, establishing the historical continuity of the new regime and legalizing the country's claim to all lands of St. István's realm. Supported by Hungary's neighbors, the great powers informed Hungary officially that no member of the House of Habsburg was acceptable to them as head of state. In general, they feared that a Hungarian king, whoever he might be, would lead to the reestablishment of the old Hungarian imperium and possibly even of the Dual Monarchy.

Under these circumstances, the throne had to remain empty. The new law, however, following medieval tradition, stipulated that the highest office of state be occupied by a regent. Horthy was the only possible candidate for this honor. He was supported by the great powers, primarily Great Britain, and by the army, ready to do whatever was needed to get its candidate elected. To show their determination, they murdered two Social Democratic journalists who had criticized the white terror. Those who opposed Horthy had no viable candidate. With the building occupied by officers of the national army, the members of the assembly elected Horthy regent on March 1, 1920, with 131 votes out of 141.

Horthy, who had served in the Dual Monarchy's navy as its commander-in-chief and for four years been the adjutant of Francis Joseph, had remained apolitical until the summer of 1919. The most salient features of his conservative political views were his hostility towards the Soviet Union, his dread of all revolutions, and his insistence that Hungary's borders be altered, irrespective of the means. He came to power with the support of the army and the extreme right, but his election pleased the great powers also. He retained his office because he was able to accommodate the interests of the traditional ruling circles while keeping the various political trends in check. After Adolf Hitler came to power in Germany, Horthy was unwilling to give up Hungary's sovereignty. Facing National Socialism and its Hungarian representatives, he represented constitutional continuity and the system of law and thus gained even the support of the leftist opposition.

The election of the regent was a temporary measure as far as the members of the National Assembly were concerned. They considered him a head of state forced on the country by external forces and hoped that when these changed a final solution would become possible. For this reason the law did not stipulate how long the regent could serve and under what conditions the office could be abolished. Nevertheless, bowing to the army's and Horthy's wishes, his powers were broadly defined. These included the right to dismiss Parliament, to act as commander-in-chief, and several other important functions. The legislature was subordinate to the wishes of the regent and those of the prime minister. The question of a king was not solved, in either the constitutional or the political sense, by the election of the regent.

The Peace Treaty of Trianon

On March 4, 1920, a new coalition government under Sándor Simonyi-Semadam's leadership came to power, in which the Smallholders and the CNUP cooperated. The Liberals and Social Democrats were excluded and formed the opposition. The new government had to sign the peace treaty.

The Hungarian treaty was an integral part of the Paris peace plan, in the preparation of which Hungary, like the other losers, was not consulted. The text was ready by the spring of 1919. Led by Count Albert Apponyi, the Hungarian delegation reached Paris in January 1920. It demanded the alteration of the borders and, in disputed regions, the holding of plebiscites. The government, while safeguarding its British connections, offered important economic advantages to Paris to gain the sympathies of the hostile French politicans. In spite of British misgiving, the conditions of the treaty were not changed because alterations would have hurt the interests of the other successor states and destabilized the situation. The president of the peace conference, the French prime minister Alexandre-Étienne Millerand, handed the final treaty text to the Hungarian delegation on May 6, 1920. With it, he also presented a letter of explanation that raised unfounded hopes in Hungary because it spoke of possible border rectifications as subjects of discussion in the future League of Nations.

In the Trianon Palace in Versailles, two representatives of the Hungarian government signed the treaty on June 4, 1920. Hungary had to cede 70 percent of her territory, and 60 percent of her total population, including 28 percent of the Hungarian speakers. About half of the three million Hungarians who came under foreign rule lived in compact masses along the new borders, mainly in Czechoslovakia and Romania. The territory of Hungary was reduced from 282,000 square miles to ninety-three thousand and her population from eighteen million to under eight million. The peace treaty forbade compulsory military service and limited the country's army to thirty-five thousand officers and men. While the amount was not fixed, Hungary had to pay reparations. Next to Austria, Hungary became the most ethnically homogeneous successor state because the Treaty of Trianon detached practically all its non-Magyar people. In 1920, 89.5 percent of the population was Hungarian with the largest minority group, the Germans, amounting to 6.9 percent. The occupational structure of the population also changed slightly. The number of those living from agriculture diminished somewhat, but was still 52 percent of the total. Industry and trade employed 32 percent.

Territorial changes brought about corresponding changes in the economic structure. The country retained only 11 percent of its iron production, 16 percent of its forests, 38 percent of its railroad network, and 56 percent of its food processing industry. Practically all industrial raw materials and machines had to be imported. On the other hand, agriculture and the alimentary industry could not exist without exports. The economy depended on foreign trade and, consequently, reacted to every change in the world economy. These changes influenced political decisions too.

Hungarian society was deeply disturbed by the Treaty of Trianon. The country had not suffered losses of this magnitude since the sixteenth century. What made the situation worse was that the new states did not respect the rights of the Hungarian minorities guaranteed by the peace treaty. All social strata and every political party, including those of the workers, rejected the treaty but were divided concerning the rectification of the country's borders. Those who aggressively demanded the borders of pre-war Hungary did not see eye-to-eye with the Social Democrats and the bourgeois Left, which demanded a settlement along ethnic lines. The Communists hoped that a new

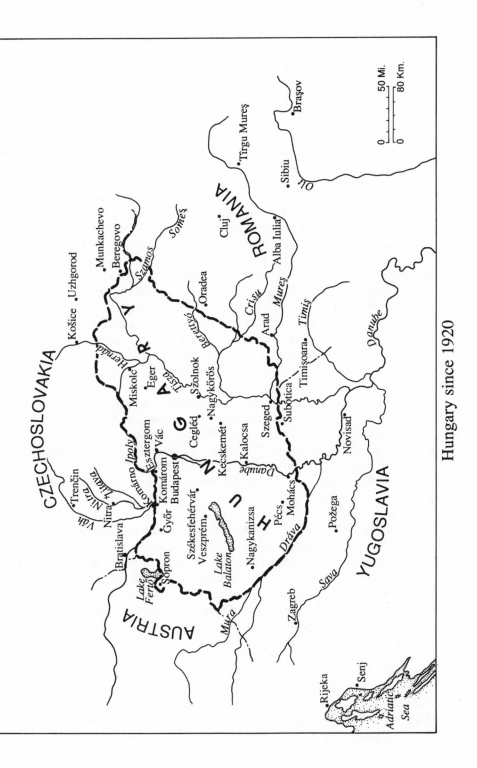

Hungary since 1920

revolution would put an end to the Trianon settlement. For a quarter century the main goal of the regime was the revision of the treaty, which it blamed for all social and economic problems.

Concepts of Stability

In the power struggle that began in the summer of 1919, three different major ideas concerning the structure of the state and the system of government clashed. These divisions were reflected, by 1922, in the composition of political parties. The old ruling circles (estate owners and important capitalists) and the majority of the middle class, including a portion of the lower middle class, sought to reestablish the old economic, social, and political system. They believed that the parliamentary form of government was the only acceptable one, provided that certain safeguards were introduced which made a turn either to the left or to the extreme right impossible. The best known representatives of this trend were the counts István Bethlen and Pál Teleki.

Another group believed that those who advocated the reintroduction of a capitalist-bourgeois society were working for a redistribution of power in their own favor. This aggressive group was composed of state and administrative employees, army officers, and owners of medium-sized landholdings, backed by an important segment of the Christian lower middle class. Based on the events of 1918–19, these people felt that the traditional parliamentary system had outlived its usefulness and that the old ruling circles were incapable of government. They demanded a strong centralized state, a dictatorship, in which neither the socialists nor the bourgeois Left had a voice, and in which Christian Hungarians were to take over the economic and other functions of the Jews. This faction was led by the future prime minister, Gyula Gömbös and his "race-protector" comrades. They propagated their ideas as members of the Smallholders and CNUP parties, as well as through the extreme Right mass movements they first established during these years: The Hungarian National Defense Association and the Association of Awakening Hungarians.

The representatives of the third faction were united in their opposition to the reestablishment of the unlimited power of the old ruling circles and also rejected the replacement of the parliamentary system with a rightist dictatorship. They wanted to rejuvenate the bourgeois-capitalist system with liberal and democratic reforms and with the broadening of democratic institutions and practices. Nevertheless, these Social Democrats, liberal bourgeois parties, and Smallholders could not agree on the extent to which various social strata were to profit from these reforms.

The traditional ruling circles feared the Smallholders the most because of their large representation in the National Assembly and because, supported by the peasant masses, they worked for land reform. They also attacked vehemently the coalition of Social Democrats and liberals that represented the urban middle class, which, with the help of those abroad, opposed not only the extreme, but also the conservative Right. The members of the coalition did not believe that the democratic great powers or Hungary's neighbors, especially Czechoslovakia, would long tolerate a rightist-nationalist system of the Horthy type.

The Beginnings of Consolidation

The survival of the system demanded consolidation and the reintroduction of the rule of law. The international power relations favored the concepts of the rightist, traditional ruling elements. On July 19, 1920, Count Pál Teleki formed his government. He was the scion of an old Transylvanian family and a well-known geographer. He advocated territorial revision out of deeply felt convictions and his ingrained conservatism turned him against liberalism and the extreme Right. He lacked the ability to maneuver and compromise, especially in his dealings with the Left. His government ended the depredations of the officers and banned the activities of certain extreme rightist armed groups, which were producing a bad impression abroad and endangering his plans for stabilizing the country. Important extremists, nevertheless, found employment in state and other administrative offices. Because, as everywhere else, the relative power of the executive grew at the expense of the legislature, the influence of these officials was subsequently an important factor.

The Teleki government, in 1921, for the "more efficient protection of the security of the state and society," outlawed the Communist Party. Already, in the fall of 1920, legal action had been taken against numerous well-known communists. Several were executed, and others wound up in the Soviet Union.

The government also introduced land reform to calm the discontented peasant masses and to disarm the Smallholders. The 1920 law required the distribution of 1,346,000 acres, and 411,000 people, 75 percent of whom were landless peasants, were given land. (Members of the Order of Heroes established by Horthy also received land. These were individuals who had backed him during the counterrevolution and on his road to power.) However the long drawn out process did not significantly increase the number of new self-sufficient landowners, who were required to indemnify the old owners. In short, the division of land and the structure of society remained practically unchanged. Nevertheless, about two million people (if entire families are counted) got small plots, reinforcing pride in ownership, the illusions which it engendered, and loyalty to the regime. In the neighboring states land reform was more thorough, expropriating large Hungarian estates but excluding Hungarian peasants from the distribution of plots.

The *numerus clausus* law of 1920 was the result of pressure exercised by the anti-Semitic Christian middle class, which faced serious economic problems. This law stipulated that universities and law schools could only admit Jews in proportion to their percentage of the country's population. (Of the students in institutions of higher learning that year, 12.5 percent were Jewish—more than twice their representation in the population.) This law represented a serious regression from the liberal legislation of the nineteenth century, making anti-Semitism constitutional for the first time in the history of modern Hungary.

While the admission requirements were changed in 1928, discrimination did not end.

The First Royal Coup d'État

The struggle over the ways and means of consolidation affected the question of the throne as well. The legitimists worked for the return of Charles IV, believing that this would ensure the reestablishment of the constitutional and legal order. Those who advocated the free election of a king and the disestablishment of the Habsburgs strengthened Horthy's position. Most of these people worked for a regime which would exclude the extreme Right from power and prevent the realization of the plans of the military.

The royalty problem provoked a crisis that forced the government out of power in February 1920. The members of the coalition, mainly the Smallholders, voted against Teleki, who, while a legitimist, was opposed to tackling the problem immediately. He and his followers left the coalition, and the CNUP became the meeting ground of legitimists. The Smallholders stood for free royal elections. They lost those who, within the party, demanded more thorough liberalizing internal measures than the leadership. These former Smallholders founded a new, left-leaning opposition party with the attorney Károly Rassay as their leader. Within a few years, he and his party became the most prominent representatives of the bourgeois-liberal opposition. The new party joined the newly formed Coalition of Citizens and Workers, which included other middle-class parties and groups and the Social Democrats. Their aim was to reform the political institutions of the country "in the spirit of the Western Bourgeois democracies." It was under these circumstances that Charles IV left Switzerland, where he lived under the supervision of the great powers, and appeared in Hungary during Easter week of 1921 to assume power. He believed that he had the backing of certain French interests and the Vatican and that his followers had made the needed preparations. Horthy, who was considered the king's supporter, and the Gömbös group that stood behind him, firmly rejected Charles' claims. The appearance of the former monarch produced sharp international protests. The neighboring countries mobilized and were ready to prevent, by force if necessary, the resumption of the royal regime. The great powers informed the Hungarian government that a Habsburg restoration was unacceptable. Thus, the first attempt of Charles IV to regain his throne ended in failure, and he left the country on April 5.

Horthy and his regime gained strength and international prestige by preventing the return of Charles IV, but they were not yet able to end the legitimist agitation. Teleki was compromised by the failed coup d'état and had to resign with his cabinet on April 13, 1921.

XVII

THE EARLY INTERWAR YEARS, 1921–1938

Mária Ormos

The Government of Count István Bethlen, 1921–1931

Political Consolidation

On April 14 Horthy asked Count István Bethlen, who had lost his Transylvanian estates, to form a new government. The new prime minister had inherited a liberalizing conservative outlook from the prewar years. He had learned his political tactics from Count István Tisza, and the events since the end of the war had convinced Bethlen that liberalism had to be strictly controlled.

Bethlen began by constructing a solid majority in Parliament and by taking steps to improve the country's international position. Among other things, he opened negotiations with the Entente powers to reach a settlement in the *Burgenland* (the western border region) question and to arrange the evacuation of the southern regions of the country around Pécs, still under Yugoslav occupation. He also applied for Hungary's admission to the League of Nations.

In August 1921, the Yugoslavs evacuated the regions that the peace treaty had awarded to Hungary. In the *Burgenland* tension continued between Austria and Hungary, and Hungarian paramilitary units occupied the disputed area. With British and French blessing, the two countries' representatives finally met in Venice on October 11. With the help of Italian mediators, they agreed that in the city of Sopron and its immediate neighborhood they would hold a plebiscite, while the Hungarians agreed to hand over the rest of the *Burgenland* to Austria.

Even before this plebiscite could be held, the peace was again disturbed by Charles IV's second attempt to regain his throne. He landed in a plane on October 20 in the disputed areas that were under the jurisdiction of legitimist officers. This made it possible for him to start his march to the capital at the head of an army. Near Budaörs regular troops blocked his way, his followers handed over their weapons, and Charles was arrested.

The Czechoslovak and Yugoslav governments tried to take advantage of this incident, but the Entente powers supported only one of their demands, the official dethronement of the House of Habsburg. The Hungarian National Assembly complied on November 3, and the allied powers interned Charles on Madeira, where he died six months later. The plebiscite in and around Sopron turned out in Hungary's favor, and in September 1922 Hungary became a member of the League of Nations.

The attempt to restore the king made it possible for Bethlen to reach agreements with the anti-Habsburg political groups. With a few of his followers, Bethlen joined the Smallholders' Party in February 1922. While István Szabó Nagyatádi remained the party's president, Bethlen became its "leader," and Gyula Gömbös made his political debut as the "managing president" of the party. Officially, the party became the Christian Smallholders and Bourgeois Party, but it was known simply as the Party of Unity.

Slightly earlier, the government had reached an agreement with the Social Democrats. In the so-called Bethlen-Peyer pact, the socialists agreed to refrain from organizing public officials, promised not to start new organizations among agricultural workers, and undertook to avoid politically motivated strikes. The government legalized the party's activities and proclaimed a limited amnesty. The Hungarian Social Democratic Party acted, from that time on, as a national party and promised to represent the Hungarian point-of-view in its international activities.

The mandate of the National Assembly was about to expire, and Bethlen did not wish to hold elections while universal suffrage was the law of the land. He issued a decree regulating the right to vote. While the regulations of 1919 gave about 40 percent of the population the right to vote, Bethlen's decree enfranchised only 28.4 percent. For rural voters the worst feature of the new decree was that voting was again made public, only the capital and the ten largest cities were granted secret balloting.

At the election, the Party of Unity gained 143 seats out of a total of 245 and within the party the number of the "booted" (peasant) deputies fell from thirty-one to sixteen. The number of deputies who came from the free professions also declined while that of the landowners and bureaucrats increased. The three parties which followed the Christian Socialist line gained thirty-five, the liberal bourgeois parties twenty and the Social Democrats twenty-five mandates. The election assured the government of a solid and comfortable majority. Thus, in 1922, one of the main characteristics of Hungary's internal policy emerged. The government accepted a legal political opposition, yet made true parliamentary life impossible by preventing the opposition from representing a serious alternative capable of assuming power. This made the work of the government much easier, but also diminished everybody's sense of political responsiblity.

The Stabilization of the Currency

The economic, commercial, and financial difficulties of the country did not improve in 1921–22. Finance Minister Loránt Hegedűs attempted to stabilize the currency without resorting to foreign help. After his failure and demission, his successor Tibor Kállay tried to find other means to solve the problem. He consciously increased the previously modest and self-generated rate of inflation. He hoped to increase economic activity in the country by this measure, but also to prove to the outside world that the country's finances precluded the paying of reparations. The government agreed on the following plan: it would request foreign loans to stabilize the currency and the budget and would demand that national assets sequestrated as security be returned and that reparations be diminished if not eliminated.

On May 4, 1923, Bethlen presented his plan in Paris before the Reparations Commission. With this a long drawn out series of negotiations began, which influenced the further developments in domestic power relations also. The radical right wing of the Party of Unity, led by Gömbös, was opposed to foreign credits and also disagreed with Bethlen about the so-called "Jewish question." The prime minister knew very well that without the collaboration of Jewish capitalists, the national economy could not be placed on secure footing and that no foreign credits could be negotiated. Gömbös and his followers accused the prime minister of betraying "Christian ideology," and of once again placing the country at the mercy "of domestic and international Jewish capital." Horthy had to decide, and he took Bethlen's side. As a result the Gömbös group became isolated. When Gömbös drew the obvious conclusions and left the governmental party, only six other deputies followed him. These men established the racist Party of Hungarian Independence.

The government was not bothered by Gömbös' defection. On the contrary, it gave Bethlen a freer hand because he had gotten rid of his anti-Semitic right wing. Nevertheless, it took additional months before the needed loan materialized. Finally, the great powers granted the government a loan of 250,000,000 gold crowns to eliminate budgetary deficits. To supervise the manner in which the loan was used, the League appointed a control commissioner. At the same time, the question of reparations was also settled. Hungary was obliged to pay 200,000,000 gold crowns over the next twenty years.

These results were not what Bethlen had hoped to achieve, but they still represented success on the international scene. Because the sequestered assets were also returned, additional sums became available for investment purposes. Inflation came to an end; the budgetary deficit disappeared within a few months; and the amount of reparations demanded was reasonable. The new currency, the pengő, introduced in 1927, proved to be stable.

Up to 1931 Hungary obtained long-term loans of 1.3 billion pengő and short and medium-term loans amounting to 1.7 billion. The borrowers were mainly the central, county, and city governments. Most of the investments were not productive because most of the money was not used to increase production, but to build up the infrastructure, cultural activities, etc. After the second half of 1925 Hungarian society began to feel the effects of the influx of capital.

The various financial changes also resulted in ending the country's isolation on the international scene. Bethlen negotiated not only with British, French, and Italian statesmen and financiers, but in the fall of 1924 he also held several talks with the leaders of the Little Entente. The government even tried to normalize Hungarian-Soviet relations. The first contact was established at the Genoa Conference in 1922 between Foreign Minister Count Miklós Bánffy and the commissar for foreign affairs, Georgii Vasilievich Chicherin. A diplomatic agreement was signed on September 5, 1924 and a commercial one seven days later. Although the Soviet government finally dropped these agreements, contacts between the two governments did not cease.

The prime minister wanted to take advantage of the more settled conditions and make the rules governing parliamentary action more stringent. The opposition reacted by leaving the legislature and starting a campaign directed against the government and the regent. It tried to prove that Horthy had been responsible for the murder of two Social Democratic newspapermen, Béla Somogyi and István Bacsó. However, information about the case had been vague even in 1920 and had become more so. Thus the publicity campaign of the Left proved to be a weak weapon.

In May 1925, the government organized municipal elections in Budapest and submitted to Parliament the electoral bill it had decreed three years earlier. Because the Social Democrats and liberals were interested in both issues, they ended their passive resistance. The Left won the municipal elections, and in Parliament they succeeded in raising the number of localities where the secret ballot was to be used to sixteen. In the second half of 1925, a peaceful mood pervaded the country. The economy began to function; unemployment was diminishing; political debates became less violent; the postwar anti-Semitic wave had almost run its course; and little was heard about the activities of the extremists.

Just at this moment, the counterfeiting scandal broke. In December at The Hague, a Hungarian army officer was arrested when he tried to change a false one thousand franc note. It soon became obvious that he was not alone, and several thousand counterfeit banknotes were found. In February 1926 a number of prominent people received jail sentences of one to four years, among them Prince Lajos Windisch-Graetz, who was one of the leaders of the counterfeiters, and two commanders of the Cartographic Institute (part of the Chief-of-Staff's establishment), who were involved in the printing and distributing of the fakes. Also sentenced was Imre Nádasy, the chief-of-police, who had used his contacts with the Ministry of Foreign Affairs to get courier passports for the distributors. The story was never fully uncovered because the investigators and those running the trial carefully avoided following those leads that pointed to the chief-of-staff and Gömbös.

This unpleasant incident proved that while Bethlen was able to get rid of Gömbös politically, the symbiosis of the conservative and radical Right, which had occurred during the counterrevolution, nevertheless played an important role in public life. This affair, not too important, made it clear that right wing extremism had become an integral part of the Horthy regime. Bethlen was able to push it out of the limelight, but he was unable to get rid of it in spite of the chance which the affair offered.

The franc scandal had not yet been settled when, during the summer of 1926, the League of Nations recalled its financial commissioner. Paradoxically the franc affair did not weaken the government; rather it was the opposition that lost strength. The death of Vilmos Vázsonyi, one of the liberal leaders, contributed considerably to this. His party fell to pieces, and several of its deputies joined the Party of Unity.

Conservative Reforms

The last action of the 1922–26 second National Assembly was to reestablish the upper house. Until the end of the war, the Hungarian parliament had had two chambers, but this system had not been reestablished after the fall of the Hungarian Soviet Government. Bethlen now argued that to assure calm and safe working conditions, the legislature needed a "safety brake," and that only an upper house organized along new lines could play this role. New elections were to be held on December 14–15, 1926. In the electoral campaign, the Party of Unity was joined by the moderate Christian Democrats and a few individuals without party affiliations. The rightist opposition was composed only of the racists (calling themselves "race-protectors") and a very few independents. The Left was composed of the National Democratic Party of Károly Rassay, the 48er and Independence Party, the Social Democrats, and the new Socialist Workers' Party of Hungary.

The Socialist Workers' Party of Hungary had been established in April 1925 by left wing Social Democrats and Communists under the leadership of István Vági. Unlike the Social Democrats, the new party intended to become active among the rural poor and to organize stronger mass movements. The government permitted the establishment of the party but limited its ability to make itself heard. When the new party was organized, the parliamentary Left was advocating passivity, so the government considered it a possible counterweight to the Social Democrats. It also hoped that this semi-legal party would give the police a chance to put its hands on Communists. The political considerations that dictated the toleration of this party became moot with the return of the Social Democrats to Parliament, and the police descended on the SWP. Its leaders were tried in 1926 and the Communists among them, including Mátyás Rákosi and Vági, received one-year prison sentences.

Under these circumstances the position of the SWP in the elections was hopeless. The Left, in general, lost heavily. The Social Democrats obtained only fourteen mandates, the liberals nine, and the 48er and Independence Party only one. The rightist race-protectors also lost three of their seven seats in the lower house. An almost monolithic Party of Unity majority in Parliament gave the government a rock-solid base for its operations. Nothing changed in the next elections in 1931. The results can only partly be explained by the limited franchise and electoral manipulations. After all, the Social Democrats suffered their losses in the cities, where the vote was secret. The results showed clearly that the urban masses were ready to desert the Social Democrats, who had proved incapable of defending the interests of the workers. The failure of the race-protectors was also significant, proving that the urban middle classes preferred Bethlen's realpolitik to turbulent racism. The Party of Unity had become almost exclusively the party of conservative gentlemen, landowners, and members of the upper middle class. It lost its extreme right wing, as well as its "booted" members.

In 1926 István Bethlen ended what he considered his work of consolidation. The state had played an important role in creating the conditions for economic revival and in assuring that the revived economy did not neglect the interests of the large estates and their continuing capitalist transformation. Bethlen created a solid conservative majority, allowing him to govern for a few years almost as if Parliament had not existed. The massive loans had produced a modest economic boom, resulting in a slow increase in the living standards of the wage and salary earners. The moment had arrived when the government could think of beginning to realize some of its reform concepts and change its foreign policy. The most noteworthy reforms of the Bethlen period were land reform (see chapter 16), health insurance, and the educational reforms tied to the name of Count Kunó Klebelsberg.

The extension of health insurance began in 1927 as new social classes were insured. Those covered could draw benefits for a year instead of the previous limit of twenty weeks. Sick pay was raised from 50 percent of wages and salaries to 60–75 percent, and accident insurance benefits were also raised. In 1928 the government made obligatory old age, disability, widow, and waif insurances. The weakness of the system was that the still considerable masses of the peasantry and the rural proletariat were not insured.

In 1927 the government felt strong enough to change the *numerus clausus* law (see chapter 16). It did not fit into Bethlen's political and economic concepts and also caused him numerous difficulties abroad. The new proposal continued to limit the number of those admitted to institutions of higher learning to prevent the growth of an intellectual proletariat, but it changed the method of admission. It eliminated as criteria racial and nationality considerations and instead paid more attention to social origin, trying to assure that the young of all classes got a chance. This did not mean that either discrimination or anti-Semitism were eliminated. The hatred that had been so virulent right after the war had not been forgotten, and social and class distinctions continued to be strongly felt. Nevertheless, the reestablishment of political and economic order and the general improvement in the standard of living offered hope that the peaceful coexistence that had begun in the nineteenth century could be further developed, provided the internal peace of the country was not disturbed. Unfortunately, this hope was not to be realized.

Klebelsberg, the minister of culture, began his reforms by reestablishing in Pécs and Szeged the universities of Pozsony and Kolozsvár, cities Hungary had lost after World War I. In the second half of the 1920s, he added modern clinical facilities and institutes of natural science to the university at Szeged. After 1923 Klebelsberg expanded the medical facilities of the university at Debrecen and also built there new facilities for the College of Humanities and Social Sciences. The construction of the Budapest Observatory started in 1923, and the Biological Institute at Tihany was erected in 1926–27.

Klebelsberg established scholarships for study abroad, and it was his plan to build, practically everywhere in Europe, Hungarian Institutes to serve as homes for students studying abroad and travelling scholars. While he was in office such institutes were built with Hungarian money in Berlin, Vienna, and Rome. The most important of his reforms was the construction of about thirty-five hundred new elementary school classrooms as well as fifteen hundred new homes for elementary school teachers. This program was completed by 1930.

All these reforms were expensive, and the Ministry of Culture's share of the budget increased considerably. According to the views of several people, the cultural expenditures were beyond the country's means. However, some peculiar political conceptions assured that the needed funds were made available: the extension of state-supported education was supposed to assure increased ideological conformity. The often stressed "Hungarian cultural superiority" was the basis on which the revision of the Trianon treaty was justified, and the politicians hoped that their cultural policy would attract not only the Hungarians, but even the non-Hungarians living in the lost territories across the borders.

Intellectual Life

The broadening of the institutional basis of cultural life was paradoxically paralleled by the regression of intellectual activities. After the war and the revolutions, Hungarian scientific and artistic life had to operate in an intellectual climate in which practically every modern or progressive trend was outside the officially accepted norm and made its followers suspect.

While various shades of right-wing conservatism dominated the political scene, a unified "Christian-nationalist" ideal did not develop. On some important questions, however, even Bethlen, Gömbös, and the Christian Socialists agreed in spite of their numerous differences.

The deputies inclined to fascism demanded a totalitarian state, much more thorough social and land reforms than what the regime proposed, and far-reaching anti-Semitic laws. Bethlen's followers, the real representatives of the trend intellectuals faced, tried to rid liberalism of its "faults and weaknesses" and to construct an authoritarian state, which would settle the most pressing socio-economic problems and introduce some reforms but would limit its influence in social and economic matters and would not become openly dictatorial. The ideology based on liberalism's critical evaluation was presented by the historian Gyula Szekfű in his study, *Three Generations*. In the name of Catholic universality, some Catholic bishops propagated this philosophy.

Philosophy produced nothing new. As has been seen in chapter 16, Károly Mannheim, the famous sociologist, had left the country in 1919 as did the well-known economic historian Károly Polányi. Freud's friend, the psychiatrist Sándor Ferenczi, lost his university position after 1919. History and linguistics were relatively better off because research in these subjects was considered less sensitive. Szekfű, mentioned above, and his co-author Bálint Hóman began in 1929 to publish their massive, seven-volume *Hungarian History*, parts of which are still useful today. Sándor Domanovszky and István Hajnal were among the other noted historians. Zoltán Gombócz was the leading linguist. Antal Szerb, a historian of literature of great talent and stature, never became professor and died in a concentration camp. In literary scholarship János Horváth, who concentrated mainly on analyzing nineteenth century Hungarian literature, was the outstanding figure.

"The Christian course" was especially detrimental for the natural scientists. János Neumann, one of the greatest mathematicians of his time, was forced to emigrate. He developed, among other things, the theories of sets and games and was a pioneer in the development of computers. Leó Szilárd and Jenő Wigner, the famed nuclear physicists, also worked abroad, as did Dezső Mihály, one of the inventors of television.

Among the scientists working in Hungary, the following achieved results recognized all over the world: József Varga, whose inventions in the petrochemical industry made him famous; Géza Zemplén, who did important work in organic chemistry; and the Nobel prize-winning biochemist, Albert Szent-Györgyi, who has resided in the United States since 1949. In mathematics Lipót Fejér, Frigyes Riesz, and Gyula Nagy Szőkefalvi achieved fame.

In the arts, state subsidies and honors went to mediocre and often bad artists, who expressed the official ideology in their works. In literature, all the honors went to those who understood what was expected. The best literature continued to be published in the magazine *Nyugat (The West)* edited by Miksa Fenyő. Hungary's most notable writers and poets of the 1920s, Mihály Babits, Dezső Kosztolányi, and Zsigmond Móricz belonged to the *Nyugat* circle. Besides these and those writers who followed the political fashion, a third group operated independently, including the popular Sándor Márai, Lajos Zilahy, Jenő Heltai, and Ferenc Molnár.

In the 1930s important changes occurred in all scientific and artistic endeavors, closely connected with world-wide political and economic events. The most spectacular of these was the Great Depression, which influenced the intellectuals, going beyond their purely economic interests, and weakened the self-confidence of the dominant conservatives. At the same time, certain social effects of industrialization and modernization became visible for the first time. A small number of individuals, sons of petty rural intellectuals, of peasants, and of urban slum dwellers, began to find their way into higher classes and better occupations. When, with the appearance of National Socialism in Germany, the international political constellation took on new shapes, the intellectuals were forced to take a stand and decide where they belonged.

The important beginnings of new social sciences date from these years. The history of ideas became a popular field, and a small group of intellectuals began to be interested in Marxism, including Eric Molnár, Gábor Gaál, and Pál Justus. History and popular historical writing became a battlefield on which fascists and anti-fascists fought. Sociology, ably represented by Ferenc Erdei, became popular, and a new "science," "Hungarology," made its appearance to fight fascism, with László Német as its main spokesman.

A sociographic experiment called village exploration, not truly scientific, was also popular in the 1930s. A segment of the new generation of writers presented the economic and intellectual poverty of village life to the general public. The best "village writers" were Imre Kovács, Gyula Illyés, and Géza Féja.

In the literary world proper, new figures emerged from among the populist and urbanist writers. The best prose and poetry produced by the populists was that of Gyula Illyés, while the urbanists produced two giants of world literature, Attila József, a poet of working class origin, and Miklós Radnóti, a sensitive poet who died in a concentration camp.

It is characteristic of the intellectual climate of the Horthy period that while Béla Bartók's works earned ever-growing recognition all over the world, the opposition to modern and intellectually open art in Hungary was so strong that Bartók finally decided to emigrate in 1940. The Hungarian musical world of this period also produced Zoltán Kodály and Ernő Dohnányi.

One of the giants of twentieth century painting, Tivadar Kosztka Csontváry had died early in the century and remained unappreciated for several more decades both in Hungary and abroad. Several important avant-garde painters worked outside Hungary, including László Moholy Nagy, who taught at the Bauhaus School before moving to the United States, and Béla Uitz, who worked first in the West and later in the Soviet Union. Some of those painting in Hungary, including József Rippl-Rónai and Ernő Czóbel, worked in the impressionist–post-impressionist tradition or followed the avant-garde like Lajos Kassák, who was also an important poet and novelist. István Szőnyi, József Egry, and János Kmetty tried to find a new, more modest, and realistic way to paint. The greatest of all the painters of the period was the highly original Gyula Derkovits.

Changes in the Foreign Policy

Between 1921 and 1926, the foreign policy aims of István Bethlen were to secure the international position of the country, to create the preconditions for economic recovery, and to improve diplomatic and economic relations with the outside world. He tried to cooperate with the great Western powers and was satisfied with finding a *modus vivendi* with Hungary's neighbors. When it became clear, in 1921, that France was basing her Central European policy on collaboration with the Little Entente, Bethlen turned to the political and economic circles of Britain. He soon discovered that Great Britain's interest in Central Europe was diminishing. Indications of this lack of interest appeared in 1924-25 and became more numerous as time passed.

A formal normalization of relations was all that Bethlen could achieve with Czechoslovakia and Romania. In 1924 it seemed as if an agreement with Yugoslavia were possible. (The Hungarian minority in that state was smaller than in the other two countries, making talks easier.) A treaty of friendship was under discussion, and the Yugoslavs were even willing to talk about a Hungarian free port on the Adriatic and a revision of the peace treaty. By September 1926, the foreign ministers had worked out the details of the treaty and communicated these to their partners and the great powers. Yugoslavia's allies objected to the Yugoslav-Hungarian rapprochement, and Mussolini, too, intervened. Through the Italian ambassador in Budapest, he let Bethlen know that he was opposed to the treaty but ready to conclude a broad agreement with Hungary.

For the first time since 1918, an important power had offered a treaty to Hungary. Bethlen had to take advantage of the offer. The Yugoslav-Hungarian treaty negotiations petered out. On April 4, 1927, Bethlen arrived in Rome, and on the next day he signed the Italian-Hungarian agreement. Valid for ten years, it proclaimed "permanent and eternal peace" between the two countries and stipulated that future disagreements that could not be solved diplomatically would be submitted to arbitration. An additional secret agreement was concluded between Mussolini and Bethlen, in which they agreed to cooperate closely politically and consult on a regular basis concerning issues of common interest. The talks revealed that both men considered the status quo in Central Europe temporary and believed that Germany would play an important role in changing it. They also agreed that in the long run, Austria's annexation by Germany was unavoidable.

The agreement was a great success for Bethlen although it made further talks with Yugoslavia impossible and brought the closer collaboration of the Little Entente powers who had already begun thinking about dissolving this alliance. In possession of the Italian trump card, Bethlen proclaimed officially that he did not consider the Trianon treaty final. The Hungarian government floated a trial balloon indicating that it was ready to negotiate with anybody about the peaceful revision of the treaty. Nothing happened. While in both France and Britain smaller or larger groups were ready to support Hungary's cause, these were not significant enough to influence their governments.

It was under these circumstances that the second Bethlen-Mussolini meeting was held in Milan on April 2–5, 1928. Though he signed nothing, Bethlen accepted more far-reaching obligations. Among other things, the heads of government agreed to support the *Heimwehr* in Austria and the Croatian separatists, and Bethlen also agreed to help Mussolini in organizing his Tripartite Pact, aimed at bringing Italy, Greece, and Bulgaria together in order to encircle Yugoslavia.

Of the Milan plans, very little was realized. The promised military loan to Hungary was not made available, and up to 1939 the country was allowed to purchase only two hundred mostly dated planes for its air force. The important sums invested in a *Heimwehr* coup d'état were lost, and the *Heimwehr* later joined the Austrian government under different sponsorship. The Tripartite pact was never concluded, but in 1929 the support of the Ustaşa movement organized by the Croatian separatists began. The talks in Milan finalized the change in Hungary's foreign policy. After his return to Hungary from his second Italian visit, Bethlen declared publicly that he doubted that peaceful border changes were possible. In May 1929, the Ministry of Foreign Affairs took a stand opposed to Central European economic cooperation and rejected negotiations dealing with redrawing the borders along ethnic lines.

The increased involvement of Bethlen in international affairs beginning in 1928 is well illustrated by the number of trips he took. He sought rapprochement with Greece, Turkey, Poland, and was especially eager to build up contacts with Germany. He hoped to solve the export problems of Hungarian agriculture by opening the German market to it, and he believed that it was Germany, joined by Italy, that would solve the problems of Central Europe. For this reason he hoped to play a role in bringing Germany and Italy together. His November 1930 visit to Berlin brought only meager results, however. He had to be satisfied with promises concerning the agricultural export and revisionist issues, and the German politicians did not wish to cooperate with Italy.

The Italian success was not followed by other foreign policy gains, and in October 1929, when the Great Depression hit Hungary, the grave economic difficulties forced the government to turn its attention once again to dealing with the internal problems of the country.

The Economy and the Economic Crisis

The capitalist industrialization of Hungary that had begun in the last third of the nineteenth century made big strides until 1918. After the war, the economy regressed due to raw material shortages, the interruption of international commercial ties, and the various monetary problems. The economy revived only during the second half of 1925 under new conditions resulting from the peace treaty. Postwar Hungary's population density was higher than it had ever been, and industry, commerce, and transportation played a greater role within the economy. While this structural change by itself was favorable, the lack of most raw materials and the disappearance of the large market of the Dual Monarchy kept the economy from regaining its earlier dynamism, even after 1925. Agriculture stagnated; the yield of wheat per acre did not increase and livestock production, even as late as 1938, was behind that of 1911. The large-scale railroad construction of the late nineteenth and twentieth centuries came to an end, and the country was among the least developed as far as the introduction of motor transportation was concerned. The same was true of everything else that would have contributed to modernization, including the building of canals, roads, and public transportation.

The meager economic results achieved by 1929 had required massive efforts from the Bethlen government. To keep the balance of payments in hand and to service the foreign loans required further and further loans. The prime minister tried to obtain in 1927–28 another large, long-term loan that would have stimulated the entire economic complex. The negotiations were still in progress when the economic crisis began. This brought, first of all, dramatic changes in agricultural exports. The main export items of the country, wheat and animal products, registered price losses of 65 and 50 percent respectively, amounting to a loss of 60 percent of the total exports-generated national income. This decline promptly influenced and limited imports and affected the domestic market. Industrial production had to be curtailed by 28 percent between 1929 and 1934.

As in the rest of Central Europe, the crisis in Hungary reached its nadir in the summer of 1931. This was caused by the collapse of the great Viennese bank, the Credit-Anstalt, whose short-term credits were recalled. The entire banking system collapsed. Simultaneously, the entire foreign currency and bullion reserves of the Hungarian banks were exhausted, and even the National Bank was saved from bankruptcy only by an emergency loan it received in June 1931 from the Bank of International Settlements. In Hungary as elsewhere, the economic crisis produced political difficulties as Bethlen was forced to get involved more and more in economic matters. Capital was dissatisfied with the decrees issued to help it, and agrarian dissatisfaction grew steadily.

The problems of agriculture induced Gaston Gaál to form a new Smallholders Party, which opposed the government's economic policy. With the steady erosion of belief in Bethlen's infallibility, the race-protectors too became more active politically. Although Gyula Gömbös, after five years in opposition, had dissolved his own party and rejoined the Party of Unity, becoming first undersecretary and then minister of defense, he had not given up his political ambitions. The regent felt the pressure of both the agrarians and the race-protectors, and in 1930–31 he too began to move away from Bethlen. Horthy wanted to introduce summary jurisdictional procedures to protect the interests of the large estates and to control the growing unrest of the workers. In the summer of 1931, Bethlen realized that running the government would force him to introduce further unpopular measures. He felt that a government that promulgated them would be committing political suicide. He refused to do this and offered his resignation on August 19. Horthy accepted his resignation and five days latter asked Count Gyula Károlyi to form a new government.

The Transition Government of Károlyi, 1931–1932

In 1919, Károlyi had been the president of the government that was formed at Arad and later functioned at Szeged. He had retired from politics and devoted his energies to his estates, which he managed in exemplary fashion. Reputed to be thrifty and puritanical, he belonged to the circle of Horthy's closest friends.

Within the governmental majority, several groups began to take shape. One of these was under Bethlen's leadership and represented the interests of the leading capitalists and the capitalistically managed large estates. Another spoke for the discontented agrarian population, while a third segment of the party followed Gömbös. The government could not act without being opposed by one or another group within its own party. National discontent was increased first by the reduction of the salaries of public employees and then by the elimination of the already low unemployment compensation. The weakening of the governmental coalition was also made plain when the deputies of the Christian Party left those committees which discussed questions related to the crisis and a minister of the same party gave up his governmental post, feeling that he could no longer represent agrarian interests. A group belonging to the extreme Right even attempted a coup d'état.

A wave of strikes much larger than anything experienced under Bethlen also hit the country. The movement reached even the villages and was ruthlessly repressed by police terror. Mass arrests followed, and the gendarmes in the countryside even opened fire on the demonstrating masses. The administration's mass arrests and investigations led the authorities to the leaders of the illegally active Communist Party of Hungary. Four Communist leaders were arrested in mid-June 1932, and two of these, Imre Sallai and Sándor Fürst, were court-martialed on July 28 and executed the following day.

The government's foreign policy produced only meager results, and Hungary was forced to return to her Western European orientation in hopes of financial help. In February 1932, the French prime minister, André Tardieu, published his plan to bring order to Central Europe's economic and fiscal affairs. Nothing better proves how critical the situation had become in Hungary than its government's willingness to begin negotiations in accordance with the stipulations of this plan, although these included close cooperation among all Central European states. This might have been why Bethlen, who had tried to create an Italian-Austrian-Hungarian customs union, turned against the prime minister.

Another cause for Bethlen's action was the steady splintering of the Party of Unity. In June 1932, Zoltán Meskó left the party and founded The Hungarian National Socialist Peasant and Workers Party. This was the first party in Hungary that followed a foreign fascist model in its program and organization.

The "steward," as Bethlen was called, thought that the moment had come to grasp the reins again and introduce a program aimed at the reestablishment of order. In a letter dated September 3, he asked the prime minister to resign. Károlyi was certainly beyond help, but Bethlen found that, looking to the future, Horthy was beginning to prefer Gömbös to him. When, on September 21, 1932, Károlyi resigned, Bethlen accepted the task of making Gömbös acceptable to the Party of Unity. Negotiations lasted for days. On the 29th, Horthy asked Gömbös to form a government, and it took power on October 1.

The Attempt of Gyula Gömbös to Organize a Totalitarian Fascist State

The First Political Attack and Its Failure

The regent, the majority party, and the leaders of the economy agreed to accept Gömbös as prime minister only after he had promised to maintain the existing governmental system and refrain from propagating racist ideas. Furthermore, the majority on which Gömbös relied followed not him, but Bethlen. Nevertheless, at the beginning of his tenure in office, Gömbös believed that it was possible to eliminate all obstacles with one bold stroke and to establish a fascist state system.

He began by making public a governmental program consisting of ninety-five points, which his contemporaries promptly dubbed Gömbös' "dreambook." The "National Work Plan" promised everybody everything imaginable. First of all, it promised the maximal satisfaction of the "national interest," and the creation of a "state working for national goals," which was to be created by "national cooperation." He denied that he wanted to rule as a dictator, but stressed that the nation needed a leader. He promised far-reaching social and economic measures, which were to benefit all classes and social strata. During the first few weeks of the new government's tenure, relative peace reigned in the country. Until the fall of 1934, the government's prestige was buttressed by a few successes in foreign affairs. Most important were those which helped to increase export sales. The month after taking office, Gömbös visited Rome. His talks with Mussolini were politically fruitless, but Mussolini promised to initiate economic negotiations aimed at an Italian-Hungarian-Austrian agreement, and these talks brought an increase in Hungarian wheat exports.

In June 1933, Gömbös visited Germany too, but returned disappointed. Hitler and his foreign minister were cool to the idea of a German-Italian-Hungarian-Austrian alliance and refused to promise tolerance of Austria. Nor were they eager to reach a political understanding with Hungary. Hitler told his visitor that Hungary would have to be satisfied with the planned German destruction of Czechoslovakia and could not count on his support of Hungarian claims against Romania and Yugoslavia. Hitler's offer of Hungary's former Czechoslovak lands did not appease Gömbös, who hoped to gain Transylvania. In economic matters, the Germans made some vague promises included in the economic agreement of July, but there was no important increase of Hungarian exports until February 1934, when a supplementary agreement was signed.

During 1933, the governments grew stronger, thanks to the improvement of world markets, increased exports, relief offered to the indebted producers, and Gömbös' success in reorganizing the majority party. After Gömbös became prime minister, Bethlen resigned from the presidency of the party, and Gömbös took his place. Gömbös began by renaming the party the Party of National Unity and undertaking a nationwide campaign of reorganization. In the same year, however, it also became evident that the dictatorial ambitions of the party leadership were opposed by the leaders of the various segments of the economy. Gömbös had to give up his plans to create the post of vice-prime minister and a new powerful economic ministry. Everybody understood that these measures would have led to increased personal power for Gömbös, and the new ministry would also have allowed his interference in economic affairs. In early 1934, the government's proposal to terminate the capital's right to govern itself was defeated. All that Gömbös was able to achieve was a law extending the powers of the regent. His first attack on the existing state structure ended in failure.

Temporary Victory

The apparent successes in party reorganization did not prevent the majority of the members from defeating the prime minister's plans. Therefore, Gömbös sought parliamentary allies who would back him in his fight with Bethlen and his followers. He found one ally in the Smallholders Party, whose current leader, Tibor Eckhart, was a race-protector.

Until 1933, the Smallholders had been the government's staunchest opponents. They changed their position when Bethlen ceased to support the government. He first turned against it early in 1934, when Parliament was debating the municipal autonomy proposal, and then, in a speech made in Debrecen, Bethlen sharply criticized the entire governmental program. This speech amounted to a declaration of war, and the leaders of the Smallholders recognized the chances it offered them. They also realized that due to the supplementary economic agreement with Germany, Gömbös' position had improved. Gömbös registered further foreign policy successes when in March he signed the Italian-Hungarian-Austrian Danubian Agreement in Rome. It had mainly prestige value because Hungary was not ready to become a guarantor of Austria's independence, and Austria was in no position to support Hungary's revisionist claims. Nevertheless, the creation of the block created a favorable impression. It influenced the attitude of Hungary's population and produced discontent in German governmental circles.

Gömbös' successes and Bethlen's challenge induced the Smallholders to approach the prime minister. The struggle and realignment was arrested for a while because Horthy did not agree to the dissolution of Parliament in the fall of 1934, and because the government found itself deeply involved in an unpleasant foreign situation.

In October 1934, the king of Yugoslavia was murdered at Marseille. It soon became evident that the Ustaşa had played a crucial part in the event, and Yugoslavia demanded an international investigation and the punishment of those governments who harbored them. The Ustaşa leaders lived in Germany and Italy, but they had numerous camps in Italy and also some in Austria and in Hungary, where they had two training camps and about forty men. In the spring of 1934, these camps were closed at the request of the Foreign Ministry, and the Ustaşa began to leave in groups of two and three. The affair was nevertheless embarrassing because several of those involved in the murder had, indeed, lived in Hungary for certain lengths of time and because some well-known Ustaşa were in Hungary during and after the event. The government's position was made even more difficult by the Yugoslavs' wish not to embarrass Germany and the desire of the French to spare Italy.

The storm was hardly over when Gömbös moved again on the domestic front. In January 1935, he forced Béla Imrédy, whom he did not like, and Bethlen's supporter, Miklós Kállay, to resign from the government. He also retired twenty-two generals, replacing them with his friends. He even dared to submit a plan to transform Hungary into a corporate state on the Italian model. What Gömbös proposed was a combination of fascist labor law and corporate law, mixed with some Hungarian conservative ideas. The proposal aimed to organize employers and workers into "corporations," and to make strikes illegal. Neither the Social Democrats nor the labor unions could accept this proposal, and the industrialists were opposed too. They might have welcomed the anti-strike aspects of Gömbös' plan, but had to oppose his attempt to gain control of factories and businesses.

At the same time, the extreme Right, which followed Gömbös and the Smallholders, began their united attack on Bethlen and his clique. The dispute became so sharp that Horthy himself attempted to make peace and summoned both Bethlen and Gömbös. Bethlen demanded that Gömbös break with the Smallholders, that he discuss his proposals with his party's leaders, and that he keep Parliament in session until its mandate expired. Gömbös made many promises and kept none of them. On March 4, the government resigned, but within two hours Horthy appointed a second Gömbös government. This tactical move absolved the new government from keeping the promises made by the old. It promptly demanded the dissolution of Parliament and Horthy acted accordingly.

Bethlen promptly left the majority party and joined the opposition. In the interview in which he explained his action, he stated that he was against demagogues, the methods employed by the government, and the "leader" principle. He added that he was afraid that the country would "witness further flirting with the principles of National Socialism, with totalitarian party rule, and with additional innovations like the formation of SA and SS units, economic planning, and the corporate system, all of which endanger the country's peace, calm, credit, and security."

The Elections and Gömbös' Isolation

According to contemporaries, the 1935 election was the most corrupt and violent in Hungary's history. The Party of National Unity gained 170 of the 245 seats in Parliament. Gömbös' real victory was not his party's unprecedented majority, but the appearance of ninety-eight deputies in the party's parliamentary block who had never been elected before and most of whom belonged to the extreme Right. Bethlen was reelected as an independent, but his followers gained only thirty or forty seats. Counterrevolutionaries from 1919, Gömbös' military comrades, and activists from extreme Right organizations were now dominant in Parliament. Thus the stage seemed set for the realization of Gömbös' plans.

Because the economic situation had improved, industry and trade were more opposed than ever to the government's intervention in their affairs. Gömbös' followers attempted to organize new mass movements and to take control of old ones, thus hurting numerous special interests. The corporate system was so unpopular that Gömbös did not even mention it again. Although Parliament enacted into law his settlement and entailed estates proposals, they satisfied neither the large landowners nor the small agrarian interests.

In early 1935, Hungary's "most reliable partner," Italy, began to collaborate with France. Italy even tried to convince Hungary to guarantee Austria's independence as part of the three countries' so-called Danubian Agreement. Since late 1934, the relations between Germany and Hungary were also deteriorating; the Germans were trying to gain Yugoslavia's and Romania's friendship and therefore distanced themselves from Hungary's revisionist claims. Hungary's international position became even worse when, in the fall of 1935, Mussolini embarked on his Ethiopian campaign. The leading circles had no doubt that, with the Italian forces tied down in Africa, there was nobody left in Central Europe who could stand up to Germany. The consequences soon became evident. In 1936, Mussolini agreed to a German-Austrian pact that stipulated that the two countries would follow "parallel" policies. He thus gave up his protection of Austria. This meant that Germany did not need Hungary's good will for her Austrian and Central European policies and therefore had no reason to make serious concessions to the Hungarian government.

An impotent foreign policy, combined with a tense domestic situation, began to transform the political power relations. First the Smallholders broke with Gömbös, who had "betrayed them" during the elections, and began to work with Bethlen. Bethlen's followers within the Party of National Unity and members of the opposition agreed on a common platform and attacked the government. Gömbös also faced unexpected new opposition from about sixty extreme right-wing deputies who had formed their own parliamentary block. These people felt that Gömbös was not enough of a fascist or, in any case not a successful one. The result was that the government no longer had a consistent majority.

Gömbös became isolated and Horthy's confidence in him diminished. The regent made peace with Bethlen, who, together with several others, tried to convince him to dismiss the prime minister. However, in March 1936, Gömbös became seriously ill, and Horthy waited until he died on October 6, 1936 in a hospital in Münich.

The Darányi Government, 1936-1938

Horthy and his circle wanted to replace Gömbös with a man who would reestablish the old order in politics, control the turbulent elements on the Right and Left, and cease to compromise the country in the West with pro-Germany and pro-Italian propaganda.

The realistic, calm, and conservative Kálmán Darányi appeared to be this man. Two circumstances were to determine, to a considerable extent, his choices and actions; he had to face considerable fascist activities at home, and, the German government began to put considerable pressure on Hungary.

Darányi wanted to cleanse his party of Gömbös' followers. They reappeared, however, in the many new fascist parties, organized along foreign models, which multiplied, dissolved, regrouped, and reorganized constantly after 1932. One of these was the Party of the National Will established in 1935 by a cashiered major, Ferenc Szálasi. He succeeded in establishing contact with certain German circles and tried to gather the various factions into one party.

The other main meeting place of the fascists was the Hungarian National Defense Association (MOVE). Once restricted to military officers, it disregarded its own by-laws and also began to admit civilians. It became the most dangerous organization because it possessed large quantities of weapons, and by March 1937, the rumor circulated that with German support MOVE was planning a coup d'état. Although the government did not believe the rumor, the German ambassador was, nevertheless, recalled, and most of MOVE's weapons were confiscated. Subsequently, a considerable number of the organization's members joined fascist parties.

German political pressure mostly affected the country's German minority. If the assimilative efforts of the Horthy regime cannot be condoned, the German demands served the interest of these people even less. With money, publications, and all other means, the German government supported the Nazi wings of the various German ethnic organizations, and disguised as tourists or cultural envoys, Nazi agitators appeared everywhere in the country.

It was under Darányi that a new way of facing German blackmail was devised, the so-called "take the wind out of their sails" policy. It offered more or less determined opposition but at the same time made concessions. For example, MOVE's activities were strictly limited, but the organization was not dissolved. In 1936–37, Szálasi was arrested twice, but on each occasion, although he was tried and condemned, he was let go. Darányi even made some concessions to the Germans in introducing changes in the schools of the minorities, but his measures did not satisfy the Nazis.

The "take the wind out of their sails" policy characterized Darányi's April 18, 1937, speech at Szeged. To help rural unemployment, he promised to begin a reforestation and irrigation program. He proposed to alleviate unemployment among the educated by "constitutionally" limiting the number of Jews in the professions to their percentage in the total population. This was the first time since the *numerus clausus* law of 1920 that the Hungarian government officially declared itself in favor of discriminatory measures.

The government's attempt to settle the country's constitutional problems was followed with great interest both in Hungary and abroad. The dethronement of the Habsburgs left unresolved the country's legal governmental status (a kingdom without a dynasty), and the question of the regent's successor was unclear. The latter issue had to be settled to prevent possible German intervention, so in 1937 the regent was given extended powers and the right to suggest his successor.

The steady advance of the fascists and the government's ambivalent attitude induced the left to change its tactics and to attempt the creation of new organizations. The illegal Communist Party opted for Popular Front tactics favoring the joint struggle of all anti-fascist forces. Though the party tried to operate within legal organizations to enhance its influence, under the circumstances it could not be effective. The legal Social Democrats' policy was also sterile, and the party's influence among the masses was diminishing. Union membership, which had reached 200,000 in 1922, fell to 125,000 over the next three years, and the Socialists received only 112,000 votes in 1939, compared to 270,000 in 1922. This decline undermined the prestige of the old leadership, and new people took its place including Eliás Mónus, an important anti-fascist, Pál Justus, the poet and translator, and the practical politician, Árpád Szakasits. The party's youth organization (National Youth Committee) included some Communists. In principle the Social Democrats favored Popular Front tactics, but refused to collaborate with the Communists, whom they considered weak but dangerous. They tried to ally themselves with the democratic middle class.

This desire made the party consider joining a new political block, the March Front, organized by the populist writers who made their appearance in the 1930s. The Front published its twelve point program on March 15, 1937. It demanded bourgeois democracy, the nationalization and distribution of estates over seven hundred acres, resistance to Nazi influences, and the cooperation of the Danubia people. In the long run, however, neither the Social Democrats nor the Independent Smallholders' Party gave their support to the Front, which became isolated and was dissolved early in 1938. Some of its adherents established the leftist National Peasant Party in the summer of 1939, including Ferenc Erdei, others sought to find a "special Hungarian way" following László Németh, and the rest turned to the fascists. While the Left failed to organize, the fascists took an important step towards unity. On October 23, several fascist organizations merged into Szálasi's new party, the Hungarian National Socialist ("Arrowcross") Party, leaving only a few small splinter groups.

In the fall of 1937, it became evident that Great Britain would not declare war in response to a limited German reorganization of Central Europe. Knowing this, Hitler not only decided to annex Austria but also made up his mind to intervene militarily in Czechoslovakia. He at once asked the Hungarian prime minister and foreign minister to visit him. They made no objections to Austria's annexation and, in exchange for a share of Czechoslovakia, promised to establish friendly relations with Yugoslavia and Romania. While the Germans did not specify what Hungary was to receive for joining the German military moves, the Hungarians left satisfied. Horthy even wrote a letter to Hitler explaining that he considered Austria part of Germany.

This new foreign policy demanded the expansion and modernization of the armed forces. The army of eighty-five thousand men was far greater than the thirty-five thousand men stipulated by the peace treaty, but its equipment was insufficient and dated. On March 15, 1938, Darányi announced a one billion Pengő rearmament program. His and subsequent governments spent this amount and organized the planned military structure, but the modernization of equipment did not take place.

The annexation *(Anschluss)* of Austria occurred on March 12–13, 1938. It speeded up Hungary's turn to the Right and created panic in leftist, liberal, and conservative circles. Szálasi's Arrowcross Party was delighted and plastered the cities with leaflets and posters proclaiming "1938 is our year," and "Szálasi is coming." This induced Darányi to contact one of Szálasi's followers. In exchange for his promise that the fascists would observe parliamentary rules, the prime minister allowed the reorganization of the just-banned Arrowcross movement under the name Hungarist Movement and even assured them of a fixed number of seats in Parliament. The news of this agreement stunned political circles. Szálasi was unacceptable not only to the opposition, but also to Horthy and the "gentleman fascists." Darányi's position was badly shaken, but Horthy allowed him to take care of some pending affairs before dismissing him. One of these was the project of extending the secret ballot to the entire country. This old democratic demand was made law at the demand of and to the advantage of the radical Right.

The second debate Darányi was allowed to terminate concerned the passing of a law "designed to assure more effectively the proper balance in the social and economic life" of the country. This was the first anti-Jewish law. Germany was not exerting that kind of pressure at the moment, and the Arrowcross movement was still mainly active in the streets rather than in politics. Darányi's attempt to reach a compromise with the radical right and please the Germans could not be stopped due to the anti-Semitism that had become prevalent in Hungarian society. This law limited the number of Jews in the free professions and clerical jobs to 20 percent. Legalized discrimination was attacked in Parliament by liberals, Social Democrats, and some conservatives, and several representatives of political, scientific, and artistic circles issued a declaration of protest. Among those who signed it were Béla Bartók, Zoltán Kodály, Zsigmond Móricz, Aladár Schöpflin, and Louis Zilahy. The fascists, on the other hand, rejected the law as too mild.

The conservatives, by then, had had more than enough of Darányi's shift to the right. A group of conservative aristocrats and, in the background, some captains of industry, which the fascists began to label "Horthy's gang," wanted to get rid of Darányi. In an audience on May 10, the regent reprimanded his prime minister, who resigned the following day. On May 13, it became known that Horthy had asked Béla Imrédy to form a new government.

XVIII

THE LATE INTERWAR YEARS AND WORLD WAR II

Loránd Tilkovszky

The Last Years of Peace

The incorporation of Austria into the Third Reich, the *Anschluss* of March 1938, meant, on the one hand, the dangerous strengthening of German pressure and, on the other, the first possibility of expanding the borders at the expense of Czechoslovakia. The latter hope tended to lessen awareness of danger although numerous indications counseled prudence.

The Darányi government in its negotiations with the Germans had stressed with good reason the military weakness and unpreparedness of the country and had begun to work on an armament program. The Imrédy government, which took over in May 1938, felt that some social reforms had to be introduced to facilitate the incorporation of people who were living under better circumstances in Czechoslovakia. The government considered it dangerous to take part in German military planning directed against Czechoslovakia because Britain and France had taken a rather firm stand during the so-called May Crisis. Coupled with the fear of possible action on the part of Czechoslovakia's Little Entente partners, Yugoslavia and Romania, the government felt obliged to initiate negotiations even with the Little Entente to gain recognition of Hungary's right to rearm and to achieve a settlement of the problems of the Hungarian minorities. In exchange, it offered not to use force in working for territorial readjustments. The agreement signed at Bled, which was never ratified, also allowed Hungary to avoid accepting the one-sided demands presented by the Germans during the discussions held at Kiel during the same months, which would have involved Hungary in the aggressive political plans of the Reich.

The renewed Czechoslovak crisis in September found the British and French ready to make concessions. They began negotiations with Hitler, who demanded the ceding of the German-inhabited Sudeten districts of Czechoslovakia. What he had in mind was the total liquidation of Czechoslovakia. In secret, Hitler offered Hungary all of Slovakia and Ruthenia, provided that it attacked

Czechoslovakia, thus opening the door to German military intervention. The Imrédy government rejected this suggestion, but demanded that, based on the same ethnic claims that Germany advanced in connection with the Sudeten districts, the Hungarian-inhabited regions of Czechoslovakia be handed over to Hungary. The Münich agreement of September 29, 1938 that handed the Sudetenland over to Germany also stipulated direct Czechoslovak-Hungarian negotiations dealing with the Hungarian claims. These talks were fruitless. A four-power arbitration should have been the next step, but Britain and France indicated that they were not interested in the issue. Consequently, only Germany and Italy acted as arbiters and it was their decision, reached in Vienna in November 1938, that brought Hungarian revisionism its first success: the retrocession of the Hungarian-inhabited southern border districts of Slovakia and Ruthenia. During the same month, the Imrédy government planned to occupy militarily the less well defended Ruthenian lands in their entirety, based on historical claims. At the last moment the Axis powers prevented this move, which contradicted the ethnic principle on which both the Münich and Vienna decisions had been based.

The first revision was a "half-success." This fact and the temporary failure of the planned action in Ruthenia became strong propaganda for the extreme Right, which saw in the total and unreserved adherance to the Axis "the road leading to Hungary's resurrection." Nor had it forgiven Imrédy for having moved against the Right at the beginning of his premiership. Although those in power hoped to calm the agitation of the extremists by promulgating, in May, 1938, the first anti-Jewish law (which the Darnyi government had prepared), the extreme Right expressed its dissatisfaction and agitated for a new, more stringent anti-Semitic law. To out-maneuver the extremists, Imrédy announced his own "marvelous revolution," using all the methods of demagoguery to sell a proposal opposed by the major landowners and leading capitalists.

Imrédy's attempt to get permission from parliament to govern the regained regions by decree independently of Parliament produced, in November 1938, a political crisis. So many deputies left his party that it lost its majority and a vote of no confidence toppled the government. This was unprecedented in the Horthy regime. Horthy reacted by asking Imrédy to form a new cabinet, and he tried to erect a solid basis for his next government by creating a mass movement uniting "all healthy right-wing forces." His model was the Patriotic Front (Vaterländische Front) which, during the last years of Austria's independence, had succeeded in dissolving all parliamentary parties and in introducing the Austro-fascist system. Furthermore, Imrédy made several gestures designed to please Germany. He made it possible for the pro-Nazi elements among the German minority in Hungary to organize themselves by establishing the *Volksbund,* and he dismissed Foreign Minister Kálmán Kánya, whom the Germans did not like because he had signed the Bled agreement. Kánya's successor, Count István Csáky, made two promises to Hitler in January 1939 that indicated Hungary's willingness to cooperate more closely with Germany in foreign affairs: he agreed to join the Anti-Comintern Pact and to quit the League of Nations. The first of these concessions led to the breaking of the recently established diplomatic relations with the Soviet Union.

The so-called "Christian Rightist Opposition," which had been organized to protect constitutionalism and national independence but rejected the support of the Social Democrats, succeeded in forcing Imrédy's resignation in February 1939. The new prime minister, Count Pál Teleki, tried to stabilize the situation through contradictory measures. On the one hand, he put an end to the mass organization of the fascists, but, on the other, he avoided cooperation with all those who, by their mass resignation, had produced the crisis in the first place, in November 1938. At the end of May 1939, new elections were held, based on the new electoral law passed under Darányi, which introduced the secret ballot even in the villages. The party of the government, now called the Party of Hungarian Life, emerged with an immense parliamentary majority that could not be voted down. While the Independent Smallholders Party and the Social Democrats lost a considerable number of mandates, the various Hungarian national socialist parties, united under the joint emblem of the Arrowcross, proved unexpectedly successful. It was quite possible that the extreme right wing of the governmental party would cooperate with them. A considerable number of the deputies who were invited (not elected) to represent the regained territories were inclined in this direction.

Although Teleki had stiffened the provisions of the second anti-Jewish law prepared by Imrédy and promulgated it before the elections, it proved to be insufficient to quiet anti-Semitic agitation. Imrédy had planned to give Hungary's Germans and, on the basis of reciprocity, the Slovaks, "ethnic group" autonomy. He had proposed to solve the "Jewish question," by recognizing the Jews as an "ethnic group" not entitled to equality before the law but possessing certain rights. The Hungarian extreme Right and its German sponsors demanded that the Jews be placed outside the law, and the majority of the Jews stuck to the principle of equal rights for all citizens and rejected the legal discrimination inherent in the "ethnic group" solution. Teleki rejected the entire "ethnic group" concept, in which he saw a retreat from the traditional Hungarian political nation concept and which he considered dangerous because it made foreign intervention possible. Despite the fact that the Jews were loyal to the idea of Hungarian national unity and that Teleki knew that his action would have numerous, especially economic, bad consequences, he legitimized discrimination by identifying them as an alien race.

Teleki's prestige was enhanced by succeeding where Imrédy had failed. In March 1939, he occupied Ruthenia seemingly by an independently initiated military action. In fact, the latest revisionist territorial gains were a planned phase of the final liquidation of Czechoslovakia, for which the time was ripe according to German calculations. Bohemia and Moravia became a German protectorate, while Slovakia, in the guise of an independent state, became a German satellite. Britain and France apparently accepted the fate of Czechoslovakia, and the emboldened Hitler began his preparation for the invasion of Poland. Teleki, who had some illusions concerning possible cooperation with

Poland, now Hungary's neighbor, would have loved to play the role of mediator. Hitler, however, had no use for mediators. The Hungarian prime minister, who saw that a European war might result from the Polish conflict, informed Hitler that Hungary would not be a part of anti-Polish moves, in spite of the country's basic solidarity with Germany. Hungary adopted a policy of armed neutrality.

"Neutral" Hungary

Germany attacked Poland on September 1, 1939. The world finally had had enough of Hitler's aggression, and World War II began. In March certain defense-related laws had been promulgated in Hungary that restricted liberties in case of danger of war. The Teleki government now used these laws to ensure internal order, curbing the extreme Right and even more stringently the Left. Teleki refused the requests of the German and Slovak governments to grant free passage through Hungary to their troops, arranged the sheltering of the large refugee masses, and helped Polish soldiers move on to France, where a Polish Legion was being organized. The Germans retaliated by suspending military deliveries to Hungary, provoking a concentrated attack on Teleki by the military circles and the extreme Right. The prime minister had to agree, in January 1940, to satisfy Germany's increasing economic demands.

In the second half of September 1939, the Soviet Union took advantage of the situation in Poland and occupied the Ukrainian-inhabited portions of Poland. Instead of a border with Poland, Hungary now had one of about ninety-five miles with the Soviet Union. This fact bothered the Hungarian ruling circles greatly. They were afraid that this common border would revitalize the Communist Party, suppressed and persecuted since 1919, and that the Soviets would demand the ceding of Ukrainian-inhabited Ruthenia. The Soviets did all they could to reassure the Hungarians and even reestablished diplomatic relations. For its part, the Hungarian government also tried to establish good neighborly relations and even signed a commercial agreement with the Soviet Union. Nevertheless, when, in November 1939, the Finno-Soviet war began, Hungary backed Finland and permitted units of volunteers to fight for her.

The next aim of the Hungarian revisionists was to make good their claims against Romania. Teleki was certain that sooner or later the Soviets would demand that Romania give up at least the Ukrainian-inhabited parts of Bessarabia, which she had annexed in 1918. He wanted to coordinate his own diplomatic and, if necessary, military action to regain Transylvania when the Soviets acted. In the spring of 1940, the German staff contemplated the occupation of the Romanian oil fields in case a Soviet-Romanian conflict should develop. The Hungarian military circles advocated not only the free passage of the needed forces through Hungary, but even military cooperation with the Germans. Teleki was afraid that granting passage to German troops would force Hungary to become belligerent. He sounded out London, and the warning he received confirmed his fear. He decided not to risk the fate of the entire country for revision-ist gains in Transylvania, to oppose the passage of German troops again, and, should the Germans force him to grant the needed permission, to establish a Hungarian government in exile in the United States. The forces of the extreme Right, supported by the right wing of the government party under the leadership of former Premier Béla Imrédy, continued to attack Teleki. The German victo-ries in the West encouraged them tremendously. The Arrowcross Party recog-nized that Hungary belonged to the German zone of influence and began, in cooperation with the *Volksbund,* to work on a plan designed to solve the na-tionality question in accordance with the privileges claimed by the German "ethnic group." They also worked to prevent Teleki from following his own nationality policy, including the granting of territorial autonomy to Ruthenia. For reasons of security, however, this idea was soon dropped by the government anyway.

For Teleki, the nightmare of the German demand for troop passage was lifted when Berlin decided, in May 1940, that it did not have to undertake military action in Romania. Because the Germans stressed repeatedly that they did not want Hungary to upset the quiet in southeastern Europe, Teleki could exert pressure on them after the Romanian government promptly satisfied the June demands of the Soviet Union, relinquishing Bessarabia and northern Bukovina. He sent a message to the German capital that Hungary would have to use force should Romania not accept her claims peacefully. Teleki also indicated that, under the circumstances, he would be satisfied with Northern Transylvania and the Székely districts only. Because he wanted to avoid a Romanian-Hungarian military confrontation, Hitler was ready to force the Romanians to the negotiat-ing table with the Hungarians. When these negotiations failed, the Axis powers arbitrated the dispute, and the second Vienna decision, in August 1940, gave Hungary the regions that Teleki had indicated would be an acceptable compro-mise. Romania, now led by the right-wing dictator, General Ion Antonescu, renounced the "useless" British guarantee of her independence and invited Ger-man "training" troops into the country. The Hungarian government agreed that these could use the Hungarian railroads. No international complications resulted.

The Hungarian politicians paid for the second Vienna decision by accepting an ethnic group agreement proposed by the Germans. In essence they handed over to the *Volksbund* Hungary's Germans. This organization could now openly proclaim that it was a National Socialist ethnic association. Teleki was also forced in Vienna to make concesssions to the Hungarian Nazis. Under the leadership of Ferenc Szálasi, who was given amnesty, their unity was achieved and their Arrowcross Party emerged as the strongest opposition party. Some of the governmental party's right-wing deputies left it and organized, under Im-rédy's leadership, their own party, the Party of Hungarian Regeneration. Teleki was constantly pushed towards the Right by extremist pressure. He agreed to begin preparations for a third anti-Jewish law and for constitutional reforms in accordance with the Nazis' wishes.

Slovakia and Romania, the states that had suffered from the two Vienna decisions, and Hungary, still dissatisfied with "half solutions" joined in November 1940 the Tripartite Pact that had been concluded in September by Italy, Germany, and Japan. They were induced to take this step by the promise that it would assure them a voice in the territorial reorganization of Europe that was to follow the victory of the fascist powers. That Hungary took this step a few days before her rivals brought no advantages and represented instead the grave danger of total commitment. The treaty of "eternal friendship" concluded in December between Yugoslavia and Hungary was not a realistic counterweight to membership in the Tripartite Pact, but it served as a means to allow Hungary to encourage Yugoslavia to join the pact, something that Hitler wanted. When the coup d'état in Belgrade in March 1941 seemingly reversed the Yugoslav decision to adhere to the pact, Hitler decided to liquidate Yugoslavia by force. By offering Hungary the return of her erstwhile southern provinces, Hitler convinced Horthy, the military leaders, and the government (which was under tremendous rightist and popular revisionist pressure) to disregard the months-old treaty and not only allow the transit of German forces but also ensure the participation of Hungarian units in the contemplated attack.

The acquisition of southern Transylvania had been the prime aim of Hungarian revisionism. The treaty with Yugoslavia served to neutralize that country in case of military action directed against Romania. The new turn of events completely upset Teleki's calculations. The violation of the treaty, the danger of involving the country in the war, and self-accusation for the turn of events induced the despondent Teleki to commit suicide. His successor, László Bárdossy, ordered the army into action in April, 1941. Because the only immediate reaction was the breaking of diplomatic relations by Britain, the conviction was strengthened that a close alliance with Germany would lead to the realization of Hungary's national goal, the recovery of its former territory. With the exception of the Banat, occupied by German forces, Hungary took possession of her pre-Trianon southern provinces. Yet, now she faced German satellite states on her southern borders too—Serbia and Croatia—and the impression was created that the country was, once again, surrounded by a sort of Little Entente dominated by Germany. None of these states, Józef Tiso's Slovakia, Ion Antonescu's Romania, Milan Nedić's Serbia, and Anton Pavelić's Croatia, accepted the revisionist territorial gains that Hungary had made at their expense. Germany used these tensions between her allies to increase her influence.

Political Trends in the 1930s

The contradictions in Hungarian society became more pronounced as a result of the Great Depression. Under the influence of intensified societal stresses, the previously repressed but nonetheless virulent racist, rightist, and fascist tendencies in the political ideology of the Horthy regime became more pronounced. These elements demanded the modernization of Hungary along the lines indicated by the success of National Socialism in Germany. The more moderate among the would-be reformers tried to gain the support of the so-called "gentlemanly" middle class, whose right wing supported them and to whom they promised an economic and political "changing of the guard." The extremists courted the agrarian and industrial proletariat, mainly with unbridled and provocative anti-Semitic propaganda.

Under these circumstances, an anti-liberal neo-conservative attitude began to dominate the ideology of the regime, which reacted to the new demands of the extreme right by introducing some moderate reforms. (The more autocratic conservatives, the aristocrats, and the upper bourgeoisie, who cooperated with the liberals also, stuck to their anti-democratic program in opposition to the rightist and fascistic tendencies.) The various cabinets appointed by Horthy feared the competition of the extreme Right and became more and more rightist themselves. They took stronger and stronger measures to suppress the activities of the liberal, bourgeois-democratic, and radical movements, which aimed to make the system more democratic by introducing liberal reforms and were opposed to anti-Semitism and National Socialism.

The regime also sharpened its war against the Social Democrats, who saw in the realization of bourgeois democracy the precondition for solving social problems. In the second half of the 1930s, the illegal communist movement gave up its sectarian stand and adopted the Popular Front approach, which made it possible for it to cooperate with the Social Democrats and the leftist bourgeois parties in an anti-fascist block. Lingering mutual distrust and the bad impression created by the personal cult surrounding Stalin, the purge trials, and the internal problems of the Communist movement made this cooperation difficult.

The most clearly formulated of those ideologies that, while anti-capitalistic could not accept socialism either and looked for a "third road," was the so-called Populist Movement, represented by those intellectuals who concentrated on the peasantry. Some of its leaders were of peasant origin. This movement rejected not only the conservatism of the Horthy regime, but also liberalism, democracy, and bourgeois radicalism. The socialists' solutions for the burning problems of society were considered by the populists as unsatisfactorily dogmatic, schematic, abstract, and unsuitable from a populist-nationalist point of view. They stressed the importance of special national characteristics, which they believed were retained in the purest form among the inhabitants of villages, and they were hostile to those who had accepted the ways of the city. The populist ideology had some elements resembling those advocated by the racists and anti-Semites, and the right wing of their movement was easily absorbed by the Arrowcross Party. The core of the movement, however, distanced itself from fascism and attempted to find ways to achieve a democratic synthesis of "Hungarianness" and "Europeanness." The left wing of the movement found a common denominator in the problems of peasants and workers and cooperated not only with the Social Democrats but also with the Communists.

The so-called populist writers, at first taken in by the reformist demagoguery of Gömbös, believed that the government would support their efforts to dismantle large estates, to introduce land reforms and the resettlement of peasants, and to limit the activities of the great capitalists. Their realization that their New Intellectual Front, which supported the government, profited only the authorities was a very important element in the very positive development which culminated in 1937 in the establishing of the March Front. This movement produced a democratic, national, and anti-fascist program. The March Front and the Populist Movement were finally destroyed by the intimidating lawsuits brought against the so-called village explorers, the growing influence of the extreme Right among the masses, and, last but not least, by the wave of nationalistic enthusiasm which swept the country in 1938–41 as a result of the territorial gains achieved with German help.

This new virulent nationalism found various ways to express itself. On the eve of the Second World War, in 1938, Hungary celebrated by holding a Saint István year to mark his death nine hundred years earlier and the entry into Slovakia. This was followed, in 1939, by another celebration which commemorated the twentieth anniversary of the counterrevolution and the success of revisionism in Ruthenia. Nineteen-forty was the five hundredth birthday of King Matthias Corvinus. This was used to celebrate not only territorial gains in Transylvania, but also to propagate the concept of the Hungarian imperium. The year of the expansion southward was the commemorative year of Count István Széchenyi, who had been born one hundred fifty years earlier. The numerous articles and speeches stressed the importance of the "greatest Hungarian's" conservative reformism and his tolerance in nationality questions, pointing to the continued importance of these qualities in the present for both the regained lands and the country as a whole.

Hungary in World War II

Hitler's Germany attacked the Soviet Union in June 1941, disregarding the non-aggression pact of August 1939. The Bárdossy government broke diplomatic relations with Moscow and intended to participate in the anti-Bolshevik struggle by sending volunteer units to the front, following the pattern established during the 1939–40 Soviet-Finnish War. The Arrowcross and the *Volksbund* were organizaing these units when, under pressure from the military circles, the Bárdossy government decided to follow the example of the Slovaks and Romanians and send regular troops to the front. The provocative bombing of Kassa, for which the government blamed the Soviet Union, was used as the pretext to declare war unconstitutionally, without consulting Parliament first. The Hungarian units, called the Carpathian Group, reached the Dniester early in July. The Rapid Army Corps, consisting of some units of the group, advanced to the Dnieper by October and to the Donets by November. Following these advances, the Corps was withdrawn. Only an Eastern Occupation Group remained on Soviet territory to fight partisans. The chief of staff, who urged further Hungarian military efforts, was dismissed by Bárdossy.

These measures induced Germany's secret efforts to get deeply involved in Hungary's internal affairs in the fall of 1941. These efforts produced a realignment of the Hungarian fascist movement. The Hungarian National Socialist Party of Count Fidel Pálffy, more inclined to serve German interests than Szálasi, who was chasing Hungarian imperialist dreams, left the short-lived Arrowcross coalition. On the recommendation of the Germans, Pálffy's party allied itself with Imrédy's Party of Hungarian Regeneration. The resulting Hungarian National Socialist Party Union subsequently became the most effective tool of German intervention in Hungary. The new alliance began to attack most vehemently the Social Democrats, who could not be tolerated in "new Europe," and the Independent Smallholders Party, whose leader, Tibor Eckhardt, proclaimed in the United States that the Hungarian government was no longer master of its own decisions and proposed the establishment of a Hungarian Independence Movement. In Hungary proper an independence movement began to develop as early as April 1941. After Hungary's entry into the war, this movement organized several significant demonstrations protesting against the war and fascism, using the slogan "for an independent, free, and democratic Hungary." Circumstances in Hungary testified that just the contrary was the case: the country was tied hand and foot; democracy and even basic human rights were ruthlessly suppressed. In August 1941, the third anti-Jewish law was promulgated. In the name of race protection it forbade marriages between Jews and non-Jews.

By the end of 1941, it became obvious that instead of a victorious "Blitzkrieg," the aggressors were facing a long and hard struggle. The German foreign minister, who visited Budapest in January 1942, and the commander-in-chief of the German forces, who followed him, demanded the intervention of the entire Hungarian army. The negotiations ended with the commitment of one-third of the army. Bárdossy also agreed to the recruiting by the SS of a volunteer corps among Germans living in Hungary, up to a limit of twenty thousand men.

The recruitment was to begin under a new head of government, Miklós Kállay. In March 1942, Bárdossy was dismissed. He had stunned those leading Hungarian circles who believed it important to keep the doors to the West open when he succumbed to German pressure and, in December 1941, declared that Hungary was at war with Great Britain and the United States. Furthermore, while Bárdossy was able to prevent the execution of the military leaders' plan to resettle the Ukrainians of Ruthenia in the German-occupied Ukraine (the Jews were shipped out and perished), he could not prevent military and gendarmery units from organizing a veritable mass slaughter in the south, especially around Ujvidék (Novi Sad), in which thousands of Serbs and Jews lost their lives as supposed "partisans." This act not only proved that the country's equitable minority policy was anything but that, but also damaged Hungary greatly when the deed became known worldwide. The bloodbath was perpetrated because the Hungarian military wanted to prove, first of all, that it was strong enough to break Serb resistance, to control Jewish subversion, and to eradicate Communist organizations, thus convincing the Germans to hand the Banat over to Hungary.

Also, primarily with southern Transylvania in mind, the same circles wanted to keep Hungarian forces away from the Russian front by drastically demonstrating to the Nazis that they were needed at home to maintain order.

Finally, Bárdossy had compromised himself when the question of a successor to the aged and sickly Horthy appeared to need a prompt solution to prevent possible German intervention. Bárdossy paid too much attention to the opposition of the extreme Right on the one hand and, on the other, to the reservations of the legitimist and Catholic circles, who hoped to place Otto, the son of the last king, on the throne one day. Therefore, he made certain that Horthy's older son, István, was elected Deputy Regent without right to succession in February 1942. This was yet another reason for the regent to oust Bárdossy. (The deputy-regent died six months later on the Soviet front in an airplane accident. The position remained unfilled.)

Bárdossy was replaced by Miklós Kállay. In the spring of 1942, the Kállay government dispatched the promised military units to the Soviet front. This was the Second Hungarian Army, whose task it was to hold an extremely long segment of the front along the Don. The SS recruitment also continued. Those who volunteered lost their Hungarian citizenship. One after the other, the *Volksbund* established a series of organizations and institutions with the purpose of placing directly at the service of the German war effort Hungary's German intellectuals and productive capabilities. Hitler had promised Horthy repeatedly that after the war he would conclude an agreement with Hungary dealing with the resettlement of Hungarian Germans in those Polish lands that were to be Germanized. This plan had been officially announced in October 1939. Like Teleki and Bárdossy before him, Kállay, too, tried to calm the agitation of the *Volksbund,* and he promised them that during the resettlement, the families of *Volksbund* members, SS volunteers, and those who did not wish to belong to the Hungarian political nation would receive preference. Not without success, he argued in Berlin that the curbing of *Volksbund* activities, which threatened the country's internal order and war effort, was in Germany's interest also.

The persecution of the anti-war leftist elements not only continued, but was stepped up. The secretary of the illegal Communist Party, Zoltán Schönherz, was arrested, condemned, and executed. The functionaries of the Social Democratic Party and of the trade unions were sent to the front as members of special penal battalions. Jews, barred from military service, were also sent to the front in labor battalions, where they were treated in the most cruel manner, one designed to kill them. There was an obligatory labor service for the minorities too. Slovaks, Romanians, and Southern Slavs were forced to work in factories and on the large estates for starvation wages.

Kállay dropped Teleki's idea of constitutional reform. Parliament continued to legislate as before. The anti-democratic nature of the regime was further enhanced by a law that replaced elected public officials with those nominated by the government. The law of 1942, which nationalized land owned by Jews, was used as an excuse to postpone further the settlement of the country's most pressing social problem, land reform. This problem remained basically unchanged in spite of the entailment and settlement reforms of the Gömbös years and the laws of 1940 dealing with tenancy and the allotment of building sites. The Jewish lands did not solve the issue either because these lands were handed over not to those who needed them but to high-ranking officials and military leaders.

Events on the various fronts at the end of 1942 and the beginning of 1943 brought changes in Kállay's policy. He ceased to proclaim that "this war is our war," adopted the stance of an "unwilling satellite," and began to sound out the West about the possibility of getting out of the war. Since the Anglo-American landing in North Africa in November 1942, Kállay expected a further landing in the Balkans and sent secret envoys, including the Nobel prize-winning scientist György Szent-Györgyi, to Turkey, Switzerland, the Vatican, and Sweden to hold preliminary talks with Anglo-American authorities.

In January 1943, a powerful Soviet attack around Voronezh destroyed the defensive line of the Second Hungarian Army along the Don, and in February the surrounded German forces surrendered at Stalingrad. The remnants of the almost totally destroyed Second Army were withdrawn, and Kállay even asked the Germans to agree to the withdrawal of the Hungarian occupation troops. In exchange, the Germans demanded that the Hungarian forces perform similar duties in the endangered Balkans. Because the Hungarian government feared that these troops would have to fight Anglo-American forces, it decided to leave the occupation troops in the East.

When, in October 1942, the Germans demanded that Hungarian Jews be forced to wear the yellow Star of David and that their deportation, which had already begun in the neighboring countries, be organized, Kállay refused to comply. His new minister of defense, Vilmos Nagy, even tried to improve the treatment of Jews serving in labor battalions. Although Kállay agreed to the recruitment of an additional twenty thousand men for the SS, he secretly supported those Germans who were opposed to this move and instituted some propaganda measures in their favor. He ordered a fair settlement of the problems of the Slovak and Romanian minorities, irrespective of the treatment Hungarians received across the borders, but the chauvinistic local authorities sabotaged his decrees. His emissaries tried to open negotiations with the minister of defense of the Yugoslav government in exile and the commander of the Četnik forces, Draža Mihajlović, with the pro-Anglo-Saxon leader of the Romanian opposition, Iuliu Maniu, and even with the head of the Slovak state, József Tiso, who was much more reasonable than his prime minister, Vojtech Tuka. All these men demanded the retrocession of the territories annexed by Hungary before entering into serious talks. Kállay was ready not only to pay compensation to the relatives of those who were massacred in the Ujvidék bloodbath, but also to punish the major culprits. Horthy ordered the suppression of the indictments. The domestic policy of the prime minister became more lenient towards the Left. He gave somewhat more freedom to the Social Democrats and began to talk about the need for a more democratic way of governing. To this, even his pro-Anglo-Saxon minister of the interior, Ferenc Keresztes-Fischer was opposed.

In April 1943, Hitler accused Kállay of defeatism and asked Horthy to replace him. When Horthy refused, the Germans mobilized the National Socialist Party Union to bring about the government's downfall. To make the Union's carefully prepared attacks impossible, Parliament was prorogued. German agents in Hungary asked all rightist organizations to work for the maintenance of order and for the prevention of economic sabotage. While the government operated on the principle that it was better "to give the Germans wheat than blood," it also took steps to hide from its allies the true economic position and production figures of the country and attempted to build reserves. The impression that Kállay was a "resister" who sought ways to get the country out of the war gave birth to widely held illusions. The bourgeois wing of the Hungarian Independence Movement as well as the Social Democrats began to show more understanding for Kállay's policy. Only the Communists continued to criticize him sharply.

July 1943 brought further changes in Hungary's position. The Allies' landing in Sicily, the fall of the fascist government in Italy, and the Italian armistice supplied an important legal argument which those working for independence could use against those who were unwilling to turn against the Germans: the Axis had been destroyed and with it also the Tripartite Pact. Hungary could leave the nefarious alliance without violating any treaty. The memorandum handed to Kállay, which had been prepared for the Independent Smallholders Party by Endre Bajcsy-Zsilinszky, not only demanded the reestablishment of equality before the law, which had been violated by anti-Jewish legislation and the regulation of the nationality problem, but even suggested that a temporary German occupation of the country was acceptable as a price for leaving the war. The Social Democratic Party accepted the demands and arguments of this memorandum and formed an alliance with the Smallholders. When the deputies of the two parties not only made the content of the memorandum public by referring to it at meetings, but also managed to get it into the foreign press, Kállay moved against them, using mainly the services of his propaganda ministry. He accused the two parties of trying to come to power by destroying the existing state system and by mobilizing worker and peasant masses with their demands for independence. Kállay was trying to save the existing system. Even in the camp of the Hungarian Independence Movement, several people were violently opposed to cooperation with the Social Democrats. They tried to separate the Smallholders from the Social Democrats and to induce them to join a planned Democratic Bourgeois Alliance. The Communists were favoring the Smallholder–Social Democrat cooperation. The fact that the Communist Party of Hungary had changed its name, in July 1943, to the Peace Party made it easier for it to establish contact with those elements within the Independence Movement that had strong anti-Communist feelings. Although not legally recognized, the Peace Party was able to propagate its views quite successfully. More and more people began to listen to the Hungarian broadcasts of the British Broadcasting Corporation and to the Kossuth radio broadcasts maintained by the Hungarian Communists in Moscow.

Neither Horthy nor the prime minister had the courage to turn against the

Germans. When it became clear that the British and the Americans would not land in the Balkans and the Soviet troops' advance continued relentlessly, they tried to get German permission to withdraw Hungarian forces to the Carpathians. They imagined that if the mountains were defended only by Hungarians, the Soviets would march around Hungary. They not only refused to return some of Hungary's territorial gains but also maintained the remaining revisionist claims in spite of the fact that the Allied Powers had made it clear that the victims of fascism, Czechoslovakia and Yugoslavia, would be reestablished within their old borders. They finally agreed, in December 1943, to try those mainly responsible for the massacres around Ujvidék but did not prevent them from escaping into Germany.

Since the fall of 1943, the Germans had worked on secret plans for the occupation of Hungary and the establishment of a puppet government. In March 1944 they moved. Hitler called Horthy to Germany and informed him that the occupation was unavoidable. By threatening him with the use of troops from the rival satellite states should he object, he gained Horthy's agreement. The occupation occurred on March 19 with practically no resistance. Horthy remained in his position as regent. After negotiating with Edmund Veesenmayer, German ambassador and plenipotentiary, he appointed Döme Sztójay, Hungarian ambassador in Berlin, as head of the new government.

With the exception of the extreme right-wing parties, which the Sztójay government worked in vain to unite, all political parties, including the Smallholders and the Social Democrats, were outlawed, and the trade unions were placed under supervision. The Gestapo arrested numerous politicians and leading figures in public life. The policy of the Germans was to retain a semblance of Hungarian sovereignty, making it easier for them to gain the authorities' cooperation. They therefore appeared to be satisfied by changes in the leadership of the administration and army. The First Hungarian Army was ordered to the Soviet front. The SS could draft Germans living in Hungary now, and those who previously had lost their citizenship by volunteering had it restored. The loyalty-to-Hungary movement was forbidden. Those who refused to appear before the draft boards were brought there by Hungarian gendarmes. This time the Germans sought sixty to eighty thousand men. The Sztójay government helped in the economic plundering of the country. The export of foodstuffs was increased. Anglo-American and Soviet planes began to bomb Hungary after the country's industry was directly subordinated to the German war production authorities. The largest Hungarian armament factory, the Csepel Works, passed directly into the hands of the SS, who made it possible for its Jewish owners to leave for a neutral country.

The Sztójay government introduced the wearing of the yellow Star of David and concentrated the Jews in ghettos in the towns and in camps in the countryside. The deportation of Jews began, and although officially they were handed over to the Germans as additions to their labor force, it was obvious that they would be exterminated. In spite of the protests of the kings of Sweden and England, President Roosevelt, and the pope, the deportation of the Jews outside

Budapest was completed. Plans for those of Budapest had also been completed when Horthy, fearing a coup d'état by the gendarmery concentrated in Budapest for this purpose, forbade further deportations.

The Hungarian Front, illegally formed in May 1944, organized the resistance movement opposing the Germans and their accomplices. Its members were the Peace Party, the Social Democrats, the Smallholders, the National Peasant Party, and the Blood Brotherhood of the legitimists, whose emblem was the apostolic cross. After the opening of the second front in June, even Horthy tried to get rid of Sztójay. Before he could succeed, Romania denounced her alliance with Germany and declared war on it in August, while in Slovakia an anti-fascist revolt broke out. The regent appointed Colonel-General Géza Lakatos prime minister in September. Lakatos attempted to stop the advance of the Soviet and Romanian troops by sending the Second and Third Hungarian Armies into southern Transylvania. The attempt failed, and soon thereafter the Soviet-Romanian forces appeared on the eastern rim of the Hungarian plain.

Horthy, who until then had only tried to negotiate an armistice with the Western powers, finally decided to send a secret mission to Moscow. On October 11, this mission signed a preliminary armistice agreement, which obligated Hungary to give up the territories annexed since 1937 and to declare war on Germany. This step required careful political and military preparations. The memoranda which the Hungarian Front sent to Horthy stressed this point. The Peace Party, again called the Communist Party, insisted on armed action and organized its own military commission. On October 10, the Communists and Social Democrats agreed to organize a united front. While Horthy's emissaries established contact with the Hungarian Front, cooperation between it and the government was impossible because the regent was not willing to make the needed political concessions demanded by the parties of the Hungarian Front. Simultaneously, the Germans and their stooges, including the Legislators' National Alliance, the grouping of rightists and extreme rightists in Parliament, did all they could to prevent Horthy's "coup d'état" from succeeding. Miklós Horthy Jr., the political leader of the forces preparing the change, and the commander of the army corps stationed in Budapest who was responsible for military arrangements were kidnapped by the Germans. Szálasi, the last political trump card of the Nazis, was kept in readiness to take power. When Horthy's armistice proclamation was broadcast over the radio on October 15, it was soon followed by an explanation which, in fact, negated it, and by the treason of the military leadership. On the next day the totally unsuccessful Horthy was forced to resign in favor of Szálasi, and on the 17th he was sent to Germany under "protective custody." Szálasi became simultaneously prime minister and head of state, with the title "Nation Leader." Members of the Arrowcross Party, other Nazis, followers of Imrédy, and deputies of the extreme right wing of the former governmental party received cabinet posts, but in fact the country was ruled dictatorially by the Arrowcross Party. The "constitution" of the fascist state had long ago been prepared by the party's State-Building Office. Numerous law projects had been worked out in the most minute detail. However, except for a few hastily issued decrees, none could be realized because the advancing Soviet troops occupied ever-increasing portions of the country. The Germans did not help because only the total military mobilization and economic exploitation of the country interested them. They had no interest in Szálasi's "specifically Hungarian" total fascism.

Under the leadership of Bajcsy-Zsilinszky a new organization, the Liberation Committee for the Hungarian National Uprising, was created in November 1944 to organize the resistance. It was made up of the parties who had united in the Hungarian Front and of a variety of civilian and military resistance groups. Lieutenant-General János Kiss headed the military staff of the Committee. The intention was to issue a proclamation to the nation, to the Soviet Government, and to the commander of the Soviet forces in Hungary and to establish contact with the Soviet troops nearing the capital. The Committee was betrayed, and its leaders were executed by the Arrowcross. Communist partisans continued to be active both in Budapest and in the countryside, and they registered a few small successes. When, on Christmas 1944, Budapest was finally totally surrounded, the Arrowcross organized a senseless "persistence" (as they called it) which brought a month and a half of suffering and destruction to the capital. The fate of the Jews massed in Budapest's ghetto was horrible beyond description. The party's armed units committed mass murder, pillaged, and behaved in the most inhumane manner.

Szálasi transferred his capital to the western borders of the country, from whence he ruled his "Hungarist Empire," consisting of the northern and western counties of Transdanubia. His regime's dissolution could not be prevented either by his demagoguery or his terror. Of the planned five divisions, he was able to organize only one as well as a Hungarian SS division. Szálasi made great efforts to transfer to Germany everybody able to work or bear arms, as well as food reserves, animals, industrial equipment, and everything else of value. When he left Hungary on April 4, a few days before the total liberation of the country, he even took the Crown with him.

The War of Minds

When Hungary got enmeshed in the Second World War on the side of the Axis, the consequences were deeply felt in the country's intellectual life too. Efforts were increased to create and to propagate a "Hungarian world view" aimed at inculcating a uniform way of thinking in accordance with the fascistic *Zeitgeist.* The "education of the nation" in the schools, in the various other educational institutions, and in the numerous patriotic associations was conducted in conformity with this spirit. The Boy Scout movement, which used to play an important role in education among the children of the elite, was deemphasized due to its Anglo-Saxon orientation. The obligatory training of youth was entrusted to the paramilitary youth organization, *levente,* organized on Italian and German fascistic models. The "social policy" and "national policy" propaganda and organizational departments of the prime minister's office were soon transformed into an independent "National Defense Propaganda Ministry." The Hungarian press became more and more controlled and centrally directed. Its work was heavily influenced by the introduction of censorship, by the suspension of several papers, and by the requirement that newspapermen be members of a press association established when the anti-Jewish laws were promulgated. Racial discrimination and political considerations greatly damaged artistic life. This was visible in programs offered by the theaters, movies, and the radio. The military leadership demanded control over the country's intellectual life, and it was the chief of staff who organized a conference of writers and told them what he expected from them in the service of military patriotism. In scientific circles, the breaking of international contacts except with fascist states had crippling results.

A unified "Hungarian world-view" did not develop, and the government's efforts were opposed from both left and right. The extreme fascist movements that worked for Germany felt that the program did not sufficiently follow the fascist *Zeitgeist*. Those who opposed the Nazi-German trend and worked for "spiritual national defense" were able to make their voices heard even under extremely difficult circumstances until the German occupation of Hungary. They made their views public in the Social Democratic newspaper *Népszava (People's Voice)*, in the liberal's *Magyar Nemzet (Hungarian Nation)*, and in the peasant-oriented *Szabad Szó (Free Word)*. These papers received some support from those elements of the ruling elite with Anglo-American sympathies, and, in exchange, these publications backed the same circles' efforts to get out of the war. Other means were also found to oppose the propagation of the new, official world view. In 1942, the "Hungarian Historical Memorial Committee" was established, which not only based itself on the traditions of the War of Independence of 1848–49 and the spirit of its impassioned poet, Sándor Petőfi, but also organized imposing anti-fascist demonstrations. Another association, the "Attila József Memorial Committee" was formed with the specific aim of using the recently deceased proletarian poet's guiding principles in the struggle for human rights, intellectual freedom, and the freedom of the country. The historian Gyula Szekfű, whose anti-liberal and neo-conservative writings created an entire school of followers and advocated the German-Hungarian community of fate, admitted in one of his newspaper articles that "somewhere we lost the right road." The conferences he organized every year on Lake Balaton, attended by young people of peasant, middle class, and worker origins, and those who belonged to religious organizations, became an important forum where the "problems of the Hungarian national fate" and social and national issues were debated in a progressive spirit. While one of the giants of Hungarian music, Béla Bartók, emigrated to the United States, Zoltán Kodály became active in the literary gatherings and theatrical performances organized to foster the spirit of national resistance. Kodály brought to a high artistic level the old Hungarian folksong tradition, utilized the poetry of the greatest poets for his choral compositions, and mobilized large numbers of people for his "singing Hungary" program.

Hungarians living in the United States and Great Britain followed and supported to the limits of their ability the struggle for an independent, free, democratic Hungary. They were unswayed by the government's efforts to gain their support by promising meaningless "democratic" reforms to be introduced after the war. Oscar Jászi, Rustem Vámbery, and Mihály Károlyi were among those Hungarian leaders living in the United States and Britain whose activities proved the true aim of the Hungarian government's efforts. They showed the futility of working to gain territory instead of attempting to find a democratic way of co-existing with neighboring countries after the war. Some of the unrepentant revisionists continued to speak of the viability and even the extension of the concept of "Saint István's Empire."

XIX

THE HUNGARIAN ECONOMY IN THE INTERWAR YEARS

György Ránki

The Hungarian economy underwent drastic change in the years between the two world wars. While the preceding chapters have made references to these developments, a short, systematic survey of these changes will help to explain Hungary's weakness not only in the economic but also in the political realm between 1918 and her entry into the Second World War.

Agriculture

Before the First World War, agriculture had played a crucial role in Hungarian economic development. After recovering from the catastrophic harvests of 1918–20, which yielded grain crops of only 60 percent of prewar figures, a long and slow recovery began, but even in 1921 yields were still about 30 percent lower than in the 1910s. When, in the middle of the 1920s, agricultural recovery appeared to have been accomplished, the prevailing view in Hungary, shared by government, landowners, and the business community, was that the prewar pattern had to be reestablished with continuing industrialization backed by constant export-oriented agricultural growth. However, this concept proved to be wrong, since the division of labor between western and eastern Europe, which had worked relatively well before the war, was jeopardized by the overwhelming competition on the western markets from American agricultural goods. This competition had been strong even before the war, and when, after the war, eastern European agriculture was unable to produce the necessary surplus, the Americans took over the western markets, including the Hungarian one. Thus, even if Hungarian agriculture had been able to produce growing export surpluses, the markets for them no longer existed. Consequently, agriculture was increasingly unable to fulfill its prewar functions. First of all, it no longer produced the large export surpluses that could cover the import demands of industrialization. Second, since production did not increase, agriculture was unable to provide a steadily growing market for industrial products.

The first and most important feature of Hungarian agricultural production was its relative stagnation during the two decades of the interwar period. Net agricultural output actually declined between 1911–13 and 1928–31 at a rate of 0.7 percent annually. In the late 1920s and 1930s, some improvements could be observed as production reached its interwar peak, but even at this time agricultural output was 7 percent below the 1911–13 level. The peak of 1934–38 was slightly better for wheat (22.2 million quintals), corn (12 million), and potatoes (21.3 million), slightly worse for rye and barley, and substantially worse for sugar beet and oats compared with 1911–13. The trend, characteristic of many countries in Europe, that weaknesses in crop-farming were compensated for by livestock-breeding was not observable in Hungary— the losses in livestock suffered at the end of the First World War were never overcome. Even if we take into account the improvements in animal breeding, higher milk production, the increase in the proportion of pigs raised for meat production, and the most impressive growth in poultry, these were only partly able to compensate for the stagnation and decline of the main crops.

Before the war, threshing was the only process to rely extensively on machinery. Horse-driven threshing machines had all but disappeared, while the number of threshing machines with combustion engines increased by 50 percent. The number of tractors increased as well, from 1,200 to 6,000. However, in neither case was there the slightest improvement after the depression; bank credit was no longer available, landowners used cheap labor, and none of the very small revenues was actually used for domestic investment. The number of tractors remained almost the same between 1929 and 1938, but only two-thirds were in actual operation—it simply did not pay to use them, given the presence of 200,000 unemployed agricultural laborers. Of course, small estates, relying on family labor anyway, were unable to take advantage of this situation. Since wages were low in Hungary, one would expect the cost of labor to have been relatively low, but this was not the case, even on the large estates. The share of wages was around 65 percent of the gross national product. The large estates were better off, but even in their case wages were over 50 percent of gross national product. This means that labor-saving processes were still far from being fully employed even on large estates.

For the most part, agricultural techniques were based on traditional implements and simple machines. Although on the average there was one plough for every holding, there were very few cultivating machines, and hauling was done by animal-drawn wagons. Hoeing, harvesting, and other operations were performed almost entirely by hand. The maintenance of the special production structure was equally the consequence of cheap labor, since large estates were mainly oriented toward gross output. In small holdings, labor-intensive production might have shifted production from cereals to vegetables, but here tradition and household orientation (due to which a relatively large part of production never entered the market) contributed to the continued dominance of cereals. Limited progress was made in the mechanization of farming in the 1920s, but the promotion of higher yields was barely considered. The use of fertilizers had reached Hungary only in the early twentieth century. In 1913 around nineteen pounds were used per acre. Of course this figure showed a sharp decline during the war and afterwards, but remarkable increase was observed again between 1925-29, approaching an average of twenty-four pounds per acre in 1930. Following the onset of the depression, however, the use of chemical fertilizers plummeted to three pounds per acre in 1933, and even by 1938 it had not reached ten pounds again. Needless to say, the use of these fertilizers was more frequent on large estates than on peasant holdings. The basic contradiction of Hungarian agricultural production was that its gross output was too great for the market, yet due to its technical backwardness prices were too high compared with international levels. All these contradictions were still partly hidden in the 1920s, when market problems were just beginning to be felt and when prices were improving or remaining relatively high. During the depression, the situation became clear. First of all, the value of exported goods dramatically decreased. Second, the gap between agricultural prices and industrial prices caused a decline in the purchasing power of agriculturalists. The real value of this purchasing power in 1932-33 was down to 53 percent of the 1927-28 level and slowly climbed to 73 percent in 1938-39. It is no wonder that improvement was slow during the 1930s, and the government took measures to relieve the burden of debts by adjusting the annual burden of repayment to the new price level, and to create new export markets and other supporting measures.

However, many of these trends were not apparent as capital formation. For example, horses were gradually replacing oxen as the principal means of draft power, and they were certainly more efficient. Of course, the question remains whether draft animals did not take too much from the scant resources of small farms by diverting a large proportion of land to growing fodder.

Truck gardening expanded and the amount of land planted with tomatoes, onions, cabbages, and peppers increased. There was a marked growth in their role in agricultural exports as well. Progress was even more substantial in fruit-growing. Orchards spread considerably during the later 1920s, so that by 1935 there were 50 percent more fruit trees in the country than at the beginning of the century. The growth of poultry-raising was also an indicator of progress during the 1930s, mainly on peasant holdings, and contributed to exports of meat and eggs.

As late as 1940 half of the Hungarian labor force was still engaged in agriculture, but agriculture's contribution to the national product had declined from around 50 percent to 32 percent. If this had been the consequence of rapid industrialization, this change might have been welcomed; however, the fact that agricultural production never reached the pre–First World War level is probably the best indicator of the basic problems of the Hungarian economy during the interwar period.

Industry

All the data indicate that industry was the driving force for economic development in the interwar period. During these years of moderate economic growth, industrial development, though far behind its prewar level was able to show considerable progress. The territorial changes following the Trianon Peace Treaty and the entirely new circumstances resulting from the collapse of the Austro-Hungarian Empire deeply modified both internal and external conditions for Hungarian industrial development. A program of industrialization was for various reasons—military concerns, overpopulation, and import substitution—promoted even more firmly than before. The peculiar industrial structure in Hungary—to some extent formed in the framework of the Austro-Hungarian Empire's division of labor—was characterized by the dominance of agriculture and by relatively strong metal-processing and engineering industries, supported by the state through different measures, among others a commission to provide goods to the fast-developing railway system. On the other hand, textile manufacture was hardly able to grow beyond the rudimentary stage, owing to strong competition from Austrian and Bohemian textile mills. The new boom of the textile industry, protected from foreign competition by high customs duties during the 1920s and other protective measures, was not strong enough to counterbalance the stagnation of the more traditional branches of the economy. While agricultural output was below the prewar level in the late 1930s, industrial production was actually 10–15 percent higher in 1929 than before the war and about one-third higher in 1938.

In spite of this growth, development was uneven. The traditional leading sectors were unable to function as the main economic movers, many operating at considerably less than full capacity during the 1920s. The closing of factories or the selling-off of excess capacity became everyday phenomena, and new investments were relatively scarce. Disregarding the reduction of the domestic market and the food industry's loss of foreign markets, we have to take into consideration the fact that almost half of this period, the years 1919–24 and 1929–34, were years of depression, when consumption was far below the prewar level. Last but not least, another element must also be taken into account—with few exceptions, such as bauxite, the most valuable raw materials were to be found in those territories that no longer belonged to Hungary. A large number of industries (concentrated mainly in the Budapest area) were cut off from their supplies of raw materials, and post-1920 Hungary was very poorly provided with them. The supply of brown coal (or lignite) was better, but during the 1920s Hungarian coal was not yet used for household purposes and could not be used for metallurgy, so coal production hardly reached the prewar level. It improved in the 1930s when protective measures prompted households to switch to domestic coal, and its use increased in the heavy industries. The three basic coal fields of Hungary—the small black-coal basin in the southwestern part of the country, the large brown-coal deposits around Tatabánya in the northwest, and the poor-quality lignite deposits in the northern part of the country—produced around seven to nine million tons a year altogether.

The new frontiers had created enormous difficulties by cutting off the Hungarian iron and steel industries, located partly in the northern part of the country (Diósgyör, Ózd, and, near Budapest, Csepel) from the iron ore mines. The ore mines left in Hungary were poor in quality and far too few. They never supplied more than 25–30 percent of domestic consumption. Crude iron output increased in the 1920s after the construction of a sixth furnace in the country. But most of this capacity was unused during the depression, when production dropped to almost 20 percent of the former peak.

There were very few branches in the iron and metal industries where significant growth occurred, the exceptions being bauxite production and the foundation of an aluminium industry. During the 1920s one of Europe's richest deposits of bauxite was discovered in Transdanubia. Since the aluminium industry was regarded as having a good future, German capital became involved at the very beginning of the exploitation of bauxite ores and helped to establish a new company to promote bauxite production. Output reached half a million tons by 1929. After the decline during the depression, the peak of 1938 did not quite reach 600,000 tons.

In spite of the rapid increase in the use of electricity, the per capita consumption was still very low in Hungary—less than a quarter of that in the more highly developed industrial countries. The machine industry belonged to those branches of the economy in which the adjustment process created tremendous difficulties in technology, and the productive capacity of Hungarian engineering was far above the general level of economic development of the country. Machine industry production had hardly returned to 1913 levels by 1938 because even in the 1920s more than the half of the output was concentrated in the older sectors like agricultural machines, railway carriages, and shipbuilding. Efforts had been made to introduce new products, and perhaps due to a tradition of good engineers and skilled workers, technological problems were always more or less successfully overcome; in spite of all this, however, costs were usually too high and the market too small to be truly competitive with foreign firms working with more advanced technology in larger markets. Large-scale investment was needed, but credit was scarce or unavailable, and almost all new branches of the industry failed after a few years.

The most significant structural change in the machine-building industry was the growing share of the electro-technical sector, but the readjustment process was far from complete. Also it was a significant trend of Hungarian industrial development that while in the more highly developed countries the trend was to increase the share of the machine-building industry in total output, in Hungary the reverse was true, and the share of machine-building actually shrank.

The development of the chemical industry required large-scale capital investment, which was not available during the 1920s. One of the most remarkable successes, however, was the rapid development of the pharmaceutical industry, as small plants were replaced by large factories. One of them, Chinoin, gained an international reputation for its products. The further development of the industry was greatly aided by the discovery of oil in the southwestern part of Hungary. Production was started by an American firm. Altogether the accomplishment of the chemical industry was remarkable, since its total output grew by more than 50 percent between the wars.

The big losses during this period were all in the traditionally dominant food industry. Its three main branches—milling, sugar refining, and brewing and distilling—all faced particular difficulties. While the mills' grinding capacity amounted to over nine million tons, the average harvest of the country was only around 2.5 million tons. It is no wonder that the impressive achievements of Hungary's early industrialization were dismantled one after the other.

Tremendous international competition ruined the sugar industry as well. In the 1920s output was around 80 percent of pre–World War I levels, but during the depression sugar refiners were forced to accept an agreement for further limitation of exports. In the 1930s they never achieved more than 50 percent of their prewar output. Distilleries were working at only about one-quarter or one-third of their production capacities.

The long tradition in the food industry was disrupted by new demands and new consumption patterns that emerged slowly as part of Hungary's adjustment to new circumstances. Important new products were developed only in the 1930s. In the forefront was the canning industry (particularly of fruit and tomatoes), which grew into a modern high-capacity industry, even by world-market standards. On the whole, however, the output of the food industry in 1938 was still 20 percent below that of the 1913 level.

Hungary's economic growth—slow as it was—relied upon the industrialization process. Industrialization, taking the form of import substitution with all its possibilities and limitations, was mainly carried out in the traditionally less developed branches of industry.

The prime mover of this process was the textile industry, which, due to strong Austrian and Bohemian competition, was unable to cover more than 40 percent of domestic consumption. Prospects for industrialization by import substitution were good. Textile factories established in the 1920s absorbed one-third of all investment in Hungarian industry. The government protected the growing textile industry in the beginning with prohibitive measures and later with high customs duties as well. The industry's expansion was facilitated by the relatively low cost of investment. Textile production had already trebled during the 1920s, and damage from the depression was relatively mild. Foreign exchange controls and other new prohibitive measures helped to limit further import competition and enabled indigenous production to take over the domestic market. In 1938 textile production was four times as great as in 1913, and with a few exceptions—mainly high quality goods—the textile industry became capable of satisfying domestic demand. Its work force grew rapidly to nearly five times its former size (from 13,000 to 64,000 workers) and the textile industry became the second largest in the country.

Other branches of the consumer-goods industry followed almost the same line. Production in the leather industry doubled, and production in the paper industry, in spite of a shortage of timber, rose by 250 percent. In both cases, the domestic market was by and large taken over by domestic industries. Nonetheless, there were a few inherent contradictions in this industrialization, oriented as it was toward light consumer goods. It was very much dependent on borrowed technology, and its technical efficiency was low, depending on heavy and prolonged protection against foreign competition.

The growth rate between 1913 and 1938 was, on the average, far from impressive: scarcely over 1 percent per annum (compared with an annual increase of over 5 percent in the early years of the century). This growth rate was well below that of the Western European countries during the same period, in spite of the fact that their accomplishments were not remarkable. Only a few countries in Europe, like Spain, Austria, and Poland, did not surpass Hungary in their industrial development. Hungarian industrial output only reached 43 percent of the average level of production of the European countries, a slightly poorer showing than the prewar figure of 44 percent.

At the same time, a relatively moderate tempo of development was accompanied by important changes in the structure of industry. Especially significant was the decline in the dominance of the food industry, once the hallmark of Eastern European industrial structure. The changes, however, did not reflect the technological demands of the age, but bore the peculiar, new Eastern European stamp: the primacy of light industry.

In 1938 the food industry accounted for less than 29 percent of industrial production, against more than 42 percent in 1913 (reckoned in terms of the frontiers of 1920). Nevertheless its share of total output still ranked it among the strongest industries in the country. Textiles became the second largest branch of industry, responsible for almost 18 percent of industrial production.

In part, these were positive changes, for besides reducing the unhealthy preponderance of the food industry, they marked the appearance of hitherto missing industries. Nonetheless, in Europe between the two World Wars, the course of modern industrial development lay in the rapid advance of heavy industry (especially its processing lines), until it accounted for nearly 50 percent of all production. By contrast, the share of heavy industry in Hungarian production did not increase at all. In 1913, the output of the iron and steel, engineering, electrical, and chemical industries (calculated in terms of the frontiers of 1920) was 38 percent of the total, but by 1938 it was less than 36 percent. If, then, structural changes acted to reduce the former severe disproportions among its various branches, Hungarian industry as a whole still remained, due to the backwardness of its heavy industry, outmoded and underdeveloped, and fell far short of the demands of the modern era.

Among the factors that contributed to the flourishing of the Hungarian economy before the First World War, the development of an adequate infrastructure had a decisive role. Twelve thousand kilometers of railway track and the necessary rolling stock kept the economy moving with its enormous demand for iron, steel, machines, and labor, not to mention the unification of the Hungarian market. Since a large part of the railway system was under the control of the state, government demand and budget subsidies had an important role in this growing industry. However, after the war, the need for transportation had obviously declined. The railway system was fully developed before the war, and actually no new railway construction was required for it. Hungary ranked seventh in density of its railway network in Europe (ninety-three kilometers of track per 1,000 square kilometers). Modernization and maintenance in time were badly needed, but not given high priority. With the budget permanently in trouble, relatively small sums were allocated for the railroads even in peak years, with the result that transport and communications belonged to those sectors whose growth was far below the optimum level. Investments were kept on a low level permanently, and with the sole exception of the electrification of the Hungarian part of the Budapest-Vienna line in the 1930s, no major investments were carried out.

Finance and Banking

Following the stabilization of 1924, the newly created Hungarian National Bank became the center of the Hungarian credit system. The bank was established on the model of the Bank of England, and with its financial help. The English bank's chief adviser was sent to Hungary when the Hungarian National Bank took over the cash transactions of the state, but its governing board came from representatives of different branches of business life. The state laid down as a general rule that the bank might only discount three-month bills, and it did not deviate from this position, in spite of strong pressure from agricultural interests, who saw themselves excluded from the direct credit available from the National Bank. The bank was supposed to handle all receipts and payments of the government and function as a lender of last resort. Its currency-issuing policy was very conservative, with a minimum cover of 40 percent in gold or foreign currencies.

During the depression the bank underwent a serious crisis. Its gold and foreign currency reserves, due to the sudden withdrawal of short-term credit, decreased to a trifling amount. It became a serious danger, and cover was below the prescribed minimum of 25 percent on December 4, 1931. With foreign exchange controls and the suspension of transfers, the crisis was temporarily overcome, and the function of the bank was extended to controlling and executing all sales and purchases of foreign currencies.

The scarcity of capital in pre–World War I Hungary and the important role of capital import may have been the most important factors contributing to the dominant role of banks in the Hungarian economy. The special activity of the banks, particularly in industry but also as the main movers behind capital accumulation, caused a lot of discussion before 1913. After the break-up of the Austro-Hungarian Empire and the collapse of historical Hungary, the banks should have been able to strengthen their influence and power, since the 674 financial institutions within the new frontiers had controlled 1,517 million pengős out of 2,288 million in capital and 9,568 million out of 12,723 million in savings. The disproportionate role of six banks and the financial institutions of Budapest was well known. The six most important banks were able to control a huge portion of the economy through their affiliates and other institutions related to them. Fifty-seven percent of all capital was concentrated in the banking system. Inflation was a severe blow, and shrinkage of the banks' assets was significant: their own capital declined by 77 percent.

However, when inflation ended assets at the banks grew rather fast, but a part of this growth was due to money that had been withdrawn from the banks during the inflationary period and converted into foreign currency, or used for shortening interest, and was not returned to savings or current accounts. During the first few years growth was actually far from impressive, and was well behind that of the growth of savings before the war. The 713 million pengő increase in savings accounts between 1925 and 1929, and 893 million pengő increase in current accounts was about 40 percent behind that of the prewar rate. It is noteworthy that an important part of current account growth was either foreign credit or just deposits made by the banks themselves, so it cannot be regarded as net accumulation.

The recovery of the banking system in the 1930s was very slow, and its assets did not actually reach the pre-depression level until 1938. Among the many reasons for this were the heavy losses from agricultural credits. Also during these years very little foreign capital came to the country, whereas during the 1920s the top banks were important intermediaries of foreign credits, and a part of their own capital increase came from foreign sources. (Of the leading banks in the Credit Bank, French capital had 20 percent, and Austrian another 20 percent interest; around 20 percent of shares at the Commercial Bank were controlled by American financial groups. The Anglo-Hungarian Bank was partly controlled by British, the Italo-Hungarian Bank by Italian financial interests.)

The characteristic features of the Hungarian credit system were the following: 1) The overwhelming importance of the two leading institutions, the Pester Hungarian Commerical Bank and the Hungarian General Credit Bank. These two institutions actually controlled over one-third of the capital of the entire credit system. 2) The weakness of the provincial credit institutions, whose assets were less than one-fifth of the assets of the banks in Budapest. 3) The ever closer involvement of banks with the most important industrial companies of Hungary. Both the Commercial Bank and the Credit Bank controlled leading industrial and financial groups that consisted of some of the largest industrial companies in key industries like coal mining, iron and steel, engineering, and electrical, along with a few leading factories in the food, textile, and chemical industries. The Commercial Bank formed a business interest group, with the top steel and engineering works of Weiss Manfréd Company, the Rimamurányi Iron Works, and the Salgótarján Coal Mining Company, to control eighty-three other important industrial enterprises. The Credit Bank and its leading business partner, the Hungarian General Coal Mining Company, included 101 enterprises in its group, among others Ganz and other top factories. These two groups actually controlled around 50 percent of Hungarian industry.

Foreign Trade

The importance of foreign trade substantially increased for Hungary as a direct result of the Trianon frontiers. The country became smaller, more dependent on international forces, and consequently more vulnerable. And although according to the classical economic view, a nation's size should not matter, the problem of Hungary's smallness was quickly perceived in the early 1920s. The loss of a large and secure domestic market meant not only that Hungary became more exposed to international competition but also that it had to overcome the disadvantages of a relatively small domestic market, higher unit costs of production, limited resources, a relatively narrow export base, and a larger proportion of foreign trade in the national product. Additionally, there were increasing difficulties with the balance of payments and instability in foreign trade, rendering the economy highly sensitive to international cyclical changes and an easy target for trade discrimination or restrictions by larger countries. Hungary was obliged to increase its exports in a period when, unlike the prewar era, international trade was growing slowly.

During the early 1920s the ailing Hungarian economy was not able to satisfy the domestic market for goods, despite its shrunken purchasing power. In a country where agriculture and industry were not able to meet basic needs, where even agricultural goods had to be imported, it was inevitable that an enormous import surplus would occur. The import surplus continued until 1929 because part of the imported foreign capital came to the country in the form of investment goods or consumer articles. Rather than an actual increase in exports, the pattern was reversed following the Great Depression. From 1929 to 1938 Hungarian foreign trade was able to produce a certain and, to some extent, growing surplus each year.

The dramatic change that occurred in foreign trade during the 1930s exhibited the following three main trends: 1) Because of the shrinkage of foreign trade and changes in the terms of trade, even though after 1930 Hungary produced an export surplus, the country became more dependent on foreign trade than ever. 2) The decreasing significance of neighboring countries in Hungarian foreign trade reached a new stage during the 1930s. Mutual protectionism, harmful as it was to all of the countries involved, reached new peaks, including custom wars during the depression. When all efforts to limit these hostilities and to elaborate some kind of common economic or customs policy had failed, Germany became the most important trade partner for all of the countries in this area, and, as it happened, for Hungary as well. All these changes brought an increase in the distances of export markets. While in 1920 the average distance of the markets from Budapest was around 400 km, this figure increased in 1924 to 464, rose to 612 in 1928, and passed the 1,000 km mark in 1935. 3) Finally, important changes took place in the structure of Hungarian foreign trade. The share of finished industrial goods in imports fell sharply between 1913 and 1937 from 62 percent to 27 percent, and the proportion of raw materials and semi-processed goods rose from 38 percent to 73 percent. Industrialization by import substitution, along with foreign exchange controls, reduced the importation of consumer goods to a very low level. The volume of investment goods imports was also low. Foreign trade policy, striving for a kind of autarky, achieved it in spite of Hungary's weakness in industrialization. Raw materials became its main import items.

Hungary's ratio of exports to the national income was relatively high in 1929—around 20 percent. This openness of the economy made Hungary extremely vulnerable in the interwar period and even more so because of the lack of flexibility in the production structure. This slowed response to changes in terms of trade inasmuch as the home market was unable to absorb the surplus when world market prices turned against Hungary.

National Income and Growth

On the whole, Hungary's economic performance was better than modest in the interwar period. Yet the process of growth had been interrupted and even reversed twice, first by World War I (and postwar readjustment), then by the Great Depression. For about half of the interwar period production and income were below prewar levels. A slow process of reorganization, or depressionary decline, alternated with rapid growth for short periods, such as 1925–29 and 1935–38. Moreover, the interwar years brought about only fragmented and scattered development, mostly in industry, while other sectors, and particularly agriculture, were neglected.

The most optimistic growth figure for the twenty years between the wars is 30 percent, an annual rate of about 1.1 percent, far behind that of the prewar 3 percent annual growth rate. Since the population increased from 7.9 million to 9 million (9.3 million in 1940) the *per capita* yearly average growth was even less, around 0.7 percent. This slowdown of Hungarian economic growth affected not only the long process of Hungary's economic modernization, but also its international performance and its place in the European economy.

While in the prewar period Hungary belonged to those countries whose growth rate was higher than the European average, the interwar performance lagged behind it in spite of the fact that Europe's growth had slowed down considerably as well.

Per capita national income, the most comprehensive index of a country's level of economic development, amounted to $120 in 1937–38 (reckoned in 1937 dollars). This was scarcely more than half the $200 average *per capita* national income of twenty-four European countries and only one-quarter to one-third the average of the most advanced countries in western and east-central Europe. The slow growth also reflects some major structural modifications in the occupational distribution of the population and in the distribution of national income.

During the whole period not more than four years produced a capital formation over 10 percent of the national product; during the depression years it was reduced to around 5 percent, and even in the 1930s it did not increase over 9 percent.

During the interwar years, the contribution of industry to national income exceeded 35–40 percent in several European countries (Austria, Denmark, and Norway), and even reached 40–45 percent in others (England, Sweden, Germany, and Belgium). In the less developed countries like those of the Balkans, the share of industry on the eve of the Second World War reached 20 percent. In that sense, Hungary was between the two extremes, but certainly closer to the less developed countries than the more developed ones. While Hungary accounted for 2.2 percent of Europe's population, its industrial production was only 0.9 percent of the European total. The difference was clear and meant that per capita industrial production was around half that of Austria and Czechoslovakia and about a quarter or even less than the per capita industrial production in Germany and England. When the war broke out, Hungary was still an agricultural industrial country in terms of its economic structure, its technological production, and its income level, and it was among Europe's economically backward countries.

After the introduction of the Györ Program based on massive German investments, Hungary witnessed an economic boom. This was simply the result of her inclusion in the German war economy and did not represent a true change in the fundamental weaknesses outlined in this chapter. The war-oriented economy not only subjected Hungary to total German domination but also brought the drastic and large-scale involvement of the Hungarian government in the country's economy to the point where it is not an exaggeration to say that the nationalization of the Hungarian economy began during World War II. This made its completion after 1945 easier than it would have been under other circumstances.

XX

FROM LIBERATION TO REVOLUTION, 1945–1956

Charles Gati

From the time the first postwar (provisional) government was formed in December 1944 to the revolution of 1956, Hungarian history—with its ups and downs, sharp turns, and sudden plunges—followed a roller coaster course. This was a decade of hope and despair, exhilaration and fear, change and stagnation, democracy and terror. Three years of political and economic pluralism (from December 1944 to the winter of 1947–48) were followed by five years of growing Stalinist terror (from 1948 to the spring of 1953), followed by three years of gradual decompression called the New Course (1953–56) that culminated in a short-lived nationalist, anti-Soviet uprising in October 1956—an uprising whose echoes were to be heard worldwide for decades to come.

Democracy in the Soviet Shadow, 1944–1947

The shape of the postwar Hungarian political order had emerged in Moscow even before World War II came to an end. In the fall of 1944, three series of secret meetings dealing with Hungary's future took place in the Soviet capital.

One was between the Soviet government, whose delegation was usually led by Foreign Commissar Vyacheslav Molotov, and a delegation of Hungarian officials led by Lieutenant-General Gábor Faraghó. The Hungarian delegation had been sent to Moscow by Horthy to negotiate an armistice with the allied powers. The agreement sought by the Hungarians would have involved the immediate cessation of hostilities, combined with safe exit for the occupying German forces and participation by British and American, as well as Soviet, troops in the country's occupation. But the Soviet government—speaking for Great Britain and the United States, too—insisted on harsher terms: Hungary was to evacuate in ten days all territories regained since 1938 (including Transylvania) and thus return to "Trianon Hungary," and it was to declare war on Germany at once. As the Hungarian delegation lacked any leverage that would have made a better deal possible, the preliminary armistice along the lines proposed, or dictated, by Moscow was signed on October 11, 1944.

A second set of secret negotiations treating Hungary's postwar orientation had begun on October 9, 1944 with a meeting between British Prime Minister Winston Churchill and Soviet leader Iosif V. Stalin. Their meeting produced the controversial "percentage agreement" regarding the postwar distribution of Western and Soviet influence over five East European countries, including Hungary. According to the rather curious and certainly vague understanding reached that day, British and Soviet influence in postwar Hungary was to be evenly divided. However, during the course of two days of subsequent bargaining on October 10 and 11, 1944, with British Foreign Secretary Anthony Eden, Molotov managed to revise the fifty-fifty deal so that the final agreement provided for 80 percent Soviet and only 20 percent British influence over Hungary's postwar political order. There was no discussion, then or later, about what these percentages actually meant.

The third, almost equally surrealistic, series of meetings held in Moscow in the fall of 1944 was the gathering of Hungarian Communists in exile. Over two dozen such "Muscovites" met on at least four occasions in September and October to hammer out their program for and define their role in postwar Hungary. They included such Hungarian-born veterans of the international Communist movement as Mátyás Rákosi, Ernő Gerő, József Révai, Zoltán Vas, György Lukács, and others who would soon return to Hungary and assume important positions in the new government. They were exhilarated by the prospect of returning to their homeland, not as conspirators and agitators facing certain arrest and imprisonment, but as free citizens of a new Hungary. However, what they apparently did not know yet was Stalin's precise plan for Hungary's postwar political order. Therefore, all the "Muscovites" could do at this time was to compose an Action Program that stressed such broadly acceptable themes as the need for national unity against Nazi Germany, speedy reconstruction, and the urgency of land reform. For now, they certainly made no plans to seize power; after all, they did not even know whether the Soviet Union would keep Horthy as the country's regent after the war (to provide for a sense of legitimacy and continuity) or whether a new Hungarian republic would be proclaimed in which the Communist Party could play a role (together with other anti-Nazi, anti-fascist political parties).

Some of the uncertainties these three sets of meetings suggested were resolved in a few months. In December 1944, Hungary's first postwar Provisional Government came into being in the East Hungarian city of Debrecen. It was a broadly based coalition government headed by one of Horthy's senior generals, Béla Miklós, and composed of representatives of the Smallholders Party, the Social Democratic Party, and the National Peasant Party, as well as the newly formed Hungarian Communist Party. In addition to Prime Minister Miklós, a few representatives of the Horthy regime stayed on in positions of some responsibility, but the establishment of the Provisional Government signified the end of the Horthy regime itself. With the regent still abroad (he had been kidnapped by the Germans in October 1944), the Provisional Government presently assumed the right to govern the country.

In fact, however, the Provisional Government was to share power with the Soviet occupying forces and with the Communist-controlled political police. This curious distribution of authority was the consequence of Stalin's decision in the winter of 1944–45 to maintain the semblance of parliamentary democracy in Hungary for several years and at the same time prepare for the eventual Communist seizure of power. Indeed, given the presence of the Red Army and the absence of a countervailing Western presence, Stalin could have directed the Hungarian Communist Party to seize power immediately. Had he chosen to do so, the Hungarian Communists almost certainly could have gained and held power without significant popular resistance. But Stalin decided on the coalition formula for the time being because of what came to be known as his "Polish trade-off"—an attempt to encourage pluralism in Hungary (and in Czechoslovakia) in order to divert Western attention from the immediate Sovietization of Poland (as well as of Bulgaria and Romania). Put another way, Stalin's response to anticipated Western protests about Poland was Soviet "acceptance" of democracy in Hungary, and that is why he had informed the Hungarian Communists that their country's pluralistic phase might last as long as ten to fifteen years.

During its tenure—from December 1944 to November 1945—the Provisional Government rather successfully dealt with many of the pressing problems of the country's war-torn economy. Compared to the neighboring states, including Austria, the government rapidly improved such essential services as health care, transportation, and education. One by one, the old bridges spanning the Danube in Budapest and elsewhere were being rebuilt. Despite the devastation in the countryside, by mid-1945 there was almost an adequate supply of food in the cities. In all areas of economic activity, private enterprise was strongly encouraged. The one major innovation introduced by the Provisional Government was the Land Reform Act of 1945, which provided for the expropriation of estates larger than one thousand *hold* (1,420 acres) and the seizure of some smaller estates as well. For a few short years, before they were forced into the collective farms in the early 1950s, Hungarian peasants could cultivate their own land and thus realize the old dream of Hungary's landless peasantry.

The Hungarian Communist Party supported these popular measures; its leaders actively and energetically participated in the country's reconstruction. At the same time, the political police under their command—the notorious AVO—committed many atrocities, often claiming that the victims were enemies of the new democracy. With the knowledge or concurrence of the Ministry of Justice, the AVO arrested, imprisoned, and tortured thousands of innocent people, especially in smaller cities and in the countryside, partly to establish its prerogatives and partly to intimidate the population. In protest against the AVO's arbitrary and indeed illegal measures, the Social Democratic minister of justice, Ágoston Valentiny, resigned his post in July 1945.

Seeking to legitimize their role in Hungarian politics, the Communists called for general elections in the expectation that the population would reward them at the polls for their apparent commitment to pluralism in general and to the cause of reconstruction in particular. So confident were some of their leaders that they publicly predicted an overwhelming Communist victory; Révai, for example, expected his Party to receive 70 percent of the popular vote. But the results of the almost completely free November 1945 elections proved that the population remained both profoundly anti-Soviet and quite skeptical of the Communist Party's ultimate goals. In the end, the Smallholders Party received a stunning 57 percent of the vote, the Social Democrats and the Communists 17 percent each, and the National Peasant Party 7 percent.

Acting through the Allied Control Commission and its chairman, Klimenti I. Voroshilov, the Soviet Union grudgingly accepted the election results, but it insisted that the Ministry of Internal Affairs portfolio—which controlled both the police and much of the administrative apparatus—be held by a Communist. That demand led to deep divisions in the Smallholders Party. Eventually, the Smallholder leadership, fearful of the responsibility of either governing the country by themselves or further arousing Moscow's anger, decided to form a coalition government in which they would hold half of the portfolios, including the Prime Ministry. But the crucial Ministry of Internal Affairs went to a Communist, Imre Nagy, who—when proved to be too weak or ineffective—was soon replaced by László Rajk, another Communist who turned out to be unscrupulous in his efforts to intimidate the Communist Party's real or imagined political adversaries.

Despite the outcome of the elections and the subsequent selection of Smallholder leader Zoltán Tildy as the first president of the Hungarian Republic on February 1, 1946, the next two years witnessed an ever-growing Communist offensive against the country's non-Communist parties and politicians. Ranging from persuasion to intimidation and coercion, the techniques the Communists applied became known as the "salami tactics," which signified the Communist Party's demands to remove step-by-step—or slice-by-slice—elements it deemed undesirable from the coalition. In 1945, it was the leftovers of the Horthy regime; in 1946, the so-called Right Wing of the Smallholders Party led by Dezső Sulyok and of the Social Democrats led by Károly Peyer; in 1947, Béla Kovács, the popular secretary-general of the Smallholders Party, followed by different factions in the same party around Zoltán Pfeiffer, Ferenc Nagy, and others. In each case, the Communist Party reiterated its commitment to democracy and to the coalition, adding, however, that first these "reactionary" or "antidemocratic" politicians must disappear from the political arena. The "salami tactics" turned out to be effective, not only because the Communists could claim the support of the Soviet occupation forces, but also because some of the non-Communist leaders rather easily acquiesced in the removal of a competing faction within their parties.

Operating in the shadow of Soviet power, then, Hungarian democracy barely survived for a few short years. As late as mid-1947, the press was still all but free; Parliament openly debated controversial issues; the stock market flourished.

Inflation had been brought under control, and the country's reconstruction had taken less time than expected. Despite the activities of the AVO and the Communists' political offensive, most Hungarians seemed to believe that the coalition formula would last. After all, every significant political force in the country, including the dominant Smallholders Party, supported a policy of friendship and cooperation with the Soviet Union. Under these circumstances, why would it serve Moscow's interests to end the coalition era and impose one-party rule on Hungary? In short, there was reason to hope, even in 1947, that Hungary (and Czechoslovakia) could avoid the fate of some of the neighboring "people's democracies," where the processes of Sovietization had advanced at a more rapid pace.

Only in the winter of 1947–48, after the founding of the Communist Information Bureau (Cominform) in September 1947, did Stalin's impatience and indeed dissatisfaction with his Hungarian comrades' relatively gradual approach to power become clear. The Hungarian Communist Party was informed at that time that the era of "parliamentary pirouetting" must come to an end. The Cold War between East and West, between the Soviet Union and the United States, was now under way, and Stalin was eager to consolidate his hold over all of the countries of East-Central Europe, including Hungary, irrespective of how this measure would affect Soviet relations with the West. The 1944–47 coalition era thus turned out to be a "democratic interlude," shorter than planned, and it was but a transition from the right-wing authoritarianism of the Horthy era to left-wing Communist totalitarianism.

The Era of Stalinist Terror, 1948–1953

Beginning with the "winter of discontent" of 1947–48, for five seemingly endless and certainly hopeless years, the Hungarian people were mobilized to lay the "foundations of socialism." As political pluralism was liquidated and the Communist Party's monopoly of power achieved, they were told to work harder for the benefit of all, emulate the Soviet model in every possible way, praise the "great Stalin" and his "wise Hungarian pupil," Mátyás Rákosi, march for or against all sorts of officially determined causes, and above all maintain eternal vigilance in the face of machinations by American imperialism and such traitors to socialism as Marshal Tito of Yugoslavia and his cohorts.

With the leaders of non-Communist parties already abroad, under house arrest, or imprisoned, and the Social Democratic Party absorbed by the Communists in mid-1948, the Communist Party—renamed the Hungarian Workers' Party—became the repository of all power and wisdom. Nevertheless, following Stalin's new theory—according to which the "class struggle" would actually sharpen after the consolidation of Communist authority—the Hungarian Communists continued to pursue the "class struggle" against their real or imagined adversaries.

In the countryside, the "class struggle" took the form of extraordinarily harsh

measures against the peasantry. Copying Stalin's pattern of forceful collectivization in the 1930s, Rákosi ordered an unrelenting struggle against kulaks (peasants having twenty-five *hold* or more) and against the so-called middle peasants
(ten to twenty-five *hold*), declaring that "the peasant must be forced to make
greater sacrifices for the building of socialism." But force did not produce economic results. Despite, or perhaps because of, all the threats, intimidation, and
terror, combined with incredibly high compulsory delivery quotas and a tax
system that actually discouraged production, collective farms accounted for no
more than one-fifth of the country's arable land in the early 1950s—while the
average independent peasant produced less than his own family needed. So
poorly did the collective farms perform, and so little were they paid for their
products by the state, that by 1952 the average income of peasant families
belonging to such farms dropped to 30.8 percent of what it had been as late
as 1949.

Elsewhere in the economy, the nationalization of factories employing ten
workers or more was ordered in 1949; by the following year essentially all
private enterprise ceased to exist. Barbers and plumbers, newspaper vendors and
psychiatrists all worked directly for the state or in state-controlled cooperatives.
The Communist Party's proudly acclaimed objective was to turn Hungary into
"a country of iron and steel." In 1949, the People's Economic Council and the
State Planning Office, both run by the Party, ordered an increase in the output of
heavy industry of over 200 percent in five years, an unrealistic target that was
further raised to 380 percent in 1951. The Party also decided to build a new
metallurgical complex at the newly named town of Sztálinváros (Stalin City),
neglecting to consider the fact that the needed iron ore and coking coal, as well
as other raw materials, were locally unavailable. Rákosi claimed that "the new
socialist man" could overcome all such technical obstacles and difficulties. By
1952–53, the Hungarian economy—burdened with immense investments, extraordinary defense expenditures, and inefficient and highly politicized central
decision-making—was on the verge of bankruptcy.

The vicious purges during the era of high Stalinism included the show trial of
József Cardinal Mindszenty, who was arrested in December 1948 and tried in
February 1949. Having been drugged and tortured by the ÁVO, the Cardinal
confessed to "anti-state" conspiracy and received a sentence of life imprisonment. (He was freed during the 1956 revolution.) Archbishop József Grósz was
tried in 1951, together with hundreds of other Catholic and Protestant clergymen as well as leaders of the small Jewish community.

A series of purges against Communist leaders and their left-wing Social Democratic supporters got under way in 1949 too. Many though by no means all of
them were "home Communists" (rather than "Muscovites") who had stayed in
Hungary during World War II, participating in the country's small anti-Nazi resistance movement. The most prominent Communist leader to be tried and executed in 1949 was László Rajk, the former minister of internal affairs. Another to
be tried and imprisoned, in 1951, was János Kádár, who succeeded Rajk as minister of internal affairs. Thousands of loyal Communists were arrested and tried

between 1949 and 1952, accused of such fantastic crimes as spying for the United States and Yugoslavia, and for leading "anti-people" conspiracies.

The country was shocked and indeed terrorized by the spectacle of Stalinist show trials. What was their purpose? How could this predominantly Catholic country so humiliate its spiritual leader? Even more puzzling were the trials of Communists, who had dedicated their lives to the cause of socialism, adored the Soviet Union and Stalin, and who had dutifully supported every twist and turn in the Party line. Why were the Communists killing off their own kind as well? Why was Rákosi decimating his own party?

These questions still cannot be answered. It may be that Rákosi and his closest aides were simply such ideological fanatics that they felt compelled to prove their loyalty to the Communist cause by doing *more* than even Stalin had expected of them. It may be that they were sadists deriving pleasure from the sufferings they ordered and witnessed. A more complex interpretation is that Rákosi, fearing that Stalin would punish him for having allowed the "democratic interlude" to last as long as it did and thus concerned about his own political fate, presently tried to make up for the "parliamentary pirouetting" of the coalition era by demonstrating his vigilance and abiding loyalty.

Whatever its cause, the reign of terror turned out to be harsher and more extensive than it was in the neighboring "people's democracies" of East-Central Europe and even the Soviet Union itself. The number of those who perished during these years was in the thousands. Tens of thousands were imprisoned or taken to what amounted to slave labor camps. Although the number of those who were deported from their homes in the cities in 1951–52 has never been determined, it was almost certainly even higher. Indeed, the total number of purge victims is thought to have reached 200,000 people.

But numbers cannot adequately describe the atmosphere of terror that permeated all aspects of everyday life. In his memorable "One Sentence on Tyranny" written in the early 1950s and published during the 1956 revolution, Gyula Illyés wrote that tyranny was present "Not only in the gun barrel,/ Not only in the prison cell,/ Not only in the torture rooms,/ Not only in the nights,/ In the voice of the shouting guard"; it also affected the way acquaintances avoided each other, the way friends discussed only apolitical topics, the way parents feared to reveal their private beliefs to their own children. Precisely because it was impossible to find out why one's relative, friend, or neighbor disappeared from one day to the next, all expected the worst. Guided by fear, some joined the chorus of denunciations of the alleged agents of imperialism and Titoism; most remained quiet. No one dared to ask questions about the promise of pluralism and democracy, about the purpose of terror and intimidation, about the fate of the victims. More than anything else, this period of Hungarian history was marked by an extraordinary gap between popular hatred for the regime and professed solidarity with it and between conditions of anxiety and fright and the officially proclaimed euphoria about the new order. Wrote Illyés: "Where there's tyranny/ Everyone is a link in the chain;/ It stinks and pours out of you,/ You are tyranny itself."

The Post-Stalin Thaw, 1953–1956

Stalin's death on March 5, 1953 opened a new chapter in Hungary's postwar history. In parallel with the processes of de-Stalinization in the Soviet Union, Hungary also experienced a period of "thaw"—a gradual relaxation of totalitarian controls. During this increasingly hopeful era called the New Course, thousands of political prisoners were released, hundreds of collective farms disbanded; the country's economic priorities shifted so as to emphasize light industry and the production of food and consumer goods, and at least some of the powers of the dreaded AVO were curtailed. These measures were undertaken by the same Communist Party which had beaten the country and its people into submission during the era of high Stalinism, and the Party was still led by "Stalin's best Hungarian disciple," the wily Mátyás Rákosi.

But at meetings, small and large, held throughout the country, it was no longer obligatory to jump up before, during, and after each proceeding and applaud the speaker with the rhythmic chant, "Long live Rákosi! Long live the Party!" Indeed, the first sign of change that every Hungarian could understand in 1953 was the gradual disappearance of what was euphemistically called the "personality cult." Rákosi was still at the helm, but in the new spirit of "collective leadership" he was no longer infallible.

What happened was that, just prior to the short-lived uprising in East Berlin on June 17, 1953, the new Soviet Politburo told Rákosi and a few of his colleagues to come to Moscow. In no uncertain terms, the Hungarians were told that they had mismanaged the economy and relied too extensively on terror rather than persuasion. Without even pretending to be merely concerned advisors, they actually ordered Rákosi to change his ways or else. The "wise leader of the Hungarian people" was instructed to keep his position as the Party's secretary-general but to relinquish his prime ministership. Worse, the Soviet comrades, there and then, selected Imre Nagy, who was not one of Rákosi's acolytes, to be the new prime minister.

After the delegation returned to Budapest, the Party's Central Committee in a secret resolution condemned Rákosi, Gerő, Farkas, and Révai—the "foursome" who had run the country—for bringing Hungary to the brink of disaster. Rákosi dutifully exercised self-criticism, admitting responsibility even for the purges and promising to observe "socialist legality." Nagy became prime minister, and Rákosi assumed the new title of first secretary (rather than general-secretary as he used to be).

At first, the personnel changes at the top did not appear to be significant. After all, Nagy was also a "Muscovite" who had lived for more than a decade in the Soviet Union and later on played an important role in the implementation of the Party's dreadful campaign of forced collectivization. That during secret deliberations of the Politburo in 1947 and again in 1949 he had questioned Rákosi's policies was unknown to all but a handful of high-ranking insiders. To most Hungarians, even Nagy's public promise in July 1953 to abolish internment camps, respect civil rights and liberties, and reform the economy sounded all but unbelievable; why would the Communists undo their own policies? At least initially, the public was highly skeptical.

Yet Nagy, if not his colleagues, took the Soviet-ordained "New Course" seriously. Within a year, some five hundred collective farms were allowed to fold. There was a substantial decrease in investments in heavy industry (over 40 percent lower in 1954 than in 1953). In the same year, the standard of living rose by about 15 percent. By 1954, many of the victims of Rákosi's purges were released; others had to be "rehabilitated" posthumously. In what amounted to a political earthquake, it was announced in March 1954 that Gábor Péter, the AVO's former chief, was sentenced to life imprisonment.

Nagy's "New Course"—this attempt to reform the Communist system—had two major consequences. One was the development of deep divisions in the Communist Party. The other was the alienation of intellectuals from the system, especially writers, journalists, and university students.

Divisions within the Party were complex and at times obscure. What was clear was the difference between Nagy and Rákosi: something of a "national Communist," Nagy genuinely believed in the necessity and urgency of the reform, while Rákosi feared the erosion of his authority and therefore sought to postpone the implementation of the "New Course." Undoubtedly, the Party apparatus was solidly behind Rákosi, who managed to pay lip service to the new program and yet at the same time convey his doubts to the Party faithful.

What made this factional struggle so complex was the post-Stalin factional struggle concurrently being waged in the Kremlin itself. The relationships between different Soviet factions and the two Hungarian contenders were truly Byzantine, with Georgi Malenkov and perhaps Lavrenti Beria supporting Nagy, while Molotov and at times Nikita Khrushchev implicitly backing Rákosi. But after Beria was shot in late 1953 and Malenkov demoted in 1955, the Kremlin line-up seemed to have changed, with Khrushchev and Anastas Mikoyan eventually leading the anti-Stalinist faction (and, presumably, lending support to the Hungarian reformers around Nagy) and Molotov heading the orthodox forces (and, presumably, signaling his support to Rákosi). Even the Twentieth Congress of the Soviet Communist Party, which was held in February 1956 and which in no uncertain terms condemned the "crimes" of the Stalin era, failed to convey a clear-cut Soviet preference for the Communist reform movement in Hungary.

More than anything else, then, mixed Soviet signals made it possible for Rákosi in the spring of 1955 to accuse Nagy of "right-wing deviations" and engineer his ouster. Having no doubt obtained Soviet approval to do so, Rákosi accused Nagy of nationalist tendencies, of neglecting the importance of the class struggle, and of disregarding the leading role of the Communist Party in the country's political life. The more scholarly Nagy, who was an inept in-fighter under all circumstances and presently ill with a heart ailment, could not marshal the necessary political strength to convince either the Kremlin or the Hungarian Politburo of the importance of the "New Course" and the falsity of Rákosi's charges.

Only in the summer of 1956 did the Soviet Politburo recognize that Rákosi had become a liability; by then even his most orthodox Hungarian supporters had also ceased to believe that he was irreplacable. On July 16, the desperate Rákosi made a last-ditch effort to reinforce his position. He recommended to his Politburo colleagues the arrest of Imre Nagy and four hundred other Communists for anti-Party conspiracy. How the pro-Rákosi Hungarian Politburo would have voted on this proposal—an incredible proposal, indeed, in this era of "socialist legality" in the immediate aftermath of the Twentieth Soviet Party Congress—will never be known because the Kremlin once again imposed its will on the Hungarian Communists. This time, Moscow quickly dispatched Mikoyan to Budapest and ordered Rákosi's dismissal. Claiming ill health, Rákosi immediately left for the Soviet Union. His replacement, Ernő Gerő, was all but indistinguishable from Rákosi. A former functionary of the Communist International and fluent in Russian, Gerő had participated in every decision in the postwar era that brought the Hungarian Communist Party to its present predicament. Clearly, Moscow still believed that order and stability could be reestablished by following more or less the same policies Rákosi pursued—without Rákosi himself. That is why there was no talk of Nagy's reinstatement, not yet. But in October, after Marshal Tito of Yugoslavia made Nagy's "rehabilitation" the condition for holding talks with Gerő, Nagy was readmitted to the Party.

Although the timing of Nagy's partial rehabilitation was due to Tito's intervention, there was ever-growing domestic pressure for such a move as well. For while the fragmented Party leadership had for three years engaged in personal intrigues and in a seemingly permanent debate about the "New Course" and its ramifications, the country's intellectuals—writers and journalists in particular—presented an almost united front against Rákosi's neo-Stalinist resurgence and for Nagy's reformist course. As in previous times in Hungarian history, intellectuals were among the first to voice the conscience of the nation. While Nagy was prime minister between 1953 and 1955, but also after his dismissal, the writers managed to speak up on behalf of his ideas. The official monthly of the Writers' Association, *Irodalmi Újság (Literary Gazette)* became the primary vehicle for the intellectuals' outcry against the abuses of the totalitarian past and its remnants, calling for a "socialist renewal." Most of the writers participating in the "revolt of the mind" since 1953 were party members and indeed loyal Communists. They had joined the Party after World War II out of genuine conviction, believing in the ideals of socialism and impressed by Soviet achievements. Some did not know about the wave of terror that had swept the Soviet Union in the 1930s, others apparently did not want to believe what they knew, and still others managed to tell themselves that it could not and would not happen in Hungary. That is why so many found it possible to idolize Stalin and revere Rákosi.

Precisely because their faith was so deep and so blind, their disillusionment turned them into angry and indeed unrelenting opponents of Communist orthodoxy after 1953. Having at first cautiously expressed support for Nagy's new program, they gradually gained courage from the proclaimed atmosphere of "socialist legality" which made their arrest or imprisonment both untimely and unlikely. In one article after another, they offered devastating descriptions of prevailing conditions in the Hungarian countryside. They kept demanding that the authorities allow the performance of such classical dramas as "The Tragedy of Man" by Imre Madách, even though the play made light of socialist utopias.

Critical of themselves for having believed that Rajk and his comrades were guilty of conspiracy and other fabricated charges, many of the country's leading writers and poets publicly asked for their readers' forgiveness. One young Communist high school teacher went even further. At a large gathering of Party activists, with Rákosi in the chair, he asked for the floor. He introduced his question by recalling that in 1949 Rákosi had boasted of "discovering" the so-called Rajk conspiracy "during many a sleepless night." Turning to the red-faced Rákosi, the high school teacher demanded that Rákosi tell the gathering, then and there, what he was actually doing during those "sleepless nights." Although the teacher was subsequently warned that such provocative statements and questions would not be tolerated, neither he nor the writers were arrested. The regime of the "bald murderer," as the intellectuals now called Rákosi, was on the verge of disintegration.

The unity of the opposition and the impotence of the regime was even more in evidence in the summer and fall of 1956. In the late spring and early summer, the intellectuals joined university students in forming the Petőfi Club, named after the hero of the 1848–49 war of independence, which held irregular meetings for discussion and debate. The topics varied from the state of philosophy to the role of the judiciary, and more. The widow of László Rajk, Júlia, spoke up at one of the sessions, calling for the purification of the ideals of socialism in Hungary and adding that it would not be achieved as long as the "murderers of my husband occupy ministerial seats." On June 27, the final debate on the media drew over four thousand participants and lasted till the early hours of the morning. In a mood of defiance, Hungary's leading writers and journalists explicitly demanded freedom of expression and the ouster of the Party's orthodox leaders. When the recently released Géza Losonczy, still bearing the physical and emotional scars of severe beatings received from the AVO, took to the podium to call for Nagy's reinstatement, he received a standing ovation. Although the Petőfi Circle was suspended, no one was arrested, and Losonczy retained his seat on the editorial board of the daily *Magyar Nemzet (Hungarian Nation)*.

In the fall, with Rákosi already in Soviet exile, the intellectuals' campaign for a humane socialist order continued. In the cultural weekly *Művelt Nép (Educated People)*, a young journalist, publicly expressing for the first time the frustration of university students, asked for a revision of regulations that required every student to study the Russian language; why not allow for a choice of Russian, English, French, or German he wanted to know. In another weekly, *Hétfői Hirlap (Monday Herald)*, Miklós Vásárhelyi demanded the public trial of Mihály Farkas, the man in the Party leadership most directly responsible for the AVO and all the trials of the Stalinist era.

Then, on October 6, under considerable public pressure, those in power agreed to the reburial of Rajk and three of his colleagues. Tens of thousands of people marched to the cemetery in Budapest, among them many of the survivors of the purges, writers, students, Party members, and others. This Communist politician, who was once quite willing to treat his adversaries brutally, now became the symbol of the opposition. His reburial was a political event, used by the authorities to show their commitment to the elimination of past "errors and mistakes." Even the Party daily *Szabad Nép (Free People)* headlined its front page editorial "Never Again!" For its part, the opposition used the event to demonstrate the guilt and corruption of the Party leadership and to reach out to the public at large.

The Revolution of 1956

What had began in 1953 as an intra-Party struggle between the reformist, national Communist faction around Nagy and the orthodox, Stalinist faction behind Rákosi, combined with a growing ferment among the country's intellectuals, turned into a nationalist, anti-Soviet revolution on October 23, 1956. On November 4, Soviet armed forces intervened and crushed the revolt. But for thirteen short days Hungary made history.

The First Day (October 23). Students at the engineering school of the University of Budapest call for a peaceful demonstration. In mid-morning tens of thousands begin to move toward the statue of Petőfi when around 1:00 p.m. the minister of internal affairs prohibits the march. But when no one pays attention to the minister's order, it is promptly revoked. In a dignified, happy atmosphere, the crowd walks from Petőfi's statue to Józef Bem's to express solidarity with Poland's ongoing upheaval. (A Polish general, Bem assisted the Hungarian revolutionaries of 1848–49.) Speeches are made, all calling for Nagy's reinstatement. Some of the demonstrators go on to the Parliament building, others to the headquarters of Radio Budapest. After Radio Budapest's director refuses to receive a delegation from the crowd and the radio broadcasts Gerő's harsh and, in effect, provocative speech at 8:00 p.m., the first shots are exchanged. By 9:30 Stalin's large statue is toppled. The AVO is helpless. Army units are called in to protect the radio building, the headquarters of the Party daily, and a few other office buildings. But the army, instead of following orders and attacking the crowd, provides the demonstrators with its own weapons. The revolution begins.

The Second Day (October 24). During the night of October 23–24, the Party's Central Committee meets in a long, extraordinary session. By then the Party leaders, perhaps Gerő, have requested Soviet military assistance. The Central Committee, after coopting Nagy and a few of his apparent supporters, "recommends" to the Presidential Council the appointment of Nagy as Prime Minister. As Soviet army units reach Budapest, martial law is declared. The Party's labeling of the revolution as "counterrevolution" rapidly inflames the situation; the insurgents—sensing the confusion and weakness of the regime—occupy several of the Party's local offices. Sounding puzzled by the rapid turn of events, Nagy asks them to trust him and let him proceed towards the full implementation of the "New Course." In vain, he also asks them to turn in their weapons. But by now, with anarchy ruling the streets, Nagy begins to lose his once enormous popularity. The people no longer think in terms of the Party and its factions. At issue is not "socialist legality" or the end of the era of the "personality cult." Years of suppressed hostility suddenly find expression in new slogans, of which one more than any other can be heard again and again: "Russians, Go Home!"

The Third Day (October 25). The Kremlin sends Mikoyan and Mikhail Suslov to Budapest. At Party headquarters, to which they are escorted in Soviet tanks, they order Gerő's replacement as the Party's first secretary by János Kádár. A cautious centrist who spent several years in Rákosi's jails, Kádár seems to be the right man both to represent Soviet interests and also to pacify the population. But the Hungarian people are no longer paying any attention to such cosmetic changes in the leadership of the Party. That which would have been seen a week or two earlier as a dramatic step signaling the end of totalitarian rule is now but a barely noticed, empty gesture. What does matter today is the shooting at thousands of demonstrators in front of the Parliament building. Over one hundred unarmed demonstrators are reported to have been killed by AVO officers positioned on nearby rooftops. In the country's chaotic atmosphere, one in which both fury and jubilation prevail, Gerő's dismissal means too little and comes too late. New passions have been released.

The Fourth Day (October 26). More of the same. The Party, offering amnesty, calls for a cease-fire. It promises a new, more broadly based government. But throughout the country the insurgents begin to form "revolutionary committees," which take over the functions of local government. In Budapest, Soviet soldiers seem less in evidence, but it is not clear where they are. Prime Minister Nagy is seen leaving Party headquarters and walking over to the Parliament building. His supporters spread the news that Nagy, having just freed himself from the influence of his Party comrades, is finally beginning to understand what has been happening around him and will act accordingly.

The Fifth Day (October 27). Still following rather than leading his people, Nagy announces the composition of his new government. As some of the Stalinists are gone, two former Smallholder leaders—Zoltán Tildy and Béla Kovács—are coopted to become minister of state and minister of agriculture, respectively. By the new standards of the capital and the countryside as well, these are but cosmetic changes. Armed groups roam the streets. In Vác, freedom fighters release political prisoners held in one of the country's largest jails. If anything, the gap widens between the government and the insurgents.

The Sixth Day (October 28). In the early morning hours, the Central Committee appears ready to adopt a hard-line approach calling for an attack by loyalist Hungarian and Soviet forces against key areas in Budapest controlled by the revolutionaries. Nagy, on the verge of resignation, succeeds not only in cancelling the plan but in altering the composition of the Party leadership. A six-member presidium takes over the functions of the Central Committee, chaired by Kádár and staffed by some of the less discredited Communist leaders. Significantly, Gerő and other Stalinist diehards are denied positions of responsibility. In the evening Nagy finally meets a few of the insurgents' demands. He announces the removal of Soviet military units from Budapest, dissolution of the hated AVO, plans to restore Hungary's traditional national emblem, and his intention to negotiate with Moscow about the removal of Soviet troops from the whole country.

The Seventh Day (October 29). The Party daily *Szabad Nép*, now in the hands of Nagy's followers, issues an editorial entitled "Response to *Pravda*," which rejects firmly but politely Soviet charges about the Hungarian "counterrevolution" having been instigated by "British and American imperialists." The editorial asserts that all Hungarians seek freedom and independence, and once these goals are achieved everyone wants to have peaceful and friendly relations with the Soviet Union. As the government and even the Communist Party thus begin to identify with the causes of the revolution, some of the insurgents appeal for an end to the bloodshed. They are not yet prepared to turn in their arms, but the authorities seem to be gaining a small measure of respect.

The Eighth Day (October 30). Dozens of new dailies appear, and a variety of revolutionary councils and committees issue demands and appeals. "The Hungarian National Revolutionary Council," led by József Dudás, claims the government lacks legitimacy. In the meantime, the political parties of the postwar coalition era announce plans for reorganization. One group of armed insurgents, after several hours of fighting, occupies the Budapest city headquarters of the Communist Party, while another group in Nógrád County liberates Cardinal Mindszenty from detention. Unnoticed by insurgents but studied with care by political insiders is this morning's *Pravda* editorial. It offers to reexamine Soviet relations with the countries of Eastern Europe "on the basis of respect for sovereignty, equality, and mutual advantage." Mikoyan and Suslov return to Budapest and stay overnight. Two topics under discussion are the establishment of a pluralist, multi-party political system and the country's withdrawal from the Warsaw Pact. In point of fact, at least a few Soviet military forces are in the process of leaving Hungary.

The Ninth Day (October 31). The previous day seems to have been a watershed. In the battle for the Budapest Party headquarters, it turns out that hundreds of Communists—mainly AVO officers and agents—were killed or even lynched. One result is that Party members lose whatever confidence they had to regroup; many seek refuge in friends' apartments. Another is the growing isolation of the most radical elements among the insurgents. The country's new hero is General Pál Maléter, who has deserted to the revolutionary forces. Opposed to summary executions, Maléter's call for order and support for the Nagy government gains adherents both in Budapest and in the countryside.

The Tenth Day (November 1). As new Soviet military divisions are reported to enter the country, Nagy declares Hungary's immediate withdrawal from the Warsaw Pact and the country's neutrality. On behalf of the renamed Hungarian Socialist Workers' Party, Kádár voices the Communists' admiration for "our people's glorious uprising" and the Party's full support of "the government's demand for the complete removal of Soviet forces." Then, under mysterious circumstances, Kádár and five or six other like-minded Communists leave Budapest with Soviet assistance for the Ukrainian city of Uzhgorod near the Hungarian border. Unaware of Kádár's disappearance, however, the public is relieved to learn that even the Communists have come to endorse the government's latest measures. Reflecting the almost jubilant mood of the day, the insurgent daily *Igazság (Truth)* carries this headline the following morning: WE ARE INDEPENDENT! WE ARE NEUTRAL! But those who know of the scope of Soviet troops movements and of Kádár's vanishing act begin to feel that the end may be in sight.

The Eleventh Day (November 2). Soviet troop movements continue; Soviet forces occupy or surround the country's airports. In New York, the U.N. acts on Nagy's request and votes to place the Hungarian issue on its agenda. In the meantime, the government is replaced by a small cabinet headed by Nagy and composed of three Smallholder, three Social Democratic, two Petőfi (National Peasant) Party, and two Communist representatives as ministers of state and of General Maléter as minister of defense. (Kádár is still listed as one of the two Communist cabinet members.) In effect, the new multi-party government more or less accurately reflects the results of the free parliamentary elections of November 1945. At long last, nearly all of the insurgents, including Dudás' maverick group, are satisfied. In Budapest, there is peace. The streets are safe. The new National Guard, which is made up of military units loyal to the democratic government and of various groups of insurgents, keeps order. Representatives of workers agree to return to the factories on Monday, November 5. Schools are scheduled to reopen that day, too. Completely unknown to all, however, Soviet leaders Khrushchev and Malenkov make a secret trip to Yugoslavia this day. From subsequent accounts it appears that Moscow has definitely decided, perhaps on the previous day, to crush the Hungarian revolution, and the Soviet leaders seek—and somewhat grudgingly receive—Tito's seal of approval.

The Twelfth Day (November 3). There is a hubbub in the Parliament building all day. The bad news is that the undeclared invasion of Hungary by Soviet military units continues unabated. Except for Budapest, the Soviet army controls all key positions. But there is good news, too. A Hungarian-Soviet joint military commission meets during the day in the Parliament building to work out the details of Soviet withdrawal from the country. While the meeting is adjourned for the afternoon, two cabinet members (Tildy and Losonczy) hold a press conference for Western reporters. Apparently still unclear about Moscow's intentions, they project a cautiously optimistic outlook. They go to great length to assure the Soviet Union of the Nagy government's desire for harmonious and indeed friendly relations. At 10:00 p.m. Cardinal Mindszenty makes a radio speech, expressing his support for the revolution and reserving judgment about the government. At about the same time, the joint military commission is scheduled to resume its deliberations at a Soviet base in Tököl, on the outskirts of

Budapest. But officers of the Soviet secret police, personally led by KGB head Ivan Serov, arrest the Hungarian negotiators. On this fateful Saturday night, the Soviet invasion of Budapest is under way.

The Thirteenth Day (November 4). It is still dark when Radio Budapest broadcasts Nagy's speech to his countrymen: "This is Imre Nagy speaking, the president of the Council of Ministers of the Hungarian People's Republic. Today at daybreak, Soviet troops attacked our capital with the obvious intent of overthrowing the legal Hungarian democratic government. Our troops are in combat; the government is at its post. I notify the people of our country and the entire world of this fact." The radio repeatedly calls for the return of the Hungarian military delegation to Budapest. It also broadcasts the Writer's Union's dramatic appeal for Western aid: "To every writer in the world, to all scientists, to all federations of writers, to the intelligentsia of the world: Help Hungary!" In the meantime, Soviet tanks enter Budapest and surround the Parliament building. (There is scattered fighting here and there but no organized resistance; for, in point of fact, Nagy declined to authorize Béla Király, Maléter's deputy, to organize one.) Nagy and his supporters receive asylum in the Yugoslav embassy. Radio Budapest goes off the air, while, using the facilities of a provincial station, the Soviet-sponsored "Hungarian Revolutionary Worker-Peasant Government" announces its existence and declares its claim to be the government of Hungary. Headed by János Kádár, it speaks of ending the "counterrevolution."

On November 7, a Soviet armored car delivers Kádár and his associates to the Parliament building.

XXI

CONTEMPORARY HUNGARY, 1956–1984

Iván T. Berend

Socialist Reconstruction

On November 4, 1956, the second intervention of the Soviet army, the armed suppression of the uprising, and the establishment at Szolnok of the Revolutionary Workers' and Peasants' Government under the leadership of János Kádár defeated the struggle against Hungarian Stalinism and Soviet domination. The new government declared that the Imre Nagy government's withdrawal from the Warsaw Pact was null and void. Hungarian foreign policy was thus determined for the coming decades. The Hungarian socialist system erected in the 1940s, which had practically collapsed after October 23, was reconstructed with the help of Soviet weapons and, subsequently, with substantial political and ideological pressure from outside. During the armed struggle all those forces which had rejected Soviet-type socialism had been defeated. The new government began, on November 11, to reorganize its own armed forces and law enforcement detachments and introduced martial law. Important anti-government demonstrations continued, however, including the women's march in early December in Budapest and the confrontation in Salgótarján during which several people lost their lives and about one hundred were wounded. The Workers' Council of Greater Budapest, organized on November 14, acted practically as a counter-government and called for a general strike against the Kádár government. The Hungarian Writers' Union took similar action.

The struggle was very bitter, and the reestablishment of central power began with extremely harsh measures. The Presidential Council of the People's Republic issued a decree on December 11 introducing summary jurisdiction, and possession of illegal arms was a capital crime. This decree remained in force until the middle of November 1957. Until the end of March, no parades or assemblies could be organized without special governmental permission, and until mid-April a curfew was in force from the late evening throughout the night. The counter-government of the Central Workers' Council and the locally organized workers' councils of cities and boroughs were declared illegal by the government on December 9, and in January it suspended the activities of the Writers' Union. Gyula Hay, Tibor Déry, and many other writers and newspapermen were arrested. Legal procedures were set in motion, and the leaders of various military groups, such as József Dudás and János Szabó, were executed "for the leading role they had played in counter-revolutionary crimes." On June 17, 1958, the people learned from the Ministry of Justice that Imre Nagy and Pál Maléter had been executed and that Ferenc Donáth and Zoltán Tildy had received life sentences.

With consistent harshness, the government reestablished socialist power and reorganized the political and social structure of the country. The several dozen political parties, most of them liberal democratic, Christian democratic, or conservative in orientation, which had been established in the fall of 1956, were dissolved, and the road leading to a multi-party system was closed. The political pluralism that could have been achieved through the workers' councils was also ended. The regionally organized workers' councils that aimed at the elimination of the Kádár government were dissolved, and even the councils that worked legally in the various factories until November 1957 disappeared one by one during local political battles.

The Hungarian Socialist Workers' Party (HSWP), which had replaced the Party of Hungarian Laborers (PHL), began to reorganize its ranks. In place of the PHL's one million members, the reorganized 3,327 local units of the HSWP had only 103,000 members by the end of 1956. By the next spring, when party reorganization was completed, the party membership had risen to over 400,000 and the hegemonic political leadership of the party was assured. After February 1957, the party organized its own armed militia, the Workers' Guard.

While political power was established within its previous structure, it did not function in the same manner or with the same purpose. Defeated during the armed struggle were not only those who had attacked Soviet-type socialism, but also the power-wielding group associated with Mátyás Rákosi and Ernő Gerő, who, during the fifties, had destroyed the legal system with show trials and established a dictatorial regime. The old leadership and its policy were not reestablished; indeed, on the contrary, the prominent figures of the previous leadership were eliminated from the political scene. It was certainly no accident that the new leaders of HSWP and the government, János Kádár, Gyula Kállay, György Marosán, György Aczél, and several others had spent years in jail during the early fifties as the victims of the Rákosi group.

The new political directive of the HSWP was presented as a two-front struggle. On the one hand, the party wished to maintain the earlier direction established by socialism, including the continuation of the country's industrialization, the transformation of farms into cooperatives, the maintenance of the property relations determined by the supremacy of state ownership, and the persistence of the political structure based on the one-party system. At the same time the party wanted to eliminate the distortions, crimes, and errors which had characterized the system in the fifties: prefabricated trials, illegal law suits, compulsory artistic norms, and poor economic policy decisions.

The changes that took place after 1957 within the party-state framework are illustrated by the fact that the new government made it possible for rich peasants (kulaks) to join the reorganized cooperatives. The government rejected the earlier policy of liquidating the well-to-do peasants, and sought instead peace in the villages and the cooperation of those who knew best how to produce. This measure was also needed to change the general political climate. What the government did, in fact, was to replace the steady intensification of class warfare with a peace policy on the internal front while still pursuing a very strict political line based on traditional ideology.

In the 1950s the former landowners, manufacturers, and officers had been deported from Budapest together with their families, and their children were barred as "class aliens" from registering at universities. In 1962 the government ended the classification of people at universities according to their class origin, and all young people could register, provided their previous accomplishments warranted it.

In 1961 János Kádár coined the slogan of national reconciliation, "All those who are not against us are with us." He thus reversed the "enemy hunting" political theory and practice of the 1950s. Although the earlier institutional framework had not been changed, important advances were made in making political life less repressive and more liberal. Arbitrary legal action became a thing of the past, and no proceedings were conducted which did not follow legal lines. Another great change was that there was no more interference in the private lives of individuals. In sharp contrast to the fifties, after 1961 anyone could obtain a passport and, within the limits of available currency, could freely travel. In short, the government tried to gain widespread popular support through respecting the individual's rights. In accordance with this principle, a policy of tolerance was introduced in the artistic and cultural spheres too. While certain basic ideologies and goals were retained, new conditions were established for creative activities.

Economic Changes

The new political conditions produced important changes in economic policy-making too. The most important change in economic policy-making concerned continued industrialization. During the first session of the meeting of the Provisional Central Committee of the HSWP in December 1956, a resolution was passed that stipulated that improving the living standard had to be the central principle of economic policy. The committee rejected a policy that sacrificed the interests of those alive for the sake of an imaginary future. The approach to socialism had to be paralleled, as time passed, by the improvement of the population's situation during every phase of the development. The living standard became the determinant factor in economic policy making. The 20 percent increase in wages introduced at the end of 1956 and early the next year was in keeping with this decision. Naturally, at that time, political imperatives were also taken into consideration; in the midst of intense political struggles, winning over the masses was essential. This prompt wage increase was followed by a long-term policy that made certain that price increases did not follow and that people would find goods on which they could spend their money. The government made it one of its main tasks to have the market well supplied with merchandise. This was not easy, however, due to the destruction wrought by the heavy fighting, the strikes that had taken place in the fall and winter, the substantial decrease of the national income, the decrease of agricultural production, and the widespread shortage of consumer goods. It took about a decade before meat shortages ceased, long lines before stores disappeared, and a satisfactory food supply was assured. To achieve this, the economic policy-makers had had to address this question: What is the proper ratio between capital accumulation, investments, and consumption?

Within the new framework of economic policy, it was impossible to maintain the earlier forced level of accumulations at 35 percent of the gross national product, which had resulted in a declining living standard. After reaching a nadir in 1957, the level of accumulation remained steady at about 20–25 percent of GNP. This moderation did not change the basic policy of industrialization. The former forced rate of growth had been unsustainable and had kept the economy under constant strain. Between 1950 and 1956, periods of significant growth were always followed by ones of decline in a pattern of extreme and harmful fluctuations. After the introduction of a reasonable growth rate in 1957, these fluctuations disappeared. Due to massive reconstruction, the GNP grew by 23 percent in 1957. It dropped to 6 percent in 1958 and remained at a high but tolerable rate (compared to the rest of the world) of 5–6 percent per year until the end of the 1970s.

With the exception of cyclical changes, the living standard in Hungary had not improved since the beginning of the twentieth century. This stagnation for three generations and the serious decline that had characterized the 1950s were followed, after 1957, by a decade during which the per capita real wage and consumption increased by 50 percent.

The economic policy responsible for this was naturally based on a thorough examination and revision of earlier policy. The already mentioned session of the Provisional Central Committee included in its first resolution the following demands: the thorough reexamination of the economic principles of the past; the acceptance of the guiding principle that the new economic policy had to be focused on the country's economic abilities, its economic traditions, and the establishment of a balance between the various sectors of the economy; and the recognition that industrialization cannot be pursued at the expense of agricultural development. The same resolution also stressed that the planning process had to be revised and had to move away from the previous practice of issuing directives which had the force of law. Finally, the document underlined the importance of letting self-interest play a role in the economy. Planning had to be limited, concentrating its efforts on outlining the major directions of development. It was not to involve detailed instructions issued for each individual enterprise.

The Economic Committee, the highest-ranking economic organ of the government, assembled on December 10, 1956. It organized a committee of about two hundred specialists and asked it to establish for the government the conceptual framework of the new economic policy and to work out the new methods of planning and directing it. The president of this committee was Professor István Varga, who had filled numerous important positions for decades before he was shunted aside in the 1950s. The leading positions on the committee were given to experts from whom the government expected a speedy but thorough and radical reform plan and whose past performances promised that they would produce it. Work on economic reform began in Hungary during a time of crisis, when it was a political necessity to change economic policy and planning procedures.

In its final proposition, the committee suggested a system that attempted to combine the positive aspects of central planning with the stimulation produced by the market. It tried to replace the Soviet model, which had been introduced into Hungary in the 1950s, and to direct the economy with compulsory planning and direct non-economic means. The plan's important contribution would have involved the introduction of a pricing system which reflected the true input and value ratios and which, consequently, would have made the producers interested in manufacturing goods whose quality and diversity satisfied the buyers' needs. A buyers' market had to replace a sellers' market. While the comprehensive reform plan was under consideration, several steps had to be taken immediately because they could not be delayed even for the few months which the committee needed for its work. At the beginning of 1957, the economy could not have been restarted without changing first a few of its functional and systemic features. For example, for political reasons the disastrous agrarian policy could not be maintained even for a single additional day.

Agrarian Reform

Compulsory deliveries of farm products and obligatory sowing plans were two basic features of the pre-1956 agrarian policy that the peasantry hated with a vengeance. Because individual peasant households or cooperatives were involved, rather than state-owned enterprises, they could not be managed by obligatory instructions based on the central plan. These instructions were replaced by the delivery obligations, which had the force of law. During some years of bad harvests, the prescribed deliveries were higher than the effective yield of the land, and the peasantry was left without seed grains or enough cereals to feed its families. The government did not pay market prices, but unrealistically low fixed prices sometimes were even lower than cost. In November 1956, the government abolished obligatory deliveries. (Politically this was necessary because the Imre Nagy government had already taken this step.) At the same time obligatory sowing plans were also terminated. Thus, in 1957, obligatory directives were automatically replaced by the market in regulating the relationships between peasants, agriculture, the state, and nationalized industry. Consequently, the prices had to be higher than cost prices because otherwise the peasantry would either not produce or not bring its harvest to the market. Prices had to stimulate production. Step by step, the prices of agricultural products increased. The price differences which considerably favored industrial over agricultural goods existed for several more years, but the gap diminished steadily. The state began to regulate agriculture indirectly by pricing and taxation and gave up direct control in the form of orders and prescriptions.

This change had historical significance in East European socialism. It became obvious for the first time that planning and a centrally directed economy were also possible when market forces were considered and when indirect economic guidance was applied. This resulted in larger yields, and the state was able to purchase the quantities it wanted to buy without using force or turning to the courts.

This new method of planning and guidance, however, was put into effect in only one important sector of the economy— agriculture. The transformation of the economy at large, as suggested in the spring and summer of 1957 by the committee of experts, was not implemented.

The Fate of the Economic Reform Plan

The idea of comprehensive radical reform had been rejected by the time the committee submitted its report. The main reason for this decision was that by late summer of 1957 the economic and political situation had changed drastically. Consolidation had progressed with unexpected speed. The massive May Day celebration, which followed similarly well attended meetings in April, showed clearly that the Kádár government was master of the streets of Budapest, where a few months earlier its enemies were in charge. The rapid consolidation of the system gave the upper hand to those who favored continuity and stability, and the political necessity of reforms was no longer strongly felt.

The international Communist movement was suspicious of reform, condemned the so-called national Communist line, labeled revisionism as the main danger, and, once again, ostracized Yugoslavia. During the summer and fall of 1957, Hungarian politics adjusted to this line. The conviction gained ground that in order to secure the continuity and stability of the socialist order, it was necessary to assure the continuity of the planning and guidance mechanisms also. Based on this belief, real reform in the planning-guidance system of the country's industrial and other state-owned economic sectors were rejected, and the government was satisfied with smaller, gradual corrections. While the principle of state-issued directives was retained, they were to be limited in scope and number. The leaders believed that former mistakes could be avoided if the state would refrain from issuing directives excessively and would regulate only the main tasks. While previously dozens, in some case even hundreds, of obligatory directives had been issued, the new plan permitted only five to fifteen directives, limited to the most important issues. The practice of obligatory plan-directives was retained not only because of the inertia of old ideological habits, but also because the decision-makers were convinced that without compulsory directives planning was impossible and that the introduction of a free market would reestablish capitalism.

It was assumed that comprehensive reforms were not needed. What was required was to assure the better functioning of the old system by applying some corrective measures. Among these was the introduction of profit-sharing and, for some of the greatest enterprises, the right to handle their export business themselves. These partial reforms did not change the economic system of the country. It is, nevertheless, important to note that at the end of 1956 began the transformation of the Soviet-type socialist economic system which, until then, was considered to be the only one possible. Up to this time, socialism had been equated with central planning, obligatory directives, and obligatory delivery quotas. While the new policies were far from radical, in agriculture, at least, they brought basic changes.

The New Agrarian Collectives

The HSWP and the government made it crystal clear from the moment they came to power that, in the long run, the collectivization of agriculture was the only possible guarantor of its development. At the same time, the government also indicated that it did not wish to establish collectives by force and hoped to induce the peasantry to join them voluntarily. The stipulations of the agrarian policy program issued by the Party during the summer of 1957 aimed to achieve two goals.

The Party declared that collectives could be established only if the required financial and social support was made available. The program also indicated that the reforming of collectives and the improvement of production had to be achieved simultaneously. Therefore, the existing collectives had to be supported to transform them into enterprises which would produce higher yields and assure larger incomes to their members than individually worked lands. The expectation was that the few existing collectives, which at that time owned only about 10 percent of the arable land, would be transformed into modern large-scale enterprises and would attract the peasantry. When this plan was worked out, at the beginning of 1957, it was assumed that truly voluntary collectivization would take fifteen or twenty years and that production would correspondingly grow as well. This assumption was soon reexamined, and December 1958 brought a new decision. It was not possible to allow collectivization to take decades; collectivization would begin at once where and when political circumstances were favorable. This speeding up of agricultural transformation coincided with similar decisions taken by other socialist countries.

The policy established by the Central Committee of the HSWP brought unexpectedly rapid success within two years. In 1959–60, the collectivization of

Hungarian agriculture was completed. Only 5 percent of the arable land remained in private ownership. This rapid collectivization was often achieved by pressure, threats, and harassment, but the brutality typical of the 1950s was avoided. Resistance did not resurface this time because the peasants realized that the wait-and-see policy they had pursued in the 1950s was hopeless and that the process of collectivization was unavoidable. Furthermore, the new policy offered them better conditions. The collectives were no longer organized along unrealistic doctrinal lines, but based on a recognition of peasant interests. Within each large collective, each member was assured of a household plot of about 2.5 acres, and his animals could be kept out of the collective. Rent was paid to everybody for the land they brought to the collective, and the members received free health insurance and were entitled to old age pensions. (Individual productive activities were fitted into those of the collective in a flexible manner.) New flexibility was introduced into the wage system, which previously had been rigid and tied to a work system which did not offer incentives. The new collectives received substantial aid from the state, and investments in them were considerable. The members elected their own leaders, and the agricultural collectives became the only self-managing sector of the Hungarian economy. Rapid collectivization would have been impossible without these basic changes. While massive collectivization was in keeping with the demands of traditional Soviet agrarian policy, there were also important differences. The manner in which the collectivization was carried out, the new organizational framework of the collectives based on real conditions, and the stimulation of the peasantry's self-interest made possible an impressive agrarian development which followed collectivization.

Industrialization

The changes in policy were also felt elsewhere in the economy. The government gave up the unrealistic concept of "the country of iron and steel" and the policy of forced industrialization, and a better balanced industrial complex became the aim. It should be noted that in these years the transformation of industrial policy was not as successful as were, for example, the new agrarian policy or the attempt to raise the living standard. The attempt to achieve autarky was not abandoned, but the proposed solutions were somewhat more reasonable. For example, the mining of expensive hard coal was given up, and plants were fueled instead by low-quality lignite, which made it possible to increase the available electric power and at a lower cost. Chemical industries were replacing metallurgy as the preferred industrial sector; especially rapid was the growth in the production of plastics, chemical fertilizers, and other basic items. While this change appeared more reasonable than the previous metallurgy-centered policy, it required a considerable increase in the importation of oil. While in some cases industrial policy became more realistic, in general it failed to create an industrial complex that allowed local forces to come to the fore. The policy failed to identify those industries which would have permitted a small country, whose economy reacted sharply to the changes on the world market, to react flexibly to these changes and thus create favorable conditions for international trade.

Because industrialization in general was pursued with vigor, the country was an industrial state by the mid-1960s. By about the same time the pool of potential workers had been exhausted, and new labor-intensive industries could not be established. The only way to assure further growth was to increase productivity and improve the available technologies. The needed changes required that the methods of management, the system of stimulants, and the organs which operated with the help of obligatory plans and directives, disregarding the market, be revamped. This realization was also based on the repeated occurrence of economic problems. There were serious imbalances in the economy, and the load of amortizing the national debt grew (because of limited export possibilities) to about two-and-a-half times the hard currency income of the country in 1964–65. Other unfavorable indicators which reappeared included wasteful production, resulting in a growing stock of poor quality unuseable goods, the typical consequence of the producers' lack of interest in the market. These useless stockpiles grew to 7–8 percent of the GNP, about twice the amount spent on national defense.

All these phenomena turned attention again to the economic reforms which had been postponed in 1957. The government, having learned a lesson from the events of 1953–56, ordered a reexamination of its earlier position without waiting to be forced to do so by political unrest and visible discontent.

The New Economic Policy

The reform process began in the summer of 1964, when a critical review of the functioning of the Hungarian economy was set into motion. Once again specialists of all kinds were mobilized and entrusted with a task which was supposed to take two years. Based on their work, the Central Committee of the HSWP decided in May 1966 to introduce a new set of reforms. The most crucial measure was the new price system, which became effective on January 1, 1968. The most important aspect of this change was that while central planning was retained, obligatory plan directives were abolished. The central plan still bound the government, but not the various plants. The newly independent enterprises were to be regulated by the government through indirect economic means, the so-called regulators, including taxes, price regulations, and wage guidelines. Rather than simply fulfilling 100 percent of the obligations placed on them by the planners' obligatory directives, plants now had to concentrate on the profits they could make by selling their products in the market.

The end of planning by obligatory directives was a turning point in the history of East European socialist economies and offered a new model. What had existed previously only in Hungarian agriculture now became the basis of the entire planning system. The majority of prices were no longer fixed by the state but fluctuated in accordance with supply and demand in the marketplace. The state continued to supervise and control the main economic processes, and prices remained fixed for basic foods and raw materials, allowing the government to react to rising prices and to limit the effects of inflation.

The principles of the proposed reforms were not fully followed when the measures of 1965–68 were promulgated. Compromises and certain safety measures were built into the system, mainly to minimize the difficulties resulting from changing over to a new way of running the economy. The debates that preceded the reforms pointed to two main dangers: unemployment and inflation. Companies interested in the market and profits could easily have fired those workers they did not need, and the influence of the world market could easily have driven up prices.

Both of these consequences of economic reform hit Yugoslavia in the middle of the 1960s. The government, consequently, did not wish to follow the principles of rentability and competitiveness at the price of creating unemployment. It wanted to maintain full employment and to retain control over prices to permit it to slow down inflation. It found the means of control by instituting a wage regulatory system which tied the companies' hands. The price paid for avoiding unemployment was a somewhat expensive and less competitive production. Inflation was controlled by fixing the prices of basic foods and raw materials, often with the help of subsidies paid to the producers. There was no serious inflation following the 1968 reforms. For years prices rose on the average by only 2–3 percent annually, while those on the world market increased much more steeply. However, a price had to be paid for low inflation also. The government protected industries by supplying them with raw materials at a price which was lower than what the state paid. Therefore, these enterprises did not feel the effects of the world market and did not adjust to them.

In spite of these problems, the changes produced significant results. The policy centered on the standard of living adopted earlier now came to full fruition because both individuals and enterprises could pursue their own interests. From the mid-sixties to the mid-seventies, Hungary's economy lived through its "golden decade," during which the real wages of workers and salaries of employees grew yearly by 3–4 percent. Including the advances made since 1957, the per capita real wage and consumption level of the population was three times greater at the end of the 1970s than it had been in 1956–57.

Agriculture too reacted favorably to the new situation. Between 1950 and 1967, the entire pre-reform period, the average yearly production growth of Hungarian agriculture was 0.7 percent. Between 1968 and the early 1980s, the yearly growth rate jumped to 3–4 percent. The significance of this becomes clear when it is compared to the growth rate of world agriculture. After 1968 the growth of Hungarian agriculture was double the world's average, and in the decade 1972–82, it was the second highest in the world after the Netherlands. The pricing policy and the connected agrarian policy made the establishment of large-scale "industrialized" agriculture possible, placing Hungary third in the world in per capita grain and meat production.

The so-called infrastructural and service sectors of the economy were also considerably altered, particularly in transportation, in the building of apartments and construction in general, and in the mass services of health and education. These once stagnating sectors grew the most rapidly after the introduction of the reforms. The construction industry, with its 8 percent yearly growth rate, became the most rapidly developing branch of the entire Hungarian economy.

In the 1970s, the number of those employed in industry began to diminish. The earlier labor-intensive industrial growth was gradually replaced by growth based on technological modernization and higher productivity. The minor reforms introduced after 1956 and the comprehensive reform of 1968 transformed the developmental strategy of the 1940s, an imitation of the Soviet model, into a specifically Hungarian economic model. The philosophy of the reform, however—combining the advantages of central planning and a market system—was basically a failure.

Societal Changes

Industrialization has always resulted in radical changes in social structure and introduced new lifestyles. In Hungary this tendency was reinforced by the various experiments aiming to create a specifically Hungarian socialist society.

One of the greatest changes that occurred in the social stratification of the country was the disappearance of former strongly hierarchical structure. The census of 1949 still registered 56 percent of the gainfully occupied population in agriculture. Within three decades, by the early 1980s, their number was reduced to 12–13 percent (to 20 percent if those are included who did industrial work in the agricultural sector). Most of the people had become either blue or white collar workers and earned approximately the same wages. Before 1968 the highest paid 10 percent of the population earned only three times as much as the lowest paid 10 percent. In a large factory, an unskilled laborer was paid two-thirds of the general manager's salary, and a skilled worker earned only 10–15 percent less than an engineer. The peasantry, which in the past had its own hierarchy (consisting of the landless, the holders of small plots, and the rich peasants), was transformed into a unified group of members of collective farms, whose income by the 1970s was as high as that of the urban workers or employees.

The urban population, which had been 38 percent of the total during the Second World War, made up over 50 percent of the inhabitants of the country by 1968. While Budapest with its 2.2 million inhabitants remained the only metropolitan center, Szeged, Miskolc, Győr, Pécs, and Debrecen, cities of 200,000 or so inhabitants, became the true economic, administrative, and cultural centers of their regions.

While the villages lost inhabitants for a while, this process ceased in the mid-1960s. About half of the industrial workers continued to live permanently in their villages and sought employment in nearby industrial centers. The percentage of the population which lived in isolated homesteads or settlements with less than five hundred inhabitants shrunk to 14 percent. Living conditions improved, and the use of household appliances and the improved communication system altered the former primitive and isolated living conditions of most rural families.

Another important feature of social equalization was universal and practically free social and health insurance. Before the war only one-third of the population was covered. By 1960, the number of those covered had doubled and ten years later these services were extended to all as part of their rights as citizens.

Tremendous inequalities caused by social stratification had long existed in the Hungarian educational system. Within thirty years after the war, great progress was made in equalizing the educational level of the population. Before the war, 200,000 children entered school each year, but less than a fifth reached the eighth grade. Even more important was the increase in the number of high school students. Before the war only children of the elite, about 10 percent of those aged fourteen to eighteen, attended these schools. By the 1970s, 90 percent of this age group entered high school and 50 percent finished. In 1980, young people finished, on the average, eleven years of schooling. University education, although far behind the level of the advanced industrial countries, was attracting 10 percent of those between eighteen and twenty-four instead of the 1–1.5 percent before the war. Education on all levels was free, and half of those attending universities came from worker or peasant families.

This cultural leveling and social equalization was paralleled by the rapid increase of the living standard and consumption. Real wages, which had fallen by 22 percent between 1949 and 1953, tripled, as already mentioned, between 1956 and 1978. Within twenty-five years somewhere between two-thirds and three-fourths of the population made the transition from village life to an urban-industrial existence. Television, which spread rapidly only after 1957, changed the way in which people spent their free time and ended the isolation of entire regions. In 1960, a washing machine was still a rarity and electric refrigerators were practically unknown. Within two decades, three-quarters of the households were fully equipped. The triumphal march of the automobile also began in 1960. By 1980, every third family owned a car.

In 1950, there were 260,000 families who could not find an apartment, and in 1960 340,000. The one million units built between 1960 and 1975 serve one-third of the country's inhabitants. The shortage of housing, however, remains the most important social problem, especially for young people and families.

According to reliable surveys, one-third of Hungarian families read regularly. In a country with fewer than eleven million inhabitants, museums are visited yearly by eighteen million people. Before the war, about 100–200,000 people traveled outside Hungary every year, but during the 1950s the country was practically closed. In the 1970s and 1980s, the yearly average of those who visited foreign countries rose to one million.

The Sciences and the Arts

After the ideologically determined "compulsory" artistic taste had been terminated, science and the arts began a new life. Significant technological achievements remained a rarity, but theoretical mathematics, on the other hand, remained a strong point, due to succeeding generations of men like Lipót Fehér, Frigyes Riesz, Pál Turán, Pál Erdős, and their pupils. Social sciences began to develop in the 1960s. György Lukács and some of his school, along with historians, sociologists, and psychologists whose fields were banned in the 1950s, and especially the Hungarian school of economics played an important part not only in presenting a true picture of society, but even in changing it. In the mid 1970s, however, Lukács's best pupils were purged and forced to emigrate.

To a considerable extent, the social sciences took over both the traditional function of art and literature—to recognize and publicize social problems—and the typically East-European function of literature—to act as the nation's "prophet." This does not mean, however, that the arts did not retain their social and political importance. After the limits imposed on expression by the pre-1956 regimes, it was quite understandable that people developed a passion for the depiction of reality, even if it took the form of documentary presentation. Literature and the motion picture industry did a great deal to satisfy this demand and, to some extent, to create and popularize it. Several successful Hungarian film makers, among them Miklós Jancsó, István Szabó, Pál Gábor, and Károly Makk, played a leading role in exploring and artistically explaining the early 1950s and the present.

Gyula Illyés, the dean of generations of Hungarian poets, continued the strong tradition of Hungarian poetry. The strength and renewal of the "queen of arts" was also demonstrated by the original and revolutionary populist-surrealistic voices of Ferenc Juhász and László Nagy. Poetry devoted to eternal values and the problems of mankind, such as the works of Sándor Weörös, János Pilinszky, and Ágnes Nemes-Nagy, however, represented the continuity of the best humanistic tradition of Mihály Babits and Dezső Kosztolányi. Poetry, nevertheless, lost its leading position and characteristic prophetic mission after the 1960s due to the modern social-political transformation of the country and the development of the social sciences.

The demand for realism determined the work of artists. It is interesting and ironic that in the 1950s, when the cultural policy-makers constantly preached "realism," the artistic "production" had nothing to do with reality, and indeed presented facts in a falsified manner. When cultural policy tolerated truth and stated that it could be expressed in various ways, then the depicting of reality created its own genre of expression in the arts. It is worth noting that the great variety of styles that suddenly flourished did not concentrate exclusively on presenting reality, but, after long years when one could only talk about things in superlatives, the typically East and Central European grotesque depiction of everyday life also reappeared.

Obviously, there is no direct relationship between the economy and the arts. Yet, it might have been more than pure coincidence that the major economic changes coincided with equally significant innovations in the arts, such as the epoch-making art of István Örkény. His first important play appeared in 1967. It was followed by his greatest theatrical works and by his "one minute short novels," which were unusual, even grotesque, yet accurately presented simultaneously several aspects of historical events in a manner both conducive to laughter and moving.

Probably the least mentioned yet most important Hungarian art form of the
period was post-Bartók music, which developed rapidly in the works of Sándor
Balassa, Endre Szöllösi, and Zsolt Durkó. This music was a hallmark of the
country's new social-intellectual orientation and prosperity.

Social Stresses in the 1970s

The economic, social, and intellectual processes which followed the reforms of
1968 caused certain social conflicts. As already indicated, before 1968 the ratio
between the lowest and highest salaries was 3:1; it quickly changed after that year
to 9:1. The values of socialism preached earlier, including financial equality, fixed
prices, and a modest but comfortable guaranteed living standard appeared to be
endangered. Social stresses developed, and the workers complained that peasants
and intellectuals profited more from the reforms than they did. The bureaucracy,
in turn, felt that its influence and privileges were disappearing.

Based on these complaints, the reforms were criticized for favoring petty
bourgeois values, growing acquisitive tendencies, and individual and company
self-interest at the expense of collective interest and socialism. At the end of
1972, a well-organized attack was launched against the reforms. While the new
organizational structure could not be changed, and planning enforced by directives could not be reintroduced, several steps were taken backward in the direction of recentralization. The ancillary industrial plants of agricultural
cooperatives, the peasantry's household plots, and the secondary activities of the
intellectuals came under attack and were regulated by new ordinances. The
independence of industrial enterprises was restricted by more determined intervention by the central organs, special regulations for the fifty largest enterprises,
the introduction of numerous exceptions to the general regulations, and, most
frequently, through informal intervention. To counteract the growing social differentiation, all wages were raised by 15 percent in 1974, and young workers
were admitted to universities even if they had not finished high school. Ideological purification was carried out. In the midst of this retreat from reform, Hungary had to face the oil crisis of the fall of 1973 and the world-wide economic
crisis it unleashed.

The Consequences of the Economic Crisis

The economic crisis affected Hungary powerfully. Hungary had to import great
quantities of fuels and raw materials and had difficulties in exporting her industrial
products, which faced growing international competition while often being of
inferior quality. After 1973, the prices of raw materials increased sharply, while

those of Hungarian exports rose much more slowly. As with all small states, Hungary is very sensitive to international markets, realizing about half of her GNP by foreign trade. Hungary lost 20 percent of its trade within a few short years.

The government, nevertheless, did not slow the economic growth rate between 1973 and 1978. This decision was based, in part, on the conviction that the crisis would not be of long duration, and, in part, on the fact that the authorities wished to maintain a rapid growth rate for ideological reasons. Thus the required yearly GNP growth rate of 5-6 percent required a yearly increase of foreign trade of 10-12 percent. The result was that the growing trade deficit produced a loss equivalent to one year's national income in the decade following 1973. This was the equivalent of Hungary's losses during World War II! The positive trade balance of the early 1970s became, by 1978, a foreign debt of about eight billion dollars. The amortization obligation was a heavy load on the economy, which began to show the signs of being out of balance.

In the resulting emergency, it became necessary to limit the percentage of the national income that could be invested or consumed domestically, and imports had to be reduced drastically. Between 1979 and 1984, the share of the GNP used for new investments was drastically reduced from 25-27 percent to 10-12 percent. The living standard–based economic policy pursued for some twenty-five years also suffered a setback, and during the same years the average per capita real wage declined by about 10-11 percent. The restrictions succeeded in reestablishing a balance in foreign trade and assured that the country was able to pay its bills and debts even in the most difficult years. This fact by itself, however, did not supply the answer to the question of how the country would be able to manage its affairs in the long run.

Certain people argued that when the situation is unfavorable on the world market, the country should withdraw from it and adopt a policy centered on economic autarky, at least within the CMEA framework. This outdated policy, however, given the country's possibilities, could no longer be considered seriously. After the slowdown of the economy and considerable uncertainty, lengthy debate and serious theoretical work gradually produced new solutions to the country's problems. The first result was a new economic policy decision taken in October 1977 by the Party and the government, concerning long-range foreign trade strategy. For the first time the strategy of import-substituting industrialization was given up. Its place was taken by an export-oriented development, which aimed to make the strongest sectors of the economy, which really decided the tempo of its development, capable of export even if its products had to be judged by the strictest measures applied on the world market. Obviously, it was not enough to declare a new policy. It was necessary to create the preconditions for its realization.

The New Economic Reform Debate

This need to create an export industry capable of competing on the world market made the continuation of economic reforms (that is, the return to the principles of the 1968 reform) the major issue beginning in the late 1970s. After 1979, the first task became the restoration of the 1968 reforms by reestablishing their crippled organizational and operational framework. To achieve this goal, in the summer of 1979 and again in 1980, factory and consumer prices were revised. Consumer prices were raised by about 20 percent, which increased the rate of inflation. In these years, the general price level rose by about 10 percent, something which had not happened since 1946. This inflation rate declined temporarily to 5 percent, but rose again to 8–9 percent in 1983–84. In 1980–81, the factory prices, designed to create new export-inducing conditions, tied domestic prices of numerous industrial sectors to those of the world market, for the first time in the history of socialist states. All those industries which sold at least 5 percent of their production abroad had to calculate their domestic prices according to their export profits. This change was paralleled by the substantial lowering of state subsidies, which had, once again, proliferated after 1973.

The prices of many services, including rents, transportation, and cultural events, continued to be heavily subsidized, but in industry, where the adjustment to the world market was most important, the enforcement of real values began. The pressures exercised by the world market were felt more and more by the enterprises as the government shielded them less and less. In other sectors of the economy the radicalization of reform also made progress.

One of the contradictions of the 1968 reform was that while the government had hoped to force the companies to compete by allowing fluctuation of prices in accordance with market conditions, it left the structure of the enterprises unchanged. Immense industrial monopolies continued to exist, some of them controlling the total production of an entire industrial sector. This fact excluded any possible competition. Early in the 1980s, the government began to break up these monopolies, to transform structurally the over-centralized enterprises, and to establish numerous small and middle-sized companies. This transformation was not limited to industry, but touched the service sectors as well, and included a change in management too. The industrial branch ministries were abolished and replaced by a single Ministry of Industry. The ministry was put in charge only of industrial policy-making, whereas the old branch ministries had played a direct role in managing the various enterprises. Thus, this structural change contributed significantly to the independent decision-making on the plant and company level.

The post-1979 reform process included the steady encouragement of private undertakings—the legalization of the so-called "second economy." In the 1980s, a larger role was assigned to small cooperatives, which could be organized in the most diverse branches and sectors of industrial production and service industries. People were encouraged to join these cooperatives as their second place of work or could make them their sole occupation with special permission. These cooperatives and also private shops have improved services in all kinds of repair-oriented occupations, trucking and taxi services, and nursery schools, to give only a few examples, by utilizing the means in private hands at a time when the state was unable to make them available. In the state-owned large industrial enterprises, worker-engineer cooperatives were established. Members sign contracts with their own companies, whose machinery and tools they use. They do overtime work on their own for considerably higher pay, increasing labor input significantly. The result is that while legal working hours had been curtailed to 40 hours per week, the activities of these cooperatives and individuals increased the total working hours on a voluntary basis. Previously this phenomenon was observable only in agriculture, where half the number of those employed in industry contributed the same number of working hours as the industrial work force. This resulted in part from the voluntary extra working hours devoted to the cultivation of the household plots, but mainly from the labor of the entire family and often that of "marginally available" workers. The latter involved the help of family members employed in industry or services, as well as of those living on pensions, etc. In agriculture, one-third of the country's production came from household plots, and in services about the same percentage came from the new cooperatives and private initiatives. The percentage of work done by the new work groups in industrial production and construction also increased rapidly. Both increased substantially the income of the population. According to some calculations about 40–50 percent of the population's income was earned in these supplementary activities.

This newly legal activity influenced income differentiation much more significantly than wage and salary levels did, depending on who was either capable of or willing to undertake supplementary work. While nearly two-thirds of the population was able to increase its income with supplementary activities at a time when real wages were declining, the living standard of the remaining one-third deteriorated significantly in comparison.

Changes on the domestic economic front were paralleled by those in the international sphere. The Hungarian government did not begin to respond to the world economic crisis that began in 1973 until 1979, and it spent the next five years trying to adjust its policies piecemeal. By the early 1980s it was obvious that limited reform had failed. It was also recognized that economic change could not be introduced successfully without abolishing the monolithic political system. János Kádár rapidly lost his earlier popularity and his regime's legitimacy was challenged. Opposition groups, becoming stronger and more outspoken, urged the establishment of political democracy. The reform wing of the ruling party became radicalized as well, and a sense of moral crisis contributed to the further erosion of the system. The Party Congress that was called in April 1985 to face these problems was charged with producing a blueprint for a new, thoroughgoing reform program. Its answer, however, was an ineffectual effort to mobilize the crisis-ridden economy.

EPILOGUE, 1985–1990

George Barany

János Kádár survived the 1985 Party Congress, but most observers agreed that in spite of his retention in office this meeting ended the Kádár period that had begun in 1956. The restructuring of the Politburo, the emergence of Károly Grósz and Imre Pozsgay as leading figures in the party, the admission that the economic reforms of 1968 were cut short too early and that the party/government had to initiate a new reform program to undo the harm which this partial ending of reforms brought with it, and the warning to the population that living standards would decline and life would become more difficult before new reforms could bring a new period of relative well being—added up to an admission that the leadership had made serious mistakes. Thus, a restructured Politburo, a new prime minister (Károly Grósz), and the admission that economic reform was impossible without social and political changes signaled the end of the Kádár period.

Following the 1985 congress, measures were introduced aimed at creating a more flexible economic mechanism to develop export-oriented production. Changes in price structure, a gradual elimination of subsidies, and a change in the managerial structure were planned by the regime. In place of an overcentralized economy operating with the help of obligatory plan-directives, indirect state guidance, based on a combination of planning and market forces, was introduced. It was not, however, an economy based on the free play of market forces.

These changes were important, but they did not go far enough. One example will illustrate the considerable difficulties that remained. According to Hungarian economists, the paperwork connected with the new state guidance policy was still so cumbersome that on the average it occupied about twenty percent of a given enterprise's work force. Eliminating these procedures would lower prices and increase export potential, argued the party and the government, but at the same time it would increase unemployment to an unacceptable level. Consequently, the expected advantages did not materialize, while the burden placed on the population by the gradual elimination of subsidies increased.

A clear indication of the socio-economic problem and the declining living standard was the government's admission, in 1987, that the inflation rate had reached seventeen percent. The true rate was probably double this figure. Salaries, and especially pensions, did not increase proportionally. As a result about two million people, twenty percent of the population, lived at the subsistence level or below it. The resulting social pressures led in 1988 to the replacement of Kádár by Grósz as general secretary of the party and the appointment of Miklós Németh, an advocate of more drastic reforms, as prime minister.

These same social pressures, combined with the changes introduced in the Soviet Union by Mikhail S. Gorbachev, speeded further changes in Hungary. The Hungarian equivalent of *glasnost* and the obvious need for *perestroika* in Hungary were two important factors. Even more critical, the Soviet president's apparent rejection of the Brezhnev Doctrine and his admission that each social-ist country had a right to go its own way removed a major restraint on those who demanded change; they did not have to fear Soviet intervention any longer.

When in July 1987 the government announced further austerity measures, the astoundingly rapid and very exciting transformation of Hungary began making headlines all over the world. The strikes of printers and coal miners were the first manifestations of discontent and popular demand for fundamental change. Independent trade unions such as the Scientific Workers Democratic Union began to appear. Opposition groups and later opposition parties such as the Democratic Forum also emerged, and long-suppressed parties such as the Small-holders reappeared.

The forces that produced these first visible signs of discontent unleashed in rapid sequence numerous dramatic changes. All of these had social, political, and economic implications, but for simplicity's sake they will be grouped under various headings.

As regards the party, the first major change occurred only a year after Grósz became first secretary. In mid 1989 he was replaced by a quartet consisting of Németh, the prime minister; Grósz; Imre Pozsgay, the best-known and most popular "reform communist"; and Rezső Nyers, the author of the 1968 reforms. Nyers became the presiding officer of this new ruling body of the party. This measure failed to regain even a modicum of popularity and credit for the party which, on October 7, 1989, proclaimed its own dissolution and reconstituted itself as the Hungarian Socialist Party. Grósz and other hardliners left the new party and formed their own. Mass defections from both parties followed, and neither had as many as 120,000 members at the end of 1989.

On the broader political front the acceptance by the then still-intact Commu-nist Party of multi-party elections (February 13, 1989) and the necessary change in the Hungarian constitution enacted by parliament, removing the party's posi-tion as the constitutional leading force in the country, made the various opposi-tion forces legal and equal, irrespective of whether they called themselves parties or movements. Hungary became, officially, a multi-party state, comparing itself with Western democracies.

The new political realities required a reevaluation of the country's history since World War II. Looking back to the years from 1945 to 1962, Prime Minis-ter Németh admitted that "over one million peasants had been sentenced, in-terned or otherwise punished in some way." He referred to the two collectivization drives. There were, obviously, people from other walks of life who also suffered during the Stalinist years and those following the revolution of

1956. It was not enough to acknowledge that 1956 was a true revolution and to rehabilitate Imre Nagy and those condemned with him. Nagy's reburial in the summer of 1989 was a celebration of the courage and martyrdom of those who suffered because of the roles they played during this revolution. The monuments planned in their honor did not give full due to Hungarians who were victims of the previous regimes. Still, at the end of the 1980s the government was restoring Hungary as a *Rechtsstaat*, in which the human and civil rights of every citizen were guaranteed.

That in spite of all these monumental changes the population at large was still distrustful of the country's government was illustrated by the November 27, 1989, elections, in which voters rejected the government's plan to elect the country's president in spite of the fact that the rather well-liked Pozsgay was the government's candidate. The selection of a president was postponed until after the free multi-party parliamentary elections scheduled for the spring of 1990.

In the international sphere the most dramatic and visible change was the removal in the fall of 1989 of the electronic warning system on the Austrian-Hungarian border. This measure followed the granting of free travel rights to all Hungarians and the removal of visa requirements by the Austrian and Hungarian governments for travel by the citizens of their respective countries. Less dramatic and visible were the numerous attempts of the government to join the various international financial and commercial organizations to bring Hungary not just politically, but also economically into the democratic Western world. The Socialist Party of the German Federal Republic even promised to sponsor the admission of Hungary into the West European Common Market. The United States Congress and several Western governments promised economic help to Hungary in an effort to facilitate this transformation.

As the 1980s drew to a close, Hungary appeared to have broken with the Communist decades since 1945 and to be well on the way to a democratic society and a free market–oriented economy. Yet the problems and difficulties that the country faced were still enormous. No socialist country had ever tried to move from a collectivist to a free market economy and from a one-party dictatorship to a multi-party democracy. Hungary, like the other countries of Eastern Europe, had no model to follow. It had to start from scratch in trying to reorganize and rebuild itself.

In the economic realm the country faced enormous difficulties in spite of the help promised by the Western democracies. It had the largest per capita foreign debt of any debtor country but could not go to the extremes of austerity that Ceauşescu imposed in Romania to repay that country's foreign obligations. Hungary was no longer a dictatorship, and her population would not tolerate further autocratic decisions. On the contrary, whoever became responsible for the country's well being after the spring 1990 election would have to face a further deterioration of the living standard, continuing inflation, and the unavoidable, growing unemployment that would result from the restructuring of the country's economy.

The new government's strength and composition appeared unpredictable as

1989 ended. The number of political parties and associations was constantly increasing; more than fifty existed at the end of 1989. While most of these were too small to be of significance, even the "big" parties could not boast of sizable memberships. In most cases, membership remained under 50,000. A coalition government appeared to be the most likely outcome of the 1990 elections. Such governments have proven rather weak historically, whereas the emerging new Hungary would certainly need a democratic but nevertheless strong government, enjoying the backing of a majority of the voters.

The economic and political uncertainty was heightened by the reemergence of some old problems. These included a nationalism going beyond the understandable and justified pride in the country's history and recent accomplishments as well as a legitimate interest in the fate of Hungarians living in the neighboring states, especially Romania. There were signs of a chauvinism inimical to the country's minorities. No reliable figures were available, but the number of non-Magyars in Hungary was estimated at between 4.5 and 9 percent of the population. While the new freedom of expression included discussions of the minorities' needs, the growing chauvinism would have to be checked before the minorities could feel that the new Hungary was their country, too.

Although no one questioned that any democracy, the emerging new Hungary included, must guarantee freedom of religion, debates about the role of churches and church-state relations raised serious problems and brought the reemergence of anti-Semitic statements and manifestations.

Unemployment and austerity made it easy to blame minorities, including the Jews. Hungary's new government would have to combat this tendency, whatever the combination of parties forming the coalition turned out to be. National unity would be needed to face a difficult future and to retain the good will of the West.

Hungarians could certainly be proud of what they had accomplished at the end of the 1980s. Together with Poland, Hungary not only took advantage of the loosening of Soviet controls but became a model for other "socialist" states, including the Soviet Union, on their way to a new, free form of government. Nevertheless, it would be fatal to forget that serious domestic problems still demanded solution. It should also be remembered that Hungary was not living in a vacuum and that much of the future development in that country would also depend on the changes in the international situation, including developments in the Soviet Union. Thus, while this Epilogue ends on a much more optimistic note than did the preceding chapter, numerous questions remain unanswered.

SOME SUGGESTED
ADDITIONAL READINGS

General Works

Czigány, Loránt, *The Oxford History of Hungarian Literature* (Oxford, 1984).
Eckhart, Ferenc, *A Short History of the Hungarian People* (London, 1931).
Helmreich, Ernest C. (ed.), *Hungary* (New York, 1957).
Kelleher, Patrick J., *Holy Crown of Hungary* (Rome-New York, 1951).
Kosáry, Dominic G., *A History of Hungary* (Cleveland, 1941).
Lengyel, Emil, *1000 Years of Hungary* (New York, 1958).
Macartney, Carlile A., *Hungary* (London, 1934).
Pamlényi, Ervin (ed.), *A History of Hungary* (London, 1975).
Sayous, Édouard, *Histoire générale des Hongrois* (Paris, 1900).
Sinor, Denis, *History of Hungary* (New York, 1959).

Chapters I–IV

Alföldi, András, *Der Untergang der Römerherrschaft in Pannonien* (Berlin-Leipzig, 1924).
Bartha, Antal, *Hungarian Society in the 9th and 10th Centuries* (Budapest, 1975).
Bogyay, Thomas von, *Stephanus Rex* (Vienna, 1975).
Dienes, István, *The Hungarians Cross the Carpathians* (Budapest, 1972).
Dóbó, Árpád, *Die Verwaltung der römischen Provinz Pannonien von Augustus bis Diocletianus* (Budapest-Amsterdam, 1968).
Fodor, István, *In Search of a New Homeland: The Prehistory of the Hungarian People and the Conquest* (Budapest, 1982).
Győrffy, György, "Die Entstehung der ungarischen Burgorganisation," *Acta Archeologica Academiae Scientiarum Hungaricae* XXVIII (1976), pp. 323–58.
———, "Formation d'États au IXe siècle suivant les 'Gesta Hungarorum' du Notair Anonyme," *Nouvelles Études Historiques,* I (Budapest, 1965), pp. 27–54.
Hóman, Bálint, *Geschichte des ungarischen Mittelalters*, II (Berlin, 1940–43).
———, *King Stephen the Saint* (Budapest, 1938).
Kniezsa, István, *Ungarns Völkerschaften im IX. Jahrhundert* (Budapest, 1938).
Kosztolnyik, Zoltán J., *Five Eleventh Century Hungarian Kings* (Boulder, 1981).
———, "The Church and the Hungarian Court under Coloman the Learned," *East European Quarterly,* XVIII/2 (1984), pp. 130–41.
Macartney, Carlile A., *The Magyars of the IXth Century* (Cambridge, 1930).

Mályusz, Elemér, *Geschichte des ungarischen Volkstums von der Landnahme bis zum Ausgang des Mittelalters* (Budapest, 1940).

Mócsy, András, *Die Bevölkerung Pannoniens bis zu den Markomannenkriegen* (Budapest, 1959).

Móor, Elemér, "Studien zur Frühgeschichte und Urgeschichte des ungarischen Volkes," *Acta Enthographica Academiae Scientiarum Hungaricae,* II/1–4 (Budapest, 1951), pp. 25–142.

Moravcsik, Gyula, "Byzantine Christianity and the Magyars in the Period of their Migration," *American Slavic and East European Review,* XIV (1946), pp. 29–45.

———, "The Role of the Byzantine Church in Medieval Hungary," *American Slavic and East European Review,* XVIII–XIX (1947), pp. 134–51.

Simonyi, Dezső, "Die Kontinuitätsfrage und das Erscheinen der Slawen in Pannonien," *Studia Slavica Academiae Scienciarum Hungaricae,* I/4 (Budapest, 1955), pp. 333–61.

Vajay, Szabolcs, *Der Entritt des ungarischen Stämmebundes in die Europäische Geschichte* (Mainz, 1968).

Chapter V

Bak, János M., *Königstum und Stände in Ungarn im 14.–16. Jahrhundert* (Wiesbaden, 1973).

De Ferdinandy, Michael, "Ludwig I von Ungarn (1342–1382)," *Südost-Forschungen,* XXI (1972), pp. 41–80.

Hóman, Bálint, *Gei Angioni di Napoli in Ungheria, 1290–1403* (Rome, 1938).

Komjáthy, Anthony, "Hungarian *Jobbágyság* in the Fifteenth Century," *East European Quarterly,* X/1 (1976), pp. 77–111.

Chapter VI

Atiya, Aziz S., *The Crusade of Nicopolis* (London, 1934).

Bak, János M. and Béla K. Király (eds.), *From Hunyadi to Rákóczi: War and Society in Medieval and Early Modern Hungary* (Brooklyn, 1982).

Birnbaum, Marianna, *Janus Pannonius* (Zagreb, 1981).

Bónis, György, "The Hungarian Feudal Diet," *Recueils de la Société Jean Bodin,* XXV (1965), pp. 287–307.

Fraknói, Vilmos, *Matthias Corvinus, König von Ungarn* (Freiburg, 1891).

Fügedi, Erik, *Castle and Society in Medieval Hungary* (Budapest, forthcoming).

———, "Hungarian Bishops in the Fifteenth Century," *Acta Historica Academiae Scientiarum Hungaricae,* XI (1965), pp. 375–91.

Gabriel, Astrik L., *The Medieval Universities of Pécs and Pozsony* (Frankfurt/ M., 1969).

Gerevich, László, *The Art of Buda and Pest in the Middle Ages* (Budapest, 1971).

Mályusz, Elemér, "Die Entstehung der ständischen Schichten im mittelalterischen Ungarn," *Études Historiques Hongroises*, I (1980), pp. 101–32.

―――, *Die Zentralisationsbestrebungen König Sigismunds in Ungarn* (Budapest, 1960).

Szakály, Ferenc, "Phases in Turco-Hungarian Warfare before the Battle of Mohács," *Acta Orientalia Academiae Scientiarum Hungaricae* XXIII (Budapest, 1979), pp. 65–111.

Chapters VII–VIII

Benda, Kálmán, "Der Haiduckenaufstand in Ungarn und das Erstarken der Stände in der Habsburgermonarchie, 1607–1608," *Nouvelles Études Historiques*, I (Budapest, 1965), pp. 285–94.

Daniel, David P., "The Fifteen Years War and the Protestant Response to Habsburg Absolutism in Hungary," *East Central Europe/L'Europe du Centre-Est*, I–II (1981), pp. 38–51.

Fekete, Lajós, *Buda and Pest under Turkish Rule* (Budapest, 1976).

Hengelmüller, Ladislaus, *Hungary's Fight for National Existence; The History of the Great Uprising Led by Francis II Rákóczi, 1703–1711*, II (London, 1913–14).

―――, *Franz Rákóczi und sein Kampf für Ungarns Freiheit* (Stuttgart-Berlin, 1913).

Káldy-Nagy, Gyula, "The Administration of the Sanjāq Registrations in Hungary." *Acta Orientalia Academiae Scientiarum Hungaricae*, XXI/2, (Budapest, 1968), pp. 181–223.

Köpeczi, Béla, "The Hungarian Wars of Independence in the 17th and 18th Centuries in Their European Context," in Ránki, György (ed.), *Hungarian History—World History* (Budapest, 1984), pp. 31–40.

Maksay, Ferenc, "Ungarns Landwitschaft zur Zeit der Türkenherrschaft," *Agrártörténti Szemle*, Supplement to Vol. X (Budapest, 1967), pp. 10–37.

McGowan, Bruce, *Economic Life in Ottoman Europe: Taxation, Trade and the Struggle for Land, 1600–1800* (Cambridge-New York, 1981).

Pillias, Étienne, *Études sur François II Rákóczi* (Paris, 1939).

Sinkovics, István, "Der Angriff der Osmanen im Donautal im 16. Jahrhundert," *Études Historiques Hongroises*, I (Budapest, 1975), pp. 347–81.

Sugar, Peter F., *Southeastern Europe under Ottoman Rule, 1354–1804* (Seattle-London, 1977).

Szabó, István, "Les grands domaines en Hongrie au début des temps modernes," *Revue d'Histoire Comparée*, XXV/2 (1947), pp. 167–92.

Szakály, Ferenc, "The 1526 Mohács Disaster," *The New Hungarian Quarterly*, XVIII (Budapest, 1977), pp. 43–63.

Székely, György, "Décadence du pouvoir Ottoman et les deux Miklós

Zrinyi," *Annales Universitatis Scientiarum Budapestinensis de Roland Eötvös nominatae, Sectio Historica,* IX (1967), pp. 31–59.

Székely, György and Fügedi Erik (eds.), *La Renaissance et la Reformation en Pologne et en Hongrie* (Budapest, 1963).

Várkonyi, Ágnes, "Hapsburg Absolutism and Serfdom in Hungary at the Turn of the XVIIth and XVIIIth Centuries," *Nouvelles Études Historiques,* I (Budapest, 1965), pp. 355–88.

Chapter IX

Depner, Maja, *Das Fürstentum Siebenbürgen im Kampf gegen Habsburg* (Stuttgart, 1938).

Foisel, John, *Saxons through Seventeen Centuries. A History of the Transylvanian Saxons* (Cleveland, 1936).

Hungarian Historical Society, *Siebenbürgen* (Budapest, 1940).

Kosáry, Dominic G., "Gabriel Bethlen; Transylvania in the 17th Century," *The Slavonic and East European Review,* XVII (1938), pp. 162–74.

Makkai, László, *Histoire de Transylvanie* (Budapest, 1946).

Molnár, Andrea, *Fürst Stefan Bocskay als Staatsmann und Persönlichkeit* (Munich, 1983).

Pascu, Ștefan, *A History of Transylvania* (Detroit, 1982).

Polish Academy of Sciences and Hungarian Academy of Sciences, *Étienne Batory. Roi de Pologne, Prince de Transylvanie* (Kraków, 1935).

Trocsányi, Zsolt, "Dignitätsadel und Beamtenintelligenz der Regierungsbehörden in Siebenbürgen des 16.-17. Jahrhunderts," *Études Historiques Hongroises,* I (Budapest, 1980), pp. 255–78.

Chapter X

Bárány, George, "Hoping against Hope: The Enlightened Age in Hungary," *American Historical Review,* LXXIX (1971), pp. 319–57.

Bernard, Paul B., *Jesuits and Jacobins. Enlightenment and Enlightened Despotism in Austria* (Urbana-Chicago-London, 1971).

————, *Joseph II* (New York, 1968).

————, *The Origins of Josephinism, Two Studies* (Colorado Springs, 1964).

Blanning, T. C. W., *Joseph II and Enlightened Despotism* (London, 1970).

Fejtő, François, *Un Habsbourg révolutionaire. Joseph II. Portrait d'un despot éclairé* (Paris, 1953).

Haselsteiner, Horst, *Joseph II und die Komitate Ungarns* (Vienna-Köln-Graz, 1983).

————, "Enlightened Absolutism and Estates Politics in Hungary at the Time of Joseph II," in Ránki, György (ed.), *Hungarian History—World History* (Budapest, 1984), pp. 51–58.

Heckenast, Gusztáv, "Les routiers intellectuels en Hongrie, 1780–1848," *Revue d'Histoire Comparée* XXVI/1 (1948), pp. 53–76.

Kann, Robert A., *A Study in Austrian Intellectual History from Late Baroque to Romanticism* (New York, 1960).

Kecskeméti, Károly, "Notes et rapports français sur la Hongrie au XVIIIème siècle," *Fontes Rerum Historiae Hungaricae in Archivis Extraneis*, IV (Brussels, 1963).

Király, Béla K., *Hungary in the Late Eighteenth Century* (New York, 1969).

Macartney, Carlile A., "Hungary" in Goodwin, Albert (ed.), *The European Nobility in the Eighteenth Century. Studies of the Nobilities of the Major European States in the Pre-Reform Era* (London, 1953), pp. 118–35.

Marczali, Henrik, *Hungary in the Eighteenth Century* (Cambridge, 1910).

McGill, William J., Jr., *Marie Theresa* (New York, 1972).

Mitrofanov, Paul von, *Joseph II*, II (Vienna, 1910).

Padover, K. Saul, *The Revolutionary Emperor, Joseph the Second* (London, 1934).

Révész, Imre, *Esquisse de l'histoire de la politique religieuse hongroise entre 1805 et 1860* (Budapest, 1960).

Révész, Imre and J. Stephen Kováts, *Hungarian Protestantism: Its Past, Present and Future* (Budapest, 1927).

Roider, Karl A. Jr., *Maria Theresa* (Englewood, N.J., 1973).

Sugar, Peter F., "The Influence of the Enlightenment and the French Revolution in Eighteenth Century Hungary," *Journal of Central European Affairs*, XVII/4 (1958), pp. 331–55.

Valjavec, Fritz, *Der Josephinismus* (Brno-Munich-Vienna, 1945).

Varga, János, *Typen und Probleme des bäuerlichen Grundbesitzes in Ungarn (1767–1849)* (Budapest, 1965).

Wandruszka, Adam, *Leopold II*, II (Vienna-Munich, 1965).

Chapter XI

Andics, Erszébet, *Metternich und die Frage Ungarns* (Budapest, 1973).

Arató, Endre, "Die verschiedenen Formen der nationalen Unterdrückung in Osteuropa und die Madjarisierung in der ersten Hälfte des 19. Jahrhunderts," *Studien zur Geschichte der Österreichisch-Ungarischen Monarchie* (Budapest, 1961), pp. 423–44.

Bárány, George, *Stephen Széchenyi and the Awakening of Hungarian Nationalism* (Princeton, 1968).

Csáky, Moritz, *Von der Aufklärung zum Liberalismus. Studien zum Frühliberalismus in Ungarn* (Vienna, 1981).

Deme, László, "Writers and Essayists and the Rise of Magyar Nationalism in the 1820's and 1830's," *Slavic Review*, XLIII/4 (1984), pp. 624–40.

Gottas, Friedrich, "Liberalismus and Nationalismus im ungarischen Reformzeitalter," *Österreichische Osthefte*, XVIII/1 (1976), pp. 26–43.

Iványi, Béla G., "From Feudalism to Capitalism: The Economic Background to Széchenyi's Reform in Hungary," *Journal of Central European Affairs*, XX/3 (1960), pp. 270–88.

Kállay, I., *Management of Big Estates in Hungary between 1711 and 1848* (Budapest, 1980).

Katona, Anna, *Mihály Vitéz Csokonai* (Boston, 1980).

Kosary, Dominic G., *Napoléon et la Hongrie* (Budapest, 1979).

Mérei, Gyula, "Der Aussenhandel des Königreiches Ungarn (1790–1848)," *Études Historiques Hongroises*, I (Budapest, 1980), pp. 429–59.

———, "Über einige Fragen der Anfänge der kapitalistischen Gewerbe-entwicklung in Ungarn," *Études Historiques Hongroises*, I (Budapest, 1960), pp. 721–75.

Sándor, Pál, *Deák und die Frage der Hörigen auf dem Reichstag der Jahre 1832–1836* (Budapest, 1977).

Schlitter, Hanns, *Ungarn*, Vol. III of *Aus Österreichs Vormärz* (Zürich-Leipzig, 1920).

Silági, Denis, *Ungarn und der geheime Mitarbeiterkreis Kaiser Leopolds II* (Munich, 1961).

Szabad, György, *Hungarian Political Trends between the Revolution and the Compromise (1849–1867)*; *Studia Historica #128* (Budapest, 1977).

Urbán, Aladár, "Attempts at Reform and the Lessons of History—Constitutional Models and the Beginnings of Political Journalism in Feudal Hungary, 1841–1842," *Études Historiques Hongroises*, I (Budapest, 1980), pp. 463–90.

Wagner, Francis S., "Széchenyi and the Nationality Problem in the Habsburg Empire," *Journal of Central European Affairs*, XX/3 (1960), pp. 289–311.

Chapter XII

Bődy, Paul, *Joseph Eötvös and the Modernization of Hungary, 1840–1870: A Study of Ideas of Individuality and Social Pluralism in Modern Politics*. In *Transactions of the American Philosophical Society*, LXII/2 (1972).

Deák, István, *A Lawful Revolution. Louis Kossuth and the Hungarians, 1848–1849* (New York, 1979).

Deme, László, *The Radical Left and the Hungarian Revolution of 1848* (Boulder, 1976).

Despalatović, Elinor M., *Ljudevit Gaj and the Illyrian Movement* (Boulder, 1975).

Engels, Friedrich, "Germany: Revolution and Counter-Revolution," in Leonard Krieger (ed.), Engels, *The German Revolutions* (Chicago, 1967), pp. 123–240.

Fejtő, François (ed.), *The Opening of an Era—1848: An Historical Symposium* (New York, 1966).

Görgei [sic], Arthur, *My Life and Acts in Hungary in the Years 1848–1849*, II (London, 1852).

Klapka, General George, *Memoirs of the War of Independence in Hungary*, II (London, 1850).

Pulszky, Theresa, *Memoirs of a Hungarian Lady* (Philadelphia, 1850).

Rath, R. John, *The Viennese Revolution of 1848* (Austin, 1957).

Robertson, Priscilla, *Revolutions of 1848. A Social History* (Princeton, 1852).
Rothenberg, Gunther E., *The Army of Francis Joseph* (West Lafayette, In., 1976).
_____ , *The Military Border in Croatia, 1740–1881* (Chicago, 1966).
Spira, György, *A Hungarian Count [Széchenyi] in the Revolution of 1848* (Richard E. Allen, trans.) (Budapest, 1974).
Sproxton, Charles, *Palmerston and the Hungarian Revolution* (Cambridge, 1919).
Stiles, William H., *Austria in 1848–49*, II (New York, 1852, reprinted in 1971).
Stroup, Edsel W., *Hungary in Early 1848* (Buffalo, 1977).

Chapter XIII

Barany, George, "Ungarns Verwaltung, 1848–1918," in Wandruszka, Adam and Peter Urbanitsch (eds.), *Die Habsburgermonarchie*, 6 vols. to date (Vienna, 1973–), II, pp. 304–468.
Bödy, Paul, *Joseph Eötvös and the Modernization of Hungary, 1840–1870* (Boulder, 1985).
Eisenman, Louis, *Le compromis Austro-Hongrois de 1867* (Paris, 1904).
Hidas, Peter I., "The Peasants in Hungary between Revolution and Compromise," *East European Quarterly*, XIX/2, pp. 191–200.
Király, Béla K., *Ferenc Deák* (Boston, 1975).
László, Peter, "The Dualist Character of the 1867 Hungarian Settlement," Ránki, György (ed.), *Hungarian History—World History* (Budapest, 1984), pp. 85–164.
Révész, László, "Die Bedeutung des Neoabsolutismus für Ungarn," *Der Donauraum*, XIV/3 (1969), pp. 146–54.
Sándor, Vilmos, *Die Hauptmerkmale der industriellen Entwicklung in Ungarn zur Zeit des Absolutismus, 1849–1867* (Budapest, 1960).
Schwarzenberg, Adolph, *Prince Felix zu Schwarzenberg, Prime Minister of Austria, 1848–1852* (New York, 1946).
Vantuch, Anton and L'udovit Holotik (eds.), *Der Österreichisch-Ungarische Ausgleich, 1867* (Bratislava, 1971).
Walter, Friedrich, "Von Windischgrätz über Welden zu Haynau," in his *Die Nationalitätenrage im alten Ungarn* (Munich, 1959), pp. 70–90.
Winter, Eduard, *Revolution, Neoabsolutismus und Liberalismus in der Donaumonarchie* (Vienna, 1969).

Chapters XIV–XV

Barany, George, "Magyar Jews of Jewish Magyars," *Canadian-American Slavic Studies*, VIII/1 (1979), pp. 1–44.

Berend, T. Iván and György Ránki, *Hungary: A Century of Economic Development* (New York, 1974).

Bridge, R. F., *Great Britain and Austria-Hungary, 1906-1914* (London, 1972).

Diószegi, István, *Hungarians in the Ballhausplatz* (Budapest, 1983).

Gottas, Friedrich, *Ungarn im Zeitalter des Hochliberalismus. Studien zur Tisza-Ära, 1871-1890* (Vienna, 1976).

Hanák, Péter (ed.), *Die nationale Frage in der Österreichisch-Ungarischen Monarchie, 1900-1918* (Budapest, 1966).

———, *Ungarn in der Donaumonarchie* (Vienna-Budapest, 1984).

Janos, Andrew C., *The Politics of Backwardness in Hungary, 1825-1945* (Princeton, 1982).

Jászi, Oscar, *The Dissolution of the Habsburg Monarchy* (Chicago, 1929).

Jeszenszky, Géza, "Hungary and *The Times* during the Political Crisis of 1904-1906," *Acta Historica Academiae Scientiarum Hungaricae*, XXI (1975), pp. 377-410.

Kann, Robert A., *A History of the Habsburg Empire, 1526-1918* (Berkeley-Los Angeles-London, 1974).

———, *The Multinational Empire*, II (New York, 1950).

Kann, Robert A. and Zdenek V. David, *The Peoples of the Eastern Habsburg Lands, 1526-1918* (Seattle-London, 1984).

Kann, Robert A., Béla K. Király and P. S. Fichtner (eds.), *The Habsburg Empire in World War I* (Boulder, 1977).

Kohn, Hans, *The Habsburg Empire* (Princeton, 1961).

Macartney, Carlile A., *The Habsburg Empire, 1790-1918* (London, 1968).

McCagg, William O., Jr., *Jewish Nobles and Geniuses in Modern Hungary* (Boulder, 1972).

May, Arthur J., *The Hapsburg Monarchy, 1867-1914* (Cambridge, Ma., 1951).

———, *The Passing of the Hapsburg Monarchy, 1914-1918* (Philadelphia, 1966).

Miskolczy, Gyula, *Ungarn in der Habsburger-Monarchie* (Vienna, 1959).

Plaschka, Richard G. and Karlheinz Mack (eds.), *Die Auflösung des Habsburgerreiches* (Munich, 1970).

Redlich, Joseph, *Emperor Francis Joseph of Austria* (New York, 1929).

Sándor, Vilmos and Péter Hanák (eds.), *Studien zur Geschichte der Österreichisch-Ungarischen Monarchie* (Budapest, 1961).

Seton-Watson, Robert W., *Racial Problems in Hungary* (London, 1908).

Sugar, Peter F., "An Underrated Event: The Hungarian Constitutional Crisis of 1905-06," *East European Quarterly*, XV/3 (1981), pp. 281-306.

Szekfű, Julius, *État et Nation* (Paris, 1945).

———, *Three Generations* (Budapest, 1920).

Taylor, A. J. P., *The Habsburg Monarchy, 1815-1918* (London, 1949).

Vermes, Gábor, *Count István Tisza* (Boulder, 1985).

Wandruszka, Adam and Urbanitsch, Peter (eds.), *Die Habsburgermonarchie, 1848-1918*, 6 vols. to date (Vienna, 1973-).

Winter, Stanley B. and Joseph Held (eds.), *Intellectual and Social Developments in the Habsburg Empire from Maria Theresa to World War I* (Boulder, 1975).

Zwitter, Fran, *Les Problèmes Nationaux dans la Monarchie des Habsbourg* (Belgrade, 1960).

Chapter XVI

Deák, Francis, *Hungary at the Paris Peace Conference* (New York, 1942).

Hajdu, Tibor, *The Hungarian Soviet Republic* (Budapest, 1979).

Jászi, Oscar, *Revolution and Counter-Revolution in Hungary* (London, 1924).

Károlyi, Michael, *Faith without Illusion* (London, 1956).

Tőkés, Rudolf L., *Béla Kun and the Hungarian Soviet Republic* (New York, 1967).

Völgyes, Ivan (ed.), *Hungary in Revolution, 1918–19* (Lincoln, Neb., 1971).

Chapters XVII–XVIII

Ádám, Magda, Gyula Juhász, and Lajos Kerekes (eds.), *Allianz Hitler-Horthy-Mussolini. Dokumente zur ungarischen Aussenpolitik (1933–1944)* (Budapest, 1966).

Barany, George, "The Dragon's Teeth; the Roots of Hungarian Fascism," in Peter F. Sugar (ed.), *Native Fascism in the Successor States, 1918–1945* (Santa Barbara, 1971), pp. 73–82.

Batkay, William A., *Authoritarian Politics in a Transitional State; István Bethlen and the Unified Party in Hungary, 1919–1926* (Boulder, 1982).

Berend, T. Iván and György Ránki, "Die Struktur der ungarischen Gesellschaft nach dem ersten Weltkrieg," *Acta Universitatis Debreceniensis,* IV (1965), pp. 95–131.

———, *The Hungarian Manufacturing Industry; Its Place in Europe (1900–1938)* (Budapest, 1960).

Braham, Randolph L., *The Destruction of Hungarian Jews* (New York, 1963).

———, *The Hungarian Labor Service System, 1939–1945* (New York, 1977).

Deák, István, "Hungary," in Rogger, Hans and Eugene Weber (eds.), *The European Right* (Berkeley, 1965), pp. 364–407.

Diószegi, István, "Die Aussenpolitik Ungarns zwischen den beiden Weltkriegen," *Annales Universitatis Scientiarum Budapestinensis, Sectio Historica,* XVII/1–2 (1976), pp. 239–58.

Fenyő, Marius D., *Horthy and Hungary. German-Hungarian Relations, 1941–1944* (New Haven-London, 1972).

Juhász, Gyula, *Hungarian Foreign Policy, 1919–1945* (Budapest, 1979).

Kállay, Miklós, *Hungarian Premier* (New York, 1958).

Kertész, Stephen, *Diplomacy in a Whirlpool* (Notre Dame, 1953).

Kis, Aladár, "Die Aussenpolitik der Imrédy Regierung (Nov. 1938–Feb. 1939)," *Annales Universitatis Scientiarum Budapestinensis, Sectio Historica*, III (1961), pp. 235–86.

Kónya, Sándor, "To the Attempt to Establish Totalitarian Fascism in Hungary," *Acta Historica Academiae Scientiarum Hungaricae*, XV/3–4 (1969), pp. 299–334.

Lackó, Miklós, *Arrow-Cross Men, National Socialists, 1935–1944* (Budapest, 1969).

Macartney, Carlile A., *Hungary and Her Successors, 1919–1937* (London, 1937).

———, *October Fifteenth. A History of Modern Hungary, 1929–1945*, II (Edinburgh, 1956–57).

Márkus, László, "Über den Charakter der herrschenden Elite des Horthy Regimes," *Acta Historica Academiae Scientiarum Hungaricae*, XVIII/1–2 (1972), pp. 119–47.

Nagy-Talavera, Nicholas M., *The Green Shirts and the Others* (Stanford, 1970).

Ránki, György, "The German Occupation of Hungary," *Acta Historica Academiae Scientiarum Hungaricae*, XI/1–4 (1965), pp. 261–83.

———, "The Problem of Fascism in Hungary," in Peter F. Sugar (ed.), *Native Fascism in the Successor States, 1918–1945* (Santa Barbara, 1971), pp. 65–72.

Rothschild, Joseph, "Hungary" in his *East Central Europe between the Two World Wars* (Seattle-London, 1974), pp. 137–99.

Sakmyster, Thomas, "From Habsburg Admiral to Hungarian Regent. The Political Metamorphosis of Miklós Horthy," *East European Quarterly*, XVII/2, (1983), pp. 129–48.

———, *Hungary, the Great Powers and the Danubian Crisis, 1936–1939* (Athens, Ga., 1981).

Szinai, Miklós and László Szücs (eds.), *The Confidential Papers of Admiral Horthy* (Budapest, 1965).

Tilkovszky, Loránt, *Nationalitätenpolitische Richtungen in Ungarn in der gegen-revolutionaren Epoche (1919–1945)* (Budapest, 1975).

———, *Pál Teleki, 1879–1941* (Budapest, 1974).

———, *Ungarn und die deutsche "Volksgruppenpolitik"* (Köln-Vienna, 1981).

Zsigmond, László, "Ungarn und das Münchner Abkommen," *Acta Historica Academiae Scientiarum Hungaricae*, VI/3–4 (1959), pp. 251–86.

Chapters XX–XXI

Aczél, Tamás and Tibor Méray, *The Revolt of the Mind* (New York, 1960).

Antal, Endre, "Der ungarische Aussenhandel," *Südosteuropa Mitteilungen*, XVIII/2 (1978), pp. 11–31.

———, "Ungarns Wirtschaftsplanung bis 1985," *Südosteuropa Mitteilungen*, XXI/4 (1981), pp. 15–33.

———, *Das Wirtschaftslenkungssystem des ungarischen Socialismus. Entwicklung seit 1968* (Munich, 1976).

Balassa, Béla A., *The Hungarian Experience in Economic Planning* (New Haven, 1959).

Bessenyei, István, "Konsumideologie in einer Mangelwirtschaft," *Südosteuropa Mitteilungen*, XXIV/4 (1984), pp. 23–31.

Gati, Charles, "Eastern Europe before Cominform: The Democratic Interlude in Post-War Hungary," *Survey*, XXVIII/2 (1984), pp. 99–134.

Kertész, Stephen, *Between Russia and the West: Hungary and the Illusions of Peacemaking, 1945–1947* (Notre Dame–London, 1984).

———, *The Last European Peace Conference: Paris, 1946—Conflict of Values* (Lanham-New York-London, 1985).

Kovrig, Bennett, *Communism in Hungary; From Kun to Kádár* (Baltimore-London, 1970).

László Rajk and His Accomplices before the People's Court [publication of the Budapest People's Court] (Budapest, 1949).

Nagy, Imre, *On Communism* (New York, 1957).

Raducziner, Zsuzsa, *Die ungarische Wirtschaftsordnung heute* (Bern-Frankfurt/M., 1982).

Szász, Béla, *Volunteers for the Gallows; Anatomy of a Show Trial* (London, 1971).

Toma, Peter A. and Ivan Völgyes (eds.), *Politics in Hungary* (San Francisco, 1977).

Töns, Heinrich H., *Ungarns Wirtschaftsorganismus in Wandel zwischen Plan und Markt* (Frankfurt/M.-Bern-New York, 1982).

United Nations, General Assembly, *Report of the Special Committee on the Problems of Hungary* (New York, 1957).

Vali, Ferenc A., *Rift and Revolt in Hungary: Nationalism versus Communism* (Cambridge, Mass., 1961).

Zinner, Paul E., *Revolution in Hungary* (New York, 1962).

NOTES ON CONTRIBUTORS

Janos M. Bak, Professor of History at the University of British Columbia, is the author of several articles and handbook chapters dealing with medieval Hungary. Together with other scholars he is preparing a Latin-English edition of the medieval laws of Hungary.

George Barany, Professor of History at the University of Denver, is the author of *Stephen Széchenyi and the Awakening of Hungarian Nationalism, 1791-1841; The Anglo-Russian Entente Cordiale of 1697-1698* and other books and numerous articles on Hungary and East Central and Southeastern Europe.

Iván T. Berend is a member and former President of the Hungarian Academy of Sciences and Professor of Economic History at the Economics University in Budapest. He has been a visiting scholar at several English and American institutions. Together with György Ránki he published many works including *Economic Development in East Central Europe in the 19th and 20th Centuries; Underdevelopment and Economic Growth;* and *The Economic Periphery and Industrialization, 1780-1914.*

István Deák is Professor of History at Columbia University. His publications include *Weimar Germany's Left-wing Intellectuals; "Die Weltbühne" and Its Crisis; The Lawful Revolution: Louis Kossuth and the Hungarians, 1848-1849;* and *A Social and Political History of the Habsburg Officer Corps, 1848-1918.*

Pál Engel is Senior Research Fellow and Section Chief at the Institute of History of the Hungarian Academy of Sciences. His major work is *Királyi hatalom és arisztokrácia viszonya a Zsigmond-korban, 1387-1437* [The Relationship between Royal Power and the Aristocracy in the Age of King Zsigmond, 1387-1437].

Tibor Frank is Associate Professor of History at Eötvös Loránd University in Budapest and has had visiting appointments at Oxford and the University of California, Santa Barbara. His publications include *The British Image of Hungary, 1865-1870; Marx és Kossuth* [Marx and Kossuth]; and *Egy Emigráns alakváltásai: Zerffi Gusztáv pályaképe, 1820-1892* [The Metamorphoses of an Emigrant: Gustavus G. Zerffi, 1820-1892].

Charles Gati is Professor of Political Science at Union College and Senior Research Scholar at Columbia University's Research Institute on International Change. Besides numerous articles and edited volumes his publications include *Caging the Bear; Containment and Cold War; Hungary and the Soviet Bloc;* and *The Bloc That Failed: Soviet-East European Relations in Transition.*

416

Tibor Hajdú is Senior Research Advisor at the Institute of History of the Hungarian Academy of Sciences. His best known works are *The Hungarian Soviet Republic* and *Károlyi Mihály: Politikai Életrajz* [Michael Károlyi: A Political Biography].

Péter Hanák is one of the founders of the Institute of History of the Hungarian Academy of Sciences, where he is Senior Research Advisor and Head of Section. He has taught at universities in Hungary, other European countries, and the United States. His numerous publications include *Ungarn in der Donaumonarchie: Probleme der bürgerlichen Umgestaltung eines Vielvölkerstaates* [Hungary in the Danubian Monarchy: Problems of the Bourgeois Transformation of a Multinational State].

Horst Haselsteiner is Professor and Chairman of the Department of Southeast European History at the Karl-Franzens University in Graz. His books include *Die Serben und der Ausgleich: Zur Politischen und Staatsrechtlichen Stellung der Serben Südungarns in den Jahren 1860-1867* [The Serbs and the Compromise: The Political and Constitutional Position of the Serbs in Southern Hungary in the Years 1860-1867]; and *Joseph II und die Komitate Ungarns: Herrscherrecht und ständischer Konstitutionalismus* [Joseph II and the Hungarian Counties: Royal Prerogatives and Estate-based Constitutionalism].

Géza Jeszenszky is Dean and Professor of History at the Economics University and member of the Institute of History of the Hungarian Academy of Sciences. His major work is *Az elveszett presztízs: Magyarország megítélésének megváltozása Nagy-Británniában, 1849-1918* [The Lost Prestige: The Changing Image of Hungary in Great Britain, 1894-1918].

László Makkai (d. 1989) was a member of the Hungarian Academy of Sciences and one of the founders of the Institute of History of the Hungarian Academy of Sciences. He was also Professor of History at the Calvinist Theological Academy in Debrecen. Among his numerous books are *Histoire de Transylvanie* [History of Transylvania]; *Magyar-Román közös mult* [The Shared Past of Hungary and Romania]; *I. Rákóczi György birtokainak gazdasági iratai* [The Economic Documents of the Estates of György Rákoczi I]; and *Agrarian Landscapes of Historical Hungary in Feudal Times*.

Zsuzsa L. Nagy is Senior Research Advisor at the Institute of History of the Hungarian Academy of Sciences. Among her numerous works are two in English, *The United States and the Danubian Basin (1919-1939)* and *The Liberal Opposition in Hungary, 1919-1945*.

Mária Ormos is a member of the Hungarian Academy of Sciences and Professor of History at and Chancellor of the Janus Pannonius University at Pécs. Her numerous publications include *Franciaország és a keleti bisztonság, 1931-1936* [France and the Eastern Security, 1931-1936]; *Faschismus und Krise: Über einige theoretischen Fragen der europäischen Faschistischen Erscheinungen* [Fascism and Crisis: Considerations of Some Theoretical Questions of the European Fascist

Phenomena]; and *Pádovától Trianonig, 1918–1920* [From Padova to Trianon, 1918–1920].

Katalin Péter is a member of the Institute of History of the Hungarian Academy of Sciences. Her most recent publications include *A magyar romlásnak századában* [During the Century of Hungarian Decline]; and *A csejtei várúrnő: Báthory Erzsébet* [The Lady of Csejte Castle: Elizabeth Báthory].

György Ránki (1931–1988) was a member of the Hungarian Academy and Director of its Institute of History. He served as Vice-President of the International Historical Association, as Professor of History at the Lajos Kossuth University at Debrecen, and as Visiting Professor at several European and American universities. He was the first holder of the Hungarian Studies Chair at Indiana University. In addition to the books coauthored with Iván T. Berend mentioned above, his publications include *The Development of the Manufacturing Industry in Hungary, 1900–1944; Hungary: A Century of Economic Development; East Central Europe in the 19th and 20th Centuries; The Hungarian Economy in the Twentieth Century;* and *The Struggle of the Great Powers for Hegemony in the Danube Valley, 1919–1939.*

Éva Somogyi is Senior Research Fellow and Head of Department at the Institute of History of the Hungarian Academy of Sciences. Her publications include *Abszolutizmus és kiegyezés, 1849–1867* [Absolutism and Compromise, 1849–1867]; and *Vom Zentralismus zum Dualismus: Der Weg der deutschösterreichischen Liberalen zum Ausgleich von 1867* [From Centralism to Dualism: The Road of the Austro-German Liberals to the Compromise of 1867].

Peter F. Sugar is Professor of History and International Studies at the University of Washington. Besides numerous articles and edited volumes his publications include *Industrialization of Bosnia-Hercegovina, 1878–1918* and *Southeastern Europe under Ottoman Rule, 1354–1804.*

Ferenc Szakály is Senior Research Fellow and Head of Department at the Institute of History of the Hungarian Academy of Sciences. His works include *Parasztvármegyék a XVII. e–s XVIII. században* [Peasant Counties in the 17th and 18th Centuries]; *A mohácsi csata* [The Battle of Mohács]; and *Magyar adoztatás a török hódoltságban* [Hungarian Taxation in Ottoman-held Hungary].

Lóránt Tilkovszky is Senior Research Advisor at the Historical Institute of the Hungarian Academy of Sciences and Professor of History at Janus Pannonius University. His books include *Revizió és nemzetiségpolitika Magyarországon (1938–1941)* [Revisionism and Nationality Policies in Hungary, 1938–1941]; *Pál Teleki (1879–1941): A Biographical Sketch; Ez volt a Volksbund: A német népcsoportpolitika és Magyarszag, 1938–1945* [This Was the Volksbund: German Ethnic Policies and Hungary, 1939–1945]; and *Die Weimarer Republik und die Deutschen Minderheiten im Donaubecken* [The Weimar Republic and the German Minorities in the Danubian Basin].

INDEX